Yiddish Cuisine

YIDDISH CUISINE

A Gourmet's
Approach to Jewish Cooking

Robert Sternberg

JASON ARONSON INC.
Northvale, New Jersey
London

The author gratefully acknowledges permission to quote from the following sources:

"The Immortal Orange" by Zalman Schneour used by permission of James Clarke & Co., Ltd.

From That Place and Time by Lucy Dawidowicz. Copyright © 1989 by Lucy S. Dawidowicz. Used by permission of W. W. Norton & Company, Inc., and Georges Borchardt, Inc.

Map of Jewish Eastern Europe adapted from *The Shtetl Book* by David J. Roskies and Diane K. Roskies. Copyright © 1975 by Ktav Publishing House, Inc. Used by permission of David Roskies.

Design by Pamela Roth.

This book was set in 11 pt. Times by Lind Graphics of Upper Saddle River, New Jersey, and printed by Haddon Craftsmen in Scranton, Pennsylvania.

Copyright © 1993 by Robert Sternberg

10 9 8 7 6 5 4 3 2 1

Library of Congress Cataloging-in-Publication Data

Sternberg, Robert.
    Yiddish cuisine : a gourmet's approach to Jewish cooking / by
  Robert Sternberg.
      p.   cm.
    Includes index.
    ISBN 0-87668-156-9
    1. Cookery, Jewish.   2. Cookery, European.   3. Cookery—Europe.
  Eastern.   I. Title.
  TX724.S75   1993
  641.5'676—dc20

                                                          93-14848

Manufactured in the United States of America. Jason Aronson Inc. offers books and cassettes. For information and catalog, write to Jason Aronson Inc., 230 Livingston Street, Northvale, New Jersey 07647.

In loving memory of
my grandmother Miriam Brizman,
my mother, Doris Brizman Sternberg,
and my aunts
Ann Brizman
and
Rose Wolfson

The Brizman family. Top (*left to right*): Doris, Grandfather Berel, Rose, Grandmother Miriam, Ann.
Bottom (*left to right*): Morris, Alex.

Contents

Preface

Dear Readers,

Throughout time, food has been elaborately described by Jewish writers in stories, poetry, humor, and song. Food plays a vital role in Jewish ritual, in holiday and Sabbath celebrations, in life-cycle events, and in any ordinary social occasion. Many beautiful Jewish religious and cultural traditions have evolved out of the preparation and consumption of various kinds of foods.

I have written this book as a personal testimony to the style and spirit of the Jewish kitchens of eastern Europe. Some of the recipes I offer here are familiar and known throughout the world to people acquainted with Jewish cooking. Other are less-known regional specialties. A few dishes were originated or adapted by the children of Jewish immigrants as they learned how to work creatively with materials found in the new markets and kitchens of America. All of the recipes are part of the traditional cuisine of a culture and life-style that, to a degree, have disappeared. Nevertheless, just as the Jewish people has survived the Holocaust, traditional Jewish foods, in a modified form, have survived in the new Jewish communities that have been built outside eastern Europe.

Although rooted in the traditions and customs of a hundred or more years ago, all of the recipes in this book have been adapted, refined, and modernized for today's cooks. The procedures are detailed but kept simple. Ingredients and menu suggestions rely on what is in season. All of the recipes are kosher, just as they were in the culture in which they were created.

With the exception of the Jews of Hungary, Yiddish was the language of the Jewish immigrants whose cuisine is featured in this book. It was also the language spoken in my home when I was a child. I try, wherever possible, to give for each recipe both the Yiddish name and the English name.

Among people in this country there is renewed interest in exploring their ethnic roots. There is also a growing respect among the American people in general for ethnic and cultural differences. I am reminded of an old Yiddish folk saying: "*A barg mit a barg zich nit tzuzamen kumen, ober mentschen kennen.*" ("A mountain is a thing that is fixed in its place. It can never be joined together with another mountain. But people are not immobile like mountains. They are always capable of bringing themselves closer together.") I would like this cookbook to be something that helps to draw closer together people of different cultural backgrounds and, in this way, to contribute something of value toward pluralism and cultural diversity in our country.

If you are a Jewish reader of this book, I hope that by reading and using it, you will discover new and different ways to connect with your own culture and your roots. If you are not Jewish, I hope that this cookbook will help you in gaining insight into and appreciation of Jewish culture and tradition as they relate to food. And if I succeed completely in what I have set out to do, then Jewish dietary customs and traditions will also be less mysterious, less confusing to the general public, and easier to work with joyfully and creatively. May your exploration into the world of Yiddish cuisine be fun and rewarding!

Mit a guten appetit!
(A good appetite!)

Robert Sternberg

Acknowledgments

A special thank you to the following people who were helpful to me in the preparation of *Yiddish Cuisine*:

Bob Cohn, editor of the St. Louis *Jewish Light*, for his friendship, writing insights, and many other forms of personal assistance.

Shirley and Dr. Julius Snitzer for their friendship, support, and assistance with the Montreal photographs.

My friend Jane Timmons, president of the St. Louis Evening Herbalists, for the use of the picnic basket and handmade quilt.

My friends Louise Legare and Sarah Woodfield for their very helpful suggestions for making *Yiddish Cuisine* understandable and appealing to non-Jewish readers.

St. Louis author Julie Heifetz-Klueh for her valuable suggestions on writing and writing style.

Beth Jacob Congregation in Carbondale, Illinois, for the use of the *shofar*.

The St. Louis Center for Holocaust Studies Archives for the use of the *Machzor* from Poland.

Dr. Lucjan Dobroszycki and Marek Web of YIVO, Mara Vishniac-Cohen, the International Center for Photography, and Duane Snedeker of the Missouri Historical Society, for their assistance with historical photographic material.

All of our many friends in St. Louis; Carbondale, Illinois; and Montreal, who helped us test recipes over the years and who gave me good, specific kinds of critique and suggestions for improving recipes.

Mary Gerstein and Dobbe Schapiro, both of blessed memory. Dear friends of my in-laws from Vilna, who have no way of knowing how helpful they were to me in putting together a composite picture of Vilna cuisine.

My mother-in-law, Nelly Komras, who has been my most helpful guide to the Jewish cuisine of Vilna and whose insights, cooking tips, and stories of her own experiences in prewar Poland with foods were of tremendous importance.

My wife, Henrietta, professional photographer and partner in the entire endeavor of creating *Yiddish Cuisine*.

Baltic *Sea*

RUSSIA

Riga

KOVNE

Kelem · Ponevizh ·

VITEBSK

Duna

Vitebsk ✦

Niemen · Kovne

Königsberg ★

GERMANY

SUVALK

Suvalk ✪

Danzig ■

Grodne ✪

Vilne ✪

Smorgon ·

Valozhin ·

VILNE

Minsk ✪

Mir ·

Kletsk ·

Lyadi ·

Shklov ·

Mohilev ✪

MOHILEV

Lomze ✪

PLOTSK

Plotsk ✪

LOMZE

Zambrev · Yablenke

Bialestok ★

Zabludeve ·

GRODNE

Slonim ·

Kapule ·

Bobruysk ★

Kutne · Varshe ·

Vengreve ·

VARSHE

Ger ·

Vurke ·

Pruzhene ·

Shedlets ✪

Kartuz-Bereze ·

Kobrin ·

Pinsk ★

Karlin ✦

Pripet

Slutsk ·

MINSK

Homel ■

CHERNIGOV

Chernigov ✪

KOLESH

Kolesh ✪

Zdunska-Volye ·

Aleksander ·

Lodz ✪

Piotrkov ·

PIOTROKOV

Pshiskhe ·

Shedlovtse ·

RUDEM

Rudem ✪

SHEDLETS

Kotsk ·

Lublin ✪

Khelm ·

Lubomle ·

Kovle ·

Trisk ·

VOLIN

Mezritsh ·

Chernobl ·

Kiev ✪

POLTAVE

Pereyaslev ·

KELTS

Kelts · Apt ·

LUBLIN

Yuzefov ·

Goray · Zampshtsh ·

Rubishoyv ·

Shebreshin ·

Tomashov ·

Sokal ·

Lutsk ·

Rovne ·

Dubne ·

Korets ·

Ostre ·

Zvihil ·

Zhitomir ·

Rizhin ·

Poltave ·

Dnieper

Kroke (Cracow) ★

Lezhensk ·

Zholkve ·

Belz ·

Brod ·

Kremenets ·

Barditshev ★

Shpole ·

KIEV

GALICIA

Nay Sandz ·

Rimanov ·

Pshemishl ·

Lemberg ★

Tarnopol ·

Strusov ·

Satanov ·

Mezhbizh ·

Khmyelnik ·

Letitshev ·

Nemirov ·

Bar ·

Talne ·

Uman ·

Tultshin · Bratslav ·

Carpathian *Mts*

HUNGARY

Munkatsh ·

Horodenka ·

Kolomay ·

Husiatin ·

Chortkov ·

Sadeger ·

Chernovits ·

Kamenets Podolsk ✪

PODOLIA

Chichelnik ·

Satmer ·

Sighet ·

ROMANIA

BESSARABIA

Prut

Dniester

Yas ·

Kishinev ·

KHERSON

Nikolayev ·

Odessa ✪

Danube

Black *Sea*

**JEWISH EASTERN EUROPE
1830-1914**

✪ Provincial Capital   ★ Major City   · Settlement

—·—·— Border   ·········· Provincial Border

▨ Congress Poland   ▨ Pale of Settlement

0   100   200 km

Glossary of Yiddish Language Terms

Most of the recipes in this book are given Yiddish as well as English names. There are also Yiddish folkloric sayings about food that appear throughout the book in both the Yiddish language and English translation. This glossary of Yiddish language terms does not include any words in either of these categories. Nor does it include any words whose meanings ae clearly explained in the text of the book (e.g., *schmaltz*). Although an attempt has been made to make sure every Yiddish word used in this cookbook is translated and explained, there are a few words that appear over and over again—enough to warrant a separate glossary that highlights and explains them in one consolidated list so that the book will be user friendly to every reader who is not familiar with Yiddish. It should be pointed out as well that all words of Hebrew origin are given the Ashkenazic pronunciation, which was used by the Yiddish-speaking world, rather than the more familiar Sephardic pronunciation, which was popularized by the use of modern Hebrew. Thus the word for "Sabbath" is *Shabbos* rather than *Shabbat*, and the word for the dietary laws is *Kashrus* rather than *Kashrut*. Following is a guide to the pronunciation of the transliterated Yiddish and an alphabetical listing and explanation of the Yiddish words that appear most often in this book.

Pronunciation Guide

Sound	Example in Text	English Equivalent	Sound	Example in Text	English Equivalent
Vowels			Consonants		
a	*schmaltz*	part	ch	*kreplach*	Bach (gutteral)
e	*shtetl*	pen	kh	*kheder*	same as "ch"
i	*milchig*	pin	g	*fleischig*	give
o	*lokshen*	born	sch	*schav*	mash
u	*kugel*	hood	ts	*tsallat*	guts
ai	*knaidel*	pain	tsch	*mentsch*	chair
ey	*sheyn*	pain			
oy	*shoyn*	boy			

Glossary of Words

blintzes — Crepes.

fleischig — Meat, foods made of meat and meat products.

gebakte — Baked.

gebrotene — Roasted.

gedempte — Stewed, braised.

gehockte — Chopped.

gekochte — Cooked.

gepregelte — Sautéed.

kashrus — The Jewish dietary traditions, also called the "kosher" laws.

kichel — Cookie (pl., *kichelach*).

knaidel — Dumpling (pl., *knaidelach*).

kottlet A patty, made from meat or fish (pl., *kottletten*).

krepl A Jewish form of stuffed pasta similar to ravioli and tortellini (pl., *kreplach*).

kugel A pudding made from eggs and noodles, grains, vegetables, or fruits.

lekach Usually means "sponge cake" but can also be a generic Yiddish word for cake.

lokshen Egg noodles.

maichollim Dishes (as in "spicy dishes" or "sweet dishes").

marinirte Marinated or pickled.

milchig Dairy, foods made of dairy products.

pareve Foods that are neither dairy nor meat.

prakkes Stuffed vegetables; in the Yiddish world, usually meant stuffed cabbage; also called *holishkes* and *golubtses*.

rebbe Teacher.

shpeiz Food (pronounced like "pies") (pl., *shpeizen*).

shtetl A village in eastern Europe that was mostly or 100 percent populated by Jews (pl., *shtetlach*).

t'viess Grains.

Yiddish The language of the Jews of eastern Europe and most of central Europe. The Yiddish language is almost 1,000 years old; its origins are in the Rhineland among Jews who spoke a Germanic vernacular that incorporated words from biblical Hebrew, Aramaic, Old French, Italian, and some Slavic languages, such as Polish, Russian, and Ukrainian. Yiddish is written using the letters of the Hebrew alphabet.

yoich Soup stock.

The Kitchen of the Yiddish World

Most Jews in eastern Europe at the turn of the century were very poor. It is a known fact that many dishes that are today considered a part of gourmet cuisine originated in the kitchens of poor people. Poor people throughout the centuries have had to be much more creative and inventive than the well-to-do in order to make their everyday meals interesting. Expensive prime cuts of meat can always be simply roasted or grilled and thus provide satisfying nourishment without much adornment or alteration. Less-tender (and therefore less-expensive) cuts require more ingenuity, such as a slow braising in wine with aromatic herbs and seasonings or a period of marination before baking or roasting. A cook might also wish to extend a piece of meat, for example, a chicken, in order to make it produce three meals instead of one. A piece of beef, too, can be extended by grinding it and using it to stuff vegetables. Or it can be wrapped in dough. Or it can become a loaf or *kottletten* (patties) by adding eggs, bread crumbs, and seasonings. A soup can be cooked with the beef that also serves as a meat course. These techniques help creative cooks to turn even a small piece of meat into at least two tasty and satisfying meals. That is how some of the most delicious foods in the Italian, French, Chinese, and Jewish kitchens came into being.

For Jews all over the world, food has always been seen as a blessing from God, and eating it has always been accompanied by religious ceremony. Each meal is blessed twice—once before the meal and again afterward. Yiddish literature abounds in stories about food, where it is described with a kind of passion reserved in some cultures for things that are usually considered more romantic. Food is the topic of many Yiddish proverbs and folk sayings, either as the main subject or as a metaphor for something else. For example, a common Yiddish put-down used against a lazy person was "*Essen, kenst du!*" ("Eating,

you can do!"), which meant simply that the only thing the person had a talent for was eating!

A chasidic story sums up the Jewish attitude toward food: A *chasid* once went to visit his teacher, who immediately brought out food and drink to be served. The *chasid* said, "Rebbe, I didn't come here to eat and drink."

"*Naar* [fool]," said the *rebbe*. "The *neshama* [soul] doesn't come into this world to eat and drink either. But if it doesn't get any food and drink, it leaves the world very fast!"

A man who could keep his family fed regularly and also have something special to eat for the Sabbath was considered wealthy in eastern European villages, which were called *shtetlach*. There is an old Yiddish saying: "*Az du host broit, zich nit kein lekach!*" ("When you have bread, don't look for cake!") Bread has always been regarded with great respect by Jews and is the central feature of a proper Jewish meal. The main blessing made on eating a meal is "*Baruch Atoh Hashem Elokeinu Melech ha-olam Ha-motzi lechem min ha-aretz*" ("Blessed be You, oh Lord our God, who brings forth bread from the earth.") This blessing over bread exempts the diner from making any of the other special blessings over food. A meal is blessed on the Sabbath and festivals by first making a blessing over the bread. During the workweek, if there were nothing else in the house, most eastern European Jews made do with bread—rich, dark rye or pumpernickel spread with butter or *schmaltz* (chicken fat)—and maybe some onions or potatoes. All the other courses in a good Jewish meal are or should be accompanied by good, wholesome, flavorful bread.

The other blessed ingredient in Jewish cooking is wine. With wine as well as with bread, every Sabbath and every holiday is ushered in with a special blessing—the *Kiddush*. The Talmud says, "*Ain simcha eloh b'yayin*" ("No celebration can be called joyous unless there is wine.") And good wine in gourmet cuisine is a natural accompaniment to a good meal.

I have never read a Jewish cookbook that treats Jewish food as gourmet cuisine. That may have something to do with the fact that the largest number of Jewish immigrants to the United States came from eastern Europe between 1880 and 1917, and the vast majority of them were extremely poor. The Jewish cuisine of that people was essentially an unsophisticated peasant fare developed by people who did not have the financial means or the leisure time to concern themselves with elegance and finery. Whatever there was in the way of a "gourmet" approach to eating was reserved for the meals that were served on the Sabbath and on holidays.

In the decades immediately prior to the outbreak of World War II, the Jews of eastern Europe began to move in larger numbers into the cities. Many opened successful businesses. A substantial merchant class developed, as did a more urbanized culture. There were more educational and economic opportunities for Jews; with those opportunities came more time and money to devote to cultural pursuits that included the development of a sophisticated, uniquely Jewish cuisine. In those Jewish homes, weekday meals as well as those served on holidays were more interesting and varied. There were also good-quality kosher restaurants in large cities like Warsaw and Vilna. Several of them were even frequented by wealthy Polish aristocrats who enjoyed eating "something different" once in a while.

In America, Jewish immigrants and their children were busy becoming part of the American melting pot, and this meant (as it did for all immigrant groups) speaking English rather than Yiddish and eating American rather than Jewish foods. The results were that Jewish cuisine remained essentially what it had been for the immigrant generation and that the best Jewish cooking in America was that prepared by the Yiddish mothers and grandmothers at home on Friday nights and festivals.

Despite this, serious Jewish cooks in this country and in Europe have always treated their art with loving attention. They are as careful and meticulous about the technical details of food preparation as are their French and Italian counterparts. And they have just as many theories and trade secrets as the gourmet cooks within every other culture. My grandmother, an immigrant from a small village in northern Poland located in what was at that time called the *Grodno gubernye* (province of Grodno), worked for a kosher caterer and was at the same time a consummate home cook. She passed on many of her cooking secrets to her daughters—my mother and my aunts—who in turn passed them on to me. Helping my grandmother in her kitchen as a young boy stimulated my interest in Jewish cooking, turning it into a lifelong labor of love.

Jewish dishes can be refined and subtle. And, as in every great cuisine, they taste best when prepared with fresh ingredients and good-quality seasonal produce. The making of stock, for example, is as much a sine qua non of good Jewish cuisine as it is of good French and Italian. Jewish *kreplach* and *knaidelach* can be every bit as challenging and interesting to make as French quenelles and Italian cappelletti, and the correct procedures for making these dishes are every bit as tricky. A *cholent*, when properly prepared as a gourmet dish, is not very different from a French cassoulet. A *shikkereh babka* is as rich and satisfying a dessert as a Sicilian cassata.

As with French and Italian cuisine, Jewish foods are, to a degree, regionalized. The following gives a general summary of how Yiddish regional cooking is categorized.

Litteh (Lithuania and Northern Poland)

The cooking styles of the Jews of both northern Poland and Lithuania are similar. Dill and sorrel are popular cooking herbs, and the flavors of dishes tend to be rather subtle. There is an emphasis on natural flavor and taste. Fish, especially salmon and herring, are much loved by people from this region. The Baltic was famous for its smoked and cured fish, all of which were popular with Jews from these areas. Potatoes in many forms were eaten with practically every meal. It was the Jews of this region who developed the best-tasting potato *kugels* and the famous potato bread, made with the starch-laden water in which potatoes had been previously boiled. Fruit soups were popular in Lithuania and northern Poland during the summer. The cooking style of this region was influenced by that of Scandinavia as much as that of Russia.

The Ukraine

The Ukraine has always been known as the breadbasket of eastern Europe. The best breads came from the Ukraine, especially dark breads, *bialys* (a kind of flat, round roll that is actually a regional specialty of the Bialystok area just to the north and west of the Ukraine), bagels, and *challahs*. Fermented beet soup, *rozl*, is a Ukrainian dish, as are some of the main dish winter soups, such as *Ukrainishe kroit borscht*. Savory meat roasts and braised meat dishes were popular here. *Mandelbroit* is called *kamishbroit* by Ukrainian Jews. *Prakkes* (stuffed cabbage) are called either *holishkes* or *golubtses*. My recipe for roast veal breast stuffed with *kasha* is also Ukrainian. The most distinctive characterisic of Ukrainian Jewish cooking is that it is rich and full of robust flavors.

Galitzia and Southern Poland

Galitzia is the southernmost part of Poland. It borders the Ukraine, Hungary, Romania, and Germany. The Galitzian style of cooking is an interesting mixture of all of these influences. The cooking of central Poland resembles that of Galitzia more than it does that of Litteh. *Galitzianer gefilte fisch* has a sweet, sugary taste as compared with that of *Litteh* (where the seasoning did not include enough sugar to impart a sweet flavor but did include black pepper to make it "sharp"). Sweet-and-sour pickled carp made with sugar, lemon juice, raisins, and various spices was masterfully executed in this region. The rich, sweet *challas* and baked beet salad with cherry brandy of Galitzia are absolutely mouth watering. Caraway seeds are used frequently in roasts, braised red cabbage, and other dishes. Juniper berries, popular in German cooking, were used by cooks from Galitzia in braising sauerkraut and in marinating beef for roasting. Desserts from Galitzia resemble those of Hungary and Vienna—they are elegant and refined. (*Galitzia* is a variation of *Galicia*.)

Hungary and Czechoslovakia

Hungarian cooks, especially those from Budapest, have a reputation of being extraordinarily gifted in the kitchen. The Jewish foods of Czechoslovakia resemble those of Hungary. Specialties include a variety of *knaidelach*, *goulashes*, *palaschinken*, and *paprikash* vegetable and meat dishes, such as *lecso*. Hungarian Jewish cooks have developed kosher versions of all the best-known Hungarian dishes. The baked goods of Hungary have always been world renowned. Hungarian flourless tortes are exquisite works of art. Hungarian sour cherry soup is considered the queen of all the fruit soups. Hungarian cooks have a distinctly individualistic style when combining wine, stock, herbs, and spices to make sauces for roasts and stews. Extensive use is made of seasonings, such as paprika, marjoram, and caraway seed. The Hungarian sweet tokay wine (if you can get it) is an unsurpassable accompaniment to desserts and fruit dishes.

Bessarabia, Romania, And the Carpathian Mountain Region

Bessarabia is present-day Soviet-Moldavia, whose capital city is Kishinev, notorious for violent anti-Jewish pogroms in 1648 and 1903. At various times during its history, it was governed by Poland, Hungary, Romania, or the Soviet Union all of which border it. Its cuisine is much more like that of Romania than of any of its other neighbors. The cuisines of Bessarabia and Romania are only vaguely related to those of the other regions. In fact, they have much more in common with those of the Balkan countries than with those of other parts of eastern Europe. I include dishes from Bessarabia and Romania in this cookbook primarily because the language of those Jews was Yiddish and because culturally they had a great deal in common with other Yiddish-speaking Jews. Dishes like *mamaliga*, eggplant salad, *ghivetch*, and roasted-pepper salad were virtually unknown in the other regions of the Yiddish-speaking world. Zesty spices, liberal use of garlic, and many varieties of savory fresh vegetables characterize the cuisine of this region. Only the Jews of Bessarabia and Romania ever cooked meats and fish on outdoor grills. Their smoked and cured meats (like *pastrami*), however, were similar to those of the other regions.

What is important to remember about the foods of the various Yiddish-speaking Jewish communities is that they really were quite different from one another. Yet they were also closely related, because a common culture, religion, and language bound the people of these regions together despite the overall dissimilarity of their respective cuisines.

Jewish meals, like those of any gourmet cuisine, can be elegant, attractive, and satisfying as well as light and balanced. All of the recipes in this cookbook treat Jewish cuisine this way. Every recipe contains suggestions for other foods to serve with it and for the best ways of incorporating the particular dish into a menu.

Every gourmet cook knows about using foods that are in season when preparing a meal. In this cookbook, the menu suggestions encourage using produce in season and cooking with a style suited to the season. Spring menus emphasize spring vegetables, such as spinach, asparagus, fresh green peas, and herbs such as chives, dill, and sorrel (called by Jews *schav* leaves). Cold beet *borscht*, *schav*, and cold fruit soups are an important part of summer menus. Hearty soups and stews as well as substantial dishes are recommended for the colder seasons of autumn and winter. The book contains a large number of Jewish fish dishes, vegetable side dishes, vegetarian and dairy main dishes, and fruit compotes—all typically served and enjoyed in the Jewish kitchens of eastern Europe.

Methods of preparing the food (e.g., whether it should be braised in the oven or simmered on top of the stove) are explained in detail in the book. I do this in order to guide readers to which cooking methods work best with a particular recipe. Even though many of the recipes are old and traditional, handed down from generation to generation, I have adapted them for the modern kitchen, incorporating the use of appliances such as the microwave oven, the food processor, and the pasta machine to help simplify difficult and time-consuming processes. However, I try never to sacrifice quality and flavor for the sake of convenience. For this same reason, I avoid using processed foods and food products in my recipes, preferring those that are fresh, the way my mother, my grandmother, and my aunts did.

Aesthetics, meaning the setting in which food is served and the way foods are paired and garnished, represents an important part of enjoying what we eat. Even food made of the best ingredients and well prepared cannot be fully enjoyed or appreciated if it is presented in an indifferent or tasteless manner. An ordinary meal can be transformed into a memorable experience when served on an attractively set table and when foods are combined with compatible colors and tastes. In Jewish traditon, we bless food before we partake of it. When we recite a blessing, we should do so in an atmosphere that enhances the recitation of a blessing. In this book, menus are developed with a total aesthetic experience in mind.

It is not realistic to think that every meal we eat, given today's hectic pace and multitude of leisure time attractions, will be turned into a total gourmet experience. However, a balance between more formal and more casual meals of fine quality is not out of the realm of possibility. It actually takes very little effort to cultivate an appreciation for these things. An enjoyment of the process of working with food, together with an extra measure of patience and persistence, is really all anyone needs to become a good home cook. This is an attitude that can be nurtured and developed. What results from learning how to enjoy cooking at home cannot be measured in dollars and cents, nor can it be purchased in any store or restaurant.

A Word about *Kashrus*

The character of any great cuisine is determined by three things—the raw materials provided for the cook by the environment, the ways in which the ingredients are blended together, and the manner in which the dishes and courses are presented. Good cooks work creatively by manipulating all three of these elements. The gourmet cook elevates the entire process to an art form. These same three principles apply no matter what the country or culture of origin of the food being prepared.

A minority of cuisines, such as those of India, for example, are also influenced by a fourth factor—the customs and traditions that place restrictions on the foods that are eaten and the special controls over how food is prepared. In Jewish cuisine, this fourth factor is of primary importance.

There is an old rabbinic story told about a Roman emperor during the period of the Second Temple who once asked the rabbi, Yehoshua ben Chananiah, "Why do the foods you Jews cook for the Sabbath smell so wonderful?"

"We have one special ingredient," said the rabbi. "It is called *Shabbos*. This gives them a special aroma."

"Give it to us, too," demanded the emperor. "We would like to use it in our food."

"I can't," said the rabbi. "It works only for those who observe the Sabbath. It isn't of any use to anyone who doesn't."

Kashrus, like *Shabbos*, is a special ingredient in Jewish cooking. *Kashrus* is the Hebrew word used to describe the dietary customs and traditions of the Jewish religion. A basic understanding of the philosophy of *kashrus* and a knowledge of some of its fundamental rules may be helpful to the cook who wants to work with Jewish cuisine. They provide insight into how some of the dishes were created. They also offer a framework for putting together a menu that is of importance to the cultural experience of eating a Jewish meal.

At least since the time the Torah was given on Mount Sinai, Jews have practiced *kashrus*. Rabbinic tradition teaches that the original human beings, Adam and Eve, were vegetarian. "And God said to Adam: 'Behold! I have given you every herb yielding seed which is seen on the face of the earth, and every tree in which exists the fruit of a tree yielding seed; to you they shall be for food'" (Genesis 1:29). Jews believe that it was not until God made a covenant with Noah after the great flood that meat eating became a common human practice. "Every moving thing that lives shall be for you for food; just as I gave you the green herb, I give you all" (Genesis 9:3). This idea is mentioned again in the Book of Deuteronomy. ". . . for cattle, for sheep, for wine, or for liquor, or for whatever your soul craves, you shall eat it there before the Lord your God" (Deuteronomy 14:26). The Talmud explains the verse in Deuteronomy to mean that a person may eat what the soul craves as long as it is eaten before God (meaning that one must bless the food before partaking of it). In addition to this, a person may eat or drink meat or wine or liquor only if the soul craves it. If one's soul does not crave these things, one should not eat them or drink them. And, if one does eat them or drink them, it should happen only occasionally and sparingly. The Talmud further explains that the longevity of the generations of people from Adam to Noah was due to their vegetarian diet. In another place, however, the Talmud contradicts itself on the subject of eating meat and drinking wine and liquor by saying, "*Ain simcha eloh b'bossar. Ain simcha eloh b'yayin.*" ("There is no joyous occasion unless there is meat or wine.") One can only conclude that rabbinic tradition is ambivalent about the subjects of eating meat and drinking wine or liquor.

The kosher laws (*kashrus*) did not formally become a part of Jewish tradition until the Torah was given to Moses on Mount Sinai. It therefore seems that Jewish tradition respects vegetarianism and may even consider it an ideal while at the same time acknowledging that at least in an evolutionary sense, it has become a natural thing for people to eat meat because sometimes they "crave it." Therefore, why not elevate those cravings, as the Scripture itself suggests, and use them for joyous religious occasions like Sabbath and holiday meals?

Kashrus is a series of rules that creates a framework for Jews to deal with their natural human cravings for meat. By eating meat within the context of *kashrus*, Jews sublimate and dignify the act of doing so.

It is interesting that the proscribed Jewish blessing over meat is the generic blessing over any food: *Baruch Atoh Hashem . . . shehakol ni'hieh bid'voro* (Blessed are you, oh Lord . . . for giving us all things which were created according to Your command). The blessings over fruits, vegetables, and grains are each specific blessings and not covered by the generic blessing of *shehakol*: *Baruch Atoh Hashem . . . Borei p'ree ho'etz* (Blessed are You, oh Lord . . . Creator of the fruit of trees); *Baruch Atoh Hashem . . . Borei p'ree ho-adamah* (Blessed are You, oh Lord . . . Creator of the fruits of the earth); and *Baruch Atoh Hashem . . . Borei minay m'zonos* (Blessed are You, oh Lord . . . Creator of the species of grains). This seems to elevate the eating of plant products to a position higher than the eating of animal products. It is ironic that in everyday practice, people do just the opposite and make a meat course the "main dish," and vegetables the "side dishes."

Many attempts have been made by historians and other scholars to find a rational explanation for the laws of *kashrus*. Some speculate that *kashrus* was created by the rabbis as a response to health problems and diseases caused by bacteria-laden food. On the surface this appears to make sense. Disease and starvation are serious threats to human survival when there is no refrigeration or other method of preserving food from decay. However, traditional rabbinic literature says nothing about *kashrus* having a medical basis. The rabbis discuss *kashrus* only in spiritual terms, in the ways I have previously described. The idea of there being a relationship between *kashrus* and good health can, therefore, never be completely substantiated, however interesting it might be.

Whatever the reasons for these practices, we do know that *kashrus* has been the driving force behind all Jewish culinary tradition. A basic knowledge of the dietary traditions and practices, therefore, is really quite important for the cook who wishes to work with Yiddish cuisine. The following list of General Principles of *Kashrus* is quite simple and at the same time very thorough. Use it as a handy reference, not only for the recipes in this book but also for developing your own Jewish recipes. This is exactly what countless generations of Jews have done.

General Principles of *Kashrus*

The rules of *kashrus* that cooks need to know fall into two general categories:

1. A listing of the animal products that may be eaten and those that may *not* be eaten.
2. A description of which foods may be combined and which must be kept apart.

Knowledge of other areas of *kashrus* (e.g., the ritual procedure for slaughtering and butchering animals) is not required.

Following are the general rules of *kashrus*.

Meat

1. Meat must come from an animal that chews its cud and has split hooves. (This excludes pigs, which do not chew their cud.)
2. Meat must be slaughtered by a *shochet* (ritual slaughterer) according to a specific ritual procedure.
3. The permissible parts of the animal must be soaked for one hour and salted for thirty minutes with coarse (kosher) salt in order to remove the blood before the meat is cooked. Liver is broiled for a few minutes to remove its blood.

Poultry

1. Only domesticated fowl may be eaten by Jews. Birds of prey are not allowed.
2. Poultry is treated exactly like meat in terms of ritual slaughter and ritual procedures so as to remove blood before cooking.

Fish

1. Fish must have fins and scales. (This excludes shellfish and fish without scales, such as eels and catfish.)
2. Fish do not need to be slaughtered by a *shochet*, nor do they need to be soaked and salted to remove blood.
3. There is a tradition not to combine meat and fish in the same dish.

Dairy Products

1. Dairy products may not be cooked with or eaten together with meat. (This excludes eating meat dishes with sauces that contain butter, cream, or cheese.)
2. A kosher kitchen has separate sets of cooking utensils, cutlery, and dishes—one for meat (*fleischig*) foods and one for dairy (*milchig*) foods.
3. There is a waiting period, after one eats meat, before one can eat dairy foods. There are various customs concerning the length of this waiting period:

   eastern European tradition—5 hours plus a minute

   German tradition—3 hours

   Amsterdam tradition—72 minutes

Pareve Products

Foods that are neither dairy nor meat are called *pareve* and can be eaten together with either. These foods include all vegetables, fruits, nuts, and grains, as well as fish and eggs. Jewish vegetarians do not have to be concerned about separate utensils, dishes, and cutlery, but like other Jews, they are required to have one extra set of each for use on Passover. Glass is a nonabsorbent material, and dishes made of glass are always *pareve*. Drinking glasses are always *pareve*, and only one set is required in the kosher home.

Passover

On Passover there is an additonal *kashrus* requirement: the prohibition on the eating of bread or any other product leavened with yeast or other leavening agents such as baking powder and baking soda. Because of this, observant Jews have additional sets of utensils, cutlery, and dishes for the eight days of Passover. Eggs are not considered leaven according to rabbinic tradition and are therefore used extensively to facilitate the rising of baked goods in Passover cooking.

The whole rationale of Jewish food culture can be understood if these basic rules are understood. In this cookbook there are no recipes containing pork or shellfish and no recipes that combine butter, cream, or cheese with meat. Menus are either for meat meals, for dairy meals, or for *pareve* meals. There are recipes using food materials and food combinations specifically developed by Jews for use in the Jewish kitchen. There are also recipes that have been so popularized (the one for bagels, for example) that they are considered American as much as they are Jewish.

Let me emphasize that you do not have to observe Jewish tradition to be able to put together a Jewish meal. As you experiment with the recipes in this book, however, it is possible that you might decide, as have many who have worked with Jewish food for years, that something is "missing" if you do not use kosher ingredients to cook with. The same possibility exists with respect to planning menus. The choice, of course, is yours to make.

Is *kashrus* like *Shabbos*—an elusive ingredient that gives Jewish food a special aroma and flavor? Try it yourself when you work with these Jewish recipes and see if you notice any difference.

Entertaining in the Jewish Home

Entertaining in the Jewish home takes many different forms. Casual dinners usually consist of three courses—a *forspeis* (appetizer), which can be either a soup, a salad, or another dish; a main dish; and a dessert. Formal dinners traditionally include four or five courses: the *forspeis*, the soup, the entrée, the salad, and a light fruit dessert. At formal dinners, pastry is served following the fruit dessert a little while after the meal is over, together with tea, coffee, chocolates, and liqueurs.

Buffets, tea tables, Sunday brunches, and Sabbath or holiday lunches are other ways of sharing hospitality. Sabbath and holiday lunches generally feature a variety of cold dishes and one hot main dish, like a *cholent*, which is set to cook slowly at a low temperature before the onset of the Sabbath or holy day (when cooking is not allowed). The dish cooks very slowly and is kept warm in the oven for many hours until it is ready to be served upon return from the synagogue.

When celebrating a life cycle event, such as a *bris* (the ritual circumcision of a baby boy), the meal usually served is in the form of a buffet. Buffets can be either *milchig* or *fleischig*. Sunday brunches are an American tradition that began in this country, primarily because unlike in the old country, Sunday was not considered a workday for anyone, including Jews. Sunday brunches generally include bagels, lox and other smoked or pickled fish, cheeses, salads, and pastries, with coffee as the main beverage. Tea tables are more of an eastern European tradition in which a variety of sweet rolls, pastries, cheeses, and fresh fruit are served together with tea.

Appendix B offers sample menus for all of these kinds of meals. Suggestions for which foods combine well in terms of flavor, color, texture, and richness are also given at the end of each recipe in the book. Use all of this information as a guideline, but be creative and invent some of your own menus as well. There are only a few basic rules you ought to follow.

1. For a formal or casual dinner, try to include no more than one starch in each meal. For example, if you serve a soup like chicken soup with *kreplach*, do not follow the soup course with another rich, heavy starch dish like a *kugel*. Think of *kugels* and grain dishes as Italian cooks think of pasta (or risotto, or polenta). Only one dish of this kind is served in an Italian meal, and only one needs to be served in a Jewish meal. Besides being lighter in calories, a meal served with only one starch will give you and your guests a greater appreciation of the flavor of the dish.

2. Serve with your entrée vegetables that are in season and whose flavor, color, and texture complement the entrée. You may serve one or two vegetables with most entrées.

3. Salads may be served American style (before the entrée) or European style (after the entrée) depending on what precedes or follows the salad. Make this decision based on the overall blending of flavors, colors, and textures in the entire menu. Some salads are good served together with the entrée. In central and eastern Europe, salads of this kind are served in side dishes made of glass. Serving suggestions are given with each salad recipe in this book. Several salad dressing recipes are in the chapter on salads.

4. Bread is an important component of Jewish meals. It should be served with every course except dessert. You may wish to have more than one kind of bread served during a meal. Work with breads as you would with any other element. Color, flavor, and texture should determine your choice of breads as they do side dishes, salads, and courses.

5. For wines and liqueurs, follow the traditional rules that apply to all gourmet cuisine. Some general

wine recommendations are given with many of the recipes in the book.

6. When you serve a fish *forspeis*, such as *gefilte fisch*, and plan to follow it with a meat entrée, it is a Jewish tradition to serve a shot of brandy, vodka, or whiskey after the fish course as a way of keeping the flavors of the fish and the meat separate. I include recipes in this book for *vishnyek* (a cherry-flavored vodka that was made at home by Jews from Lithuania and northern Poland specifically for this purpose) and other flavored, vodka-based cordials that were popular among eastern European Jews.

Sabbath welcome dinner for Jewish immigrants. St. Louis, 1920s. (Courtesy of Missouri Historical Society.)

Stocking Your Pantry

Most of the basic ingredients for Jewish recipes are found in a typical kitchen. There are some things, however, that need to be specified, as follows. Because these foodstuffs are used so frequently, keeping a regular supply of them in your pantry, refrigerator, or freezer is essential. A few of the items in the list are specialties that are for the most part easy to obtain. It would be impossible to authentically reproduce the cooking of the Jews of eastern Europe in your kitchen without these ingredients.

Flours and Yeast
Mehl und Heiven

Several kinds of fresh flour should always be kept on hand. For *challahs*, *bialys*, *bulkes*, bagels, *pletzel*, and potato bread, unbleached white flour (ideally, bread flour) is needed. Unbleached white bread flour is also an ingredient in Jewish rye and pumpernickel breads. The other kinds of flour to keep in your pantry are rye flour, whole wheat bread flour, unbleached white cake flour, white and yellow cornmeal, and potato flour (or potato starch). Unbleached white cake flour is used for pastries that are leavened without yeast. If it is difficult to obtain separate bread and cake flours, you may use all-purpose unbleached white flour, but there will be a slight loss overall in the unique properties of the individual flours. Rye flour, whole wheat bread flour, and cornmeal are used for baking the "black" breads—rye and pumpernickel. Cornmeal is also used for *mamaliga*. The last flour, potato starch, is used in potato bread, *kissel* (a fruit dessert), and as a thickener for sauces. American cooks generally use cornstarch for this purpose, but potato starch was

the one used by eastern European Jews. That is why it is still marketed widely by kosher food distributors (although most of the potato starch bought today by kosher consumers is for Passover use).

It is also a good idea to have a regular supply of freeze-dried yeast so that you are free to bake bread or make a supply of yeast pastry dough whenever you are in the mood. (I am in the mood often. Nothing relaxes me more than the process of working with yeast dough.) Although some professional bakers say there is a difference between bread baked with fresh yeast and bread baked using freeze-dried yeast, I have not found this to be the case. And since the freeze-dried yeast is much easier to obtain and keep until you are ready to use it, I strongly advocate freeze-dried yeast.

Matzoh

Matzoh is a large cracker made exclusively of flour and water. It is rolled very, very thin and baked for precisely 18 minutes. *Matzoh* is eaten by Jews on Passover instead of bread. It is said to replicate the unleavened bread baked by the Hebrews as they fled Egypt. Good-quality *matzoh*, which can be enjoyed all year long as well as during Passover, should be very crisp, dark around the edges, hard, and very flavorful. If good-quality *matzoh* was available all year round, I would recommend that it always be kept in the pantry and enjoyed all year as well as on Passover.

Unfortunately, this is not usually the case. Most commercially baked *matzoh* that is not made specifically for Passover use contains additives and preservatives to extend shelf life. The 18-minutes-in-the-oven formula specified by rabbinic tradition is not strictly adhered to either, except at Passover time. The result is *matzoh* that lacks proper crispness, is vapid and uninteresting in flavor, and crumbles instead of cracks when you break it apart. *Matzos* made in Israel are generally better in flavor and texture than the American products, and sometimes one can find Israeli-made *matzos* that are good even if they are not Passover *matzos*. However, these are not widely distributed except in large cities with sizable Jewish communities, like New York. I personally buy large quantities of Passover *matzoh* at Passover time and enjoy the *matzoh* box by box until it is all gone. Then I wait until the next Passover to stock up again.

Matzoh Meal

Matzoh meal is a finely ground meal made of *matzoh*. Unlike other made-for-Passover products, *matzoh* meal is available year-round. Even though the product at Passover time seems to be better than that available during the rest of the year, the discrepancy between the two is not quite as great as that between Passover and non-Passover *matzoh*. It is also necessary to have *matzoh* meal in your kitchen all year because it is an important ingredient in many kinds of *knaidelach*, *kugels*, *latkes*, and sometimes *kottletten* and *schnitzel*. Stock up on the made-for-Passover *matzoh* meal but if you run out of it before the year is up, don't hesitate to buy the year-round type.

Eggs

Ayer

Fresh eggs are used in such a variety of ways in the Jewish kitchen that they should be considered a fixture. For poor Jews in the Old Country, eggs were the cheapest and sometimes the only source of protein. It is not at all surprising that Jews devised many special uses for eggs (in *kugels*, in *lokshen*, in *latkes*) because often entire meals were made of these kinds of dishes. The recent medical research on eggs is full of contradictions about whether they are beneficial or detrimental to one's health. I personally believe that they are a natural product that, when used

wisely and judiciously and eaten in moderation, are no cause for concern. The recipes and menus in this book provide a sensible framework for using and enjoying eggs without overindulging.

Fats and Oils

Schmaltz, Putter, und Beimel

Oils and cooking fats are essential elements in every kind of cooking. The one ingredient that has the greatest effect on how a dish tastes is the oil or fat that is used to prepare it. Rancid, poor-quality, or bad-tasting oil or fat has ruined many a recipe. Old-fashioned Jewish cooks used only three kinds of fat—sweet butter for dairy dishes, *schmaltz* (rendered chicken fat) for meat dishes, and some kind of oil for putting into *challah* and *pareve* baked goods. My recipes use the first two of these and several kinds of monounsaturated and polyunsaturated vegetable oils. Following is a list of all of them together with their special properties and uses.

Sweet Butter (*Zisse Putter*)

There is no substitute in flavor for sweet butter. Medical research has demonstrated clearly that butter and margarine are equivalent when it comes to things like cholesterol, and even though butter is a saturated fat, in several important ways it is healthier than margarine. Margarine is a hydrogenated vegetable fat. The process of hydrogenation prevents spoilage but at the same time changes the polyunsaturates into a form called trans-fatty acids. Trans-fatty acids are more damaging to the heart and to the arteries than either saturated fat or cholesterol. In my opinion, most margarines also have a terrible flavor, or at best, they contribute absolutely nothing to the taste of food. I therefore never use margarine. I use sweet butter whenever I feel a recipe requires it. I also like to use sweet butter for much of my baking because I like the flavor it gives to sweets. Therefore, a good many of my recipes for baked goods are *milchig* (dairy) rather than *pareve*.

Chicken *Schmaltz*

The word *schmaltz* in Yiddish means "fat," but by implication at least, it means "flavorful fat." *Schmaltz* is a very favorable term, and if something smelled or tasted of *schmaltz*, to the Jews of the Yiddish-speaking world it simply glowed with a heavenly aroma or flavor. In American colloquial English, the word *schmaltz* has come to mean either "having pizzazz" or "being melodramatic and overexuberant". (One chooses the definition one prefers based on whether or not one likes *schmaltz*, I guess.) There is absolutely no substitute in flavor for chicken *schmaltz*. Chicken *schmaltz* has also been erroneously given a bad rap in terms of its health properties. It is important to know that chicken *schmaltz* is not a saturated fat (unlike other animal fats) and therefore is closer in its chemical structure to vegetable oils. Poultry fats, because they are highly unsaturated, are liquid at room temperature and are therefore closer in chemical structure to vegetable than to animal fats. The other thing about chicken *schmaltz* is that you make it yourself, so you know exactly what goes into it (no chemical preservatives or additives). It keeps very well in the refrigerator for months and months at a time without going rancid. I prefer to make my own chicken *schmaltz* rather than purchase that which is sold in kosher butcher shops. (My recipe for chicken *schmaltz* appears in chapter 1 in the section on sauces and sauce components.)

Corn Oil

Corn oil is an excellent polyunsaturated cooking oil with a high smoking point (about 440 degrees) and a delicate flavor. I prefer the unrefined corn oil found in health food stores because it has a slight flavor of corn instead of the refined version sold in supermarkets, which is virtually tasteless. I like to use corn oil in all of the *mamaliga* recipes that are not dairy dishes as well as in salads when I want something other than olive oil.

Olive Oil

I keep two kinds of olive oil in my kitchen—virgin olive oil for use in salads and pure olive oil for use mainly in cooking. If olive oil had been easy for Jews in eastern Europe to obtain, it would have been used extensively. Very expensive olive oil was available to light the Chanukah *menorah* but because of its prohibitive cost, its use would have been restricted to doing only what was required for the *mitzvah* of lighting the oil-burning Chanukah lamp. I use olive oil very often to sauté vegetables, and I always use it

for fresh tomato sauce. Olive oil is monounsaturated, which makes it extremely healthy. The Talmud even mentions that it was used as a cure for many ailments. (The tractate *Broches* says that because it is used as a medicine, when you partake of it by itself, you do not recite a blessing over it.) Olive oil has a distinct, fruity flavor and aroma and should not be used for a dish in which it is desirable that the cooking fat or oil be flavorless.

Peanut Oil (*Fistaschkeh Beimel*)

Peanut oil is my favorite all-purpose "flavorless" cooking oil. Peanut oil is what I use for sautéeing *latkes* when I cannot or do not wish to use butter. Peanut oil is also what I mix with butter for some sautéed dishes if I do not want the taste of pure butter or if I am afraid the butter will burn. I always use peanut oil to sauté *kottletten* or *schnitzel*. Because it is very bland, peanut oil neither lends nor subdues any flavor when you cook with it. It is at home with both sweet and savory dishes. Peanut oil is polyunsaturated and has a high smoking point.

Sunflower Oil

Sunflower oil is light, polyunsaturated, and very delicate in flavor. It has always been popular in Romanian cooking and in the cooking of the Balkan countries. I use sunflower oil as a general-purpose oil when I cook dishes of Romanian origin (with the exception of *mamaliga*).

I do not, as a rule, use any oils with generic labels like "salad oil" or "vegetable oil" in my kitchen. Most of these mixtures are highly chemicalized and poor in flavor. The only thing that can be said in their favor is that they are cheap.

Vinegars and Lemon Juice
Essig und Lemon Essig

Three types of acid ingredients are used as flavoring agents in Jewish recipes—red wine vinegar, cider vinegar, and fresh lemon juice. Cider vinegar was once the only vinegar used by Jews when kosher wine vinegar was unavailable. Distilled white vinegar is excellent for one purpose—as a household cleaning and deodorizing fluid. I like to use freshly squeezed lemon juice in most recipes that call for vinegar because it is milder and more delicate in flavor. I therefore recommend always having an ample supply of fresh lemons on hand.

Herbs and Spices

Kreitechtzen und Gewirtzen

Herbs and spices are very important in Jewish cooking, and a fresh supply of the necessary ones is essential. The following list is in alphabetical order.

1. Allspice: Allspice contains the flavors of cinnamon, cloves, and nutmeg, hence its name. It is used in making beef stock, some meat dishes, pickled fish, and baked goods. Have a supply of whole and ground allspice.

2. Bay leaves: Choose whole, unbroken, dried bay leaves when you buy them. This pungent herb is essential for bouquet garni in stocks and soups and for many braised meat dishes.

3. Caraway seeds: Caraway seeds, called *kimmel* in Yiddish, are very important in making the Jewish black breads (rye and pumpernickel). They are also used in many of the dishes that come from Hungary, Galitzia, and central Poland. They impart a taste that is cool and nutty.

4. Chives: Chives are a delicate herb with a mild onion flavor. They are popular in Lithuanian and northern Polish cooking. Chives are one of the first fresh herbs to be harvested in the spring. They can be grown outdoors or indoors in pots on a sunny windowsill and snipped whenever they are needed. They are extremely easy to grow and I strongly advocate trying it. Dried chives lose a great deal of flavor in the drying process.

5. Cinnamon (*Tzimring*): Cinnamon imparts a sweet, spicy flavor and aroma to baked goods, desserts, and fruit compotes. It is especially compatible with apples. Keep both cinnamon sticks and ground cinnamon on your spice rack.

6. Cloves (*Neigelach*): Cloves are pungent and sweet. They are used, stuck into onions, for beef stock and also in some desserts. Have a supply of both whole and ground cloves.

7. Dill (*Kropp*): Dill is the most important herb in the cuisine of the Jews of Lithuania and northern Poland. In the cooking of this region, fresh dill leaves are chopped into just about every dish that calls for

herbs. Dill sprigs provide the "different" taste of Jewish chicken stock and chicken soup. Dill goes into kosher dill pickles, fish dishes (especially those with salmon), potato dishes, vegetable sautés, and salads. Dill seed gives a good flavor to baked bread. Dill grows very easily in temperate climates from seed, either outdoors or in pots. Keep it in a sunny window and snip as needed, as with chives. Dill freezes well but when removed from the freezer, it is unattractive in appearance. However, thawed, previously frozen dill is fine for use in cooking as long as it is not snipped into chicken soup or used as a garnish. Dried dill leaves lose a great deal in flavor in the drying process, so I do not recommend them.

8. Garlic (*Knobel*): Fresh garlic is used in large quantities in Jewish cooking. Never substitute garlic powder or preminced garlic packed in glass jars for the fresh whole cloves. The minimal amount of flavor these commodities impart is decidedly ersatz. Garlic cloves are easy to peel, and a little bit of garlic goes a long way. Garlic is used both raw and cooked in stews, goulashes, braised dishes, vegetable sautés, and soups.

9. Ginger (*Ingber*): Ground dried ginger is an important ingredient in some desserts, sweet-and-sour meatballs, Polish *prakkes*, and *essig fleisch*. In some of the meat dishes I use, with tremendous success, peeled fresh ginger root instead of the dried ground ginger. Only the dried, however, needs to be kept as a household staple.

10. Horseradish (*Chrain*): Fresh horseradish root is very important in Jewish cooking. It is the primary ingredient in *chrain* and in *Ukrainishe gedempte brustfleisch*. Do not substitute any form of bottled horseradish for the fresh. This substance is considerably weaker in its bite and it is drenched with the flavor of the poor-quality white vinegar it has been soaking in. If your supermarket is temporarily out of fresh horseradish root, plan a different menu and eat dishes with horseradish in them only when you are able to get the fresh root.

11. Juniper berries: Juniper berries are used in only two recipes in this book. Both come from Galitzia, which was influenced by German cooking, in which juniper berries are popular. Keep a supply of these berries on your spice rack if you enjoy the taste of these dishes.

12. Marjoram: Marjoram is a savory herb that is essential to Hungarian cooking. It is a somewhat difficult herb to grow but the result is well worth it if you succeed. Fresh marjoram has a pungent burst of

flavor that is not present in the dried version. Be sure to keep a supply of dried marjoram for making goulashes and other Hungarian dishes.

13. Mushrooms (dried) (*Getrukente Schvammen*): Dried gourmet mushrooms (either from Poland or from Italy) are essential in several dishes, including *krupnik zupp* and *schvammen zupp*. Fresh, cultivated mushrooms are no substitute for the woodsy flavor of the dried, whose taste is highly concentrated. This will probably be the most expensive pantry ingredient in your kitchen.

14. Nutmeg (*Moshkat*): Nutmeg is sweet, slightly nutty, and delicious with baked goods featuring apples and plums. Purchase whole nutmeg and grate your own whenever you need it.

15. Paprika: Paprika goes into practically every entrée. In 1937, the Hungarian-born American scientist Dr. Albert Szent-Györgyi, working with the Rockefeller Foundation, earned the Nobel Prize for discovering that paprika contains more vitamin C than any citrus fruit. This, of course, makes paprika extremely healthy as well as delicious. When you buy paprika, always buy the Hungarian kind, and keep both sweet and hot varieties handy. You will use them often and in large quantities. Spanish paprika is not nearly as tasty as Hungarian paprika.

16. Parsley (*Petrushka*): Parsley is a crisp, savory, all-purpose herb needed for bouquet garni, soups, and many other dishes. Always use fresh parsley and use it often. Don't relegate it to being a decorative garnish that doesn't get eaten. It tastes too good! Parsley is also an excellent mouth freshener.

17. Peppers (*Pfefferen*): Whole dried red chili peppers are used in kosher dill pickles and a few other dishes.

18. Poppy seeds (*Mohn*): A very large quantity is essential in Jewish cooking because they are used in many desserts (e.g., *makos*, *mohn torte*, *hamantaschen*) as well as sprinkled over breads and *lokshen*. Do not purchase poppy seeds in the little containers found in the spice section of your supermarket. Buy them in bulk from a Jewish merchant or at a natural foods store in quantities of one pound or more.

19. Sesame seeds: Sesame seeds are also needed for breads and desserts but not in as large quantities as poppy seeds.

20. Vanilla bean: Vanilla bean is used for making vanilla sugar, which is used in baking. Vanilla bean is far superior to vanilla extract. A recipe for making vanilla sugar is found chapter 1 in the section on sauces and sauce components.

21. Coarse salt: Coarse salt is sometimes called kosher salt. This is because it was once used in every Jewish home to salt meat to remove the blood before cooking. Because this process is now usually done by kosher butchers, coarse salt is generally used today for making dill pickles. It is also better than ordinary table salt for baking bread, bringing water to boil for cooking *lokshen* and *knaidelach*, and for making stock.

Lokshen

Lokshen is the Yiddish word for noodles. *Lokshen* is not synonymous with pasta, however. Italian pasta is generally made with semolina flour that is specially grown for that purpose. *Lokshen* is made with regular white bread flour. The coming into being of the electric pasta machine has made *lokshen* making simple. The process is described in detail in chapter 8. There are four kinds of packaged, dried *lokshen* that you should always have on hand. These are thin egg noodles (for chicken soup and *Yerushalmi kugel*), medium egg noodles (for use in *kugels*), wide egg noodles (for *lokshen* dishes), and bow tie noodles (for the American version of *kasha varnishkes*).

Kasha

Kasha is buckwheat groats and it is sold in boxes marked "whole grain," "coarse grind," "medium grind," and "fine." Forget the fine and medium grinds (unless you enjoy eating cream of wheat), and stock both whole grain and coarse grind in your pantry. Whole grain is used for making plain *kasha* and *kasha varnishkes*. Coarse-grind *kasha* is used for *knishes*, stuffings, and chicken soup. *Kasha* can be found in the kosher section of any supermarket or in any natural foods store.

Pearl Barley

Perlgroipen

Pearl barley is used in *krupnik zupp*, in stuffings, and as a grain dish.

Cheeses

Kayzen

There are three types of cheese that are used in the Jewish kitchen—farmer cottage cheese, cream cheese, and *brynza*. Farmer cottage cheese is an all-purpose cheese used for making *blintzes*, *kreplach*, and many other dishes. It is also delicious eaten by itself. Farmer cottage cheese is light, low in fat, and natural. There is no substitute for it in flavor. It is generally available in Jewish grocery stores and delicatessens and even in some supermarkets. Cream cheese is the familiar accompaniment to lox and bagels as well as the main ingredient in American-style cheesecakes. *Brynza* is a soft, white goat cheese that is popular in Romania, Bessarabia, and the Carpathian Mountain region. It is milder and sweeter than Greek feta and firmer in texture than French chevre. It is used on its own with *mamaliga* or mixed into Romanian salads and cheese spreads.

Dried Fruits and Nuts

Getrukente Frucht und Niss

Dried fruits and nuts are used extensively in Jewish cooking for baked goods and many other kinds of dishes. Keep the following kinds of dried fruits and nuts on hand:

dark raisins (*Schwartze rozinkes*)
golden raisins (*Goldene rozinkes*)
pitted prunes (*Getrukente flommen*)
almonds (whole and in pieces) (*Mandlen*)
walnuts (whole and in pieces) (*Weltschanner niss*)
hazelnuts (*Hazzen nisselach*)

Lekvar

Lekvar is a thick prune butter. Excellent, commercially produced *lekvar* can be purchased in European specialty or gourmet shops, especially those that specialize in Hungarian products. Or you can make your own. I include a recipe for *lekvar* in chapter 13.

Honey

Honig

Honey is an important ingredient in many Jewish recipes. The better the quality of honey used, the better the flavor of the dish. I like to keep two kinds of honey in my pantry—a good-quality dark honey for all-purpose cooking and baking and a light, orange blossom honey for use in dishes that have a citrus-based sauce, such as *hendel mit marantzen*.

Herring

Fresh herring is practically impossible to obtain in most places. Because herring is a fatty, oily fish, it goes rancid very quickly after it is removed from the water. For this reason, most of the herring catch taken on fishing boats is almost immediately processed into salt herring in order to preserve it. All of the herring recipes in this book can be made with salt herring, but if you are lucky enough to be able to get fresh herring where you live, buy it and enjoy it fresh for all of the baked herring dishes. Fresh herring should not be used for the pickled and marinated herring dishes.

In Yiddish, salt herring is called *schmaltz* herring. It must be soaked in several changes of cold water to remove all of the salt in which it has been preserved before it can be used in a recipe. Detailed instructions on how to do this are given in chapter 3. *Matjes* herring is a kind of salt-preserved herring that does not require as long a soaking period as *schmaltz* herring. It comes from the Netherlands. *Matjes* herring has a delicious and distinctive flavor and is wonderful in marinated and pickled herring dishes. Smoked herring that is ready to eat immediately is a specialty of the Baltic countries and is rather difficult to obtain unless you live in a city that has a Russian deli. Look for it in gourmet shops specializing in Russian foods and enjoy it by itself. The ordinary "herring marinated in wine sauce" that is found in most supermarkets tastes absolutely nothing like any of the herrings previously mentioned. About the only thing I do with it is make herring in sour cream sauce, and then I rinse it and dry it first to remove the flavor of the poor-quality white vinegar mixture in which it has been soaking.

Sour Cream and Yogurt

Smetane

Sour cream is used in many of the dairy dishes of Yiddish cuisine, including *borscht*, *schav*, fruit soups, *blintzes*, and many types of baked goods and sauces. Plain yogurt may be interchanged with sour cream for a lighter dish in many of the recipes. In some, however, I feel that sour cream is a real necessity. I have indicated in each recipe that calls for sour cream where I feel yogurt may be substituted. I also include, in chapter 2, a recipe for making homemade sour cream.

In addition to all of the ingredients already mentioned, it is advisable to always have on hand a good supply of carrots, onions, and potatoes (and probably celery, turnips, parsnips, and leeks) because these "aromatic" vegetables, especially onions, are used frequently and in large quantities in Jewish cooking.

Kitchen Equipment

Last but not least are the cooking utensils. Your kitchen should be equipped with the following pots and pans:

A large stockpot that can hold 10 to 12 quarts of ingredients for making stock (including 6 quarts of water).

Several deep, round or oval-shaped casseroles for braising (the best, in my opinion, are made of heavy enameled cast iron).

At least one good-quality roasting pan with a rack.

A fish poacher.

At least two heavy, deep sauté pans, with lids.

A 6-inch crepe pan for making *blintzes* and an 8-inch one for making *palaschinken*.

Skillets and one or two Chinese woks (which are wonderful for sautéeing vegetables).

Two or three stockpots that will comfortably hold at least 4 quarts of liquid. These are used for cooking soups and boiling water for making *knaidelach* and *lokshen*.

Various assorted baking pans, cookie sheets, pie pans, cake pans, and loaf pans for baking and for making breads and *kugels*. Some of the cake and pie pans should be springform. Also have one *kugelhopf* or *bundt* cake pan for making *babka*.

Electric appliances such as a blender, a food processor, and a good-quality mixer.

A pasta maker (either hand or electric) for making *lokshen* and *kreplach*.

Various boards for chopping vegetables and fruits and for kneading dough.

An assortment of fine-quality sharp knives of various sizes, including one small serrated knife and one large serrated bread knife.

An efficient peeler for peeling potatoes and other vegetables and a good zester for lemon and orange peel.

Ladles, spatulas, sieves, colanders, a salad drier, a meat pounder, wooden spoons, wire whisks, funnels, and a skimmer.

A cherry pitter and an apple corer.

A small hand grater for grating nutmeg.

A good pepper mill.

Metal boxes for storing cookies, *mandelbroit*, and *macaroons*.

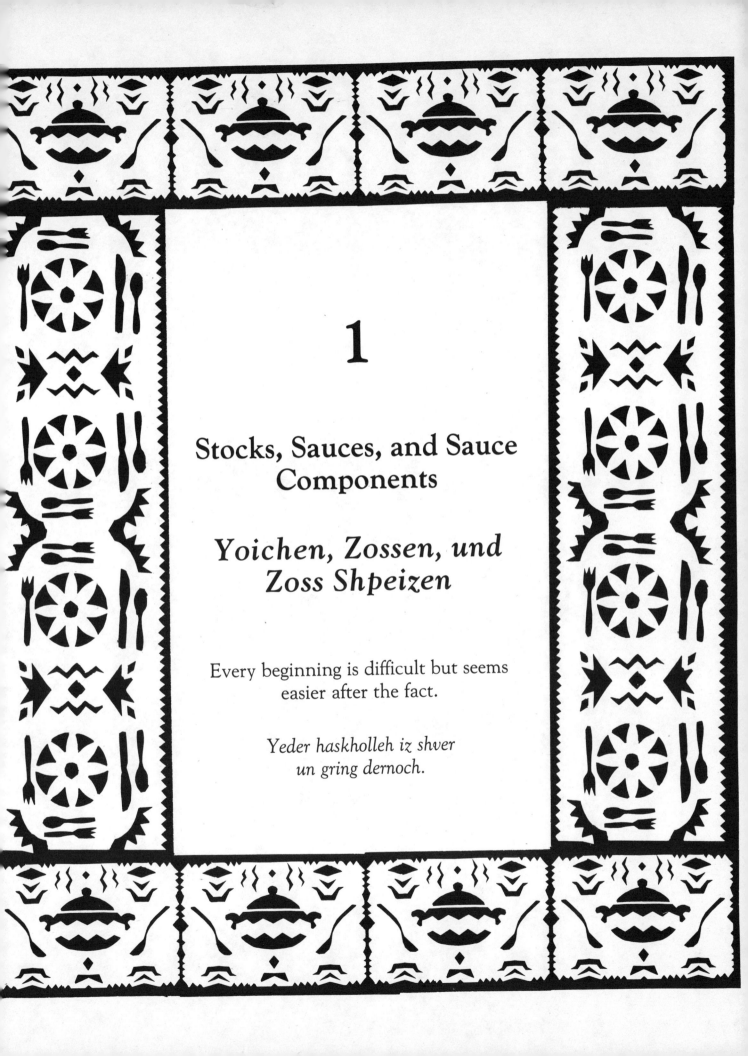

1

Stocks, Sauces, and Sauce Components

Yoichen, Zossen, und Zoss Shpeizen

Every beginning is difficult but seems easier after the fact.

*Yeder haskholleh iz shver
un gring dernoch.*

Chicken Stock

Hinner Yoich

I like to make chicken stock in two stages, generally over a two- or three-day period. It is not a difficult or time-consuming job, and if the work is spaced over this period of two or three days, it can be done leisurely and will never interfere with other activities. Each stage of the process gives you something that can be used for other meals in addition to the stock itself. Stage 1 provides cooked bits of chicken, which can be used in salads or sandwiches. This meat can also be ground and used in fillings for *kreplach*, *knishes*, or *chremslach*. Stage 2 results in a wonderful poached chicken dinner that I call Jewish Poule-au-Pot. The folllowing recipe lays out the making of chicken stock over a two-day period.

Day 1: Stage 1 – The Basic Stock

4 to 5 lb. chicken parts (wings, backs, necks, gizzards, hearts, and, if you can get them, feet)
2 large onions (white or yellow), peeled and left whole
4 large carrots, peeled and cut into large chunks
4 stalks celery, cut into large chunks
1 bouquet garni, consisting of the following: 6 to 8 sprigs fresh parsley, 4 to 6 sprigs fresh dill, 1 large bay leaf, 4 stalks fresh thyme (if available; do not substitute dried), and two large pieces of greens from one leek. Wrap all these herbs together in the leek greens and tie with kitchen string.
10 whole black peppercorns, wrapped in cheesecloth and tied with kitchen string
2 Tblsp. coarse or kosher salt
cold water to cover (approximately 6 to 7 quarts)

1. Wash and dry chicken parts and place them in a large stockpot. Cover with cold water that rises at least two inches above the meat. You will probably need 6 to 7 quarts.

2. Bring to a boil uncovered over medium heat. Skim off scum with a skimmer as it rises to the surface. Try to skim off as much as you can before the water comes to a boil so that the resulting stock will be clear.

3. You will probably be almost through skimming when the water comes to a boil. When you are through skimming, lower the heat to simmer and add the rest of the ingredients. Cover the pot, leaving the lid slightly ajar, and let the stock simmer 2 1/2 hours. Check occasionally and skim if necessary.

4. After 2 1/2 hours, remove pot from heat and let cool with lid still left slightly ajar. This is to make sure the stock will not sour or form a skin as it cools.

5. When stock is cool, remove bag of peppercorns and pieces of chicken with a slotted spoon. Set the chicken aside for later use in salads, sandwiches, or as filling for *kreplach*, *knishes*, or *chremslach*. Strain the stock through a fine sieve, pressing down on the vegetables to get as much of the flavor as you can. Discard vegetables, bouquet garni, and peppercorns. Place stock in refrigerator in covered pot and leave overnight.

Day 2: Stage 2 – Finishing the Stock and Making Jewish Poule-Au-Pot

On this day you will complete the making of the stock and at the same time prepare an excellent poached chicken dinner called Jewish Poule-au-Pot. Poule-au-Pot is a Provincial French dish that is generally eaten when a cook is preparing a pot of soup stock. This Jewish version differs from the French in only three ways:

1. The absence of butter poured over the vegetables when they are served.
2. The absence of any kind of stuffing for the chicken.
3. Jewish Poule-au-Pot is served with *chrain* (recipe p. 8).

1 4- to 5-lb. chicken (a stewing chicken is best), washed, dried, trussed, and tied with kitchen string
3 carrots, peeled and cut on the bias into 2-inch lengths
3 stalks celery, cut on the bias into 2-inch lengths
2 leeks (white part and 1 inch of greens), carefully washed and quartered and then tied together with kitchen string
2 parsnips, peeled and cut on the bias into 2-inch lengths
stock from previous day's preparation
4 to 6 medium-size red potatoes, unpeeled and whole
***chrain* (recipe p. 8)**
kosher dill pickles (recipe p. 291)

1. Remove stock from refrigerator. Fat should have risen to the top in a solid mass. Remove it carefully with a slotted spatula and discard it. Bring stock to a boil. Gently place trussed chicken into the pot. Reduce the heat to simmer after 3 or 4 minutes and cover, leaving lid slightly ajar. Simmer 1 hour undisturbed. (You should probably not have to do any skimming this time, but keep your eye on the pot and skim off scum if necessary.)

2. After chicken has simmered 1 hour, uncover pot and add all vegetables except potatoes. Replace lid and continue simmering undisturbed 30 to 35 more minutes.

3. While stock is simmering, boil potatoes on top of the stove or in the microwave oven until soft and cooked through (about 30 minutes on the stove or 15 in the microwave).

The stock is now made and ready to use or freeze for later use. If you desire a less fatty stock, refrigerate the stock after it cools, as you did in stage 1. Remove the fat the next day with a slotted spatula and freeze the stock in 1/2-, 1-, 2-, or 4-cup containers. Stock will keep in refrigerator without freezing for up to a week.

To serve the Poule-au-Pot, gently remove the chicken and place it on a carving board. Carve into portions and serve with vegetables and boiled potatoes laid out attractively on a serving platter or on individual dinner plates. Serve *chrain* and dill pickles in separate dishes. Good bread (any kind will do) completes the meal.

Serving suggestions for Jewish Poule-au-Pot

This meal is traditionally preceded by a steaming bowl of the soup stock, garnished with soup *mandlen* (recipe p. 55). Any seasonal fruit compote makes an excellent dessert. For wine, serve a medium-dry white such as chardonnay, white burgundy, or Chablis. I prefer a medium-dry white wine to a fruity one with this dish despite the sharpness of the horseradish in the *chrain*.

Beef Stock and Jewish Pot-Au-Feu

Fleisch Yoich

Beef stock is generally used in Jewish cooking as a base for various sauces and in braised meat dishes.

You will make this stock less often than you do chicken stock. It is also not necessary to make the stock in two separate stages, as it is for chicken stock. The making of beef stock results in a traditional boiled beef dinner, which I call Jewish Pot-au-Feu (after the Provincial French dish of the same name). The Jewish Pot-au-Feu differs from the French in the following ways:

1. Jewish Pot-au-Feu is made with brisket and not any other cut of meat.
2. Butter is not poured over the vegetables, as in the French dish.
3. *Chrain* rather than Dijon mustard, and kosher dill pickles rather than cornichons, accompany the meat when it is served.
4. The vegetables used to prepare the Jewish beef stock differ somewhat from those used to prepare the French.

For Beef Stock

4 lb. beef marrow bones
4 lb. beef brisket (in one piece)
3 large yellow onions, one peeled and stuck with 6 whole cloves and the other two unpeeled and cut in half (the brown onion skins add color as well as flavor to the beef stock)
2 large garlic cloves, peeled
2 large carrots, peeled and cut in large chunks
1 large white turnip, peeled and cut in large chunks
4 stalks celery, cut in large chunks
1 parsley root, peeled (if available)
1 bouquet garni made with the following: 6 to 8 sprigs fresh parsley, 4 sprigs fresh thyme (if available), 1 large bay leaf, and the greens of one leek. Wrap the herbs in the leek greens and tie together with kitchen string.
10 whole black peppercorns and 6 whole allspice berries wrapped in a cheesecloth and tied with kitchen string. If fresh thyme is unavailable, use 1 1/2 tsp. dried thyme wrapped together with the peppercorns and allspice.
2 Tblsp. coarse or kosher salt
cold water to cover (about 6 to 7 quarts)

Vegetables for Jewish Pot-au-Feu

6 carrots, peeled and cut on the bias into 2-inch lengths

4 leeks, quartered, carefully washed and
   trimmed of all but 1 inch of their greens.
   Tie leeks together with kitchen string.
6 medium-sized red boiling potatoes, washed,
   unpeeled, and left whole

1. Put marrow bones and salt into stockpot and
cover with cold water. Water should cover meat by
at least 2 inches. Add more, if necessary. Cover pot
and bring to a boil over medium heat. Using a
skimmer, skim the scum as it rises to the surface.
Most of it should be removed before the pot actually
comes to a boil.

2. Add the brisket while the liquid is boiling.
Reduce the heat to simmer after 3 or 4 minutes. Skim
the surface for scum again.

4. After the liquid returns to a gentle, rolling
boil, add all of the other ingredients except the
vegetables for the Pot-au-Feu, reduce heat to simmer, and cover the pot, leaving the lid slightly ajar.
Simmer over low heat for 3 1/2 hours.

5. After stock has simmered for 3 1/2 hours, add
carrots and leeks for Pot-au-Feu. Cook for an additional 30 minutes.

6. As Pot-au-Feu simmers, boil potatoes on top
of the stove or in the microwave oven in salted water
(30 minutes on top of the stove or 15 minutes in the
microwave).

Remove pot from heat. Remove carrots, leeks,
and brisket from the stockpot. Transfer the brisket
to a carving board. Carve into portions and serve
with carrots, leeks, and potatoes on a platter or on
individual dinner plates. Serve with *chrain* (recipe p.
8), kosher dill pickles, and dark bread (rye or pumpernickel). Some people like the taste of the marrow
from the marrow bones. Serve the bones to those
who enjoy the marrow.

Serving suggestions for Jewish Pot-au-Feu

This dish can be preceded with a steaming bowl of
the stock, garnished with soup *mandlen* (recipe p.
55). Any seasonal fruit compote makes an excellent
dessert. For wine, serve a dry red burgundy or
bordeaux, a cabernet sauvignon, or an Italian Chianti.

To prepare the stock for storage

Proceed as with chicken stock. Cool the stock in the
stockpot with the lid left slightly ajar. Remove the
marrow bones (if you have not already done so) and
the cheesecloth spice bag. Strain the stock through a
fine sieve and refrigerate. The next day, remove any
fat with a slotted spatula and ladle stock into 1/2-,
1-, 2-, and 4-cup containers and freeze for later use.

Fish Stock
Fisch Yoich

Fish stock is used for making fish soups and for
poaching fish other than *gefilte fisch*. This dish has a
stock of its own, which is different from the one in
this recipe. I generally prefer to make fish stock fresh
each time I use it but it can be made in advance and
frozen, just like chicken and beef stock.

2 lb. fish heads, tails, and bones
2 cups white wine
1 large onion, peeled and stuck with 2 whole
   cloves
2 carrots, peeled
2 ribs celery
1 bouquet garni of 8 sprigs fresh parsley, 6
   sprigs fresh dill, and 1 large bay leaf, all tied
   together with kitchen string
3/4 Tblsp. coarse or kosher salt
8 black peppercorns
6 cups cold water

Put everything into a stockpot and bring to a boil
over high heat. Reduce heat to simmer, partly cover
the pot, and cook for 1 hour. Strain stock through a
fine sieve and discard all solid ingredients. Makes 6
to 7 cups of fish stock. Use as directed in recipes.

Vegetable Stock
Greener Yoich

Vegetable stock has many different uses in the
kitchen. It is the base ingredient primarily for soups
when the meal will be either *pareve* or dairy. It is also
excellent to use when you desire a lighter soup base
for all dishes that call for chicken or beef stock. For
vegetarians, this stock replaces the meat stocks and
is a very acceptable substitute, even in terms of
flavor. Vegetable stock takes very little time to make
and, like all the other stocks, it can be made ahead

and frozen for later use. Despite the fact that I give a specific recipe here for vegetable stock, there is nothing wrong with saving odds and ends of vegetables and using them up at one time by making a vegetable stock out of them. Many vegetarian cookbooks advocate doing this.

3 large onions, peeled and chopped
3 large carrots, peeled and chopped
6 to 8 stalks celery, chopped
2 parsnips, peeled and chopped
2 large turnips, peeled and chopped
3 leeks, well washed, trimmed, and chopped
1 bouquet garni of 6 fresh parsley sprigs, 3
   fresh thyme branches, and 1 bay leaf, tied
   together with kitchen string (1/4 tsp. dried
   thyme can be substituted)
6 Tblsp. peanut oil
10 cups cold water
3/4 Tblsp. salt

1. Heat oil in stockpot over medium heat and sauté onions until wilted but not brown. Add remaining vegetables and sauté 10 minutes.

2. Add salt, bouquet garni, and water. Cover pot and bring to a boil. Uncover pot slightly and simmer 45 minutes or longer until vegetables are soft and have rendered their flavors.

3. Strain stock through a fine sieve, pressing down hard on the vegetables to remove all flavor and moisture before discarding. Use as directed in recipes and/or freeze in 1/2-, 1-, 2-, and 4-cup containers for future use.

Chicken *Schmaltz*

Es iz gut tzu banoient tzu a teppeleh schmaltz—efsher vel es opraybentzich!

It is good to get close to a pot of *schmaltz*—some of it is sure to rub off!

— Yiddish folk saying

1 lb. chicken fat plus a few pieces of chicken
   skin
1 small onion, chopped
cold water

1. Cut fat into small pieces and put them in a heavy saucepan. (Enameled cast iron is excellent.) Cover the fat with cold water.

2. Bring the pot to a boil over medium heat and reduce to simmer. Cook uncovered until almost all of the water has evaporated.

3. Add the chopped onion and reduce the heat to the lowest simmer. Continue cooking until all of the fat is rendered and the bits of fat, called *gribenes*, are crisp and brown. Do not raise the heat too high or the *schmaltz* will burn. Cooking time will be 3 to 4 hours or even more. *Schmaltz* can be left to cook basically untended, so it is really not at all difficult to make. Check it from time to time just to make sure that none of the solid pieces of fat are sticking to the bottom of the pan.

4. When the *schmaltz* is through cooking and the *gribenes* are nice and brown, remove the pan from the heat before straining the *schmaltz* into a clean glass jar. *Schmaltz* will keep, covered tightly, in the refrigerator for months. *Gribenes* can be eaten mixed into chopped liver, chopped egg and onion dishes, *fleischig lokshen kugel*, *knishes*, or mashed potatoes.

Fresh Tomato Sauce
Pomidoren Zoss

Fresh tomato sauce is an essential ingredient in many recipes, including *goulash* and *paprikash* dishes, sweet and sour meatballs, *prakkes*, stuffed peppers, and many other things. Canned tomato sauce of any kind is not a satisfactory substitute for this sauce. If you do not wish to make your own tomato sauce in large quantities and can it yourself, use this recipe and substitute good-quality canned tomatoes for the fresh ones. Directions for making this sauce with canned tomatoes are given immediately following the one for making it with fresh tomatoes.

I make fresh tomato sauce in the summertime, when the locally grown tomatoes are in season and their flavor is at its peak. I make it in large quantities and can it for use all during the year. This is indeed a time-consuming task, but it is very much worth the extra effort.

Do not substitute out-of-season store-bought fresh tomatoes for those that are in season. The resulting product is not worth the time and effort you put into preparing it. All gourmet chefs recommend using canned tomatoes over the insipid-tasting off-season variety that is sold year-round in supermarkets.

Don't be intimidated by the lengthy procedure involved in making fresh tomato sauce. Once you've tried it and tasted it, I am willing to bet you won't be satisfied with anything else.

The recipe below is for making 2 cups of sauce. When you are canning, increase the proportions by at least 7 times the amount given and double all the cooking times. The recipe will then yield 4 quart-size jars of tomato sauce, which can then be processed by normal canning procedures.

For sauce made with fresh tomatoes

3 lb. fresh tomatoes
1 large carrot, chopped
1 medium-large onion, chopped
2 stalks celery, chopped
1/2 tsp. sugar
1/2 cup oil (I use olive oil)
salt to taste

1. Cut tomatoes into chunks and place in a stockpot. Cover pot, leaving lid slightly ajar, and cook over medium heat for 1 hour, stirring occasionally, especially at the beginning of cooking, to make sure nothing sticks to the bottom of the pot.

2. Strain the contents of the pot through a sieve, pressing down hard until all the pulp and liquid from the tomatoes is separated from the seeds and skin. Discard the residue left inside the sieve.

3. Heat oil in the bottom of a stockpot (the same one can be used after it is rinsed out) and sauté onions, carrots, and celery until they are soft. Transfer tomato mixture back into the pot. Add sugar and bring to a boil over medium heat. Reduce the heat to low and cook this mixture for 1 hour, covered, with lid left slightly ajar.

4. Remove pot from heat, add salt to taste, and cool until tepid. Strain contents of pot through fine sieve, pressing down hard on the vegetables. The pulp will come out beautifully pureed as it passes through the sieve. Practically all the solids will go through except that which is solid cellulose. Discard whatever residue is left in the sieve.

The sauce is now ready to use or to be canned. For canning the sauce, sterilize enough quart-size mason jars to hold the quantity of sauce you have prepared. Running them through one cycle in the dishwasher does this very well. If you do not have a dishwasher, wash them carefully with soap and hot water and then pour boiling water into and over the jars. Dry the jars thoroughly. You are now ready to can the sauce.

Fill the jars with the finished sauce and cover tightly with the mason jar lids. (These should have been carefully washed and dried using very hot water.) Process in a canning pot according to the directions given by the manufacturer or, alternatively, place a wire rack in a large stockpot and fill it with very hot water. Bring the water to a boil and place the jars on top of the rack. (The pot will hold four jars at a time.) The water should completely cover the jars. Bring the water to a gentle boil and cover the pot. Cook over medium heat for 15 to 20 minutes. Remove jars of sauce from the pot and store on your pantry shelf in a cool, dry place. This sauce will keep well for a year and even longer.

To make tomato sauce with canned tomatoes (makes 2 cups sauce)

Substitute 2 1/2 28-oz. cans of tomatoes for the fresh. Drain the tomatoes and cut into chunks. Puree in blender or food processor and strain through a sieve. (Seeds will be all that is left in the sieve after tomatoes have been strained.) Proceed as directed in step 3. It is possible that you will not have to add salt to this recipe because canned tomatoes already contain salt. Taste the sauce to see if you need any salt after you have completed step 4. This tomato sauce is easier and faster to prepare and is certainly sufficient for using in most of the dishes in this book. However, it is still not a substitute for the sauce made with fresh tomatoes.

Chrain

Gefilte fisch on chrain iz genug a klolleh!

Gefilte fish without *chrain* is enough of a curse!
—Yiddish saying

When some people think of *chrain*, they think of grated horseradish root mixed with sugar, salt, vinegar, and a tablespoon of beet juice for color. Properly speaking, however, this is not *chrain*. *Chrain* is really a beet and horseradish condiment, the essential ingredient of which should be baked beets whose flavor is sharpened by the addition of freshly grated horseradish. In this old, traditional recipe for *chrain*, each of the flavors harmonizes with the others, and none is so dominant that it overpowers any of the others. This *chrain* is the perfect condiment to accompany *gefilte fisch* as well as boiled and plain roasted meats. It is also excellent with *kottletten* and *schnitzel*.

1 1/2 lb. medium-sized beets
1/3 lb. fresh horseradish root
4 Tblsp. red wine vinegar or fresh lemon juice
2 tsp. coarse or kosher salt
1 heaping tsp. sugar

1. Cut off tops of beets, leaving 1/2 inch of the stems. Scrub beets under cold running water and then wrap them in aluminum foil with only the 1/2 inch of stems showing.
2. Preheat the oven to 350°. Bake the beets for 1 hour and remove from oven. Cool to room temperature. When beets are cool, peel them and discard the stems and root ends. Cut into chunks.
3. Peel horseradish root and cut into small pieces.
4. Put horseradish and beets into the food processor or blender together with the other ingredients and process until the mixture achieves a "grated" texture. Alternatively, you'll have to do it the old-fashioned way, grating everything by hand, which, with sharp horseradish, is not fun to do.
5. Refrigerate tightly covered for at least 24 hours before serving to allow flavors to develop fully.

Brown Butter

Broine Putter

Brown butter is a simple kind of sauce used for fish. It is particularly good on grilled or baked fish and in various special fish preparations. It has a subtle, nutty flavor and is quite easy to make.

To make brown butter, melt a quantity of butter over the lowest possible heat and continue to cook it until it is as brown as a nut. Allow 2 teaspoons butter per portion of fish. The most important thing to remember about making brown butter is that it must

cook at an extremely low temperature or it will scorch and burn.

Serve brown butter with any plain grilled, broiled, or baked fish or use it as directed in the recipes in this book that specify it as an ingredient.

Mushroom Duxelles Sauce

Schvammen Zoss

2 Tblsp. corn or peanut oil
1 large onion, peeled and very finely chopped
1 lb. fresh mushrooms, wiped clean with a
    damp cloth and very finely chopped
1/2 cup finely chopped fresh parsley
1 cup beef, chicken, or vegetable stock
1/2 cup dry red wine
1 tsp. Dijon mustard
1 Tblsp. potato starch mixed with 1/4 cup cold
    water (optional)
salt and black pepper to taste

1. Heat oil in a 12-inch skillet over medium heat and sauté onions until soft and translucent.
2. Add mushrooms and continue sautéing until mushrooms start to give off liquor.

Mix together the stock, mustard, and wine and add to the skillet. Reduce the heat slightly and cook 5 to 6 minutes.

Add the parsley, salt, and pepper, and cook 1 minute longer. If the sauce does not seem thick enough, stir in the potato starch mixture to thicken. Remove from the heat and serve immediately.

Serving Suggestions

This sauce is delicious with *kottletten* or poured over potato or *lokshen kugel*. When made with vegetable stock it is *pareve* and can be served with a vegetarian meal.

Fresh Apricot or Plum Sauce

Frucht Zoss

This sauce is delicious with pastries, particularly *shtrudel*, and various kinds of cakes like Jewish apple cake. Your choice of which fresh fruit to use is determined by the season—spring and early summer for apricots, late summer and autumn for plums. This recipe can be used to create sauces out of other fresh fruits as well.

1 1/2 lb. fresh apricots or plums, halved and pitted
1 1/2 cups cold water
3/4 cup sugar
1/3 cup brandy, apricot brandy, or crème de cassis

1. In a saucepan, dissolve the sugar into the water and bring it to a boil over high heat. Boil it rapidly for 5 minutes and remove it from the heat. Cool to lukewarm.

2. Place the fruit into the sugar syrup and bring to a boil again over medium heat. Cook 5 to 10 minutes or until the fruit is cooked through.

3. Remove the fruit from the syrup with a slotted spoon and place it into a sieve over a mixing bowl. Pass the fruit through the sieve, pressing down hard to separate the pulp from the skins, which will remain in the sieve as the cooked fruit pulp passes through.

4. Discard all but 1/2 cup of the sugar syrup in the saucepan and add the fruit puree to it. Add the liqueur to the saucepan (apricot brandy for apricots, crème de cassis for plums, brandy with either) and bring it to a boil again, very gently. Cook 2 minutes and remove from heat. The sauce may be served warm or cooled to room temperature.

Serving Suggestions

This sauce is delicious with *shtrudel* or any kind of cake with which it is compatible. It is excellent as an alternative to the brandied apricot preserves sauce usually served with apple *schalet* or the traditional brandy or rum sauce that accompanies *challah* bread pudding. It is also wonderful with cheese *kreplach* and Hungarian cottage cheese *knaidelach*. Try it as a less-fattening alternative to melted butter.

Einbren

Einbren is the Yiddish word for roux and it is used as a thickening agent for sauces with roasted and braised meats. *Einbrennen* can be made with flour and oil or flour and *schmaltz*. I have always found it

interesting and curious that a Jewish *einbren* is very similar to the brown roux that was invented by America's great Creole chefs in New Orleans. The logic behind the preparation of the *einbren* is to remove the "floury" taste of the flour before it is used for making a sauce.

To make a proper *einbren*, take 1 tablespoon of oil or *schmaltz* for every tablespoon of flour called for in the recipe and mix this together in a small skillet or saucepan. Turn on the heat to medium and stir constantly. When the *einbren* begins to bubble, reduce the heat to its lowest point and cook for 30 minutes, stirring every once in a while. After 30 minutes have passed, the *einbren* is ready to be used. Use as directed in the recipe.

Vanilla Sugar

Vanilla sugar is used in baking. It is very simple to make. Just bury a vanilla bean in one pound of granulated sugar. Store this in a glass jar or metal container with a tight-fitting cover and leave it alone for 2 to 3 weeks. At the end of that time, the fragrance and flavor of the vanilla bean will have permeated the sugar. The vanilla sugar can be used in any of the recipes in this book that call for a vanilla flavor. The bean lasts for at least one year, continuing all that time to impart its taste and aroma to the sugar. Replenish the container with fresh granulated sugar as you use it up. Stir the sugar a little whenever you add to it so that the more highly flavored grains are pushed closer to the top. Replace the bean every year or so to keep the vanilla sugar at its maximum flavor.

Homemade Sour Cream
Haimische Smetane

Homemade sour cream has become popular again and is called *crème fraîche* in gourmet cookbooks. But my grandmother made it all the time and called it simply *smetane*, which is Yiddish for "sour cream." It is easy to make, delicious, and less caloric than the commercially made sour cream. Many people like to use yogurt in place of sour cream because it is lighter. This, of course, is fine. Plain yogurt is really quite good. It is just that plain yogurt does not taste like sour cream. This homemade sour cream really does!

4 cups heavy or whipping cream
2 cups buttermilk

Mix the buttermilk and whipping cream in a large 2-quart mason jar or canning jar with a tight-fitting clamp-on lid. Shake the jar vigorously for a minute or two. Let it stand at room temperature for 24 hours. The mixture will then be quite thick and the sour cream extremely flavorful. Refrigerate and use it for every recipe in this book that calls for sour cream.

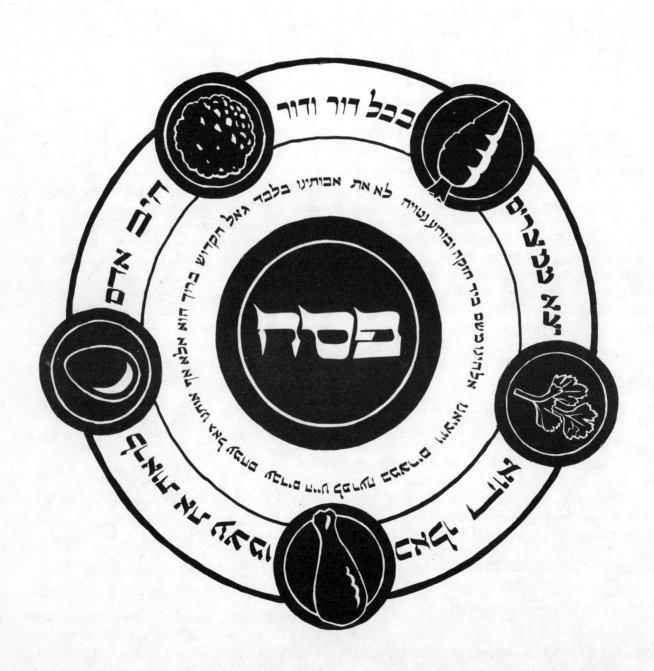

Traditional Passover Seder Menu

Matzoh

Litvishe gefilte fisch with *chrain*

Passover brandy

Chicken soup with *knaidelach*

Roast Cornish hen with Passover *matzoh* stuffing

Baked fresh asparagus   Sautéed carrots with chives

Chardonnay

Tossed field green salad with fresh herb vinaigrette

Fresh strawberry compote with almond macaroons

2

Bread

Broit

Where there is no flour, there is no Torah.
And if there is nothing in the cooking pot,
there is nothing in the head.

Im ain kemakh, ain Torah.
Az es iz nit do ken topf, iz nit do ken kopf.

Challah

The word *challah* is mentioned in the Bible (Numbers 15:17–21) and was the name given to the portion of dough set aside by each Hebrew bread maker from each fresh batch of dough to give to the Temple priest. The custom of separating a small piece of dough from every batch, wrapping it in tinfoil, and "burning" it in the oven in remembrance of the biblical practice is still a tradition among observant Jews. This practice is followed for baking every kind of bread, not only *challah*.

Challah in culinary terms refers to the white, egg-enriched bread that is prepared by Jews for the Sabbath and festivals. Eastern European Jews made two types of *challah*—regular and sweet. The sweet *challah* was eaten during the autumn holiday season.

There is a tremendous amount of folklore and religious custom surrounding *challah*. The shaping of the bread is as important as the ingredients that go into it or on top of it. The seeds that are sprinkled on top of the bread are said to symbolize the manna, which fell from heaven to feed the Hebrew people during their years of wandering in the Sinai desert. Two whole, uncut loaves of the bread are blessed before each Sabbath and holiday meal to symbolize the double portion of manna that was provided on these days. Some Jews sprinkle sesame rather than poppy seeds on their Sabbath *challas* because of the traditional belief that the color of the manna was white. A wooden board is placed under the *challas* and they are covered with a white cloth before they are blessed because of the belief that dew lined the manna both above and below it to keep it fresh.

During the Middle Ages, the shaping of *challah* was developed by Jews into a high folk art. Some of these medieval traditions survive. The most common of these is the "braided" shape, but there are many other shapes as well, each having a religious or folkloric significance. A section on shaping *challas*, complete with diagrams and illustrations, is included immediately following the *challah* recipes.

Regular *Challah*

10 1/2 cups unbleached white bread flour (plus 1 additional cup as needed)
1/2 cup plus 1/4 tsp. sugar
1/2 cup peanut oil
1 Tblsp. coarse or kosher salt
2 pkg. freeze-dried yeast
2 1/4 cups lukewarm water
4 jumbo eggs at room temperature, beaten
1 egg yolk mixed with 1 Tblsp. cold water (egg wash)
poppy or sesame seeds for sprinkling

1. Dissolve 1/4 tsp. sugar in the lukewarm water. Stir in yeast crystals and set aside in a draft-free place to proof (about 10 minutes).

2. Mix together 10 cups flour, salt, and the remaining sugar by hand or in a food processor equipped with a dough blade.

3. If preparing by hand, make a well in the center of the flour mixture. Add the beaten eggs, oil, and the proofed yeast mixture.

4. Mix and knead by hand, with dough blade in food processor or with dough hook in an electric mixer. If using the mixer or food processor, add additional flour until dough forms a sticky ball and pulls away from the sides. I recommend completing the final kneading of the dough by hand. Place it on a floured board and continue to knead by hand, adding flour as you work, if necessary. Dough should be blistered from kneading and feel moist and slightly sticky, but it should not stick to either the board or your fingers. It can be tricky to judge the readiness of dough but the more you work with it, the more you will develop a sense of how it is supposed to feel. Be careful not to add too much flour (which many cooks have a tendency to do in order to get rid of the "sticky" feeling), or you will end up with a bread that is too heavy in texture.

5. When kneading is completed, place the dough into an oiled pan and cover it with a damp kitchen cloth. Set it aside in a draft-free place (e.g., an unlighted oven) for 2 1/2 to 3 hours to rise. Dough will be doubled in bulk when it has completely risen.

6. When dough has risen, punch it down and knead it again. To be certain that the first rising is finished, test dough by pushing it in with your finger. If it does not spring back, it is ready for its second kneading. Knead it again, doing the same thing you did in step 4. Dough should feel similar to what it felt like at the end of the first kneading.

7. Set it aside to rise again, covered with a damp kitchen cloth, in the same draft-free spot. The second rising should take no longer than 1 to 1 1/2 hours.

8. Now it is time to shape the *challah*. Divide it into 2 or 3 parts, depending on how large a loaf you wish to make. This recipe makes 2 large *challas* or 3 regular-sized ones. Choose what shape you wish to

Jewish bakery in Cracow, 1937. The sign reads: Very good and beautiful *challas* for the Sabbath. Egg *challas* also. (Photograph by Roman Vishniac.)

make the *challas* and follow the instructions given at the end of this recipe for making the various shapes.

9. After you finish shaping your *challas*, place them on the cookie sheets or in the pans in which they will be baked and cover them with moist kitchen cloths. Allow them to rise until they are doubled in size (about 35 to 45 minutes). Preheat the oven to 350°. While the oven is warming, brush the egg wash over each of the *challas*, using a pastry brush. Sprinkle with poppy or sesame seeds. Bake 35 to 45 minutes. Loaves are finished baking when they are golden brown and sound hollow when tapped on the bottom. Cool *challas* on wire racks before serving.

Sweet *Challah*

The recipe for sweet *challah* differs from that for regular *challah* in the following ways:

1. Add 1/2 cup honey to the rest of the ingredients in step 3.
2. Add 1/2 cup raisins to the recipe. Knead them in by hand during step 6.
3. Add 1 tsp. honey to the egg wash.

With the exception of these three things, there is no difference between sweet *challah* and regular *challah*. Prepare and bake sweet *challah* using the procedure in steps 1 through 9.

Shaping *Challah*

The following are various methods of shaping *challah*:

The Braided *Challah*

Braided *challas* are the most common and the most familiar. Some Jews followed a custom of braiding their *challas* so that 6 humps would show at the end of the braiding of each loaf. Then 2 *challas* together, when placed next to each other on the Sabbath table, would have 12 humps. The 12 humps would symbolize the 12 tribes of biblical Israel and the 12 loaves of "showbread" (*lechem hapanim*) that were displayed in the ancient Hebrew Temple in Jerusalem and eaten by the priests each Sabbath.

To make braided *challah*, first divide each quantity of *challah* dough that you are going to make into one loaf into 3, 4, or 6 pieces and roll them between the palms of your hand until you have a rope shape approximately 12 inches long. The ends of the ropes should be thinner than the centers. Vertically line up the ropes as shown in the photographs below.

The Three-Rope Braid

This is the easiest braid to make, but the loaf is slightly flatter than the four- or six-strand braid. The trick to making a perfectly braided *challah* is to start the braiding in the middle of the loaf rather than at one of the ends. Follow the sequence shown in the photographs on page 18.

Set the *challas* aside to rise and bake as directed in step 6 of the recipe.

The Four-Rope Braid

Follow the same procedure as for the three-braid *challah*, using the directions shown in the sequence of photographs on page 18. The four-braid *challah* is one of the most beautiful loaves of all.

The Six-Rope Braid

This is the most complex of the braided *challas*. To make an attractive six-braid *challah*, you will need more dough than to make the other two braided shapes. One recipe of *challah* dough makes 2 beautiful six-braid *challas* or 3 slightly smaller and flatter loaves. To make a six-rope braid, follow the directions shown in the sequence of photographs on page 19.

Faiglan

Faiglan is the Yiddish name given to the round, spiraling loaves that are baked for Rosh Hashanah and Sukkos. The spiral symbolizes the ascendance of the soul into higher spheres and levels of consciousness in its search for a meaningful relationship with God. It is traditional to use sweet *challah* dough to make *faiglan*.

Braided *faiglan* for Rosh Hashanah (yields 3 loaves)

Divide the entire *challah* dough recipe into 3 equal pieces. Divide each of the 3 pieces into 3 pieces of equal size. Using the palms of your hand and a bread board, roll each of them into a rope no shorter than 24 inches in length. *Faiglan* dough must always be rolled longer than that for regular braided *challah* so that it will be long enough to spiral attractively. Braid the three strands together as directed in the recipe for braided *challah*. Then wind the entire loaf into an ascending spiral. Follow the directions

The Three-Rope Braid

Step 1

Step 2

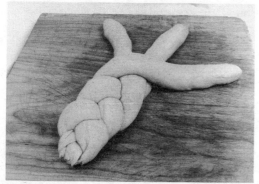

Step 3

Step 4

The Four-Rope Braid

Step 1

Step 2

Step 3

Step 4

The Six-Rope Braid

Step 1

Step 2

Step 3

Step 4

shown in the sequence of photographs on page 20. Cover the bread and let it rise. When the *challah* has risen, bake as directed in step 6 of the recipe. You will repeat these same steps for all 3 of the *faiglan*.

Faiglan for Sukkos (yields 3 loaves)

Divide the entire recipe of *challah* dough into 3 parts. Roll each part into a 24-inch-long rope with one end slightly thicker than the other. Wind each rope into an ascending spiral. Follow the directions shown in the sequence of photographs on page 20. Let rise and bake as directed in step 6 of the recipe.

Luchos Habris (Tablets of the Law) Pattern for Shevuos

One recipe of *challah* dough makes 2 *luchos habris*—shaped loaves. Use the sequence of photographs on page 21 to help you make this beautiful and interesting shape. Take enough dough for one loaf of *challah* and divide it into 3 pieces—two of equal size and the third very small (about 1/5 the size of the other two). Take the 2 pieces of equal length and shape them into long, oval loaves. Place them into a well-oiled 8-inch-wide baking pan next to each

other. Take the very small piece of dough and divide it into 8 pieces. Shape these lengthwise into 4-inch-long "pencils" by rolling them between the palms of your hands. Twist the pencils of dough around one another as shown in the photographs. Lay the pencils across the two tablets as shown in the diagram. Cover and let rise until doubled in bulk. Before baking, sprinkle seeds (sesame, poppy, or a combination of both, alternating row by row) only over the sections in between the pencil dividers. The divisions symbolize the breaking points for the Ten Commandments, which were printed on the tablets. Bake as directed in step 6 of the recipe.

Galitzianer Potato Bread

Galitzianer Kartoffel Broit

This specialty from Galitzia, probably of German origin, is a delicious, all-purpose white bread that goes well with sandwiches and soups and makes delicious *bulkes* (dinner rolls). The crisp, nutty taste

Braided *Faiglan* for Rosh Hoshanah

Step 1

Step 2

Step 3

Step 4

Faiglan for Sukkos

Step 1

Step 2

Step 3

Luchos Habris (Tablets of the Law)

Step 1

Step 2

Step 3

Step 4

of the caraway seeds is a sharp contrast to the mellow, earthy texture of the dough in this bread.

**6 cups unbleached white bread flour plus more
     as needed
1 pkg. freeze-dried yeast
2 Tblsp. corn oil
1/2 tsp. sugar
1 Tblsp. coarse or kosher salt
1/3 cup potato starch
1 cup lukewarm water or potato water (water
     that is left over after boiling potatoes)
1 1/2 cups mashed potatoes (about 2 or 3
     medium-size potatoes)
1 1/2 Tblsp. caraway (*kimmel*) seeds plus seeds
     to sprinkle
1 egg white mixed with 1 Tblsp. cold water
     (egg-white wash)**

1. Mix the yeast, sugar, and water together and set in a draft-free spot to proof (approximately 10 minutes). When the mixture is ready to use, yeast will be bubbly.

2. In a food processor or electric mixer with dough attachment or in a deep mixing bowl, place the flour and salt. Mix in the yeast mixture, salt, oil, potato starch, potatoes, and *kimmel* seeds.

3. Knead for about 15 minutes by hand, by machine, or by a combination of the two to achieve the correct consistency and texture and to activate the yeast molecules. Add flour, if necessary, as you knead. The dough should be smooth and moist and only slightly sticky. Do not use too much flour or the bread will be too heavy.

4. Set dough aside in a well-greased bowl in a draft-free place. Cover with a damp kitchen cloth and allow to rise. Rising should take approximately 2 1/2 to 3 hours. At the end of rising, dough will be doubled in size. To test for doneness, gently press dough with one finger. If it does not spring back, dough has risen and is ready for the next step.

5. Punch down the dough and cut it in half with a serrated bread knife. Roll each half into a round or an oblong shape. Set on greased baking sheets or in greased loaf pans. Cover again with the damp kitchen cloth and allow to rise again. After about 1 hour, the dough should have risen again to double its bulk.

6. Preheat oven to 350°. Using a serrated knife, make diagonal slits in the bread if it is oblong in

shape or cut a cross into the top if it is round shaped. Brush each loaf with egg-white wash and sprinkle with *kimmel* seeds.

7. Bake at 350° for 40 to 45 minutes or longer until bread is nicely browned. To test for doneness, lift up one loaf and tap it lightly. If it sounds hollow, it is done. Cool before slicing and serving. Recipe yields 2 loaves.

Lithuanian Potato Bread

Litvishe Kartoffel Broit

This rich potato bread is delicious with any kind of meal or by itself, spread with sweet butter. The optional dill leaves and dill seed add a sweet herbal fragrance.

5 1/2 to 6 cups unbleached white bread flour, or more if needed
1 pkg. freeze-dried yeast
1 cup lukewarm potato water (the water that is left over after boiling potatoes)
1 1/2 cups mashed potatoes (about 3 medium-size potatoes)
1/3 cup potato starch
1 extra-large egg, beaten
2 Tblsp. corn or peanut oil
1/4 cup sugar
2 1/2 tsp. coarse salt
1 small egg beaten with 1 Tblsp. cold water (egg wash)

1. Mix 1 tsp. sugar with potato water and yeast and set aside in a draft-free place to proof (about 10 minutes).

2. In a food processor or electric mixer with dough attachment or in a deep bowl, mix together the flour, remaining sugar, and salt. Add oil, potato starch, potatoes, beaten extra-large egg, and yeast mixture. Knead by machine, by hand, or by a combination of the two for 20 minutes until dough achieves correct consistency and texture. Add flour as needed. Dough should feel soft, spongy, smooth, moist, and only slightly sticky. Do not add too much flour or bread will be too heavy.

3. Place dough in a greased bowl, covered with a damp kitchen cloth, in a draft-free spot and allow to rise. Rising time will be approximately 2 1/2 to 3 hours. Dough will be double in bulk when rising is complete. To test for doneness, gently poke the dough with a finger. If it doesn't spring back, rising is complete.

4. Punch dough down and cut in half with a serrated bread knife. Knead again and shape into oblong or round shapes. Place on greased baking sheets or in greased loaf pans. Cover again with the damp kitchen cloth and set aside to rise a second time. Rising will be completed in approximately 1 hour.

5. Preheat oven to 350°. Using a serrated knife, make slits in the oblong-shaped loaves or cut a cross into the round loaves. Brush with egg wash and bake in the oven for 40 to 45 minutes or until bread is nicely browned. To test for doneness, lift up one loaf and tap the bottom. If it sounds hollow, it is finished baking. Cool before slicing and serving. Yields 2 loaves.

Variation

For a delicious variation on this recipe for *Litvishe kartoffel broit*, add 1 1/2 Tblsp. dill seeds and/or 1/2 cup finely chopped fresh dill leaves to the dough during step 2 and continue as directed above.

Vienna Bread

Weinerbroit

Vienna bread is the ordinary, everyday loaf of bread eaten in Austria and in the area of Hungary that is close to the Austrian border. This particular recipe is a specialty of Budapest. American Vienna white bread may be a variation of this bread, which was brought here by Hungarian or Austrian immigrants. This bread is, in fact, a basic sourdough white bread and it is extremely tasty, especially when accompanying goulash and *paprikash* dishes. The sourdough starter used to make *weinerbroit* is also used for making the sourdough variation of Jewish rye bread. The ingredients in this bread are as basic as can be—essentially nothing more than flour and water. To make it, you must first make a sourdough starter.

For sourdough starter

1 cup unbleached white bread flour
1/2 cup lukewarm water
1 tsp. freeze-dried yeast

For bread

1 cup sourdough starter
7 to 8 cups unbleached white bread flour
2 cups lukewarm water

1. First, you have to make the sourdough starter. Mix together all the ingredients for the starter in a deep ceramic or glass bowl with a tight-fitting lid (or alternatively, use plastic wrap). After mixing the ingredients, cover the bowl tightly and place it in a draft-free place, such as an unlit oven, to ferment overnight. Leave the starter alone and forget about it for at least 12 hours. Sourdough starters are a little unpredictable, so give it longer if after 12 hours bubbles have not yet appeared in the starter. Starter is ready to use when the mixture has risen in the bowl and bubbles appear all over it. To make the first batch of bread, use all of your starter.

2. Mix the starter with the lukewarm water and add 2 cups of flour. Set aside this mixture, tightly covered, in the draft-free spot and leave it alone for several hours. If you do this in the morning, check it in the afternoon to see if a bubbly sponge of dough has formed. If it has, at this point you are ready to make the bread. Before doing this, separate 1 cup of the sponge. This will be your sourdough starter for your next batch of bread. Put it in a tightly covered jar and keep it in the refrigerator. Sourdough starter can be used and refreshed several times before it begins to lose its punch. Try to use the starter to make bread every 2 to 3 weeks to keep the starter at its maximum operating point.

3. Knead in the remaining flour by hand or by machine. Dough will feel moist and very slightly sticky and will have a wonderful sourdough aroma. When you have finished kneading, place the dough in a well-greased bowl in a draft-free spot to rise. Cover with a damp kitchen cloth. Rising time for sourdough bread takes a little longer than for regular yeast dough. Allow about 3 to 3 1/2 hours before testing. To test for doneness, press a finger into the dough. If it does not spring back, rising is complete.

4. Punch down the dough and divide into two or three pieces. Knead again and shape into round or oblong loaves. Place on well-greased baking sheets. Cover again with damp kitchen cloths and set aside to rise until double in bulk (about 1 hour).

5. Preheat oven to 400°. Using a serrated knife, cut diagonal slits into the loaves if they are oblong shaped, or cut a cross into the loaves if they are round. Place a shallow baking pan filled with cold water on the bottom rack of the oven and then put the bread in the oven on the middle shelf. Bake 10 minutes, then lower heat to 375°. Bake an additional 25 to 30 minutes. Bread is ready when it is golden brown in color and when it sounds hollow on the bottom when tapped. The water-filled pan helps to provide a crisp, hard crust on the bread as it bakes. Recipe yields 2 to 3 loaves of bread.

Jewish Rye Bread

Rye bread is one of the basic breads of Jewish cuisine. It tastes good with any kind of sandwich—cold cut, chicken or tuna salad, *liptavsky kayz*, chopped egg and onion, or anything else. It is also an excellent bread to serve with any of the main-dish soups. Real Jewish rye bread is made with lots of caraway (*kimmel*) seeds and a combination of rye and white flour. It is not a heavy-textured bread when properly made. Rye bread requires a longer kneading than white bread and a slightly heavier touch in order to get the yeast molecules to work at their maximum. It should also be understood almost from the outset that rye flour, unlike wheat flour, is very sticky. Do not add extra white flour to the recipe, as you might to a white flour bread, in order to alleviate the stickiness of the dough. Too much flour will result in a bread that is too heavy and solid in texture.

2 cups lukewarm water
2 pkg. freeze-dried yeast
2 tsp. sugar
1 Tblsp. coarse or kosher salt
3 1/2 cups rye flour
3 1/2 cups unbleached white bread flour
1/4 cup cider vinegar
2 Tblsp. corn oil
1/3 cup yellow cornmeal
3 Tblsp. caraway (*kimmel*) seeds
1 egg white mixed with 1 Tblsp. cold water
**   (egg-white wash)**

1. Dissolve sugar into water. Stir in yeast and set aside in a draft-free place for 10 minutes to proof. Yeast is proofed when bubbles rise to the surface.

2. Mix together 3 cups white flour and 3 cups rye flour, salt, and *kimmel* seeds in a deep bowl or in the food processor or electric mixer with dough attachment.

3. When yeast is proofed, add vinegar, yeast mixture, and oil to the flour mixture and knead by hand, by machine, or by a combination of the two. Kneading should take 15 to 20 minutes. Remember that the dough will be rather sticky. Knead in the remaining 1/2 cups of white and rye flour. Add white flour only if the dough is so sticky that a coating of it sticks to your fingers as you knead. When you are through kneading the dough, place it in a greased bowl and cover it with a damp kitchen towel. Put it in a draft-free place to rise until doubled in bulk. This will take about 2 hours.

4. To test for doneness, push a finger into the dough. If it does not spring back, rising is complete. Punch the dough down and cut it in half. Knead each piece again and shape it into an oblong or round loaf. The dough will not be as sticky this time. Grease two baking sheets (or loaf pans, if you wish) and spread the cornmeal over the bottom (and sides, if using loaf pans). Place the loaves on the sheets or in the pans and cover again with the damp kitchen towel. Set aside to rise. Second rising should take from 45 minutes to 1 hour. Rye bread does not rise as high as white bread, so do not be concerned if the bread does not seem to puff up as much as you would like it to.

5. Preheat oven to 350°. Using a serrated knife, cut diagonal slashes into oblong-shaped loaves or a cross into round ones at 2-inch intervals. Slashes should not be more than 1/2 inch deep.

6. Using a pastry brush, brush egg-white wash across the top of the breads. Bake 35 to 40 minutes or until loaves are nice and brown and sound hollow when tapped on the bottom. Cool on wire racks before serving. Rye bread freezes very well. Recipe yields 2 loaves.

Variation 1: St. Louis *Tzitzel* Rye

To make this St. Louis Jewish specialty rye bread, sprinkle yellow cornmeal all over the bread after it has risen a second time and been placed on a bed of cornmeal on its baking sheet. The cornmeal should be a thin coating rather than a sprinkling. Make slashes as you would for regular Jewish rye before you coat with cornmeal. The finished bread has a crunchy coating of cornmeal all around it and tastes absolutely delicious!

Variation 2: Sourdough Jewish Rye

You can make an excellent sourdough Jewish rye bread by replacing the yeast mixture, vinegar, oil, and salt with a simple sourdough starter (see recipe for Vienna bread, p.   ). Use the same proportion of rye flour and wheat flour and the same quantity of *kimmel* seeds. Follow the instructions given for Vienna bread, which are standard for making any sourdough bread.

Pumpernickel Bread

Schwarzebroit

Pumpernickel bread is called in Yiddish *schwarzebroit* or "black bread" because of its dark color. It is not only the healthiest of the Jewish breads but also the most flavorful. Some people think of *schwarzebroit* as having "everything in it except the kitchen sink," which, in *shtetl* terms, meant that it was generally made out of various odds and ends that were left over in bakeries, food stores, and pantries. It is ironic but not difficult to understand that in the *shtetl*, bread made from white flour was given a very high status and considered "rich person's bread," whereas the much tastier and healthier dark breads were considered "peasant" or "workingman's" breads. Many Jewish homes would adopt the custom of serving the dark breads on weekdays and the white bread, usually *challah*, on Sabbaths and festivals. It was probably a blessing from God that the poorer people ate black bread instead of white bread every day because it is so much more nourishing. The rich black bread was often the only food the poorest people had to make a meal of.

Today, black breads have really come into their own and are accorded a much higher status due to the healthy, fiber-laden ingredients that go into them. Jewish pumpernickel is, in my opinion, the tastiest of any of the dark breads. It is especially delicious with main-dish soups and salads or in various kinds of sandwiches. It is beautiful to look at as well as delicious. We had an elderly neighbor whose idea of a "little piece of heaven" was nothing more than a slice of rich *schwarzebroit* spread with *schmaltz* and topped with some thinly sliced raw red onion. And he lived to be a healthy 96 years old!

3 1/2 to 4 cups unbleached white bread flour
2 cups whole wheat bread flour
4 cups rye flour
2 pkg. freeze-dried yeast

1/2 cup lukewarm water
2 cups strong black coffee
1 Tblsp. coarse or kosher salt
2 Tblsp. sugar
1/3 cup dark molasses
1/3 cup corn or peanut oil
1 Tblsp. cider vinegar
1/4 cup unsweetened cocoa
2 Tblsp. caraway (*kimmel*) seeds
1 very small finely grated onion
cornmeal for sprinkling top and bottom of
   bread
1 egg white mixed with 1 Tblsp. cold water
   (egg-white wash)

1. Mix the water and 1 tsp. sugar together with the yeast and set aside in a draft-free spot to proof (about 10 minutes).

2. Mix together the coffee, molasses, salt, oil, remaining sugar, vinegar, cocoa, and grated onion in a small bowl.

3. In a large mixing bowl or in a food processor or in an electric mixer with dough attachment, mix the rye, whole wheat, and 2 cups of the white flour together. Mix in the coffee and yeast mixtures and *kimmel* seeds and knead together by hand, by machine, or by a combination of the two. Add the remaining white flour as you knead the dough. Keep on adding flour until you are able to knead the dough without having large amounts of it sticking to your fingers. Even if you begin the kneading process for this bread by machine, I recommend that you finish by hand. The dough will be heavy and rather sticky. Do not add too much white flour or you will have loaves that are too heavy and dry. Pumpernickel dough, like that for rye bread, is quite a bit stickier than the one for white bread or potato bread. The more times you make this bread, the more you will develop a feel in your hands for when to stop adding flour. Don't get discouraged if it doesn't work perfectly the first few times.

4. Pumpernickel dough needs about 20 minutes of kneading before it can be turned out into a well-greased bowl. Cover the dough with a damp kitchen cloth and set it aside in a draft-free place to rise. Allow at least 3 hours for the first rising. Pumpernickel dough will not rise as high as dough made of white flour. Test for doneness by gently pushing a finger into the risen dough. If it doesn't spring back, rising is completed.

5. Punch the dough down with your fist and cut it into two parts. Shape the dough into round or oblong shapes. Place them on baking sheets that are well greased and spread with yellow cornmeal. If you wish to bake the loaves in loaf pans, grease them well first and spread cornmeal along the bottom and sides of the pans. Cover the loaves again with the damp kitchen cloth and set aside to rise. Second rising will take 1 hour.

6. Preheat oven to 350°. Using a serrated knife, slash diagonal slits into oblong loaves or cut a cross into round loaves. Brush with egg-white wash and, if you wish, sprinkle yellow cornmeal over the tops. Baking time is approximately 1 hour. After 45 minutes, test for doneness by tapping the bottom of one loaf. If it sounds hollow, bread has finished baking. If not, give it another 10 or 15 minutes and test again. Cool before slicing and serving. Recipe yields 2 loaves.

Bialys

Bialys are delicious round, rather flat, sort of *pletzel*-shaped rolls. They are named after the city of Bialystok in northeastern Poland and were a specialty of the Jews of this region. *Bialys* are one of the best sandwich breads ever created. To make sandwiches out of them, they are simply sliced in half across the middle lengthwise and filled with any sandwich filling desired—cold cuts and vegetables, *liptavsky kayz*, lox and cream cheese, chopped egg and onion, and the like. The closest food I have ever found to resemble *bialys* is the flat, crusty, round miniloaves of Italian bread made in New Orleans and used to make those wonderful New Orleans deli sandwiches called "muffalattas."

My grandmother made two kinds of *bialys*—one with an onion and poppy seed topping and one with a sugar topping. The *bialys* with the onion topping were generally used for meat sandwiches (salami, corned beef, pastrami), lox and cream cheese, chopped egg and onion, or smoked fish sandwiches. The sweet *bialys* with the sugar topping were for the kind of sandwiches served with tea—plain farmer cottage cheese, cream cheese, or just sweet butter and jam.

1 recipe *challah* dough (see p. 16)
1 egg beaten with 1 Tblsp. cold water (egg wash)
4 cups chopped onion (for onion *bialys*)

3 Tblsp. corn or peanut oil (for onion *bialys*)
poppy seeds for sprinkling (for onion *bialys*)
1/3 cup granulated sugar (for sugar *bialys*)
1/4 tsp. cinnamon (optional; for sugar *bialys*)

1. Divide the dough into 16 pieces and shape each piece into a round ball. Flatten one ball in the palm of your hand and roll it out to 1/4-inch thickness. Place the flattened roll on a well-greased baking sheet. You will need 4 baking sheets. Repeat this procedure with all 16 pieces of dough. When you have finished, you should have 4 baking sheets with 4 rolls on each. Cover the breads with damp kitchen cloths and leave to rise for 30 to 45 minutes. Breads will be double in size. To test for doneness, press one *bialy* with a finger. If it doesn't spring back, rising is complete.

2. If making onion *bialys*, sauté the onions in the oil until translucent. Set aside. Preheat oven to 350°.

3. After the breads have risen, brush egg wash over them and top with one of the two toppings. Onion *bialys* are topped with a little of the sautéed onions and sprinkled with poppy seeds. Sugar *bialys* are sprinkled with sugar or with a mixture of sugar and cinnamon.

4. Bake the *bialys* at 350° for 20 to 25 minutes or until rolls are nicely browned and sound hollow when tapped on the bottom. Cool before serving. Do not bake sugar *bialys* and onion *bialys* in the same oven or at the same time because they will absorb aromas from each other and both will taste bad. Recipe makes 16 *bialys*.

Serving Suggestions

To make sandwiches from *bialys*, simply cut them in half across the middle lengthwise and insert sandwich filling. Sandwiches may then be cut in half, in quarters, or into 6 or 8 wedges as tea or luncheon sandwiches. These are wonderful on party or buffet trays. Onion *bialys* also make excellent hamburger buns. To do this, just make the *bialys* half the size of that given in the recipe above. One recipe of *challah* dough will yield about 30 hamburger-bun-size onion *bialys*.

Pletzel

Pletzel is a flat, hard, cracker-like onion-and-poppy-seed bread that is delicious served with sweet butter or cream cheese. It is equally wonderful as an accompaniment to *forspeissen* like chopped liver, chopped egg and onion, or *liptavsky kayz*. *Pletzel* is traditionally made with *challah* dough. Both home cooks and professional Jewish bakers make their *pletzel* out of dough that is left over from a batch of *challah*.

The word *pletzel* in Yiddish means "wooden plank," and the shape of *pletzel* is similar to this. People who don't like *pletzel* say that it also tastes like a wooden plank. Nothing, of course, could be further from the truth! What strange notions these people have who have been reared on corn flakes and white bread! *Pletzel* is also a humorous generic term in the Yiddish language for anything "flat as a board" (a flat-topped hat, a flat-topped hairdo, a cake that did not sufficiently rise, etc.). Once you have had your first *pletzel*, you'll be permanently addicted to it and if you eat it often, I promise you'll never have to buy a set of false teeth.

1 recipe *challah* dough (p. 16)
4 cups onions
2 Tblsp. poppy seeds
3 Tblsp. corn or peanut oil
1 egg, beaten with 1 Tblsp. cold water (egg wash)

1. Sauté the onions in the oil until tender and translucent.

2. Cut dough into four parts. Using a rolling pin, roll out each piece of dough on a floured board into a flat rectangular or oval shape to no more than 1/4-inch thickness (less thick is even better!). Place each piece of dough on a well-greased baking sheet.

3. Preheat the oven to 350°. Brush the beaten egg over each piece of dough. Top with 1 cup sautéed onions and sprinkle with poppy seeds. Pierce each *pletzel* all over with the tines of a fork.

4. Bake each *pletzel* for 35 to 40 minutes or until onions are nicely browned and bread is crisp and golden brown at the edges. Cool before serving.

Serving *Pletzel*

Pletzel does not break apart into neat, even-shaped pieces. A properly baked *pletzel* never crumbles apart, either. It cracks just like a crisp cracker. To serve *pletzel* you may either place it unbroken on a large, flat bread board or platter and pass it around for each diner to break off a piece, or you may presnap pieces of *pletzel* and serve it in a breadbasket.

Bagels

Az me esst op di gantzeh bagel, bleibt in di kesheneh di loch!

If you eat up the entire bagel at once, all you'll have left in your pocket is the hole!

— Yiddish proverb

No Jewish bread or, for that matter, no Jewish food is as well known or as popular as the bagel. Many Americans who have never met a Jewish person know all about bagels and eat them regularly. Bagels are as much standard American fare as hot dogs, hamburgers, and pizza. I would not be surprised if a large number of Americans have no idea that bagels are a Jewish food that was brought to this country by Yiddish-speaking immigrants from eastern Europe.

The word *bagel* is German for bracelet or ring, and less than a century ago in some parts of eastern Europe, bagels were considered *mazeldik* ("full of God-given good luck") because they were round— the perfect form, with no beginning and no end. Bagels were often used as amulets that were reputed to have amazing protective powers. Bagels were said to ward off demons and evil spirits, particularly the *ayin hora* (the "evil eye"). They were also said to be a blessing for prosperity for whoever ate them.

One of the first historical mentions of bagels is found in the community ledger of regulations for the city of Cracow, Poland, in the year 1610. There it states that bagels should be given to a woman in labor. Today bagels are still eaten with hard-boiled eggs after a funeral because their shape is said to symbolize the eternal cycle of life.

In the *shtetlach* of eastern Europe, there were special bagel sellers who carried long sticks with bagels strung over them through their holes. These bagel sellers would work the streets and market-places of the villages peddling their bagels. Among the many Jewish immigrants who came to America were bagel makers and bagel sellers who plied their trade from pushcarts on the Lower East Side of Manhattan and in similar neighborhoods across the country. In Israel today, you can still see bagel peddlers, but the bagels themselves taste very different from the eastern European variety. Israeli *bagellim* are really a Middle Eastern snack rather than the more familiar eastern European Jewish bread.

During the 10-year period of my life that I lived in Montreal, Quebec, I got to know and taste what I consider the best bagels I have ever eaten. There were two different bagel bakeries there that manufactured these bagels. Each claimed to be the city's first bagel bakery. Both were open during the wee hours of the morning, when customers would line up outdoors even in the most frigid, below-zero weather to buy their bags of freshly baked bagels and bring them home. The aromas that wafted out into the street from these two wonderful business establishments were sumptuous and enticing beyond description. And you could watch the entire process of bagel making right there from where you stood, including seeing the bakers remove the finished bagels from the deep clay ovens in which they had been baked. Ahhh!

If you do not live in Montreal or in a city where bagels of similar fine quality are available, you must try to bake your own. Not only is it lots of fun, but the difference in flavor and texture will make you permanently hooked!

The following recipe is actually two recipes in one. The optional eggs are used in making egg bagels. To make plain bagels, just leave the eggs out of the dough.

5 to 5 1/2 cups unbleached white bread flour
2 tsp. salt
2 pkg. freeze-dried yeast
1/4 cup sugar
2 large eggs (egg bagels only)
3 Tblsp. corn or peanut oil (egg bagels only)
1 cup lukewarm water or potato water
1 egg white mixed with 1 Tblsp. cold water
  (egg-white wash)
poppy or sesame seeds for sprinkling
3 quarts boiling water

1. Mix 1 tsp. sugar with the water or potato water and stir in the yeast. Set aside in a draft-free place to proof (about 10 minutes).

2. Mix together the flour, salt, and remaining sugar in a food processor or electric mixer with dough attachment or in a large mixing bowl.

3. Add the yeast mixture (and eggs and oil, if using) and knead by machine, by hand, or by a combination of the two about 15 minutes or until the dough has the right consistency. It should feel moist and spongy but not sticky. If necessary, add flour to achieve the correct consistency. Place it in a well-greased bowl and cover with a damp kitchen cloth. Let rise in a draft-free place until the dough is double in bulk (about 1 1/2 hours).

Peddling bagels on a street that is off limits to Jews. Warsaw, 1937.
(Photograph by Roman Vishniac.)

4. Punch down the dough and knead again until all air is pressed out and the dough is smooth.

5. Divide the dough into 12 equal parts and roll each into a ball. Poke a hole with your thumb through the center of one ball. You now have a small, tight-fitting ring of dough. Twirl the ring of dough around your finger to widen the hole. With two or more fingers of one hand placed inside the ring of dough, rub and roll it with both hands to produce a nice, rounded cylindrical shape, something like a doughnut. Do not be too fussy about getting a perfect doughnut shape, however. Real bagels do not have to be perfectly doughnut-shaped. Repeat this procedure with every ball of dough and set the finished bagels aside to rise for 1 hour. Cover with a damp cloth.

6. After the water has come to a boil, slide 3 or 4 bagels into it and boil them for 1 minute. Turn them over and boil them 1 minute longer. Remove the bagels with a slotted spoon and put them on a board to dry. Repeat this procedure with the rest of the bagels. The boiling gives the bagels their characteristic chewy texture. Do not boil too long or bagels will be too chewy.

7. Preheat oven to 425°. Place bagels on well-greased baking sheets. Brush with egg-white wash and sprinkle with poppy or sesame seeds. Bake 20 minutes or until golden brown. Cool before serving. Recipe makes 16 to 18 bagels.

Variations

Bagels can be made of any of the other bread doughs as well. Just follow the instructions above for shaping, boiling, and baking given in this recipe, steps 5 through 7.

The Man from Outer Space

A man from outer space once landed in the middle of a city and was found staring into the window of a bakery shop, fascinated. The owner of the bakery invited him to come in and asked him, finally, what he found so interesting.

Freshly baked bagles at the St. Viateur Bagel Bakery. Montreal, 1992.

"What are those little round wheels sitting in the window?" asked the visitor.

"Wheels? What wheels?" asked the puzzled shopkeeper. The spaceman pointed toward a display shelf. "Oh, those! Those are called bagels. We eat them. Here. Try one."

The spaceman bit into a bagel and smacked his lips happily. "Mmmm . . . delicious. I bet they'd taste wonderful with cream cheese and lox!"

Bulkes

Bulke is the Yiddish word for "roll." These instructions are for making dinner rolls out of any of the Jewish bread recipes that appear in this cookbook (other than the recipe for bagels, which must be treated separately). To make *bulkes*, all you have to remember is that any of the bread recipes will produce between 16 and 20 *bulkes*. The following diagrams are for various-shaped *bulkes*.

Knot-Shaped *Bulkes*

Use the photograph sequence below to help you shape the *bulkes*. Take pieces of dough that are approximately 8 inches long and 1 inch wide (Fig. 1). Cross one side over the other. You are left with a small hole in the middle (Fig. 2). Take the tip of the higher half and bend it toward the lower half, filling the hole and sticking it up a little at the top (Fig. 3). Try making this type of *bulke* with *challah*, pumpernickel, *weinerbroit*, or potato bread dough.

Cloverleaf-Shaped *Bulkes*

Follow the directions in the photographic sequence on page 31 to make these bulkes. Take small pieces of dough, each about 8 inches long and 1 inch wide, and divide them into three parts. Roll each part into a ball and place it in a greased muffin tin (Fig. 1). Three balls, after rising and baking, produce one cloverleaf-shaped *bulke*. Try making this out of each of the potato breads or out of *weinerbroit*.

Minibraids

The photographic sequence found on p. 18 under the directions for shaping a three-rope braid can be

Knot-Shaped *Bulkes*

Step 1

Step 2

Step 3

Cloverleaf-Shaped *Bulkes*

Step 1

Step 2

Step 3

used to help you shape minibraids. Take small pieces of dough approximately 9 inches long and 1 inch wide and divide them into three parts. Shape into ropes, and braid as you would for braided *challah*. Make this kind of *bulke* out of any of the bread recipes, but especially *challah*.

Miniature *Faiglan*

The sequence of photographs on p. 20 for making regular *faiglan* for Sukkos may be used to help you learn how to shape miniature *faiglan*. Take small pieces of dough 8 inches long and 1 inch wide and roll them into ropes approximately 8 to 10 inches

long, with one end wider than the other. Take the thicker end and wind the rest around it two or three times, making a round, spiral shape. This *bulke* is delicious made with any of the bread recipes (*challah*, potato bread, rye, *weinerbroit*, or pumpernickel).

To bake *bulkes*, cover the baking pans or, in the case of cloverleaf *bulkes*, the muffin tins full of rolls with damp kitchen cloths and allow 20 to 30 minutes for them to rise. You may brush them with either egg wash or egg-white wash if you wish, and you may sprinkle them with poppy, sesame, or *kimmel* seeds. Bake *bulkes* for 20 minutes at 350°. Like all breads, they are done when they sound hollow after being tapped on the bottom.

Photographic still life by Henrietta Komras Sternberg.

Lag B'Omer Picnic

Chilled *schav* (fresh sorrel soup)

Finger wedge sandwiches on onion *bialys* made of

liptauer cheese, smoked fish, and summer chopped egg salad

Beet and cucumber salad

Assorted fresh fruit

Three kinds of Aunt Ann's cookies:

Sugar cookies

Oatmeal cookies

Peanut butter cookies

Iced tea and iced coffee

3

Appetizers

Forspeizen

Another person's appetizer tastes good.

A fremdeh forspeis shmekt ziss.

Gefilte Fisch

There are no dishes more closely linked in the minds of European Jews with celebrating the Sabbath than chicken soup and *gefilte fisch*. In turn-of-the-century Jewish homes, no Friday night ever went by without every family member having a taste of *gefilte fisch*.

The tradition of eating fish on the Sabbath goes back to Jewish mystical teachings. There it was taught that fish are metaphysically linked to the coming of the Messiah. An old legend recounts that the Messiah will come to the people of Israel in the form of a giant fish from the sea, called the Leviathan, and that every righteous person will be able to eat of its flesh.

Over the centuries, the practice of eating a piece of fish as part of the Sabbath meal has become an accepted ritual—a kind of culinary declaration of hope for peace and harmony in the days to come, when every day of the week will be as peaceful and joyous as the Sabbath.

The actual recipe for *gefilte fisch* grew out of poverty. Fresh fish, in eastern Europe, is difficult to come by, even in the Baltic countries, and what is available is very expensive. Even the poorest Jews wanted to have a piece of fish every week in honor of the Sabbath. So a recipe was developed over time as a kind of "fish stretcher" in which the meat of the fish is ground together with onions and mixed with eggs, seasonings, *matzoh* meal or crumbs, and maybe a little grated carrot. Then it would be shaped into patties and cooked. In this way, a small quantity of fish could be made to go a long way and create enough food to give everybody at least a taste of fish for Sabbath. In medieval times, the making of *gefilte fisch* was very elaborate, and the medieval recipe, in fact, is the one that gave the dish its name. In this recipe, a whole carp would be boned, with the head and part of the tail left intact. The meat would be scraped from the skin and then ground and mixed with the other ingredients. This mixture would then be stuffed back into the skin of the fish before cooking. Hence, the name *gefilte fisch*, which means stuffed or filled fish.

Even in more recent times, some elaborate and attractive versions of *gefilte fisch* have been prepared. An eastern European recipe for *chasseneh fisch* ("wedding fish") called for boning a large pike, leaving its head attached, stuffing it with a traditional *gefilte fisch* mixture, and then poaching the whole fish in stock in the usual way. The fish would then be sliced into attractive portions and regally displayed on a large platter before being served as a *forspeis* at a wedding dinner.

It is unfortunate that the art of preparing homemade *gefilte fisch* is neglected by today's cooks. Far too many young American Jews have never had the opportunity to taste the authentic version of this old beloved Jewish dish. The main problem is that *gefilte fisch* had become so popular in the 1940s and '50s that commercial suppliers began packaging it in jars and cans and it was turned into a kind of Jewish convenience food. Canned and jugged *gefilte fisch* is readily available today in any supermarket where kosher foods are sold. The taste of these products, however, cannot be compared with the homemade. What a pity—especially since homemade *gefilte fisch* is really so easy to make if you buy the ground-fish mixture from a reliable Jewish supplier like your neighborhood kosher butcher.

I have a special childhood memory of *gefilte fisch* being made in my grandmother's house. Thursday was her day for making the *Shabbos* fish. Up until the time I was 6 or 7 years old, I remember her bringing home live fish on Thursday morning and putting them into the bathtub. She would begin the cooking process by taking one live fish after the other out on to the back porch while it was still writhing and flopping around and give it a "klop" over the head with a hammer to stun it. She would then proceed to clean, gut, and scale the fish, wrapping the discarded material into old newspapers. After washing and drying the cleaned and scaled fish very carefully, she would bone them and separate the meat from the skin. The bones, heads, and tails would be put into a large stockpot with celery, onions, and carrots and made into *fisch yoich*. My grandmother had a special hand-operated meat grinder attached to a huge enameled tub that was large enough to double as a baby's bathtub. The fish and onions were ground into this tub, and then all the other ingredients were mixed into it. My job was handing her pieces of fish and onion to grind, and sometimes, if I was lucky, she would let me help her shape the fish into patties.

Here are two different recipes for *gefilte fisch*. The first, which is the nonsweet version, is my grandmother's recipe and was made by the Jews who came from *Litteh* and the Ukraine. The second, or sweet, version comes from *Galitzia* and was popular among the Jews of southern and central Poland as well as those of Budapest and Vienna. Both are delicious.

Recipe 1: *Litvishe Gefilte Fisch*

For the stock

4 stalks celery, cut in pieces
2 large onions, peeled and quartered
6 carrots, cut in pieces
several heads and bones of fish, preferably carp
2 Tblsp. coarse or kosher salt
1 Tblsp. sugar
4 whole black peppercorns
cold water to cover all the ingredients by 1 to 1
    1/2 inches

Bring contents of the stockpot to boil over medium heat. Reduce heat and partially cover the pot. Cook for 45 minutes at a steady simmer. Strain stock and discard everything except the fish heads. These are considered a delicacy by those who enjoy them, so refrigerate them and serve together with the *gefilte fisch.*

For the fish patties

3 lb. carp or buffalo, boned and skinned
1 1/2 lb. pike, boned and skinned
1 1/2 lb. whitefish, boned and skinned
4 onions, peeled
1 Tblsp. coarse or kosher salt
1 tsp. black pepper (some like white pepper
    because the color disappears into the patties)
1 tsp. sugar
4 eggs
1 cup *matzoh* meal
3/4 cup stock from the fish stock just made
2 large carrots, peeled

1. Grind fish in meat grinder using the fine blade or in the food processor using a pulse/chop motion. Do not grind it too finely. Place into a large mixing bowl.

2. Grate onions and one of the carrots in the same way and add to the fish.

3. Add the remaining ingredients, except for the last carrot. Blend by hand very carefully and thoroughly. Some cooks prefer to begin chopping the fish in the Cuisinart and to finish by hand using an old-fashioned *hockmesser*, which is a kind of chopping blade or knife similar to a cleaver. This is, of course, more work and, in my opinion, not really necessary as long as you are careful not to create too fine a texture when you process it in the food processor.

4. Peel the remaining carrot and slice it very thinly into rounds.

5. Pour the fish stock into the fish poacher or large stockpot. Bring it to a gentle boil and cover the pot. Have a bowl of cold water next to you. Wet your hands and take 1/2 cup of the fish mixture into your wet hands. Shape it into a fat, oval-shaped patty. Press a thin round of carrot into the center of the patty and then lay it onto a large platter. Repeat this procedure until all the fish mixture is used up. You will have between 20 and 24 patties. If you are using a stockpot, there is a good chance that the decorative slice of carrot that was placed into the fish patty will fall out during cooking. Do not worry about this because it will not lose its shape as it cooks and can be retrieved and replaced after the fish balls have cooked completely. Also, you may have to cook the fish in two batches if using a fish poacher. If you do, refrigerate the uncooked patties until you are ready for the second round of cooking.

6. Lower the patties into the fish poacher. Be sure that the liquid in the fish poacher covers the patties. Add water if it does not. If using a stockpot, gently lower each patty into the simmering stock.

7. Reduce heat to simmer, and cover the fish poacher or stockpot. Simmer gently for 2 hours. Remove pot from heat and cool, partly uncovered, to room temperature. Remove *gefilte fisch* from the pot and arrange attractively on a platter. Replace any carrot rounds that have fallen off during cooking. Ladle a small amount of stock over the patties— enough to lightly glaze them without overflowing off the platter. Chill in the refrigerator before serving. Ladle the stock into a container and chill in the refrigerator separately. When chilled, it makes a lovely aspic to serve alongside the fish.

Serving Suggestions

Gefilte fisch may be served directly from the platter on which it has chilled or on individual serving plates. Serve some of the aspic with the fish. *Gefilte fisch* is traditionally served with *chrain* (see recipe p. 7). Serve the *chrain* in a glass container and pass it around the table, allowing diners to take their own portions.

Recipe 2: *Galitzianer Gefilte Fisch*

Galitzianer gefilte fisch differs from *Litvishe gefilte fisch* in the following ways:

1. More sugar is used in the fish stock. Increase the sugar from 1 tsp. to 3 Tblsp.
2. No pepper is used in *Galitzianer gefilte fisch*. Delete it from the recipe when making this version.
3. *Galitzianer gefilte fisch* patties are sweet. Increase sugar in recipe from 1 tsp. to 1/3 cup.

Prepare *Galitzianer gefilte fisch* in every other respect the same way you prepare *Litvishe gefilte fisch* and serve it the same way.

Herring *Forspeizen*

B'mokom she'eyn ish iz a herring oich a fisch!

In a place where people don't live, a herring is also a fish!
— Yiddish witticism

Herring was so inexpensive and so popular in eastern Europe that practically everybody ate it at least once a week. For the poor in particular, it was often the only kind of fish that was affordable. This was probably the condition that gave birth to this caustic witticism. Despite this, herring is delicious, if somewhat an acquired taste.

The following *forspeizen* all feature herring in some form. Herring was popular throughout eastern Europe, but it was most popular in Litteh. All of the herring *forspeizen* in this book are recipes from Litteh, my grandmother's place of birth. These herring dishes can be served as single appetizers, or you may combine two or three different kinds in one meal as long as the flavors are compatible with each other and with whatever else is being served. A *milchige* buffet table, for Lithuanian Jews, always has at least two kinds of herring dishes on it. The best drink to serve with these dishes is an ice-cold double shot of vodka, schnapps, or *vishnyek*. For something a little different, try one of the Polish or Russian flavored vodkas or Scandinavian aquavit with a glass of beer.

Litvishe Marinated Herring

4 *schmaltz* herrings
2 medium-size sweet red onions, peeled and thinly sliced
2 tart green apples, cored and thinly sliced
1 large lemon, washed and thinly sliced
2 cups cold water
3/4 cup cider vinegar
1/2 cup sugar
12 whole allspice
8 whole black peppercorns
2 bay leaves
2 tsp. mustard seeds
2 tsp. dill seeds

1. Soak the herring in cold water to cover in the refrigerator for at least 48 hours, changing the water several times to remove the salt that has preserved the herring. Then wash and dry the herring.
2. Mix water, vinegar, and sugar in a deep saucepan and bring to a boil. Boil 5 minutes and remove from the heat. Set this marinade aside to cool to room temperature.
3. Meanwhile, prepare the herring by cutting it into 1 1/2-inch pieces. You may fillet the herring before cutting it or leave it whole with bones in. There is no difference in flavor, only in visual effect.
4. Layer the herring, onions, apples, and lemon slices in a deep glass bowl or a large glass preserving jar that will hold it all. Conclude the layering with onions and lemon slices rather than with herring. Sprinkle each layer with some of the whole pickling spices. End with a layer of onions and lemon slices at the top of the jar. Pour the marinade over all of this. Marinate in the refrigerator for at least 24 hours before serving. The marinated herring keeps well for at least 1 week in the refrigerator. Recipe serves 10 to 12 people as a *forspeis*.

Serving Suggestions

Serve this dish exactly as it is in a deep glass bowl when serving it as part of a buffet. When serving as a *forspeis*, place 2 or 3 fillets on each serving plate. Garnish with pickled beet slices (p.   ) and thinly sliced fresh red onion rings, and serve rye or pumpernickel bread on the side. Leave the onions, apples, and lemon slices from the jar in the jar. They render their flavor into the marinade and are not meant to be eaten.

Sweet-and-Sour Marinated Herring

Ziss und Zoyer Marinirte Herring

3 *schmaltz* herrings
2 cups cold water
2 large sweet red onions, peeled and thinly sliced
2 large tart green apples, cored and thinly sliced
1/2 cup dark raisins
1/3 cup brown sugar
1 stick cinnamon
1 large lemon, washed and thinly sliced
1 2-inch piece fresh ginger, peeled and thinly sliced into rounds

1. Soak the herrings for 48 hours in cold water to cover in the refrigerator, changing the water several times. This is to remove the salt in which it has been preserved. Then wash and dry the herrings, fillet them, and cut the fillets into 1-inch pieces.

2. Mix together the sugar and water in a deep saucepan and bring it to boil. Add cinnamon, ginger, and raisins. Cook about 10 minutes and remove from the heat. Cool to room temperature.

3. Layer a large glass preserving jar or a deep glass bowl with the herring slices, apple slices, lemon slices, and raisins. Pour the marinade over them. Cover tightly and refrigerate for at least 24 hours before serving. The herring keeps fresh in the refrigerator for at least a week. Recipe serves 10 to 12 people.

Serving Suggestions

This marinated herring may be served exactly as it is in a deep glass bowl as part of a buffet table. When serving as a *forspeis*, place 4 or 5 pieces on each serving dish and garnish with thinly sliced pieces of fresh lemon.

Herring in Sour Cream Sauce

Recipe 1: Herring in Sour Cream with Apples (*Herring mit Smetane und Eppl*)

2 *schmaltz* or *matjes* herrings

2 medium-size mild red onions, peeled and very thinly sliced
1 large tart green apple, peeled and thinly sliced or chopped
1 cup sour cream
1 tsp. dry mustard
1 Tblsp. sugar
1/4 cup fresh lemon juice

1. If using *schmaltz* herring, soak in cold water to cover in the refrigerator for at least 48 hours, changing the water several times. This removes the salt in which it has been preserved. If using *matjes* herring, salt-removal time is much shorter. Cover the herrings with cold water for 3–5 hours in the refrigerator. After this process is completed, wash and dry the herrings and fillet them. Cut the fillets into 1-inch pieces.

2. In a small bowl, mix together the sugar, mustard, lemon juice, and 1/3 cup of the sour cream. Blend it together by stirring vigorously until the sour cream begins to foam. Add the remaining sour cream and whip with a wire whisk.

3. In a deep glass or ceramic bowl, mix together the herring pieces, onion slices, and apple pieces. Pour the sour cream mixture over this and stir with a wooden spoon until thoroughly mixed. Cover and chill several hours before serving. Recipe serves 8 to 10 people as a *forspeis*. Serve exactly as is on a buffet table. No garnish is needed.

Recipe 2: Herring in Sour Cream with Dill (*Herring mit Smetane und Kropp*)

2 *schmaltz* or *matjes* herrings
2 small red onions, peeled and very thinly sliced
1 cup sour cream
1/4 cup fresh lemon juice
1 Tblsp. sugar
1/4 cup chopped fresh dill leaves

1. Prepare herrings as directed above in recipe 1.

2. Using a wire whisk, whisk together sugar, lemon juice, and sour cream until thoroughly blended. Add dill leaves and whisk again until all ingredients are well combined.

3. In a deep glass or ceramic bowl, mix together herring fillets and onion slices. Pour sour cream mixture over all and stir with a wooden spoon until

blended. Chill at least 3 hours before serving. Serves 8 to 10 people as a *forspeis*.

Serving Suggestions

Follow the instructions given in recipe 1.

Variations

Acceptable variations of these two dishes can be made with the herring in wine sauce that is sold in most supermarkets. Simply substitute 2 16-oz. jars of this herring for the *schmaltz* or *matjes* herring in the recipe. To make herring in sour cream sauce this way, first separate the herring pieces completely from the rest of the contents of the jars and place them in a colander. Discard everything else that was in the jars. Wash and dry the herring pieces to rid them of the taste of the vinegar in which they have been marinating. After you have dried the herring pieces, proceed as directed in the recipes above.

Tomato Herring

Herring in Pomidoren Zoss

3 *schmaltz* herrings
2 tart green apples, cored, peeled, and chopped
1 1/2 cups fresh tomato sauce
2 medium-size onions, peeled and very thinly sliced
1 bay leaf
black pepper to taste

1. Soak herrings in cold water to cover in the refrigerator for 48 hours, changing the water several times. When this process is complete, wash and dry the herring and fillet it.
2. Put apples, onions, bay leaf, and tomato sauce in a saucepan. Bring to a boil over medium heat. Cook 10 to 15 minutes or until onions soften and apples begin to disintegrate. Remove from heat and cool to room temperature. Add freshly ground black pepper to taste.
3. Put herring pieces into a deep ceramic or glass bowl or a large glass preserving jar with a tight-fitting lid. Pour tomato marinade over herring, sprinkle with black pepper, mix this in, and chill 3 to 4 hours before serving. Tomato herring keeps well in the refrigerator for about a week. Serves 8 to 10 people as a *forspeis*.

Serving Suggestions

Tomato herring may be served by itself as part of a buffet table or on individual plates as a *forspeis*. If you wish, garnish with thinly sliced English cucumber. Pumpernickel bread is an excellent accompaniment.

Matjes Herring in Olive Oil

3 *matjes* herrings
2 red onions, peeled and very thinly sliced
12 black peppercorns
2 bay leaves
olive oil to cover

1. Soak herrings in cold water to cover for 3 or 4 hours. Rinse and dry, fillet, and cut fillets into 1-inch pieces.
2. Place herring pieces and onions in layers in sterilized mason jars with tight-fitting lids. Place 6 peppercorns and 1 bay leaf in each jar and fill with olive oil up to the top, until fish is covered. Cover each jar tightly and marinate in the refrigerator at least one week before serving. This herring will keep a very long time in the refrigerator. Recipe makes 2 quart-size jars of herring and serves 10 to 12 people as a *forspeis*.

Serving Suggestions

Herring in olive oil is very versatile and can be served on its own or in combination with one of the other herring dishes. Pieces of herring in olive oil together with a small portion of beet greens salad (p. 225) make a wonderful hors d'oeuvre, especially to precede an entrée of baked or broiled fish.

Chopping Herring With Apples

Gehockte Herring

2 *schmaltz* herrings
2 slices pumpernickel bread
1/4 cup fresh lemon juice

2 Tblsp. cold water
1 medium-size red onion, peeled
2 tart green apples, peeled, cored, and chopped
2 hard-boiled eggs
1 Tblsp. sugar
4 Tblsp. corn oil
black pepper to taste

1. Soak herrings in cold water to cover in the refrigerator for at least 48 hours, changing the water every few hours. This removes the salt used to preserve the herring. After doing this, wash, dry, and fillet the herring. If you wish, you may remove the skin of the fish before proceeding to the next step.

2. In a food processor or blender or in a meat grinder with a fine blade, grate the onion. If you do not own any of these appliances, grate the onion by hand. Process the remaining ingredients in the food processor, blender, or meat grinder and mix everything together. Make sure that the mixture is chopped rather than pureed. Chopped herring, like chopped liver, should have a rather coarse texture.

3. Refrigerate at least 3 hours before serving. Chopped herring keeps at least a week in the refrigerator. Recipe serves 8 to 10 people.

Serving Suggestions

Garnish each portion of chopped herring with thinly sliced, unpeeled tart green apple slices and serve with pumpernickel bread. Chopped herring is also a good buffet table dish or cocktail spread.

Chopped Egg Salad with Onion and *Schmaltz*

Gehockte Ayer Mit Tzibbeles

6 hard-boiled eggs
2 medium onions, finely chopped
3 scallions, including 1 inch of greens, finely
    chopped
4 Tblsp. *schmaltz*
salt and black pepper to taste
1 Tblsp. *gribenes* (optional)

1. Chop eggs by hand (do not use food processor) into small chunks and set aside in a bowl.

2. Heat *schmaltz* in a skillet over medium heat, and sauté onions until translucent and slightly browned.

3. Gently mix eggs and sautéed onions and stir in the remaining ingredients until just combined. Do not overmix. Recipe serves 6 people.

Serving Suggestions

This *forspeis* is excellent with *pletzel*, pumpernickel, *challah*, or *matzoh*. If you wish, you may garnish each portion with fresh tomatoes (in season) and thinly sliced English cucumber or with kosher dill pickles (p. 291) and pickled beets (p. 291).

Summertime Chopped Egg And Vegetable Salad

Zummerdige Gehockte Ayer Mit Tzibbeles

This variation on chopped egg and onion was made by Lithuanian Jews during the summer months, when fresh herbs and green beans were in season. It is a perfect light luncheon dish as well as a *forspeis*.

4 hard-boiled eggs
1 large onion, finely chopped
2 stalks celery, finely chopped
2 cups cooked fresh green beans
4 Tblsp. corn or peanut oil
2 Tblsp. chopped fresh parsley leaves
2 Tblsp. chopped fresh chives
2 Tblsp. chopped fresh dill leaves
salt and black pepper to taste

1. Sauté onions over medium heat in oil until translucent. Add celery and continue sautéing until celery begins to soften (about 10 minutes). Remove from heat and set aside.

2. Pulse/chop eggs and green beans in food processor or blender until nicely chopped.

3. In a mixing bowl, mix together the egg mixture, the onion mixture, and the herbs and seasonings until well blended. Refrigerate covered until ready to serve.

Serving Suggestions

This dish can be refrigerated in a mold and unmolded before serving. Its molded presentation is particularly attractive on a buffet table. When serving as a *forspeis*, garnish with fresh tomatoes (in season) or pickled beet slices (p. 291).

Russian Eggs

Russische Ayer

This dish is a carryover into Yiddish cuisine from czarist Russia. It is an elegant and somewhat rich presentation that was often part of the Russian appetizer course called *zakuskie* (a variety of appetizers served at once).

6 large hard-cooked eggs, shelled
4 oz. smoked sprats or kippered herring
2 Tblsp. freshly squeezed lemon juice
1 tsp. Dijon mustard
1/4 cup finely snipped chives
1/3 cup mayonnaise
1/4 tsp. hot paprika

1. Cut the eggs in half lengthwise and remove the yolks. Leave the whites alone, as they will serve as shells for the stuffing mixture.

2. Mash the yolks together with the sprats. Mix in the remaining ingredients.

3. Stuff this mixture into the egg-white shells. Each stuffed egg will have a heaping mound of the stuffing in it. Serve immediately or refrigerate until ready to serve.

Serving Suggestions

This dish is an excellent *forspeis* with just about any entrée. It is also marvelous as a cocktail appetizer or buffet dish. The eggs should be garnished with kosher dill pickles (p. 291), pickled beet slices (p. 291), anchovy fillets, and a thin slice of lemon.

Old Country Chopped Liver

Gehockte Leber

This *forspeis* is so simple and straightforward that it is underappreciated as the gourmet dish it really is. My general rules for making chopped liver are:

1. Use only chicken liver to make this dish. Do not use beef or calf liver. Their flavors are too strong.

2. Use *schmaltz*. Do not substitute oil or any other fat. If you are concerned about cholesterol, eat chopped liver less often, but eat the uncompromised version. Anyway, the amount of *schmaltz* per portion of chopped liver in this recipe is the equivalent of no more than one pat of butter.

3. Chop all the ingredients by hand rather than by machine. Chopped liver should not look like a puree or a pâté. In texture it resembles French pâté du campagne or the Quebecois rillets du gran'mère, coarse and rustic.

4. Eat it in small portions—it is very rich—and make it only for special occasions. Then you eat it less often and enjoy it more when you do.

1 lb. chicken livers (fresh, not previously frozen)
2 cups finely chopped onions
3 hard-boiled eggs
6 Tblsp. *schmaltz*
salt and black pepper to taste
a few *gribenes* (optional)

1. Preheat broiler to 500°. Broil livers on broiler rack 4 inches from the heat source for 3 minutes on each side. Remove from oven and finely chop livers.

2. Melt 6 Tblsp. *schmaltz* in skillet and sauté onions over medium/low heat until soft and just beginning to brown. Add chopped liver pieces and sauté 1 minute more. Remove from heat.

3. Pour contents of skillet into a mixing bowl. In a separate bowl, chop the eggs and add them to the liver mixture. Mix in the salt, pepper, and *gribenes* (if using). Mix everything together until well blended. Chill at least 3 hours in the refrigerator before serving.

Serving Suggestions

Serve small portions of chopped liver garnished with kosher dill pickles and pickled beet slices (p. 291)

during the winter. Garnish the liver with fresh tomato and English cucumber slices in the summer.

A medium-dry white wine, such as chardonnay,
goes very well with chopped liver. So does a white
zinfandel.

Liver Pâté à La Rothschild

The *shtetlach* of eastern Europe were full of very poor
people who resembled the famous characters of Yiddish literature, like Sholom Aleichem's Tevye and I.
L. Peretz's Bontsche Schweig. These hardworking
people literally struggled through life from meal to
meal. Most of them had very simple aspirations,
such as having a day just once in a while when they
could put a full three-course meal on the table for
their family. This was what they aspired to. Anybody who could do things like this more than once
in a while was considered "as rich as Rothschild."
Who was Rothschild?

The Rothschild family was a famous German
Jewish banking family that originally hailed from
Frankfurt. They were great philanthropists and
great patrons of the arts and sciences. The founder of
the Rothschild dynasty, Mayer Amschel Rothschild
(1744–1812), made his fortune dealing in antiques
and old coins. In 1769, the landgrave (a kind of
German nobleman or aristocrat) William IX of Hesse-
Kassel gave the title of baron to Rothschild, who
served as his financial adviser. This was the first time
in European history that a person of the Jewish faith
received such a title, the honor at that time being
reserved exclusively for Christians. The name *Rothschild* became a positive symbol in the Jewish community of what a Jew might hope to achieve in the
post-Renaissance Enlightenment—wealth, status,
and the ability to be involved in philanthropy on a
large scale.

The Rothschild symbol was particularly important to the Jews of eastern Europe, where entry into
non-Jewish society at any level was strictly denied
them. The Jew in Poland who moved from a *shtetl* to
a large city and built up a modest business was often
considered by old friends and acquaintances to have
become "as rich as Rothschild." A Yiddish-speaking
Jew who got a secular education and was able to
enter one of the professions (e.g., law, medicine,
science), however middle-class the income or life-

style might have been, was considered by peers a
part of the "intelligentsia" and, as such, "living the
life of a Rothschild." Any Jew who immigrated to
America, about which myths were circulated that
there was so much gold they actually paved streets
with it, was said to have become "another Rothschild." The word *Rothschild* became symbolic of
everything that was opulent, prestigious, and ex-
ceedingly rich. In Yiddish cuisine, the term "à la
Rothschild" connoted recipes that were ultrarefined
and developed in the homes of middle- and
upper-middle-class "city" Jews at the turn of the
century.

Some of these wonderful "à la Rothschild"
recipes, almost neglected and forgotten by modern
Jewish cooks, are reintroduced here. These dishes
are characterized by refinement of both techniques
and presentations and often by the judicious
inclusion of wine, liquor, or liqueurs in the recipes.
A few of the dishes are kosher variations of czarist
Russian or aristocratic Hungarian, Viennese, and
Polish dishes. I have given some of them distinctive
appellations like "à la Rothschild" to highlight their
origins. Liver pâté à la Rothschild is one of those
dishes.

**1 1/2 lb. chicken livers (fresh, not previously
  frozen)**
2 medium-size onions, peeled and chopped
**1 tart green cooking apple, peeled, cored, and
  chopped**
4 hard-boiled eggs, peeled and cut in pieces
salt and black pepper to taste
2 or 3 gratings fresh nutmeg
1/4 cup brandy or cognac
6 Tblsp. chicken *schmaltz*
**very thin slices of green and red apple for
  garnish**

1. Preheat the oven broiler to 500°. Broil the
livers 2 inches from the heat source for 1 1/2 minutes
on each side to make the liver kosher. Remove from
the oven and set aside to cool.

2. Melt the *schmaltz* in a skillet over medium
heat and sauté the onions until soft and translucent.
Add the apples and continue sautéing until the
apples soften (about 5 or 6 minutes).

3. Chop the livers into pieces, add them to the
onions and apples, and cook until heated through,
stirring constantly to make sure nothing gets too
brown.

4. Put the contents of the skillet into the food processor with the eggs, nutmeg, salt, and pepper, and process into a smooth puree. Add the brandy or cognac and process again until the liquor is incorporated and the puree is very smooth.

5. Put the contents of the food processor into a well-oiled mold or mixing bowl. Chill several hours before serving. Serve garnished with the apple slices.

Serving Suggestions

Liver pâté à la Rothschild is very rich and should be served in small portions with *challah*. It is a rich, elegant *forspeis* to serve on special occasions and goes particularly well with a meal whose main entrée is poultry. Try it as a *forspeis* with any of the following:

Hendel mit marantzen (p. 103)
Hendel mit getrukeneh flommen (p. 109)
Shtadlan's hendel (p. 114)
Roast duck with apples and pears (p. 121)
Roast turkey or goose with potato stuffing (p. 122)

Hungarian-Style Liver *Blintzes*

Ungarische Leber Blintzes

Liver *blintzes* are a rich and scrumptious Hungarian *forspeis* that should be enjoyed infrequently enough to warrant special commendation by your family or your guests whenever they are served. This is the perfect *forspeis* to accompany veal steaks *paprikash*, roast chicken with prunes, and many other elegant dishes. The liver *blintzes* taste wonderful with or without the poached apple sauce.

For *blintzes*

4 eggs
1/2 tsp. salt
1 cup water
1 cup unbleached white flour
peanut oil for sautéing

1. Mix together flour and salt. In a separate bowl, beat the eggs with a wire whisk and add the water. Beat thoroughly until water and eggs are completely mixed together.

2. Add flour mixture slowly, beating constantly with a wire whisk to make a smooth, thin batter.

3. Lightly grease a 6-inch skillet or crepe pan with oil and place over a moderately high heat. Pour 1/3 cup batter into a pan and spread quickly to make a rather thin crepe (*blintz*). If you find that 1/3 cup batter makes *blintzes* that are too thin or too thick, increase or decrease quantity accordingly.

4. Sauté *blintz* on one side only. When *blintz* begins to blister and the edges begin to curl away from the skillet, it is done. The center of the *blintz* may be slightly moist, but do not be concerned about this.

5. Turn *blintz* onto a cookie sheet or clean kitchen board with the moist side facing up and repeat this process until all the batter is used up. Lightly grease pan after every third *blintz*. Recipe should make about 16 to 18 *blintzes*.

For filling

1 1/2 lb. sliced calf liver
1 large onion, peeled and very finely chopped
6 Tblsp. *schmaltz*
salt and black pepper to taste

1. Broil liver for 3 minutes on each side to remove blood. Take out of the oven and cut into cubes.

2. Melt *schmaltz* in skillet and sauté onions until translucent and soft. Add liver cubes and sauté 5 minutes longer. Remove from heat and add salt and pepper.

3. Transfer the entire contents of the skillet to food processor or blender and puree until smooth. Set aside.

To Make the Blintzes

1. Place 1 heaping Tblsp. of filling slightly down from the center of each *blintz* and spread it lengthwise into a long, oval shape. Do not let the filling come too close to the edge of the *blintz*. Raise one flap of the dough over the filling lengthwise and cover it. Fold in the flaps on either side of the first fold, and roll the *blintz* into a cigar shape, jelly-roll fashion, toward the outer edge of the flap that has never been folded. When you are finished rolling the *blintz*, the never-folded flap will have been rolled to

the bottom. Place the rolled *blintz* into a well-greased baking dish.

2. Repeat this procedure with all the *blintzes* until they are all filled, folded, and rolled. Lightly brush the *blintzes* with peanut oil just before they are to be put into the oven.

3. Preheat oven to 425° and bake *blintzes*, uncovered, until they are brown (about 15 to 20 minutes). Serve immediately, either as they are or with the sauce.

For poached apple sauce

2 tart green apples, peeled, cored, and cubed
1/2 cup cold water
1/4 cup sugar
1 Tblsp. calvados or apple brandy

In a small saucepan, mix water and sugar together and bring to boil over high heat. When sugar is well dissolved, add apple cubes and reduce heat to medium. Cook until apples are soft and just beginning to disintegrate. Remove from heat and add calvados or apple brandy.

Serving Suggestions

Serve 2 *blintzes* per portion on individual serving dishes. Ladle sauce delicately across the center of the *blintzes* before serving. Recipe serves 8 to 10 people.

Liver *blintzes* are a very elegant hors d'oeuvre and very rich. This *forspeis* should be followed by something more simple and straightforward. It is not a good *forspeis* to precede a braised meat dish or a substantial one like a *tzimmes*. The exceptions to this rule are veal steaks *paprikash* and roast tongue in raisin sauce. When you serve liver *blintzes* with veal steaks *paprikash*, do not use the poached apple sauce. Try liver *blintzes* before any of the following:

Hungarian Style Stuffed Roast Chicken (p. 113)
Roast Chicken with Prunes (p. 109)
Hendel mit Marantzen (p. 103)
Roast Tongue with Raisin Sauce (p. 162)
Roast Veal with *Kimmel* (p. 142)
Veal Steaks *Paprikash* (p. 144)

A good-quality chardonnay is an excellent wine to serve with this *forspeis*.

Calf's Foot Aspic

P'tcha

P'tcha is an old-fashioned dish that originally comes from Russia but was popular all over Yiddish-speaking Europe. The nonkosher version was made with pig's feet, but the Jewish version used calf's feet, which makes a beautiful and tasy aspic. Although *p'tcha* can be served any season of the year, I rather like it in the summertime, when the body craves cool, delicate flavors.

2 lb. calf's feet
1 medium onion, peeled and left whole
1 large carrot, peeled and left whole
1 bay leaf, 6 whole allspice berries, and 8 whole black peppercorns, wrapped in cheesecloth and tied with kitchen string
1 very small calf's tongue, preboiled and skin removed (see p. 161 for technique for doing this)
1 Tblsp. salt
juice of one large lemon
2 Tblsp. sugar
cold water to cover
2 jumbo hard-boiled eggs, chopped

1. Place the calf's feet, the tongue, and the salt in a large stockpot and cover with cold water by 1/2 inch. Bring to a boil and skim off the scum as it rises to the top.

2. Reduce the heat to a simmer, add all the remaining ingredients except for the hard-boiled eggs, cover the pot, and simmer for at least 2 1/2 hours.

3. Remove the meat from the pot and set it aside. Strain the contents of the pot through a fine sieve and discard all the solids.

4. Cut the meat off the bones of the calf's feet and grind it coarsely in the food processor. Place it at the bottom of a flat glass or Pyrex rectangular-shaped pan. Cover it with half the liquid from the stockpot and refrigerate for 1 1/2 hours.

5. While the calf's foot meat is chilling and solidifying, cut the meat of the tongue into fine dice.

6. Remove the aspic from the refrigerator. The first layer should be fairly well jelled. Spread the diced tongue and chopped hard-boiled egg over the aspic and cover with the remaining liquid from the stockpot. Return to the refrigerator, cover with plastic

wrap, and chill for at least 2 more hours or until ready to serve.

7. To serve *p'tcha*, cut into small squares and garnish with thinly sliced English cucumber and lemon. Recipe serves 8 to 10 people as a *forspeis* and 4 to 6 as an entrée.

Serving Suggestions

P'tcha is an elegant *forspeis* that goes well with just about any entrée. Do not serve a soup following *p'tcha*, since the aspic is actually like a chilled, jelled soup. *P'tcha* also makes a wonderful light summer main-dish entrée.

Liptauer Cheese
Liptavsky Kayz

Liptavsky kayz is a Hungarian and Austrian specialty. It is good not only as an appetizer before dinner but also as a spread for sandwiches and cocktail snacks and a dip for vegetables. It is also very much at home on a *milchig* buffet table. *Liptavsky kayz* is made several different ways. I offer three variations here. The first comes from Budapest and Vienna. The second, which uses *brynza*, is in the style of Munkacs and Szeged, which are in eastern Hungary on the Romanian border. The third is an American variation developed by Hungarian Jewish cooks using American cream cheese.

Liptavsky Kayz 1: Budapest Style

1/2 lb. farmer cottage cheese
1 quarter-lb. stick sweet butter, cut into bits
1 Tblsp. Hungarian sweet paprika
2 tsp. caraway (*kimmel*) seeds
1 tsp. Dijon mustard
1 tsp. capers, drained and rinsed
1 small onion, peeled and chopped
1/3 cup sour cream
salt and black pepper to taste

1. Using a food processor or blender, grate the onion very finely. Add the butter bits, mustard, capers, and sour cream and process until thoroughly blended.

2. Add the remaining ingredients and blend again until all is completely mixed together and has the consistency of a very thick, spreadable, smooth paste that holds its shape without going flat. (This part is a little tricky. You may need to increase the quantity of cottage cheese. But don't worry too much as the butter will solidify the mixture again once it is refrigerated.)

3. Shape the *liptavsky kayz* into a ball or mound, or fill an enameled porcelain or glass bowl with the mixture. Refrigerate at least 2 hours before serving. *Liptavsky kayz* keeps well in the refrigerator for at least a week.

Liptavsky Kayz 2: Munkacs Style

1/2 lb. *brynza* cheese
1 Tblsp. Hungarian sweet paprika
2 tsp. caraway (*kimmel*) seeds
1 tsp. dry mustard
1 small onion, peeled and chopped
3 heaping Tblsp. sour cream
salt and black pepper to taste

1. Place onion and sour cream in food processor and blend until onion is finely grated and mixture is completely blended.

2. Add the remaining ingredients and process thoroughly until all is mixed together. Mixture should have the consistency of a very thick, smooth paste.

3. Roll into a ball or mound, or fill an enameled porcelain or glass bowl with the mixture. Refrigerate at least 2 hours before serving. Cheese keeps at least a week in the refrigerator.

Liptavsky Kayz 3: American Version

Substitute 1 8-oz. pkg. American cream cheese for the butter in version 1, delete capers, and proceed as directed in the previous recipes. Plain yogurt may be substituted for the sour cream in this recipe without loss of flavor.

Serving Suggestions

Liptavsky kayz may be served in any of the ways described above or as an appetizer before a dairy or *pareve* meal. To serve as an appetizer, make a small mound of cheese in the middle of each serving dish and garnish with thinly sliced English cucumber. Serve with *pletzel*, pumpernickel, or rye bread.

Romanian *Brynza* Spread

This appetizer is good served alone with black bread or as part of a *milchige* buffet table. Serve it as well with *mamaliga* and a variety of Romanian salads for a light lunch or dinner.

1/2 lb. *brynza* cheese
1 large clove garlic
1 extra-large hard-boiled egg
3 Tblsp. chopped fresh dill
2 Tblsp. chopped fresh chives
1/4 cup sour cream or plain yogurt
salt and black pepper to taste

Blend all the ingredients together in a blender or food processor or by hand. Place mixture in a glass or enameled porcelain bowl and refrigerate overnight before serving. When serving as a *forspeis*, garnish with good-quality black olives (e.g., Niçoise), fresh tomatoes (in season), and triangles of pumpernickel bread. Recipe serves 6 to 8 people.

Knishes

Knishes are an appetizer that was devised to use up leftover potatoes, meat, or *kasha*. They can also be eaten as cocktail hors d'oeuvres or snacks at any time.

2 cups unbleached white flour
1 tsp. baking powder
1/2 tsp. salt
2 Tblsp. cold water
1 Tblsp. corn or peanut oil
2 eggs, well beaten
filling (see recipes below)
1 egg yolk mixed with 1 Tblsp. cold water (egg wash)

1. Mix flour, salt, and baking powder together. Make a well in the center and add water, oil, and beaten eggs. Mix with a wooden spoon until smooth and then knead for 6 to 8 minutes. Place dough in a greased bowl, cover with a damp towel, and let rest for 1 hour.

2. On a flour-dusted pastry board, roll half of the dough out to a 1/8-inch thickness. Using a small glass or a cookie cutter with a 3-inch diameter, cut the dough into rounds. Place 2 Tblsp. filling (see recipes below) in the center of each round. Fold over and pinch the ends of each round together to form a *knish*. Secure the seal by pressing the pinched dough with the tines of a fork all along the edge of the seal. Place on a well-greased baking sheet.

3. Repeat this procedure with the rest of the dough until it is used up. Reroll the ends that are left after making rounds, and cut this dough into new rounds. If you have filling left after assembling the *knishes*, put it away for some other purpose. Do not exceed or decrease the amount of filling recommended for the *knishes*.

4. Preheat the oven to 350°. Brush each *knish* with egg wash and bake for 25 minutes or until golden brown. Recipe makes 18 to 20 *knishes*. *Knishes* may be served hot or at room temperature.

Filling for *Knishes*

Potato Filling

2 cups mashed boiled potatoes
2 medium-size onions, peeled and finely chopped
3 Tblsp. *schmaltz*
salt and black pepper to taste

Melt *schmaltz* and sauté onions until golden brown. Mix with potatoes, salt, and pepper. Fill *knishes*.

Kasha Filling

1 cup coarse ground *kasha*
3 Tblsp. *schmaltz*
2 medium onions, peeled and finely chopped
1 egg
1 cup boiling water
salt and black pepper to taste

Toast *kasha* grains in a saucepan over medium/low heat. Beat egg and add to *kasha*. Stir constantly until egg is completely incorporated into the *kasha*. Add water and cook over medium heat 10 to 15 minutes until *kasha* is cooked through. Sauté onions in *schmaltz* in a skillet until golden brown. Add to *kasha*. Add salt and pepper to taste. Fill *knishes*.

Meat Filling

Meat filling for *knishes* is the same as for *kreplach*. See recipe for *kreplach* (p. 59).

Serving Suggestions

Knishes may be served as a cocktail snack, as a *forspeis*, or on their own as a light meal. As a *forspeis*, it is interesting to make knishes with more than one filling. I recommend making *knishes* with all three fillings and serving one of each to each diner as a portion. *Knishes* may be served with just about anything. Just remember not to serve any vegetable starch with your meat entrée when you serve *knishes* as a *forspeis*. You can make this course especially elegant by serving a nice red or rosé wine with it. On the *fleischig* buffet table, *knishes* can have an honored place as a hot dish among a series of cold dishes. If serving *knishes* alone as a light lunch or supper, serve nothing more than a tossed salad alongside them. *Knishes* are also a traditional accompaniment to main-dish soups, both *milchig* and *fleischig*. *Knishes* freeze very well and can be made ahead of time, whenever it is convenient, and merely defrosted before serving.

Cheese *Knishes*

Cheese *knishes* are both a cocktail hors d'oeuvre and a lunch, tea, brunch, or dairy buffet dish. My grandmother made cheese *knishes* in a triangular shape to distinguish them from the *knishes* with *fleischig* fillings. The dough used to make cheese *knishes* is also different.

3 cups unbleached white flour
2 1/2 tsp. baking powder
1 tsp. salt
2 Tblsp. sugar
1 cup sour cream or plain yogurt, at room
    temperature
2 eggs, beaten
4 Tblsp. sweet butter, melted

filling (see recipe following)
1 egg yolk mixed with 1 Tblsp. cold water (egg
    wash)

1. Mix dry ingredients together. In a separate mixing bowl, mix sour cream, butter, and eggs. Combine wet and dry ingredients into a dough, and knead for 6 to 8 minutes.

2. Preheat oven to 350°. On a floured pastry board, roll out half the dough to a 1/8-inch thickness. Cut into 4-inch squares. Put 2 Tblsp. filling on each square and fold into a triangle. Pinch edges together and secure seal by pressing with the tines of a fork.

3. Repeat this procedure with each *knish* until all the dough has been used up. Place the *knishes* on well-greased baking sheets. Brush each *knish* with egg wash. Bake 30 to 35 minutes or until *knishes* are golden brown. Recipe makes 18 to 20 *knishes*. Serve warm or at room temperature.

For filling

1/2 lb. farmer cottage cheese
1/2 lb. cream cheese
1/3 cup sugar
1 egg, beaten
2 Tblsp. sour cream or plain yogurt
1/4 cup raisins (optional)

Mix together all the ingredients and use as directed to fill the *knishes*.

Serving Suggestions

Cheese *knishes* are delicious served with drinks or as part of a *milchig* buffet. When serving as a *forspeis*, serve 1 or 2 per person. A small portion of carrot-and-raisin salad (p. 227) makes an excellent accompaniment. A dry white wine such as Riesling or gewürztraminer is a good drink to accompany cheese *knishes*.

Baltic-Style Summer Harvest Dinner for Shevuos

Challah shaped like Tablets of the Law

Summer green pea soup with fresh herbs

Kulebiaka (salmon en croûte with fresh sorrel and spinach)

Creamy beets with fresh dill

Sauvignon blanc

Rhubarb compote and *blintzes* with sour cream

Egg-enriched coffee

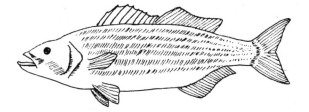

4

Soups

Zuppen

Troubles with soup are easier to bear
than troubles without soup.

*Tsores mit zupp iz gringer tzu fartrogen vi
tzores on zupp.*

Seven Variations on Chicken Soup

Chicken soup is one of the best known of Jewish dishes, and there are many ways to prepare it. All begin with the basic chicken stock recipe given in chapter 1. At the end of each recipe, suggestions are given for what to serve the soup with. If you follow the general guidelines on which these suggestions are based, you can fully enjoy each type of chicken soup, follow it with a meat entrée, and never feel that your meal is too heavy in carbohydrates. Think of the heavier variations of chicken soup as the equivalent of a pasta course in an Italian meal, and plan your menu accordingly. You will be pleasantly surprised at how much more you will enjoy eating each of the courses. Most chicken soups can be eaten at any time of the year, but I like to have the chicken soup with *kasha* and the chicken soup with *lokshen* only during the colder seasons because they are more substantial.

Variation 1: Chicken Soup with *Mandlen*

Chicken soup with *mandlen* is the most basic of the chicken soups. It is also very light and can be followed by a meat course that is served with potatoes or some other kind of starch. To make chicken soup with *mandlen*, simply warm up enough of the chicken soup stock for your guests, fill each soup bowl with the stock, and garnish it with finely chopped parsley. Either pass a bowl of soup *mandlen* around and let everyone take some, or place a few of the *mandlen* into each bowl before you serve. The recipe for soup *mandlen* is given below.

For soup *mandlen*

3 eggs
3 Tblsp. corn or peanut oil
1 tsp. salt
1 1/2 to 2 cups unbleached white flour

1. Preheat oven to 350°. Lightly grease two baking sheets. Mix together the eggs, oil, and salt. Add 1 1/2 cups of the flour and knead. Dough should be soft but not sticky. Gradually knead in up to no more than 1/2 cup flour to achieve correct texture.

2. Divide dough into 8 pieces. Roll each piece into a rope about 1/2 inch thick. Cut each rope into 1/2-inch pieces and place on baking sheets. Bake 20 to 25 minutes on the middle shelf of the oven, shaking the baking sheet occasionally. It is important that this be done on the middle shelf in order to prevent the *mandlen* from burning. They are done when they are golden brown and firm to the touch. Cool and store in airtight metal containers (such as used cookie tins). Soup *mandlen* keep fresh this way for weeks and weeks and are available anytime you are in a hurry and want to make a soup that won't take too much time to cook. Soup *mandlen* are also good used in place of crackers for other types of soups.

Serving Suggestions

This soup is excellent served with just about anything, but it is particularly appropriate when you are serving a substantial, heavier entrée. It is also the correct soup to serve when you wish to serve a starch with your meat course.

Variation 2: Chicken Soup Consommé

This is one of the most elegant ways of serving chicken soup as well as the lightest. Jewish chicken soup stock makes a superb consommé.

The most important thing to remember about making consommé is that it must be very clear and totally fat free. To do this correctly, after you have finished stage 2 of making the regular chicken stock (see p.   ), take as much of the stock as you wish to turn into consommé and separate it. I usually make 2 quarts of consommé when I make a pot of stock. Separate 3 quarts of stock before putting the remainder into containers for freezing, and ladle it into a separate pot. Then put it into the refrigerator overnight. In the morning, the fat will have risen to the top. Remove as much of this as you can with a skimmer while it is still solid and place the pot of stock on the stove. Bring the stock to a boil on top of the stove and boil it down until it is reduced to about 2 quarts. Then strain it through a cheesecloth to remove any lingering traces of fat.

To clarify the stock, beat 1 egg white to a froth together with the crushed eggshell. (Separate the yolk from the white and use it for some other purpose.) Reduce the heat to medium and beat in the egg white and shell with a wire whisk. When the stock comes to a boil again, the egg white will rise to the surface, gathering any solid material with it. When this happens, stop stirring and remove pot from the heat. Allow it to settle for 5 minutes and strain it through a fine sieve lined with several thicknesses of cheesecloth. Do this very slowly and do not rush the process, or you will not have perfectly clarified consommé. The liquid should just drip through the cheesecloth into the pot or bowl underneath it. When you have finished this, you have chicken soup consommé. The consommé can be reheated and served anytime after that. It also freezes very well. This recipe makes about 10 cups of consommé. Four cups of consommé serves 6 people at a meal because it is served in very small consommé bowls.

Serving Suggestions

This light, elegant dish is really the essence of chicken soup. You may serve it in one of two ways. Garnish it with a light sprinkling of fresh, finely chopped herbs such as dill, chives, or parsley. If you like, place one tablespoon of dry sherry in each consommé bowl and fill the bowl with consommé. Then sprinkle the herbs into the soup. This soup is perfect to serve with a rich entrée like *Shtadlan's hendel* (p. 114), Polish-style roast duck with apples and pears (p. 121), or roast stuffed goose (p. 122). It is also good before any grilled or plain roasted meat like beef.

Variation 3: Chicken Soup with *Knaidelach*

Di Haggadah iz nit der ikker, der ikker iz der knaidelach!

The Haggadah is not the most important part of the Passover Seder, the most important part is the *knaidelach*!
— Yiddish Saying

Good *knaidelach* are as tricky to make as a good soufflé or good homemade pasta. This dish is underappreciated as a gourmet food. There are several schools of thought on making *knaidelach*, and Jewish home cooks have debated the subject endlessly. Some people prefer *knaidelach* that are very firm textured; others like them light. Some cooks use *schmaltz* in their *knaidelach*; others do not. My grandmother never put *schmaltz* in her *knaidelach* and as for texture, hers always seemed to be balanced somewhere in between being so light that they did not need to be chewed and so firm that they had to be cut with a knife. She passed away when I was 14 years old, long before I had ever given any thought to writing down treasured family recipes. Try as I

may, I have never been able to replicate the taste and texture of her *knaidelach*. But in my many attempts to reconstruct the recipe, I have developed a few tricks and preferences of my own, which I offer here as my personal contribution in the Great *Knaidelach* Debate.

4 large eggs
1/2 cup seltzer or club soda
1 cup *matzoh* meal
salt and pepper to taste

1. In a glass or ceramic bowl, beat eggs to a froth. Stir in seltzer, salt, and pepper. Gradually stir in the *matzoh* meal until mixture is completely blended. Cover bowl and refrigerate mixture for at least 1 1/2 hours.

2. Bring 3 to 4 quarts of salted water to a boil. Have the *matzoh* meal mixture and a bowl of cold water ready on the counter next to the stove.

3. Reduce the heat under the water and maintain it at a medium simmer. Moisten your hands. Take approximately 2 Tblsp. of the *matzoh* meal mixture and form it into a ball. Drop it very gently into the simmering water. Repeat this procedure until all the *matzoh* meal mixture is used up. Cover the pot, reduce the heat again, and simmer for 30 minutes. *Do not uncover the pot while it is simmering.*

4. After 30 minutes, the *knaidelach* will have risen to the surface and are ready to be served. This recipe makes between 15 and 16 *knaidelach* and will serve 5 to 7 people.

To serve *knaidelach* in chicken soup, bring 2 quarts of chicken stock (p. 3) to a medium boil together with a bouquet garni consisting of 4 sprigs of fresh dill, 4 sprigs of parsley, a piece of green from 1 leek, and a small piece of celery. Have 1/2 cup freshly chopped dill leaves ready. When stock has cooked for 15 minutes, remove bouquet garni. Place 2 to 3 *knaidelach* in each soup bowl and pour the stock over them. Garnish each portion of soup with the chopped dill leaves.

Serving Suggestions

Chicken soup with *knaidelach* makes a delicate and very elegant soup course. It tastes best when followed by simple roasts of chicken, beef, and veal. Try it with any of the following recipes:

Hendel mit Marantzen (p. 103)
Passover Roast Stuffed Capon (p. 112)

Pesachdige Hendel (p. 102)
Braised Veal with Herbs (p. 141)
Gedempte Kalbsfleisch mit Kimmel (p. 142)
Braised Tongue with Wine Sauce (p. 161)
Hungarian-Style Braised *Flanken* (p. 135)
Brustfleisch mit Mayeren (p. 132)

Do not serve potatoes or any kind of grain dish with the roast, and do follow the vegetable suggestions given with each recipe.

Variation 4: Chicken Soup with *Lokshen*

Lokshen is the Yiddish word for noodles or pasta, and the *lokshen* traditionally served in chicken soup is so similar to vermicelli that people sometimes confuse the two. Jewish soup *lokshen* is sometimes sold in packages labeled "thin egg noodles." There is a big difference between "thin egg noodles" and vermicelli. Vermicelli is long and unbroken; "thin egg noodles" are short and twisted. Vermicelli should not be substituted for "thin egg noodles" for this reason. For the same reason, neither should cappelli d'angeli (also called "angel hair pasta") be used as a substitute. These noodles are meant for pasta courses rather than soups and, unlike "thin egg noodles," do not sit easily and attractively in a soup spoon, as properly made Jewish soup *lokshen* should do. I do not personally advocate breaking apart vermicelli or angel hair pasta to cook in a soup either, because the better varieties are made of durum wheat, which has a different texture from noodles made from regular flour.

Homemade *lokshen* is delicious and very easy to make when you use the pasta machine. I include a recipe for homemade *lokshen* in chapter 8, the chapter on *kugels* and grain dishes. Chicken soup with *lokshen* can be made with either homemade *lokshen* or packaged "thin egg noodles." All you have to do is precook it according to the instructions given in the recipe (p. 170) or on the package of noodles. When cooked, rinse the *lokshen* with cold water to remove the starch that makes it stick together, drain it, cover it, and set it aside until ready to serve the soup.

To serve chicken soup with *lokshen*, bring 2 quarts of chicken stock to a boil. Apportion the precooked *lokshen* among as many bowls as there are diners, and pour the boiling stock over it. Garnish the soup with finely chopped parsley and serve. Two quarts of stock and 3/4 lb. precooked *lokshen* will serve 5 to 7 people.

Serving Suggestions

Chicken soup with *lokshen* is a more substantial dish than chicken soup with *knaidelach* and goes very well with meat dishes that have robust flavors. Try it with any of the following entrées:

Roast Chicken with Prunes (p. 109)
Braised Sweet-and-Sour Tongue (p. 163)
Essig Fleisch (p. 131)
Litvishe Prakkes (p. 152)
Braised Brisket with Apples (p. 132)

As with chicken soup with *knaidelach*, do not serve potatoes or grains with the meat course, and do follow the vegetable suggestions given with the recipes.

Variation 5: Chicken Soup with Rice

Chicken soup with rice is similar in some ways to an Italian risotto. However, it is much more like a substantial soup than a grain dish. It is also made with regular long-grain white rice rather than short-grain arborio rice. Unlike in the Italian dish, no parmesan cheese is added to the soup.

7 cups chicken stock (p. 3)
1 1/2 cups long-grain white rice, rinsed with cold water to remove the starch and drained in a colander
1 medium onion, finely chopped
1 small carrot, grated
1 clove garlic, finely chopped
2 Tblsp. finely chopped parsley
2 Tblsp. finely snipped chives
1 Tblsp. corn oil
salt and pepper to taste

1. Heat the oil in a soup pot and sauté the onion until translucent. Add the carrot and garlic and continue sautéing until it begins to soften. Add the rice and continue to cook, stirring with a wooden spoon until all of the rice has been moistened.

2. Add 2 cups of stock and cook until all is absorbed. Continue to add the stock one cup at a time until 3 cups of stock remain at the end. The rice should have absorbed all the stock that has been added up to this point.

3. Bring the remaining 4 cups of stock to a boil in another pot. When it comes to a boil, add it to the rice and remove the pot from the heat. Stir in the herbs, salt, and pepper and serve immediately. Recipe serves 6 to 8 people.

Serving Suggestions

Chicken soup with rice is both substantial and delicate. It should be followed by a meat dish that tastes good with a rice accompaniment. Try it with any of the following:

> *Shabbosdige Hendel* (p. 101)
> Baked Lemon Chicken (p. 110)
> Hungarian-Style Braised *Flanken* (p. 135)
> My Bobbe's Meat Loaf (p. 151)
> *Gedempte Fleisch* (p. 129)

Do not serve potatoes or grains with the meat entrée, and do follow the vegetable suggestions given with each recipe.

Variation 6: Chicken Soup with *Kasha*

Kasha, like *lokshen*, is very substantial and makes for the heaviest of all the chicken soups. This soup tastes particularly good on a cold winter evening.

6 cups chicken stock (p. 3)
1 1/2 cups coarse-grind *kasha*
1 egg
3 cups cold water
1 medium onion, finely chopped
1 small carrot, grated
1 clove garlic, finely chopped (optional)
1 Tblsp. corn oil
salt and pepper to taste

1. Sauté onion in oil until translucent. Add carrot and garlic (if using) and continue sautéing until soft. Remove from heat.

2. In a saucepan, toast *kasha* grains over medium heat until they begin to give off a toasted smell. Break egg over the grains and stir it into the grains. Add sautéed vegetables and water and cover pot. Cook over medium-low heat until all the water is absorbed.

3. Meanwhile, bring the stock to a boil in a 4-quart pot. When *kasha* has absorbed all the water,

it is done. Add it to the boiling stock and remove the pot from the heat. Add salt and pepper to taste and serve the soup in deep soup bowls. Recipe serves 6 to 8 people.

Serving Suggestions

This savory and substantial winter soup is very versatile and goes well with simple roasted meats or with dishes that have a robust, flavorful sauce. Try it with any of the following:

> *Gedempte Kalbsfleisch mit Kimmel* (p. 142)
> Breast of Veal with Savory Stuffing (p. 149)
> My Bobbe's Meat Loaf (p. 151)
> Braised Brisket with *Chrain* (p. 129)
> *Gedempte Fleisch* (p. 129)

As with most of the other chicken soups, do not serve potatoes or grains with the meat courses, and do follow the vegetable suggestions given with each recipe.

Variation 7: Chicken Soup with *Kreplach*

Kreplach in a kholem iz nit ken kreplach, nor a kholem.

Kreplach in a dream are not kreplach. They are just a dream.

—Yiddish saying

Kreplach are the Jewish equivalent of Italian cappelletti or Chinese wonton. Chicken soup with *kreplach* is a very special and extraordinary dish and should be served only on special occasions. Traditionally they are served on Rosh Hashanah, at the meal before the fast on Yom Kippur, and at the Purim *seudah* (special meal for Purim) because, in rabbinic tradition, Purim is compared with and contrasted to Yom Kippur.

Kreplach are tricky to make. They are smaller in size than wonton and larger than cappelletti. Unlike in Italian pasta, the dough used for making *kreplach* is made from regular unbleached white flour. There is no reason for this other than the fact that, perhaps, Jews in eastern and central Europe did not have access to durum wheat, which produces the semolina flour used to make Italian pasta. I have tried making *kreplach* with semolina flour and the result is exquisite, but the flavor is more like cappelletti than *kreplach*. The fillings for these dishes are, of course, quite different from each other.

The two biggest complaints I have about some of the *kreplach* I have eaten are that they were too pasty and hard or that they did not retain their shape when cooked. Both of these problems are easily corrected. They occur because of five basic mistakes that the cook makes:

1. An improper ratio of flour to eggs
2. Not rolling the dough out thinly enough
3. Using too much filling in each *krepl*
4. Boiling the *kreplach* too slowly
5. Improper sealing of the *kreplach*

Making *kreplach* the right way takes a little time and patience, but the rewards are so great that after you succeed at doing it correctly the first time, you will want to do it over and over again.

I recommend using a pasta machine (hand cranked or electric) to roll out the dough for *kreplach*. This makes the recipe practically foolproof and ensures that the dough will never be too thick. *Kreplach* can, of course, be rolled by hand in the old-fashioned way, but it is considerably more time consuming and much more difficult to be precise about the thickness of the dough.

For pasta dough

2 cups unbleached white flour
2 large eggs
pinch of salt
4 tsp. cold water (or more, if needed)

For filling

1 Tblsp. *schmaltz*
1/2 cup onions, very finely chopped
1/4 lb. lean ground beef
1/2 cup cooked ground chicken
1 tsp. fresh parsley, very finely chopped
salt and pepper to taste

1. Mix the flour and salt on a large, flat working surface (preferably wood or Formica but not marble). Make a well in the center of the flour and drop in the eggs and 4 tsp. of the cold water. Stir and knead this mixture until it becomes a dough. Knead the dough by hand about 15 minutes or until it is very smooth. This step can be done in the food processor using the dough attachment, but I prefer doing it by hand so that I can feel the moment when the correct texture is achieved. It can also be done in some electric pasta machines, which saves time and is very convenient. If you are doing this, just follow the instructions that come with the machine for making pasta dough that is used for ravioli or cappelletti. It is important that the dough be smooth and not dry and crumbly. Add a drop or two of water, if necessary, to achieve the correct consistency, but do this very carefully or you will end up with a sticky dough, which will result in a pasta that is pasty and rubbery. When the kneading of the dough is finished, set it aside for an hour at room temperature in a plastic bag, plastic wrap, or wax paper.

2. While the dough is resting, make the filling for the *kreplach*. Melt the *schmaltz* in a skillet and add the onions. Sauté until translucent and add the beef. Cook this mixture until the meat is no longer pink. Remove from the heat and add the chicken, salt, pepper, and parsley. Set aside.

3. When the dough has rested for 1 hour, it is ready to roll. Divide it in half and place the half not being used back in the plastic or wax paper wrap. At this point you must follow the instructions given with your pasta maker. With a hand-cranked pasta maker, proceed as follows: Flatten the dough and, using a rolling pin, shape it into a rectangle no wider than the rolling bars on the machine. Make sure it is thin enough to fit into the widest setting of the machine. Roll the dough through this setting. Fold it in thirds and roll it again. Proceed through all of the settings in this way, making the pasta thinner and thinner until you have rolled it through the thinnest setting on the machine. This is the trickiest part of making *kreplach*. You must be patient and work until the desired thinness is achieved. Do not give up if your *kreplach* do not come out right the first time. By practicing, you will eventually develop a feel for recognizing the correct thinness and texture of the dough.

4. Cut the finished sheet into 2 1/2-inch squares. *Be precise in your measurements.* Accuracy is important in order to make the *kreplach* uniform in size and to have the right pocket size for the filling. If you are careless about your measurements, you may get *kreplach* that burst apart because they are too stuffed with filling. Use the scraps of dough that are left over after you cut the first squares to add to the rest of the dough and make more squares. Place them back in the plastic wrapping while you fill the *kreplach* you have made.

5. To fill the kreplach, use 1 tsp. of filling for each square. Place the filling in the center of the pasta square and fold over diagonally to make a triangle. Press the ends firmly together to seal. Then bend the triangular *krepl* around your finger and press the two ends of the triangle together. The shape of *kreplach* is exactly that of cappelletti. As you make the kreplach, set them out in neat rows on a clean, dry kitchen cloth.

6. Repeat this process until all the dough and all the filling are used up. The recipe makes between 18 and 20 *kreplach. Kreplach*, like their Italian cousins— cappelletti, ravioli, and tortellini—can be frozen in batches and defrosted for use at a later date, but like any fresh pasta, they are at their best when eaten right after being made. *Kreplach* may also be kept in the refrigerator for at least a week with no significant loss of flavor. If you refrigerate or freeze *kreplach*, make sure they are not pressed against each other, or they might stick together and fall apart when they cook, ruining hours of painstaking work. Wrapping each *krepl* separately in plastic wrap will prevent this from happening.

7. To cook *kreplach*, bring 4 quarts of salted water to a rapid boil. Gently drop the *kreplach* into the pot, and cook as you would any pasta, for 20 to 25 minutes. Remove them with a slotted spoon, drain, and place them in soup bowls.

8. While the *kreplach* are cooking, heat 2 quarts of chicken stock in another pot. Have ready 1/2 cup of finely chopped parsley and chives, mixed together. After the *kreplach* are cooked, put two or three in each soup bowl and ladle the soup over them. Sprinkle each portion of soup with the herbs and serve. Recipe serves 6 to 8 people.

Serving Suggestions

Chicken soup with *kreplach* is the most elegant of the chicken soups. It should be followed by an entrée that is equally elegant and refined. Try it with any of the following:

> Roast Veal with Herbs (p. 141)
> Braised Brisket with Apples (p. 132)
> Braised Brisket with Carrots (p. 132)
> Roast Cornish Hens with *Challah* Stuffing
>   (p. 110)
> Braised Tongue with Wine Sauce (p. 161)

Follow the vegetable recommendations given with each recipe. You may serve a wine with this soup. Try a white zinfandel or a rosé.

Creamy Potato Soup with Fresh Herbs

Milchig Kartoffel Zupp

3 Tblsp. sweet butter or corn oil
2 medium onions, peeled and very finely
**   chopped**
2 leeks (white part and 1/2 inch of the green),
**   carefully washed and sliced very thin**
3 lb. red boiling potatoes, peeled and cut into
**   small chunks**
2 stalks celery, thinly sliced
3 carrots, peeled and thinly sliced
3 Tblsp. old-fashioned oatmeal
5 cups vegetable stock (p. 5)
1/2 cup finely chopped fresh parsley
1/4 cup finely snipped chives
1/4 cup fresh dill leaves, chopped
2 cups whole milk
1/2 cup sour cream or plain yogurt
salt and black pepper to taste

1. Melt butter or heat oil in a large, deep soup pot over medium heat. Add onions and sauté until translucent. Add leeks, celery, and carrots and sauté an additional 10 minutes.

2. Add stock and potatoes and bring to a boil. Reduce heat to simmer and, leaving lid slightly ajar, simmer for 35 minutes. Add oatmeal and simmer an additional 15 minutes. Add milk and continue simmering until well heated through. The soup should have a moderately thick consistency. Add sour cream and herbs and simmer until just heated through. Do not let it come anywhere near a boil or sour cream and milk will curdle, ruining the recipe. Add salt and pepper and serve immediately. Recipe serves 6 to 8 people, or even 10, if the portions are small.

Serving Suggestions

This is a very rich soup and excellent to serve before a fish entrée that has a light rather than a rich sauce. Try it with any of the following:

> Sautéed flounder or sole (p. 83)
> Any of the broiled fish recipes (p. 81)
> *Scharfeh Fisch* (p. 85)
> *Botviniker Lox* (p. 87)

You may serve the same white wine with the soup that you serve with the fish.

Fresh Pea Soup with Bouquet of Spring Herbs

Zummerdige Arbess Zupp

3 cups shelled fresh peas (about 3 lb. unshelled)
 or 3 cups frozen peas
3 leeks (white part and 1/2 inch of the green),
 carefully washed and chopped
1 medium onion, peeled and chopped
3 Tblsp. sweet butter or corn oil
6 1/2 cups vegetable stock (p. 5)
1/2 cup fresh parsley, finely chopped
1/4 cup chives, finely snipped
1/4 cup fresh dill leaves, chopped
1 cup heavy or whipping cream
salt and black pepper to taste

   1. Melt butter or heat oil over medium heat in a large, deep soup pot and sauté onions until translucent. Add leeks and continue sautéing until soft (about 5 to 6 minutes).
   2. Add stock, peas, and half of the herbs. Cover pot and bring to a boil. Lower heat and, leaving lid slightly ajar, simmer 40 to 45 minutes. Remove the soup from the heat and puree in a blender or food processor. *Soup can be prepared in advance up to this point.* The last step should be done just before serving.
   3. Add the cream, and mix thoroughly into the soup. Reheat the soup slowly, being careful not to bring it to a rapid boil. Just before serving, stir in the salt and pepper and the remaining herbs. Recipe serves 6 to 8 people.

Serving Suggestions

This elegant spring or early-summer soup calls for an equally elegant fish entrée. Salmon is a particularly good choice. Try it with any of the following:

   Poached Salmon with Dill Sauce (p. 85)
   Jewish Sole Meunière (p. 82)
   Steamed Salmon with *Schav* Leaves and
     Spinach (p. 87)
   Grilled Salmon Steaks or Fillets (p. 82)
   Scharfe Fisch (p. 85)
   Kulebiaka (p. 94)

Drink the same white wine with the soup that you serve with the fish.

Wild Mushroom Soup with Sherry and Herbs

Shvammen Zupp

This is a Jewish variation on the classical European cream of mushroom soup.

1 1/2 lb. fresh cultivated white mushrooms,
 wiped with a damp cloth and chopped
1/2 lb. fresh wild or gourmet mushrooms (e.g.,
 shiitake, oyster, chanterelles) or substitute
 1/2 cup dried Polish or Italian mushrooms
 soaked for 1 hour in 1 cup boiling water. If
 using fresh mushrooms, wipe clean with a
 damp cloth and chop.
1 medium onion, peeled and chopped
2 leeks (white part only), carefully washed and
 sliced
4 Tblsp. sweet butter
6 cups vegetable stock (p. 5)
1/4 cup fresh parsley, finely chopped
1/4 cup fresh dill leaves, chopped
1/4 cup chives, finely snipped
1/4 cup fresh marjoram leaves (or substitute 2
 tsp. dried marjoram), finely chopped
1 cup heavy or whipping cream
1/3 cup port wine or sherry (optional)
salt and black pepper to taste

   1. Melt butter over medium heat in a large, deep soup pot and sauté onions until translucent. Add leeks and sauté 2 minutes more. Add fresh mushrooms and continue sautéing an additional 8 to 10 minutes or until the mushrooms start to give off their liquor.
   2. Add stock and, if using, the port or sherry and the dried mushrooms together with their soaking liquid. Be sure to chop any dried mushrooms that are larger than the fresh mushroom pieces that are already chopped.
   3. Add the marjoram and half of the other herbs. Cover the pot and bring to a boil. Reduce heat to simmer and, leaving the lid slightly ajar, cook for 40 minutes.
   4. Remove the pot from the heat and puree the soup in the blender or food processor into a coarse puree. Return the soup to the pot. *The soup may be prepared in advance up to this point.*
   5. Add the cream and stir it thoroughly into the soup. Reheat the soup slowly, being careful not to

bring it to a rapid boil. When the soup is completely reheated, stir in the remaining herbs, the salt and the pepper. Serve immediately. Recipe serves 6 to 8 people.

Serving Suggestions

Follow the suggestions given for Fresh pea soup (p. 61).

Golden Carrot Soup

Goldene Mehren Zupp

8 to 10 large carrots, peeled and sliced
1 large red boiling potato, peeled and cut into chunks
1 medium onion, peeled and chopped
6 1/2 cups vegetable stock (p. 5)
3 Tblsp. corn oil or sweet butter
1/4 cup fresh parsley, finely chopped
1/4 cup chives, finely snipped
salt and black pepper to taste

1. Melt the butter or heat the oil in a large, deep soup pot and sauté the onions until translucent. Add the carrots and sauté 5 minutes more.

2. Add the stock and potato chunks and cover the pot. Bring to a boil and reduce heat to simmer. Leaving lid slightly ajar, simmer the soup for 45 minutes or until potatoes and carrots are soft and completely cooked through. Remove from heat and puree in the blender or food processor. Puree should be very smooth.

3. Return soup to the pot. It can be prepared in advance up to this point. Reheat the soup and stir in the herbs, salt, and pepper just before serving. Recipe serves 6 to 8 people.

Serving Suggestions

This is the most versatile of any of the Jewish soups and goes well with absolutely anything except an entrée featuring carrots, like *flommen tzimmes* (p. 134) or braised brisket with carrots (p. 132). When you are not sure what soup to serve with dinner, you can choose this one and know that it will always be a hit. When serving *fleischigs*, use the oil instead of the butter. For a richer *milchig* version, take 1/3 stick

sweet butter and melt it into the soup when you reheat it. Delicious!

Bouquet of Fresh Vegetables Soup

6 cups vegetable stock (p. 5)
2 medium onions, peeled and very thinly sliced
2 large carrots, peeled and thinly sliced
2 stalks celery, thinly sliced
2 medium turnips, peeled and cut into small chunks
1 parsnip, peeled and thinly sliced
2 small zucchini, cut into small chunks
2 leeks, carefully washed and thinly sliced
1 large or 2 medium-size red boiling potatoes, peeled and cut into small chunks
1 large clove garlic, peeled and finely chopped
1/4 cup chopped fresh dill leaves
1/3 cup chopped fresh parsley
1/4 cup finely snipped fresh chives
4 Tblsp. corn or sunflower oil
salt and black pepper to taste

1. Heat the oil in a deep soup pot and sauté the onions until translucent. Add the garlic and remaining vegetables except for the potatoes and sauté an additional 7 to 10 minutes or until the vegetables begin to soften.

2. Add the stock and potatoes and bring to a boil. Partially cover the pot and reduce heat to simmer. Simmer 30 to 35 minutes or until the vegetables are tender. *Do not overcook*. Remove from the heat and stir in the herbs, salt, and pepper. Serve immediately. Recipe serves 6 to 8 people.

Serving Suggestions

This is the quintessential light, fresh vegetable soup. Any combination of vegetables, in season, can be substituted for the zucchini, parsnip, and turnips in the same proportions. Do not substitute any of the other ingredients. The other vegetables are called "aromatics" and are essential for the proper flavor and bouquet. The potatoes are essential for bulk and for thickening. Other good vegetables to use in this soup are green beans, peas, spinach, chard, beet greens, beets (if you don't mind the red color), and yellow or pattypan summer squash. This soup is extremely versatile and can be served with practically any entrée (*milchig*, *fleischig*, or *pareve*). I recommend this soup especially when you wish to serve a starch such as *kasha* or *farfel* with a meat entrée. I do not recommend serving it before a main dish that has several different ingredients combined, such as *tzimmes* (p. 134), or any of the stuffed vegetables. You should follow this soup with an entrée that is uncomplicated and straightforward, like *Shabbosdige hendel* (p. 101), baked veal chops (p. 143), or Jewish-style rib roast (p. 137).

Polish Strawberry Soup

Pozenikes Zupp

Strawberry soup is a spring and summer specialty of Polish Jews. Strawberries are the first berries that come out in the springtime, and often the first time that this soup is tasted during a particular year is at Passover. This is usually the case in St. Louis, where garden strawberries have an early blooming season. Strawberry soup is also popular on Shevuos, when dairy foods are eaten. I provide here a traditional recipe for strawberry soup and two of my own variations.

Traditional recipe

2 lb. fresh strawberries, hulled and sliced in
   half
1/2 cup sugar
4 cups cold water
sour cream (1 Tblsp. per serving)

1. In a large, deep saucepan, mix together the sugar and water and bring to a boil over high heat. Reduce the heat and add the strawberries. Cook over medium heat, partly covered, about 15 minutes. Remove from the heat and cool to room temperature.

2. Puree the soup in the blender or food processor and put it into an enamel or glass crock. Cover and chill for at least 3 hours.

3. To serve, place 1 Tblsp. sour cream in each soup bowl together with 1/2 tsp. sugar. Ladle 1/4 cup soup into the bowl and mix together vigorously with a spoon until the mixture is slightly foamy. Add the rest of the portion of soup and stir it together

before serving. If you wish to serve the soup in a soup tureen, use 3/4 cup sour cream, 2 Tblsp. sugar, and 1 1/2 cups soup to make the sour cream mixture. Whisk it together with a wire whisk. Add the remaining soup and, using the whisk again, stir the entire soup together until well blended. Recipe serves 6 to 8 people.

Serving Suggestions

Polish strawberry soup is delicious before any dairy meal or a lightly prepared fish entrée. Try it with any of the following:

Grilled or Broiled Fish with Lemon (p. 81)
Jewish Sole Meunière (p. 82)
Sautéed Flounder or Sole (p. 83)
Fish *Kottletten* (p. 93)
Cheese *Kreplach* (p. 185)
Chremslach (p. 296)
Blintzes (p. 187)

Variations

1. Substitute maple sugar (which is delicious with strawberries) for the sugar in the recipe and add 1/3 cup pure maple syrup to the puree.
2. The flavor of Grand Marnier also goes exceptionally well with strawberries. Add 1/3 cup Grand Marnier liqueur to the basic strawberry soup recipe for an extremely elegant soup.

Lithuanian Plum Soup

Litvishe Flommen Zupp

3 lb. tart red plums, pits removed
1 cinnamon stick
1/2 cup vanilla sugar (or 1/2 cup regular white
   sugar plus 1/8 tsp. vanilla extract)
2 cups cold water
1 1/2 cups zinfandel or another fruity red wine
sour cream (1 Tblsp. per portion of soup)

1. Place pitted plums, sugar, wine, water, and cinnamon stick into a large, deep soup pot. Stirring constantly to dissolve the sugar, bring the soup to a boil over high heat. Reduce heat to simmer and cover the pot, leaving the lid slightly ajar. Simmer 1

hour or until the plums start to disintegrate and separate from their skins.

2. Remove pot from the heat and set aside, covered, with the lid still ajar, to cool. After soup has cooled to room temperature, remove and discard the cinnamon stick. Pour the contents of the soup through a fine sieve, pressing down hard on the fruit to completely separate it from its skin. At the end of this process, the skins will cling to the sides of the sieve, and the soup will be an attractive, smooth puree. Refrigerate at least 3 hours before serving.

3. To serve, place 1 Tblsp. sour cream in each soup bowl together with 1/2 tsp. sugar. Ladle 1/4 cup soup over this and mix together vigorously with a spoon until the mixture is well blended and slightly foamy. Ladle the rest of the portion of soup into the bowl and mix together thoroughly. Repeat this process with each portion of soup.

If you wish to serve the soup in a soup tureen, use 3/4 cup sour cream, 2 Tblsp. sugar, and 1 1/2 cups soup for the initial mixing. Blend with a wire whisk and then blend the sour cream mixture back into the soup. Recipe serves 6 to 8 people.

Serving Suggestions

This summer fruit soup is excellent before a simply prepared fish or dairy main dish. Try it with any of the following:

> Sautéed Flounder or Sole (p. 83)
> Any of the grilled or broiled fish dishes (p. 81)
> Jewish Sole Meunière (p. 82)
> Poached Salmon with Dill Sauce (p. 85)
> Steamed Salmon with *Schav* Leaves and Spinach
>   (p. 87)
> *Gravad Lox* (p. 94)
> Cheese *Kreplach* (p. 185)
> Medley of *Latkes* (p. 211)

Baltic Blueberry Soup

Blueberry soup is a true summertime fruit soup. The best blueberries grow in cold climates like those of Russia, the Baltic states, and the Scandinavian countries. Needless to say, this recipe comes from the cuisine of the Jews of the Baltic states. Blueberries and lemon have an affinity for one another, as do blueberries and nutmeg. This recipe makes use of both fresh lemon zest and freshly grated nutmeg.

2 lb. fresh blueberries (the smallest berries have the tastiest flavor)
3/4 cup sugar
grated zest of one lemon
2 Tblsp. freshly squeezed lemon juice
1/4 tsp. freshly grated nutmeg
4 cups cold water
sour cream (1 Tblsp. per serving)

1. Mix together the sugar and water in a large, deep saucepan and bring it to a boil. Add lemon zest and blueberries and cook 15 minutes. The berries should more or less disintegrate. If this does not happen, cook a few minutes longer.

2. Remove the soup from the heat and stir in the lemon juice and nutmeg. Chill in the refrigerator at least 3 hours. To serve, place 1 Tblsp. sour cream in each soup bowl together with 1/2 tsp. sugar. Add 1/4 cup soup and stir together vigorously with a spoon until mixture foams. Add the remaining portion of soup and mix together thoroughly before serving. Repeat this process with each portion of soup. To serve the soup in a soup tureen, use 3/4 cup sour cream, 2 Tblsp. sugar, and 1 1/2 cups soup to make the sour cream mixture. Stir it together with a wire whisk, and whisk in the remaining soup before serving. Recipe serves 6 to 8 people.

Serving Suggestions

Baltic blueberry soup may be used in the same way as strawberry soup or plum soup. The flavor in blueberries is also very compatible with cornmeal. For an interesting dairy meal, begin with the blueberry soup and follow with *mamaliga* (p. 186), sautéed *mamaliga* (p. 186), or baked *mamaliga* with cheese (p. 186). If using the regular *mamaliga* or the sautéed *mamaliga*, serve *brynza* cheese and vegetables whose flavors are compatible with the entire meal, like Boston lettuce salad (p. 220), carrot-and-raisin salad (p. 227), or beet-and-cucumber salad (p. 227).

Hungarian Sour Cherry Soup

Ungarishe Karshen Zupp

Hungarian sour cherry soup is considered the queen of all the fruit soups because the season for cherries is very short compared with that of other fruits. Cherries are also rather pricey commodities, generally speaking. Practically every recipe for sour cherry soup that I have seen calls for making this dish with canned cherries. I do not understand why this practice developed unless it is because the soup itself is so delicious that people started making it with canned cherries in order to be able to have the dish outside its regular season. I strongly recommend not doing this. The best brand of canned cherries (as with any canned fruit) tastes absolutely nothing like fresh ones. Most brands of canned cherries are also full of sugary syrup that really detracts from the fresh, crisp, tart flavor of fresh sour cherries.

I have also seen recipes for sour cherry soup that call for morello cherries or Queen Anne cherries. This, too, is a serious mistake. Morello and Queen Anne cherries are neither tart nor sour.

To make a proper sour cherry soup, you should use only fresh, tart sour cherries—the kind that are called "baking" or "pie" cherries because they are used to make filling for cherry pies. Sour cherries are not always easy to obtain. Much of the American crop is bought up by the canning plants that manufacture canned cherry pie filling, an unpleasant-tasting convenience food. If you live in a temperate climate, you can grow your own sour cherries. The tree is hardy in most parts of the United States, grows quite easily, and attracts relatively few garden pests other than squirrels. I enjoy sour cherry soup so much that I have two sour cherry trees in my backyard and I harvest the cherries every year more for making soup than for making pies or jam. Once you have made sour cherry soup from the right kind of tart sour cherry, you will never again be satisfied with any substitute. And if enough consumers get out there and start buying fresh, tart sour cherries, maybe the supply will increase with the demand. Try to enjoy sour cherry soup often during its season. I'm sure you'll agree with me, once you've tried it, that there is no soup in the world quite like it!

2 lb. fresh, tart sour cherries
1 cup sugar
1 cinnamon stick
1 cup dry red wine
3 cups cold water
sour cream

1. Using a cherry pitter, remove the pits from the cherries and put them into a large, deep sauce-pan. Add sugar, water, and the cinnamon stick. Bring to a boil over medium heat.

2. Reduce the heat to simmer and add the wine. Partly cover the pot and simmer the soup for 30 minutes. Remove from the heat and, partly covered, let the soup cool to room temperature.

3. Remove and discard the cinnamon stick. Puree half of the cherries in the blender or food processor and return them to the pot. Chill in the refrigerator overnight before serving.

4. To serve the soup, place 1 Tblsp. sour cream in each soup bowl with 1/2 tsp. sugar. Ladle 1/4 cup soup into this and stir vigorously with a spoon until mixture foams. Add the remainder of the portion of soup and stir everything together completely before serving. If you wish to serve sour cherry soup in a tureen, use 3/4 cup sour cream, 2 Tblsp. sugar, and 1 1/2 cups soup for the sour cream mixture. Whisk all of this together using a wire whisk and, after it is foamy, incorporate the rest of the soup into it before serving. Recipe serves 6 to 8 people.

Serving Suggestions

A soup as elegant as this requires a very elegant entrée to follow it. Try it preceding any of the following:

Kulebiaka (p. 94)
Poached Salmon with Dill Sauce (p. 85)
Grilled Salmon Fillets or Steaks (p. 82)
Steamed Salmon with *Schav* Leaves and Spinach
    (p. 87)
Gravad Lox (p. 94)

Old Country Beet Borscht

Haimishe Burekeh Borscht

Billig vi borscht!

Cheap as *borscht!*

—Yiddish saying

Beets were a very cheap commodity in eastern Europe, hence their popularity among the Jews of the *shtetlach*. *Borscht* is the generic name that is applied to several different soups that are based on or contain beets. *Burekeh borscht* is the most basic of all of these because it is made of pure beets and very little else. Two different versions of *burekeh borscht* are given here—one for hot *borscht* and one for cold *borscht*.

3 lb. beets, peeled
1 medium onion, peeled and left whole
1 Tblsp. salt
2 Tblsp. sugar
juice of 1 large lemon
cold water
3 egg yolks (for hot *borscht* only)
sour cream (1 Tblsp. per serving)
freshly snipped chives for garnish
boiled potatoes (optional)

1. Cut all but one of the beets into small chunks. Leave one small beet whole. This is from my mother-in-law, who claims that it adds color to the *borscht*. (I haven't been able to prove or disprove this theory, but it is eccentric enough to make me a believer.) Put them in a large, deep soup pot.

2. Add enough cold water to cover the beets by 2 inches. Mix in the salt and the sugar and cover the pot. Bring the *borscht* to a boil over medium heat and then reduce it to simmer. Leaving the lid slightly ajar, simmer the soup for 45 minutes or until beets are tender. Remove from the heat, remove and discard the onion, and stir in the lemon juice.

To Make Hot *Borscht*

Beat the egg yolks in a mixing bowl and add 1 1/2 cups hot *borscht* (liquid only) into them. Whisk together with a wire whisk until thoroughly blended. Remove 4 1/2 cups additional liquid and place it in a deep saucepan. Add the egg mixture and whisk together, over low heat, until all is incorporated and the soup is hot. Do not allow it to come to a boil or the eggs will curdle. At this point, the hot *borscht* is ready to serve. For a *milchig* meal, it may be garnished with a dollop of sour cream. For a *fleischig* meal, serve it as is. Garnish each portion of *borscht* with freshly snipped chives. You may also add sliced boiled potatoes to each bowl of soup if you wish.

To Make Cold *Borscht*

To make cold *burekeh borscht*, simply chill the *borscht* in the refrigerator overnight. When you are ready to serve it, place 1 Tblsp. sour cream with 1/2 tsp. sugar in each soup bowl. Add 1/4 cup liquid to this and

stir vigorously with a spoon until mixture foams. Add the remaining portion of the soup and stir together. Cold *borscht* may be served with or without the beets, depending on how you like it. Garnish each portion with freshly snipped chives. Some people like to serve slices of hot boiled potato in cold *burekeh borscht*, but I do not like it this way.

Serving Suggestions

Serve hot *Milchig Borscht* (with sour cream) before:

My Bobbe's Baked Halibut (p. 84)
Baked Herring and Potato Casserole (p. 91)
Baked Fish Fillets, Hungarian Style (p. 88)

Serve hot *Pareve Borscht* (without sour cream) before:

Shabbosdige Hendel (p. 101)
Pesachdige Hendel (p. 102)
Braised Brisket with *Chrain* (p. 129)
Jewish Prime Rib Roast (p. 137)

Cold *Borscht*

This is especially delicious on a hot summer day served before an array of smoked fish and salads or before any of the following dishes:

Gravad Lox (p. 94)
Lox and Potato Casserole (p. 91)
Blintzes (p. 187)
Cheese *Kreplach* (p. 185)

Variation: *Chlodnik*

Chlodnik is a kind of Polish gazpacho. It is basically a cold-beet *borscht* mixed with a variety of fresh, finely diced vegetables. The non-Jewish version also calls for shrimp. To make *chlodnik*, add finely diced pieces of English cucumber, cold boiled potato, hard-boiled eggs, radishes, scallions, and fresh dill leaves to the basic *bureke borscht*. Serve with sour cream as you would cold *burekeh borscht*. *Chlodnik* is a main-dish summer soup that needs no accompaniment other than good rye or pumpernickel bread. *Chlodnik*, followed by *blintzes* or cheesecake, is a traditional Shevuos lunch of Polish Jews.

Fresh Sorrel Soup

Schav

Schav is the traditional Shevuos soup of Ukrainian Jews, and it is a popular summer soup with Jews from all over eastern Europe. *Schav* means "sour grass." It is another name for the herb "sorrel," which has a distinctive tart, lemony taste. Sorrel grows wild in the Ukraine during spring and early summer. The soup made from this herb, called *schav*, is always *milchig* and always served cold.

When I was a very young boy, I remember *schav* leaves being sold in our neighborhood grocery store. Then suddenly one year, and every other year after that, the store stopped selling them. My aunt started making *schav* out of spinach leaves because *schav* leaves could not be found anywhere. They had simply disappeared from the marketplace. My grandmother complained bitterly about the new version of *schav*, refusing to call it anything but "*shpinatz borscht*" (spinach borscht). Over the years I, too, started calling the *borscht* made out of spinach leaves "*schav*," but I never forgot that it was "not the real thing." I knew that somewhere out there was something else called "*schav* leaves" that was definitely not "spinach leaves," but exactly what it was I did not know.

When my wife and I moved to St. Louis, my work gave me the opportunity to become friendly with a Roman Catholic priest of Polish background who shared my interest in herb gardening. One day, he and I were discussing herbs, and he asked me, "Are you going to grow *schav* in your garden?"

My eyes lit up with a mixture of amazement and delight. I replied, "*Schav*? Do *you* know what *schav* is?"

"Of course I do," he said. "*Schav* is a Polish dish as well as a Jewish dish." (I realized then that *schav* was probably a Polish dish long before it ever became a Jewish dish.)

"Do you know what plant makes *schav* leaves?" I asked.

He told me that *schav* leaves were sorrel leaves from the French sorrel plant, an herb commonly sold in most herb greenhouses. I decided then and there that I was going to buy some sorrel plants, grow them in my herb garden, and see what kind of *schav* they were going to make. The plants turned out to be beautiful and very prolific. When I tasted my first bowl of *schav* made from them, I understood how right my friend had been. Memories of my grandmother's *schav* immediately came back to me. It had been almost 25 years since I had tasted real *schav*.

Now we eat it all the time. The sorrel plant is very hardy and gives me several crops of *schav* leaves every growing season. I always wondered why *schav* leaves ever disappeared from the market in the first place.

I hope that my including this recipe for *schav* will be an inspiration to Jewish cooks and to people everywhere who want to "cook Jewish" to seek out a local source of fresh sorrel leaves. Try to buy from a supplier who sells in quantity, because you will need a lot of it to make the soup. If you have the inclination, try to grow sorrel yourself. It's not much of a challenge, and the rewards are tremendous.

1 lb. *schav* leaves
6 cups cold water
2 Tblsp. sugar
1 Tblsp. salt
2 medium-size red boiling potatoes, peeled and
　　cut into small chunks
juice of one lemon
1 egg, beaten (optional)
sour cream (1 Tblsp. per serving)

1. Mix the sugar and salt together with the water in a large, deep soup pot. Bring to a boil over high heat. Reduce the heat to medium/low and add the *schav* leaves and potatoes. Cook 30 minutes or until the potatoes are tender.

2. Remove the pot from the heat and cool slightly. In a blender or food processor, pulse/chop the soup to get a coarse puree. Return the soup to the pot and add the lemon juice and egg, if using. Refrigerate the soup overnight.

3. To serve, place 1 Tblsp. sour cream with 1/2 tsp. sugar in each soup bowl. Add 1/4 cup soup and stir together vigorously until the mixture is foamy. Add the remaining portion of soup and mix together completely. If you wish to serve *schav* in a tureen, use 3/4 cup sour cream, 2 Tblsp. sugar, and 1 1/2 cups soup for the sour cream mixture. Whisk it together with a wire whisk and then add the remaining soup. Stir completely before serving. Recipe serves 6 to 8 people.

Serving Suggestions

Dark bread like rye or pumpernickel should accompany *schav*. This tart soup goes extremely well with fish. Have it precede an assortment of smoked fish and salads or with any of the following:

> *Scharfe Fisch* (p. 85)
> Poached Fish with *Chrain* Sauce (p. 86)
> Lox and Potato Casserole (p. 91)
> My Bobbe's Baked Halibut (p. 84)
> Fish *Kottletten* (p. 93)
> Any of the grilled fish recipes (p. 81)

Rozl

Rozl is a fermented beet soup that is traditional in the Ukraine and northern Poland. *Rozl* itself is the name given to the fermented beet liquor used to make the soup. In the Yiddish language the word *rozl* (which means "something reddish") came to be associated over the years with many other dishes that did not use *rozl* in them but were only reminiscent of *rozl* because of their tart, fermented taste. Some Jews called roasted meat dishes made with pickle brine as an ingredient, for example, by the name *rozl* or *rozlfleisch*. Even the dish *essigfleisch*, which is a sweet-and-sour braised beef dish containing lemon juice or vinegar, was called by some Jews *rozl*.

The *rozl* itself is not a soup. It is combined with other ingredients to make *rozl* soups. The soups can be *milchig*, *fleischig*, or *pareve*. The *fleischig* version is a main-dish soup called *rozlfleisch*.

Ukrainian Jews traditionally made *rozl* for Passover. I personally feel *rozl* works better as an autumn or winter dish, and I recommend using *rozl* during this season. The recipe for making basic *rozl* follows, and after that, the *milchig* and *pareve* versions of *rozl* soup. The recipe for *rozlfleisch* can be found in chapter 7 with the other main meat dishes.

Rozl Beet Liquor

4 lb. beets, peeled and cut into quarters
boiled water

Place beets in a deep ceramic, glass, or earthenware crock. Cover the beets with water that has been boiled and cooled to room temperature. There should be 2 inches of water covering the beets. Cover the crock with a tight-fitting lid and let stand in a warm place for 4 weeks to ferment. When fermenting is completed, skim the scum off the top of the *rozl* and, if you wish, transfer it to quart jars. The *rozl* is now ready to be used in recipes.

Pareve Rozl Borscht

6 cups *rozl*
1 Tblsp. sugar
3 eggs, beaten
1 medium onion, peeled and left whole
hot boiled potatoes, peeled and cut into small
  chunks
pepper to taste

Bring the *rozl*, sugar, and onion to boil over medium heat. Cook 40 minutes. Remove and discard onion and reduce heat to simmer. Beat eggs together in a mixing bowl and ladle 1 cup soup into them. Whisk together with a wire whisk and return the entire egg mixture to the pot of soup. Whisk together over the heat until everything is well incorporated. *Do not allow the soup to come to a boil or eggs will curdle.* Add potato chunks and pepper and remove soup from heat. Serve immediately. Recipe serves 6 to 8 people.

Milchig Rozl Borscht

Add 1/2 cup sour cream to the above recipe at the same time as you add the potatoes and pepper. Serve immediately.

Serving Suggestions

Rozl soup is served in the same way as hot *burekeh borscht*. Follow the serving suggestions given for hot *pareve* or hot *milchig burekeh borscht*.

Main-Dish Soups

The following recipes are familiar to most American Jews. They are all very substantial soups, which, in eastern Europe, were usually served as entire meals, accompanied by good, dark rye or pumpernickel bread. In my opinion, this is the way each of these soups ought to be treated in our own kitchens as well. None of them should be used as a soup course that is served before a main dish of meat or fish. They are filling and rich enough to be the main course in and of themselves.

A very elegant dinner can be made of these dishes if they are preceded by a *forspeis* that goes well with them. Suggestions are given together with each recipe.

These soups are all cold-weather dishes and should be served in the autumn or winter, when our bodies crave foods that are warm, hearty, and filling.

Ukrainian Meat and Cabbage Soup

Ukrainishe Kroit Borscht

This is a Jewish variation of a Russian and Ukrainian dish. Unlike its nonkosher counterpart, it does not contain any pork or sour cream (which cannot be mixed with meat). It is a rich, satisfying one-dish meal.

3 lb. beef flank steak, cut into 1 1/2-inch cubes
2 1/2 quarts beef stock (p. 4)
2 medium onions, peeled and coarsely chopped
5 Tblsp. corn oil
1 small celery root, peeled and chopped
1 parsley root, peeled and chopped
2 large carrots, peeled and sliced
1/2 small head white cabbage, finely shredded
1 leek (white part only), carefully washed and
    sliced
2 lb. beets, peeled and coarsely chopped
2 lb. red boiling potatoes, peeled and coarsely
    chopped
2 large cloves garlic, peeled and chopped
1 tsp. caraway seeds
1 bouquet garni consisting of 1 bay leaf, 5
    parsley sprigs, 5 dill sprigs, and the greens of
    one leek, tied together with kitchen string
3 Tblsp. brown sugar
3 Tblsp. freshly squeezed lemon juice
salt and black pepper to taste
chopped dill leaves for garnish

1. In a heavy 6-quart pot, heat the oil and brown the beef cubes, a few pieces at a time, on all sides. Be careful not to put too many pieces of meat in the pot at once or it will steam instead of brown. Remove meat as it browns.

2. When all the meat has browned, add onions and sauté until translucent. Add garlic, celery root, parsley root, and carrots and sauté for 3 minutes more. Add cabbage, leeks, and caraway seeds and sauté 3 more minutes.

3. Return the meat to the pot. Add stock, bouquet garni, and beets. Cover pot and bring to a slow boil. Lower heat to simmer and cook, leaving lid slightly ajar, for 1 hour.

4. At the end of 1 hour, add sugar, lemon juice, and potatoes and continue cooking for 1 hour longer. Remove bouquet garni and add salt and pepper to taste. Serve soup in deep, wide soup bowls, garnished with a sprinkling of dill leaves. Have plenty of good rye or pumpernickel bread and *pletzel* to serve with the soup. Recipe serves 6 to 8 people.

Serving Suggestions

This is a one-dish meal that needs no accompaniment other than bread. For a *forspeis*, try chopped egg and onion with *schmaltz* (p. 42) or chopped herring (p. 41). Any of the fruit *kissels* makes an excellent dessert. Drink a fruity zinfandel with the soup.

Meat and Cabbage Soup From Galitzia

Galitzianer Kroit Borscht

This recipe for *kroit borscht* is more typical of the Polish and Galitzianer kitchen. It, too, contains no pork or pork sausages, as its Polish counterpart would.

2 1/2 lb. beef shoulder, cut into 1-inch cubes
2 medium onions, peeled and coarsely chopped
1 small head white cabbage, cored and very
    finely shredded
1 lb. fresh sauerkraut, rinsed and dried
4 Tblsp. *schmaltz*
1 cup fresh tomato sauce (p. 6)
6 cups beef stock (p. 4)
3 Tblsp. freshly squeezed lemon juice
3 Tblsp. brown sugar
2 tart green apples, peeled, cored, and cut into
    chunks
1 bay leaf
black pepper to taste

1. Melt *schmaltz* in a heavy 6-quart pot and brown beef cubes, a few at a time. Do not crowd or meat will steam instead of brown. Remove meat and, in the same fat, sauté onions until translucent.

2. Add cabbage and continue to cook 5 to 7 minutes or until cabbage begins to soften.

3. Add tomato sauce, stock, bay leaf, and sauerkraut. Cover pot and bring to a boil. Reduce heat to simmer and cook for 1 1/2 hours, leaving lid slightly ajar. Stir from time to time to prevent any vegetables or meat from sticking to the bottom of the pot.

4. Add lemon juice, sugar, and apples. Stir into the soup. Cover pot again, leaving lid slightly ajar, and continue cooking for another 45 minutes. Add pepper, and taste for seasoning.

To serve, ladle the soup into deep, wide soup bowls. Serve with plenty of rye or pumpernickel bread and *pletzel*.

Serving Suggestions

Knishes (p. 48) go very well with this soup, either as a *forspeis* or together with the soup, in which case they take the place of bread. Potato and *kasha knishes* are preferred to meat *knishes* if you are going to serve them with the soup. *Galitzianer gefilte fisch* (p. 39) or any of the herring appetizers except those with sour cream also make wonderful *forspeizen*. For dessert, Jewish apple tart (p. 275), Jewish apple cake (p. 268), and, for something lighter, *eppl shnay* (p. 244) are excellent choices. Serve a fruity zinfandel with the main course.

Savory Mushroom and Barley Soup

Krupnik Zupp

This delicious Polish soup is traditionally made in the autumn or early spring when wild mushrooms are gathered but can be made anytime during the cold-weather season with dried mushrooms whenever you get a craving for it. The 1/2 cup port wine and the fresh thyme and marjoram are my own touches to the traditional recipe.

2 1/2 lb. beef shoulder, cut into 1-inch cubes
1/2 cup dried mushrooms (either Polish or Italian)
1 cup boiling water

1 lb. fresh cultivated white mushrooms, wiped clean with a damp cloth and sliced
1/2 lb. fresh wild mushrooms, wiped clean with a damp cloth and sliced (if unavailable, substitute 1/2 lb. cultivated white mushrooms)
1 cup pearl barley
2 medium onions, peeled and finely chopped
1 leek (white only), carefully washed and thinly sliced
2 large cloves garlic, peeled and finely chopped
2 carrots, peeled and grated
6 cups beef stock (p. 4)
3 Tblsp. corn oil
1 bouquet garni consisting of the greens of 1 leek, 1 bay leaf, 4 sprigs parsley, 5 sprigs dill, and 2 sprigs each fresh thyme and fresh marjoram (if available; 1/2 tsp. each of the dried herbs may be substituted for the fresh)
1/2 cup port wine
salt and black pepper to taste

1. Place dried mushrooms in a bowl and cover with boiling water. Set aside at least 1 hour to soak before preparing the soup.

2. Heat oil in a deep, heavy soup pot and brown the meat a few cubes at a time. Do not crowd or meat will steam instead of brown. Remove meat to a platter and sauté the onions in the same fat until translucent and just beginning to turn golden. Add fresh mushrooms and garlic and continue to sauté. After 5 minutes, add grated carrot. Sauté 5 more minutes or until the mushrooms start to give off liquor. Remove the mushrooms and vegetables from the pot, using a slotted spoon, and set aside.

3. Add stock and dried mushrooms together with the water in which they have soaked. Using a wooden spoon, scrape the bottom of the pot to remove browned bits as the stock comes to a boil.

4. Return meat to the pot, and add bouquet garni and wine. Cover pot and bring to a boil. Reduce heat to simmer and cook slowly for 1 hour, leaving lid slightly ajar.

5. After 1 hour, return mushrooms and vegetables to the pot. Add the barley. Continue simmering for 45 minutes. Remove the bouquet garni from the pot and serve the soup in deep, wide soup bowls. Recipe serves 6 to 8 people.

Note: This soup is good reheated, but the barley tends to absorb liquid if it rests for any length of time. To reliquefy, add stock or water when you reheat it.

Serving Suggestions

The best bread to serve with this meal is one of the potato breads (p. 19 and p. 22), and the best *forspeis* is green bean salad (p. 222). Poached pears in red wine (p. 241) makes an excellent dessert. Serve a full-bodied red wine with the soup like a Spanish rioja, an Italian Chianti, or a cabernet sauvignon. A good-quality dry red bordeaux is also excellent with *krupnik zupp*.

Winter Pea Soup

Vinterdige Arbess Zupp

This split-pea soup is familiar to most Europeans and Americans and is part of the cuisine of many northern European countries. The nonkosher version of this dish, however, invariably contains salt pork or a ham bone. This Jewish version is just as tasty without the pork.

2 cups yellow dried split peas
2 1/2 lb. beef chuck, cut into 1-inch cubes
3 large carrots, peeled and sliced
3 stalks celery, sliced
2 medium onions, peeled and coarsely chopped
1 small celery root, peeled and cut into small chunks
2 leeks (white part only), carefully washed and sliced
1 bouquet garni consisting of the greens from 1 leek, 6 sprigs parsley, 1 bay leaf, 3 sprigs fresh thyme, and 3 sprigs fresh savory (1/2 tsp. dried thyme and dried savory can be substituted for the fresh, if fresh is unavailable)
2 quarts beef stock (p. 4)
3 Tblsp. corn oil
salt and black pepper to taste

1. Heat oil in a deep, heavy soup pot and brown the meat, a few pieces at a time, being careful not to crowd. This makes sure that the meat browns and does not steam. Remove meat from the pot as it browns and set it aside.

2. When meat has finished browning, add onions to the fat in the pot and sauté until they begin to turn translucent. Add carrots, celery, celery root, and leeks and continue sautéing 8 to 10 minutes or until the vegetables begin to soften.

3. Add stock and, with a wooden spoon, stir up any browned bits that may have stuck to the bottom. Return the meat to the pot. Add the bouquet garni and split peas to the soup, cover the pot, and bring it to a boil. Reduce heat to simmer, and simmer the soup for 1 1/2 hours. The split peas will start to disintegrate and color the soup. Some of the peas will remain whole, and the soup will look as if it is partly pureed and partly not, which is how it is supposed to look. If this does not happen, remove 2 cups of the vegetables from the soup and puree them in the blender. Return this puree to the soup. Stir in the salt and pepper. Remove the bouquet garni before serving. Serve in deep, wide soup bowls. Recipe serves 6 to 8 people.

Serving Suggestions

This soup needs no accompaniment other than rye or pumpernickel bread and *pletzel*. For a *forspeis*, serve a tossed green salad (p. 219), a green bean salad (p. 222), or a cabbage salad (p. 230). Baked apples (p. 244) make an excellent dessert. So does citrus compote (p. 238). A dry, full-bodied red wine is the best wine to serve with this soup. Try Chianti, Beaujolais Villages, or Spanish rioja.

Bessarabian Bean Soup

Bessarabishe Bebelach Zupp

This very nutritious and savory soup is a specialty of the Carpathian Mountain region, where winters are cold and snowy. It is either *fleischig* or *pareve*, depending on whether you use beef or vegetable stock. When made *pareve*, it is an excellent vegetarian main dish. This soup tastes even better reheated than when it is fresh off the stove. There is nothing like it for warming up the body on a freezing winter day.

1 1/2 cups great northern or other white beans
2 quarts beef stock (p. 4) or vegetable stock (p. 5)
3 ribs celery, with leaves
2 large carrots, peeled and left whole
1 bouquet garni consisting of 5 sprigs parsley, 2 bay leaves, the greens of 1 leek, and 4 sprigs fresh thyme (if available), tied together with kitchen string
8 black peppercorns, wrapped in cheesecloth and tied with kitchen string

3 medium onions, peeled and coarsely chopped
2 large cloves garlic, finely chopped
2 leeks (white part only), well washed and
    sliced
2 medium-size red boiling potatoes, peeled and
    cut into chunks
1 tsp. dried thyme
1 1/2 tsp. Hungarian sweet paprika
1/4 tsp. hot paprika
1 1/2 Tblsp. red wine vinegar
3 Tblsp. corn or sunflower oil
salt and black pepper to taste

1. Soak the beans overnight covered with cold water by 2 inches. In the morning, drain and rinse them.

2. In a large stockpot, bring the stock to boil and add the celery, carrots, bouquet garni, peppercorns, and beans. Reduce heat to simmer and cover the pot, leaving the lid slightly ajar. Simmer for 2 hours.

3. Using a slotted spoon or skimmer, remove the peppercorn bag and bouquet garni and discard them. Then remove about 2/3 of the beans, the celery, and the carrots, and puree this in the blender or food processor. Return the puree to the pot.

4. In a skillet, heat the oil and sauté the onions until translucent. Add the garlic and leeks and sauté 2 minutes longer. Add the two paprikas and the thyme and sauté 3 to 4 minutes longer. Add a ladleful of the soup from the pot to the skillet and, with a wooden spoon, scrape up all browned bits. Add the contents of the skillet to the soup.

5. Add the potatoes to the soup and bring the pot to a boil. Reduce the heat, cover the pot, and leave the lid slightly ajar. Simmer the soup 30 to 35 minutes or until the potatoes are completely cooked through. Serve in deep, wide soup bowls. Recipe serves 6 to 8 people.

Serving Suggestions

This hearty winter soup can be the feature of a *fleischig* or a *pareve* meal. If *fleischig*, serve meat *knishes* with the soup and precede it with a cabbage salad (p. 230). If a *pareve* meal, serve *brynza* or farmer cottage cheese and the cabbage salad or, if you prefer, a beet-and-cucumber salad (p. 224). The *brynza* cheese spread on p. 48 is also very tasty with this soup. If you do not accompany the soup with *knishes*, then rye and pumpernickel are the breads to serve with the soup. Butter may be served at a *pareve* meal. A fruity red wine goes well with this meal. Try a Beaujolais or zinfandel.

Winter Vegetable Soup with Oat Grits

Huber Grits Zupp

Huber grits are something I have not seen in the supermarket for a long time. They are a kind of grits made out of oats and are available in some health food stores or Jewish groceries. You may substitute old-fashioned rolled oats for the *huber grits* in this recipe, but the texture of the soup will not be the same. It is a main-dish *pareve* soup that is very nutritious and wholesome.

1 cup great northern or navy beans
6 cups vegetable stock (p. 5)
1 cup fresh tomato sauce (p. 6)
3 large carrots, peeled and sliced
3 stalks celery, sliced
3/4 lb. fresh green beans, cut into 1-inch
    lengths
2 medium onions, peeled and coarsely chopped
2 turnips, peeled and cut into small chunks
2 leeks (white part only), carefully washed and
    sliced
2 large red boiling potatoes, peeled and cut into
    small chunks
1/2 cup *huber grits* or old-fashioned rolled oats
1 bouquet garni consisting of 5 sprigs parsley, 5
    sprigs dill, 1 bay leaf, 3 sprigs fresh thyme, 3
    sprigs fresh savory, and the greens of 1 leek,
    all tied together with kitchen string (1/2 tsp.
    each dried thyme and dried savory can be
    substituted for the fresh)
3 Tblsp. corn oil
salt and black pepper to taste

1. Soak the beans overnight in cold water to cover by 2 inches. Drain and wash the beans and set aside.

2. Heat oil in a large, heavy soup pot and sauté onions until translucent. Add leeks, carrots, turnips, and celery and continue sautéing 5 to 7 minutes.

3. Add stock, tomato sauce, beans, bouquet garni, and *huber grits* or rolled oats. Cover pot and bring to a boil. Reduce heat to simmer, and simmer soup for 1 hour. Add potatoes and green beans and continue simmering for an additional 35 minutes or until the potatoes have completely cooked through. Remove bouquet garni before serving. Serve in deep, wide soup bowls. Recipe serves 6 to 8 people.

Serving Suggestions

This soup is excellent served with *knishes*. For a *fleischig* meal serve meat *knishes*, and for a dairy meal serve cheese *knishes* with the soup. No *forspeis* is called for but if you wish, you may serve a tossed green salad (p. 219) or a Boston lettuce salad (p. 220) before or after the soup. A white wine is very good with this dish, and just about any kind will do.

Variation

Substitute 1 cup whole milk for the tomato sauce to create an entirely different flavor. Add the milk to the soup 30 minutes before cooking is completed.

Ukrainian Fish Soup

Ukrainishe Fisch Zupp

6 cups fish stock (p. 5)
3 lb. fish fillets (use at least three kinds; I suggest the following combination: 1 lb. boned carp or buffalo; 1 lb. whitefish, lake perch, or pike; 1 lb. halibut)
3 Tblsp. sweet butter
2 large onions, peeled and thinly sliced
3 large carrots, peeled and sliced
1 medium-size parsley root, peeled and sliced
1 medium-size celery root, peeled and cut into small chunks
2 leeks (white part only), carefully washed and sliced
6 medium-size red boiling potatoes, peeled and cut into small chunks
2 cups dry white wine
1 bouquet garni made with 2 bay leaves, 6 stalks parsley, 1 stalk celery (with leaves), and the greens of 1 leek, tied together with kitchen string
juice of 1 1/2 lemons
salt and black pepper to taste

1. Wash and dry the fish. Cut into 1-inch pieces or slices. If using carp and/or halibut, remove the skin before slicing. If the halibut has a bone in it, remove that as well. Place the fish in a bowl together with the lemon juice and cover with plastic wrap. Refrigerate for 2 to 3 hours.

2. Melt butter in a large, heavy soup pot and sauté onions until translucent. Add carrots, parsley root, celery root, and leeks and continue sautéing for 5 minutes or until vegetables begin to soften.

3. Add stock, wine, and bouquet garni and bring to a boil. Reduce heat to simmer, and partially cover the pot. Simmer 15 minutes. Add the potatoes and continue to simmer 30 minutes.

4. Remove the fish from the marinade and add it to the soup. Simmer 25 to 30 minutes or until the fish is cooked through. Remove the bouquet garni before serving. Serve in deep, wide soup bowls. Recipe serves 6 to 8 people.

Serving Suggestions

This is one of the most elegant and delicious main-dish soups. It needs nothing to accompany it other than good bread and *pletzel*. Rye or pumpernickel is best. Serve a tossed green salad (p. 219), a Boston lettuce salad (p. 220), or a green bean salad (p.222) before or after the soup. For an elegant dinner, serve a *forspeis* of herring in olive oil (p. 41) or any smoked fish like sprats or trout accompanied by baked beet salad (p. 224) or pickled beets (p. 281). A white wine like Chablis, chenin blanc, sauvignon blanc, or fume blanc is excellent with the fish soup.

Lithuanian Fish Soup

Litvische Fisch Zupp

8 cups fish stock (p. 5)
2 large carrots, peeled and finely chopped
1 parsnip, peeled and finely chopped
2 leeks (white only), carefully washed and thinly sliced
2 medium-size red boiling potatoes, peeled and finely chopped
3 lb. fresh fish (1 lb. halibut, 1 lb. pike, 1 lb. cod or lake perch), boned and cut into chunks
3 Tblsp. sweet butter or corn oil
2 large egg yolks
1/3 cup finely chopped fresh parsley
1/3 cup finely snipped chives
salt and pepper to taste
sour cream or plain yogurt (1 Tblsp. per serving)

1. Melt butter or heat oil in a large soup pot over medium heat and sauté vegetables (except potatoes) until soft. Add stock and potatoes and bring to a boil. Reduce heat to simmer, partially cover the pot, and cook for 20 minutes.

Basement storefront, Vilna. (Photograph by Roman Vishniac.)

2. Add fish and simmer for 15 minutes longer or until fish just cooks through. Remove from heat.

3. Beat egg yolks in a mixing bowl and add 1 cup soup (liquid only) to them. Whisk together with a wire whisk until thoroughly incorporated and then pour back into the soup. Return soup to the heat. Add parsley and chives and stir together with a wooden spoon until egg mixture and parsley are completely mixed into the soup. Soup should gently reheat. Do not let it come to a boil or the eggs will curdle. When soup is reheated, add salt and pepper and remove again from the heat. Serve soup in deep, wide bowls with a dollop of sour cream on top of each portion. Recipe serves 6 to 8 people.

Serving Suggestions

This soup needs no accompaniment other than good rye or pumpernickel bread, *pletzel*, and butter. Precede or follow it with a Boston lettuce salad (p. 220). For an elegant *forspeis*, serve any of the herring appetizers. A warm *challah* bread pudding (p. 246), apple schalet (p. 245), *eppl shnay* (p. 244), or Jewish apple cake completes the meal. Serve a light, delicate white wine like Riesling or Gewürztraminer with the fish soup.

American-Style Chicken Soup

When I was a child, I once saw a Campbell's Soup commercial on television. I noticed that the soup had chunks of chicken in it as well as noodles and vegetables and I asked my Aunt Ann if she knew how to make a soup like the one I saw on TV. She said, "I guess I could do it but it looks like a heavy dish. If you think you would like it, I'll try to make it for us." That was the birth of a dish that came to be called "American-style chicken soup" by my aunt. After she made it, she said she couldn't understand how you could eat a soup like that as a soup and afterward eat a roast chicken too, and of course she was right. American-style chicken soup (this was the name my grandmother gave it—*Americanishe zupp*) became one of our favorite main-dish soups, but it was always served as a main dish and never as a soup before an entrée.

This dish is a good example of how immigrants and their children respond to new and unfamiliar ways of doing things in their kitchens. Some immigrants quickly take on the new culture and abandon their old. They try, as much as they can, to become like the other people who live in their new country. Other immigrants do not see the new ways as superior to the old. They take whatever they choose to take from the new culture and assimilate it into the life-style they are most comfortable with. In the kitchen, this makes interesting things happen. From time immemorial, unusual and original dishes have resulted from the blending of diverse ingredients and different cooking styles.

My own recipe for American-style chicken soup is very much like that of my aunt. I put enough chicken pieces into the dish that it can be served as a main-dish soup, which is the way I think it presents itself best.

8 cups chicken stock (p. 3)
4 cups chicken left over from making stock (p. 3) (you may use the whole chicken that is served as Jewish Poule-au-Pot; remove the skin and cut the chicken into chunks)
2 medium onions, peeled and thinly sliced
2 large carrots, peeled and thinly sliced
2 stalks celery, thinly sliced
1 leek (white only), carefully washed and thinly sliced
1 medium turnip, peeled and cut into small chunks
3 Tblsp. corn or peanut oil
1/2 lb. thin egg noodles, precooked in boiling salted water and drained
1/3 cup fresh chopped parsley
salt and black pepper to taste

1. Heat the oil in a deep soup pot and sauté the onions until translucent. Add the other vegetables and sauté 7 minutes longer or until soft.

2. Add the stock and bring to a boil over medium heat. Partially cover the pot and reduce heat to simmer. Simmer 30 minutes. Add chicken chunks (I recommend removing the skin from the chicken before cutting it into chunks) and continue cooking until heated through (about 10 minutes). Add noodles and parsley and heat through for 1 more minute. Remove from heat and add salt and pepper. Serve in deep, wide soup bowls. Recipe serves 6 to 8 people.

Serving Suggestions

I like to serve *challah* and *pletzel* with this soup and accompany it with a buttery chardonnay wine. For an appetizer, serve one of the green salads (pp. 219–221) or a baked-beet salad (p. 224). Baked apples (p. 244) or any of the fruit *kissels* in season are good desserts.

Romanian Summer Harvest Dinner for Shabbos Nachmu

Challah

Karnotzelach with Romanian Roasted Pepper Salad

Ghivetch (Romanian veal ragout) with *mamaliga*

White St. Emilion

Kokos and *dios* pastries

Platter of fresh summer fruits

Coffee or tea

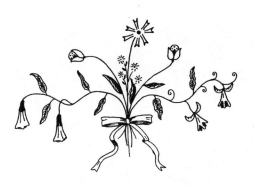

5

Fish

Fisch

Don't pat yourself on the belly
while the fish is still in the pond.

*Potsch zich nit in beichele az der
fischele iz noch in teichele.*

Broiled Fish Recipes

Broiled fish is the simplest and most basic way of preparing fresh fish. Anyone can broil fish. It is something every home cook can and should learn how to do. I personally consider broiled fish warm-weather food—something you prepare when you are enjoying the fresh air and do not wish to spend a great deal of time cooking. It is also one of the tastiest and lightest of "convenience" foods.

I include four different broiled fish recipes. The broiled fish with lemon is my Aunt Ann's recipe. The Hungarian broiled salmon was inspired by a dish made by the mother of one of my childhood friends, who came from Budapest. The broiled fish with garlic and white wine and the broiled trout are my own recipes.

Recipe 1: Broiled Fish Fillets with Lemon

Fillets of fish should generally be broiled on one side only, without turning the fish, unless the fillets are more than 1 inch thick. To broil fillets in the oven, spread a piece of aluminum foil over the entire length of the oven broiler pan that you are using and overlap a piece on each end. This will serve as a handle when you remove the fish from the pan onto a platter or serving plate. Brush the foil lightly with oil and set aside. The following recipe works well with any kind of fish fillet.

2 1/2 lb. fish fillets
1/2 cup corn oil
1 tsp. salt
freshly ground black pepper to taste
1/2 tsp. hot paprika
1 clove garlic
1/3 cup freshly squeezed lemon juice
1 Tblsp. chopped fresh parsley
1 Tblsp. freshly snipped scallion greens
lemon wedges for garnish

1. Chop the garlic clove and put it into a mortar together with the salt. Crush this mixture with a pestle until it becomes a paste.
2. Mix the garlic mixture, pepper, paprika, lemon juice, and oil together in a mixing bowl. Use a wire whisk to blend it completely. Wash and dry the fish fillets and place them into the vinaigrette. Marinate in the refrigerator for at least 30 minutes.

2. Preheat the oven to broil, or preheat your outdoor grill. Remove fish from the marinade and lay each fillet skin side down on the oiled broiler pan. If using the outdoor grill, enclose fish in a wire basket. Mix parsley and scallion greens together.
4. Broil the fish for 10 to 12 minutes or until it is done. If using the outdoor grill, you may turn the fish once, half-way through the broiling, by turning over the wire basket in which it is enclosed. Baste with the marinade every 3 minutes or until it is used up. Sprinkle each fillet with a little of the parsley/scallion green mixture before serving. Garnish the fish with lemon wedges. Recipe serves 4 to 6 people, depending on size of fillets.

Serving Suggestions

Any dairy or *pareve* soup goes well with these broiled fish fillets. Any of the sautéed vegetable dishes in chapter 9 also go well with the fish. Just choose a combination that will provide a variety of colors and textures, and serve only one starch (e.g., *milchig* potato soup, p. 60) in the meal. A mixed vegetable salad (p. 220–221), a field green salad (p. 219), or a Romanian vegetable salad (p. 220) are all good served either before or after the fish, if you do not wish to accompany it with sautéed vegetables. Any seasonal fruit compote concludes the meal. Serve a white wine, such as fumé blanc, Soave, or sauvignon blanc, with the fish.

Recipe 2: Broiled Fish with Garlic and White Wine

1/2 cup olive oil
1/3 cup white wine
2 large garlic cloves, crushed together with 1
    tsp. salt into a paste
1/2 tsp. hot paprika
black pepper to taste
2 1/2 lb. fish fillets
6 Tblsp. brown butter sauce (p. 8)

1. Mix together everything except the fish and the brown butter sauce in a mixing bowl using a wire whisk. Add the fish fillets and marinate at room temperature for 30 minutes or in the refrigerator for 1 1/2 hours.
2. Preheat the broiler in the oven or the outdoor grill. Before putting the fish up to broil, prepare brown butter sauce and keep it warm.

3. Broil fish fillets according to the instructions given in recipe 1, basting with the marinade every 2 minutes or until it is used up. Fish should be done in 10 to 12 minutes. Pour 1 Tblsp. brown butter sauce over each portion of fish before serving it.

Serving Suggestions

Do not serve lemon wedges with this fish. The brown butter sauce provides a very different flavoring accent that will be overwhelmed by the taste of lemon. Follow the serving suggestions given in recipe 1. For wine, chardonnay is an excellent choice. So is a light dry wine like Riesling or Gewürztraminer.

Recipe 3: Hungarian-Style Broiled Salmon

1/2 cup corn oil
1/3 cup lemon juice
zest of 1 lemon, finely chopped
1/2 tsp. dried marjoram
1/4 tsp. hot paprika
1/4 cup chives
1 large clove garlic, crushed with 1 tsp. salt into
    a paste
freshly ground black pepper to taste
6 large salmon steaks or fillets
6 Tblsp. melted sweet butter

1. Mix together all ingredients except for the salmon and melted butter, using a wire whisk. Add the salmon and marinate at room temperature for 45 minutes or in the refrigerator for 2 hours.
2. Preheat the oven broiler or outdoor grill. Remove the salmon from the marinade and broil as directed in recipe 1. Unlike with fish fillets, salmon steaks may be turned once if being broiled in the oven. Broil the fish 6 minutes before turning. The fish should be ready in 12 to 15 minutes. Pour 1 Tblsp. melted butter on each steak or fillet before serving. If you wish, the fish may be garnished with lemon wedges. Recipe serves 6 people.

Serving Suggestions

These salmon steaks are delicious served with sautéed mushrooms in sour cream (p. 203) or sautéed spinach in butter (p. 197). Precede with *milchig* potato soup (p. 60). If you are not serving spinach, serve a green bean salad (p. 222) before or after the fish.

For an elegant Hungarian dessert, try *palaschinken* (p. 247) or Hungarian fruit *knaidelach* (p. 248). A sauvignon blanc or a fine-quality white bordeaux like a Graves or a St. Emilion is the best choice in wine to accompany this elegant dish.

Recipe 4: Broiled Trout

Trout are delicate and delicious when broiled whole in the oven or on the open outdoor grill. This dish is one of the simplest to make.

4 to 6 whole trout
4 to 6 garlic cloves, thinly sliced
1/2 tsp. hot paprika
1/2 cup corn or olive oil
1/3 cup fresh lemon juice
salt and black pepper to taste
4 to 6 Tblsp. brown butter sauce (p. 8)

1. Cut slits in each trout on both sides and insert a slice of garlic in each slit. Mix together the salt, pepper, paprika, lemon juice, and oil and pour mixture over the fish. Marinate the fish in this for 30 minutes at room temperature or for 1 hour in the refrigerator.
2. Preheat the oven to broil or the outdoor grill. Prepare the brown butter sauce and keep it warm while you cook the fish. Broil the fish for 6 minutes on each side. Pour 1 Tblsp. brown butter sauce over each fish before serving. Recipe serves 4 to 6 people.

Serving Suggestions

I like to serve broiled trout by itself and precede it with a salad or a bouquet of fresh vegetable soup (p. 62). Paprika potatoes (p. 200) are also an excellent accompaniment to the fish if you wish to serve a vegetable with it. A light dessert like *eppl shnay* (p. 244) or a seasonal fruit compote completes the meal. A crisp white wine like fume blanc or a delicate one like Riesling goes well with the fish.

Jewish Sole or Flounder Meunière

Gepregelte Yam Tzungen

The classic French sole meunière is lightly floured and then sautéed quickly in clarified butter or a mixture of butter and oil (which can be heated to a high temperature without burning). My Aunt Ann's version of this (although she had no idea that she was making a variation of a classic French dish) is what I call Jewish sole or flounder meunière. Interestingly enough, my aunt prepared only sole or flounder fillets this way.

sole or flounder fillets, enough for 4 to 6 people
    (it is sometimes difficult to tell whether 1 or
    2 fillets are needed per portion; be your own
    judge)
1/4 cup unbleached white flour
1/2 tsp. hot paprika
salt and black pepper to taste
3 Tblsp. sweet butter
3 Tblsp. corn oil
lemon wedges for garnish

1. Mix the flour with the paprika, salt, and pepper and spread it on a platter.

2. Melt the butter together with the oil in a skillet. Heat until very hot and sizzling but not smoking.

3. Lightly coat each fish fillet with the seasoned flour and gently slip it into the sizzling fat. Cook fish until done, turning only once. Take care not to let the fish break apart. Do not crowd fillets in pan, but sauté them in batches in more than one skillet, if necessary. A good pan to own for preparing this dish is an oval-shaped skillet, which is available in gourmet shops and restaurant-supply stores. I like the idea of owning two of them and using them to prepare this dish. Serve the fish garnished with lemon wedges.

Serving Suggestions

Jewish sole meunière can be served with just about anything. I personally like delicate sautéed vegetable dishes with it, as they do not overwhelm the delicateness of the fish. Try it with sautéed spinach in butter (p. 197) and baked beets with dill (p. 203). If you do not serve beets with the fish, then hot beet *borscht* (p. 66) makes a good soup to serve with this meal. Other equally good choices are fresh pea soup (p. 61) and *shvammen zupp* (p. 61). Just about any dessert, light or rich, will do. Fumé blanc, Riesling, or Gewürztraminer is the best wine with this fish.

Old Country Sautéed Flounder or Sole

Gepregelte Fisch

This lightly breaded, sautéed fish dish may be made with any delicate white-fleshed fish. The choice is not limited to flounder or sole.

1 1/2 to 2 lb. fish fillets
1/4 cup unbleached white flour
2 eggs, beaten
1/3 cup *matzoh* meal
salt and black pepper to taste
4 to 6 Tblsp. sweet butter
4 to 6 Tblsp. corn or peanut oil
lemon wedges for garnish

1. Mix flour with salt and pepper and spread it on a platter. Beat the eggs in a deep, wide soup bowl. Spread the *matzoh* meal on a second platter. Have these three lined up in a row.

2. Lightly flour each fish fillet. Dip it into the beaten egg and coat it completely. Allow excess egg to drip back into the bowl and then coat the fillet with the *matzoh* meal.

3. As you coat each fillet, place it on a clean platter. When all the fillets have been coated, place the fish in the refrigerator and chill for 45 minutes to set coating.

4. Heat butter and oil in a skillet until very hot but not smoking. The key to making this dish well is to have the fat hot enough to cook the fillets quickly without burning them. Allow about 8 minutes' cooking time for each 1-inch thickness of the fish (which means, in most instances, you will probably cook the fish 3 to 4 minutes on each side). Slip each fillet into the sizzling fat and do not overcrowd. Turn the fillets only one time during sautéing. If necessary, drain on paper towels before serving. Garnish with lemon wedges. Recipe serves 4 to 6 people.

Serving Suggestions

My favorite combination of side dishes with this fish is *milchig* mashed potatoes (p. 199) and sautéed carrots and peas (p. 202), but just about any combination of sautéed vegetables will do. I like to serve a salad either before or after the fish. Mixed vegetable salad (p. 220) is my choice. Serve a buttery chardonnay with the fish.

Romanian-Style Sautéed Fish Fillets

Rumanishe Gepregelte Fisch

3 lb. fresh fish fillets (lake perch, red snapper, flounder, bass, or other fish that makes attractive fillets)
1/2 cup unbleached white flour
salt and black pepper to taste
3 medium-size onions, peeled and thinly sliced
4 to 6 Tblsp. sunflower oil
1 cup fresh tomato sauce (p. 6)
1/2 cup dry white wine
1 Tblsp. white wine vinegar
1 tsp. hot paprika
1 dried hot chili pepper, seeded and crumbled

1. Mix flour, salt, and black pepper together on a flat plate. Dredge the fish fillets in the seasoned flour and set on another plate.

2. Heat the oil over high heat and sauté the fish fillets until lightly browned. Do not turn them more than once. Browning will take approximately 3 to 4 minutes on each side. Do not sauté all the fillets at once but do them in batches. As you complete the sautéing, set the fillets back on the plate on which they were resting.

3. After you finish sautéing all the fillets, add more oil if necessary, reduce the heat to medium, and sauté the onions until translucent and soft. Add the paprika and crumbled hot chili pepper and reduce the heat again. Cook for an additional 5 minutes over low heat and add the wine, tomato sauce, and vinegar. Mix with a wooden spoon, scraping up any brown bits that have clung to the bottom of the sauté pan. When you have finished doing this and after the sauce comes to a bubbling boil, return fish fillets to the sauté pan and cover it tightly. Cook 10 to 12 minutes over the lowest possible heat. Serve the fish together with the sauce. Recipe serves 4 to 6 people.

Serving Suggestions

This dish does not need any vegetable accompaniment. Just serve it with good, crusty Vienna bread to dip into the sauce. Precede or follow the fish with a green bean salad (p. 222) or a tossed field green salad (p. 219), and conclude the meal with fresh fruit and *roggelach* (p. 262), cookies, or, if you prefer, a seasonal fruit compote or *kissel*. Serve a full-bodied white wine, such as a semidry Chablis or a sauvignon blanc, with the fish.

My Bobbe's Baked Halibut

This used to be one of my favorite childhood dishes. The soaking and baking in milk keeps the fish very, very moist, and the sour cream, onion, and paprika are all that are needed to add zing and richness to the sauce.

4 to 6 halibut steaks
2 3/4 cups whole milk
2 onions, very finely chopped
1 tsp. Hungarian sweet paprika
4 Tblsp. sweet butter
1/2 cup sour cream or plain yogurt
1/4 cup unbleached white flour
salt and black pepper to taste

1. Pour 2 cups milk over fish steaks and marinate in the refrigerator for 1 hour. Remove fish from milk and pat dry with paper towels. Discard milk.

2. Mix flour together with salt and pepper and spread on a platter. Lightly coat fish steaks with seasoned flour.

3. Melt 3 Tblsp. butter in a skillet and sauté fish for 1 minute on each side to lightly brown. Transfer to a baking dish that has been greased with 1 Tblsp. butter.

4. In the same butter, sauté the onions until translucent and soft. Add paprika and sauté 4 minutes longer. While onions are cooking, mix the remaining 3/4 cup milk with the sour cream or plain yogurt using a wire whisk, and preheat the oven to 350°. When onions are through sautéing, pour them into the milk mixture and mix again. Pour this over the fish.

5. Bake the fish uncovered in the oven for 20 to 25 minutes. Most of the liquid will have been absorbed by the fish. The remainder will serve as a sauce to pour over the fish when it is served. Do not be concerned if the sour cream or yogurt appears to have separated. It has a natural tendency to do that. Whisk the sauce together, using your wire whisk, before pouring it over the fish. Recipe serves 4 to 6 people.

Serving Suggestions

This is a very rich dish that is good on a cold winter or autumn day. Butter-steamed new potatoes (p. 198 and a vegetable such as sautéed green beans (p. 197) or sautéed spinach in butter (p. 197) are the best accompaniments. Carrot soup (p. 62) or bouquet of fresh vegetables soup (p. 62) makes a good starter. Any seasonal fruit compote or *kissel* is a good finish. A fruity white wine like Chablis, sauvignon blanc, or chenin blanc goes well with this fish.

Poached Spring Salmon With Dill Sauce

Frische Lox mit Kropzoss

Salmon was always considered the king of fresh fish for eastern European Jews, and each of the many salmon recipes I offer in this book would qualify for serving as the main course in an elegant and formal rather than a casual everyday dinner. Salmon and dill are a favorite combination of the Jews of *Litteh*.

3 quarts fish stock (p. 5)
4 to 6 salmon fillets
2 to 3 Tblsp. sweet butter
1 tsp. sugar
2 to 3 Tblsp. unbleached white flour
2 to 3 Tblsp. sour cream or yogurt
1/2 cup chopped fresh dill leaves
1 1/2 tsp. freshly squeezed lemon juice
salt and black pepper to taste

1. Place fish stock in fish poacher or large, deep casserole. Stir in sugar, and salt and pepper to taste. Bring to a boil over high heat and reduce heat to simmer. Add fish fillets and poach gently for 20 to 30 minutes or until fish is done.

2. While fish is poaching, melt butter in a saucepan over medium/low heat. Add flour and make an *einbren*. Stir the flour and butter together, and reduce heat to the lowest simmer. Cook, stirring occasionally, for at least 15 minutes; longer will not hurt.

3. When fish is done cooking, lift up the rack in the fish poacher holding the fish, set it aside, and remove 1 1/2 cups of the poaching liquid. Place the rack with the fish on it back into the poacher to keep warm while you prepare the sauce. If you do not have a fish poacher, remove the fish and place in a covered baking dish in the microwave oven under "keep warm" or in the regular oven on a very low flame.

4. Using a wire whisk, slowly mix the poaching liquid into the *einbren*, taking care to let it thicken without lumping. After all the poaching liquid has been added, mix in the dill leaves, lemon juice, and sour cream or yogurt. Continue to cook gently, whisking all the while, until the sauce is velvety and thick. Do not allow to come to a boil or the sour cream or yogurt will curdle, ruining the sauce. To serve, place one fish fillet on each dinner plate and gently nap it with sauce. Serve the remainder of the sauce in a sauceboat. Recipe serves 4 to 6 people.

Serving Suggestions

Butter-steamed new potatoes (p. 198) or plain boiled potatoes and spinach sautéed in butter (p. 197) are the best accompaniments for this dish. Precede the salmon with cold beet *borscht* (p. 66) or one of the fruit soups for a perfect springtime or summertime meal. In cooler weather, begin with carrot soup (p. 62) or bouquet of fresh vegetables soup (p. 62). A herring *forspeis* is nice before the soup in wintertime. *Galitzianer flommenkuchen* (p. 270), Jewish apple tart (p. 275), and apple *schalet* (p. 245) are all good choices for dessert. Full-bodied white wines like sauvignon blanc, Chablis, and white bordeaux are the best choices to serve with the fish.

Poached Salmon in Savory Lemon Sauce

Scharfeh Fisch

The sauce in this interesting recipe so closely resembles Greek avgolemono sauce that it is quite plausible that *scharfeh fisch* is an ancient Jewish recipe that was brought north into Poland and Russia with migrations of Sephardic Jews from Spain, Greece, and Turkey. *Scharfeh fisch*, however, was so much a part of the cuisine of eastern European Jews by the nineteenth century that its true origin has been obscured. The sauce in this dish is excellent for any fish that takes well to poaching. I like it with salmon, walleye pike, halibut, whole trout, or lake perch.

6 fresh salmon fillets
8 cups fish stock (p. 5)
3 egg yolks
1/3 cup freshly squeezed lemon juice
1/4 cup finely chopped parsley
salt and black pepper to taste

1. Place the fish stock in a fish poacher or deep soup pot and bring to a boil. Reduce the heat to simmer and gently lower the fish into the simmering liquid. If using a fish poacher, simply place the fish on the rack of the fish poacher and gently lower it into the pot. Cover and poach gently for 20 to 25 minutes.

2. Meanwhile, beat egg yolks and lemon juice together in a mixing bowl. When fish is done poaching, remove rack with the fish on it from fish poacher and set aside while you remove 2 cups of the poaching liquid. If you do not have a fish poacher, gently remove fish fillets and place in a covered baking dish. Place this in the microwave oven on "keep warm" or in an oven on very low heat to keep warm while you make the sauce. If using the fish poacher, simply lower the rack with the fish on it back into the poaching liquid and remove the fish poacher from the heat. It will stay warm while you make the sauce.

3. Place the 2 cups of poaching liquid in a small saucepan and turn on the heat to a gentle simmer. Ladle one ladleful of this into the egg-lemon mixture and whisk it together with a wire whisk. Pour this mixture into the saucepan and whisk together until thoroughly mixed. Heat the sauce through slowly, stirring all the time. Do not allow to come to a boil or the eggs will curdle, ruining the sauce. The sauce will gradually thicken. When it has, add the parsley, salt, and pepper and remove from the heat.

4. To serve *scharfeh fisch*, place one salmon fillet on each dinner plate and nap it with some of the sauce. Serve the remaining sauce in a sauceboat. Recipe serves 6 people.

Serving Suggestions

Serve *scharfeh fisch* with butter-steamed new potatoes (p. 198) or plain boiled potatoes and sautéed spinach in butter (p. 197) or some other combination of sautéed vegetables. *Shvammen zupp* (p. 61) or fresh pea soup (p. 61) makes a good first course. *Scharfeh fisch* is also very good cold. When serving it this way, accompany it with Baltic-style cucumber salad with dill (p. 223) and baked-beet salad (p. 224).

Precede the cold *scharfeh fisch* with *schav* (p. 67) or one of the fruit soups. Baked apples (p. 244) or a seasonal fruit compote completes the meal when you serve *scharfeh fisch* hot. For something more elegant, albeit heavier, try *palaschinken* (p. 247). When serving it cold, I prefer a warm dessert like Hungarian fruit *knaidelach* (p. 248) or the lighter cottage cheese *knaidelach* (p. 185). Practically any kind of white wine goes well with *scharfeh fisch*. I like chardonnay or a crisp sauvignon blanc.

Zesty Poached Fish with Fresh Horseradish Sauce
Gekochte Fisch mit Chrainzoss

10 cups fish stock (p. 5)
1 4- to 5-lb. whole fish (pike, bass, or salmon), cleaned and scaled with head and tail left on
1/2 lemon, sliced
3 Tblsp. sweet butter
3 Tblsp. unbleached white flour
2 tsp. sugar
1/4 lb. fresh horseradish root, finely grated
1 jumbo egg yolk
1 cup sour cream or plain yogurt

1. Fill a fish poacher with the stock and bring it to a boil over high heat. Add the lemon slices and reduce the heat to a gentle simmer.

2. Place the fish on the rack of the fish poacher and gently lower it into the simmering stock. Make sure the stock covers the fish completely. If it does not, add water.

3. Cover the fish poacher and poach the fish for 45 minutes. Remove the fish poacher from the heat.

4. While the fish is cooking, melt the butter in a saucepan and add the flour. Make an *einbren* (p. 9) and cook it over the lowest possible heat, stirring occasionally with a wooden spoon while the fish cooks.

5. When the fish is done cooking, turn off the heat, lift the rack out of the fish poacher, and remove 2 1/2 cups of poaching liquid. Return the fish to the fish poacher and cover it to keep the fish warm while you make the sauce.

6. To make the sauce, slowly add the poaching liquid to the *einbren* and whisk in thoroughly with a wire whisk to prevent lumping. When 1 cup of the liquid has been mixed in, add the sugar. Then whisk in the rest of the liquid. After all the poaching liquid has been mixed into the sauce, add the grated horseradish and let the sauce simmer very gently while you do the next step.

7. Mix the egg yolk with the sour cream or yogurt, using the wire whisk. Ladle a small amount of the simmering sauce into the sour cream or yogurt mixture, whisk it together thoroughly, and then whisk this mixture back into the simmering sauce. Cook a few minutes longer until the sauce heats through and thickens sufficiently, but do not let it come anywhere near a boil or the sauce will curdle.

8. To serve the fish, remove it from the fish poacher and apportion it among 6 to 8 plates. Nap each portion with some of the sauce before serving. Serve the remaining sauce in a sauceboat. If you wish to present the fish whole before serving it, skin it on one side and nap this side with the sauce. Then serve the portions of fish at the table. Recipe serves 6 to 8 people.

Serving Suggestions

This delicate but very rich dish goes well with butter-steamed new potatoes (p. 198), spinach sautéed in butter (p. 197), and sautéed carrots and peas (p. 202). Precede it with one of the lettuce salads (pp. 219–221). If you wish to begin with soup, try *milchig* potato soup (p. 60) or hot *milchig borscht* (p. 66) and do not serve potatoes with the main course. Baked apples (p. 244) or any seasonal fruit compote makes a good finish to the meal. For wine, serve a dry Chablis, a sauvignon blanc, or a dry white bordeaux.

Fillets of Spring Salmon with Fresh Sorrel and Spinach

Lox in Botvinikerzoss

Botviniker lox is a variation on the Russian fish soup called *botvinia*. It was a popular dish among the Jewish upper classes in the Baltic cities at the turn of the century but lends itself very well to a thoroughly modern American menu.

4 to 6 salmon fillets, each 6 to 8 oz.
1/3 cup corn oil
1/3 cup freshly squeezed lemon juice
salt and black pepper to taste

For the sauce

3 cups tightly packed *schav* (sorrel) leaves
3 cups tightly packed fresh spinach leaves
1/2 cup chopped fresh parsley leaves
1/2 cup chopped fresh dill leaves
1/2 cup scallions, thinly sliced
2 cups heavy or whipping cream
1/2 cup dry white wine
2 Tblsp. freshly squeezed lemon juice
3 Tblsp. sweet butter
salt and black pepper to taste
thin lemon slices for garnish

1. Mix together oil, 1/3 cup lemon juice, salt, and pepper and pour over the fish in a deep mixing bowl. Cover with plastic wrap and marinate in the refrigerator for 1 hour.

2. Remove fish from the marinade and arrange in a steamer set over simmering water. A Chinese wok and the accompanying bamboo steamers work exceptionally well. To use these, simply place two or three fish fillets in deep soup bowls and place in the bamboo steamers. Set these into the wok over boiling water and cover with the wok cover. Steam the fish for 18 to 20 minutes. Fish is ready when it is opaque and flakes easily when prodded with a fork.

3. While fish is steaming, prepare the spinach and *schav* leaves. Cook the leaves in a pot in a small amount of water for 4 to 5 minutes or until leaves are limp but spinach is still a bright green. Drain leaves and completely squeeze dry. Puree in a food processor or blender using a pulse/chop motion to produce a coarse puree. Remove this from the blender or processor and transfer to a saucepan. Stir in the scallions, herbs, and half of the whipping cream.

4. Add the wine and the remaining whipping cream and heat over a low flame, stirring constantly with a wooden spoon. Stir in the butter 1 Tblsp. at a time. Remove from the heat and add the lemon juice, salt, and pepper. The mixture should be smooth and thick.

5. To serve, ladle some of the spinach mixture onto a serving plate and spread attractively. Place one fish fillet on top of the puree. Garnish with a thin slice of lemon.

Serving Suggestions

No vegetable accompaniment should be served with this dish. Just serve it as is with slices of Lithuanian potato bread (p. 22) and sweet butter. Carrot soup (p. 62), *milchig* potato soup (p. 60), and hot *milchig borscht* (p. 66) are good starters. For a change of pace, serve potato *latkes* (p. 211) with sour cream instead of soup as a *forspeis*. Apple *schalet* (p. 245), baked apples (p. 244), or apple compote (p. 245) concludes the meal. For wine serve a crisp fumé blanc, a Chablis, or a sauvignon blanc.

Hungarian-Style Baked Fish Fillets

Ungarische Gebakte Fisch

4 to 6 large fish fillets (scrod, lake perch, and bluefish are particularly good prepared this way)
1/2 lb. fresh mushrooms, sliced
1 oz. dried gourmet mushrooms, soaked in 3/4 cup boiling water for 1 hour
4 Tblsp. sweet butter
1 medium onion, thinly sliced
1 leek (white only), thinly sliced
2 tsp. Hungarian sweet paprika
1/2 tsp. dried marjoram (or 1 tsp. fresh)
pinch hot paprika
1/2 cup dry white wine
1 cup heavy or whipping cream
1/2 cup sour cream or plain yogurt

1. Melt 2 Tblsp. butter, and sauté the onions until translucent and soft. Add sweet paprika and hot paprika and continue sautéing 5 minutes more over very low heat. Meanwhile, melt the remaining 2 Tblsp. butter, and sauté the fresh mushrooms and leeks until they are soft and the mushrooms start to give off liquor. Add the soaked dried mushrooms, chopping them into small pieces if necessary. Add the marjoram, and sauté 1 minute more.

2. Combine the mushroom mixture and onion mixture in a saucepan. Add the soaking liquid from the dried mushrooms, the wine, and the heavy cream to this and cook over low heat until heated through.

3. Lay the fish fillets in a baking dish (one that can be used on top of a burner on the stove) greased with sweet butter, and pour the contents of the saucepan over the fish. Cover with aluminum foil and bake in the oven at 350° for 15 minutes. Uncover the pan and raise the heat to 400°. Bake uncovered for 6 to 7 minutes or until mixture is bubbling and fish fillets are beginning to brown. Remove from the oven.

4. Remove the fish fillets from the baking dish. Add the sour cream or yogurt to the contents of the baking dish and, stirring with a wooden spoon over low heat, heat through until warm and thick. Pour this sauce over each portion of fish before serving. Recipe serves 4 to 6 people.

Serving Suggestions

This elegant dish may be accompanied by sautéed paprika potatoes (p. 200) or roast potatoes (p. 197) and spinach sautéed in butter (p. 197) or asparagus baked in butter (p. 201). Two good soups to serve before this entrée are carrot soup (p. 62) and bouquet of fresh vegetables soup (p. 62). Galitzianer potato bread (p. 19) and Vienna bread (p. 22) are the breads to serve with this meal. Any seasonal fruit *kissel*, a fruit compote, or plain fresh fruit completes the meal. For wine, serve sauvignon blanc, chenin blanc, or a good-quality white bordeaux.

Polish-Style Carp

Poilisher Karp

This dish from central Poland is a universal favorite with eastern European Jews. It can be served hot or cold as a main dish or a *forspeis*.

4 lb. carp, in one piece
2 large carrots, peeled and sliced
1 medium-size celery root, peeled and sliced
2 parsley roots, peeled and sliced
1 parsnip, peeled and sliced
6 medium-size onions, peeled and thinly sliced
1 stalk celery, with leaves, left whole
1 bay leaf
6 whole black peppercorns
4 whole cloves
4 whole allspice berries
3 tsp. sugar
salt to taste
cold water to cover

1. Wrap the peppercorns, allspice berries, bay leaf, and cloves in a piece of cheesecloth and tie together with kitchen string.

2. In a fish poacher, make a bed of all the vegetables except the celery. Place the celery and spice bag underneath the fish and sprinkle with the sugar. Lay the fish on top of the rack of the fish poacher and place this on top of the vegetables. Cover with cold water.

3. Bring to a boil over medium heat and reduce to simmer just as it begins to come to a boil. Cover the fish poacher and cook for 45 minutes. Fish may be served immediately with some of the vegetables on the side, or it may be chilled in the refrigerator and served cold (which is how I prefer it). To do this, remove the fish from the fish poacher and lay it on a large platter or in a Pyrex baking dish. Cover it with some of the poaching liquid and then cover this with plastic wrap before refrigerating. Discard the spice bag and the celery stalk. Separate the vegetables from the liquid by draining through a colander. Regrigerate the vegetables and the liquid separately. Serve the carp in individual portions with some of the jellied aspic, some of the vegetables, and *chrain*. Recipe serves 8 to 10 people as an entrée or 16 as a *forspeis*.

Serving Suggestions

The dish is very versatile as a *forspeis* and may be treated as an alternative to *gefilte fisch*. Follow it with a soup and a meat entrée. Practically any will do, provided that the flavors complement each other in the overall menu. If it is to be an entrée, serve a side dish of cucumber salad with dill (p. 223) and either *challah*, pumpernickel, or Vienna bread. Follow the fish with one of the sweet *lokshen* dishes in chapter 8, cottage cheese *knaidelach* (p. 185), or Hungarian fruit *knaidelach* (p. 248). A light white wine, such as Riesling or Soave, may be served with both courses. Conclude the meal with tea or coffee and *mandelbroit* (p. 255), cookies, or cinnamon toast (p. 257).

Sweet-and-Sour Pickled Fish

Ziss und Zoyer Marinirte Fisch

This dish, like *Poilisher karp*, may be served as either a *forspeis* or an entrée.

3 lb. whole pike, carp, buffalo, lake perch, or whitefish
3 carrots, peeled and sliced
1 parsnip, peeled and sliced
2 large onions, peeled and sliced
salt and pepper to taste

Pickling Mixture

1/2 cup freshly squeezed lemon juice
1 cup cold water
1/2 cup sugar
1 small onion, very thinly sliced
1/3 cup raisins
1 carrot, peeled and thinly sliced
2 bay leaves
one 1-inch-piece fresh ginger, peeled and sliced
4 whole garlic cloves, peeled
1 tsp. whole allspice
1 tsp. whole coriander seeds
1 cinnamon stick
5 whole cloves
5 whole black peppercorns
coarse or kosher salt to taste

1. Cut the fish into steaks or fillets and place on the rack of a fish poacher. Place the parsnip, carrots, sliced onions, salt, and pepper into the fish poacher. Lay the rack with the fish on top of this and cover with cold water. Cover the poacher and bring to a boil over medium heat. Reduce to simmer and poach 15 to 20 minutes or until fish is tender but firm. Cool to room temperature. Remove the fish and discard the poaching mixture.

2. While the fish is cooling, make the pickling mixture. Combine all ingredients except the lemon juice in a saucepan and bring to a boil. Remove immediately from the heat and add lemon juice. Cool to room temperature.

3. Arrange fish attractively in a glass or Pyrex dish or, alternatively, in pickling jars. Pour the pickling mixture over the fish. Refrigerate the fish 24 hours before serving. Serve chilled or at room temperature. Pickled fish will keep in the refrigerator for a week. Recipe serves 6 people as an entrée or 12 as a *forspeis*.

Serving Suggestions

If this fish is a *forspeis*, it should be accompanied or followed by a shot of *vishnyek* (p. 299), brandy, vodka, or whiskey. It may be served as a *forspeis* preceding any dish with whose flavors it does not clash. Either of the tongue dishes (pp. 162–163), brisket with *chrain* sauce (p. 129), and *essig fleisch* (p. 131) are all good choices. If serving sweet-and-sour pickled fish as an entrée, accompany it with a side dish of baked-beet salad (p. 224) or carrot and raisin salad (p. 227) and pumpernickel bread. Follow it with one of the sweet *lokshen* dishes in chapter 8. Do not serve wine with this meal.

Sautéed Herring in Sweet Cream

Gepregelte Schmaltz Herring

This dish comes from Lithuania, where herring is a favorite fish. Fresh herring may be used instead of *schmaltz* herring, if you can get it. If using fresh herring, skip step 1 in the recipe.

3 *schmaltz* herrings
2 cups whole milk
1/2 cup bread crumbs
3 medium-size onions, peeled and very thinly
    sliced
6 Tblsp. sweet butter
1 cup heavy or whipping cream

1. Soak the herrings in cold water to cover at least 48 hours (I prefer to do it for 3 days) in the refrigerator to remove the salt in which the fish has been preserved. Change the water at least 3 times daily during this period.
2. Rinse and dry the herrings and fillet them. Discard the carcasses and everything else that is left of the fish except the fillets.
3. Place the herring in the milk and return it to the refrigerator for 2 hours to marinate.
4. Remove the fish from the milk and discard the milk. Pat dry with paper towels and roll the fillets in the bread crumbs.
5. Melt the butter in a sauté pan and sauté the onions until golden brown. Transfer to a bowl using a slotted spoon. Sauté the herring fillets in the same butter, turning over only once, until each side is golden brown. Place each fillet on its individual serving plate or on a platter.
6. Return the onions to the pan and add the cream. Simmer for 2 to 3 minutes or until heated

through and thickened. Pour this over the fish and serve. Recipe serves 6 people.

Serving Suggestions

Gepregelte herring should be accompanied by potatoes. Serve butter-steamed new potatoes (p. 198), sautéed potatoes with onions (p. 199), or plain boiled potatoes. For a vegetable to go with this, serve honey-glazed carrots (p. 202), baked-beet salad (p. 224), or *Galitzianer* beet salad (p. 225). Precede or follow the fish with a Boston lettuce salad (p. 220). Any dessert made with apples tastes very good with this meal. Drink beer rather than wine with the entrée.

Baked Herring with Sour Cream

Gebakte Schmaltz Herring Mit Smetane

This is a variation of *gepregelte* herring, also from Lithuania. Fresh herring, again, may be used instead of *schmaltz* herring. If you use fresh herring, skip step 1 of the recipe.

3 *schmaltz* herrings, prepared as in steps 1 and
    2 for *gepregelte* herring (p. 90)
2 medium onions, peeled and very thinly sliced
3 Tblsp. sweet butter
1 cup sour cream

1. After you have prepared the herrings by soaking and filleting, lay them in one row in a rectangular baking dish greased with butter.
2. Place the onion slices in a small saucepan and cover them with water. Bring this to a boil and remove immediately from the heat. Drain the onions and spread them over the herring fillets. Preheat the oven to 350°.
3. Cut the 3 Tblsp. butter into bits and scatter all over the herring. Bake in the oven 35 to 40 minutes, or until the onions begin to brown.
4. Remove from the oven and spread the sour cream over the fish. Bake another 10 minutes. Place each fillet on an individual serving dish or on a platter. With a wooden spoon, mix together the sour cream mixture remaining in the baking dish, if it has

separated, and pour it over the fish before serving. Recipe serves 6 people.

Serving Suggestions

Follow the same serving suggestions as given for *gepregelte* herring. Paprika potatoes (p. 200) are also quite good with this dish.

Herring and Potato Casserole

Gebakte Herring mit Kartoffel

This baked herring dish, which combines the *schmaltz* herring and the potatoes in one dish, was standard fare in the Lithuanian Jewish home, particularly in the *shtetlach*, where fresh meat and fish were always at a premium. The brown butter sauce finish elevates this dish from a simple peasant casserole to gourmet fare.

3 *schmaltz* herring, prepared as directed in
    steps 1 and 2 for *gepregelte* herring (p. 90)
4 large baking potatoes, peeled and thinly sliced
2 medium onions, peeled and very thinly sliced
3 eggs, beaten
2 cups whole milk
3 Tblsp. sweet butter
bread crumbs
6 Tblsp. brown butter sauce

1. Grease a deep, rectangular baking dish with butter and sprinkle bread crumbs over the bottom and sides.
2. Melt the butter in a skillet and sauté the onions until they are golden brown. Remove from the heat and set aside.
3. Spread half the potatoes over the bottom of the baking dish. Cover this with half the sautéed onions. Lay the herring fillets over this. Cover with the remaining onions and finish with a layer of the remaining potatoes.
4. Preheat the oven to 350°. Beat the eggs together with the milk and pour it over the contents of the baking dish. Bake at 350°, uncovered, for 45 minutes or until the potatoes are nice and brown.
5. While the herring is baking, make the brown butter sauce according to the instructions on p. 8.

6. To serve, spoon out a portion of the casserole onto each serving plate. Top with 1 Tblsp. brown butter sauce. Recipe serves 6 people.

Serving Suggestions

Serve baked beet salad (p. 224) or beets with dill (p. 203) with the casserole. Carrot soup (p. 62) or a Boston lettuce salad (p. 220) is a good starter. Finish the meal with a dessert made with apples, and drink beer instead of wine with the meal.

Lox and Potato Casserole

Gebakte Lox mit Kartoffel

3 large white baking potatoes, peeled and
    thinly sliced
1 medium-size onion, peeled and very finely
    chopped
1/2 lb. lox (lox pieces, which are much cheaper,
    work very well in place of the more
    expensive lox)
3/4 cup chopped dill leaves
ground allspice and black pepper to sprinkle
2 cups heavy or whipping cream
1 Tblsp. sweet butter plus 4 Tblsp. melted
    sweet butter

1. Preheat the oven to 350°. Place a third of the sliced potatoes in a layer in a round or rectangular-shaped casserole that has been well greased with sweet butter (1 Tblsp. should be sufficient for this).
2. Sprinkle half of the chopped onions over the potatoes. Sprinkle this with black pepper and allspice.
3. Top this with half of the lox or lox pieces. Sprinkle half of the dill leaves over the lox. Pour 1 Tblsp. melted butter over this.
4. Make a second layer with another third of the potatoes and the remainder of all the other ingredients, topping the last of the dill leaves with 1 more Tblsp. melted butter.
5. Spread the remaining third of the potatoes over all, sprinkle this with allspice and pepper, and pour the last 2 Tblsp. melted butter over the potatoes.
6. Pour the heavy cream along the sides of the casserole into the casserole, and bake for 1 hour and

15 minutes in the oven. The top will be a crispy golden brown. Serve immediately. Recipe serves 6 to 8 people.

Serving Suggestions

This casserole can be served with one or two salads on the side, like baked-beet salad (p. 224) and cucumber salad with dill (p. 223). Or it can be preceded with one of the lettuce salads in chapter 9. Drink a light white wine such as Riesling or gewürztraminer with the main dish.

Romanian Fish Casserole
Romanishe Gedempte Fisch

This rich, flavorful dish comes from Bessarabia. Although it is traditionally made with carp and other freshwater fish, I have substituted some ocean fish, which I think taste better than the freshwater fish when prepared this way.

3 lb. firm, white-fleshed fish fillets (I like a
    combination of 1 lb. halibut, 1 lb. cod or
    haddock, and 1 lb. lake perch), cut into
    1-inch pieces
1/2 cup sunflower oil
1/4 cup freshly squeezed lemon juice
1 large red bell pepper, roasted, peeled, seeded,
    cored, and cut in strips
3 large cloves garlic, peeled and chopped
2 medium onions, peeled and very thinly sliced
1 lb. fresh mushrooms, wiped clean with a
    damp cloth and sliced
1 cup fresh tomato sauce (p. 6)
1 1/4 cups dry white wine
1/4 cup chopped fresh dill leaves
1/4 cup chopped fresh parsley
1/2 tsp. hot paprika
1 cup *brynza* cheese, cut into chunks
salt and black pepper to taste

    1. Mix 4 Tblsp. oil and the lemon juice, salt, and black pepper together and pour over the fish in a large, deep mixing bowl. Marinate 30 minutes at room temperature or 1 1/2 hours in the refrigerator.

    2. Heat the remaining oil in a deep, wide sauté pan and sauté the onions until translucent. Add the garlic, mushrooms, and the hot paprika and sauté an

additional 5 to 6 minutes or until mushrooms begin to give off liquor.

    3. Add the peppers, tomato sauce, and wine and continue to cook until the mixture begins to thicken and achieve a saucelike texture.

    4. Preheat the oven to 375°. Pour fish, together with the marinade, into a deep baking dish and add the mixture from the sauté pan. Mix thoroughly and bake for 15 minutes. Sprinkle the *brynza* cheese over the fish and bake an additional 10 to 15 minutes, or until the casserole is bubbly and slightly browned. Serve in deep, wide soup bowls. Recipe serves 6 to 8 people.

Serving Suggestions

The traditional accompaniment to this dish is *mamaliga* (p. 186), but Vienna bread (p. 22) is also quite good. Precede the fish with a field green salad (p. 219) or a green bean salad (p. 222). Conclude the meal in the traditional Romanian manner with fresh fruit and *mandelbroit* (p. 256) or *makarrondelach* (p. 258). A good-quality dry white wine like Chablis or a white bordeaux like a Graves or a St. Emilion is excellent with this dish.

Hungarian-Style Quenelles In Fresh Tomato Sauce

This is an elegant Hungarian dish from Budapest that contains all the refinement and sophistication that are typical of the cuisine of this region.

2 lb. cod or haddock, cut into small chunks
grated zest of 1 lemon
1/2 tsp. dried marjoram
1/4 cup finely chopped fresh parsley plus
    chopped fresh parsley for sprinkling
1 extra-large egg, beaten
2 slices of *challah*, crust removed
1 to 2 Tblsp. bread crumbs
1 large onion, very thinly sliced
2 Tblsp. sweet butter plus 1/2 stick (4 Tblsp.)
1 Tblsp. coarse salt
2 1/2 cups fresh tomato sauce (p. 6)

    1. In a food processor or a meat grinder (using the fine blade), grind the fish into a puree. Put fish in a mixing bowl.

2. Cut the *challah* into very small pieces and soak in water for a few minutes. Drain and squeeze dry and add to the fish.

3. Add all remaining ingredients except the onion, bread crumbs, coarse salt, tomato sauce, and butter to the fish mixture. Add 1 Tblsp. bread crumbs to the fish mixture. It should be able to hold its shape nicely in a spoon. If it does not, add 1 more Tblsp. bread crumbs to achieve the correct consistency.

4. Fill a large soup pot with cold water and add the coarse salt. Bring to a boil. Meanwhile, sauté the onion in the 2 Tblsp. butter until soft and translucent. Add to the boiling water in the soup pot. Reduce heat to a gentle simmer.

5. Have a bowl of cold water next to you as you proceed with this step. Moisten your hand in the cold water and take approximately 1/4 cup of the fish mixture into them. Using a light touch, roll this into a ball and gently drop it into the simmering liquid. Repeat this procedure until all the fish mixture is used up. Cover the pot and simmer the fish balls for 30 minutes.

6. Meanwhile, prepare the sauce. Heat the fresh tomato sauce in a saucepan and add the 1/2 stick butter. Melt this, stirring from time to time. The sauce will thicken attractively as it cooks.

7. To serve, ladle some of the sauce into a deep, wide soup bowl and add 3 or 4 fish balls to it, carefully removing them, with a slotted spoon, from the pot in which they have been cooking. Sprinkle with a little chopped parsley. Recipe serves 4 to 6 people.

Serving Suggestions

This dish calls for no vegetable accompaniment. Serve it with *challah* or Vienna bread. The potato breads are also very nice with this dish. Precede the fish with a green bean salad (p. 222) or a field green salad (p. 219). *Palaschinken* (p. 247) or one of the cheesecakes (pp. 281–283) makes an elegant and tasty finish. Drink sauvignon blanc, chenin blanc, or fumé blanc with the fish.

Herbed Fish Cutlets

Fisch Kottletten

These are popular all over eastern and central Europe, but this particular recipe comes from northern Poland.

1 1/2 lb. fish fillets (I like a combination of flounder and cod or haddock)
8 to 10 Tblsp. peanut or corn oil
2 medium-size onions, peeled, one thinly sliced and one quartered
4 slices *challah,* cut into small pieces
1/2 cup whole milk
1 large egg, beaten
1/4 cup chopped fresh dill leaves
1/4 cup chopped fresh parsley
2 Tblsp. freshly squeezed lemon juice
1/2 cup bread crumbs
salt and black pepper to taste
lemon wedges for garnish

1. Heat 3 Tblsp. oil in a skillet and sauté the sliced onion until golden brown. Remove with a slotted spoon and set aside to cool in a mixing bowl.

2. Mix the milk and *challah* in another mixing bowl and let soak 3 or 4 minutes. Drain and squeeze dry.

3. In a food processor or meat grinder (using the fine blade), process the fish and remaining onion until finely ground. Transfer to the bowl containing the sautéed onions.

4. Add the lemon juice, dill, parsley, egg, *challah,* salt, and pepper to the fish mixture and cover the mixing bowl. Chill in the refrigerator for 1 hour or until firm.

5. Spread the bread crumbs on a flat plate. Form the fish mixture into patties and dredge in the bread crumbs. Heat 6 to 7 Tblsp. of the oil in a sauté pan over medium/high heat until sizzling but not smoking. Sauté in the oil until golden brown on both sides. Turn only one time during cooking. Add more oil as needed to sauté all the *kottletten.* Drain on paper towels before serving. Garnish with lemon wedges. Recipe serves 6 to 8 people.

Serving Suggestions

These fish *kottletten* may be served any season of the year, and the season will determine what to serve with them. Try any of the following combinations:

1. Sautéed carrots and peas (p. 202) and sautéed cauliflower (p. 197)
2. Sautéed spinach in butter (p. 197) and sautéed mushrooms in sour cream (p. 203)
3. Romanian salad (p. 228)
4. Beet green salad (p. 225) and beet-cucumber salad (p. 224)

The season will also determine what kind of soup to serve before the fish. Just about any of the *milchig* or *pareve* soups is a good starter. Conclude your meal with a seasonal fruit compote, and drink a light white wine such as Riesling or gewürztraminer with the fish.

Gravad Lox

Gravad lox is a Scandinavian dish that I fell in love with the first time I tasted it. Surprisingly enough, it was never a part of any Jewish cuisine, even in the Baltic countries, but logically it should have been. I include a recipe for it in this book because it tastes so good with Jewish dishes and is truly light as well as low in calories.

**4 lb. fresh salmon, center cut, cleaned and
    scaled
1 very large bunch fresh dill
1/3 cup coarse or kosher salt
1/3 cup sugar
1 Tblsp. coarsely ground black pepper**

1. Divide the salmon in half lengthwise and remove the backbone and as much as you can of the rest of the bones.
2. Place half of the fish, skin side down, in a glass or enameled porcelain baking dish or casserole. Sprinkle the top with half of the sugar and half of the salt and pepper, and lay the bunch of dill leaves across it. Sprinkle the remainder of the salt, sugar, and pepper over this and cover it with the other half of the fish.
3. Cover the salmon in plastic wrap and set several plates on top of it to weight it down. Refrigerate the fish for 3 days, turning it once every morning and once every evening. Baste the fish with the liquid that accumulates at the bottom of the casserole every time you turn the fish. Replace the weights every time you turn and baste the fish.
4. To serve *gravad lox*, remove it from its marinade and discard the dill. Pat it dry with paper towels and lay it on a carving board. Slice it into very thin slices on the diagonal and serve it with the mustard/dill sauce that follows. Recipe serves 6 to 8 people as a main course and 14 to 16 people as a *forspeis*.

Mustard/Dill Sauce for *Gravad Lox*

**4 Tblsp. Dijon mustard
1 tsp. dry mustard
3 Tblsp. sugar
2 Tblsp. white wine vinegar
1/3 cup corn or peanut oil
1/3 cup chopped fresh dill leaves**

In a small mixing bowl, mix together the Dijon mustard, dry mustard, and sugar. Using a wire whisk, whisk in the oil and vinegar. Stir in the dill leaves. The sauce may be refrigerated. It keeps for at least a week.

Serving Suggestions

To serve *gravad lox*, lay 2 slices (for a *forspeis*) or 4 or 5 slices across a dinner platter. Dribble the sauce attractively across the center of the fish. Serve with pumpernickel bread, cucumber salad with dill (p. 223), and baked-beet salad (p. 224). Have extra mustard/dill sauce and sweet butter on the table as well. A *forspeis* of *gravad lox* needs no garnish other than the mustard/dill sauce. I can think of no more perfect, elegant light summer dinner than this one. Precede the *gravad lox* with a bowl of Hungarian sour cherry soup (p. 65) or with *schav* (p. 67). A fumé blanc or a sauvignon blanc is a superb wine accompaniment for *gravad lox*.

I like to conclude a meal of *gravad lox* with a warm dessert. Any of the following are nice:

Blintzes (p. 188)
Cheese *Kreplach* (p. 185)
Hungarian Fruit *Knaidelach* (p. 185)
Varenikas (p. 247)
Hungarian Cottage Cheese *Knaidelach* (p. 248)

Either of the cheesecake recipes (pp. 281–283) is also a terrific finale to this meal.

Kulebiaka

Kulebiaka is one of the most elegant salmon dishes ever to have been invented. It was created in czarist Russia by the chef of one of the czars and was subsequently incorporated into the national cuisines of all of the countries that fell under Russian influence, including those where there were Jews in the region. In some very prosperous Jewish homes, this dish was featured as part of the Shevuos menu, when dairy dishes and spring herbs are highlighted. *Kulebiaka* is, of course, rather time consuming to make and it is therefore something not to be considered everyday fare. But don't let that deter you from trying it. Once you taste it, you'll want to enjoy it at least once a year!

Step 1: Pastry Dough

4 cups unbleached white flour
2 sticks (1/2 lb.) sweet butter
1 tsp. salt
10 to 12 Tblsp. ice water

In a large, chilled bowl, combine flour, salt, and butter cut into bits. Crumble together with your fingertips. Work quickly, blending the flour and butter together until they form crumbs of coarse meal. Pour 10 Tblsp. ice water into this mixture and knead it lightly. Gather it up into a ball. If the dough still seems too crumbly, add more water until it reaches the correct consistency. Divide the dough in half. Dust each half with flour and wrap each half separately in wax paper. Refrigerate at least 3 hours.

Step 2: Salmon Filling

3 lb. salmon, in one piece
2 quarts fish stock (p. 5)

Bring fish stock to boil in a fish poacher over medium heat. Place the salmon, skin side down, on the rack of the fish poacher and lower into the simmering stock. Lower the heat to simmer and cover the pot. Simmer fish gently for 15 to 20 minutes or until it feels firm to the touch. Remove to a platter and set aside to cool. Fish stock may be reused for another purpose.

Step 3: Barley Filling

3/4 cup pearl barley
1 1/2 cups vegetable stock (p. 5)
1 1/2 Tblsp. corn oil
1 small onion, finely chopped
2 Tblsp. chopped fresh dill leaves
1 Tblsp. chopped fresh parsley
1 Tblsp. snipped fresh chives

salt and black pepper to taste
1 large egg, beaten
2 Tblsp. *matzoh* meal or bread crumbs

1. Sauté the onion in oil in a saucepan until translucent. Add the barley and stir until barley is coated with oil.
2. Add vegetable stock and cover the pot. Bring to a boil and reduce the heat. Cook 15 to 20 minutes or until all the stock is absorbed. Remove from heat and add the herbs, salt, and pepper and set aside to cool.
3. Mix the egg and *matzoh* meal or bread crumbs together and add to the barley after it has cooled to room temperature.

Step 4: Spinach Filling

1 1/2 lb. fresh spinach leaves
1/2 lb. *schav* (sorrel) leaves
1 small onion, finely chopped
2 Tblsp. sweet butter
salt and pepper to taste
1 large egg, beaten

1. Wash spinach and *schav* leaves and cook in a pot in the water clinging to the leaves until the leaves wilt but the spinach is still bright green. Drain in a colander, pressing down to extract all the liquid.
2. Melt the butter in a small skillet and sauté the onion until translucent and soft. Set aside to cool.
3. Put the onion and greens into a food processor or blender and, using a pulse/chop method, process this mixture into a coarse puree. Put it into a mixing bowl and add the egg, lemon juice, salt, and pepper.

Step 5: Assembling and Baking the *Kulebiaka*

1. Remove half of the dough from the refrigerator and place it on a floured board. Roll it out into a rough rectangle about 1 inch thick. Dust it with flour and roll it again until it is about 1/8 inch thick. Trim it to a perfect rectangle shape that is 7 inches wide and 16 inches long.
2. Grease a large baking sheet very well with sweet butter. Drape the pastry rectangle over the rolling pin and gently unroll it onto the greased baking sheet.

3. Remove the second piece of dough from the refrigerator and roll it into a rectangle 9 inches wide and 18 inches long, following the same procedure outlined in step 1. The two pieces need to be different in size because the second piece is placed over the filling and needs the extra length to fit properly.

4. Place the barley filling on top of the dough in the greased baking pan. Spread it out over the dough, leaving a 1-inch border all around the pastry.

5. Gently remove the skin from the salmon and whatever bones it is possible to remove without causing the fish to separate. Top the barley filling with the fish.

6. Spread the spinach filling over the salmon, making sure that none of it goes over the 1-inch border left by the barley filling.

7. Drape the top layer of dough gently over the filling. Using your fingertips, seal the dough all the way around the *kulebiaka*. Then, using the tines of a fork, or more attractively, a pastry crimper, make an attractive border all around the outside edges of the *kulebiaka*. This is not only for the sake of beauty; it ensures that the seal will hold while the *kulebiaka* bakes.

8. Gather together the scraps of dough and shape them into leaves or other attractive shapes. If the dish is for Shevuos, a pattern of the two tablets of stone on which the Ten Commandments were written makes a beautiful decoration to complement the leaves. This is in keeping with the tradition of Shevuos.

9. Cut a round circle 3/4 inch in diameter out of the top of the *kulebiaka*. This is to allow the steam to escape during baking.

10. Make an egg wash using one egg, beaten, mixed with 1 Tblsp. cold water. Brush the entire *kulebiaka* with the egg wash and put it in the refrigerator. Chill the *kulebiaka* for 20 minutes.

11. Preheat the oven to 375°. Melt 1 Tblsp. sweet butter and pour it into the opening at the top of the *kulebiaka*. Bake the *kulebiaka* on the middle shelf of the oven for 1 hour or until it is golden brown. Serve at once. Cut into slices at the table.

Serving Suggestions

Kulebiaka is traditionally served cut into slices with sour cream on the side and accompanied by a sauceboat of melted sweet butter. It may be served this way or with a vegetable accompaniment of sautéed mushrooms in sour cream (p. 203) or beets with dill (p. 203). The soup you start the meal with will determine which, if any, of the two vegetable accompaniments you use. I like to start this meal with either a hot *milchig borscht* (p. 66), a *schvammen zupp* (p. 61), or a fresh pea soup (p. 61). For an extremely elegant Shevuos dinner, follow the *kulebiaka* with strawberry compote (p. 237) or rhubarb compote (p. 240) and conclude the meal with *blintzes* (p. 188) or one of the cheesecakes (pp. 281–283). Serve a fine-quality white bordeaux like a Graves or a St. Emilion, a sauvignon blanc, or a Chablis with the meal.

Rosh Hashanah Dinner from Galitzia

Sweet *faiglan* bread

Galitzianer gefilte fisch with *chrain*

Cherry brandy (*vishnyek*)

Chicken soup with *kreplach*

Brisket in cider marinade with apples

Honey-glazed carrots   Sautéed brussels sprouts with lemon

Red bordeaux

Poached pears in red wine with hazelnut macaroons

After-Dinner Sweet Table

Honey *medyvnik*   Glazed lemon *mohn* torte

Taigelach

Tea or coffee

6

Poultry

Oifes

If a poor man eats a chicken,
one of them is sick!

*Az an oremen esst a hun,
iz er krank oder iz der hun krank!*

Shabbosdige Hendel

Shabbosdige hendel is my grandmother's name for a basic Jewish-style pot-roasted chicken. This dish was our "ordinary" Friday-night family dinner when nothing "out of the ordinary" was being planned. If it were a Friday night without company or without anything else to distinguish the meal other than the fact that it was *Shabbos*, I could almost predict without fail that the main course would be *Shabbosdige hendel*. My Aunt Ann used to say that all a person needed to make a *Shabbosdige hendel* was a chicken and that anybody who knew how to cook knew exactly how to make it. Maybe this dish was considered ordinary because it was so easy to prepare. Or maybe it was ordinary because it was made out of things you always had in the house, even if you hadn't done any shopping. Whatever the case, *Shabbosdige hendel* is really not an "ordinary" dish at all.

My wife and I once served *Shabbosdige hendel* to some friends on a Friday night when we both had had a lot of emergencies to deal with in our offices earlier that day and had come home late, with practically no time to prepare for our company. When our guests arrived, we apologized in advance for what we were sure would be a dinner not up to our usual standard. The response of our friends to the *Shabbosdige hendel* was unbelievable. They not only raved about it; they request it in advance every time they are invited over.

Shabbosdige hendel is tasty and very versatile and goes well with just about any vegetable accompaniment and any *forspeis* you wish to serve it with. Make a *Shabbosdige hendel* for dinner any night of the week, and you are guaranteed to make that night feel just like *Shabbos*!

1 4- to 5-lb. roasting chicken, pullet, or capon
(giblets and liver set aside for another use)
3 to 4 Tblsp. *schmaltz*
1 large onion, peeled and sliced
1 clove garlic, peeled and chopped
1 stalk celery, sliced
1 carrot, peeled and sliced
2 cups chicken stock (p. 3)
salt, black pepper, and hot paprika to taste
6 to 8 small white baking potatoes, peeled and
left whole (optional)

1. Crush the garlic together with the salt in a mortar, using the pestle until it has the consistency of a paste. Spread it all over the inside and outside of the chicken. On a rack that just fits it, place the chicken into a roasting pan that has a cover or in a Dutch oven or casserole. Sprinkle it all over with black pepper and hot paprika. Surround the chicken with the potatoes, if using. Sprinkle them as well with salt, pepper, and paprika. Preheat the oven to 450°.

2. Melt *schmaltz* in a small skillet or saucepan and pour it over the chicken and potatoes. Place the chicken in the oven, breast side up, and roast uncovered for 15 minutes. Turn the chicken over so that the underside faces upwards, and sprinkle this side with salt, pepper, and paprika as well. Put the chicken back in the oven and roast it again for 15 minutes. Remove the pot from the oven and reduce the heat to 350°.

3. Set the chicken and potatoes on a platter and remove the rack from the pan. Make a bed of the sliced onions, carrots, and celery on the bottom of the roasting pan. Place the chicken, breast side up, on top of the bed of vegetables. Pour the stock over the chicken and cover the pan tightly. If necessary, cover first with aluminum foil and then with the cover of the pot.

4. Return the chicken to the oven and braise for 45 to 55 minutes, at 350°, depending on whether you are cooking a 4- or a 5-lb. chicken.

5. Remove the chicken from the oven and uncover it. Surround it with the potatoes, if using. Return it to the oven to roast, uncovered, for an additional 30 minutes.

6. To serve, set the chicken on a carving board and carve it into attractive portions. Nap each portion with gravy from the pan. If you cooked the potatoes with the chicken, serve with one potato per diner on the side. Serve in a sauceboat any gravy that remains. You may strain the gravy from the vegetables through a sieve, if you wish. Recipe serves 6 to 8 people.

Serving Suggestions

Shabbosdige hendel is very versatile. It may be preceded by any of the soups other than those that are *milchig* or those that are main-dish soups. It is naturally paired with the chicken soup variations. Do not serve the heavier versions if you are roasting potatoes with the chicken.

You may accompany the chicken with just about any of the sautéed vegetable side dishes except those sautéed in butter. I also do not recommend serving *Shabbosdige hendel* with any of the vegetables that are cooked in tomato sauce. *Fleischig lokshen kugel* (p. 170) and potato *kugel* (p. 178) also go well with *Shabbosdige hendel* instead of the roasted potatoes. If you serve the chicken with one of these, precede or follow it with one of the lettuce salads (pp. 219–221), and for a soup, serve chicken soup with *mandlen* (p. 55) or chicken soup consommé (p. 56). Conclude your meal with a seasonal fruit compote or *kissel* (pp. 237–244). Any white wine goes well with *Shabbosdige hendel*. I personally like a buttery chardonnay.

Baked Chicken for Passover

Pesachdige Hendel

2 3 1/2-lb. chickens, cut in quarters (giblets, backs, and livers removed and set aside for another use)
2 eggs, beaten
1/2 cup cold chicken stock (p. 3)
2 cloves garlic crushed in a mortar into a paste together with 1/2 tsp. salt
black pepper and hot paprika to taste
2 to 2 1/2 cups *matzoh* meal
lemon wedges for garnish (optional)

1. Preheat the oven to 375°. Beat eggs and mix together with the stock and the garlic paste. Mix the *matzoh* meal with the black pepper and paprika and spread it onto a flat plate.

2. Dip each piece of chicken into the egg mixture and allow the excess to drain back into the mixing bowl. Then dip it into the *matzoh* meal mixture. Make sure the breading sticks to the chicken by patting it gently into place. As you prepare each piece of chicken, place it onto a well-oiled baking sheet or into a well-oiled baking pan.

3. Bake the chicken 55 minutes to 1 hour or until it is crisp and brown. Turn over once during baking after the first 30 minutes. If desired, serve garnished with lemon wedges. Recipe serves 8 people.

Serving Suggestions

This is an extremely versatile dish and goes well with just about any soup, *forspeis*, and vegetable side dish. Because it does not contain a sauce, I like to serve it with one of the vegetable side dishes that is made with one. Hungarian-style green beans (p. 207), *lesco* (p. 208), Romanian-style sautéed eggplant (p. 207), Galitzianer-style red cabbage (p. 204), or Litvishe-style red cabbage (p. 205) are all good choices. Chicken soup with *knaidelach* (p. 56) or chicken soup with rice or *kasha* (p. 57 or p. 58) is a good soup choice. Conclude the meal with a seasonal fruit compote or *kissel* and, if it is Passover, a *Pesachdige lekach* (p. 272). Drink chardonnay with the baked chicken.

Chicken *Paprikash*

Chicken *paprikash* is the Hungarian equivalent of coq au vin. This Hungarian Jewish version leaves out the sour cream, making it kosher. The fresh marjoram added at the end makes a big difference in the taste and aroma of the dish, if you are able to get it.

2 3 1/2-lb. frying chickens, cut in eighths, with giblets, necks, and backs removed and set aside for another use
3 large onions, peeled and very thinly sliced
8 Tblsp. corn oil
3 green bell peppers, roasted, peeled, seeded, and thinly sliced (see directions, p. 228)
1 cup fresh tomato sauce (p. 6)
1 cup dry white wine
1 cup chicken stock (p. 3)
1 1/2 Tblsp. Hungarian sweet paprika
1 tsp. hot paprika
2 tsp. dried marjoram
1 tsp. fresh marjoram leaves (if available)
1 large bay leaf
2 large cloves garlic, peeled and finely chopped
1/4 cup chopped fresh parsley
1/4 cup freshly squeezed lemon juice
1/2 cup unbleached white flour
salt and black pepper to taste

1. Mix the salt and black pepper into the flour and spread it on a flat plate. Dredge the chicken

pieces in the seasoned flour and set them on a clean platter.

2. Heat 4 Tblsp. oil over fairly high heat in a deep, wide sauté pan that has a tight-fitting lid. Brown the chicken pieces a few at a time, turning with kitchen tongs. Set them back on the platter as they brown.

3. Add the remaining 4 Tblsp. oil to the skillet and reduce the heat to medium. Add the onions and sauté until translucent and soft. Reduce the heat and add the two paprikas and the garlic. Cook an additional 6 to 7 minutes, stirring from time to time with a wooden spoon.

4. Add the dried marjoram, bay leaf, tomato sauce, chicken stock, wine, and roasted pepper strips and bring to a gentle boil. With a wooden spoon, scrape up any browned bits from the bottom of the sauté pan as you stir the ingredients together. Add the chicken pieces and mix everything together with the wooden spoon. After the ingredients are thoroughly mixed together, cover the pan with aluminum foil and then with the lid of the pan. Reduce the heat to the lowest simmer and simmer undisturbed for 1 1/2 hours.

5. Uncover the pan. Remove the aluminum foil and discard it. A lovely herbal aroma should greet you the second you remove the foil. Add the parsley, lemon juice, and fresh marjoram (if using) and stir this into the chicken *paprikash*. Cover the pot and simmer an additional 5 to 7 minutes before serving. Serve in deep, wide soup bowls. Recipe serves 6 to 8 people.

Serving Suggestions

The traditional accompaniment to chicken *paprikash* is plain boiled rice or rice *pilav* (p. 182). It is, of course, delicious served this way. For a less-traditional menu, precede the chicken with a pasta course featuring *lokshen* with onions and poppy seeds (p. 173) and accompany the chicken with nothing but crusty Vienna bread to mop up the sauce. Chopped liver (p. 43) makes an excellent *forspeis* as well. Follow the chicken with a field green salad (p. 219), and conclude the meal with a seasonal fruit compote or fresh fruit and *makos*, *dios*, or *kokos*. Serve a good-quality chardonnay, Chablis, or white burgundy with the dinner.

Variation

For a lighter version of this dish, substitute 8 skinless, boneless chicken breasts for the chicken pieces.

Golden Orange Roasted Chicken

Hendel mit Marantzen

Oranges were hard to get and very expensive in eastern Europe. Therefore they were eaten only on special occasions or they were given as a special "healing" gift to a person who was ill. (Obviously, the benefit of the vitamin C in citrus fruit was not unknown to the Jews who lived in poor *shtetlach*.)

The ready availability and low cost of oranges and other citrus fruit in America made a deep impression on my grandmother when she emigrated to this country. The idea of America being a *goldene land*, in her mind, was as much connected to America's abundant resources as it was to the ability to get ahead by working hard. She was not alone in her beliefs. To many turn-of-the-century Jewish immigrants like her, eating an orange a day made them feel like kings and queens in their new *goldene haim*, even if they possessed no gold at all!

I think you can understand, given this explanation, why *hendel mit marantzen* was considered a rather opulent dish in our home and was reserved for very special occasions. My grandmother made it every year for *Shabbos Shira*, the Sabbath that falls during the week of *Tu B'Shevat*. She chose that Sabbath (which actually occurs at the height of the citrus season) because she knew that oranges grew in abundance in *Eretz Yisroel* (the land of Israel), a place she prayed for the well-being of every day of her life but never had the privilege to see.

Hendel mit marantzen is really a very simple dish that evokes the essence of the orange itself. The recipe allows very few other flavors and aromas to intrude on the spicy fresh flavor of the fruit itself, which underscores its preciousness.

2 3 1/2-lb. roasting chickens, trimmed of fat
    (necks, wing tips, giblets, and liver set aside
    for some other purpose)
2 large seedless navel oranges
2 cups freshly squeezed orange juice
1 cup dry white wine
1/3 cup honey plus 2 Tblsp.
salt and black pepper to taste

1. Season each chicken inside and out with salt and black pepper to taste. Take each orange and poke holes in it with a toothpick or a metal skewer. Roll the oranges between the palms of your hands to soften them, and place one in the cavity of each chicken. Truss and tie the chickens with kitchen string.

2. Place the chickens on a rack, breast side up, in a roasting pan. Preheat the oven to 450°. Spoon 1 Tblsp. honey over each chicken, and roast them in the oven for 20 minutes. Meanwhile, mix the orange juice, wine, and 1/3 cup honey together in a mixing bowl with a wire whisk.

3. Lower the oven temperature to 350°. Remove the chickens from the oven and ladle some of the orange juice mixture over them. Return them to the oven to roast 20 minutes more.

4. Remove the chickens from the oven and turn them over on their other side, with wings upward. Ladle some of the orange juice mixture over them and return to the oven. Roast another 20 minutes.

5. Remove the chickens from the oven again and turn them over so the breast side is once again facing up. Baste with orange juice mixture and return to the oven. Roast the meat an additional 45 minutes, basting every 10 to 12 minutes with orange juice mixture. To test for doneness, pierce one thigh with a toothpick or a skewer. If the juice that runs out is yellow, the chicken is ready. Remove from the pan and set on a carving board.

6. You should still have approximately 1 cup of orange juice mixture left. If you do not, add white wine to whatever is left and remove the rack from the roasting pan. Place it on a burner on top of the stove and turn on at medium heat. Add the remaining orange juice mixture to the pan and deglaze it. Use a wooden spoon to scrape the browned bits from the bottom. Cook this sauce down until you have approximately 1 cup of sauce.

7. To serve the chicken, carve into attractive portions and serve on individual serving plates, napped with a little sauce. Serve the remaining sauce in a sauceboat. The meat may also be carved at the table if you wish and the sauce served separately. Recipe serves 8 people.

Serving Suggestions

This elegant and flavorful roast chicken is very versatile and goes well with many different vegetable accompaniments and *forspeizen*. My grandmother would make a special fruit and *matzoh* meal *kugel* that contained orange peel and fresh orange juice to go with *hendel mit marantzen*. The recipe for this *kugel* is found on p. 181. For an elegant Sabbath dinner, I recommend a *forspeis* of liver pâté à la Rothschild (p. 44) or chopped liver (p. 43). Follow this with chicken soup with *mandlen* (p. 55) or a lighter chicken soup consommé (p. 56). Serve the chicken with the *matzoh* meal fruit *kugel* (p. 181) and baked asparagus with lemon (p. 201), sautéed brussels sprouts with lemon (p. 197), or sautéed broccoli with garlic (p. 197). If you do not wish to serve the *kugel*, any of the simple roasted or sautéed vegetables will do, as long as their flavors, textures, and colors complement both the dish and the meal. Follow the entrée with a field green salad (p. 219) or a green bean salad (p. 222). To end the meal, serve a cranberry compote (p. 241), pineapple compote (p. 239), or citrus compote (p. 238). A good-quality white burgundy or a chardonnay goes very well with this meal.

THE IMMORTAL ORANGE
DER UMSHTERBLICHER POMERANTZ

Zalman Schneour
Translated from the Yiddish by Hannah Berman

Two boxes of oranges going across the blue ocean. The oranges are Algerian, globular, juicy, heavy, with a glowing red peel—the color of African dawns.

The oranges in the first box boast: "We are going to Warsaw, the ancient Polish capital. Oh, what white teeth will bite into us, what fine aristocratic tongues will relish us!"

The oranges in the second box keep silent; snuggle one against the other, and blush for shame. They know—thanks be to God—that their destination is a little village somewhere in Lithuania, and God knows into what beggarly hands they will fall. No, it was not worth drinking so thirstily the warmth of the African sun, the cool dews of the Algerian nights, the perfumes of the blossoming French orange groves. Nimble brown hands of young mulatto girls cut them down off the trees, and flung them into bamboo baskets. Was it worthwhile?

But we shall see who came off best: the oranges that went to Warsaw, or those that arrived late at Shklov—a remote village in Lithuania. And we shall draw the moral.

So the first lot of oranges arrived at Warsaw and the fruit merchants set them out in pyramids. They glowed like balls of fire out of the window. But that did not last long. They were sold the same day. The tumultuous, thirsty street soon swallowed them up. Tired folk thrust them into their pockets, pulled off their juicy, golden peel with dirty fingers, and flung it on the slush-covered pavements. They swallowed the oranges as they walked along, like dogs, without saying grace. The refreshing juice bespattered dusty beards, greasy coats. Their place in the shop is already taken by other fruits and even vegetables. No feeling for birth and breeding! Only bits of their beautiful peel still lay about in the streets, like the cold rays of a far-off, glowing sun. But no one understood that these were greetings from distant sunny lands, from eternally blue skies. They were trampled underfoot, horses stamped on them, and the street sweeper came with his broom, and swept them, ruthlessly, into the rubbish box. That was the end of the oranges! The end of something that had flourished somewhere, and drawn sustenance between perfumed leaves, and fallen into bamboo baskets under a hot, luxuriant sky.

The second box of oranges arrived a few days later at Shklov. They were dragged along in little peasant wagons, and jolted in Jewish carts, until they had the honor of being shown into their new surroundings.

The wife of the spice-merchant of Shklov called over her husband:

"Come on, my smart fellow. Open the oranges for the Purim presents."

Eli, the spice-merchant, despite his wife's sarcasm, was an expert at unpacking. He worked at the box of oranges for a couple of hours. Patiently, carefully he worked around the lid with his chisel, like a goldsmith at a precious case of jewels. His wife stood beside him, giving advice. At last the box was opened, and out of the bits of blue tissue paper gleamed the little cheeks of the oranges, and there was a burst of heavy, festive fragrance.

In a little while, the oranges lay set out in the little shop window, peeping out on the muddy market-place, the grey, lowering sky, the little heaps of snow in the gutters, the fur-clad, White Russian peasants in their yellow-patched, sheepskin jerkins. Everything around them was so strange, northern,

chilly, half-decayed. And the oranges with their festive perfume and their bright color were so rich and strange and new in such an unfamiliar, poor *milieu*, like a royal garment in a beggar's tavern.

Aunt Feiga arrives with her woollen shawl about her head, and a basket in her hand. She sees the freshly unpacked fruit, and goes in to buy. Purim gifts. And here begins the *immortality* of the orange!

Poor and grey is Lithuanian life. And the little natural wealth that sometimes falls into this place is used up a little at a time, reasonably, and with all the five senses. Not a drop goes to waste of the beautiful fruit that has strayed in here. No, if the orange had been no more than the wandering spirit of a sinful soul it would have found salvation at the home of Aunt Feiga.

II

"Then you won't take eight *kopecks* either? Good day!"

The spice-merchant's wife knows full well that Aunt Feiga has no other place where she can buy; yet she pulls her back by the shawl:

"May all Jews have a pleasant Purim as surely as I am selling you golden fruit . . . I only want to make a start."

"We only want to make a start!" repeats Eli, the spice-merchant, the experienced opener of orange boxes.

A *ruble* more or a *ruble* less. Aunt Feiga selects the best, the heaviest orange, wraps it up, and drops it carefully into the basket, between eggs, onions, goodies for Purim, and all sorts. Aunt Feiga comes home, and the little ones clamor round her, from the eleven-year-old *Gemara* student to the littlest one who is just learning the alphabet, and who have all been given a holiday from school for the eve of Purim. They immediately start turning out their mother's basket.

"Mother, what have you brought? What have you brought?"

The mother silences them. One gets a smack in the face, because of the holiday; another a thump; and a third a tweak of the ear.

"What has happened here! Look at the locusts swarming around me!"

Yet she shows them what she has brought.

"There! Look, you devils, scamps!"

Among the small town Lithuanian goodies, *the orange* glows like a harbinger of wealth and happiness. The children are taken aback. They still remember last Purim, a shadow of the fragrance of such a fruit. Now it has come back to life with the same fragrance and roundness. Here it is! They will not see the like of it again till this time next year.

They snatch at it with the thin little hands; they smell it; they marvel at it.

"Oh, how delicious!" cries the youngest child. "Oh, how it smells!"

"It grows in Palestine," puts in the *Gemara* student, and somehow feels proud and grave.

Aunt Feiga locks it into the drawer. But the round, fragrant, flaming fruit lives in the imagination of the children, like a sweet dream. It shines rich and new among the hard green apples and pickled cucumbers that the children have been seeing all the winter.

When the Purim feast begins, the orange sits at the head of the table, among a host of little tarts and jellies, and figs and sweets, and shines like a huge coral bead in a multi-colored mosaic.

Aunt Feiga covers it with a cloth, and gives it to the Purim gift-bearer to take away. The orange sticks the top of its head out of the cloth, as one might say: "Here I am. I am whole. A pleasant festival, children!" The children follow him on his travels with longing eyes. They know that it will have to pass through many transmigrations, poor thing, until it is brought back to them by the beadle.

And so it was. One aunt exchanges the orange for a lemon, and sends it to another relative. And Aunt Feiga has the lemon. So she sends the lemon to another relative, and there it again meets the orange, and they exchange places. And Aunt Feiga gets her precious orange back again.

The cloth is removed. The orange, the cunning devil, sits in his former place, like the *King of Bagdad*, and rules over little cakes, and sweets and raisins. The cold of the Purim night lies on him like a dew. He seems to be smiling a little wearily, a little chilled after his long journeyings in so strange, snow-covered, and unfamiliar a night:

"You see, children, I've come back! You needn't have been afraid."

III

When Purim is over, the orange lies in the drawer, still whole, and feels happy. If relatives call, and Sabbath dainties are served up, the orange has first place on the table, like a prince among plebeian apples and walnuts. People turn him over, ask how

much he cost, and give their opinion about him, like wealthy folk who are used to such fruits, and he is put back on his plate. The apples and the nuts disappear one by one, and the orange always escapes from the hands of the relatives, and remains whole. Relatives in Shklov are no gluttons—God forbid! They know what must be left for good manners.

"When the month of *Adar* comes we have jollifications . . ." About ten days after Purim there is a betrothal contract drawn up in Aunt Feiga's home. Aunt Feiga has betrothed her eldest daughter to a respectable young man. And again the orange lies on top, right under the hanging lamp, just as if he were the object of the whole party. True, one cheek is a bit withered by now, like that of an old general, but for all that, he still looks majestic. He lights up the table with his luxuriant, exotic strangeness. The youngsters, from the ABC boy to the eleven-year-old *Gemara* student, have already hinted repeatedly to their father and their mother that it is high time they had a taste of the orange. . . . Say the blessing for a new sort of fruit—that was all they wanted, only to say the blessing on a new sort of fruit. . . . But Aunt Feiga gave them a good scolding: "Idlers, gluttons! When the time comes to say the blessing over new fruit, we shall send a special messenger to notify you. . . . Your father and mother won't eat it up themselves. You needn't be afraid of that."

The youngsters were all atremble at the betrothal party lest the bridegroom should want to say the blessing for new fruit. Who can say what a bridegroom might want at his betrothal party? Mother always gives him the best portions.

But the bridegroom belongs to Shklov. He knows that an orange has not been made for a bridegroom to eat at his betrothal party, but only to decorate the table. So he holds it in his hand just for a minute, and his Adam's apple runs into his chin and runs out again. And the orange again is left intact.

But at last the longed-for Friday evening arrives. The orange is no longer so globular as it had been, nor so fragrant. His youth has gone. But it does not matter. It is still an orange. After the Sabbath meal the mood is exalted. No notification has been sent by special messenger; but the youngsters know instinctively that this time *the blessing over the new fruit will be said*. But they pretend to know nothing. One might think there was no such thing as an orange in this world.

Said Aunt Feiga to Uncle Uri:

"Uri, share out the orange among the children. How long is it to lie here?"

Uncle Uri, a bearded Jew with crooked eyes, an experienced orange-eater who has probably eaten half a dozen oranges, or more, in the course of his life, sat down at the head of the table, opened up the big blade of his pocket-knife—an old "wreck"—and started the operation. The children stand round the table watching their father with reverend awe, as one watches a rare magic-maker, though they would love to see the inside of the orange and taste it as well. They are only human beings, after all, with desires. . . . But Uncle Uri has lots of time. Carefully and calmly he cuts straight lines across the fruit, from "pole" to "pole." First he cuts four such lines, then eight, one exactly like the other. (You must admit that he is a master at that sort of thing!) And then he begins to peel the orange.

Everybody listens to the crackling of the fleshy, elastic peel. Slowly the geometrically true pieces of red peel come off. But, here and there, the orange has become slightly wilted, and little bits of the juicy "flesh" come away with the peel. Uncle Uri says "Phut!" just as if it hurts him, thrusts the blade of his knife into the orange, and operates on the danger spot. The orange rolls out of its yellowish-white, fragrant swaddling-clothes, and is artistically divided up by the Uncle into equal half-moons, piece by piece.

"Children," cries the newly engaged girl, placing a big glass on the table, "don't forget the pips. Throw them in here. They will be soaked and planted. . . ."

She addresses her little brothers, but she means her father as well.

The youngsters undertake to assist their sister in her housekeeping enthusiasm, which seems to hold out a promising prospect. And they turn their eyes on the tender, rosy half-moons on the plate.

The first blessing is the prerogative of Uncle Uri himself. He chews one bite, and swallows it with enthusiasm, closing one crooked eye, and lifting the other to the ceiling, and shaking his head:

"A *tasty* orange! Children, come over here. . . ."

The youngest-born goes first. This is his privilege. Whenever there is anything nice going, he is always first after his father. He says the blessing at the top of his voice, with a little squeak, flings the half-moon into his mouth, and gulps it down.

"Don't gulp!" says Uncle Uri very patiently. "No one is going to take it away from you."

"And where is the pip?" asks his betrothed sister, pushing forward the glass.

"Yes, that's right. Where is the pip?" Uncle Uri backs her up.

"Swallowed it . . ." says the youngster, frightened, and flushes to his ears.

"Swallowed it?"

"Ye-e-s."

And the tears come into the little one's eyes. He looks round at his older brothers. . . . They keep quiet.

But it is too late. . . . He knows. . . . No father can help him now. They will tease the life out of him. From this day on he has a new nickname: "Little pip."

Then the remaining portions of the orange are shared out in order, from the bottom upwards, till it comes to the turn of the *Gemara* student. He takes his portion, toys with it a while, and bites into it, feeling that it tastes nice, and also that it is a sweet greeting from Palestine of which he has dreamed often at *Cheder*. Oranges surely grow only in Palestine. . . .

"And a blessing?" says Uncle Uri, catching him out, and fixing him with his crooked eyes.

"Blessed art Thou . . ." the *Gemara* student murmurs, abashed; and the bit of orange sticks in his throat. His greeting from Palestine has had all the joy taken out of it.

But Uncle Uri was not yet satisfied. No. He lectured the *Gemara* student to the effect that he might go and learn from his youngest brother how to say a blessing. Yes, he might take a lesson from him. He could assure him that he would one day light the stove for his youngest brother. Yes, that he would, light his stove for him. And . . .

But he suddenly remembered:

"Feiga, why don't you taste a bit of orange?"

It was a good thing that he remembered; otherwise, who knows when he would have finished his lecture?

"It doesn't matter," Aunt Feiga replied. Nevertheless, she came up, said the blessing, and enjoyed it: "Oh, oh, what lovely things there are in the world!" And then they started a discussion about oranges.

Aunt Feiga said that if she were rich, she would eat every day—half an orange. A whole orange was beyond her comprehension. How could anyone go and eat up a whole orange costing eight and a half *kopecks*?—But Uncle Uri did things on a bigger scale.

He had after all been once to the Fair at Nijni-Novgorod. So he smiled out of his crooked eyes: No, if he were rich he would have the juice squeezed out of—three oranges at once, and drink it out of a glass. There!

His wife and children were astounded at the richness of his imagination, and pictured to themselves a full glass of rosy, thick orange juice, with a white froth on top, and a pip floating about in the froth. . . .

They all sat round the table in silence for a while, gazing with dreamy eyes at the yellow moist pips which the betrothed girl had collected from all those who had a share of the orange. She poured water over them, and counted them through the glass, one, two, three, four. . . . She had nine in all. Yes. Next week she would plant them in the flower-pots; and after her wedding, she would take them with her to her own home. She would place them in her windows, and would let them grow under inverted glasses. . . .

You no doubt think that this is the end. Well, you have forgotten that an orange also has a peel. . . .

IV

One of the youngsters made a discovery—when you squeeze a bit of orange peel over against the lamp, a whole fountain of transparent, thin little fragrant drops squirts out, and when you squirt these into the eyes of one of your brothers, he starts to squint. . . . But before he had time to develop his discovery, he got a smack on his hand. And all the bits of peel vanished into Aunt Feiga's apron.

"There is no trick too small for them to play, the devils. Just as if it were potato-peelings. . . ." If she could only get a little more, she could make preserves. . . . Yes, preserves. . . .

But that was only talk. By the time she could collect enough orange peel to make preserves the Messiah would have come.

So she placed the peel overnight in the warm stove to dry. The golden red bits of peel, that only yesterday had looked so fresh and juicy, were now wilted, blackish-brown, curled up and hard, like old parchment. Aunt Feiga took her sharp kitchen-knife, and cut the peel into long strips, then into small oblongs. . . . She put them into a bottle, poured brandy on them, strewed them with soft sugar, and put it away to stand. The brandy revived the dried-up bits of orange peel, they swelled out, blossomed forth, took on again their one-time

bloom. You pour out a tiny glassful, sip it, and taste the genuine flavor and bouquet of orange peel.

Relatives come to pay you a visit, they pronounce a blessing, take a sip, and feel refreshed, and it is agreed unanimously that it is very good for the stomach. And the women question Aunt Feiga how she came to think of such a clever thing. . . .

"Look," said Uncle Zhama to Michla, his wife, "you let everything go to waste. Surely you had an orange as well for Purim! Where is the peel? Nothing. Thrown it away."

Uncle Uri interrupts him:

"Don't worry, Zhama, let us have another sip."

And he smiles out of his crooked eyes at his "virtuous woman," Aunt Feiga.

The bottle is tied up again with a piece of white cloth about the cork, so that it should not evaporate. And it is put away in the cupboard so that it should draw for a long time. And the bottle stands there, all alone, like a pious woman, a deserted wife, in a hood. . . .

Passover comes, and Jews go through the formality of selling their leaven to Alexieka the water-carrier, with the dirty, flaxen hair; so the bottle of orange-brandy-water too falls into Gentile hands. All that week it stands there, sold, a forbidden thing, and scarcely lives to see the day when it is once more redeemed, so that Jews with grey beards and Jewish women in pious wigs should pronounce the blessing over it, and tell each other about Aunt Feiga's amazing capacity.

Sometimes a bottle like that stands for years. From time to time you add fresh brandy, and it is tasted very rarely, until the bits of orange peel at the bottom of the bottle begin to lose their strength, become sodden and pale. Then Uncle Uri knocks them out on a plate.

This is always done on a Saturday night, after the blessing at the termination of the Sabbath, when the spirit of exaltation has vanished, and the weekday drabness creeps out of every little corner. Then Uncle Uri looks for something of a pick-me-up, and remembers the faded, brandy-soaked, sugared bits of orange peel.

He turns the wide, respectable bottle bottom up—begging your pardon, and smacks it firmly but gently on the bottom.

"Phut, phut, phu-ut . . ." the bottle resounds complainingly, penetrating with hollow dullness all over the room, into the weekday, post-Sabbath shadows.

There is a sound, like a deep, frightened sigh, an

echo from a dried-up ancient well. The bottle seems to cry aloud that the soul is being knocked out of it, its last breath. . . . And at the same time, sticky, golden-yellow, appetizing bits of peel fall out of the neck.

Then all is silent. Uncle Uri pronounces the blessing over the leavings, tastes, and then hands them round.

The children agree that though they are a little harsh, one still detects the taste of the one-time Purim orange, peace unto it.

But at the very moment that the last vestige of the famous orange is disappearing from Uncle Uri's house, the heirs of the orange—the sodden, swollen-up little pips—have long since shot up in the flower-pots at the home of Uncle Uri's married daughter. Three or four spiky, sticky little leaves have sprouted out from each little pip.

The overturned, perspiring glasses were removed long ago. They are getting accustomed quite nicely to the climate of Shklov, and are sprouting slowly, with the reserved, green little smile that they had brought with them and secreted within themselves.

The young wife looks after them, waters them daily. And *God knows what may grow out of them one day*.

Savory Roast Chicken with Red Wine and Prunes

Gebrotene Hendel mit Getrukente Flommen

1 4 1/2- to 5-lb. roasting chicken or capon
  (giblets and liver removed and set aside for
  another purpose)
1 lb. pitted prunes
3 cups dry red wine
2 cups chicken stock (p. 3)
grated zest of 1 orange and 1 lemon
1 1/2 tsp. Hungarian sweet paprika
2 Tblsp. corn oil
salt and black pepper to taste

1. Soak prunes in red wine to cover for 1 hour at room temperature.

2. Rub the cavity of the chicken inside with the salt, pepper, and half the grated citrus zest. Drain prunes and reserve the liquid. Loosely fill the cavity of the chicken with prunes and close the opening tightly with small metal skewers. Not all of the prunes will fit into the chicken. Reserve in a separate bowl from the reserved liquid those that remain. They will be added to the roast at a later point. Truss and tie the chicken with kitchen string. Massage the rest of the orange and lemon zest into the outside of the chicken. Sprinkle the chicken all over with the paprika and with more pepper and salt. Set it on a rack in a roasting pan, breast side up.

3. Preheat the oven to 450°. Pour the oil over the chicken. Put the chicken in the oven and roast it for 20 minutes.

4. Remove the chicken from the oven and lower the heat to 350°. Mix the prune liquid together with some of the chicken stock and ladle some of this mixture over the chicken. Return it to the oven and roast it for another 20 minutes.

5. Remove the chicken from the oven and turn it over so the wings are facing up. Ladle some of the prune liquid over the chicken and return it to the oven. Roast another 20 minutes.

6. Remove the chicken from the oven and turn it over again so that it is once again breast side up. Surround the chicken with the remaining prunes. Roast an additional 45 minutes, basting the chicken every 12 minutes with prune liquid. You should use up all but approximately 3/4 cup liquid in the basting.

7. After 45 minutes, test for doneness by piercing a thigh with a toothpick or metal skewer. If the juice that runs out is yellow, the chicken is ready. Set it on a carving board while you finish the sauce.

8. Remove the rack from the roasting pan but leave the prunes in it. Place it on the stove over medium heat and add the remaining prune liquid. Using a wooden spoon, scrape up the browned bits from the bottom of the roasting pan and remove from the heat.

9. To serve, carve the chicken into attractive pieces and place portions on individual serving plates. Garnish each portion of meat with some prunes from the roasting pan and with some that were stuffed into the chicken. Nap each portion of the meat with the gravy and serve in a sauceboat that which remains.

Serving Suggestions

This is an autumn or winter dish that is filling and satisfying on a cold evening. Roasted winter vegetables (p. 205) are good with the chicken. Honey-glazed carrots (p. 202), sautéed cauliflower (p. 197), or sautéed kohlrabi (p. 197) is also quite good, as is either of the braised cabbage dishes. A chicken soup should be served before the entrée. My favorite choice is chicken soup with *lokshen* (p. 57). Conclude the meal with cranberry *kissel* (p. 243), apple compote (p. 240), citrus compote (p. 238), pineapple compote (p. 239), or baked apples (p. 244). Rosé or a medium-dry red burgundy is a good wine choice for this dish.

Baked Lemon Chicken
Hendel Mit Lemmen

This was one of my Aunt Ann's special recipes. She loved the taste of lemon and never tired of using it in baking and cooking. This is one of those dishes that seem to have universal appeal, and everybody who has tried it tells me they love it.

2 3 1/2-lb. chickens, cut in eighths (backs, giblets, and livers set aside for another use)
the juice of 2 lemons
the grated zest of 2 lemons
1/2 cup flour
1 heaping tsp. hot paprika
salt and black pepper to taste
6 Tblsp. corn or peanut oil
1/3 cup sugar
1 cup chicken stock (p. 3)

1. Marinate the chicken in the lemon juice 2 or 3 hours in the refrigerator.
2. Mix flour, paprika, salt, and pepper together and spread it on a flat plate.
3. Remove chicken from the marinade but do not wipe dry. Coat each piece in the seasoned flour and set it on a clean platter. Preheat the oven to 350°.
4. Heat the oil in a sauté pan to a fairly high temperature. Brown the chicken in the oil on all sides, a few pieces at a time. Do not crowd; be sure the meat is browned and not steamed. As each piece browns, transfer it to a shallow baking pan.
5. Mix 2 Tblsp. of the lemon juice used for the marinade into the chicken stock and pour it into the sauté pan. With a wooden spoon, scrape up the browned bits that cling to the bottom. Add the

lemon zest and sugar. Cook a few minutes until all the browned bits are mixed into the stock and the ingredients in the sauté pan are turned into a sauce. Pour this over the chicken pieces in the baking dish.

6. Bake uncovered in the oven for 40 to 45 minutes. To test for doneness, pierce one thigh and see if the juices run yellow. When meat is completely cooked, serve immediately. Recipe serves 8 to 10 people.

Serving Suggestions

My aunt used to serve this dish with a simple rice *pilav* (p. 182), which really is one of the best accompaniments. For an elegant dinner, precede the chicken with carrot soup (p. 62) and follow it with one of the lettuce salads. For an alternative menu, you may begin the meal with chicken soup with rice (p. 57) and accompany the meat with sautéed brussels sprouts with lemon (p. 197) and honey-glazed carrots (p. 202). Any seasonal fruit compote or *kissel* completes the meal. Serve white wine with the chicken. Chardonnay, Italian Soave, and white burgundy are all good choices.

Variation

For a light version of this dish, substitute 6 to 8 skinless, boneless chicken breasts for the chicken pieces and follow the recipe step-by-step as outlined above.

Roast Chicken with *Challah* Stuffing
Haimishe Gefilte Hendel

This savory traditional stuffing (*gefillachts*) may be used with capon, turkey, and Rock Cornish game hens as well as with chicken.

1 5-lb. roasting chicken
1/2 loaf stale *challah*, broken into fairly small pieces
3 Tblsp. chicken *schmaltz*
2 small onions, peeled and chopped
1 cup fresh chopped parsley
1/2 cup chopped celery
1 clove garlic, finely chopped

1/2 tsp. hot paprika
1 extra-large egg, beaten
1 tsp. sugar
salt and black pepper to taste
3 cups chicken stock (p. 3)
2 cups dry red wine
1 *einbren,* made with 2 Tblsp. *schmaltz* and 2
    Tblsp. unbleached white flour (p. 9)

1. Soak the *challah* in cold water to cover for 5 minutes. Squeeze out water with your hands until the bread is almost dry. Place it in a large mixing bowl.

2. Melt 1 Tblsp. *schmaltz* in a skillet over medium heat and sauté the onions until translucent and soft. Reduce the heat slightly and add the celery. Cook an additional 5 minutes. Add the paprika and the garlic and cook 5 minutes longer. Remove from the heat and cool to room temperature.

3. While the vegetables are cooling, rub the chicken inside and out with salt and black pepper.

4. When the vegetables have cooled sufficiently, add them to the *challah.* Add the sugar, beaten egg, and salt and pepper to taste to the stuffing.

5. To stuff the chicken, begin by gently loosening the skin on the bird with your hands. Take 1/3 of the stuffing mixture and put it between the skin and the meat that covers the breasts and thighs. Do not put too much or the stuffing will spill out, ruining the appearance of the dish. Gently spread it all around the chicken by massaging the skin. Stuff the cavity of the bird from both ends with the remainder of the stuffing mixture. There should be just enough to loosely fill the cavity, which is exactly what you want to do.

6. Secure the stuffing inside the cavity of the bird with toothpicks or metal skewers. Truss and tie the chicken with kitchen string. Preheat the oven to 450°.

7. Rub the remaining 2 Tblsp. *schmaltz* all over the chicken. Place it on a rack in a roasting pan, breast side up, and roast it for 20 minutes at 450°. Meanwhile, mix the wine and stock together in a mixing bowl.

8. After 20 minutes of roasting the chicken at 450°, reduce the oven temperature to 350°. Ladle some of the wine/stock mixture over the chicken and roast another 20 minutes.

9. Remove the chicken from the oven and turn it over carefully onto its other side. Ladle some of the wine/stock mixture over it and return it to the oven. Roast 20 minutes longer.

10. Roast the chicken an additional 30 to 45 minutes, basting with the wine/stock mixture every 10 or 12 minutes. Be sure to leave 2 cups of the wine/stock mixture for making the gravy. During this time, also prepare the *einbren* in a saucepan according to the directions on p. 9. After 30 minutes, test for doneness by poking a thigh with a metal skewer or toothpick. If the juices run yellow, the chicken is ready. Remove it from the oven and place it on a carving board to rest while you make the gravy.

11. To make the gravy, divide the remaining wine/stock mixture in half. Use half to deglaze the roasting pan. Remove the rack and place the roasting pan on a burner on top of the stove. Add the wine/stock mixture and, over medium heat, use a wooden spoon to scrape up the browned bits that cling to the pan. When this is finished, add this back into the wine/stock mixture that has not yet been used. Using a wire whisk, add the wine/stock mixture slowly to the *einbren.* Stir constantly to prevent lumping. When all the wine/stock mixture has been added and the gravy is smooth and of the proper texture, transfer it to a sauceboat.

12. To serve the chicken, carve it into portions at the table or in the kitchen onto individual dinner plates. Give some of the stuffing to each diner and nap each portion of meat with a small amount of gravy. Pass the remaining gravy around the table. Recipe serves 4 to 6 people.

Serving Suggestions

This elegant traditional roast is meant for special occasions. It should be garnished with 2 or 3 sautéed vegetables. Choose from among those listed in chapter 9. Precede the roast with chicken soup with *kreplach* (p. 58), chicken soup with *mandlen* (p. 55), or chicken soup consommé (p. 56). Liver pâté à la Rothschild (p. 44), chopped liver (p. 43), or either of the *gefilte fisch* recipes (pp. 38–39) are all appropriate *forspeizen,* depending on the occasion and the rest of the menu. Follow the roast with a salad. I personally like either a field green salad (p. 219) or a Boston lettuce salad (p. 220). A seasonal fruit compote or *kissel* (pp. 237–244) completes the meal. Serve a good-quality dry white wine with this meal. A white bordeaux like Margaux, St. Emilion, St. Estephe, or Cotes do Beaune is excellent.

Roast Stuffed Capon with Passover *Matzoh* Stuffing

Pesachdige Gefilte Kapon

This kosher-for-Passover version of *haimishe gefilte hendel* actually has a different kind of stuffing. Although I give a recipe here for capon, the same stuffing also works very well with roasting chicken, turkey, and Rock Cornish game hens. I prefer the lighter gravy with this dish, made without the *einbren*, but the same gravy that was made for *haimishe gefilte hendel* (p. 111) works very well with *Pesachdige gefilte hendel* too (not for Passover, though!).

For stuffing

2 whole *matzohs*
1 large onion, peeled and finely grated
1 large white baking potato, peeled and finely grated
2 eggs, beaten
1/4 cup *matzoh* meal
2 stalks celery, with leaves, finely chopped
1 large clove garlic, finely chopped
2 Tblsp. *schmaltz*
1/4 tsp. hot paprika
salt and black pepper to taste

1. Break *matzoh* into small pieces and soak in hot water for 1 minute. Drain and squeeze thoroughly dry with your hands and place in a mixing bowl.

2. Melt *schmaltz* over low heat and sauté celery and garlic until soft. Add this to the *matzoh*.

3. Grate the onion and the potato in the food processor, in the blender, or by hand. Add this to the *matzoh* mixture, together with the remaining ingredients. Mix together thoroughly. Recipe makes about 4 cups stuffing.

For roast

1 6-lb. capon
1 recipe stuffing (above)
2 Tblsp. *schmaltz*
1 large onion, peeled and coarsely chopped
1 stalk celery, chopped
1 large carrot, peeled and chopped
2 cups chicken stock (p. 3)
2 cups dry white wine
salt, black pepper, and hot paprika to taste

1. Rub the capon with salt and black pepper both inside and out. Stuff as much of the stuffing into the cavity of the bird as you can without overfilling it. It should be loosely stuffed. Any stuffing that remains should be baked in a well-greased, covered baking dish at 350° for 45 minutes to 1 hour.

2. Secure the filling inside the cavity of the bird with metal skewers or toothpicks. Truss and tie the capon with kitchen string. Preheat the oven to 450°.

3. Put the capon on a rack in a roasting pan. Rub the 2 Tblsp. *schmaltz* all over it and sprinkle it with hot paprika. Roast, breast side up, in the oven for 20 minutes. Meanwhile, mix the wine and chicken stock together.

4. After 20 minutes, reduce the heat to 350° and remove capon from the oven. Surround it with the chopped onions, celery, and carrots. Ladle some of the wine/stock mixture over it and return it to the oven to roast for another 20 minutes.

5. Remove the capon from the oven and turn it over on its other side. Ladle some more of the wine/stock mixture over it and return it to the oven. Roast another 20 minutes. Remove it from the oven and turn it back to its original position.

6. Continue to roast the capon an additional 45 minutes to 1 hour, basting with the wine/stock mixture every 10 to 12 minutes. Test for doneness by inserting a metal skewer into a thigh. If the juices run yellow, the meat is done. Remove it from the oven and place it on a carving board to rest.

7. Deglaze the pan with whatever remains of the wine/stock mixture or, if none remains, with 1/2 cup cold water. Remove the rack from the pan and place it on a burner on top of the stove. Turn on the heat and add the wine/stock mixture or the water. Using a wooden spoon, scrape the brown bits up from the bottom of the pan. Strain the gravy through a sieve, pressing down hard on the vegetables to extract their juices.

8. To serve, carve the meat into portions. Serve some of the stuffing with each portion of meat and nap it with the sauce. Serve the remaining sauce in a sauceboat. Recipe serves 6 to 8 people.

Serving Suggestions

This is the traditional roast served for the Passover *seder*. The capon should be accompanied by your choice of vegetables. I like baked asparagus spears (p. 201) and sautéed carrots with chives (p. 197). For a complete traditional seder menu featuring this dish, see p. 12. Any of the chicken soups other than chicken soup with *lokshen* or chicken soup with *kasha* goes well with this dish. Any seasonal fruit compote completes the meal. Drink a good-quality dry white wine with the capon. Chardonnay, Chablis, white bordeaux, and white burgundy are all excellent choices.

Hungarian-Style Stuffed Roasted Chicken

1 4 1/2- to 5-lb. roasting chicken (giblets and neck removed and set aside for another use) or 3 1 1/2- to 2-lb. Rock Cornish game hens, plus livers from the chicken or hens
1 medium-size onion, peeled and chopped
6 Tblsp. corn oil
6 slices Vienna bread (p. 22)
2 1/2 cups chicken stock (p. 3)
2 jumbo eggs, beaten
2 Tblsp. fresh chopped parsley
1 cup dry red wine
salt, black pepper, and hot paprika to taste

1. Cut or tear the bread in small pieces and pour 1/2 cup chicken stock over them. Mix together thoroughly and set aside.

2. Preheat the broiler in the oven to 500°. Broil the liver(s) of the chicken or Cornish hens for 1 minute on each side. Remove from the oven and set aside.

3. Heat 3 Tblsp. oil in a skillet over medium heat and sauté the onions until translucent and soft. Chop the liver into very small pieces and add to the onions. Cook 3 minutes longer and add to the bread mixture. Add to the stuffing the parsley, beaten eggs, and salt and black pepper to taste.

4. Stuff the stuffing into the cavity of the chicken (or divide it into 3 parts and stuff it into the

The Passover *seder* of the Max and Fanny Weiner family. St. Louis, 1934.
(Courtesy of Missouri Historical Society.)

Cornish hens). Truss the bird(s) and tie it (them) with kitchen string. Mix the wine, stock, and remaining 3 Tblsp. oil.

5. Rub the bird(s) with salt and black pepper to taste and sprinkle it (them) with hot paprika. Lay it (them) on a rack, breast side up, in a roasting pan. Preheat the oven to 450°. Roast the chicken 20 minutes (15 minutes for Cornish hens). Lower the oven temperature to 350°.

6. Remove the meat from the oven and ladle some of the wine/stock mixture over it. Return to the oven and roast an additional 20 minutes (15 minutes for Cornish hens). Turn the meat over onto its other side, ladle some more of the wine/stock mixture over it, and roast 20 minutes longer (10 minutes for Cornish hens).

7. Turn the meat back over onto the breast-up side and roast the chicken 40 minutes longer (30 minutes for Cornish hens), basting every 10 minutes with the wine-stock mixture. To test for doneness, prick a thigh with a metal skewer. If the juices run yellow, the meat is ready. Set on a board while you deglaze the pan.

8. Use whatever remains of the wine-stock mixture to deglaze the pan, or add up to 1/2 cup of cold water to make 3/4 cup liquid for deglazing. Remove the rack from the roasting pan and place it on a burner. Add the liquid to the pan over medium heat and scrape up the browned bits with a wooden spoon.

9. To serve, carve the chicken into attractive portions. Serve some of the stuffing with each portion of meat. If making this dish with Cornish hens, split them in half and serve half a hen and half of its stuffing to each diner. Nap the meat with the sauce and, if any sauce is left, serve it separately in a sauceboat. Recipe serves 6 people.

Serving Suggestions

This dish is excellent when accompanied by one of the Hungarian-style vegetables with a sauce. Try green beans or zucchini in tomato sauce (p. 207), Galitzianer-style red cabbage (p. 204), or lesco (p. 208). Precede the meat with chicken soup with rice (p. 57), chicken soup with mandlen (p. 55), or chicken soup consommé (p. 56). Carrot soup (p. 62) is also a good starter. Any seasonal fruit compote or kissel (pp. 237–244) accompanied by makos, dios, or kokos concludes the meal. In terms of wine, this dish is extremely versatile. Most white wines are good with it but I like chardonnay the best. This dish is also excellent with rosé wine.

Brandied Cornish Hen with Wild Mushrooms

Shtadlan's Hendel

A shtadlan, in English a "court Jew," was an important figure in Poland and in the Austro-Hungarian Empire. The shtadlanim were usually business people or professionals (lawyers, physicians, scientists, literary figures) who knew Christians in prominent positions in the government. Their job was to use their friendship to assist the Jewish community (who were mostly disadvantaged) with various matters, like repealing burdensome taxes, getting a permit to open a business, preventing pogroms, alleviating situations of tension between Jews and their Christian neighbors, and so forth. The tragedy of the court Jews was that they were often unwitting agents of the government officials they thought were their friends, who sent them back to their communities to recommend policies that benefited no one but those in power. The "influence" the court Jews had with the nobility was, in reality, rather minor and unimportant. Sadly, some of the shtadlanim earned the enmity of the entire peasant class, Christian and Jewish alike. The greatest tragedy of all was the way this system of government pitted Jews against Christians and Christians against Jews, creating an atmosphere of tension and deep-rooted prejudices between the two groups. The shtadlanim themselves, however, lived a rather prosperous life, by bourgeois eastern European standards, and were among the small number of Jews who succeeded in escaping the poverty of the shtetl.

This dish that I call shtadlan's hendel, made with Rock Cornish game hen, is my own variation of an old, historical recipe that comes out of Franz Josef's Austro-Hungarian Empire. It is very elegant and delicious—one of the best and yet one of the simplest recipes I have ever used for preparing Cornish hen. It is also very low in calories, despite the use of chicken schmaltz.

4 to 6 whole Rock Cornish game hens (giblets, necks, and livers removed and set aside for another purpose)
4 to 6 Tblsp. chicken schmaltz
2 medium onions, peeled and very finely chopped

8 shallots (don't confuse shallots with scallions; scallions are green onions; shallots are a small, purple-colored member of the onion family that are sold in most supermarkets)

2 large carrots, peeled and finely chopped

1/2 lb. fresh brown gourmet mushrooms, chopped (if your supermarket doesn't carry these, substitute regular white button mushrooms; the flavor of the mushrooms will not be quite as pronounced but it will still be delicious)

1 oz. dried mushrooms, soaked in 1 cup boiling water for 1 hour

1 cup Tokay wine (substitute Madeira or cream sherry if you cannot get Tokay)

1 tsp. dried thyme

1 bay leaf

1. Truss and tie the hens with kitchen string so they will hold their attractive shape during cooking. Melt the *schmaltz* over fairly high heat in a large, oval-shaped casserole or Dutch oven that has a tight-fitting lid. Brown the hens in the *schmaltz* and set them on a platter. Reduce the heat to medium.

2. Saute the onions in the *schmaltz* remaining in the casserole until they are translucent and soft. Add the shallots, carrot, and fresh mushrooms. Continue sautéing an additional 10 minutes. The mushrooms will be just beginning to give off their liquor.

3. Chop the dried mushrooms, if necessary, and add them, together with the remaining ingredients, into the casserole. Bring to a gentle boil. Preheat the oven to 350°.

4. Lay the hens breast side up on top of the vegetables. Cover the casserole with aluminum foil and then with the lid of the casserole. Braise in the oven for 45 minutes, undisturbed.

5. Remove the casserole from the oven. Place one Cornish hen on each dinner plate. Discard the bay leaf and strain the contents of the casserole through a fine sieve to separate the vegetables from the gravy. Do not press on the vegetables. There should be just enough of the sauce to nap each portion of meat with it. If there is more, serve it separately in a sauceboat. The vegetables are saved to mix in with the rice pilav (p. 182) that accompanies the meat. When you put the meat in the oven to braise, put the rice in together with it. Mix the vegetables into the rice and serve a portion of rice *pilav* together with each hen. Recipe serves 4 to 6 people.

Serving Suggestions

This elegant dish needs no accompaniment. Precede or follow it with a field green salad (p. 219) or a green bean salad (p. 222). Carrot soup (p. 62) or chicken soup consommé (p. 56) is the best soup to serve with the meal. For an especially elegant dinner, fit for a *shtadlan*, begin with liver pâté à la Rothschild (p. 44), liver *blintzes* (p. 45), or *Galitzianer gefilte fisch* (p. 39). (*Litvishe gefilte fisch* would not do at all with an entrée that is so Austro-Hungarian and undoubtedly popular with all the *shtadlanim* in Galitzia!) Serve with the meal the best-quality white wine you can find. (I still like chardonnay or white burgundy best with poultry.)

Stewed Chicken for *Erev* Yom Kippur

Gedempte Hendel

Gedempte hendel, the Yiddish name for "stewed chicken," was the traditional meal served in our home before beginning the fast of *Yom Kippur*. My grandmother claimed it was easy on the digestion and because it is rather bland, it would not stimulate the taste buds and make a person hungry during the fast. The dish itself somewhat resembles Jewish Poule-au-Pot and therefore it may seem repetitive to include it in this cookbook. I include it anyway because of my desire to document and preserve it as something of folkloric and cultural interest. This dish was an important tradition in my own and many other Jewish homes. It is also very tasty.

1 4- to 5-lb. stewing chicken, cut in eighths, with its giblets and neck. Save the liver for another use. (A stewing chicken is not easy to obtain today; you may substitute a roasting chicken, but the texture and, to a degree, the flavor will not be the same.)

2 Tblsp. corn or peanut oil

3 stalks celery, preferably those that have some leaves, sliced

2 large carrots, peeled and cut in pieces

1 large onion, peeled and quartered

one bouquet garni consisting of 5 sprigs fresh parsley, 5 sprigs fresh dill, the greens of 1 leek, and 1 bay leaf, tied together with kitchen string

salt and black pepper to taste
6 cups boiling water

1. Heat the oil to a fairly high temperature in a heavy casserole or soup pot with a tight-fitting lid. Brown the chicken pieces and set on a platter. Reduce the heat to medium, and brown the onions, carrots, and celery in the same oil. Return the chicken to the pot together with any juices that have accumulated on the platter and add the boiling water and bouquet garni.

2. Reduce heat to simmer and cover the pot. Simmer for 1 1/2 to 2 hours undisturbed. Recipe serves 6 to 8 people.

Serving Suggestions

My grandmother would serve the stock that the chicken cooked in together with *lokshen* or *kreplach* as a first course. The chicken would be served, moistened with a spoonful of the soup stock, with a plain rice *pilav* (p. 182) or boiled potatoes and carrot-and-parsnip *tzimmes* (p. 203).

Grilled Rock Cornish Game Hen, Romanian Style

Romanishe Gebrotene Hendel

This unusual Romanian-style grilled chicken is very good made with squabs or small fryers as well as with Rock Cornish game hens. The birds should be no more than 2 lb. each.

3 Rock Cornish game hens or squabs, split in
    half with backbones and necks removed
    (save these together with the giblets for
    making stock)
1/3 cup sunflower oil plus 4 Tblsp.
1 small onion, peeled and finely chopped
1 small green bell pepper, roasted, peeled,
    seeded, and chopped
4 cloves garlic, peeled and finely chopped
6 scallions, finely chopped
1/3 cup fresh chopped parsley
1 tsp. hot paprika
1/2 cup bread crumbs

1/2 cup shelled, roasted sunflower seeds,
    ground in a blender or food processor
1 1/2 tsp. Dijon mustard
salt and black pepper to taste

1. Heat 4 Tblsp. oil in a skillet over medium heat and sauté the onions until soft and translucent. Transfer them to a mixing bowl and cool to room temperature.

2. Add the garlic, chopped green pepper, parsley, sunflower seeds, and scallions to the onions. Thoroughly mix together. Add the mustard, bread crumbs, and salt and pepper to taste to this mixture and stir together until well blended.

3. Gently lift the skin of the chicken off the meat and stuff this mixture underneath it. Spread it with your fingers, leaving enough of a margin to prevent any stuffing from leaking out during the grilling of the chicken.

4. Preheat the oven broiler to 500° or prepare the outdoor grill according to the instructions. Season the chicken halves on both sides with salt and black pepper. Mix the remaining 1/3 cup oil with the paprika.

5. When the oven or grill is ready, place the meat on the rack of the oven broiler pan (or, if using the outdoor grill, place it on the rack of the grill). If using the oven, place the meat skin side up. If using the outdoor grill, place it bone side down. Before doing this, brush with the paprika oil the side of the meat that is exposed to the heat first. Grill 10 minutes.

6. Turn the meat over, brush the other side with paprika oil, and grill another 10 minutes. Brush and turn the meat two more times and grill an additional 5 to 10 minutes. Test for doneness after 5 minutes by inserting a metal skewer into a thigh near the bone. (Be careful to avoid breaking the skin when you do this or the stuffing will leak out.) If juices are still pink, continue to grill the meat, basting and turning from time to time until the juices run yellow. Brush with whatever paprika oil is left before serving. Serve half a chicken per diner. Recipe serves 6 people.

Serving Suggestions

This wonderful warm-weather dish tastes delicious with Romanian-style sautéed eggplant (p. 207) and sautéed *mamaliga* (p. 186). Precede the entrée with Romanian roasted-pepper salad (p. 228) or Romanian salad (p. 228). For a particularly elegant *forspeis*, accompany the salad with Vienna bread and thin slices of garlicky kosher dry salami, brushed with a small amount of oil and sprinkled with freshly ground black pepper. A platter of fresh fruit and *mandelbroit* (p. 256) or *makarondelach* (p. 258) concludes the meal. Several different kinds of wines go well with this meal. Rosé, white zinfandel, and chardonnay are all excellent choices.

Chicken Breast or Turkey *Schnitzel*

Hendel Schnitzel; Indig Schnitzel

Schnitzel is basically an Austro-Hungarian dish but it was popular with Jews in some of eastern as well as central Europe, particularly central Poland and Galitzia. The trick to making good *schnitzel* lies in pounding the meat thin enough and sautéing it quickly without burning it. It is also very important to chill the meat after it is breaded in order to make sure the breading adheres to the meat.

2 lb. skinless, boneless chicken breasts or slices
    of turkey breast cut into 1/2-inch cutlets
hot German or Creole mustard
2 jumbo eggs, beaten
1/2 cup bread crumbs or *matzoh* meal
1/3 cup flour
salt, black pepper, and hot paprika to taste
lemon wedges for garnish
10 to 12 Tblsp. corn or peanut oil

1. If using chicken breasts, remove the small piece of meat that adheres to the underside of each breast. These can be dipped in the same breading mixture, sautéed at the end, and served, if you wish, as "chicken nuggets." Or they can simply be put away and used for some other purpose. (I like to save them to sauté with tofu and Chinese vegetables in my wok for a totally different meal.) They should not be used when making *schnitzel*. If using the turkey cutlets, of course, this step is unnecessary.

2. Place each piece of meat between two pieces of wax paper, and pound with a kitchen mallet until very thin and flat.

3. Spread a small amount of the mustard on one side of each *schnitzel*.

4. Have two flat plates, a large platter with a rectangular rack set on top of it, and a mixing bowl next to you while you work. On one plate, put the flour and season it with salt, black pepper, and hot paprika to taste. Mix it together well and spread across the plate. On the second plate, spread the bread crumbs or *matzoh* meal. Beat the eggs in the mixing bowl with a wire whisk.

5. Dip each *schnitzel* in the seasoned flour and coat it thoroughly. Next dip it in the beaten egg. Let the excess drain back into the mixing bowl after the *schnitzel* is coated. Next dip it in the bread crumbs or *matzoh* meal. Lay it on the rack, which is on the large platter. Repeat this until all of the *schnitzels* are breaded. Place the platter in the refrigerator for 45 minutes to set the coating.

6. Heat the oil in a deep, wide sauté pan until it is bubbling but not smoking. Gently slip 2 or 3 *schnitzels* into the oil and sauté about 5 minutes on one side. Turn over and sauté 4 to 5 minutes longer. Be sure not to crowd the *schnitzels* or they will not sauté properly. If you wish, drain on paper towels before serving, but serve as promptly as possible. The beauty of a good *schnitzel* is when it comes to the table very crisp and hot. Serve 1 *schnitzel* per person. Garnish with a lemon wedge. Recipe serves 6 people.

Serving Suggestions

Schnitzel is very versatile and works itself well into many different kinds of menus. In warm weather, it goes well with cold vegetable salads. In cooler weather, I like to serve it with one of the vegetables that has a sauce. Try any of the following combinations:

Baked Beet Salad (p. 224) and Cucumber Salad
    with Dill (p. 223)
Galitzianer Beet Salad (p. 225) and sliced English
    cucumber
Carrot-and-Raisin Salad (p. 227) and thinly
    sliced tart green apples or pears
Beet Greens Salad (p. 227) and Potato Salad (p.
    229)
Cabbage Salad (p. 230) and Pickled Beets (p. 291)
Lesco (p. 208)
Green Beans or Zucchini in Tomato Sauce
    (p. 207)
Galitzianer Braised Red Cabbage (p. 204)

For a *forspeis*, my favorite is carrot soup (p. 62). Any seasonal fruit compote or *kissel* completes the meal. A dry white wine is good with this dish. I rather like Italian Soave or a dry white burgundy.

Chicken Giblet Fricassee

8 chicken gizzards
8 chicken wings, sliced in half into drummettes
      and wings
6 chicken livers
1/2 lb. ground beef
1/2 lb. ground veal
3 Tblsp. *matzoh* meal
1 large egg
4 onions, peeled (1 large, quartered; 2 medium,
      thinly sliced; 1 small, grated)
3 stalks celery with leaves, chopped
2 medium-size green peppers, roasted, peeled,
      seeded, and sliced lengthwise into very thin
      strips
1 bouquet garni consisting of 5 sprigs fresh dill,
      5 sprigs fresh parsley, and 1 bay leaf, tied
      together with kitchen string
1 1/2 cups fresh tomato sauce (p. 6)
2 cloves garlic, peeled and finely chopped
1/4 tsp. ground allspice
pinch ground cloves
1 1/2 tsp. Hungarian sweet paprika
2 Tblsp. unbleached white flour
3 Tblsp. corn or peanut oil
salt and black pepper to taste

1. Mix together the ground beef, ground veal, egg, *matzoh* meal, allspice, cloves, grated onion, and salt and pepper to taste. Set aside in the refrigerator while you prepare the giblets.

2. Preheat the oven broiler to 500° and broil the livers for 1 1/2 minutes on each side to make kosher for use in the dish. Remove from the oven and set aside.

3. Place the gizzards, wings, and a small amount of salt in a large saucepan and cover with cold water by 2 inches. Bring to a boil and skim the scum as it rises to the surface. Reduce the heat to simmer and add the quartered onion, the celery, and the bouquet garni. Cover the saucepan with lid left slightly ajar and simmer gently for 45 minutes.

4. Remove the beef-and-veal mixture from the refrigerator and shape into meatballs. Add to the saucepan and cook an additional 30 minutes.

5. Cut the livers in half and add to the saucepan. Cook an additional 15 minutes.

6. In another large saucepan or casserole with a lid, heat the oil over medium heat and sauté the onions until translucent and soft. Reduce the heat and add the garlic and paprika. Cook an additional 5 minutes. Sprinkle the flour over the onion mixture and cook an additional 10 minutes, stirring constantly with a wooden spoon to prevent anything from sticking to the bottom.

7. Add very slowly 1 cup broth from the saucepan in which the meat is cooking, stirring constantly with a wooden spoon or wire whisk to prevent lumping. Add enough additional broth so that you have what appears to be a "thinnish" sauce. Add the green peppers, the tomato sauce, and the meat from the other saucepan. Simmer the fricassee for at least another 20 to 25 minutes, partially covered. Stir from time to time. The resulting fricassee should be thick and savory at the end of cooking. If necessary, add a little more of the broth from the other saucepan.

8. At the end of cooking, add the chopped fresh dill leaves and taste for seasoning. Add salt and black pepper, if necessary. After adding the dill, cook 2 or 3 minutes more and then serve. Recipe serves 6 to 8 people.

Serving Suggestions

This dish is usually accompanied by plain boiled rice or rice *pilav* (p. 182), but I rather like to eat it by itself with plenty of crusty Vienna bread or one of the potato breads to mop up the sauce. In any event, do not serve it with vegetable accompaniment. Precede it with a salad like green bean salad (p. 222), field green salad (p. 219), or Boston lettuce salad (p. 220). Jewish apple tart (p. 275) or *palaschinken* (p. 247) is a good dessert to follow a fricassee. A medium-dry red or white burgundy or a sparkling rosé goes well with the fricassee.

Roast Turkey with Savory Potato Stuffing

Gebrotene Indig mit Kartoffel Gefilachts

Have you ever thought of serving a Jewish recipe for Thanksgiving turkey? I created this recipe myself based on an old recipe for roast goose, which I acquired from a Galitzianer cook. Curiously enough, the stuffing ingredients are almost the same as those used in making potato *kugel* (p. 178). The ingredients are simple and subtle and do not overwhelm the natural taste of the turkey. The freshness and lack of complexity in the stuffing allows the full flavor of the turkey gravy and cranberry relish (p. 292) to be appreciated—more so, I think, than with the usual stuffing made out of bread, nuts, fruits, and spices.

Turkey and stuffing

1 10- to 12- lb. turkey
2 cups onions, finely chopped
2 1/2 lb. white baking potatoes, peeled, grated, and drained
1 stalk celery, very finely chopped
2 eggs, beaten
1/3 cup *matzoh* meal
1/2 tsp. hot paprika plus hot paprika for sprinkling
10 Tblsp. chicken *schmaltz*
3 cups chicken stock (p. 3)
3 cups white wine
salt and black pepper to taste

1. Remove giblets, neck, wing tips, and liver from the turkey and set aside for making the sauce.

2. Melt 3 Tblsp. of the *schmaltz* in a skillet over medium heat, and sauté the onions and celery until soft and translucent. Add the grated potatoes and cook 6 to 7 minutes more. Transfer to a mixing bowl and cool to room temperature. Add the *matzoh* meal, 1/2 tsp. paprika, eggs, and salt and pepper to taste.

3. Rub the turkey all over, inside and out, with salt and black pepper. Stuff the cavity of the bird loosely with the potato-onion mixture. There should be just enough stuffing to fit inside the bird, but if you find that you have too much, bake the rest in a covered baking dish for 45 minutes at 350°. Seal up the ends of the cavity of the turkey with metal skewers. Truss and tie the bird with kitchen string and sprinkle it all over with hot paprika. Preheat the oven to 450°. Slather the turkey with the remaining 7 Tblsp. of *schmaltz*. This may seem excessive, but remember that turkey is a relatively dry meat and requires more fat to keep it moist than other fowl do. Place it on a rack in a roasting pan breast side up.

4. Roast the turkey for 30 minutes at 450° and then lower the heat to 325°. Mix the chicken stock and wine and ladle some of this over the turkey. Roast an additional 20 minutes.

5. The turkey will need to roast an additional 3 to 3 1/2 hours, depending on its size. Baste it with the wine-stock mixture every 15 minutes. Turn the turkey over onto its other side after the first hour or so of cooking and roast it on this side for 1 hour before turning back onto its original side. Do not be concerned if you use up the wine-stock mixture. Continue to baste the turkey with juices from the pan once you run out. While the turkey is roasting, prepare the gravy.

For gravy

reserved giblets, wing tips, and liver from the turkey
1 onion, peeled and stuck with 3 whole cloves
1 bay leaf
1 large carrot, peeled and cut into chunks
2 stalks celery, cut into chunks
1 parsnip, peeled and cut into chunks
5 sprigs fresh thyme
peel of 1 small orange, cut into thin strips
1 1/2 cups red wine
1/2 cup sherry or brandy
3 Tblsp. unbleached white flour
3 Tblsp. chicken *schmaltz*
salt and black pepper to taste
1 1/2 Tblsp. plum jelly

1. Preheat oven broiler to 500° (before you put the turkey in to roast), and broil the liver 1 1/2 minutes on each side. Remove it and set it aside.

2. Place giblets, neck, and wing tips in a saucepan with a small amount of salt. Cover them with cold water that rises over them by 2 inches. Bring to a boil and skim the scum as it rises to the surface. Reduce the heat to simmer and add all the ingredients except the wine, brandy, plum jelly, flour, and *schmaltz*. Chop the liver into small pieces and add it to the stock. Partially cover the pot and simmer for 2 hours undisturbed. When stock is through simmering, remove the meat and strain it through a sieve, pressing down hard on the vegetables to extract all their juices.

3. One hour before the meal is ready to be served, make an *einbren* out of the *schmaltz* and the flour in a heavy saucepan. Cook it over the lowest

possible heat for at least 30 minutes before you proceed in making the gravy.

4. Add 2 cups of the turkey stock to the *einbren*. Stir in slowly with a wire whisk to prevent lumping. Then add the wine and the brandy, stirring all the while. Let the gravy simmer while you finish preparing the turkey.

5. When the turkey is finished roasting, remove it from the oven and let it rest on a carving board. To test for doneness, insert a metal skewer into a thigh. If the juices run a pale pink, the turkey is ready. (I prefer to remove the turkey from the oven while the dark meat is slightly underdone so that the white meat is not overcooked. Be sure that the juices are pale pink, and not pink, which will mean that the meat is still not sufficiently cooked through.)

6. Remove the rack from the roaster and place it on a burner on top of the stove. Turn on the heat to medium and add a ladleful of the turkey stock. With a wooden spoon, scrape up any browned bits that cling to the bottom of the roasting pan and add this to the gravy.

7. The gravy should have a nice smooth consistency. If it is too thick, add more stock. If too thin, raise the heat and, stirring all the while with a wire whisk, cook it down until the correct consistency is achieved. Then add the plum jelly and whisk it in.

8. To serve the turkey, carve it carefully, placing one piece of white meat and one piece of dark meat on each dinner plate. Spoon out some of the stuffing and nap the meat with the gravy. Serve the remaining gravy in a sauceboat and the rest of the turkey and stuffing on platters. Recipe serves 8 to 10 people.

Serving Suggestions

This delicious Thanksgiving turkey should be accompanied by cranberry-orange relish (p. 292) and two or three vegetable side dishes. I like to serve sautéed brussels sprouts with lemon (p. 197) and honey-glazed carrots (p. 202). If you like the taste of them, my recipe for caramel-glazed sweet potatoes (p. 210) goes just as well. Begin the meal with a green bean salad (p. 222) and conclude it with poached pears in red wine (p. 241). Serve your pumpkin pie and coffee after you are well rested from the main meal. Or, instead of pumpkin pie, do what we do and serve Aunt Ann's lemon meringue pie (p. 285) for a joyous all-American finish. Rosé or a fine-quality fruity, medium-dry red burgundy, like Beaujolais Villages, is the best wine to serve with the turkey.

Leftover Turkey *Kottletten*

These *kottletten* are a great way of using up leftover turkey. I think it is so good I sometimes cook a whole turkey breast or leg just to make this dish!

3 cups leftover cooked turkey
1 large or 2 medium-size white baking potatoes, peeled and cut into cubes
1 onion, peeled and cut into chunks
2 medium-size beets, baked and peeled (see recipe for baked-beet salad, p. 224)
1/4 cup bread crumbs or *matzoh* meal
2 eggs
salt, pepper, and hot paprika to taste
8 to 10 Tblsp. peanut oil for sautéing

1. In a food processor or blender or using the coarse blade of a meat grinder, grind the meat into a coarse puree and transfer into a mixing bowl. If using the food processor or blender, puree the meat with a pulse/chop movement on the machine.

2. Cut the beets into a fine dice and add to the turkey.

3. Finely grate the potato and onion in the food processor or blender (or by hand, if necessary) and add to the meat and beets.

4. Mix in all the remaining ingredients except the oil, and form into *kottletten*.

5. Heat the oil in a large, deep sauté pan until hot and sizzling but not smoking. Sauté the *kottletten* a few at a time in the sizzling oil, being careful not to crowd them. Sauté on one side for 6 to 7 minutes and turn with a spatula. Sauté an additional 4 to 5 minutes or until the ingredients are completely cooked through. Drain on paper towels and keep warm in a low oven or in the microwave until all the *kottletten* have been sautéed.

6. When you have made all the meat mixture into *kottletten*, they are ready to be served.

Serving Suggestions

Serve *kottletten* with cranberry-orange relish (p. 292) and a tossed green salad (p. 219) or a green bean salad (p. 222) on the side. Recipe serves 6 to 8 people. If you wish to serve wine, chardonnay and rosé are both compatible. A seasonal fruit compote or *kissel* completes the meal. Apple compote (p. 240), citrus compote (p. 238), and dried fruit compote (p. 242) are all excellent choices.

Polish-Style Roast Duck with Brandied Apples and Pears

Poilische Gebrotene Katschke Mit Eppl Und Barness

Duck is a succulent, delicious, and rich-tasting meat. It is somewhat neglected because it contains a lot of fat. The trick to preparing duck is to roast it in such a way as to eliminate most of the fat (which is rendered during the roasting and siphoned off with a bulb baster for reuse later as an alternative to chicken *schmaltz*) while keeping the meat moist and not allowing it to dry out. There is an ingenious Chinese technique used in making Peking duck which I have incorporated into this recipe precisely for the purpose of achieving this. The technique can be applied to any roast duck or goose recipe and, of course, works very well with this Jewish one.

2 4- to 5-lb. ducklings (giblets, necks, wing tips, and liver set aside)
2 medium-size onions, peeled and chopped, plus 1 small onion, peeled and left whole and stuck with 3 whole cloves
2 or 3 large, tart green apples, peeled, cored, and cut into chunks
2 or 3 large Anjou pears, peeled, cored, and cut into chunks
2 large carrots, peeled and cut into chunks, plus 1 small carrot, peeled and cut in half
2 stalks celery, cut into 2-inch pieces
1 medium-size turnip, peeled and cut into chunks
1 small parsnip, peeled and cut in half
1 3-inch piece fresh orange peel plus the juice and grated zest of 2 oranges
3 Tblsp. honey
1 bouquet garni consisting of 1 bay leaf, 5 stalks parsley, 2 pieces leek green, and 5 sprigs fresh thyme (substitute 1/2 tsp. dried thyme if fresh is unavailable), tied together with kitchen string
1 1/2 cups dry red wine
1/3 cup pear brandy
salt and black pepper to taste

1. Prepare duck stock using the giblets and liver. Cover the giblets with cold, salted water by at least 2 inches and bring to a boil. Skim the scum as it rises to the surface. Then lower the heat to simmer and add the small carrot, parsnip, turnip, whole onion stuck with cloves, orange peel, and bouquet garni. Partially cover the pot and let it simmer.

2. Preheat the oven broiler to 500° and broil the liver for 1 1/2 minutes on each side. Add this to the stock. Simmer the stock for at least 2 hours. Remove the meat and strain it through a fine sieve, pressing down hard on the vegetables to extract all the juices. You should have about 2 1/2 to 3 cups of stock.

3. To prepare the duck for roasting using the Chinese method, try to cut off and remove as much of the fat as is visible. Then bring a pot of water to boil on top of the stove. Put one duck into this and cook it for 7 to 10 minutes. Remove it from the pot and repeat with the second duck.

4. Drain the ducks and thoroughly dry them with paper towels. The preboiling opens the pores of the skin, allowing fat to flow out more easily during roasting. Ironically, the meat also does not dry out if the ducks are preboiled before roasting.

5. The ducks are now ready to roast. Season them both inside and out with salt, pepper, and grated orange peel. Place some of the chopped onion into each bird. Preheat the oven to 450°. Place the ducks on a rack in a roasting pan and roast for 20 minutes. Using a bulb baster, remove as much as you can of the fat that has accumulated in the bottom of the roasting pan and transfer it to a glass canning jar with a tight-fitting lid. Lower the oven temperature to 350°.

6. Roast an additional 20 minutes and remove fat again in the same way. This is about all the duck fat you will be able to render during the roasting, because at this stage, you should scatter the remaining onions, carrots, apples, and pears around the bottom of the roasting pan. Return the roast to the oven and roast an additional 15 minutes. Spoon 1 1/2 Tblsp. honey over the top of each duck. This provides a beautiful glaze. Remove fat with the bulb baster once again, but this time you will have to discard it.

7. Mix together the stock, wine, and orange juice. Ladle some of this over the meat and return to the oven. Roast the meat an additional 45 to 55 minutes, basting every 10 minutes with the wine-stock mixture. You will probably use up all but about 1 1/2 cups of liquid in this way.

8. When the meat is through roasting, place it on a carving board to rest while you prepare the sauce. Remove the rack from the roasting pan and strain its contents through a fine sieve, pressing down hard to extract the juices from the fruit and

vegetables. Using a bulb baster, skim off as much of the fat from the top of this as you are able.

9. Place the roasting pan on top of the stove and turn on the heat to medium. Using the wine-stock mixture that remains, deglaze the pan, scraping up any browned bits with a wooden spoon. Pour off and discard any excess fat before you deglaze. Pour this into the saucepan containing the strained sauce ingredients. Add the pear brandy and bring to boil on top of the stove. Reduce this to about 2 cups of sauce.

10. To serve the meat, cut each duck into 4 quarters with poultry shears (if the ducks are particularly small, cut them in half). Serve a quarter or a half duck per diner, depending on its size, napped with a little of the sauce. Serve the rest of the sauce in a sauceboat. Recipe serves 4 to 8 people.

Serving Suggestions

Roast duck is an elegant, festive, and very rich entrée, and I like to reserve it for special occasions. For a rich gourmet dinner featuring roast duck, try the following menu:

> Liver Pâté à la Rothschild (p. 44)
> Chicken Soup Consommé (p. 56)
> Roast Duck with Apples and Pears (pp. 121–122)
> Sautéed Turnips (p. 197)
> Honey-glazed Carrots (p. 202)
> Field Green Salad with Herb Vinaigrette (p. 219)
> Cranberry *Kissel* with Hazelnut *Makarondelach* (pp. 243 and 258)

Serve a fruity, full-bodied wine with the meal. There are both whites and reds that would go well with it. For a white, try a good-quality white burgundy or a chardonnay. For a red, a Beaujolais Villages, a medium-dry red burgundy, or a cabernet sauvignon is nice. Rose also goes well with this meal. Sometime after the meal has been digested, serve coffee, tea, liqueurs, chocolates, and, if your guests can consume it, a lemon *mohn* torte (p.   ), whose flavors nicely complement the entire meal.

Roast Goose with Two Varieties of Stuffing

Gebrotene Ganz

At the turn of the nineteenth century (and for many centuries before that), goose was the most popular kind of meat to serve on the Sabbath and holiday tables of Jewish families. It was goose fat rather than chicken fat that was made into *schmaltz*, the kosher alternative to the commonly used lard. Today, of course, very few chefs cook with lard, and very few Jewish cooks make *schmaltz* out of goose fat. The goose itself has become somewhat of an exotic item in America, rarely tasted by the average consumer. In Europe and Israel, it is popular but still more neglected as a meat source than it has ever been. This is too bad. The excellent Chinese technique for rendering fat works just as well with goose as it does with duck. This method enables a chef to prepare goose in a much less fattening way and still render some of the fat for use as *schmaltz*. Roast goose is magnificent as a special treat, particularly during the coldest winter days, when the body craves something substantial and just a little fatty. I like to make roast goose for *Shabbos Chanukah* (the Sabbath that falls during Chanukah). I include two different recipes for stuffing the goose, both of which are delicious and traditionally Jewish.

1 10-lb. goose (neck, wing tips, and giblets removed and used for stock; liver removed and used for stuffing)
1/2 cup brandy
3 cups red wine
3 cups stock made from goose giblets
1 recipe stuffing 1 or 2
salt and black pepper to taste

For goose stock

1 carrot, peeled and cut into chunks
1 celery stalk, cut into chunks
1 onion, peeled and stuck with 3 cloves
1 parsnip, peeled and cut into chunks
1 bay leaf
6 sprigs parsley

1. Prepare stock according to the method outlined in step 1 of recipe for roast duck (p. 121). Simmer goose stock at least 2 hours before straining it for use in the recipe.

2. Prepare the goose for roasting according to the Chinese technique, outlined in steps 3 and 4 of recipe for roast duck (p. 121).

3. Rub the goose all over, inside and out, with salt and pepper. Stuff it with stuffing 1 or 2 (recipes are given for these at the end of this recipe). Truss

the goose and tie it with kitchen string. If necessary, seal the cavity with metal skewers and place it on a rack in a roasting pan. Preheat the oven to 450°.

4. Place the goose in the oven and roast it for 30 minutes. Using a bulb baster, remove all fat that has accumulated at the bottom of the pan and place it in a glass canning jar with a tight-fitting lid. Turn the oven down to 350°.

5. Roast the goose another 20 minutes, and with the bulb baster, remove the fat once again. Roast another 20 minutes, and once again, remove the fat.

6. Mix the stock and wine together and ladle some over the goose. Return it to the oven and continue roasting. Siphon off fat with a bulb baster as you roast the meat. The fat rendered at this point should be discarded. Roast the goose an additional 1 1/2 hours, basting with the wine-stock mixture every 15 minutes.

7. When the meat is through roasting, remove it from the oven and place it on a carving board. To test for doneness, insert a metal skewer into one thigh. If the juices run yellow, the meat is ready.

8. Use the remaining wine-stock mixture to deglaze the roasting pan. Remove the rack from the pan and place it on the stove over medium heat. Pour off any excess fat. Add the wine-stock mixture and, using a wooden spoon, scrape up the browned bits. Pour this into a saucepan and add the brandy. Cook until the mixture is reduced to about 1 1/2 cups.

9. To serve, apportion the stuffing onto individual dinner plates or pull all of it into a bowl. Carve the goose into attractive slices and arrange some on each plate or on a platter. Nap the meat with a little of the sauce and serve the rest of the sauce in a sauceboat. Recipe serves 8 to 10 people.

Serving Suggestions

The best vegetable to serve with roast goose is braised cabbage. I like the Litvishe recipe with stuffing 2 and the Galitzianer with stuffing 1. Either cabbage dish provides a good counterpoint to the flavor of the meat. Precede the meat with carrot soup (p. 62) and precede the soup with a *forspeis*. Chopped herring (p. 41) followed by a shot of *vishnyek* (p. 299) and liver pâté à la Rothschild (p. 44) are both good choices. *Helzel* (p. 187) is the best *forspeis* if you can get it. Conclude the meal with an apple compote (p. 240) or poached pears in red wine (p. 241) and *makarondelach* (p. 258) or *mandelbroit* (p. 256). Drink a good-quality, full-bodied red wine with the meal, such as Chianti and Barolo, or a full-bodied, dry red bordeaux or burgundy.

Recipes for Stuffing

Stuffing 1: *Galitzianer* Potato Stuffing

1 1/2 cups finely chopped onions
the liver of the goose, broiled in a 500° oven
    for 2 minutes on each side and then finely
    chopped
3 cups peeled white baking potatoes, finely
    grated
1 large stalk celery, finely chopped
1 jumbo egg, beaten
1/3 cup *matzoh* meal
1 tsp. caraway seeds
1/2 tsp. hot paprika
4 Tblsp. chicken *schmaltz* or rendered goose
    fat

1. Melt the *schmaltz* or goose fat in a skillet over medium heat and sauté the onions until they are translucent and soft. Add the celery and cook an additional 5 minutes. Lower the heat and add the caraway seeds and paprika and cook 5 minutes more. Add the chopped goose liver and cook 2 more minutes. Remove from the heat and cool to room temperature.

2. Mix this with the remaining ingredients and stuff the goose. Precede with the stuffed goose recipe as indicated in step 3 above.

Stuffing 2: Hungarian Sweet *Challah* Stuffing

1 1/2 cups chopped onion
1 cup chopped celery
6 Tblsp. chicken *schmaltz* or rendered goose
    fat
3/4 loaf of raisin *challah* (p. 17)
the liver from the goose, broiled in the oven at
    500° for 2 minutes on each side and finely
    chopped
1/2 cup Tokay or red wine
1/2 cup chicken stock (p. 3) or goose stock
    (aforementioned recipe)
2 Tblsp. brandy

1 jumbo egg, beaten
3 Tblsp. bread crumbs (if necessary)
salt, black pepper, and hot paprika to taste

1. Melt the *schmaltz* or goose fat in a skillet over medium heat and sauté the onions until translucent and soft. Add the celery and sauté 5 minutes longer. Add the liver and sauté 2 minutes more and remove from the heat.

2. Cut or tear the *challah* into small pieces and put into a mixing bowl. Pour the wine, brandy, and stock over it and mix together. The bread should be well moistened but not soggy.

3. Mix the ingredients in the skillet with the *challah*. Add the egg and the seasonings and mix together well. If the texture seems a little too soggy, add bread crumbs to help it achieve the correct consistency.

4. Stuff the goose and proceed with the recipe as indicated in step 3.

Photographic still life by Henrietta Komras Sternberg.

My Grandmother's Erev Yom Kippur Prefast Dinner

Sweet *challah* with honey

Polish-style carp

Chicken soup with *kreplach*

Gedempte hendel (lightly poached chicken)

Rice *pilav*   Carrot-and-parsnip *tzimmes*

Poached apple compote with glazed honey *lekach*

7

Meat

Fleisch

Where there is meat and fish,
there is a happy table!

Vi iz fleisch un fisch iz a freilicher tisch!

Old Country Pot Roast

Gedempte Fleisch

This is the most basic beef pot roast prepared by Jews. In my childhood home, this was treated like *shabbosdige hendel* (p. 101) and served on Sabbaths when we were having an "ordinary" *Shabbos*.

1 4- to 5-lb. beef shoulder roast
1/4 cup plus 2 Tblsp. unbleached white flour
2 large onions, peeled and finely chopped
4 garlic cloves, peeled and finely chopped
1 large carrot, peeled and finely chopped
2 medium-size green peppers, roasted, peeled, seeded, and chopped
4 large stalks celery (with leaves), chopped
1/3 cup chopped fresh parsley
1 1/2 tsp. hot paprika
1 1/2 cups beef stock (p. 4)
1 cup dry red wine
4 to 5 Tblsp. corn or peanut oil
1 bay leaf
salt and black pepper to taste

1. Season the 1/4 cup flour with salt and black pepper to taste. Dredge meat on all sides in the seasoned flour.

2. Heat 4 Tblsp. of the oil in a deep heavy casserole (one that has a tight-fitting lid) on top of the stove over fairly high heat, and brown the meat on all sides. Transfer it to a plate.

3. Reduce the heat to medium, and sauté the onions until soft and translucent. Add the carrot and celery, and sauté 7 minutes more. Reduce the heat slightly, add the garlic and paprika, and sauté 5 minutes longer.

4. Sprinkle this mixture with the remaining 2 Tblsp. flour and cook 5 minutes longer, stirring constantly with a wooden spoon to prevent sticking.

5. Add the green peppers, stock, bay leaf, and red wine slowly. Stir with the wooden spoon to prevent lumping as you add the liquid. Preheat the oven to 325°.

6. Return the meat to the casserole, and cover with aluminum foil and then with the cover of the pot. Place the casserole into the oven and braise undisturbed for 2 1/2 hours.

7. The braising ingredients are the sauce for *gedempte fleisch*. To serve, carve the meat into attractive slices and serve on individual dinner plates or a platter, napped with some of the braising sauce ingredients from the pot. Remove and discard the bay leaf. Serve the remaining sauce from the pot in a sauceboat. Recipe serves 6 to 8 people.

Serving Suggestions

Gedempte fleisch is very versatile and goes well with many different vegetable accompaniments. Some of the starchy dishes that can go with it are *kasha* (p. 182), *kasha varnishkes* (p. 183), roast potatoes (p. 198), *fleischig* mashed potatoes (p. 199), and yellow rice *pilav* (p. 182). If you serve one of the heavier soups, like chicken soup with *kasha* (p. 58) or chicken soup with rice (p. 57), accompany the meat with one or two plain sautéed vegetables from chapter 9 and good *challah* or potato bread to enjoy with the sauce. Any seasonal fruit compote or *kissel* concludes the meal. Drink a dry cabernet sauvignon, a merlot, a dry red burgundy, or a Spanish rioja with the meal.

Ukrainian Pot Roast With Horseradish

Ukrainishe Gedempte Fleisch Mit Chrain

This Ukrainian Jewish pot roast is hearty and savory and contains the favorite drink of Ukrainian Jews (particularly the Lubavitcher *chasidim*), vodka!

1 4- to 5-lb. brisket or rolled beef shoulder roast (this is prepared by any kosher butcher; the meat is rolled attractively and tied with heavy kitchen string)
2 large carrots, peeled and cut into thick chunks
1 parsley root, peeled and cut into thick chunks
1 small celery root, peeled and cut into chunks
1 large parsnip, peeled and cut into large chunks
2 medium-size turnips, peeled and cut into chunks
1 large onion, peeled and cut into chunks
6 cups beef stock (p. 4)
3 Tblsp. *schmaltz*
1/2 cup freshly grated horseradish root
3 Tblsp. unbleached white flour

1/4 cup freshly squeezed lemon juice
1/2 cup vodka
2 tsp. sugar
salt and black pepper to taste
1/3 cup bread crumbs
1/4 cup chopped fresh parsley for garnishing
    the soup

1. This dish can be prepared in two different stages. The second stage can wait until the next day. For the first stage, place the stock in a large soup pot and bring it to a boil over high heat. Add the meat and, as it starts to cook, skim off the scum that rises to the surface. Reduce the heat to the lowest simmer, add all the vegetables, and cover the pot, leaving the lid slightly ajar. Simmer undisturbed for 2 hours.

2. Remove the meat from the broth. Separate 2 3/4 cups of the stock from the vegetables and set aside.

3. The stock and vegetables that remain can be used as a soup with this meal or with a different one. To make the soup, puree the remaining soup and vegetables in a blender or food processor. Use a pulse/chop motion to make a coarse puree, which is more attractive than a smooth one. If you wish a slightly thicker soup, add one medium-size boiled potato to the stock and vegetables before you puree it. Garnish the soup with chopped parsley when you serve it. *At this point, cooking can be left off and finished the next day.* Refrigerate the meat, vegetable soup, and stock in separate containers.

4. To continue cooking, heat *schmaltz* in a saucepan and make an *einbren* with the flour according to the instructions given on p. 9. The *einbren* should cook at least 25 to 30 minutes to bring out its full flavor.

5. When the *einbren* has cooked a sufficient amount of time, add the grated horseradish, sugar, and salt and pepper to taste. Stir this together with a wooden spoon until it is well incorporated.

6. Add the stock slowly, stirring constantly with a wire whisk to prevent lumping. When the stock is all added, add the lemon juice and the vodka and mix together again. The result should be a thinnish sauce (which will cook down to the correct consistency during the next step). Remove from the heat and set aside. Preheat the oven to 350°.

7. Slice the meat attractively and arrange in overlapping rows in a deep baking dish or gratin dish. Sprinkle half of the bread crumbs over the meat. Pour the sauce over this and sprinkle with the remaining bread crumbs. Put the meat in the oven and bake for 25 minutes uncovered or until the top is brown. Serve immediately. Recipe serves 6 to 8 people.

Serving Suggestions

This is a rich dish that gives you two courses—a delicious soup and an even tastier entrée. If you wish to serve the meat with some kind of starchy vegetable, try it with *kasha* (p. 182), potato *kugel* (p. 178), or *fleishig lokshen kugel* (p. 170), and if you wish, a sautéed vegetable like brussels sprouts or broccoli. Any of the braised cabbage dishes is also very nice with this entrée. For an elegant formal dinner, a *forspeis* of chopped herring (p. 41) or chopped egg and onion with *schmaltz* (p. 42) is very appealing. If you do not serve the pureed vegetable soup that was made from the first stage of preparing the meat, then carrot soup (p. 62) goes well with this meal. For dessert, serve a seasonal fruit compote or *kissel*. Drink a fruity, full-bodied wine with the meat, like zinfandel.

Budapest-Style Pot Roast With Coffee
Ungarische Gedempte Fleisch

Budapest, like Vienna, was world famous for its coffeehouses. It is not surprising that Hungarian (and Viennese) Jews developed this unusual recipe for pot roast using extra-strong, espressolike coffee as the braising medium instead of stock or wine. It is an extraordinarily good dish.

1 4- to 5-lb. beef shoulder roast
1 very large onion, peeled and thinly sliced
2 large carrots, peeled and finely chopped
2 stalks celery, finely chopped
3 Tblsp. corn oil
2 cups espresso or very strong coffee
1/3 cup brandy or cognac
1/4 cup unbleached white flour
1 tsp. hot paprika
1 tsp. dried thyme
1 bay leaf
salt and black pepper to taste

1. Mix salt and black pepper into the flour and dredge the meat with it. Heat the oil in a deep

casserole with a tight-fitting lid over slightly high heat and brown the meat on all sides. Set it aside on a plate.

2. Reduce the heat to medium and sauté the onions until translucent and soft. Add the carrots and celery and sauté an additional 7 minutes. Add the paprika and thyme and sauté 5 minutes longer.

3. Add the coffee and brandy to the casserole and stir with a wooden spoon to mix thoroughly. Preheat the oven to 325°.

4. Return the meat to the casserole and cover with aluminum foil and then with the lid of the casserole. Braise in the oven undisturbed for 2 1/2 hours.

5. To serve, slice the meat attractively and place on individual serving plates or a large platter. Nap each portion with the sauce and serve the remainder of the sauce in a sauceboat. Recipe serves 6 to 8 people.

Serving Suggestions

This roast is very versatile. Serve with rice *pilav* (p. 182) or one of the potato dishes and a sautéed vegetable accompaniment. Any soup will do, but bouquet of fresh vegetables soup (p. 62) is one of the best choices. Conclude the meal with any seasonal fruit compote or *kissel* and serve a dry red wine like cabernet sauvignon or merlot with the meat.

Sweet-and-Sour Pot Roast

Essig Fleisch

Essig means "vinegar," and *essig fleisch* is the Yiddish name given to a traditional sweet-and-sour pot roast of beef. There are many different recipes for this classic Jewish dish. My recipe uses the nontraditional freshly squeezed lemon juice in place of vinegar, because I prefer the flavor of lemon with the seasonings used in the recipe. If you wish to use vinegar instead of lemon juice, make it cider vinegar, the flavor of which complements the rest of the seasonings.

1 4- to 5-lb. beef shoulder roast (a rolled and tied shoulder roast prepared by the butcher is the best choice)
1/4 cup unbleached white flour
1 large onion, peeled and finely chopped

2 large garlic cloves, peeled and left whole
2 bay leaves
3 Tblsp. corn or peanut oil
4 whole allspice
1 1-inch-piece fresh ginger, peeled and left whole
1/3 cup freshly squeezed lemon juice
1/3 cup honey
1/2 cup raisins
1 cup beef stock (p. 4)
2 cups fresh tomato sauce (p. 6)
salt and black pepper to taste

1. Preheat oven to 325°. Mix the flour with salt and pepper to taste. Dredge the meat in the seasoned flour. Heat oil over fairly high heat in a large, heavy casserole with a tight-fitting lid. Brown the meat on all sides and set aside on a plate.

2. Reduce the heat to medium and sauté the onions until translucent and soft. Add the rest of the ingredients and continue to cook, mixing everything together.

3. Return the meat to the casserole, spoon some of the liquid over the meat, and cover tightly with aluminum foil and then with the lid of the casserole. Place the roast in the oven and braise undisturbed for 2 1/2 hours.

4. To serve, remove meat from the pot and slice attractively on a carving board. Serve on individual dinner plates or on a platter, napped with some of the sauce. Remove the bay leaves, allspice, ginger, and garlic, and discard. Serve the remaining sauce in a sauceboat. Recipe serves 6 to 8 people.

Serving Suggestions

Essig fleisch goes very well with *lokshen*. Serve it with a *fleischig lokshen kugel* (p. 170), a *Yerushalmi kugel* (p. 172), or roasted *farfel* (p. 177). *Essig fleisch* is also quite good with yellow rice *pilav* (p. 182). Precede the meat with bouquet of fresh vegetables soup (p. 62) or carrot soup (p. 62). If you wish to serve a chicken soup before *essig fleisch*, choose chicken soup with *lokshen* (p. 57) or chicken soup with *mandlen* (p. 55). When you serve the soup with *lokshen*, serve the meat with one or two of the sautéed vegetables in chapter 9. Chopped egg and onion with *schmaltz* (p. 42), *matjes herring* marinated in oil (p. 41), or chopped herring (p. 41) all make excellent *forspeizen* for a formal dinner. Conclude the meal with a seasonal fruit compote or *kissel*. Drink zinfandel with the meal.

Spiced Braised Brisket with Carrots and Red Wine

Gedempte Brustfleisch Mit Mehren

This brisket is a traditional Sukkos dish among Jews from central and southern Poland. It is a sweet dish, in keeping with the traditional foods eaten during the autumn holiday season.

1 3 1/2- to 4-lb. beef brisket
14 large carrots, peeled and sliced
6 Tblsp. chicken *schmaltz*
1 large onion, peeled and finely chopped
3 Tblsp. unbleached white flour
3 cups beef stock (p. 4)
1 cup dry red wine
1 bay leaf
1/2 cup honey
1/2 tsp. dried cinnamon
1/4 tsp. ground allspice
salt and black pepper to taste

1. In a deep, heavy casserole or Dutch oven with a tight-fitting lid, melt 3 Tblsp. *schmaltz* over fairly high heat. Brown the meat on all sides and transfer it to a plate.

2. Reduce the heat to medium and sauté the onions until translucent and soft. Sprinkle the flour over the onions and reduce the heat to the lowest simmer. Using a wooden spoon, stir the mixture constantly and cook it for 6 to 7 minutes to remove any floury taste from the flour.

3. Add the stock very slowly, stirring constantly with the wooden spoon to prevent lumping. Add the spices, honey, and wine, and mix until thoroughly blended. Add the carrots and mix everthing together again. Preheat the oven to 325°.

4. Place the meat on top of the carrots and cover the pot first with aluminum foil and then with the lid of the casserole. Braise in the oven undisturbed for 2 1/2 hours.

5. To serve, place the meat on a carving board and slice attractively. All the sauce will more or less have been absorbed by the carrots, which should be very tender and fragrant. Serve a portion of the meat with some of the carrots. Recipe serves 6 to 8 people.

Serving Suggestions

Nothing tastes as good with this dish as a slice of *Yerushalmi kugel* (p. 172), whose peppery fragrance seems to bring out the sweetness of the carrots and the honey. If you do not like *Yerushalmi kugel*, serve the meat with a slice of *fleischig lokshen kugel* (p. 170). Precede or follow the meat course with a Boston lettuce salad (p. 220). For soup, a simple chicken soup with *mandlen* is the best choice. End the meal with a seasonal fruit compote or *kissel* and traditional Sukkos sweets, like honey *lekach* (p. 272) and *mohn torte* (p. 281). Drink a fruity zinfandel with the meal. A sparkling rosé is also quite good with this dish.

Braised Brisket in Apple Marinade

Gedempte Brustfleisch mit Eppl

1 4- to 5-lb. beef brisket, trimmed of fat
1 recipe marinade (see below)
1/3 cup applejack or calvados
1/2 cup apple juice or apple cider
6 Tblsp. corn or peanut oil
1 bay leaf
1 cup onions, finely chopped
1 cup carrots, finely chopped
1 cup celery, finely chopped
1/2 cup parsnips, finely chopped
1 large, tart green apple, peeled, cored, and
  finely chopped
3 Tblsp. unbleached white flour
1 cup crumbled leftover honeycake from the
  recipe on p. 272. Stale honey cake is
  excellent for this purpose. If you do not
  have honey cake, *tzimshterner kichelach*
  (p. 279) are a good substitute.

For marinade

1/2 cup white wine
1/2 cup cider vinegar
2 cups apple juice or apple cider (alcoholic
  apple cider is better, but apple juice is
  acceptable)
1 medium-size onion, peeled and thinly sliced
8 whole black peppercorns

10 whole juniper berries, crushed
2 bay leaves
1 1/2 tsp. coarse or kosher salt

1. Three days before you are planning to serve this dish, mix together in a saucepan all the ingredients for the marinade. Bring to a boil over high heat and then remove from the heat immediately. Cool to room temperature.

2. Place the brisket in a glass or enameled bowl and pour the marinade over the meat. Cover tightly and refrigerate for three days, turning the meat over at least twice a day.

3. On the day the meat is to be served, remove it from the refrigerator and bring it to room temperature. When it is at room temperature, remove it from the marinade and pat it dry with paper towels. Strain the marinade through a fine sieve and reserve the liquid, discarding all the solids.

4. Heat over medium-high heat 4 Tblsp. of the oil in a deep, oval-shaped braising pan or casserole that has a tight-fitting lid. Brown the meat, turning until all sides are nicely browned.

5. While the meat is browning, heat the calvados or applejack in a small, flameproof utensil and remove it from the heat. Ignite the liquor with a match and pour it, flaming, over the brisket. Remove the brisket from the heat and shake the pan. Allow the flames to burn off by themselves, which will take only a minute or two. This flambé technique imparts the essence of the liquor into the meat and gives it a delicious, distinctive flavor.

6. Remove the meat from the casserole and set it aside to rest on a platter. If necessary, add oil (up to 2 Tblsp.) and heat on top of the stove over medium heat.

7. Add the onions to the casserole and sauté until soft and translucent. Add the carrots, parsnips, apples, and celery and continue sautéing an additional 5 to 7 minutes or until the vegetables begin to soften.

8. Sprinkle the vegetables with the flour and continue sautéing, stirring constantly to prevent burning or sticking. Cook for at least 5 minutes this way. This removes any floury taste in the braising sauce.

9. Preheat the oven to 350°. Add 1 1/2 cups of the reserved marinade slowly, stirring constantly to prevent lumping. When all of this is added, add the remaining ingredients except for the leftover honey cake crumbs. The sauce should be somewhat thinnish. It will thicken slightly during cooking and will be thickened at the end with the honey cake crumbs. Therefore, if the sauce seems to be too thick, add a little more marinade.

10. Return the meat to the casserole and cover tightly with aluminum foil and then with the lid of the casserole. Place the casserole in the oven and let it braise for 2 hours.

11. When 2 hours have passed, remove the casserole from the oven and uncover it. A wonderful aroma will escape from the pot as you lift off the aluminum foil. Transfer the meat to a carving board and cover it with the foil to keep it warm while you make the sauce.

12. To make the sauce, add the honey cake crumbs to the braising pan and cook gently over medium-low heat for 10 minutes on top of the stove, stirring constantly. Strain the entire contents of the casserole through a fine sieve, pressing down hard with a wooden spoon to extract all the juices and to force as much of the vegetable pulp as possible through the sieve.

13. To serve the brisket, carve it attractively, arrange on individual serving plates or on a platter, and nap it with the sauce. Serve the remainder of the sauce in a sauceboat. Recipe serves 6 to 8 people.

Serving Suggestions

This entire dish can be prepared in advance and reheated in its own sauce. Leftovers are as good (some say even better) than the first servings. This brisket tastes good accompanied by a grain dish like roasted *farfel* (p. 177), *kasha varnishkes* (p. 183), or *galushkes* (p. 177), all of which are popular in Galitzia, where this dish originates. (The recipe is a traditional Galitzianer dish, my only additions being the calvados and the wine.) It is similar to the German sauerbraten, but the use of apples as a flavoring makes it an original recipe. Some terrific vegetable accompaniments are braised green cabbage (p. 204), honey-glazed carrots (p. 252), sautéed cauliflower (p. 197), and sautéed brussels sprouts (p. 197). For an elegant formal dinner in the Galitzianer fashion, begin with a *forspeis* of *Galitzianer gefilte fisch* (p. 39) served with *chrain*, followed by a chicken soup consommé (p. 56). My Rosh Hashanah dinner menu (p. 97) features this dish as an entrée, preceded by chicken soup with *kreplach* (p. 59). As this is obviously an autumn or winter dish, conclude the meal with a seasonal fruit compote or *kissel*. Try to avoid a dish that features apples, so that the menu won't seem redundant. Drink a full-bodied, fine-quality red wine with the meal. A good fruity Beaujolais, a zinfandel, and a fruity red burgundy are all excellent choices.

Flommen Tzimmes

Flommen tzimmes is a classical eastern European meat dish that is traditionally served on Sukkos. It is a dish of the *shtetl*, and it is composed of simple and usually inexpensive ingredients. There are many ways in which Jewish cooks have prepared *flommen tzimmes*. In my opinion, the key to making a good *flommen tzimmes* lies in the quality of the cut of meat chosen by the cook, the prodigious use of beef stock and red wine as simmering liquids instead of water, and the use of *schmaltz* and no other cooking fat. *Tzimmes* made with water and with a cooking fat other than *schmaltz* really lacks pizzazz because the traditional seasoning in the dish is minimal. When prepared acccording to these basic guidelines, *flommen tzimmes* is no longer just an ordinary peasant stew. It is a sophisticated one-dish entrée that you can serve to the most discriminating gourmet.

I deplore the American Jewish custom of adding sweet potatoes to this recipe. Sweet potatoes add a saccharine sweetness to what is already a rather sweet dish, and they do nothing to enhance the overall flavor and visual appeal. In addition, sweet potatoes do not braise very well. Unlike ordinary white baking potatoes, sweet potatoes disintegrate rapidly into a rather flaky mess when they are braised for a long time, ruining the appearance of the dish when it is served. European Jews, who were unfamiliar with the sweet potato, never used it in *flommen tzimmes*. The recipe below follows and builds upon the European rather than the American Jewish tradition.

3 lb. beef flank steak, cut into 1-inch pieces
1 large onion, peeled and thinly sliced
1/2 lb. pitted prunes
2 lb. white baking potatoes, peeled and cut into
    1-inch pieces
7 large carrots, peeled and sliced into thick
    slices
1 cup red wine
6 1/2 Tblsp. chicken *schmaltz*
1/2 cup honey

3 1/2 Tblsp. unbleached white flour
3 1/2 to 4 cups beef stock (p. 4)
salt and black pepper to taste

1. Place prunes in a mixing bowl and cover with the wine. Soak at least 1 hour before beginning the next step.

2. Melt 3 Tblsp. of the *schmaltz* in a large, heavy casserole on top of the stove over medium-high heat. Brown the meat on all sides, a few pieces at a time. Remove the meat cubes from the pot and set aside as they brown.

3. When all of the meat is browned, reduce the heat to medium and sauté the onions until translucent and soft. Remove from the pot with a slotted spoon and set aside.

4. Add the remaining *schmaltz* to the pot. Melt it and then add the flour. Make an *einbren* with the *schmaltz* and the flour according to the instructions found on p. 9. Reduce heat to simmer, and simmer the *einbren* at least 30 minutes over the lowest possible heat, stirring every once in a while. At the end of the cooking, the *einbren* should be golden brown in color.

5. Return the onions to the pot. Mix everything together with a wooden spoon and begin to add the stock slowly, stirring constantly to prevent lumping. Add 3 1/2 cups liquid and, if the sauce seems too thick, add an additonal 1/2 cup.

6. Return the meat to the casserole, cover tightly, and simmer over medium-low heat for 1 hour.

7. Uncover the pot and add the honey, carrots, potatoes, prunes, and wine, and mix everything well. Preheat oven to 350°.

8. Cover the pot tightly with aluminum foil and then with the lid of the pot. Put into the oven and braise 1 1/2 hours, undisturbed. Add salt and pepper to taste at the end of cooking.

9. To serve, simply spoon the *tzimmes* into individual deep, wide soup or stew dishes. Recipe serves 6 to 8 people.

Serving Suggestions

Flommen tzimmes needs no accompaniment other than good homemade *challah* and a fruity red wine. Although it makes for a rather heavy meal, a slice of *Yerushalmi kugel* (p. 172) goes extremely well with *flommen tzimmes*. Precede or follow the *tzimmes* with a Boston lettuce salad (p. 220). For an elegant formal dinner, start out with a *forspeis* of *gefilte fisch* (p. 38).

Either the Lithuanian or Galitzianer recipes go well with *tzimmes*. A *kissel* rather than a compote should be served for dessert. Drink wines like zinfandel, Beaujolais, or a fruity red burgundy with the meal. A sparkling rosé also goes well with *flommen tzimmes*.

Good Advice

A rabbinical student who had no experience with women went out on a date. By giving him some good advice, his more experienced friends, knowing that he was very shy, tried to help him overcome his fear of not knowing what to say.

"Remember," said one of them, "when you first meet her, start to talk about the subject of love."

"But not too much," said another. "As soon as you finish with the subject of love, talk to her about family."

"And if neither of you has too much to say about family," said a third, "change the subject fast and talk to her about philosophy."

When the two young people were finally alone, the rabbinic student remembered the advice that his friends had given him. First he asked the girl, "Do you like *tzimmes*?"

"Why shouldn't I like *tzimmes*?" she replied.

The young man decided they had talked enough about love and he went on to the subject of family. "Do you have a brother?" he asked.

"No," said the girl. "I don't."

So much, thought the young man, about the subject of family. It was now time to talk about philosophy. So he looked earnestly at the girl and said, "So, if you had a brother, do you think *he* would like *tzimmes*?"

Hungarian-Style Braised Short Ribs of Beef

Ungarische Gedempte Flanken

3 lb. beef short ribs, cut into 3-inch lengths
1 large onion, peeled and very thinly sliced
2 carrots, peeled and grated
1/3 cup corn or peanut oil
3 Tblsp. flour

4 Tblsp. Dijon mustard
3 tsp. sugar
2 bay leaves
1 Tblsp. red wine vinegar
1 1/2 cups beef stock (p. 4)
salt and black pepper to taste

1. Preheat the oven to 350°. In a heavy casserole with a tight-fitting lid, heat the oil over medium heat. Brown the meat a few pieces at a time and set aside on a platter as they brown.

2. Reduce the heat slightly, add the onions to the pot, and sauté until soft and translucent. Add the carrots and cook 5 minutes longer. Sprinkle the flour over the vegetables, reduce the heat to moderate, and cook 5 minutes longer, stirring often to prevent burning. Cook this at least 7 minutes to remove all the floury taste from the flour.

3. Add the sugar, mustard, vinegar, bay leaves, and stock, and mix together until well blended. Return the meat to the pot. Cover tightly with aluminum foil and then with the lid of the casserole. Braise for 2 hours undisturbed. To serve, apportion the meat onto individual serving plates and nap with the sauce. Remove the bay leaves and serve the remainder of the sauce in a sauceboat. Recipe serves 6 to 8 people.

Serving Suggestions

This simple stew is delicious accompanied by plain or yellow rice *pilav* (p. 182), *galushkes* (p. 177), or one of the *knaidelach* recipes on pp. 183–184. Just about any plain sautéed vegetable side dish in season goes well as an accompaniment. Precede the meat with bouquet of fresh vegetables soup (p. 62) or carrot soup (p. 62), and conclude the meal with a seasonal fruit compote or *kissel*. Drink red wine with dinner. Just about any kind will do, but I rather like a Spanish rioja.

Hungarian Goulash

Ungarische Goulash

Hungarian goulash is one of the most satisfying and tasty meat dishes ever created, when it is properly made. It is a sophisticated and elegant way of preparing beef and should not be thought of as an everyday, ordinary beef stew. The key to preparing a successful Hungarian goulash lies in using Hungarian-manufactured sweet paprika, a sufficient amount of onions (don't be alarmed by the quantity used in this recipe), a homemade rather than a store-bought tomato sauce, and the correct seasonings combined in the right proportions. The onions almost disappear into the sauce as a result of the gentle lengthy cooking, and the other ingredients merge subtly and harmoniously into a veritable culinary symphony while at the same time retaining their own distinct flavors. I like to serve goulash in deep, wide soup bowls or pasta bowls rather than on flat platters, on which the sauce tends to separate from the meat, creating an unattractive appearance. Follow these suggestions and serve Hungarian goulash when you entertain special guests. You will all be pleasantly surprised at how fabulous this dish can be.

3 1/2 lb. good-quality stewing beef, trimmed of fat and cut into 1-inch cubes
4 lb. onions, peeled and sliced very thin
1/2 cup corn oil
3 Tblsp. Hungarian sweet paprika
1/2 tsp. Hungarian hot paprika
3 large cloves garlic, peeled and finely chopped
1 medium-size green pepper, roasted, peeled, seeded, and finely chopped
1 heaping Tblsp. dried marjoram (in season, substitute 2 heaping Tblsp. fresh marjoram)
1 heaping tsp. fresh marjoram (if available)
1 heaping Tblsp. caraway seeds
2 tsp. salt
1/4 tsp. black pepper
1 cup dry red wine
1 cup fresh, homemade tomato sauce (p. 6)
1/2 cup beef stock (p. 4)
1 1/2 Tblsp. unbleached white flour
juice of 1/2 lemon

1. In a heavy, deep casserole or Dutch oven, heat the oil over medium-low heat on top of the stove. Sauté the onions, stirring often, until they are soft and translucent. Add half of the sweet paprika and reduce the heat to simmer. Cook 5 minutes, stirring constantly with a wooden spoon to prevent sticking and scorching.

2. Add the garlic, caraway seeds, and dried marjoram (if using) and cook 5 minutes longer, stirring constantly. Add the meat and cook 5 minutes more, stirring all the while.

3. Sprinkle the flour over this mixture and mix it in thoroughly. Cook an additional 5 minutes, stirring constantly to make certain that nothing burns.

4. Add the remaining paprikas, green pepper, wine, stock, tomato sauce, salt, black pepper, and all but the 1 tsp. of fresh marjoram (if using). Stir everything together, cover tightly, and simmer on top of the stove for 1 hour at the lowest possible temperature.

5. After 1 hour of cooking time has passed, add the lemon juice and check to be sure that there is sufficient liquid in the pot. This part is a little tricky. Hungarian goulash should not have a sauce that is very liquid, because it is made mostly of onion that has disintegrated in cooking. But it should still *look* as if there is a sauce. To be sure that nothing will stick to the bottom of the pot and burn, stir it thoroughly when you add the lemon juice. If the sauce seems too thick, add a little more wine (about 1/4 cup will do). Cover tightly again and cook 1 hour longer. During the last hour of cooking, check the pot periodically to make sure the consistency of the sauce is correct. Stir the goulash to prevent any scorching. If it seems necessary, add more wine or stock.

6. After 2 hours of cooking have passed, it is time for the last special touch. For this, you will need the remaining heaping tsp. of fresh marjoram. If you are unable to obtain fresh marjoram, the goulash will be delicious anyway. Do not substitute dried marjoram for the fresh in this step. Lift the cover off the pot and add the tsp. of fresh marjoram. Stir it into the goulash, cover the pot, and cook 10 minutes longer. The addition of a small amount of fresh marjoram gives an herbal freshness to the finished dish that results in a heady aroma.

7. To serve the goulash, simply apportion it into deep, wide soup or pasta bowls and serve immediately with the accompaniments suggested below. Recipe serves 6 to 8 people.

Serving Suggestions

The best vegetable accompaniment to Hungarian goulash, in my opinion, is *kartoffel knaidelach* (p. 183). Serve 2 or 3 of these with each portion of goulash. Other suitable accompaniments are *challah knaidelach* (p. 184) and *matzoh knaidelach* (p. 184). You may also use the more conventional accompaniments of plain boiled potatoes or rice, but I feel the dish needs something more sophisticated to go with it. Precede or follow the goulash with a green bean salad (p. 222). Chopped liver (p. 43) makes a delicious *forspeis*. For a fine conclusion to an elegant dinner, try *palaschinken* (p. 247) or one of the Hungarian flourless tortes in chapter 12. A fruity, full-bodied red wine goes very well with goulash. A good red burgundy, a Beaujolais, a Chianti, or an Italian Barolo are all excellent choices. For that matter, so is a California zinfandel.

Variation

For the Viennese version of goulash, in step 4, add the finely grated peel of 1 lemon to the recipe.

Hungarian Pepper Steak

This sautéed steak dish is good any season of the year. It is a quick, light, tasty meal that can be prepared almost at a moment's notice.

2 lb. beef tip steaks, cut into 3-inch-long, 1/4-inch-wide strips
1 large or 2 medium-size onions, peeled and very thinly sliced
2 cloves garlic, peeled and chopped
1 tsp. Hungarian hot paprika
1/2 lb. fresh mushrooms, wiped clean with a damp cloth and sliced
2 large green bell peppers, roasted, peeled, seeded, and cut into strips
4 Tblsp. corn or peanut oil
salt and freshly ground black pepper to taste

1. Heat oil in a deep, wide sauté pan over high heat and brown meat strips, a few at a time. Set meat on a platter after it has browned.

2. Reduce heat to medium and sauté onions until soft and translucent. Add mushrooms and continue sautéing until they start to give off liquor.

3. Reduce heat again to medium-low and add the garlic and paprika. Cook 5 minutes.

4. Add the pepper strips and return the meat to the pan together with the juices that have accumulated around it. Reduce the heat to its lowest point. Cover the sauté pan tightly with aluminum foil and then with its lid. Simmer 30 minutes before uncovering. Season the steak with salt and freshly ground black pepper before serving.

Serving Suggestions

This dish is traditionally served with rice *pilav* (p. 182), but there are some excellent nontraditional ways of serving it as well. It can be served on its own with nothing but Vienna bread and a good wine to accompany it. Potatoes in any form also go well with it. My first choice would be paprika potatoes (p. 200). Sautéed sweet potatoes (p. 204) are also an unusual but tasty accompaniment. A dry red wine tastes good with pepper steak. My favorite is Spanish rioja. Precede with a *forspeis* of chopped eggs and onions with *schmaltz* (p. 42), and conclude the meal with fresh fruit or a seasonal fruit compote.

Jewish-Style Prime Rib Roast

Vos ken men foon an oks farlangen mer vi oksnfleisch?

What more can you expect from an ox than beef?
— Yiddish witticism

Everyone likes a good roast beef once in a while. Although Jewish cuisine is much better known for its braised meat dishes and stews, this method of preparing roast beef has been popular with Jewish cooks in Europe and in America. It differs from the classical roast beef in its seasonings, which give it a kind of "je ne sais quoi" that makes it uniquely Jewish. Roast beef lovers will love this dish.

1 5-lb. standing rib roast
3 cloves garlic, peeled and cut into thin slices
coarse or kosher salt
freshly ground black pepper
Hungarian hot paprika
2 to 2 1/2 cups beef stock (p. 4)
1 cup dry red wine

1. Cut small slits in the meat and insert a sliver of garlic into each slit. Sprinkle the fatty top of the roast (but not the flesh on its sides) with coarse salt, black pepper, and hot paprika. Refrigerate it for 2 hours.

2. Preheat the oven to 475°. Place the meat on a rack in a roasting pan and put it into the oven directly from the refrigerator without bringing it to room temperature. Sear the roast at this high tem-

perature for 20 minutes and then reduce the heat in the oven to 350°.

3. Roast the meat at 20 minutes per pound for a medium roast. Roasting time will be between 1 1/2 and 2 hours, depending on the size of the roast.

4. Mix the stock and wine together in a bowl. After the first 30 minutes of roasting, start to baste the meat with the wine-stock mixture. Do this every 12 to 15 minutes until you have used up all but 1 cup of the liquid. Reserve this for making the sauce at the end. If you run out of liquid too soon, add a little more wine.

5. When the meat is finished roasting, set it on a carving board to rest while you finish the sauce. To make the sauce, remove the rack from the roasting pan and place it on a burner on top of the stove. Turn on the heat to medium and deglaze the pan with the remaining cup of wine-stock mixture. Scrape the bottom of the pan with a wooden spoon to loosen the browned bits.

6. To serve the meat, carve it into portions and set it on individual serving plates or on a platter. Nap the slices of meat with the sauce and serve the remaining sauce in a sauceboat. Recipe serves 6 to 8 people.

Serving Suggestions

My favorite accompaniment to roast beef is potato *kugel* (p. 178). Either the Litvish or the Galitzianer recipe goes well with it. Some people like to serve roast potatoes with it. My recipe for roast potatoes appears on p. 197. Any sautéed vegetables in season are a welcome addition to the entrée. Just about any soup or *forspeis* can be eaten with roast beef. Follow the entrée with one of the lettuce salads, and conclude the meal with a seasonal fruit compote or *kissel*. Drink a fine-quality, dry red wine with this meal. Nothing beats a good French bordeaux.

Rozlfleisch

Rozlfleisch is an old traditional *shtetl* dish. The true meaning of *rozlfleisch* has become obscured as the art of making *rozl* itself has largely disappeared. Among some Jews (even those from eastern Europe), *rozl-fleisch* was a term used to describe any braised beef dish made with vinegar or that had a slightly fermented flavor. These definitions are all incorrect.

Rozlfleisch, plainly and simply, is a *fleischig* stew made with *rozl* (p. 68) as the cooking medium. *Rozlfleisch* is a one-dish meal that is as tasty as it is exotic. Trust me when I say that it is worthwhile making *rozl* once a year just to have a chance to eat *rozlfleisch*.

2 1/2 lb. brisket or **brust dekel** (also called "plate brisket")
1 medium-size onion, peeled and very thinly sliced
2 bay leaves
4 cups *rozl* (p. 68)
1 Tblsp. sugar
salt and black pepper to taste
3 eggs, beaten
2 1/2 lb. red boiling potatoes
1/3 cup fresh parsley

1. Bring the *rozl* to boil in a stock pot over high heat. Add the onions and the bay leaves and cook 5 minutes. Reduce the heat to simmer and add the sugar and the meat. Cover the pot tightly and simmer gently for 2 hours.

2. Remove the meat to a carving board and discard the bay leaves. When the meat has cooled sufficiently to carve, slice thinly. While waiting for the meat to cool, boil the potatoes in their jackets in the microwave oven or on top of the stove. When they are done, plunge them into cold water to stop the cooking. Peel the potatoes and cut them into chunks. The potatoes can also be boiled, peeled, and sliced one day in advance and then added to the *rozl* as directed in step 3.

3. Beat the eggs in a mixing bowl. Return the meat to the *rozl* and add the potato chunks. Reheat the *rozl* gently. When it has heated through sufficiently, ladle some into the eggs, and beat this together with a wire whisk. Pour this mixture into the *rozl* and heat very gently until just heated through. Do not allow it to come to a boil, or the eggs will curdle.

4. Add the parsley and salt and pepper to taste. Serve immediately in deep, wide soup bowls. Recipe serves 6 to 8 people.

Serving Suggestions

Rozlfleisch was a tradtional Passover dish among Ukrainian Jews, who served it with *matzoh*. It is delicious this way and equally delicious with *pletzel* (p. 26). A beet green salad (p. 225) or a cucumber salad with dill (p. 223) makes an excellent vegetable accompaniment. No *forspeis* is required. A dessert made with apples, such as Jewish apple cake (p. 268) or Jewish apple tart (p. 275), rounds out the menu very well. A fruity red wine like zinfandel is just fine with *rozlfleisch*.

Cholent

I am always amazed when I meet a Jewish person who has never tasted *cholent* or does not know what it is. *Cholent*, culturally speaking, is probably the most "Jewish" of any Jewish food. Jews in every part of the world created dishes by various names that are similar to this one using food products and seasonings typical of their national cuisine. A *cholent* is a one-dish hot meal consisting of a variety of meats, grains, and vegetables all cooked together in one pot, for a long time, in a very slow oven.

Cholent, or some variation of *cholent*, has always been the traditional Sabbath midday meal served upon return from Saturday-morning synagogue services. Because cooking is prohibited on the Sabbath, the *cholent* is always set to cook at the lowest possible oven temperature just before the Sabbath begins. It is left in the oven overnight and is taken out when it is ready to be served at lunchtime. *Cholent* is probably the Jewish dish that has the oldest recorded written history. It is mentioned in the Talmud, where the procedure for making it was not so different from that used today except that in those days of primitive (or nonexistent) ovens, the tightly sealed pot with the *cholent* in it was lowered into a pit in the ground and left there overnight to be cooked by the heat generated by the ground itself. Although the Talmud does not specifically state that a fire was kindled and then extinguished in the *cholent* baking pit, I cannot help but wonder whether the ancient Hebrews cooked their *cholent* (called *chamin*) the same way early Native American peoples prepared seafood and corn in their baking pits or the way ancient Hawaiians roasted pigs and taro in their *imus*. In the *shtetlach* of eastern Europe, pots of *cholent* were cooked in the communal baker's oven, which was large enough to generate and retain an incredible amount of heat. The families would go after synagogue services were over to collect their pots of *cholent* and partake of their Sabbath meal.

There are an incredible number of recipes for *cholent*, but all contain the following essential, common features: two or more kinds of meat, potatoes or legumes or both, grains, liquid of some kind to provide moisture, and seasoning. It is highly likely that the famous French dish called "cassoulet" originated as a variation of *cholent*. Needless to say, *cholent* is not exactly delicate fare for the girth conscious! I consider *cholent* a winter dish whose flavor is practically unsurpassable on a cold winter night or day. There is nothing like a hot bowl of *cholent* to warm you up after a trudge home from *shul* through the snow (or, for that matter, a drive home from work in a blizzard). And there is nothing like a brisk *shpatzir* (Sabbath walk) after your appetite has been royally sated (believe me, you'll need that walk!). Of course, you can always do what my grandfather did and fall asleep at the table immediately after you have chewed your last mouthful.

My recipe for *cholent* is different from many others in several ways: I like to use wine and stock as the cooking medium instead of water, which really elevates the dish to gourmet status and makes an incredible difference in its overall flavor. I also like to follow my grandmother's practice and prepare a *ganef* to be cooked inside the *cholent*. *Ganef* in Yiddish means "thief." The *ganef* in a *cholent* is a kind of *knaidel* (or large dumpling) that absorbs the flavors of all the ingredients in the *cholent*, hence its name. The *ganef* is cut into slices for serving when the *cholent* is served.

3 lb. **brust dekel (plate brisket) or flank steak**
1 **whole fresh or smoked veal tongue (about 3 lb.), prepared by precooking and peeling according to the instructions on p. 161**
1 1/2 **cups dried great northern, navy, or lima beans**
3/4 **cup pearl barley**
9 **medium-size white baking potatoes**
3 **large onions, peeled and very finely chopped**
1 **large carrot, peeled and finely grated**
6 **Tblsp. chicken schmaltz (do not substitute oil)**
2 **Tblsp. Hungarian sweet paprika**
1/2 **tsp. Hungarian hot paprika**
3 **large cloves garlic, peeled and left whole**
3 **Tblsp. unbleached white flour**
2 **bay leaves and 6 to 8 sprigs fresh thyme, tied together with kitchen string (1 1/2 tsp. dried thyme may be substituted)**
6 **cups beef stock (p. 4)**
2 **cups dry red wine**
1 **recipe cholent ganef (see variations at the end of the recipe)**

Housewives bringing their pots of *cholent* to the oven of the communal bakery. Poland, 1930s.
(Courtesy of YIVO Archives.)

1. One day before making the *cholent*, soak the beans overnight in cold water to cover by 2 inches. Drain and rinse the next morning. They are now ready to cook in the *cholent*. Remember that the *cholent* needs to cook a minimum of 12 hours, so if you don't begin preparations the night before you serve it, do so very early in the morning.

2. To begin cooking the *cholent*, over medium-high heat, melt the *schmaltz* in the large, large heavy casserole in which you will be cooking the *cholent* and brown the meat on all sides. Set it aside and lower the heat to medium.

3. Sauté the onions until translucent and soft. Add the garlic, the grated carrot, and the paprikas and cook an additional 5 to 7 minutes. Sprinkle the flour over the vegetables and cook 5 minutes longer, stirring and scraping with a wooden spoon to prevent sticking and scorching.

4. Add the stock and wine slowly, stirring all the time with the spoon to prevent lumping. When all of this has been added, add the bay leaves and the thyme.

5. Return the meat to the casserole and surround it with the beans, barley, and potatoes. The liquid should come up to the top of the ingredients in the pot and cover them by about 1/2 inch. If necessary, add more stock. Cover the pot and bring it to a gentle boil on top of the stove. Preheat your oven to its lowest possible temperature.

6. When the pot is gently simmering, add the *ganef* and reduce the heat to the lowest simmer. Cover tightly with aluminum foil and then with the lid of the casserole. Place the *cholent* in the oven and forget about it for at least 12 hours or until you are ready to serve it.

To serve the *cholent*: Slice the meats and the *ganef*. Arrange some of the potatoes, beans, and barley with slices of meat and *ganef* in individual deep, wide soup bowls. There will probably not be enough liquid to constitute a sauce, but if there is, ladle some of this over the *cholent* and serve. Recipe serves 8 to 10 people.

Cholent Ganef (two variations)

Variation 1: *Matzoh* Meal *Cholent Ganef*

1 1/4 cups *matzoh* meal
4 large eggs
1/2 cup water
salt and black pepper to taste

1. Mix all the ingredients together in a mixing bowl, cover with plastic wrap, and refrigerate for at least 1 hour or longer. Mixture may be made the evening before and left in the refrigerator overnight.

2. Remove the mixture from the refrigerator. Have a bowl of cold water next to you while you work. Moisten your hands in the water and lift the *matzoh* meal mixture out of the bowl. Shape it into an oblong cylinder and lay it gently into the *cholent*. Proceed with recipe, step 6.

Variation 2: Hungarian Flour *Cholent Ganef*

1/3 cup *schmaltz*
1 1/2 cups flour
1 jumbo egg
1 small onion, grated
1 tsp. Hungarian hot paprika
salt and black pepper to taste

Combine the *schmaltz* with the flour by hand. Add egg, grated onion, and seasonings, and knead together well. Shape into an oblong loaf about 5 inches long. Wrap in cheesecloth and tie both ends with kitchen string. Make sure the cheesecloth wrapping is loose to allow for expansion during cooking. Place into the *cholent* and proceed with recipe, step 6.

Serving Suggestions

Cholent is a heavy, very filling dish. In order to really enjoy it, it should be part of a menu that features only light dishes before and after. Precede the *cholent* with a salad. Green bean salad (p. 222), field green salad (p. 219), mixed vegetable salad (p. 220), and green cabbage salad (p. 230) are all excellent choices. If you like, serve kosher dill pickles (p. 291) and pickled beets (p. 291) with the *cholent*. Conclude the meal with fresh fruit or a seasonal fruit compote or *kissel*. *Cholent* needs a good-quality, full-bodied, dry red wine. Try cabernet sauvignon, Chianti, Italian Barolo, or Spanish rioja.

Braised Veal Shoulder with Aromatic Herbs and Vegetables

Gedempte Kalbsfleisch

Kalbsfleisch iz halbfleisch.

Calf's meat is half-meat.
— Yiddish saying

1 4- to 5-lb. veal shoulder roast, boned, rolled, and tied with kitchen string
2 large onions, peeled and chopped
2 large carrots, peeled and diced
1 parsnip, peeled and diced
1 turnip, peeled and diced
3 stalks celery, diced
3 large cloves garlic, peeled and chopped
1 bouquet garni consisting of 1 bay leaf, 6 sprigs parsley, and 5 sprigs thyme (1 tsp. dried thyme may be substituted if fresh is unavailable), tied together with kitchen string
1 tsp. Hungarian hot paprika
salt and black pepper to taste
2 Tblsp. unbleached white flour
6 Tblsp. corn or peanut oil
1/2 cup red wine
1 cup beef stock (p. 4)
1/4 cup brandy

1. In a large, deep casserole with a tight-fitting lid, heat 3 Tblsp. oil over medium-high heat and brown the meat on all sides. Remove it to a platter and reduce the heat to medium.

2. Add the remaining 3 Tblsp. oil to the pot and sauté the onions until translucent and soft. Reduce the heat to medium-low and add the garlic and paprika. Cook 5 minutes more.

3. Add all the remaining vegetables and sauté 10 minutes more, stirring with a wooden spoon to prevent sticking and scorching.

4. Sprinkle the flour over the vegetables and sauté 5 more minutes, stirring constantly.

5. Add the stock, wine, and brandy, and mix together well. Make sure there are no lumps. If the mixture seems too thick, add up to 1/2 cup more wine or stock.

6. Add the bouquet garni and return the meat to the casserole. Preheat the oven to 350°. Cover the pot tightly with aluminum foil and then with the lid of the pot. When pot is simmering, transfer it to the oven and braise for 2 hours.

7. Uncover the pot and remove the meat to a carving board to rest while you prepare the sauce. Discard the bouquet garni and strain the contents of the pot through a sieve into a saucepan, pressing down hard on the vegetables to extract all their juices and to puree some of the pulp. Add salt and pepper and taste for seasoning. Carve the meat into attractive slices and arrange it on individual serving plates or a serving platter. Nap it with some of the sauce and serve the remainder of the sauce separately in a sauceboat. Recipe serves 6 to 8 people.

Serving Suggestions

This attractive dish goes well with classical vegetable accompaniments like roast potatoes and sautéed vegetables chosen for their complementary flavor, color, and texture. Just about any kind of *forspeis* and soup go well with this dish except one made with herring or bouquet of fresh vegetables soup (which has too many kinds of vegetables in it and deadens the effect of the vegetable-herb sauce). Follow the entrée with a field green salad (p. 219), and conclude the meal with a seasonal fruit compote or *kissel*. A full-bodied, dry red wine goes well with this dish. My first choice would be a good French bordeaux.

Braised Veal
With Caraway Seeds

Gedempte Kalbsfleisch
Mit Kimmel

1 4- to 5-lb. veal shoulder roast, boned and trimmed of extra fat

2 Tblsp. caraway seeds
2 large onions, peeled and very finely chopped
1 1/2 tsp. Hungarian hot paprika
3 large cloves garlic, peeled and cut into thin slivers
3 Tblsp. unbleached white flour
salt and black pepper to taste
1 1/2 cups chicken stock (p. 3)
1 cup dry white wine
6 Tblsp. chicken *schmaltz* (p. 6)

1. Wash and completely dry the meat. Make small slits using a sharp knife all around the meat. Insert a sliver of garlic into each slit. Rub the meat with salt and pepper and the caraway seeds. If necessary, tie the meat with kitchen string to make sure it holds its shape well during roasting. Refrigerate for 3 hours.

2. In a large, heavy casserole that has a tight-fitting lid, melt 4 Tblsp. of the *schmaltz* over medium-high heat. Brown the meat on all sides in the sizzling *schmaltz*. Remove it and set it on a platter to rest.

3. Add 2 more Tblsp. *schmaltz* and reduce the heat to medium. Sauté the onions until soft and translucent.

4. Reduce the heat slightly and sprinkle the remaining paprika over the onions. Sauté 5 minutes longer.

5. Sprinkle the onions with the flour and continue sautéing, stirring constantly to prevent scorching and sticking. Cook 5 to 6 minutes longer.

6. Slowly add the stock and wine to the casserole, stirring all the while to prevent lumping. Scrape the bottom of the casserole with a wooden spoon to remove any bits that have clung to the bottom of the pot. When the liquid is well mixed in and the mixture in the casserole resembles a thinnish sauce, return the meat to the casserole, together with any juices that have accumulated on the platter.

7. Preheat the oven to 350°. Cover the casserole with aluminum foil and then with its own cover. Braise the meat undisturbed for 2 hours in the oven.

8. To serve, remove the meat to a carving board and carve it into attractive slices. Arrange on individual serving plates or on a platter. Nap the meat with some of the sauce and serve the rest in a sauceboat. Recipe serves 6 to 8 people.

Serving Suggestions

My favorite vegetable accompaniment to this dish, which comes from Galitzia, is Galitzianer braised red cabbage (p. 204), but other sautéed vegetables in season work just as well. Green beans or brussels sprouts are particularly nice. So is sautéed green cabbage (p. 204). You may also accompany the meat with oven-roasted potatoes (p. 197) or a Galitzianer potato *kugel* (p. 180) if you wish. Any of the chicken soups is fine and so is Bessarabian bean soup (p. 71) if you are serving this dish in the winter. Just be sure to include only one starchy vegetable or grain dish in the meal, and choose your accompaniments to the meat entrée accordingly. A seasonal fruit compote or *kissel* completes the meal. A fruity white wine is better than red with this veal dish. Try a full-bodied white burgundy, a Chablis, or a chardonnay.

Grilled Veal Chops with Garlic Sauce

The sauce in this dish emphasizes the pungency of fresh, uncooked garlic and sweet herbs. Like an Italian salsa verde, which traditionally accompanies plain stewed or roasted meats, this sauce is uncooked.

6 first-cut veal chops, each about 1/2 to 3/4 inch thick
8 large cloves garlic, peeled
1 tsp. salt or more to taste
1 tsp. Hungarian hot paprika
1/4 tsp. freshly ground black pepper
1 cup beef stock, warmed (p. 4)
1/4 cup finely chopped fresh parsley
1/4 cup finely chopped fresh dill leaves
1/3 cup sunflower oil

1. Place everything except the veal chops and 3 Tblsp. oil into a food processor or blender and blend at high speed until pureed. Or, lacking either of these appliances, mash the garlic cloves with the salt in a mortar until it turns into a paste, and mix it together with all the other ingredients. Set aside.

2. Preheat the outdoor grill or oven broiler. Brush the veal chops with the remaining oil on both sides and grill 5 minutes on each side. Spoon a little of the garlic sauce over the meat on one side, turn that side so it faces the heat of the grill or broiler, and grill 3 minutes longer.

3. Spoon more of the sauce over the meat and turn this side so it faces the heat of the grill or broiler.

Broil another 3 minutes. If you like your meat grilled until it is well done, repeat the process a second time on both sides of the meat. Serve immediately, with the remaining garlic sauce served in a sauceboat. Recipe serves 6 people.

Serving Suggestions

This tasty Romanian dish is good both summer and winter. Hungarian summer salad (p. 223), Romanian potato salad (p. 229), Romanian salad (p. 228), any of the lettuce salads, and green bean salad (p. 222) all go well with the veal chops. If you prefer a hot vegetable accompaniment with the meat, then *lesco* (p. 208) or any of the vegetables in tomato sauce are equally good. If it is winter, Bessarabian bean soup (p. 71) makes an excellent first course. Both white and red wines can be drunk with this meal. If choosing white, you will do well with a Chablis or a dry white bordeaux. For reds, go with a dry red bordeaux or a dry cabernet sauvignon.

Polish-Style Baked Veal Chops

Poilisher Gebakte Kalbsfleisch

6 second-cut veal chops, each about 1/2 to 3/4 inch thick
6 Tblsp. corn oil or more if needed
2 large onions, peeled and very thinly sliced
1/3 cup unbleached white flour
1/2 tsp. ground allspice
1/4 tsp. Hungarian hot paprika
salt and freshly ground black pepper to taste
1 clove garlic, peeled and chopped
3/4 cups beef stock (p. 4)
3/4 cups beer

1. Mix the flour with the salt, pepper, and hot paprika and spread it out flat onto a plate. Dredge the veal chops in the seasoned flour on both sides and set aside to rest for 10 minutes on another plate.

2. Heat the oil in a sauté pan over fairly high heat. Brown the veal chops two at a time and set them into a baking pan in which they will all fit in one layer.

3. When all the chops are browned, reduce the heat under the sauté pan to medium, add more oil if

needed, and sauté the onions until soft and translucent. Add the garlic and allspice and cook an additional 5 minutes. Remove the onions with a slotted spoon and spread them over the veal chops.

4. Preheat the oven to 350°. Pour the stock and the beer into the sauté pan and deglaze it, scraping up the browned bits with a wooden spoon. Pour this over the meat in the baking pan, cover the pan with aluminum foil, and bake in the oven for 20 minutes.

5. Remove the foil and bake an additional 20 to 25 minutes, basting the meat from time to time with the pan juices. Serve 1 chop per diner on individual dinner plates with some of the sauce poured over the meat. Recipe serves 6 people. If the chops bunch up unattractively during cooking, use a sharp knife to cut them in one or two places so they will lie flat on the plate when they are served.

Serving Suggestions

This is a tasty way to serve a cheaper cut of meat. That is why I recommend using second-cut rather than first-cut veal chops when making this dish. The entrée may be accompanied by any of the sautéed vegetables listed in chapter 9. I rather like sautéed green cabbage (p. 204) with this meat. Many different kinds of starches are suitable as well. A piece of *kishka* (p. 187) goes nicely with the cabbage. Or you may precede the meat entrée with chicken soup with *kasha* (p. 58) or chicken soup with rice (p. 57) and just accompany the meat with one or two vegetable side dishes. Another good choice is bouquet of fresh vegetables soup (p. 62). Your choice of soup will be determined by the other things you decide to include with the meal. For an elegant formal dinner, serve a *forspeis* of chopped egg and onion with *schmaltz* (p. 42) before the soup. A seasonal fruit compote or *kissel* completes the meal. Either red or white wine is equally good to drink. I prefer something fruity to offset the spiciness of the sauce. A medium-dry Chablis is a nice white. Zinfandel is a good choice if you wish to serve red. A sparkling rosé is also excellent with this dish.

Veal Steaks *Paprikash*

I created this dish as an alternative to Swiss steak (which is one of my favorite American dishes) when I felt inspired to do something different and give it a Hungarian type of seasoning. The veal steaks themselves are cut from the shoulder section of the veal. This is the part from which veal cutlets or scallopine are taken in a kosher-butchered animal. The main trick to successful preparation of this dish is to cut the steaks thick enough and then to pound a sufficient amount of flour into them with the edge of a dinner plate or the back of a cleaver rather than the traditional kitchen mallet used to pound *schnitzel*. To make *schnitzel*, it is desirable to get the piece of meat as thin as possible and then to sauté it as quickly as possible. With Swiss steak (and with veal steaks *paprikash* as well), the meat needs to absorb flour but retain some of its thickness. The dinner plate or the back of a cleaver achieves this because it opens some space in the meat, which is filled by the seasoned flour that goes into it. This gives the cooked meat body and makes it very tender.

Veal steaks *paprikash* is one of my favorite "company" dishes because it is rather simple to make, is not terribly time consuming, and does not require the cook to spend a great deal of time at the stove while the guests wait. The flavor of veal steaks *paprikash* is also complex, interesting, and sophisticated.

6 veal shoulder steaks, cut 2 inches thick
1/2 to 2/3 cup unbleached white flour
5 medium-size onions, peeled and very thinly
    sliced
2 large garlic cloves, peeled and finely chopped
6 Tblsp. corn oil
1 heaping Tblsp. Hungarian sweet paprika
1/2 tsp. Hungarian hot paprika
1 bay leaf
1 1/2 tsp. dried marjoram
1 tsp. fresh marjoram (no substitutes)
1/4 cup finely chopped parsley
1/4 cup finely chopped fresh dill leaves
1 cup fresh tomato sauce (p. 6)
1 cup dry red wine
3/4 cup chicken stock (p. 3)
2 Tblsp. freshly squeezed lemon juice
salt and freshly ground black pepper to taste

1. Put the steaks on a cutting board and sprinkle 2 to 3 Tblsp. flour over them. Grind some black pepper over the flour. Using the edge of a dinner plate or the back of a cleaver, gently pound the seasoned flour into the meat until it is absorbed,

working first along the width of the steak and then across the length. Pound in such a way as to make pressure marks in the meat, which makes sure that the flour gets held in place there. When you have done this on one side of the steaks, repeat the process on the other side. The size of the steaks will probably be reduced to about 1 inch in thickness when you have finished, and you will have used up between 1/2 and 2/3 cup of flour. Set the meat aside to rest on a platter.

2. In a large, deep, wide sauté pan, heat the oil over fairly high heat until it is bubbling and sizzling but not smoking. Quickly brown the meat on both sides and remove it back to the platter. Reduce the heat to medium.

3. Add the onions to the oil and sauté them until they are soft and translucent, turning from time to time with a wooden spoon to prevent burning or sticking.

4. When the onions are soft and translucent, reduce the heat to medium-low, add the garlic and the sweet and hot paprika, and cook 6 minutes, stirring frequently to prevent burning and sticking.

5. Add the dried marjoram, tomato sauce, wine, and stock to the onions. Stir everything together well and cook until it just begins to come to a boil.

6. Return the meat to the pan, together with the juices that have accumulated on the platter. Gently push the meat down into the sauce so that it is more or less covered. Cover the pan tightly with aluminum foil and then with the lid of the sauté pan. Reduce the heat to the lowest possible simmer and cook undisturbed for 1 1/2 hours.

7. Uncover the pan and pour in the lemon juice. When you first remove the foil, an incredible savory aroma will hit you. This is the aroma that needs to be preserved for your guests; it is accomplished by adding the herbs at the last minute. Stir the lemon juice into the sauce, add some salt, taste for seasoning, and add as much as you need to correct the seasoning. The dish can be prepared in advance up to this point and reheated without any loss of its flavor.

8. Just before you are ready to serve the steaks, make sure the contents of the pan are nice and hot if you are reheating. Add all the fresh herbs and cover the pot, this time without the aluminum foil. Cook 5 to 7 minutes and serve immediately. Serve one steak to each diner, smothered attractively in some of the sauce. Serve in a sauceboat any sauce that remains. Recipe serves 6 people.

Serving Suggestions

Veal steaks *paprikash* can be presented several different ways. The most traditionally Hungarian would be to serve them with a portion of rice *pilav* (p. 182). I like to serve them with a simple green vegetable sautéed with garlic, such as broccoli, green beans, and spinach and to accompany the entrée with plenty of freshly baked, crusty Vienna bread (p. 22) to mop up the sauce. If you serve it this way, precede the steaks with one of the more substantial chicken soups such as chicken soup with rice (p. 57), chicken soup with *lokshen* (p. 57), or chicken soup with *kreplach* (p. 59). A "pasta" course of fresh *lokshen* dressed with a sauce of onions and poppy seeds (p. 173) is also quite nice. Chopped liver (p. 43) makes an elegant *forspeis* if the entrée is preceded by a soup. If serving the *lokshen*, serve the steaks with broccoli and follow them with a field green salad (p. 219) or a green bean salad (p. 222). A seasonal fruit compote or *kissel* completes the meal. For a festive accompaniment to coffee and liqueurs after the meal is over, bring out one of the Hungarian-style tortes whose recipes appear in chapter 12. No wine is better than an earthy, full-bodied red. Try an Italian Barolo or a good-quality red burgundy with a full, fruity bouquet.

Weinerschnitzel

This is a Jewish variation on the classic Viennese dish. *Weinerschnitzel* was popular among Jews throughout central Europe. The trick to making a good *weinerschnitzel* lies in pounding the meat to the correct thinness and sautéing it quickly. It also helps to own three or four skillets, because in all likelihood, you will be unable to sauté more than one or two *schnitzel* at a time. They should be served piping hot immediately after their brief cooking has been completed.

4 to 6 veal shoulder steaks or cutlets, each 1/2 inch thick
2 eggs, beaten together with 2 Tblsp. cold water
1/3 cup unbleached white flour
1 cup bread crumbs
salt, black pepper, and hot paprika to taste
peanut oil for sautéing
lemon wedges for garnish

1. Place the veal steaks or cutlets between two sheets of wax paper. Using a kitchen mallet, pound them until they are flat and very, very thin. The thinner the *schnitzel*, the better it will taste. The cutlets will spread out a great deal and look very large. This is why usually only one will fit into a skillet.

2. Have a wide soup bowl, two flat dinner plates, and one large flat platter all lined up next to one another as you proceed with this next step. Spread the bread crumbs across one of the plates. Mix the flour with the salt, pepper, and paprika and spread it across another of the plates. Mix the water with the beaten egg in the soup bowl. The platter will hold the *schnitzel* while it sets.

3. Uncover the flattened cutlets and discard the top layer of wax paper. Take 1 cutlet and dredge it in the seasoned flour. Make sure that every bit of the surface is covered and then gently shake the excess back onto the plate.

4. Next, dip the cutlet into the egg mixture and allow the excess to drip off back into the soup bowl.

5. Last, dredge the cutlet in the bread crumbs and lay it on the platter. Repeat this procedure until all the *schnitzel* have been breaded.

6. Refrigerate the *schnitzel* for 20 to 30 minutes to set the coating.

7. Take the *schnitzel* out of the refrigerator. Heat 4 Tblsp. peanut oil in a 12-inch skillet over high heat. (If you have more than one skillet, do the same with the others.) Allow the oil to come to the point where it sizzles without smoking. Sauté the *schnitzel* in the sizzling oil for 3 to 4 minutes on each side. Serve immediately, garnished with lemon wedges. Recipe serves 4 to 6 people.

Variation

Weinerschnitzel is sometimes served topped with a sautéed egg sunny-side up or a poached egg and a sprinkling of capers. It is delicious plain or made with this topping.

Serving Suggestions

I like to serve *weinerschnitzel* with one of the vegetable side dishes that contain a sauce. *Lesco* (p. 208), either of the braised red cabbage dishes (pp. 204 and 205), or any of the vegetables in tomato sauce in chapter 9 makes an excellent choice. A soup such as carrot soup (p. 62) or bouquet of fresh vegetables soup (p. 62) goes well with *weinerschnitzel*. Complete

the meal with a seasonal fruit compote or *kissel*. A fruity white wine like chardonnay is the best to serve with this meal.

Veal Goulash

Szekely Gulyas

Szekely goulash in non-Jewish Hungarian cuisine is actually made with pork and, of course, the usual sour cream. This kosher version of *szekely* goulash is made with veal and is quite delicious.

2 1/2 lb. veal shoulder, cut into 1-inch cubes
3 Tblsp. corn oil
2 large onions, peeled and very thinly sliced
1 very large or 2 medium-size green bell peppers, roasted, peeled, seeded, and cut into thin strips
1 1/2 cups fresh tomato sauce (p. 6)
1 lb. fresh sauerkraut, rinsed to remove excess salt and dried with paper towels
1 large clove garlic, peeled and chopped
1 Tblsp. Hungarian sweet paprika
8 whole black peppercorns
6 whole allspice berries
2 bay leaves
1 tsp. caraway (*kimmel*) seeds
1/2 cup beef stock (p. 4)
salt to taste, if needed

1. Heat the oil over medium heat in a deep, round casserole or Dutch oven. Sauté the onions until soft and translucent. Add the paprika, garlic, and caraway seeds and cook 5 minutes longer, stirring with a wooden spoon to prevent sticking.

2. Reduce the heat to simmer and add the tomato sauce, stock, and spices except for the salt, and cook, stirring with a wooden spoon to blend everything together, until the mixture comes to a boil.

3. Add the meat and cover the pot. Cook undisturbed for 30 minutes.

4. Preheat the oven to 350°. Add the pepper strips and the sauerkraut to the pot. Stir everything together thoroughly. Cover with aluminum foil and then with the cover of the pot. Place the casserole in the oven and braise for 1 1/2 hours.

5. To serve, remove from the oven and taste for seasoning. If necessary, add a little salt. Serve the goulash in deep, wide soup bowls. Recipe serves 6 to 8 people.

Serving Suggestions

Szekely goulash should be accompanied by slices of *challah knaidelach* (p. 184), *kartoffel knaidelach* (p. 183), or plain boiled potatoes. Chopped herring (p. 41), chopped liver (p. 43), or chopped egg and onion with *schmaltz* (p. 42) makes an excellent *forspeis*. Goulash should never be preceded by a soup or followed by a compote. For dessert, serve a Jewish apple cake (p. 268), a Jewish apple tart (p. 275), a light *eppl schnay* (p. 244), or *palaschinken* (p. 247). Baked apples (p. 244) are also good if you want a light dessert. Drink a full-bodied red wine like zinfandel with this meal.

Romanian-Style Veal Ragout

Ghivetch

Ghivetch is one of Romania's national dishes, and it is prepared in both kosher and nonkosher versions. *Ghivetch* may also be prepared as a vegetarian dish if you leave out the meat, which would make it a kind of variation on ratatouille. The main thing to remember about preparing a tasty *ghivetch* is to include a variety of seasonal fresh vegetables and to braise it in a very slow oven. Because it uses a large variety of different vegetables, the best season to serve *ghivetch* is during the late summer or early autumn. The nonkosher versions use pork as well as or instead of veal, and the cooking fat is lard; the kosher version uses oil. I suspect that the kosher version is closer to the original dish, which was probably Turkish and traveled to Romania with Jewish immigrants from Turkey.

3 lb. veal shoulder, cut into 1-inch cubes
6 to 8 Tblsp. olive oil
1/2 cup unbleached white flour
salt and black pepper to taste
3 large cloves garlic, peeled and chopped
3 medium-size onions, peeled and very thinly sliced
1 small eggplant, peeled and cut into 1-inch cubes

1/2 small head of green cabbage, cored and finely shredded
3 carrots, peeled and sliced
1 large green bell pepper, roasted, peeled, seeded, and cut into thin strips (directions for roasting and peeling peppers are given on p.   )
1 large red bell pepper, roasted, peeled, seeded, and cut into thin strips
4 small zucchini squash, trimmed and sliced
1 medium-size celery root, peeled and cut into chunks
2 medium-size turnips, peeled and cut into chunks
1 lb. fresh pumpkin, peeled and cut into 1-inch cubes (or substitute 1 lb. hubbard squash)
1 lb. green beans, trimmed and cut into 2-inch lengths
2 lb. red boiling potatoes, peeled and cut into chunks
1 cup red wine
2 cups beef stock (p. 4)
2 cups fresh tomato sauce (p. 6)
1 tsp. fresh marjoram (or substitute 1/2 tsp. dried)
1 tsp. fresh thyme leaves (or substitute 1/2 tsp. dried)
1/4 cup fresh parsley
1 tsp. Hungarian hot paprika
1/2 lb. seedless green grapes

1. Place the eggplant cubes into a colander and sprinkle them with salt. Mix with your hands to make sure that salt covers them all over. Place two or three plates on top of the eggplant and let it rest for 1 hour. This removes all of the bitter juices. After 1 hour, rinse the eggplant, gently squeeze the moisture out of it, and dry it on paper towels.

2. Place the flour into a plastic bag with salt and black pepper to taste. Shake the bag until the ingredients are well mixed. Add the veal cubes a few at a time and shake the bag to coat them all over with flour. As the veal cubes are dredged in the seasoned flour, place them on a platter to rest while you dredge the rest.

3. In a very large, deep, wide casserole or Dutch oven, heat 4 Tblsp. of the oil over fairly high heat and brown the veal cubes a few at a time. Set the browned meat into a bowl or onto a clean platter. Repeat as many times as necessary to complete the process.

4. If necessary, add 2 more Tblsp. oil and brown the eggplant cubes. Add them to the meat.

5. If necessary, add up to 2 more Tblsp. oil, reduce the heat to medium, and sauté the onions until soft and translucent. Add the garlic and the paprika and cook 5 minutes longer, stirring all the while to prevent sticking.

6. Add the following vegetables one at a time to the onions and cook 1 to 2 minutes, stirring constantly with each addition: carrots, celery root, cabbage, turnips, zucchini, green beans.

7. When all of these vegetables are cooking happily, add the wine, stock, tomato sauce, thyme, and marjoram. Stir everything well with a wooden spoon, scraping up any browned bits that cling to the bottom.

8. When the ingredients in the casserole come to a boil, reduce the heat to simmer and return the meat and eggplant to the casserole, together with any juices that have accumulated around them. Mix together well.

9. Preheat the oven to 300°. Add the remaining ingredients except for the grapes. Cover the casserole tightly with aluminum foil and then with the lid of the casserole. Braise in the oven for 2 hours undisturbed.

10. Remove the casserole from the oven. Uncover it and stir in the grapes. Replace the foil and the cover and return the casserole to the oven for 30 minutes longer. Serve in deep, wide soup bowls with plenty of crusty Vienna bread (p. 22) to soak up the sauce. *Ghivetch* tastes good reheated too. Recipe serves 8 to 10 people.

Serving Suggestions

Ghivetch needs no accompaniment other than Vienna bread and a good red wine. *Mamaliga* (p. 186) is also delicious with *ghivetch*. Precede the *ghivetch* with a *forspeis* of chopped liver (p. 43). Fresh fruit is the best dessert together with *mandelbroit* (p. 256) or one of the different *makarrondelach* (p. 258). You may drink either a dry or a fruity red wine with this dish. I like cabernet sauvignon or a dry red burgundy. Italian Barolo is also nice.

Variation

For a vegetarian main-dish variation, just leave out the meat and cut the cooking time by 1 1/2 hours. Serve a good *brynza* cheese or one of the cheese *forspeizen* in chapter 2 along with the *ghivetch* and the bread. A white wine is preferable to a red with this variation. Try chardonnay or a medium-dry Chablis.

Roast Veal Breast with *Kasha* and Herbs

Gebrotene Kalbsbrust mit Kasha

Veal breast is an inexpensive cut of meat that is somewhat neglected but very delicious. It requires long, slow cooking to bring out its full flavor and give it a soft, buttery texture. This recipe and the next one are both Ukrainian in origin, and both work magic with the ingredients.

1 5- to 6-lb. veal breast
4 garlic cloves, finely chopped
1 large onion, very finely chopped
1/4 lb. fresh white mushrooms, finely chopped
1/4 cup fresh chopped parsley
1/4 cup freshly chopped dill leaves
1/4 cup freshly snipped chives
1 1/2 cups uncooked coarsely ground *kasha*
1 large egg, beaten
2 Tblsp. corn or peanut oil
1 1/2 cups chicken stock (p. 3)
salt and black pepper to taste

For sauce

1/2 cup dry white wine
3/4 cup chicken stock
salt and black pepper to taste

1. Have the butcher cut a pocket in the veal breast just above the bone, or do this youself. Make sure when you cut the pocket that you leave the meat attached to the bone on both ends.

2. Preheat the oven to 300°. In a large saucepan, heat the oil over medium heat and sauté the onions until soft and translucent. Remove with a slotted spoon and set aside.

3. Add the *kasha* to the oil remaining in the saucepan and toast it, stirring constantly with a wooden spoon. Return the onions to the pan together with any juices that have accumulated around them. Add the chopped mushrooms and keep cooking, stirring constantly to prevent anything from sticking, for 3 to 4 minutes.

4. Add the chicken stock and salt and pepper to taste. Cover the pot, reduce the heat to simmer, and cook until the *kasha* absorbs all the liquid and is soft (about 15 minutes). Remove from the heat and stir in the fresh herbs. Cool to room temperature.

5. When the *kasha* mixture has cooled sufficiently, add the beaten egg to it. Stuff the *kasha* mixture into the pocket of the veal breast. Sew the opening together with kitchen thread or pin it together with small metal skewers. Sprinkle the veal breast with salt and black pepper. Transfer the meat to a well-greased roasting pan. Add 1/4 cup cold water to the pan, cover it tightly, and roast in the oven for 2 hours.

6. Uncover the pan and roast the meat for an additional 1/2 hour. Transfer the meat to a carving board to rest while you make the sauce.

7. To make the sauce, mix the wine and the stock and deglaze the pan with this mixture. Use a wooden spoon to scrape up all the browned bits. Taste for seasoning and add salt and pepper only if necessary.

8. To serve, carve the meat into portions by cutting along the bone joints. Remove the skewers, if you have used them, before doing this. Place each portion of meat on a serving plate, nap it with some of the sauce, and serve the remaining sauce in a sauceboat, if any is left. Recipe serves 6 to 8 people.

Serving Suggestions

This is an elegant spring dish that should be accompanied by spring vegetables such as baked asparagus (p. 201) or sautéed spinach with garlic (p. 197). Precede the entrée with carrot soup (p. 62). Strawberry compote (p. 237), rhubarb compote (p. 240), and *kissel* (p. 242) all make excellent desserts. Drink a white wine with this dish. A medium-dry Chablis or a good white, medium-dry bordeaux is a good choice.

Roast Veal Breast with *Challah* and Mushroom Stuffing

Gebrotene Kalbsbrust Mit Challah Und Shvammen Gefilachts

This luscious variation of roast veal breast is an autumn dish, made with those delicious fresh wild mushrooms so beloved by eastern Europeans. It is now possible to buy fresh gourmet mushrooms that have every bit as much flavor as those gathered in the wild. Every gourmet will love this dish!

1 5- to 6-lb. veal breast
3 large onions, 2 peeled and finely chopped and 1 peeled and coarsely chopped
4 stalks celery, 2 stalks very finely diced and 2 coarsely chopped
2 carrots, peeled and coarsely chopped
1 parsnip, peeled and coarsely chopped
4 cups stale *challah*, cut into small cubes
1 1/2 lb. fresh gourmet mushrooms (I prefer a combination of shiitake, oyster, and brown mushrooms but choose whatever is available and looks good in the market), chopped
1 oz. dried mushrooms, soaked in 1 cup boiling water for 1 hour or longer
1/2 cup freshly chopped parsley
6 to 8 Tblsp. chicken *schmaltz*
2 eggs, beaten
2 to 3 Tblsp. bread crumbs
1 bay leaf
1 1/2 cups beef stock (p. 4)
1 cup dry red wine
salt and black pepper to taste

1. Have the butcher cut a pocket in the veal breast just above the bone, or cut one yourself. Be careful to leave the meat attached to the bone on both ends.

2. Melt 4 Tblsp. *schmaltz* in a skillet over medium heat and sauté the finely chopped onions until soft and translucent. Add the finely diced celery and sauté 6 minutes more.

3. Add the chopped fresh mushrooms to this and continue cooking, stirring all the while with a wooden spoon, until the mushrooms start to give off liquor.

4. Remove the dried mushrooms from their soaking liquid, chop if necessary, and add to the sauté pan. Cook until the dried mushrooms are heated through. Remove from the heat, place in a mixing bowl, and cool to room temperature.

5. Lightly season the inside of the pocket of the veal breast with salt and pepper and set it aside. Pour 1/2 cup stock over the *challah* cubes and mix thoroughly so that the *challah* absorbs all the liquid. If it seems too dry, add more stock until the correct consistency is achieved. The *challah* should be moist but not mushy. It will absorb more liquid when it is mixed with the mushroom mixture and the eggs.

6. Mix the *challah* into the mushroom mixture. Add the eggs and the parsley and mix again. Add 2 Tblsp. bread crumbs. If mixture seems too moist,

add 1 more Tblsp. bread crumbs. Season with salt and black pepper to taste.

7. Stuff the veal breast with this mixture. Spread all through the pocket by pressing over the top of the meat with your hand. Sew the opening closed with kitchen thread, or secure it with small metal skewers.

8. In a large, deep, oval-shaped braising pan or casserole, heat the remaining 4 Tblsp. *schmaltz* over medium heat. Add the coarsely chopped onions and sauté until soft and translucent. Add the celery, carrot, and parsnip and cook an additional 6 to 7 minutes or until the vegetables begin to soften.

9. Add the bay leaf, wine, remaining stock, and the soaking liquid from the dried mushrooms. Stir together with a wooden spoon and scrape up any bits that cling to the bottom. Preheat the oven to 325°.

10. Place the meat in the casserole. Cover tightly with aluminum foil and then with the lid of the casserole. Place the casserole in the oven and braise undisturbed for 2 1/2 hours.

11. After this time has passed, remove the casserole from the oven and set the meat on a carving board to rest. Strain the contents of the casserole through a fine sieve, pressing down hard on the vegetables to extract the juices and to puree some of the pulp. Discard the bay leaf. This becomes the sauce for the meat.

12. To serve, carve the meat into portions along the joints of the bone and place on a serving plate. Nap with a little of the sauce and serve the remainder of the sauce in a sauceboat. Recipe serves 6 to 8 people.

Serving Suggestions

I like to accompany this rich, savory dish with one or two sautéed autumn-season vegetables such as brussels sprouts and honey-glazed carrots (p. 202). An elegant soup like chicken soup with *kreplach* (p. 59) goes well before the entrée, and liver pâté à la Rothschild (p. 44) makes a fine *forspeis* for a formal dinner. Conclude the meal with an appropriate seasonal fruit compote or *kissel*. As for wine, red is best and dry is preferable to fruity. A fine quality red bordeaux or burgundy is just the thing to make this meal an experience worth remembering.

Carpathian-Style Braised Lamb Shoulder

This rather earthy dish is an alternative to *cholent* that was prepared by the Jews of the Carpathian Mountain region, which spans southern Poland, Hungary, and Romania. Although lamb was never as popular among eastern European Jews as beef and veal, sheep were raised in this region. The wool jackets manufactured in Zacopane, a beautiful Polish mountain resort, are still world famous. A non-kosher version of this dish was made with pork, but the Jews prepared it with lamb.

1 5- to 6-lb. lamb shoulder roast, in one piece
    and trimmed of extra fat
1 lb. great northern or navy beans
4 Tblsp. chicken *schmaltz*
2 large onions, peeled and very thinly sliced
6 to 8 large cloves garlic, peeled and left whole
1 1/2 Tblsp. Hungarian sweet paprika
1 tsp. Hungarian hot paprika
3 to 4 cups beef stock (p. 4)
1 cup fresh tomato sauce (p. 6)
1 tsp. finely chopped fresh hot red peppers (or
    substitute 1/2 tsp. seeded, crumbled, dried
    hot red peppers)
salt to taste

1. Soak the beans overnight in cold water to cover by 2 inches. Discard anything that floats to the surface. Drain and wash off the beans the next morning.

2. In a large, oval-shaped casserole or Dutch oven with a tight-fitting lid, melt the *schmaltz* over medium heat and sauté the onions until translucent and soft. Add the sweet and hot paprika and cook 5 minutes longer.

3. Add the garlic cloves, hot peppers, tomato sauce, and 3 cups of the stock. Bring to a boil and add the meat and the beans. If the liquid does not come up high enough, add up to 1 more cup stock. It is not necessary to cover everything in liquid, as the onions will turn to liquid during the slow braising in the oven. It is only necessary to have a sufficient amount of liquid to cook the beans in because they will swell during cooking.

4. Preheat the oven to 250° (or, alternatively, to its lowest setting if preparing before *Shabbos* and

leaving to cook overnight as you would a *cholent*). Cover the pot tightly with aluminum foil and then with its lid. Place in the oven and braise for 4 hours (if setting the oven at 250°). After 4 hours have passed, uncover the pot to see if it needs any more liquid. At this point, add cold water if necessary.

5. Cook an additional 45 minutes to 1 hour before serving. To serve this dish, lay the meat on a carving board and cut it into portions. Add salt to taste to the beans in the pot. Spoon some of the beans into a deep, wide soup bowl and add to it a portion of meat. Make sure that every diner gets one of the whole garlic cloves, which will keep their shape during cooking. Recipe serves 6 to 8 people.

Serving Suggestions

This dish calls for an accompaniment of cabbage of some kind as well as kosher dill pickles (p. 291). Cabbage salad (p. 230) is a very good choice, served in glass dishes alongside the entrée. Also include some *challah* or Vienna bread to mop up the sauce. Russian eggs (p. 43) and chopped eggs and onions with *schmaltz* (p. 42) make nice *forspeizen*. Conclude the meal with a seasonal fruit compote or *kissel*. A full-bodied red wine like zinfandel or Spanish rioja goes well with this entrée.

My Bobbe's Meat Loaf

This is an old family recipe that goes back at least as far as my grandmother, hence its name (which means "Grandmother's meat loaf"). It was a favorite dish in my childhood home. I have not made any changes to the original recipe.

1 1/2 lb. lean ground beef
1 Tblsp. chicken *schmaltz*
3/4 cup beef stock (p. 4)
1 clove garlic, finely chopped
1 medium-size onion, peeled and finely grated
    by hand or in the food processor
1/2 tsp. hot paprika
3 Tblsp. *matzoh* meal
1 extra-large egg
salt and black pepper to taste
4 hard-boiled eggs, peeled
2 cups fresh tomato sauce (p. 6)

1. Preheat the oven to 350°. Mix all the ingredients together by hand except the *schmaltz*, hard-boiled eggs, and tomato sauce. Form this mixture into a cylinder-shaped loaf.

2. Make slits in the center of the loaf along its length in four places and insert 1 hard-boiled egg into each slit. Enclose the eggs in the loaf by surrounding them with the meat mixture, and reshape into a loaf. The loaf will be longer than it originally was.

3. Gently roll or place the loaf into a loaf pan greased with the *schmaltz*. Bake in the oven for 1 hour and 15 minutes.

4. Heat the tomato sauce separately in a saucepan.

5. To serve, unmold the meat loaf and cut it into slices. Arrange attractively on a serving platter or on individual dinner plates. Nap with some of the tomato sauce, serving the remainder of the sauce in a sauceboat. The slices of meat loaf look beautiful with the white and yellow of the hard-boiled egg in the center. Recipe serves 6 to 8 people.

Serving Suggestions

This dish goes very well with a grain dish on the side like *kasha* (p. 182) or roasted *farfel* (p. 177). It is also wonderful with sautéed green cabbage (p. 204) or sautéed cauliflower (p. 197). If serving the meat loaf with a grain dish, precede with a bowl of carrot soup (p. 62) or chicken soup with *mandlen* (p. 55), and follow the entrée with a mixed vegetable salad (p. 220). If serving with the cabbage, precede with chicken soup with *kasha* (p. 58) or chicken soup with *lokshen* (p. 57). Conclude the meal with a seasonal fruit compote or *kissel*. For wine, drink Chianti, a dry red burgundy, or a California Pinot noir.

Stuffed Cabbage

Prakkes

Prakkes is one of the best known of the traditional Jewish dishes. *Prakkes* are also called by other Yiddish names, including *holishkes* and *golubtzes*, but my grandmother called them *prakkes*. It is quite possible that *prakkes* is the oldest name for this dish. It bears a great similarity in sound to *yaprak*, the Greek name for stuffed grape leaves. It is quite possible that Sephardic Jewish immigrants called the stuffed cabbage leaves *yapraki*, which in Yiddish would have become *yaprakkes*, or eventually, *prakkes*. Jews from all parts of Poland, the Baltic states, and the Ukraine make *prakkes* with a sweet-and-sour tomato sauce and raisins. While there are quite a few variations on the recipe, all are similar to one another in many ways. In Hungary, Slovakia, and Romania, the *prakkes* are made with a savory tomato sauce that includes fresh sauerkraut. Both kinds of *prakkes* are delicious, and I include a version of each recipe here. Some people serve *prakkes* as a *forspeis*, but I prefer them as a main dish.

Variation 1: *Prakkes* in a Sweet-and-Sour Tomato Sauce

3 Tblsp. corn or peanut oil
2 large onions, peeled and very thinly sliced
1 tart green apple, peeled, cored, and very
    finely chopped or grated
1/3 cup brown sugar
1 1-inch-piece fresh ginger, peeled and left
    whole
1/3 cup honey
2 bay leaves
6 cups fresh tomato sauce (p. 6)
1 cup red wine
1 large head green cabbage (savoy cabbage is
    also excellent)
3/4 cup raisins
juice of 1 large lemon
2 lb. lean ground beef
2 medium-size eggs
1/3 cup rice
salt and black pepper to taste

1. Place the raisins in a bowl and cover with the wine. Soak while you prepare everything else.

2. Fill a large stockpot with salted water and bring to a boil. Place the whole head of cabbage in the boiling water, cover the pot, reduce the heat, and simmer for 20 minutes. Remove cabbage from the water and drain in a colander. Pour cold water over the cabbage to stop it from cooking.

3. In a saucepan, bring another cup of salted water to a boil and add the rice. Parboil for 5 minutes. Drain in a colander and place in a mixing bowl. Cool to room temperature.

4. When the rice has cooled, add the meat, eggs, salt, and black pepper. Mix together well and set aside.

5. In a large, deep casserole, heat the oil over medium heat and sauté the onions until translucent and soft. Add the bay leaves, ginger, honey, apple, sugar, the raisins and their liquid, and the tomato sauce. Lower the heat to simmer and partially cover the pot. Simmer this mixture while you prepare the *prakkes*. The sauce should simmer at least 40 minutes, which will be just about the length of time it will take you to stuff the cabbage leaves.

6. Carefully peel off the leaves of the cabbage one by one, without tearing them. The leaves should be limp enough to enable you to do this easily as well as to fold them over after you fill them. If necessary, cut off a small bit of the stem end of some of the leaves if you think they can be folded more easily with this removed. Do not discard these ends; they will be shredded together with the small leaves at the center of the head of cabbage and added to the sauce. If you find that some of the larger, stuffable leaves toward the center of the cabbage are too stiff, they can be softened by parboiling in more salted water.

7. To stuff the cabbage leaves, place approximately 1/3 cup of the meat mixture into the center of a cabbage leaf. Spread it across so that when it is folded and rolled, it will form the shape of a cylinder or cigar. Fold the bottom (stem end) of the cabbage leaf over the stuffing. Then fold the two sides of either end across this fold. Roll the leaf, jelly roll fashion, across these folds and set it aside. It will be a nice roundish cylinder. Repeat this process with as many leaves as you can until all of the meat filling has been used up. You should be able to make between 16 and 20 *prakkes*.

8. Preheat the oven to 325°. After you have shaped and filled all the *prakkes*, finely shred the remaining cabbage except for the core, which you may discard, and add it to the simmering sauce.

9. Gently lower the *prakkes*, one by one, into the simmering sauce. Push them down as far as you can into the sauce, and make sure, after you have added all the *prakkes*, that they are as covered by the sauce as they can possibly be. Cover the casserole tightly with aluminum foil and then with the lid of the casserole.

10. Transfer the casserole to the oven and braise for 2 hours undisturbed. To serve as a main dish, serve 3 *prakkes* per person. Serve 1 or 2 as a *forspeis*.

Recipe generally serves 6 to 8 people as an entrée, more as a *forspeis*.

Serving Suggestions

Prakkes should always be served with a nice portion of their sauce to accompany them. As a *forspeis*, nothing else is required. When serving *prakkes* as an entrée, choose *fleischig lokshen kugel* (p. 170), roasted *farfel* (p. 177), or either of the potato *kugels* (p. 178 and p. 179) to go with it. I like to precede the *prakkes* with carrot soup (p. 62). For an elegant formal dinner, a *forspeis* of chopped liver (p. 43) or liver pâté à la Rothschild (p. 44) stimulates the appetite well. Conclude the meal with baked apples (p. 244) or a seasonal fruit *kissel* rather than with a compote. If you serve *prakkes* as a *forspeis*, follow it with a simple roast of beef or veal. For wine, just about any full-bodied red will do. I like Chianti.

Variation 2: Romanian-Style Stuffed Cabbage
Romainishe Prakkes

This recipe, although listed as Romanian, was actually popular in eastern Hungary and in Slovakia as well.

1/2 cup rice
1 cup cold water
2 Tblsp. corn oil
1 1/2 lb. lean ground beef
1 medium-size onion, peeled and very finely chopped
2 cloves garlic, peeled and finely chopped
1 1/2 tsp. Hungarian sweet paprika
1/8 tsp. Hungarian hot paprika
1 large egg, beaten
salt and black pepper to taste

1. Bring the water to a boil in a saucepan and parboil the rice 5 minutes. Drain it and set it in a mixing bowl.

2. Heat the oil in a small skillet over medium heat and sauté the onions until translucent and soft. Add the garlic and the paprikas, reduce the heat slightly, and cook for 5 minutes, stirring with a wooden spoon to prevent burning or sticking. Add this to the rice. Cool the entire mixture to room temperature.

3. Add the meat, salt, pepper, and egg and set aside while you prepare the cabbage.

1 large head of green cabbage (savoy cabbage works as well)
2 lb. fresh sauerkraut
3 Tblsp. corn oil
1 large onion, peeled and very thinly sliced
2 cloves garlic, peeled and chopped
1 bay leaf
1 Tblsp. Hungarian sweet paprika
1/4 tsp. Hungarian hot paprika
1/2 cup red wine
2 cups fresh tomato sauce (p. 6)
salt and black pepper to taste

1. Prepare the cabbage leaves for stuffing as directed in the previous recipe (p. 152, steps 2 and 6).

2. To prepare the sauce, first rinse and drain the sauerkraut in a colander to remove excess salt.

3. In a large, deep casserole, heat the oil over medium heat and sauté the onions until translucent and soft. Add the paprikas and the garlic, reduce the heat slightly, and cook 5 minutes longer.

4. Add the bay leaf, sauerkraut, tomato sauce, and wine and partially cover the pot. Reduce the heat to simmer, and simmer gently while you stuff the *prakkes*.

5. To stuff the *prakkes*, follow the procedure outlined in the previous recipe (p. 152, step 7). Preheat the oven to 325°.

6. Shred all that remains of the head of cabbage except the core, and add it to the pot of simmering sauce. Then gently lower the *prakkes*, one by one, into the sauce. Push down as far as you can. Make sure that after all the *prakkes* have been added, they are covered as well as possible by the sauce.

7. Cover the pot tightly with aluminum foil and then with its lid and place in the oven. Braise for 2 hours undisturbed. To serve the *prakkes*, serve 3 to each diner together with some of the sauce. In my opinion, this is best as an entrée rather than as a *forspeis* (which is how it is served in Romania). Recipe serves 6 to 8 people.

Serving Suggestions

Romanishe prakkes go well with plain boiled potatoes, *kartoffel knaidelach* (p. 183), *challah knaidelach* (p. 184), or *mamaliga* (p. 186). If serving one of the *knaidelach*, an additional side dish of *kishka* (p. 187) is actually quite good, even though it makes for a heavier meal. Chopped liver (p. 43) is an excellent *forspeis*. Conclude the meal with fresh fruit and a pastry such as *makos*, *dios*, or *kokos* (p. 275). A full-bodied red wine like zinfandel makes the best drink.

Stuffed Peppers

Gefilte Pfefferen

6 large green bell peppers
1 1/4 lb. lean ground beef
3/4 cup rice
1 medium-size onion, peeled and very finely chopped
1 small onion, peeled and finely grated by hand or in the food processor
2 cloves garlic, chopped
1 large egg
1 1/2 tsp. Hungarian sweet paprika
a pinch Hungarian hot paprika
juice of 1 large lemon
2 cups fresh tomato sauce (p. 6)
1/4 cup finely chopped parsley
2 Tblsp. corn or peanut oil
salt and black pepper to taste

1. Bring 2 cups of water to boil in a saucepan and parboil the rice for 6 minutes. Drain and set in a mixing bowl. Cool to room temperature.

2. Mix into the rice the meat, grated onion, 1 chopped clove of garlic, the parsley, the egg, and salt and pepper to taste. Set aside.

3. Slice the tops (stem end) off the peppers and set them aside. Remove cores, seeds, and white ribs from the inside of the peppers.

4. Stuff each pepper with some of the meat mixture. Do not pack in too tightly or fill completely to the top, as the rice will expand during cooking. Cover each pepper with its own stem end top, which was removed from it.

5. Heat the oil in a large, deep, round casserole with a tight-fitting lid and sauté the chopped onions until translucent and soft. Add the paprikas and the remaining chopped clove of garlic, reduce the heat, and cook 5 more minutes.

6. Add the tomato sauce and lemon juice and stir together until thoroughly mixed. Preheat the oven to 350°.

7. Place the stuffed peppers in an upright posi-

tion in the casserole with the stem ends facing upward. Ideally, all the peppers should be able to stand next to one another without being too crowded or too loose. This is rather important in order to ensure an even distribution of heat when the peppers cook. Cover tightly with aluminum foil and then with the lid of the casserole. Place in the oven and bake for 1 to 1 1/2 hours.

8. Taste the sauce for seasoning and, if necessary, add a little salt and pepper to it before serving. To serve, serve to each diner one stuffed pepper with some of the sauce. Recipe serves 6 people.

Serving Suggestions

Stuffed peppers are traditionally served with *fleischig* mashed potatoes (p. 199). Romanian Jews serve them with *mamaliga* (p. 186). Both of these are excellent accompaniments. I rather like a *Romanishe shalloteh* (p. 229) as a *forspeis*, although carrot soup (p. 62) does just as well. Conclude the meal with fresh fruit and some kind of pastry like *makos*, *dios*, or *kokos* (p. 275), or *mandelbroit* (p. 256). A zinfandel is the best wine to drink with stuffed peppers.

Sweet-and-Sour Meatballs

Ziss und Zoyer Hocktfleisch

For meatballs

1 1/2 lb. lean ground beef
1 small onion, very finely grated by hand or in the food processor
2 Tblsp. corn or peanut oil
1 large egg
2 Tblsp. *matzoh* meal
1/2 tsp. salt
1/8 tsp. coarsely ground black pepper

For sauce

2 cups fresh tomato sauce (p. 6)
juice of 1/2 lemon
3 Tblsp. brown sugar
1 1-inch-piece fresh ginger, peeled and left whole
1 bay leaf
1 cup beef stock (p. 4)
1 heaping Tblsp. potato starch mixed with 1/4 cup cold water

1. Mix together all the ingredients for the meatballs. Make sure they are well mixed. Form into 1-inch meatballs and set onto a large platter or baking sheet.

2. In a large saucepan, combine all the sauce ingredients except the potato starch mixture. Bring to a boil, stirring constantly to make sure the sugar dissolves. Reduce the heat to simmer and partially cover the pot. Cook 15 minutes.

3. Gently lower the meatballs into the simmering sauce. After all are in the sauce, reduce the heat to its lowest temperature and cover the pot tightly. Simmer over low heat for 1 1/2 hours. Check the pot from time to time and stir gently to prevent the meatballs from sticking to the bottom.

4. To thicken the sauce, stir the potato starch mixture well and add it to the pot. Stir it in gently and raise the heat slightly. When the sauce has thickened sufficiently, serve the meatballs in wide, deep soup bowls, together with some of the sauce. Recipe serves 4 to 6 people as an entrée, 8 to 10 as a *forspeis*.

Serving Suggestions

I prefer to serve sweet-and-sour meatballs as an entrée, but some people use them as a *forspeis*. If served as a *forspeis*, they should precede an entrée that does not have a tomato-based sauce and preferably one that is not made of beef. Some good entrée choices are roast chicken with *matzoh* stuffing (p. 117), baked lemon chicken (p. 110), or *Shabbosdige hendel* (p. 101).

As an entrée, sweet-and-sour meatballs go well with *fleischig lokshen kugel* (p. 170), *mamaliga* (p. 186), *kasha* (p. 182), *kasha varnishkes* (p. 183), roast *farfel* (p. 177), or any of the rice *pilaven* (p. 182). Precede or follow the meatballs with a field green salad (p. 219), a mixed vegetable salad (p. 220), or a green bean salad (p. 222). Conclude the meal with a seasonal fruit compote or *kissel*. Just about any red wine goes well with this meal. I like a zinfandel.

Aunt Rose's
Sweet-and-Sour Meatballs

This is the only recipe in my cookbook that uses processed foods. I generally shy away from using such things, because like most old-fashioned home

cooks, I feel that processed foods have an ersatz flavor and also contain additives and preservatives that I would rather avoid ingesting too much of. I make an exception with this dish because of the nice memory connected with it.

My Aunt Rose Wolfson, of blessed memory, was a consummate home cook. Her sweet-and-sour meatballs were one of my favorite dishes. One time when I was visiting her, she served what seemed to me a "new kind" of sweet-and-sour meatball dish that I proclaimed the best sweet-and-sour meatballs I had ever in my life eaten. When I asked her for the recipe, she laughed heartily and said that I would never believe what was in it. All her life, she had made sweet-and-sour meatballs according to the directions given in the preceding recipe, and then a friend had surprised her with the version below, which she also proclaimed the best ever.

1 recipe meatballs (p. 155)
1 16-oz. bottle Heinz 57 sauce
1 pkg. kosher onion soup mix
2 1/2 cups ginger ale

1. Make the meatballs as directed in the recipe on p. 155, step 1.

2. Mix the remaining ingredients together in a large saucepan and bring to a boil. Cook partially covered at a medium-low temperature for 15 minutes.

3. Add the meatballs, reduce the heat to its lowest simmer, and cook 1 1/2 hours. Serve in wide, deep soup bowls with some of the sauce. Recipe serves 4 to 6 people as an entrée and 8 to 10 as a *forspeis*. Follow the serving suggestions given for sweet-and-sour meatballs on p. 155.

European-Style
Ground Meat Patties

Kottletten

Ground meat patties, called *kottletten* in Yiddish (which is similar to "cutlets"), have always been very popular among European cooks. American hamburger patties have their origin in dishes similar to these *kottletten*, which European immigrants brought with them into this country. The difference between European and American meat patties is that for Europeans, *kottletten* were a way of stretching a small quantity of meat by adding other ingredients to it, and for Americans, most meat patties traditionally consist of meat with a little seasoning and very little else. The Jewish "meat stretcher" mixture differs from the others in its use of *matzoh* meal (which I personally prefer to the usual bread crumbs) and the finely grated onion (which I have never come across before except in traditional Jewish recipes).

Kottletten can be made of several different kinds of meat, and you may use one kind only or more than one kind whenever you make this dish. I make *kottletten* out of ground beef, ground veal, ground chicken, and ground turkey. The general rule is that if you are going to mix meats to make *kottletten*, mix beef with veal and chicken with turkey, but do not mix the poultry meat with the red meat. Their flavors are not complementary, and the flavor of the beef or veal generally overwhelms the taste of the chicken or turkey. Both veal and turkey take well to a little spicing in the mixture, hence my optional recommendation for allspice and cloves when preparing a mixture that includes either of these meats. The other thing to remember about *kottletten* is that they are sautéed rather than grilled or broiled.

1 1/2 lb. lean ground meat (beef, veal, chicken, turkey, or a combination)
2 Tblsp. chicken *schmaltz*
1 small onion, very finely grated by hand or in the food processor
3/4 cup *matzoh* meal
2 garlic cloves, peeled and finely chopped
3/4 cup beef or chicken stock (p. 3 or p. 4)
1 jumbo or 2 small eggs
salt and black pepper to taste
1/2 tsp. ground allspice (optional for veal and turkey)
1/4 tsp. ground cloves (optional for veal and turkey)
corn or peanut oil for sautéing

1. Mix the *matzoh* meal, eggs, and stock together and allow to rest for 1 hour, covered, in the refrigerator.
2. Mix the remaining ingredients into the *matzoh* meal mixture and form into patties. Lay the patties on a large platter or a baking sheet until you have formed the entire mixture into patties. The mixture should make between 6 and 8 large or 12

and 16 small patties, depending on how you like to make them.

3. Heat 6 Tblsp. corn or peanut oil in a 12-inch skillet over high heat until it is sizzling but not smoking. Sauté the patties on both sides, turning once during cooking, until they are colored golden brown on both sides.

4. To complete cooking, reduce heat to simmer, cover the pan, and cook patties 15 to 20 minutes longer. Recipe serves 6 to 8 people.

Serving Suggestions

Kottletten may be served many different ways. Lemon wedges, kosher dill pickles (p. 291), pickled beets, and warmed fresh tomato sauce (p. 6) are all fairly traditional. Veal, chicken, and turkey *kottletten* go particularly well with *Galitzianer* beet salad (p. 225) as an accompaniment. Any of the vegetables cooked in tomato sauce in chapter 9 or the cabbage dishes are also delicious with *kottletten*. Please don't ruin a good recipe like this by putting ketchup on the table with it! If you would like a simple sauce for *kottletten* that is an alternative to fresh tomato sauce, try the mushroom duxelles sauce on p. 8. Bouquet of fresh vegetables soup (p. 62) is a wonderful choice as a course to serve before the *kottletten*. Conclude the meal with a seasonal fruit compote or *kissel*. For wine, choose white with poultry and red with beef or veal. Chardonnay is a good all-purpose white wine, but a dry burgundy or bordeaux goes just as well and makes this meal something memorable. For reds, choose Chianti or a dry burgundy or bordeaux.

Karnotzl

Karnotzl is a spicy Romanian ground-meat sausage grilled on the outdoor grill. It is eaten traditionally with *mamaliga* and an assortment of Romanian salads. *Karnotzlach* are a perfect summertime dish and a delicious alternative to the usual American grilled hamburger patties. I provide two alternative seasonings for *karnotzl* in this recipe.

Meat mixture

2 lb. lean ground beef
2 large cloves garlic, peeled and finely chopped
1/3 cup beef stock (p. 4)
2 Tblsp. sunflower oil

Seasoning mix 1

1/2 tsp. ground allspice
1/2 tsp. dried thyme
1/4 tsp. ground cloves
1 tsp. salt
1/4 tsp. freshly ground black pepper

Seasoning mix 2

1 very small onion, peeled and finely grated by
    hand or in the food processor
1 tsp. Hungarian hot paprika
1 tsp. salt
a few grindings of black pepper

1. Mix together all the ingredients in a mixing bowl, choosing either the ingredients in seasoning mix 1 or in seasoning mix 2 to add to the meat mixture.

2. Have a bowl of cold water next to you as you work. Moisten your hands and take a small amount of the *karnotzl* mixture into them. Shape into a fat, stubby cylinder or cigar about 3 inches long and 1 inch wide. Repeat until everything is used up. Moisten your hands in between the shaping of each *karnotzl*. Lay them on a platter as you make them.

3. Preheat the outdoor grill (or indoor broiler in your oven) to a high temperature. Grill the *karnotzl* on the outdoor grill or alternatively on the broiler rack 3 inches from the heat source in your oven. Grilling time will be about 10 to 15 minutes. Turn the meat several times as it cooks. *Karnotzl* are ready when they are crisp and brown on all sides. Serve immediately. Recipe serves 4 to 6 people as an entrée or 9 or 10 as a *forspeis*.

Serving Suggestions

When you serve *karnotzlach* as an entrée, accompany them with *mamaliga* (p. 186) or sautéed *mamaliga* (p. 186) and a variety of the Romanian salads listed in chapter 10. An alternative to salads is one of the vegetables cooked in tomato sauce. Another way of serving *karnotzlach* is to precede them with a Romanian sautéed *lokshen kugel* (p. 172) and then accompany the meat with a vegetable cooked in tomato sauce, such as green beans, zucchini, or eggplant. *Karnotzl* also makes an interesting *forspeis*. When served this way, put 2 *karnotzlach* on an appetizer plate and accompany them with a portion of Romanian eggplant salad (p. 229) or Romanian roasted pepper salad (p. 228). The best wine to drink with

karnotzl is a full-bodied red like Italian Barolo, zinfandel, or Spanish rioja.

Sautéed Liver with Onions
Leber mit Tzibbeles Und Schmaltz

This traditional Jewish dish is so much like its Venetian counterpart that I am tempted to speculate that Venetian Jews brought it north in their migrations into Poland and Russia. The only two things that make this different from the sautéed "fegato a la Veneziana" of the Veneto region of Italy are the use of chicken *schmaltz* (which is absolutely essential in this dish) and the initial grilling of the liver to make it kosher. In fact, it is an interesting coincidence that Rumanian Jews traditionally serve this dish with sautéed *mamaliga*, which tastes exactly like Italian polenta.

Every eastern European Jewish cook knows how to make *leber mit tzibbeles*. In my childhood home, it was made only with calf liver. Beef liver and baby beef liver were used for making *eingedempte leber*. Our family recipe, which went from my grandmother to my mother and my aunts to me is undoubtedly part of a much broader based, older culinary tradition, possibly one that predates Polish Jewry altogether.

1 1/2 lb. calf liver
6 Tblsp. chicken *schmaltz*
4 medium-size onions, peeled and very thinly
    sliced
salt and black pepper to taste

1. Preheat the oven broiler to 500°. Broil the liver for 1 1/2 minutes on each side to make it kosher. Remove it from the oven and cut it into thin strips.

2. Melt the *schmaltz* in a deep, wide sauté pan or in a Chinese wok over medium heat and sauté the onions until they are soft and translucent but still white in color.

3. Raise the heat slightly and add the liver strips. Sauté, stirring constantly to prevent sticking and scorching, until everything is well cooked through. The onions will have turned a nice golden brown. Season with salt and pepper to taste and serve immediately. Recipe serves 6 people.

Serving Suggestions

All Jews from the Yiddish-speaking world except those who come from Romania traditionally serve this dish with *fleischig* mashed potatoes (p. 199). Romanian Jews serve it with sautéed *mamaliga* (p. 186). No other type of vegetable accompaniment ought to be considered. Precede or follow the liver with a salad. A field green salad (p. 219), mixed vegetable salad (p. 220), Hungarian summer salad (p. 223), or green bean salad (p. 222) is a good choice. If serving the liver Romanian style, with sautéed *mamaliga*, precede or follow with a Romanian salad (p. 228). Conclude the meal with a seasonal fruit compote or fresh fruit. Drink Spanish rioja or a dry red burgundy with the liver.

Braised Beef Liver with Apples and Onions

Eingedempte Leber mit Eppl Und Tzibbeles

This recipe was popular throughout Poland and is probably German in origin. It may have been brought into Poland by German Jews, who settled there in large numbers during the Renaissance to escape persecution in western Europe.

1 1/2 lb. beef or baby beef liver
3 large onions, peeled and very thinly sliced
4 Tblsp. corn or peanut oil
3 tart green apples, cored and sliced but
    unpeeled
3 medium-size white baking potatoes, peeled
    and thinly sliced
1 cup beef stock (p. 4)
salt and black pepper to taste

1. Preheat broiler to 500°. Broil liver on both sides for 1 1/2 minutes on each side to make it kosher. Remove from the oven and cut into 1-inch pieces.

2. In a large, deep sauté pan, heat the oil over medium heat and sauté the onions until they are soft and translucent. Remove with a slotted spoon and set aside.

3. Add liver to the sauté pan and cook an additional 3 minutes. Turn and shake frequently to prevent scorching and sticking.

4. Add the stock to the pan and, with a wooden spoon, scrape up all the browned bits from the bottom.

5. Add the apples and potatoes to the pan. Return the onions and all the liquid that has accumulated around them to the pan as well. Cover tightly and reduce the heat to simmer. Simmer the liver for 35 minutes. Serve immediately. Recipe serves 6 to 8 people.

Serving Suggestions

This is one of those dishes that does not need and should not have any vegetable accompaniment. Precede the liver with a bowl of carrot soup (p. 62). Conclude the meal with a seasonal fruit compote or *kissel*, preferably one that does not feature apples. I like to drink a rosé wine or a white zinfandel with this dish. If you prefer, you may also serve a white Rhine wine such as Riesling or gewürztraminer.

Sweet-and-Sour Braised Liver

Ziss Und Zoyer Eingedempte Leber

This recipe was popular in northern as well as southern and central Poland but the accompaniment was different, depending on what region one came from. In Galitzia and southern Poland, they ate the Jewish version of German spaetzle, called *galushkes*. In the northern parts of Poland, *farfel* was the preferred choice. The recipe for the liver itself was similar in all regions.

1 1/2 lb. beef or baby beef liver
2 large onions, peeled and very thinly sliced
3 Tblsp. corn or peanut oil
2 Tblsp. unbleached white flour
2 cups beef stock (p. 4)
1 Tblsp. sugar
1/4 cup freshly squeezed lemon juice
1 tsp. Hungarian sweet paprika
salt and black pepper to taste

1. Preheat the oven broiler to 500°. Broil the liver 1 1/2 minutes on each side to make it kosher. Remove it from the oven and cut into 1-inch pieces.

2. Heat the oil over medium heat in a deep, wide sauté pan and sauté the onions until they are soft and translucent. Add the paprika, reduce the heat slightly, and cook 5 minutes longer, stirring constantly to prevent scorching and sticking.

3. Add the liver pieces and cook 5 minutes longer, stirring all the while.

4. Sprinkle the flour over the ingredients in the sauté pan and keep cooking and stirring until it is well incorporated.

5. Pour the stock into the pan and mix together well with a wooden spoon. Make sure that there are no lumps and that the sauce looks smooth.

6. Sprinkle the sugar over the liver mixture and add the lemon juice. Stir everything together so that it is well mixed. Cover the pan tightly, reduce the heat to simmer, and cook 35 minutes. Uncover and stir the ingredients every once in a while during cooking to prevent lumping and sticking. At the end of 35 minutes, the sauce should be nice and thick and everything should be well cooked. Season to taste with salt and pepper and serve immediately. Recipe serves 6 to 8 people.

Serving Suggestions

This *eingedempte leber* may be served with roasted *farfel* (p. 177) or with *galushkes* (p. 177). Baked-beet salad (p. 224), Galitzianer beet salad (p. 225), beet green salad (p. 225), or green cabbage salad (p. 230) is good with this, served in a side dish alongside the entrée. Precede the liver with carrot soup (p. 62), and conclude the meal with a seasonal fruit compote or *kissel*. Drink rosé or a fruity red or white wine like chardonnay or zinfandel.

Romanian-Style Braised Liver

Rumanishe Eingedempte Leber

1 1/2 lb. beef or baby beef liver
2 large red bell peppers, roasted, peeled, seeded, and cut into thin strips (instructions are given for doing this on p. 228)
2 large green bell peppers, roasted, peeled, seeded, and cut into thin strips
3 medium-size onions, peeled and very thinly sliced
2 cloves garlic, peeled and chopped
2 tsp. Hungarian sweet paprika
1/4 tsp. Hungarian hot paprika
1 cup fresh tomato sauce (p. 6)
1 cup beef stock (p. 4)
2 Tblsp. unbleached white flour
4 Tblsp. sunflower oil
1 tsp. red wine vinegar
salt and black pepper to taste

1. Preheat oven broiler to 500°. Broil the liver 1 1/2 minutes on each side to make it kosher. Remove it from the oven and cut it into thin strips.

2. In a deep, wide sauté pan, heat the oil over medium heat and sauté the onions until soft and translucent. Add the paprikas and the garlic, reduce the heat slightly, and cook for 5 minutes longer.

3. Add the liver and continue cooking, stirring constantly to prevent sticking and scorching, with a wooden spoon. Cook 5 minutes and sprinkle the flour over everything. Continue cooking, mixing the flour thoroughly into the other ingredients.

4. Add the stock, the vinegar, and the tomato sauce. Stir well to prevent lumping. When this is well mixed together, add the pepper strips. Mix together well, reduce the heat to simmer, and cover the pan tightly. Cook 35 minutes. Uncover the pan once in a while and stir everything together to prevent sticking and burning. Season with salt and black pepper to taste before serving. Recipe serves 6 to 8 people.

Serving Suggestions

This dish may be served with an accompaniment of *mamaliga* (p. 186), rice *pilav* (p. 182), or entirely on its own with some crusty Vienna bread to soak up the sauce. I have also come up with an unusual but, I think, tasty nontraditional recommendation. Try serving this dish with a baked sautéed sweet potato (p. 209). The flavors, colors, and textures blend quite well. Precede the entrée with a *forspeis* of Romanian eggplant salad (p. 229), and conclude the meal with fresh fruit accompanied by *makos*, *dios*, or *kokos* (p. 275). Drink zinfandel with the meal.

Sautéed Chicken Livers on a Bed of Spinach

Leberlach mit Shpinatz

Springtime in Budapest and Vienna brings in the new crop of spinach and young spring chickens. This simple, sophisticated combination is both delicate in flavor and fragrantly aromatic.

2 lb. whole chicken livers
9 Tblsp. olive oil
2 large cloves garlic, peeled and very finely chopped
1 medium-size onion
1 1/2 Tblsp. fresh marjoram (or substitute 1 1/2 tsp. dried)
1 cup chicken stock (p. 3)
1/2 cup dry white wine
2 lb. fresh spinach leaves
salt and black pepper to taste

1. Preheat the oven to 500° and broil the livers 2 minutes on each side to make them kosher. Remove from the oven and set aside.

2. Wash the spinach carefully to remove any sand that clings and place it in a large stockpot. Cook it over medium heat in only the water that clings to it, stirring every once in a while, until all the leaves have wilted. Drain it immediately in a colander and pour cold water over it to stop the cooking. This will ensure that it retains a beautiful fresh green color.

3. Have a sauté pan and a 12-inch skillet ready at your side. Heat 5 Tblsp. oil in the sauté pan over fairly high heat and sauté the livers in batches until completely cooked through and are crisp on the outside. Set aside.

4. Reduce the heat to medium and sauté the onions in the same oil until soft and translucent. Add half the garlic and marjoram and sauté for less than a minute just to heat through. Immediately pour the stock and wine into the sauté pan and, using a wooden spoon, scrape up any browned bits that cling to the bottom. Return the liver to the pan, cover it, and let it cook a little while you sauté the spinach.

5. Squeeze any excess water out of the spinach and dry it as best you can with paper towels. Heat the remaining 4 Tblsp. oil in the skillet over medium heat. Add the garlic and sauté less than a minute just to heat through. Add the spinach and sauté, stirring

constantly, until it is well heated through. Remove from the heat and seaason with salt and pepper to taste.

6. Apportion the spinach onto 6 to 8 serving plates. Spread it to make a flat bed. Uncover the liver in the sauté pan and apportion the livers onto the plates as well, on top of the spinach. Bring the heat under the sauté pan to a rapid boil over high heat, and reduce the liquid in the pan slightly. Season to taste with salt and pepper and pour it over the liver and spinach. Serve immediately. Recipe serves 6 to 8 people.

Serving Suggestions

This wonderful springtime entrée needs no accompaniment other than good bread and wine to go with it. Precede it with carrot soup (p. 62), *pareve rozl* (p. 68), *pareve* hot beet *borscht* (p. 66), or for something more unusual, a *forspeis* of potato *latkes* (p. 211). Conclude the meal with a seasonal fruit compote or *kissel*. Serve a light, dry white wine with the meal, such as Riesling or gewürztraminer.

Braised Sweetbreads Or Brains

Sweetbreads and brains were popular in central Europe, where this recipe comes from. They are healthy and delicious as well as somewhat underappreciated as food items. Sweetbreads have to be parboiled before their final cooking in order to remove a membrane that surrounds them. Brains only need to be soaked for an hour in cold water in order to remove the membrane that surrounds them.

2 lb. sweetbreads or brains, parboiled (for 15 minutes) or soaked in water and membrane removed
1 medium-size onion, peeled and very thinly sliced
1 lb. fresh white mushrooms
4 Tblsp. chicken *schmaltz*
1/4 cup unbleached white flour
1/2 tsp. Hungarian hot paprika
1 clove garlic, peeled and thinly sliced
2 cups chicken stock (p. 3)
1/2 cup sherry or brandy
salt and black pepper to taste

1. After the membrane has been removed from the meat, cut it into 1-inch pieces. Wipe the mushrooms with a damp cloth or paper towel and slice or quarter them.

2. In a large sauté pan, melt the *schmaltz* over medium heat and sauté the onions until translucent and soft.

3. Add the garlic and paprika, reduce the heat, and cook 5 minutes longer.

4. Add the mushrooms and cook until they begin to give off liquor (about 6 to 8 minutes), stirring all the while to prevent anything from sticking to the bottom.

5. Sprinkle the flour over the vegetables and continue to cook, mixing all the while with a wooden spoon to keep everything from sticking and burning on the bottom.

6. Slowly add the stock, stirring constantly until it is well incorporated. Then add the meat and mix in carefully.

7. When the meat is mixed in, add the sherry or brandy, cover the pan, and cook 15 to 20 minutes. Stir every once in a while to make sure that nothing burns. Serve immediately on individual serving plates. Recipe serves 6 to 8 people.

Serving Suggestions

This dish needs no vegetable accompaniment. Some crusty Vienna bread to wipe up the sauce and a good white wine make the best companions. Precede or follow the entree with a mixed vegetable salad (p. 220), a Boston lettuce salad (p. 220), or a green bean salad (p. 222). If you want to serve soup, carrot soup (p. 62) is a good choice. Conclude the meal with a seasonal fruit compote or *kissel*. For the wine, drink chardonnay.

Braised Beef Tongue with Savory Wine Sauce

Gedempte Tzung mit Wein

Tongue is an underappreciated meat in America, but Jews have been eating tongue for centuries and have many different ways of preparing it. Whenever tongue is to be cooked, the skin that surrounds it has to be removed. The process is described in detail in steps 1 and 2 of the recipe. Although it may appear to be time consuming, it really isn't. It is quite simple. Tongue also takes very well to different kinds of spicing and seasoning, and that makes it a fun and creative meat to work with.

1 4- to 4 1/2-lb. beef tongue
4 Tblsp. chicken *schmaltz*
1 large onion, peeled and finely chopped
2 large carrots, peeled and chopped
2 stalks celery, peeled and chopped
1 parsnip, peeled and chopped
1 leek, white only, carefully washed and thinly sliced
1 large clove garlic, peeled and chopped
1 bouquet garni consisting of 6 stalks parsley, 1 bay leaf, 5 sprigs fresh thyme, and the greens of 1 leek (1 tsp. dried thyme may be substituted)
8 whole black peppercorns
6 whole allspice berries
4 whole cloves
1/2 tsp. Hungarian hot paprika
2 Tblsp. unbleached white flour
1 1/2 cups beef stock (p. 4)
2 cups dry red wine
1/2 cup brandy
salt to taste

1. Put the tongue in a pot with enough boiling salted water to cover it. Reduce heat to simmer and poach the tongue for 2 hours. Partially cover the pot as the meat cooks. When the tongue has finished cooking, remove it and drop it into a bowl of cold water. Discard the poaching liquid.

2. When the tongue has cooled enough to be handled, remove it from the water and peel off the skin. It should come off very easily.

3. Melt the *schmaltz* over medium-high heat in a large, deep, oval-shaped casserole with a tight-fitting lid. Brown the tongue in the *schmaltz* on all sides and set it on a platter. Reduce the heat to medium.

4. Sauté the onions until translucent and soft. Then add the rest of the vegetables and cook, stirring constantly with a wooden spoon for about 10 minutes.

5. Sprinkle the paprika over the vegetables, add the garlic, and cook 5 minutes longer, stirring constantly.

6. Add the spices and mix them into the vegetables. Sprinkle the flour over all of this and stir constantly as you cook to prevent anything from sticking and burning on the bottom.

7. When the flour is well incorporated, add the stock, wine, and brandy slowly, stirring constantly with the wooden spoon to prevent lumping. Add the bouquet garni and then the meat. Push the meat down into the simmering sauce. Preheat the oven to 325°.

8. Cover the casserole tightly with aluminum foil and then with the lid of the pot. Place it in the oven on the middle shelf and braise undisturbed for 2 hours.

9. Remove the casserole from the oven, uncover it, and place the tongue on a carving board to rest while you finish preparing the sauce.

10. Remove and discard the bouquet garni and press the remaining ingredients through a fine sieve into a saucepan. Press down hard on the vegetables to extract all juices, and then press some of the pulp through the sieve. Add salt to taste and keep warm on top of the stove.

11. To serve, carve the tongue into attractive slices and apportion it onto individual serving plates or onto a platter. Nap the slices of tongue with the sauce and serve the remainder of the sauce in a sauceboat. Recipe serves 6 to 8 people.

Serving Suggestions

Braised tongue in wine sauce calls for a savory grain dish to accompany it. Choose from among the following: *kasha* (p. 182), *kasha varnishkes* (p. 183), roasted *farfel* (p. 177), potato *kugel* (p. 178), and *fleischig lokshen kugel* (p. 170). In addition to this, you may add one or two sautéed seasonal vegetables, such as brussels sprouts, green beans, and cauliflower. Precede the meat with chicken soup consommé (p. 55), chicken soup with *mandlen* (p. 55), or carrot soup (p. 62). You may serve one of the heavier chicken soups as well, so long as you do not serve a grain dish with the meat. Either of the *gefilte fisch* recipes (p. 38 and p. 39) makes a good *forspeis*. Conclude the meal with a seasonal fruit compote or *kissel*. For wine, drink a full-bodied red like Italian Barolo, cabernet sauvignon, or Spanish rioja.

Braised Veal Tongue with Raisin Sauce

Gedempte Tzung mit Rozinkes

This tongue dish is traditionally made with veal rather than beef tongue and comes from Galitzia, although Jews all over Poland are familiar with it.

1 3 1/2- to 4-lb. veal tongue
1 cup dark seedless raisins
1 cup red wine
1 cup prune juice
1 cup beef stock (p. 4)
1 bay leaf
1 large onion, peeled and finely chopped
2 Tblsp. unbleached white flour
4 Tblsp. corn or peanut oil
salt, black pepper, and Hungarian hot paprika to taste

1. Prepare the tongue for cooking by removing the skin as directed in steps 1 and 2 of the previous recipe (p. 161).

2. While the tongue is simmering, place the raisins in a mixing bowl and cover with the wine.

3. When the tongue has been skinned, heat the oil over medium-high heat in a deep, wide, oval-shaped casserole. Brown the meat on all sides and remove to a platter.

4. Reduce the heat to medium and sauté the onions until soft and translucent. Sprinkle the paprika over the onions and cook for 5 minutes, stirring constantly with a wooden spoon to prevent anything from sticking and burning.

5. Sprinkle the flour over this and cook an additional 6 to 7 minutes, stirring constantly to prevent sticking and scorching. Then add the stock and the prune juice. Stir constantly with the wooden spoon until everything is well incorporated. Make sure, as you stir, that there are no lumps in the sauce. Preheat the oven to 325°.

6. Add the raisins and their soaking liquid and the bay leaf. Then return the meat to the casserole. Cover tightly with aluminum foil and then with the lid of the casserole. Put it into the oven on the middle shelf and braise for 2 hours.

7. Remove casserole from the oven and set meat onto a carving board. Add salt and black pepper to the sauce. Carve into attractive slices and place on individual serving plates or onto a platter. Spoon some of the sauce from the pot over the meat and serve the rest of it in a sauceboat. Recipe serves 6 to 8 people.

Serving Suggestions

The traditional and, in my opinion, the best accompaniment to this dish is either *galushkes* (p. 177) or roasted *farfel* (p. 176). In addition to the grain dish, serve one or two sautéed vegetables. Turnips and green beans are good choices. Precede the entrée with carrot soup (p. 62), chicken soup with *mandlen* (p. 55), or chicken soup consommé (p. 55). Conclude the meal with a seasonal fruit compote or *kissel*, one that does not include prunes. Drink zinfandel with the meal.

Sweet-and-Sour Smoked or Pickled Tongue

Ziss und Zoyer Tzung

This dish is made with a whole pickled or smoked beef tongue, which can be purchased at any kosher butcher shop or delicatessen. As with fresh tongue, it is possible that you will have to remove the skin before preparing it. If you do, follow the procedure outlined in steps 1 and 2 of the braised tongue with wine sauce recipe on p. 161.

1 3 1/2- to 4-lb. smoked or pickled beef tongue, skin removed
4 Tblsp. corn or peanut oil
1 large onion, peeled and finely chopped
2 Tblsp. unbleached white flour
1/3 cup freshly squeezed lemon juice
1 1-inch-piece fresh ginger, peeled and left whole
2 cups beef stock (p. 4)
3 Tblsp. brown sugar
1/2 cup dark raisins
1/2 cup red wine
black pepper to taste

1. Heat the oil over medium heat in a large, deep, oval-shaped casserole and sauté the onions until soft and translucent. Sprinkle the flour over the onions and cook 6 minutes, stirring constantly with a wooden spoon to prevent sticking and burning.

2. Slowly add the stock, stirring constantly with the spoon to prevent lumping.

3. Add the remaining ingredients except for the meat, and stir together to blend well. Preheat the oven to 325°.

4. Add the meat and push it down into the sauce. Cover the casserole tightly with aluminum foil and then with the lid of the casserole. Braise in the oven on the middle shelf for 2 hours.

5. To serve, remove the casserole from the oven and place the tongue on a carving board. Carve into attractive slices and arrange on individual serving plates or on a large platter. Nap the meat with some of the sauce and serve the remaining sauce in a sauceboat. Recipe serves 6 to 8 people.

Serving Suggestions

Follow ones given for tongue in raisin sauce on p. 162. In addition to this, a slice of *fleischig lokshen kugel* (p. 170) makes a very good grain accompaniment. The entrée almost cries out for honey-glazed carrots (p. 202), so serve this vegetable rather than a carrot soup (p. 62). I rather like a *forspeis* of *Galitzianer gefilte fisch* (p. 39) with this meal. Chopped herring (p. 41) is also quite good. Conclude the meal with a seasonal fruit compote or *kissel*. Zinfandel is the best wine to drink.

Jewish *Bigos*

Bigos is a very famous Polish dish that is made with cabbage, sauerkraut, and a variety of meats, some of them game. Since Jewish tradition prohibits hunting, Polish Jews developed their own version of this Polish dish using kosher charcuterie meats. The result is a little like an Alsatian choucroute garne and just as delicious.

1 1/2 lb. pastrami (in one piece)
1 smoked or pickled beef tongue
1 lb. smoked veal shoulder (in one piece)
6 to 8 butcher-made knockwurst or Polish sausage (available in kosher butcher shops; you may use the prepackaged kosher sausages, but their flavor is not anywhere near as good as those the butcher makes)
4 Tblsp. chicken *schmaltz*
2 large onions, peeled and very thinly sliced
1 cup sweet red or Tokay wine
1 1/2 cups fresh tomato sauce (p. 6)
1 Tblsp. Hungarian sweet paprika
1 head green cabbage, washed, cored, and very thinly shredded
1 lb. fresh sauerkraut, drained, rinsed, and squeezed dry
2 bay leaves
6 whole allspice berries
8 whole black peppercorns
2 large cloves garlic, peeled and sliced
salt to taste, if necessary

1. Over medium head, melt *schmaltz* in a very large, heavy casserole that is used for making *cholent*. Sauté the onions until they are soft and translucent. Add the paprika and cook 5 minutes longer, stirring constantly.

2. Add the shredded cabbage and the garlic and continue cooking, stirring constantly with a wooden spoon. Cook for 10 minutes.

3. Add the wine, tomato sauce, sauerkraut, bay leaves, and spices, mixing all the time with the wooden spoon to make sure that everything is well incorporated. Preheat the oven to 325°.

4. Add the meats and push them down into the vegetables. Cover the casserole tightly with aluminum foil and then with its lid. Braise 1 1/2 hours and remove to check if there is sufficient cooking liquid in the pot. If necessary, add a little cold water. Cover tightly again and cook 1/2 hour longer.

5. To serve, remove pastrami, tongue, and smoked veal, and slice attractively on a carving board. Spoon some of the cabbage mixture onto each serving plate and arrange the portions of meat around it. Serve each diner one knockwurst as well (light eaters may want only half a knockwurst).

Serving Suggestions

The *bigos* may be served by itself, accompanied by a variety of mustards and good dark rye and pumpernickel breads. If you wish, roast potatoes (p. 197) or plain boiled potatoes can also be served. Precede the *bigos* with carrot soup (p. 62) or hot *pareve borscht* (p. 66). Conclude the meal with a dessert featuring apples. Apple compote (p. 240) and *eppl schnay* (p. 244) are both delicious. Drink a fruity zinfandel with the meal.

Festive Holiday Dinner in the Sukkah

Faiglan bread

Liver pâté à la Rothschild

Flommen tzimmes (braised beef with autumn vegetables)

Zinfandel

Savory green bean salad with dried herb vinaigrette

Medley of 3 *shtrudels* with fresh plum sauce

Coffee or tea

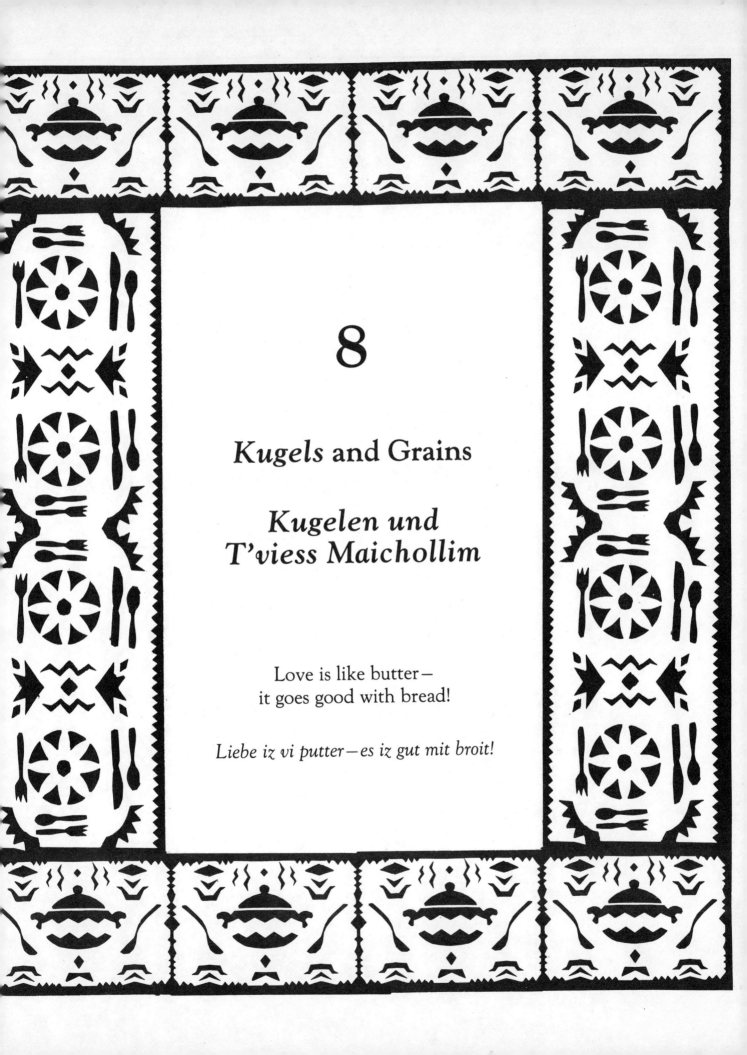

8

Kugels and Grains

Kugelen und T'viess Maichollim

Love is like butter —
it goes good with bread!

Liebe iz vi putter — es iz gut mit broit!

Lokshen

A sakh t'filles, veinik lokshen.

A lot of prayers, but few noodles.
— Yiddish commentary on *shtetl* life

Lokshen is the Yiddish word for noodles, and essentially, *lokshen* is nothing more than regular egg noodles. The main difference between *lokshen* and Italian pasta is that *lokshen* is always made out of regular unbleached white bread flour, and Italian pasta is traditionally made out of semolina flour, which gives the two different kinds of noodles very different textures and flavors.

Eastern European Jews never cultivated the art of shaping and saucing their noodles the way the Italians did, but they did develop some special noodle dishes that are unique to Jewish cuisine. As with Italian pasta, *lokshen* tastes entirely different when it is made fresh, and it is well worth the time it takes to make fresh *lokshen*. The job is much, much easier today now that we have pasta machines that can be used in the home. The marvelous pasta machine cuts time and significantly reduces labor with no loss at all to flavor and texture. Today's cooks can make *lokshen* easily at home with very little work.

I remember as a child the special occasions when my grandmother made her own *lokshen*. One time I asked her to teach me how to do it.

"What for you want to learn how to make *lokshen*?" she said to me in amazement.

"I love to eat *lokshen*. Why shouldn't I want to know how to make it? After all, I might have to make my own someday."

"What are you—a *meshuggeneh* [a crazy person]?" she replied. "Nobody but *alteh bobbehs* [old grandmothers] makes *lokshen*. Better you should go to the store and buy *lokshen*. The way some people today make *lokshen*, better they should go buy, too."

"No! Today I want to be an *alteh bobbeh* in training," I insisted, undaunted. "Teach me how to make *lokshen*."

"You know what you need to make *lokshen*? A *bezemshtecken* [broomstick]." And so began my first apprenticeship in the art of *lokshen* making.

In my grandmother's house, *lokshen* making was an all-day process that took hours and hours of hard work. In those days they did not even have the hand-cranked pasta makers on the commercial market, and the rolling of the dough was all done by hand. My grandmother, as she said herself, always used a *bezemshtecken* (a broomstick with the broom end removed) to roll out the dough for the *lokshen*. This particular broomstick used to sit in the pantry and be taken out only for making *lokshen* and *shtrudel* dough. I don't recall that it ever had an actual broom brush attached to it.

The procedure for making the *lokshen* itself was long and complicated. The first thing my grandmother would do was to spread flour all over the kitchen table. This was her working surface. Then she would put the dough on top of it. She would put the palm of her left hand on the part of the dough nearest to her and wrap the opposite end around the broomstick two or three times. Then, using the palm of her right hand, she would hold down the dough and roll the stick away from her with short, quick, jerky motions. She repeated this over and over and over again, stretching and stretching the dough until it draped more than halfway across the table. It looked to me to be as large as the American flag that hung over the blackboard at school. The amazing thing about it was that the dough never seemed to break or crack open all the while that it was being tugged and pulled at with the broomstick.

When she finally decided that she had done enough stretching, she left the dough to dry out for about half an hour. ("It shouldn't get too dry," she explained.) Then she would roll it up like a big, long jelly roll and chop it into *lokshen*. Chop, chop, chop with the *hockmesser*, that handleless cleaverlike knife that every Jewish household seemed to have! (My bobbe had two of them—a *fleischig* one for chopping liver and one that was *pareve* that she used to chop the *gefilte fisch* and the *lokshen*.) A steady, rhythmic motion, never losing a single beat. Then the *lokshen* had to dry out some more (at least an hour or two, but longer was also perfectly all right). This second drying was done on top of floured white bed sheets on the bed because there was no room to spread it out on the kitchen table or any of the counters.

Today, nobody has to do this. The modern pasta maker greatly simplifies the process and vastly cuts the preparation time, so there is no excuse for not trying it. Buy a pasta maker and go to it! Believe me, it's worth the effort.

This does not mean to say that there is anything wrong with store-bought *lokshen*. You should always have some in your pantry and save the making of fresh *lokshen* for special occasions, because you will for sure want to cook *lokshen* more often than you will want to make it fresh. There are three types of Jewish *lokshen* and they are all packaged with the following labels: thin egg noodles (for use in chicken soup, Romanian *lokshen kugel*, and *Yerushalmi kugel*), medium egg noodles (used for *milchig* and *fleischig lokshen kugel* and for some of the other *lokshen* dishes), and wide egg noodles (used mainly in *lokshen* dishes with sauces but also usable in *kugels* if you prefer their shape to the medium cut). *Lokshen* dough can also be cut and shaped in ways other than these. *Farfel* and *galushkes* are two other kinds of *lokshen*. Bow-tie-shaped *lokshen* are used for making the American version of *kasha varnishkes* (p. 183).

This recipe is for making your own *lokshen*. All of the other *lokshen* dishes follow this recipe.

2 cups unbleached white bread flour
2 large eggs, lightly beaten
1/2 tsp. salt

Mix the ingredients by hand and knead a little until they become a stiff dough. Process in your pasta maker according to the instructions for operating the appliance. There are both electric and hand-operated pasta makers on the market, and both work equally well. When you cut the pasta, keep in mind the traditional shapes of Jewish *lokshen*, and do not make spaghetti, fettuccini, or linguini, which will give you a pasta that is not *lokshen*. Allow the cut *lokshen* to dry for at least an hour before cooking. When it is dry, it can be stored in plastic bags for a short time. To cook *lokshen*, simply boil it in rapidly boiling salted water for 10 minutes, drain, and use as directed in each recipe. *Lokshen* also freezes quite well.

Kugels

Az me esst Shabbos kugel, iz men di gantzeh voch zat.

If you eat *kugel* on the Sabbath, you'll be full all week.
　　　　　　　　　　　　　　—Yiddish folk saying

A *kugel* is a rich dish made from a grain or starch, eggs, and seasonings. Among American Jews it is usually thought of as a side dish to be served with meat. In eastern Europe, however, it was often a main dish in and of itself, eaten by poorer people who were unable to buy meat. *Kugel* was a delicious and nutritious source of protein. For this reason, I personally recommend an unconventional concept for using *kugels* in a meal. *Kugels* are fine as side dishes with certain kinds of meat, but they are equally good as a course by themselves (much like an Italian pasta, which is always served as a separate course, the "primo"). *Kugels* are also excellent as a main-dish light meal in and of themselves, served with some appropriate vegetable accompaniments. Some ideas of how to use *kugels* in these new ways are given as Serving Suggestions.

I also introduce a special cooking technique of my own for preparing *kugels* that enables every diner to have a taste of the most delicious part of the *kugel*, the crisp crust. When I bake *kugels*, I always bake them in loaf pans and they are always baked twice. In this way, every portion of *kugel* that is served is encased in a crisp coating. It slices very attractively when prepared in this way, too. Much nicer, in my opinion, than when it is cut into squares like brownies.

Fleischig Lokshen Kugel

1/2 lb. medium or wide egg noodles
3 eggs, lightly beaten
1 large onion, peeled and finely chopped
4 Tblsp. chicken *schmaltz*
1/4 cup *gribenes* (optional, p. 6)
2 Tblsp. sugar
1/2 tsp. salt

1. Preheat the oven to 350°.
2. Melt 3 Tblsp. *schmaltz* over medium heat in a skillet and sauté the onions until they are translucent and soft. Transfer to a mixing bowl and cool to room temperature while you prepare the *lokshen*.
3. Bring a large pot of salted water to a rapid boil and cook the noodles until they are tender but still firm (al dente). Drain and place into the bowl with the onions.
4. Add the remaining ingredients to the mixing bowl except for the remaining *schmaltz*, and mix together well.
5. Grease a loaf pan with a small amount of the *schmaltz*. Line it with wax paper that has been cut to the size of the bottom and sides of the pan. Grease the paper with the remaining *schmaltz*.

6. Transfer the *lokshen* mixture into the pan and bake for 35 to 40 minutes or until the top of the *kugel* is golden brown. Remove from the oven.

7. Place a well-greased baking sheet over the top of the *kugel* and turn it over onto the baking sheet. The *kugel* should unmold very easily. Let it rest this way for a few minutes and then gently remove the pan. Let the *kugel* cool off until the wax paper can be removed without damaging the shape of the *kugel*. Then remove it. Up to this point, the *kugel* can be made in advance.

8. When ready (immediately after you remove the wax paper or any time thereafter), return the *kugel* to a 350° oven for final browning. Brown for 10 to 12 minutes or until the outside looks crisp and golden. Serve the *kugel* cut in attractive slices. Recipe serves 6 to 8 people.

Serving Suggestions

As a side dish, *fleischig lokshen kugel* is good served with some kind of roasted or braised meat that has a sauce. Try it with any of the following entrées:

Gedempte Fleisch (p. 129)
Essig Fleisch (p. 131)
Braised Tongue in Wine Sauce (p. 161)
Roast Chicken with Prunes (p. 109)
Stuffed Peppers (p. 154)

The *kugel* may also be served as a course on its own. If so, simply accompany the meat with nonstarchy vegetable side dishes. To serve *fleischig lokshen kugel* as an entrée, accompany it with a mixed vegetable salad (p. 220) or a green bean salad (p. 222) and, if you wish, a mushroom duxelles sauce (p. 8).

Milchig Lokshen Kugel

1 lb. medium or wide egg noodles
4 to 5 Tblsp. sweet butter
4 eggs, lightly beaten
1/2 cup sugar
1 cup farmer dry cottage cheese
1 8-oz. pkg. cream cheese
2 cups sour cream
5 tart green apples, peeled, cored, and chopped
1/2 cup seedless dark raisins

1. Fill a large stockpot full of salted water and bring to a rapid boil. Add noodles and cook until tender but still firm (al dente). Drain in a colander and place in a mixing bowl with 3 Tblsp. of the butter. Mix well and set aside.

2. Preheat the oven to 350°. Add all the remaining ingredients to the mixing bowl except the last Tblsp. of butter and mix well.

3. Grease two regular-size or one very large loaf pan with some of the butter. Line the pan(s) with wax paper cut to fit into the bottom and sides of the pan(s). Grease the wax paper lining(s) with the remaining butter.

4. Pour the *lokshen* mixture into the pan(s) and bake for 45 to 50 minutes or until the top(s) of the *kugel(s)* is (are) golden brown. Turn onto a well-greased baking sheet by placing the sheet over the pan(s). Allow to rest a few minutes before removing the pan(s). Allow to cool a little longer until the wax paper can be removed without ruining the shape of the *kugel(s)*. The *kugel(s)* should unmold easily and retain an attractive shape. Up to this point, this dish can be prepared in advance.

5. When ready, return the *kugel(s)* to the oven and bake 10 to 12 minutes longer or until the *kugel(s)* is (are) crisp and golden brown in color. Serve cut into attractive slices. This recipe serves 6 to 8 people as a main dish.

Serving Suggestions

Milchig lokshen kugel is a main-dish entrée and should not be served as a side dish. It may be served as part of a *milchig* buffet. For a delicious dairy meal, precede the *kugel* with cold beet *borscht* (p. 66), hot beet *borscht* (p. 66), any of the summer fruit soups, or a hot carrot soup (p. 62) made with vegetable instead of meat stock. Serve either a carrot and raisin salad (p. 227) or a baked-beet salad (p. 224) with the *kugel*, depending on what soup you preceded it with. No dessert is necessary. If you like, serve a bowl of sour cream or plain yogurt with the *kugel*, and diners can take their own cream. *Milchig lokshen kugel* also makes a wonderful dessert after a meal featuring smoked or pickled fish. When served this way, just serve smaller portions of *kugel*. If you would like to drink wine with the *kugel* when you serve it as an entrée, just about any white wine will do, but I like the taste of the delicate white wines like Riesling or gewürztraminer with it.

Yerushalmi Kugel

Yerushalmi kugel is not an eastern European Jewish dish, but it is deeply rooted in the same culinary traditions. *Yerushalmi kugel* is a specialty of the chasidic Jews who live in the Meah Shearim section of Jerusalem and whose roots go back to eastern Europe. This unique and special dish is right at home with every classical European Jewish recipe, and everyone who wishes to develop the ability to cook "Yiddish" needs to learn how to make it. I first became acquainted with *Yerushalmi kugel* in 1972, when I spent two years in Israel studying in a *yeshiva* (rabbinic school). I grew to love its sweet, peppery flavor and used to go to Meah Shearim every Friday to buy some and take it home with me.

The trick to making good *Yerushalmi kugel* lies in correctly doing the caramelizing process on the sugar and in long, slow baking, which is necessary in order to give the *kugel* its characteristic golden brown color.

1/2 lb. thin egg noodles
1/2 cup peanut or corn oil
3/4 cup sugar
salt to taste
1 1/2 tsp. coarsely ground black pepper
3 large eggs, lightly beaten

1. Bring a large pot of cold salted water to a rapid boil and cook the noodles until they are tender but still firm (al dente). Drain and set aside.

2. Prepare a loaf pan by greasing it with oil and lining it with waxed paper cut to fit the bottom and sides. Grease the paper as well and set the pan aside. Preheat the oven to 300°.

3. In a medium-size saucepan, heat the oil and add the sugar. Reduce the heat to its lowest possible temperature and cook this mixture, stirring constantly with a wooden spoon until the sugar caramelizes. You will know this by its brown color. The caramelizing will take about 15 minutes.

4. As soon as the sugar has caramelized, immediately remove it from the heat and add the *lokshen*. Stir it well to combine. Then add all the remaining ingredients.

5. Transfer the *lokshen* mixture to the loaf pan and place in the oven. Bake 2 hours. If it looks as if the top is starting to burn, cover it loosely with aluminum foil.

6. Remove from the oven and place a greased baking sheet over the kugel. Allow it to rest for a few minutes before unmolding. It should unmold very easily. Check the color. If it is not golden brown enough, return to the loaf pan and put it back in the oven for an additional 30 minutes. If the color is right, let it rest for a few more minutes until the wax paper can be removed easily without damaging the shape of the *kugel*. The *kugel* should look like a cake with a golden brown color. Up to this point, the dish may be prepared in advance.

7. When ready, return the *kugel* to the oven, this time set at 350°, for final browning. Brown 10 to 12 minutes, cut into attractive slices, and serve. Recipe serves 6 to 8 people as a side dish.

Serving Suggestions

Yerushalmi kugel makes an excellent side dish for roasted or braised meats with a sweet sauce. It is the perfect accompaniment for brisket braised with carrots (p. 132). It is also quite good with roast chicken with prunes (p. 109).

Romanian Sautéed *Lokshen Kugel*

1/2 lb. thin egg noodles
2 Tblsp. sweet butter or sunflower oil
1 large onion, peeled and chopped
6 to 8 Tblsp. sunflower oil for sautéing
2 large eggs, beaten
salt and black pepper to taste

1. In a large stockpot, bring a full pot of cold salted water to a rapid boil and cook the noodles until tender but still firm (al dente). Drain and set aside in a mixing bowl.

2. Heat the 2 Tblsp. oil or butter in a skillet and sauté the onions until soft and translucent and just beginning to turn golden in color. Add to the *lokshen*.

3. Add the beaten eggs, the salt, and the pepper to the *lokshen* mixture and mix everything together well.

4. In a 12-inch skillet, over medium-high heat, heat 6 Tblsp. oil until it is sizzling but not smoking. Add the contents of the mixing bowl to the skillet and sauté about 4 minutes. By this time, the bottom should be golden brown in color.

5. Slide the *kugel* out of the skillet and onto a plate. Add the remaining 2 Tblsp. oil to the skillet and again bring to a sizzling temperature.

6. Using the plate as a support, turn the *kugel* over onto its uncooked side into the skillet. You might have to turn it over onto the plate first and lose a little egg that way, but no matter. Sauté the *kugel* on this side for 3 to 4 minutes as well and slide it onto a clean plate. Serve immediately, cut into wedges. Recipe serves 4, 6, or 8 people, depending on how it is served (see Serving Suggestions).

Serving Suggestions

This *kugel* is the traditional Chanukah dish of Romanian Jews. Like *latkes*, it is fried in oil and is therefore part of an old Jewish custom to cook foods in oil on Chanukah. By doing this, we remind ourselves of the miracle of the cruse of oil that burned in the menorah in the ancient Hebrew Temple for 8 days. Romanian Jews also enjoy *latkes*, but this *kugel* is unique to the cuisine of this region of eastern Europe. It is traditionally a *milchig* dish served with sour cream and *brynza* cheese, but it may also be served as an accompaniment to meat when you sauté the onion in oil instead of butter. When served with meat, I like to have the *kugel* as a *forspeis* and follow it with the meat entrée, accompanied by vegetables. It is particularly good with sweet-and-sour meatballs (p. 154). When served as an entrée, this *kugel* serves 4 people. When served as a *forspeis* or side dish, it serves 6 to 8.

Lokshen with Savory Onion Confit and Poppy Seeds

Lokshen mit Tzibbeles und Mohn

This savory dish is really a Jewish pasta course and tastes wonderful as a *forspeis* before a meat entrée. It is also quite nice on its own as a light lunch or dinner.

1 lb. fresh *lokshen* (store-bought wide or medium egg noodles may be substituted)

2 very large onions, peeled and very thinly sliced
2 cloves garlic, peeled and cut into thin slivers
1 1/2 tsp. Hungarian sweet paprika
1 Tblsp. sugar
3 Tblsp. poppy seeds
1/2 cup corn oil
1/2 cup vegetable or chicken stock (p. 3 or p. 5)
salt and freshly ground black pepper to taste

1. Heat the oil over medium heat in a large, heavy saucepan or sauté pan and begin to sauté the onions until they are translucent and soft. Cook only 5 minutes this way and then reduce the heat to the lowest possible temperature.

2. When the onions begin to turn very soft, add the paprika, the sugar, and the garlic and continue to cook, stirring occasionally. This cooking will take between 20 and 25 minutes before the right consistency is achieved. During this time, the natural sugars in the onions will begin to caramelize slightly and sweeten the entire mixture.

3. While the onions are slow-cooking, bring a large stockpot of salted cold water to a rapid boil over high heat. When the water comes to a boil, add the *lokshen* to the pot. At the same time, add the poppy seeds and the stock to the onions and stir this in thoroughly.

4. Cook the *lokshen* until tender but still firm (al dente). With fresh *lokshen* this will take only a few minutes. With dried, store-bought *lokshen* it will take between 12 and 15 minutes. In a colander, drain the *lokshen* as soon as it has finished cooking.

5. Add salt and pepper to taste to the onion-poppy seed sauce and then put the *lokshen* into the saucepan or sauté pan. Mix everything together well and heat through. Serve immediately on individual serving plates. Recipe serves 6 to 8 people as a *forspeis* or 4 as a main-dish entrée.

Serving Suggestions

This dish is excellent with most meat entrées. I like it with *essig fleisch* (p. 131) or *gedempte fleisch* (p. 129) served as a *forspeis*. Accompany the meat with suitable nonstarchy vegetables. If serving this dish as an entrée, precede it with a mixed vegetable salad (p. 220) or a green bean salad (p. 222). If you would like a wine with this *lokshen* dish when you serve it as an entrée, choose white. Any kind will do.

Lokshen with Honey, Cream, and Poppy Seeds

Lokshen mit Honig und Mohn

This variation of *lokshen* with poppy seeds is *milchig* and is usually served as a dairy main dish. It is also excellent when served as a second course following an entrée of pickled fish. The *lokshen* serves as both a more substantial entrée and a dessert. This way of organizing courses that feature dishes like pickled fish followed by *lokshen* in a sweet sauce was traditional, particularly in Poland, where this recipe comes from.

1 lb. fresh *lokshen* (store-bought wide or
    medium egg noodles may be substituted)
1/2 cup honey
1 cup heavy or whipping cream
4 Tblsp. sweet butter
1/4 cup poppy seeds

1. In a large stockpot, bring a full pot of cold salted water to a rapid boil over high heat. Add the *lokshen* and cook until tender but firm (al dente). This will take only a few minutes with fresh *lokshen*. Dried will take between 12 and 15 minutes. When the *lokshen* is finished cooking, drain in a colander.

2. In a large sauté pan, melt the butter over medium heat. Add the honey and the poppy seeds and mix together well. Then reduce the heat to low and stir in the cream. Do not let the cream come to a rapid boil, or it will curdle. Just heat it slowly until it comes to the boiling point.

3. When the cream is heated to the right temperature, add the *lokshen* to the sauté pan and heat through well, mixing everything together thoroughly until ingredients are well incorporated. Serve immediately on individual serving plates. Recipe serves 6 to 8 people as a second course after pickled fish or 4 as a dairy entrée.

Serving Suggestions

If serving this dish as a dairy entrée, accompany it with a carrot-and-raisin salad (p. 227), a baked-beet salad (p. 224), or a Galitzianer beet salad (p. 225). The *lokshen* may also be preceded by a Boston lettuce salad (p. 220). If serving as a second course, precede with sweet-and-sour pickled fish (p. 89) or one of the herring dishes in chapter 2. Conclude this light meal in typical Polish fashion by drinking tea with the *lokshen* course and, if your sweet tooth craves something else, a nice pastry with more tea.

Lokshen with Baked Apples

Lokshen mit Eppl

This is another of those wonderful sweet Polish *lokshen* dishes. This one features the classical method of cooking *lokshen* in Poland—first boiling it, then saucing it, and then baking it in the oven to give it a nice crust.

1 lb. fresh *lokshen* (store-bought wide or
    medium egg noodles may be substituted)
4 Tblsp. sugar
1/4 tsp. ground cinnamon
1/8 tsp. ground cloves
4 large, tart green apples, peeled, cored, and
    thinly sliced
6 Tblsp. sweet butter
1 cup heavy or whipping cream
1/3 cup bread crumbs

1. Bring a large stockpot of cold salted water to a rapid boil over high heat. Cook the *lokshen* until tender but still firm (al dente). Fresh *lokshen* will take only a few minutes. Dried egg noodles will take between 12 and 15 minutes. Drain the *lokshen* in a colander.

2. In a large sauté pan, melt 4 Tblsp. of the butter over medium heat. Add the sugar and cook until it begins to caramelize (about 5 minutes). Then add the apples and the spices. Cook, stirring constantly but gently, until the apples begin to soften.

3. Lower the heat slightly and add the cream. Heat through well, but do not allow to come to a boil.

4. When the ingredients in the sauté pan are properly heated, add the *lokshen* and mix everything together well. Remove from the heat. Up to this point, this dish can be prepared in advance.

5. When ready, grease a baking dish with some of the remaining 2 Tblsp. butter. Add the entire contents of the sauté pan to the baking dish. Preheat the oven to 350°.

6. Sprinkle the bread crumbs over the *lokshen* mixture. Cut the remaining butter into bits and dot

the top of the baking dish with this. Bake in the oven about 12 to 15 minutes or until nicely gratinéed, and serve immediately. Recipe serves 4 as a dairy entrée and 6 to 8 as a second course following pickled fish.

Serving Suggestions

Follow those given for *lokshen* with honey and poppy seeds (p. 174).

Lokshen with Sweet Cream, Prunes, and Wine

Lokshen mit Getrukente Flommen

This dish, like the previous two, is Polish in origin and served as either a dairy entrée or a second course following pickled fish.

1 lb. fresh *lokshen* (store-bought wide or
    medium egg noodles may be substituted)
1/2 cup pitted prunes
1 cup red wine
1/2 cup prune juice
1/2 cup heavy or whipping cream
6 Tblsp. sweet butter
2 Tblsp. sugar mixed with 1/4 tsp. ground
    cinnamon
1/3 cup bread crumbs

1. Cut the prunes into small pieces and soak in the wine for 1 hour.

2. When the prunes have finished soaking, bring a large pot of cold salted water to a rapid boil over high heat and cook the *lokshen* until it is tender but firm (al dente). Fresh *lokshen* will take only a few minutes. Dried egg noodles will take between 12 and 15 minutes. Drain in a colander when the *lokshen* is ready.

3. Melt 4 Tblsp. of the butter over medium-low heat in a large sauté pan and add the prunes, drained of their soaking liquid. Cook 5 minutes.

4. Add to this the wine in which the prunes had been soaked and the juice and bring to a boil. Reduce the heat and add the cream. When this is heated through, add the *lokshen*. Mix everything

together well and remove from the heat. Up to this point, this dish may be prepared in advance.

5. Grease a baking pan with some of the remaining butter, and preheat the oven to 350°. Pour the contents of the sauté pan into the baking dish.

6. Sprinkle the bread crumbs over the *lokshen* and then sprinkle the cinnamon-sugar mixture over this. Cut the remaining butter into tiny bits and scatter these over the top of the *lokshen*. Bake 12 to 15 minutes or until nicely gratinéed. Serve immediately. Recipe serves 4 as a dairy entrée and 6 to 8 as a second course after pickled fish.

Serving Suggestions

Follow those given for *lokshen* with honey and poppy seeds (p. 174).

Lokshen with Farmer Cheese and Yogurt

Lokshen mit Kayz

1 lb. fresh *lokshen* (store-bought wide or
    medium egg noodles may be substituted)
6 Tblsp. sweet butter
1/2 lb. farmer dry cottage cheese
1 cup plain yogurt
1/2 tsp. salt

1. Bring a large pot of cold salted water to a rapid boil over high heat and cook the *lokshen* until it is tender but firm (al dente). Fresh *lokshen* will take only a few minutes. Dried egg noodles will take between 12 and 15 minutes. Drain in a colander as soon as the *lokshen* is ready.

2. Melt the butter over medium-low heat in a large sauté pan. Add the cheese and break it apart into small pieces with a wooden spoon. Add the yogurt and lower the heat to its lowest temperature. Heat through, being careful not to let it come to a boil, or the yogurt will curdle.

3. When heated through, add the *lokshen* and mix very thoroughly to incorporate everything. When the contents of the sauté pan are heated through again, remove from the heat. Mix in the salt and serve immediately. Recipe serves 4 people as a dairy entrée.

Serving Suggestions

This is one of the easiest and quickest meals you can serve when you are in a hurry. It is also very delicious and nutritious. All you need is a salad before, after, or with the entrée. You may also serve a white wine with the entrée. A light Riesling is my favorite.

Ukrainian-Style *Lokshen* With Cabbage

Lokshen mit Kroit

1 lb. fresh *lokshen* (store-bought wide or medium egg noodles may be substituted)
1 small head green cabbage, cored and very finely shredded
4 Tblsp. sweet butter or corn oil
1 medium-size onion, peeled and very thinly sliced
1 tsp. sugar
1 tsp. caraway or dill seeds
salt and freshly ground black pepper to taste

1. Bring a large pot of cold salted water to a rapid boil over high heat and cook the *lokshen* until it is tender but firm (al dente). Fresh *lokshen* will take only a few minutes. Dried egg noodles will take about 12 to 15 minutes. Drain the *lokshen* in a colander when it is ready.

2. In a large sauté pan, melt the butter or heat the oil over medium heat. Sauté the onion until translucent and soft. Add the cabbage and cover the pan. Reduce the heat. Cook over medium-low heat, stirring every once in a while, until the cabbage starts to soften.

3. When the cabbage is just beginning to turn soft, add the caraway or dill seeds and mix them in.

4. When the cabbage is soft and bubbling nicely, stir in the sugar and cook about 10 minutes more, covered.

5. Uncover the sauté pan and stir in the *lokshen*. When everything is well heated through, add salt and pepper to taste and serve immediately. Recipe serves 4 as a vegetarian entrée or 6 to 8 as a *forspeis*.

Serving Suggestions

This dish may be *milchig* or *pareve*, depending on whether you cook it in butter or oil. Generally, I like to use oil when serving this as a *forspeis* and butter when it is an entrée. It makes a wonderful *forspeis* before any meat entrée that has a nice sauce. Any of the tongue recipes, Hungarian-style short ribs of beef (p. 135), *gedempte fleisch* (p. 129), and *essig fleisch* (p. 131) are all very good choices as entrées to follow this *lokshen* dish.

Farfel

Farfel are similar to the manfrigul or achine de pepe of Italian pasta. They are small, irregularly shaped tiny balls of *lokshen* dough that are cooked similarly to rice or *kasha*. The are served as a side dish with meat or in soups and stews. *Farfel* can be eaten plain or toasted.

The method of making *farfel* varied from region to region. In *Litteh*, Jews prepared their *farfel* by chopping off tiny amounts of the dough and rolling them into balls with their fingers. In central Poland, they rolled the dough into extremely thin strips, cut the strips into tiny pieces, and rolled these pieces into tiny balls. This resulted in *farfel* that was more uniform in size. In Galitzia, a hand-held grater was used to cut the dough into tiny pieces, which were then rolled by hand. Although techniques differed, the resulting flavor of the cooked *farfel* was pretty much the same everywhere.

1 extra-large egg
2 cups unbleached white flour
1/4 tsp. salt

Beat the egg together with the salt. Mix in the flour, kneading by hand, until it forms a very stiff ball of dough. Chop the dough into very tiny pieces, and roll the pieces into balls between your fingers. Or, alternatively, roll the dough into a thin sheet using the pasta machine, cut it into thin strips, and then cut the strips into tiny squares. Roll the squares of dough into tiny balls. It does not really matter which method you use. Nor does it matter whether or not the balls of dough are the same size. Traditional *farfel* are not evenly sized, and such a task will be next to impossible anyway. Lay the balls on a clean, very lightly floured board or kitchen cloth and let them dry for at least 1 hour or until they are completely dried out. The *farfel* may then be used immediately or stored in tightly sealed glass jars almost indefinitely until ready to be used.

To make toasted *farfel*, simply spread on a dry baking sheet and toast in a 325° oven for about 15 minutes. The *farfel* will turn golden brown. Remove from the oven and cool to room temperature before storing or using in cooking. To use *farfel* in soup, simply boil it in a pot of salted water for 10 minutes as you would *lokshen*. When serving *farfel* as a side dish with a meat entrée, I like to prepare it as a *pilav* according to the instructions below.

Roasted *Farfel*

3 small onions, chopped
1 1/2 Tblsp. *schmaltz* or corn oil
2 cups chicken or vegetable stock (p. 3 or p. 5)
1 cup dry *farfel* or toasted *farfel* (prepared as
    directed above)
salt and freshly ground black pepper to taste

1. Preheat the oven to 350°. Heat the *schmaltz* or oil in an ovenproof saucepan with a tight-fitting lid over medium heat. Sauté the onions until translucent and soft.

2. Add the *farfel* and mix everything together with a wooden spoon.

3. Pour the stock over the *farfel* mixture and cover the pot. Cook in the oven for 30 to 35 minutes or until all the stock is absorbed. The *farfel* will swell to double its size.

4. Remove from the oven and stir in salt and pepper to taste before serving.

Serving Suggestions

Roasted *farfel* goes well with just about any meat dish. My favorites are braised brisket with horseradish sauce (p. 129), *gedempte fleisch* (p. 129), and *gedempte kalbsfleisch* (p. 141).

Galushkes

Galushkes are almost the same as German spaetzle except that they are made with water in the dough instead of milk. The recipe comes from Galitzia, but *galushkes* were popular among the Jews in every part of central Europe, particularly Czechoslovakia and Vienna. Hungarians make a similar dish called *nokeldy*.

2 large eggs
1 tsp. salt
1/2 cup water
2 1/2 cups flour
3 Tblsp. peanut or corn oil (optional)
1/4 cup bread crumbs (optional)

1. Beat the eggs together with the salt and the water in a mixing bowl. Add the flour slowly, beating well with each addition, until the mixture begins to become thick enough to turn into a dough.

2. Add the remaining flour by hand and knead until the mixture is doughlike in its consistency. It will be stiff but not nearly as stiff as *farfel* or *lokshen* dough.

3. Grate the dough through the large holes of a hand-held grater onto a lightly floured board; separate the pieces from one another as you grate. Or roll the dough into a very long, very thin cylinder and then chop it into small pieces of more or less equal size.

4. Bring to a rapid boil over high heat a large stockpot full of salted cold water. Drop the pieces of dough into the boiling water.

5. After all of the *galushkes* rise to the top of the pot, cook a full 10 minutes. Use the oven timer to time this exactly.

6. Remove the *galushkes* with a slotted spoon. The *galushkes* can then be served as is, or they can be sautéed with the oil and bread crumbs.

7. If serving the *galushkes* with bread crumbs, heat the oil over medium heat in a sauté pan. Add the *galushkes* and toss until well coated with oil. Add the bread crumbs and continue tossing until everything is thoroughly mixed together. Serve immediately. Recipe serves 6 to 8 people.

Serving Suggestions

Galushkes are natural accompaniments to braised-meat dishes. I particularly enjoy serving them with recipes that originated in Galitzia. Try them with sweet-and-sour *gedempte leber* (p. 158), braised brisket with apples (p. 132), braised tongue with raisins (p. 162), and Hungarian-style *gedempte fleisch* (p. 130).

Variation

A Hungarian-style *milchig* variation on this recipe can be made by substituting 1/2 cup whole milk for the water and sweet butter for the oil. When sautéing the *galushkes*, add 1/4 cup brown sugar, 1/4 cup walnuts, and 1/4 tsp. cinnamon to the bread crumbs. Serve this as a *milchig* entrée for a light dinner or lunch and follow the serving suggestions given for *lokshen* with apples (p. 174) or cottage cheese *knaidelach* (p. 185).

Potato *Kugel*

Potato *kugel* has always been one of my favorite dishes and, as with most *kugel* lovers, my favorite part of the *kugel* has always been the crisp crust. I have developed a method of my own for preparing *kugels*, which was explained in more detail in the recipe for *lokshen kugel* on p. 170. I use this method for every *kugel* I make. Each portion of *kugel*, when it is made this way, contains some of the delicious crust.

2 1/2 lb. white baking potatoes, peeled and cut into chunks
2 medium-size onions, peeled and cut into chunks
4 eggs, beaten
1 cup *matzoh* meal
1/2 cup corn or peanut oil
salt and black pepper to taste

1. Preheat the oven to 400°. Oil the inside of a 2-quart loaf pan. Line it with wax paper along the bottom and sides and then oil the paper. Set the pan aside.

2. Grate the potatoes and the onion in batches in a food processor using a pulse/chop movement or in a meat grinder using the fine-grind blade. If you do not have either of these appliances, an old-fashioned hand grater works just as well. As you grate each batch, drain it slightly and quickly through a sieve with very fine holes to remove excess moisture. The holes of the sieve should be fine enough to allow liquid to pass through them without removing any of the vegetable pulp. Put the grated vegetables into a mixing bowl.

3. Add the remaining ingredients and mix well with a wooden spoon until completely incorporated.

4. Turn this mixture into the prepared loaf pan and bake for 45 to 50 minutes, or until the *kugel* is well browned on top.

5. Remove from the oven and place a well-greased baking sheet over the loaf pan. Turn it upside down so that the baking sheet rests on the bottom and the loaf pan rests, turned over, on the top. Allow to cool slightly.

6. Unmold the *kugel* from the loaf pan. The pan should lift off very easily, leaving the *kugel* upside down and covered by the wax paper. Allow to cool down enough to remove the wax paper without damaging the shape of the *kugel*. Peel the paper off very gently. In all likelihood, the part of the *kugel* that was under the paper will not be really brown. Up to this point, this dish can be prepared in advance.

7. To finish cooking the *kugel*, replace it in the heated 400° oven and bake for about 20 to 25 minutes, or until the top and sides are brown and crusty.

8. Remove from the oven and serve immediately. Cut into attractive slices. Recipe serves 6 to 8 people as a *forspeis* or an accompaniment to meat. It may also be served as a vegetarian entrée, in which case the recipe will serve 4 people.

Serving Suggestions

There is nothing like potato *kugel* to accompany a Jewish prime rib roast (p. 137). It also goes well with just about any other meat dish. I like to serve it as a *forspeis* and follow it with the meat entrée, accompanied by one or two nonstarch vegetables. When potato *kugel* is served as a main-dish entrée, mushroom duxelles sauce (p. 8) poured over it makes it extraspecial. Accompany this entrée with a delicate white wine like Riesling.

Potato *Kugel* from Galitzia
Galitzianer Kartoffel Kugel

This variation on the traditional potato kugel comes from Galitzia. It is very rich and flavorful and at the same time light and airy.

A family of bagel peddlers. Warsaw, 1938. (Photograph by Roman Vishniac.)

5 medium-size red boiling potatoes
3 medium-size onions, peeled and finely
   chopped
1/3 cup corn or peanut oil
3 large eggs, separated
1/2 cup *matzoh* meal
salt and black pepper to taste

1. Boil potatoes in their jackets in salted water until tender (about 25 minutes on top of the stove or about 15 minutes in the microwave oven). Immediately plunge into cold water to stop cooking. Cool to room temperature.

2. Peel potatoes and mash with a potato masher or a fork in a mixing bowl. Preheat oven to 400°.

3. Prepare a very large loaf pan or two smaller ones by greasing it (them) with oil and lining it (them) with wax paper to cover the bottom and sides. Oil the wax paper lining and set the pan(s) aside.

4. Heat the oil in a skillet and sauté the onions until they are translucent and soft. Add this to the potatoes and mix in thoroughly.

5. Stir the egg yolks, the *matzoh* meal, and the salt and pepper into the potato mixture. In a separate, larger mixing bowl, beat the egg whites in an electric mixer or with a hand-held egg beater until stiff. Fold the egg whites into the potato mixture with a spatula, using a cut/foldover motion until well incorporated and until the whites are no longer showing.

6. Fill the prepared loaf pan(s) with this mixture and bake in the oven for 45 to 50 minutes or until the top(s) of the *kugel(s)* is (are) nicely browned.

7. Remove from the oven and place a baking sheet over the top of the *kugel(s)*. Turn upside down and cool slightly before unmolding. The loaf pan(s) should slide off easily, leaving a wax-paper-covered *kugel*. Cool until the wax paper is able to be peeled off the *kugel* without damaging its shape. This *kugel* is somewhat more delicate than the others, so you will have to be very careful when you peel off the paper. Peel it off as soon as you are able to. Up to this point, the *kugel* can be prepared in advance.

8. To finish baking the *kugel*, return it to the 400° oven to brown for about 20 to 25 minutes. Cut into slices and serve immediately. Recipe serves 6 to 8 as a *forspeis* or accompaniment to a meat entrée and 4 as a vegetarian entrée. Follow the serving suggestions given potato *kugel* (p. 178).

Savory Onion *Kugel*

Tzibbele Kugel

Tzibbeles is the Yiddish word for onions. This light, tasty *kugel* requires more eggs than the others to hold it together.

6 large eggs, separated
3 large onions, peeled and finely chopped
3/4 cup *matzoh* meal
1/3 cup vegetable stock
1 heaping tsp. salt
black pepper to taste
4 Tblsp. corn or peanut oil

1. Prepare a very large loaf pan (or two smaller loaf pans) by greasing it (them) with oil and lining it (them) with wax paper cut to fit the bottom and sides. Oil the paper and set aside. Preheat the oven to 350°.

2. Beat the egg yolks, oil, stock, *matzoh* meal, salt, and pepper together in a mixing bowl. Cover this mixture and allow it to rest in the refrigerator for 45 minutes. Then add the onions to it.

3. In a separate large mixing bowl, beat the egg whites in an electric mixer or with a hand-held egg beater until they are stiff. Fold into the onion mixture with a spatula, using a cut/foldover motion until well incorporated and no egg white is visible.

4. Pour this mixture into the loaf pan(s) and bake for 45 minutes. Remove from the oven and place a greased baking sheet over the top of the loaf pan(s). Turn upside down and let cool for a few minutes before unmolding. *Kugel(s)* should unmold easily. Allow to cool a few more minutes before removing the wax paper that clings to the sides and top of the unmolded *kugel(s)*. When cool enough to remove the paper without damaging the shape of the *kugel*, peel it off. Do this gently and delicately. Up to this point, this dish can be prepared in advance.

5. When ready to finish baking the *kugel*, return it to the oven and bake an additional 10 to 15 minutes or until the *kugel* is nicely browned. Cut into slices and serve immediately. Recipe serves 6 to 8 people as a *forspeis* or a side dish and 4 as a vegetarian entrée.

Serving Suggestions

Tzibbele kugel is very versatile and tastes good with fish as well as meat. It is excellent paired with my bobbe's baked halibut (p. 84), poached salmon with dill sauce (p. 85), and roast chicken with prunes (p. 109). If served as a vegetarian entrée, mushroom duxelles sauce (p. 8) poured over it makes it into something special. *Tzibbele kugel* is one of the lightest *kugel* dishes in Jewish cuisine.

Orange-Scented Fruit *Kugel*

Matzoh Meal Frucht Kugel

This was my grandmother's special *kugel* that she made to accompany *hendel mit marantzen*. She also called it *zisse kugel*, or "sweet *kugel*." It really isn't overly sweet when made correctly and is actually a delicious accompaniment to meat dishes other than *hendel mit marantzen*.

2 1/2 cups *matzoh* meal
grated rind of one orange
1/2 to 3/4 cup freshly squeezed orange juice
4 tart cooking apples, peeled and cut into very
    fine dice
2 Tblsp. sugar
1/2 cup golden raisins
6 eggs, separated
4 Tblsp. corn or peanut oil
1/4 tsp. cinnamon (optional)

1. Prepare a loaf pan by greasing it with oil and lining it with wax paper to fit over the bottom and sides. Oil the paper and set the pan aside.

2. Preheat the oven to 350°. In a mixing bowl, using a wire whisk, beat the egg yolks together with 1/2 cup of the juice, the sugar, the cinnamon if using, and the rind. Add the *matzoh* meal and mix together well, using a wooden spoon. If the mixture seems too dry, add a little more orange juice. The *matzoh* meal should be completely soaked, but the mixture should be solid. Add juice only if there does not seem to be enough liquid to soak into the *matzoh* meal.

3. Mix the apple pieces and the raisins into the *matzoh* meal mixture.

4. With an electric mixer or a hand-held egg beater, beat the egg whites until stiff. Fold the whites into the *matzoh* meal mixture with a spatula, using a cut/foldover motion until they are completely incorporated and no white is showing.

5. Place the *matzoh* meal mixture into the prepared loaf pan and bake in the oven for 45 minutes or until the top is nicely browned.

6. Remove from the oven and place a greased baking sheet over the top of the loaf pan. Turn upside down and allow to cool a few minutes before unmolding. Unmold the *kugel* by lifting out of the loaf pan. It should come off quite easily and the *kugel*, covered by wax paper, will remain on the baking sheet. Allow to cool a few more minutes before peeling off the wax paper. Peel gently so as not to damage the shape of the *kugel*. Up to this point, the *kugel* can be prepared in advance.

7. To finish baking the *kugel*, return to the 350° oven for 10 to 15 minutes to brown. Cut into attractive slices and serve immediately. Recipe serves 6 to 8 people as a side dish to a meat entrée.

Serving Suggestions

In addition to *hendel mit marantzen* (p. 103), this *kugel* tastes good when served with roast chicken with prunes (p. 109), tongue with raisin sauce (p. 162), sweet-and-sour smoked or pickled tongue (p. 163), and *essig fleisch* (p. 131).

Rice *Pilav*

I learned this method of preparing rice from my Aunt Ann, and it is infinitely superior to any other method I know for cooking rice. This rice is baked in the oven rather than cooked on top of the stove, which results in every grain's being separate rather than glued together with starch from the rice. The method also gives the grain a lovely roasted aroma. This is surprisingly true, even for ordinary white rice. Although my aunt generally used plain water as the cooking medium for her rice, I find that stock makes a dish that is much more flavorful and interesting. Anytime I want rice to go with an entrée, this is the method I use to prepare it. Here is my basic recipe, with three variations.

1 1/2 cups long-grain white or brown rice
    (brown rice, of course, is more nutritious)
2 Tblsp. peanut or corn oil
3 cups chicken or vegetable stock (p. 3 or p. 5)
salt and black pepper to taste

Preheat the oven to 350°. In a heavy ovenproof saucepan or casserole with a tight-fitting lid, heat the oil on top of the stove. Add the rice and sauté for 1 or 2 minutes, stirring with a wooden spoon to make sure all the grains are covered with oil. Stir in the salt and pepper and pour the stock in. Cover tightly and bake in the oven, 35 to 40 minutes for white rice, or 1 1/4 hours for brown rice. Remove from the oven and serve immediately. Recipe serves 6 to 8 people as a side dish.

Serving Suggestions

This basic rice *pilav* is excellent with poultry, fish, and some Hungarian-style meat dishes. Serve it with baked lemon chicken (p. 110), chicken *paprikash* (p. 102), or Romanian-style *gedempte leber* (p. 169).

Variation 1: Creole Rice *Pilav*

I created this variation on Creole green rice to serve with fish. Take 1/2 cup chopped fresh parsley, 1/2 cup chopped scallions (whites and greens), and 1/2 cup finely chopped onions and sauté them in 3 Tblsp. oil for 2 to 3 minutes. Add 2 or 3 pinches of cayenne pepper to this and mix it into the rice *pilav* after it has finished baking. Serve immediately. Delicious! Try it with any of the broiled or grilled fish (pp. 81–82).

Variation 2: Yellow Rice *Pilav*

Mix 1/4 tsp. dried saffron into 1/3 cup boiling water and let it steep for a few minutes. The water will turn a brilliant yellow. Add this with 1 bay leaf and a pinch of cayenne pepper to the rice at the same time you add the stock. Bake it as directed above. The rice comes out a beautiful yellow color. The bay leaf will have floated to the surface during cooking. Discard it and serve immediately. Aromatic and elegant! Try this with roast chicken with prunes (p. 109), braised tongue with wine (p. 161), or roast veal with wine and herbs (p. 141).

Variation 3: Barley *Pilav*

Substitute 1 1/2 cups pearl barley for the rice and prepare as directed in the recipe for rice *pilav*. Baking time is 40 to 45 minutes in the oven at 350°.

Kasha

Toireh, Toireh in keppeleh, kasha kochn in teppeleh.

Torah, Torah should fill your thoughts, and you should always have *kasha* in your pot.
      —Words taken from my grandmother's lullaby

Kasha is very popular with Jews from Russia, Litteh, and the Ukraine. To my way of thinking, it is one of the most delicious of all grains, although for some people, it is an acquired taste. *Kasha* goes particularly well with braised beef and veal dishes. Buckwheat is very nutritious and contains a large amount of fiber, recommending it for everyone's diet. The secret to making good *kasha* is in first toasting it until the grain begins to give off an aroma and then braising it in the oven instead of cooking it on top of the stove.

1 1/2 cups *kasha* (whole grain or coarse grind)
1 large egg, beaten
1 tsp. salt
3 1/2 cups chicken or vegetable stock
    (p. 3 or p. 5)
1 large onion, peeled and finely chopped
1 lb. fresh white mushrooms, wiped clean with
    a damp cloth and chopped
1/4 cup chopped fresh parsley
4 Tblsp. corn or peanut oil
black pepper to taste

1. Preheat the oven to 350°. Place on top of an oven burner an ovenproof, heavy casserole or saucepan that has a tight-fitting lid . Turn on the burner to medium heat and add the *kasha* to the pot. Toast the grains at this temperature for 2 to 3 minutes, turning with a wooden spoon. If the grains have not yet begun to give off sufficient aroma, continue toasting until this happens.

2. Immediately add the beaten egg to the pot and stir it vigorously into the *kasha*. Add the stock and stir everything together well. Cover the pot tightly and transfer to the oven. Bake 40 to 45 minutes.

3. While the *kasha* is baking, heat the oil in a large skillet or sauté pan over medium heat and sauté the onions until translucent and soft.

4. Add the chopped mushrooms and continue sautéing until the mushrooms begin to give off their liquor.

5. Add the parsley and cook 1 to 2 minutes more. Remove from the heat and stir in the salt and pepper to taste.

6. When the *kasha* is ready, remove it from the oven and mix the onion mixture into the *kasha*. Serve immediately. Recipe serves 6 to 8 people as a side dish.

Serving Suggestions

Serve *kasha* as a side dish with savory entrées like braised brisket with *chrain* (p. 129), *gedempte fleisch* (p. 129), braised veal with wine and herbs (p. 141), or braised tongue with wine and herbs (p. 161).

Kasha with Egg Noodles

Kasha Varnishkes

1 cup *kasha,* coarse grind or whole
1 egg, beaten
1 tsp. salt
2 1/2 cups chicken or vegetable stock
    (p. 3 or p. 5)
4 Tblsp. corn or peanut oil plus 1 Tblsp. for
    sprinkling
1 large onion, very finely chopped
1/2 lb. medium or wide egg noodles

1. In a heavy saucepan with a tight-fitting lid, toast the *kasha* grains over medium heat until they begin to give off an aroma (approximately 2 to 3 minutes).

2. Immediately stir in the egg with a wooden spoon until completely incorporated. Add salt and stock and cover the pot. Reduce the heat to simmer and cook the *kasha* until it absorbs all the stock (about 15 minutes).

3. Meanwhile, cook the noodles in a stockpot filled with rapidly boiling salted water until tender but still firm (al dente). Drain in a colander and place in a mixing bowl.

4. Heat the 4 Tblsp. oil in a skillet over medium heat and sauté the onions until translucent and soft. Add to the noodles.

5. When the *kasha* has completely cooked, mix it into the noodle mixture. Transfer the contents of the mixing bowl to a greased baking dish or gratin dish. Preheat the oven to 350°.

6. Sprinkle 1 Tblsp. oil over the *kasha*-noodle mixture and bake in the oven for 15 minutes. The top will be slightly brown and crunchy. Serve immediately as a side dish with meat. Recipe serves 6 to 8 people.

Serving Suggestions

Kasha varnishkes is very versatile and goes with just about anything. I am inclined to serve it with beef or tongue when I am in the mood for it.

Variation

For an American Jewish variation on this dish, substitute bow-tie-shaped noodles for the medium or wide egg noodles.

Potato *Knaidelach*

Kartoffel Knaidelach

Kartoffel knaidelach are one of my favorite "starchy" side dishes. They take a little skill to make, but the effort is well worth the slight amount of trouble. They are very popular in Hungarian and Czech Jewish cuisine, particularly as an accompaniment to braised meats.

4 cups finely grated potato
2 large eggs
1 small onion, finely grated
1/3 cup potato starch
1/2 to 2/3 cup *matzoh* meal
1 tsp. salt

1. Do the grating of the vegetables in the food processor or meat grinder. If you do not own either of these appliances, grate them by hand. Drain off the excess liquid in a sieve with very fine holes that will separate the liquid but not any of the vegetable pulp. Place in a mixing bowl.

2. Beat the eggs into the potato-onion mixture and then mix in the remaining ingredients, including 4 Tblsp. of the *matzoh* meal. If the mixture seems too liquid, add a little more *matzoh* meal, up to 1 Tblsp.

3. Bring a large stockpot of salted cold water to a rapid boil over high heat. Have a bowl of cold water next to you as you work. Reduce the heat slightly

but make sure the water is boiling at an even, rapid rhythm.

4. Wet your hands and shape 2 Tblsp. of the potato mixture into a ball. Drop it gently into the boiling water. Repeat until all the *knaidelach* batter has been used up. Boil the *knaidelach* uncovered. In about 20 minutes they will all have risen to the top of the pot and will have puffed up to twice their size. Remove with a slotted spoon and serve immediately.

Serving Suggestions

Kartoffel knaidelach are the best accompaniment I know of for Hungarian goulash (p. 136). They are also delicious with any other braised meat dish that has a savory sauce. Try them with *gedempte fleisch* (p. 129), *szekely goulash* (p. 146), Hungarian-style *gedempte fleisch* (p. 130), or braised brisket with apples (p. 132).

Hungarian *Challah Knaidel*

This, unlike other *knaidelach*, is shaped into a large, long, cylindrical *knaidel* and then cut into slices when it is served. It is a little tricky to make but, like all *knaidelach*, well worth the effort.

3 cups stale *challah*, cut into 1/2-inch cubes
2 eggs, beaten
4 Tblsp. corn or peanut oil (or more, if
**   necessary)**
1 small onion, peeled and very finely chopped
10 Tblsp. unbleached white flour
1/2 tsp. salt
1/4 cup chicken or vegetable stock (p. 3 or p. 5)
2 or 3 shakes Hungarian hot paprika

1. Heat the oil in a large skillet over medium heat and sauté the *challah* cubes until golden brown on both sides. Transfer with a slotted spoon into a mixing bowl.

2. In the same oil, sauté the onion until translucent and soft. Add oil, if necessary. When the onions are ready, add them to the *challah* cubes.

3. Beat the eggs and add them, with the stock and the seasonings, to the *challah* mixture.

4. Add the flour, a little at a time, mixing with a wooden spoon until everything is well incorporated. Let the mixture stand for 30 minutes.

5. Fill a large stockpot with salted cold water and bring to a boil over high heat. Reduce the heat

slightly and let the water boil at an even, rhythmic pace while you prepare the *knaidelach*.

6. Divide the dough mixture in half and shape each half into a sausage-shaped cylinder about 7 inches long and 2 inches thick. Gently add each of these cylinders to the boiling water, taking care not to let the water stop boiling.

7. Cook the *knaidelach* for 25 minutes, turning them once after 12 minutes have passed. Remove with a slotted spoon and drain on a cloth or paper towel before slicing to serve. Slice the *knaidelach* attractively and serve immediately, alongside a meat entrée. Recipe serves 6 to 8 people as a side dish.

Serving Suggestions

Challah knaidel is delicious with goulash, especially *szekely goulash* (p. 146). It is also wonderful alongside *Romanishe prakkes* (p. 153), Polish-style roast duck with apples and pears (p. 121), or roast stuffed goose (p. 122). In Hungary and Czechoslovakia, it is often served as an accompaniment to roast goose with cabbage and caraway seed stuffing, for which no recipe appears in this book.

Matzoh Knaidelach

These *knaidelach* are traditional for Czech Jews during Passover but are really delicious all year long provided you can obtain good-quality *matzos*. For some reason, they are not as difficult to make as potato or *challah knaidelach*, which require practice to get a feel for achieving the correct texture.

1 lb. box *matzos* (or substitute 1 lb. box
**   *matzoh farfel*)**
4 cups boiling water
1 medium onion, peeled and finely chopped
3 garlic cloves, peeled and finely chopped
1/4 cup chopped fresh parsley leaves
salt and black pepper to taste
***matzoh* meal, if needed**
1 large stockpot boiling salted water for cooking
**   *knaidelach***

1. If using the *matzos*, break them apart into small pieces about 1/2 to 1/4 inch in size. Place these or the contents of the box of *matzoh farfel* into a mixing bowl.

2. Pour the 4 cups boiling water over the *matzoh* or *matzoh farfel* and steep 3 minutes. Drain and squeeze out by hand as much water as you can. Return the *matzoh* to the mixing bowl and add the remaining ingredients except for the *matzoh* meal. Mix everything together well.

3. Bring the pot of salted water to a rapid boil over high heat. Test the consistency of your batter by dropping 1 tsp. into the boiling water. If it falls apart, it will be necessary to add a little *matzoh* meal to the batter before cooking.

4. Have a bowl of cold water next to you as you work. Take 2 Tblsp. of the batter into your moist hands and shape it into a ball. Drop it gently into the boiling water. Repeat until all the batter is used up. Cover the pot and reduce the heat to medium-low. Simmer the *knaidelach* at this temperature for about 20 minutes. Uncover the pot. The *knaidelach* should have risen to the surface. Remove with a slotted spoon and serve Immediately. Recipe serves 6 to 8 people as a side dish with meat.

Serving Suggestions

Follow those given for Hungarian *challah knaidel* (p. 184) or for potato *knaidelach* (p. 184).

Hungarian Cottage Cheese *Knaidelach*

1/2 lb. farmer dry cottage cheese
1 stick (8 Tblsp.) sweet butter
1 Tblsp. sugar plus 1/3 cup
1/2 tsp. cinnamon
1 heaping cup unbleached white flour
1/2 cup bread crumbs
1 egg

1. In a blender or food processor, place 4 Tblsp. butter cut into bits, the cheese, 1 Tblsp. sugar, and the egg. Pulse/chop until ingredients are well blended and butter is thoroughly incorporated into the cheese. If you do not have a blender, it may be done in the electric mixer or by hand. Place this mixture into a mixing bowl.

2. Mix the cinnamon with the remaining 1/3 cup sugar and set aside.

3. Add the flour to the cottage cheese mixture and form, by kneading, if necessary, into a medium firm dough.

4. Spread the bread crumbs onto a sheet of wax paper. Have a kitchen cloth or paper towels spread out next to the stove.

5. Bring a large stockpot of cold salted water to a rapid boil over high heat. Reduce the heat slightly but keep it rolling at a steady, rhythmic pace.

6. Shape the dough by hand into 1 1/2-inch balls and gently drop them into the boiling water. They will rise to the top in about 15 minutes. Turn them once with a slotted spoon as they cook. When 15 minutes have passed, remove them from the water and drain them on the cloth or paper towels.

7. While the *knaidelach* are cooking, melt the remaining butter in a sauté pan over medium heat. When the *knaidelach* have boiled, roll them in the bread crumbs and place them in the sauté pan with the melted butter. Sauté a few at a time until nicely browned. Sprinkle with the cinnamon-sugar mixture and serve immediately. Recipe serves 6 to 8 people as a dessert or 4 to 6 as a light *milchig* supper.

Serving Suggestions

When serving the cheese *knaidelach* as a dairy entrée, precede with bouquet of fresh vegetables soup (p.   ) and accompany the *knaidelach* with more melted butter or, if you prefer, sour cream or plain yogurt. As a dessert, they stand on their own. Serve 2 *knaidelach* per diner as a dessert portion.

Cheese or Potato *Kreplach*

Cheese or potato *kreplach* make a delicious dairy or vegetarian dinner entrée. To make them, just prepare the *kreplach* dough according to the instructions on p. 59 and fill them with the potato filling mixture for potato *knishes* (p. 48) or the cheese filling below.

1 1/2 cups farmer dry cottage cheese
3 Tblsp. bread crumbs
2 Tblsp. sugar
1 egg, beaten
finely grated peel of 1/2 lemon
1 1/2 Tblsp. sour cream

1. Mix all of the ingredients together and fill the *kreplach* as instructed on p. 59. Boil in salted water according to the directions given on p. 59. Drain and serve with melted butter and sour cream or plain yogurt as a dairy entrée. Accompany the *kreplach* with carrot-and-raisin salad (p. 227) or baked-beet salad (p. 224).

Mamaliga

Mamaliga is Romania's national dish and loved by Jews as much as by anyone else. It has been immortalized in the Yiddish-speaking world by being mentioned in the popular Yiddish theater song "Romania, Romania!" which is a nostalgic treatise on all the things Romanian Jews loved about their country. *Mamaliga* is exactly the same thing as Italian polenta, where the recipe is believed to have originated. *Mamaliga* can be served freshly boiled, sautéed in oil, or baked in a casserole. I provide recipes for all three kinds of *mamaliga*.

Recipe 1: Boiled *Mamaliga*

3 1/2 cups water
1/4 tsp. salt
1 1/2 cups yellow cornmeal
6 Tblsp. sweet butter or corn oil

1. Combine the salt and water in a heavy saucepan and bring to a boil. Add 2 Tblsp. cornmeal in a steady stream and whisk together with a wire whisk or wooden spoon until the water boils up again.

2. Gradually add the remaining cornmeal in a slow, steady stream, stirring constantly. Reduce the heat to simmer and cook the mixture until thickened. Keep stirring as it cooks. The *mamaliga* is through cooking when it starts to pull away from the sides of the pot.

3. When this happens, stir in the butter or oil, a little at a time, and cook for about 5 minutes longer. By this time, the *mamaliga* is pulling away nicely from the sides of the pot. Transfer it to a greased mixing bowl, a mold, or some other round container. Flatten the top of the *mamaliga* with a wooden spoon and let stand about 5 minutes.

4. Invert the *mamaliga* onto a platter and cut it into slices or wedges for serving. Serve immediately. Recipe serves 6 to 8 people.

Serving Suggestions

Mamaliga is very versatile and may be part of a dairy or a meat meal. For a dairy meal featuring *mamaliga*, sprinkle the finished *mamaliga* with melted butter when it is served and serve it with *brynza* cheese, black olives, and a Romanian vegetable salad (p. 228), a roasted pepper salad (p. 228), or Romanian-style sautéed wild mushrooms (p. 208). For a meat meal, make the *mamaliga* with corn oil instead of butter and serve it with *karnotzl* (p. 156) and any of the salads mentioned above.

Recipe 2: Sautéed *Mamaliga*

Sautéed *mamaliga* is the traditional accompaniment in Romania to sautéed liver and onions. Prepare the basic *mamaliga* recipe with corn oil and instead of using a round mold to shape the *mamaliga*, use a loaf pan. Pour the *mamaliga* into a greased loaf pan. It may be unmolded right away or saved in the refrigerator for use another day. When ready to cook the sautéed *mamaliga*, just unmold it from the loaf pan (it will slide out very easily), slice it, and sauté the slices in oil. Serve them alongside the liver or any other meat entrée you wish to accompany it. Sautéed *mamaliga* is also good with fish and, if you wish, you may prepare it and sauté it in butter to serve with a fish entrée.

Recipe 3: Baked *Mamaliga*

There are several variations of this:

1. Slice the *mamaliga* and layer it in a well-buttered casserole or gratin dish. Sprinkle each layer with crumbled *brynza* cheese and butter bits. Bake in a 375° oven for 10 minutes or until cheese is golden and bubbly. Serve with a good dry white wine.
2. Cut the *mamaliga* into slices and sprinkle with gratings of a hard yellow cheese like gruyère or mozzarella. Drizzle with melted butter and bake in a 375° oven until top is browned. Serve with a dry white wine.
3. Slice (do not grate) mozzarella cheese and layer in a buttered casserole with slices of *mamaliga*. Bake in a 375° oven until cheese is melted and browned. Serve with a good dry white wine.

Accompany each of these baked *mamaliga* with a good salad of your choice.

Stuffed *Kishke*

Kishke means "intestine" and this dish is actually a stuffed sausage casing. It is a tasty, if somewhat heavy, Jewish peasant dish that can accompany a meat entrée or be served as a course by itself. Any kosher butcher can supply you with fresh sausage casing for making *kishke*.

3 8-inch lengths of beef large intestine prepared as sausage casing and carefully rinsed
1 large onion, peeled and finely chopped
1/4 cup chicken *schmaltz*
2 stalks celery, finely chopped
1/4 tsp. Hungarian hot paprika
3/4 cup unbleached white flour
2 Tblsp. *matzoh* meal
salt and black pepper to taste

1. Melt the *schmaltz* in a skillet and sauté the onions and celery until soft and translucent. Transfer to a mixing bowl.
2. Stir in the remaining ingredients and stuff the *kishke* with this mixture. Sew up the ends and then tie them tightly with kitchen string.
3. Bring a pot of salted water to a rapid boil over high heat and boil the *kishke* for 10 minutes. Drain well.
4. Preheat the oven to 350°. Bake the *kishke* in a well-greased, shallow baking pan for 1 1/2 hours or until browned, basting frequently with the pan juices. Cut into slices and serve. Recipe makes 6 servings. *Kishke* can be reheated after it is cooked the first time. Just preheat the oven and bake it until it is warm.

Serving Suggestions

Kishke goes well with any meat entrée. It adds something special to braised brisket with carrots (p. 132) when served as a side dish with the meat.

Helzel

Helzel is an old-fashioned Jewish peasant dish that is hard to make today only because it is practically impossible to obtain a whole intact goose neck anywhere. This, of course, is what *helzel* is—stuffed goose neck. If your city has a live poultry market,

and if you flatter the butcher in the right way, the butcher may be able to obtain a fresh goose for you with the entire neck intact. If you are one of those lucky people, you are in for quite a treat!

skin of 1 goose neck (neck meat removed for another use)
1 very small onion, peeled
1/2 small carrot, peeled
1 2-inch-piece celery, chopped very finely
1/3 cup *schmaltz*
1 1/2 cups unbleached white flour
1/4 tsp. Hungarian hot paprika
salt and black pepper to taste

1. Grate the onion and carrot in the food processor or by hand and mix together with everything else except the skin of the goose neck. Sew up one end of the skin and stuff the skin with this mixture. Sew up the other end and roast the *helzel* with the goose. (Of course, you can roast it and serve it with some other kind of meat, too.) It takes about 1 1/2 hours to roast. Serve the *helzel* cut in slices either with the meat or as a *forspeis* before the soup (my favorite way). I am told one can also make *helzel* by stuffing and sewing chicken skin with the same mixture, but I have never tried it.

Cheese *Blintzes*

Cheese *blintzes* are traditionally associated with the holiday of Shevuos and were served for dessert at the festival meal by eastern European Jews. The word *blintz* comes from a Ukrainian word meaning "pancake." In America, *blintzes* are usually thought of in connection with New York City's famous Jewish dairy restaurants. Even though American Jewish cooks have tried to be creative by filling their *blintzes* with all manner of fruit and nut mixtures, I must confess that I do not care for any of the modern variations on this classical dish (with the exception of the Hungarian liver *blintzes* recipe featured on p. 45). I like *blintzes* with the traditional cheese filling, and I like to accompany them with plenty of good sour cream and a seasonal fruit compote.

Blintzes are a lot like crepes. The secret to making perfect *blintzes* in the classical manner is to make the batter thin enough to make thin pancakes without their being quite as thin and delicate as crepes. This requires precision in measuring the ingredients and a short waiting period between the mixing of the batter and the sautéing of the *blintzes*.

Batter

4 eggs
1 cup cold water
1/2 tsp. salt
2 Tblsp. peanut oil
1 cup unbleached white flour

1. Beat the eggs, water, salt, and oil together. Using a wire whisk, mix in the flour gradually, stirring all the while to prevent lumping of the batter. The batter will be on the thinnish side. In order to achieve the correct consistency, add a little more water or flour than indicated in the recipe, if needed. *Blintz* batter is similar to crepe batter, and it is important that you do not make it too thick. If you make that mistake, the *blintzes* will turn out like flat pancakes. They will be difficult to fold and will taste heavy and doughy.

2. This next step is very important. *Blintz* batter needs to rest before it can be used. It may rest up to 2 hours at room temperature or even up to 12 hours if refrigerated. Do not reduce the amount of time of this resting period. The minimum resting period is 1 hour at room temperature or 4 hours in the refrigerator.

3. When you are ready to sauté the *blintzes*, have a crepe pan, a pastry brush, some paper towels, and some melted butter ready next to the stove. A nonstick Teflon-coated 6-inch crepe pan is a perfect cooking utensil. The Teflon-coated pan uses a slightly lower cooking temperature than a regular metal crepe pan. If using a regular metal crepe pan, heat it over medium-high heat. The Teflon-coated pan may be heated over medium heat. Let the pan get good and hot and then brush it with a little melted butter. The butter should sizzle but not brown or burn. If it does, lower the heat, wipe the pan out with a paper towel, and start again.

4. The secret of a perfect *blintz* is having just enough batter to thinly coat the bottom of the pan. You will use approximately 1/4 cup batter for each *blintz*. Ladle this amount of batter onto the prepared pan and spread it by tipping the pan from side to side until the pan is completely coated.

5. Now comes the part that makes *blintzes* different from crepes. *Blintzes* are sautéed on *one side*

only, whereas crepes are cooked on both sides. *Blintzes* are also ever-so-slightly thicker than crepes.

6. Let the *blintz* cook until it looks as if it is almost totally cooked through, and then remove it onto a dish or other flat surface. The bottom of the *blintz* should be light and barely beginning to brown around the edges.

7. Repeat this procedure until all the batter is used up. Brush the crepe pan with a little melted butter before making each *blintz*. The recipe yields about 18 *blintzes*.

Filling

2 cups farmer dry cottage cheese
3 Tblsp. sugar
1 egg yolk
1 1/2 tsp. freshly squeezed lemon juice
1 tsp. finely grated lemon zest

Mash the cheese and mix everything else into it.

To prepare the *blintzes*

1. Place a heaping Tblsp. of the cheese filling onto one side of a *blintz*. Spread it out over the length of the *blintz*, leaving a 1/4-inch margin on both ends.

2. Fold the lengthwise side of the *blintz* that is closest to the filling over the filling. Fold the two shorter perpendicular ends of the *blintz* across this fold. Then roll up the *blintz* jelly roll fashion. The result will be a short, cylindrical, cigar-shaped package.

3. Repeat this step until all the filling and all the *blintzes* are used up. You may or may not have any filling left over. Do not exceed 1 Tblsp. of filling per *blintz*, or the *blintzes* may burst during cooking.

4. Arrange the filled and rolled *blintzes* in a well-buttered baking dish. Dot with bits of sweet butter.

5. Preheat the oven to 450°. Bake the *blintzes* for 10 to 15 minutes and serve immediately. (Alternatively, the *blintzes* may be sautéed in butter, but this results in a slightly heavier dish.) Recipe serves 8 people as a dessert or 4 to 6 as a dairy entrée.

Serving Suggestions

When serving *blintzes* as a dessert, accompany them with sour cream and a seasonal fruit compote. Strawberry compote (p. 237), summer berry compote

(p. 238), and rhubarb compote (p. 240) are particularly good with *blintzes*. When serving *blintzes* as a dairy entrée, accompany them with sour cream and a carrot-and-raisin salad (p. 227). A crisp white wine is absolutely delicious with *blintzes*. Gewürztraminer or Riesling is particularly good. So is a fumé blanc.

A MAASEH FUN CHELM (A STORY OF CHELM)

Chelm was the name of a little Polish village that was populated by extremely stupid people. (The Chelm of Yiddish fiction, of course, bore no resemblance to the real Polish city of Chelm.) The citizens of this little village were nicknamed the *Chachmei Chelm* (the Wise Folk of Chelm), and many humorous Yiddish stories were written about them.

This particular story concerns a poor Hebrew teacher who was a private tutor for the children of wealthy families and who lived with his wife on the top of a hill with a synagogue at the bottom. The day before Shevuos one year he was giving a lesson to a student when he smelled the aroma of freshly made cheese *blintzes* being sautéed in butter in the kitchen. The *blintzes* smelled so delicious that when the teacher went home, he asked his wife if she was also preparing *blintzes* for their holiday.

"*Vey iz mir!* [Oh, woe is me!]" said the woman. "I don't have cheese and butter in the house and we won't have enough money to buy them."

So the two of them made a pact. Beginning the day after Shevuos, each of them would save one *grosch* (the currency of the *shtetl*) of their pay (he from his teaching, she from flicking chickens) every week, so that by the end of the year they would have enough money saved to buy everything needed to make *blintzes*.

The teacher found in his house a large trunk that was mounted on wheels. He cut a slit in the left-hand side of the trunk and then in the right-hand side and then he locked it. "At the end of each week I will put my *grosch* into the right-hand slit and you will put your *grosch* into the left-hand slit," said the husband to his wife. "Two days before Shevuos we will unlock the trunk and take out all the money." To show good faith he inserted his first *grosch* into the right-hand slit and she inserted hers into the left.

The next week the teacher said to himself, "You know, I made so little money this week that I think

I'd better keep the extra *grosch*. My wife's *grosch* will still go into her slot and next week I'll start to add mine. It won't make any difference in the long run."

The wife, meanwhile, said to herself, "I don't even have enough to buy a piece of fish for *Shabbos* this week. I'll keep my extra *grosch* this week and start to put in next week. No one will notice, and we'll have more than enough at the end of the year to make the *blintzes*."

And so it went, week in, week out. The husband found another excuse to keep his *grosch* and the wife found a reason to keep hers. And neither of them put another *grosch* into the trunk. The year finally passed and the day came to open up the trunk. The husband got the key and unlocked the trunk and lo and behold, there was nothing in it but two *groschen*.

"You cheat!" exclaimed the husband. "You spent all your money on trifles all year long and expected to eat *blintzes* with my *groschen* only!"

"I a cheat? You're the cheat! Where are all the *groschen* you were supposed to put in?"

"Where are yours? What did you do with yours?"

The two of them got so angry with each other that they started to yell and scream and then wrestle with each other. Before long, the wife pushed the husband into the trunk, he pulled at her, and she came tumbling in on top of him. The trunk started to shake back and forth and to roll around on its wheels, and before either of them could get themselves out, the lid fell down on top of them and clamped shut.

They screamed and they cursed and they pushed and they pulled and the trunk rattled and rolled and rolled and rattled and finally wound its way into the open doorway and out into the street.

Now remember—the teacher lived on the top of a hill at the bottom of which was a synagogue. The teacher and his wife were making such a ruckus trying to open up the trunk that the wheels rolled down the hill—down, down, down—until it reached the door of the synagogue, where it stopped dead in its tracks. People saw the trunk rolling, heard the horrible noises and curses coming from inside it, and thought it was possessed by an evil spirit.

"Look! Look!" they cried to one another. "The trunk is possessed by a *dybbuk* [the proverbial evil spirit of the *shtetl*]!" People started to gather around the trunk and scream for mercy. Some of them tore their clothes and started to chant the prayer of penitence for their sins. Some of them asked each other for forgiveness for wrongs they had done to one another. Others began to proclaim openly all of the sins and indiscretions they had committed in secret, in the hope of ridding their community of the *dybbuk*. Meanwhile, the noises never stopped and the trunk rattled and shook and was prevented from rolling any farther only because it was stuck in its place up against the synagogue door.

The rabbi appeared and began to recite psalms. But nothing helped. The horrible noises grew louder and louder. Finally the rabbi said they would have to open the trunk and perform an exorcism. The men drew straws to see who would be given the unlucky task of opening the trunk—because everyone knew that the closer you got to a *dybbuk*, the easier it was for it to jump out, enter into you, and take possession of your body.

Finally, Yankel Shmerel, the town *schnorrer* (beggar), drew the unlucky straw and, with a crowbar, popped open the top of the trunk. And what did they see? Out fell the teacher and his wife, still yelling and cursing at each other.

The teacher had to tell the rabbi the whole story, whereupon everybody was terribly upset. So many people had confessed their secret sins and indiscretions that the town gossips wuld have plenty to talk about from this Shevuos to next Shevuos.

That evening, the day before Shevuos, the town council of Chelm met to decide what to do. They issued three edicts, which were read publicly before the congregation on Shevuos night:

1. There are to be no more trunks on wheels in Chelm.
2. No Hebrew teachers shall be allowed to live on top of the hill opposite the synagogue anymore.
3. It is strictly forbidden for any Hebrew teacher and his wife to desire *blintzes* filled with cheese and sautéed in butter on Shevuos.

Spaghetti

"American" foods were, with very few exceptions, never cooked or eaten in my grandmother's home. This was partly because she was totally unfamiliar with them and quite comfortable cooking the things she knew best. But it was also partly because she resisted what she called "Americanization" very strongly. To her, becoming more American meant becoming less "Jewish." She had left Europe, like the

majority of her contemporaries, to escape poverty, starvation, and pogroms, but had done so with mixed feelings. She had an intense love-hate relationship with the Old Country. She scorned the prejudice and poverty that had driven her from Poland, but she remembered with nostalgia the religious life and close friendships among the people she knew there. She promised herself when she left Poland that she would seek a better "material" life in America but that she would always remain a pious, observant Jew and never succumb to the temptation to abandon her Jewish roots. She stuck firmly to these principles throughout her life and tried hard to instill them in her own children.

My mother's generation was, of course, more comfortable in America, never having known any other home. Most of these Jews were easily "Americanized," and many of them abandoned the religious as well as the cultural traditions of their parents. My grandmother's children, out of respect to her, kept kosher homes and observed traditions to a greater or lesser degree, but all of them introduced American customs and American cuisine into their homes as well. This blending of the two cultures sometimes resulted in some humorously eccentric ways of doing things. My Aunt Ann's recipe for "spaghetti" is a perfect example of this. It was not only my mother and my aunt who prepared "spaghetti" this way. The mothers of some of my friends did the same thing and nobody I recall ever discussed the recipe. This dish is *milchig*. The mother of one of my friends made a *fleischig* version using ground beef in place of farmer cheese and sour cream. My Aunt Rose, the most "Americanized" of the three sisters, actually took a quantum leap and made a wonderful version of "real spaghetti and meatballs." But what I remember best from my childhood when I think of "spaghetti" is the dish featured in this recipe.

I think if I were to ask my aunt today to explain to me how she came to make spaghetti this way, she would probably say that "baking it in a pan in the oven" was the "only way I ever learned how to make *lokshen*, and spaghetti is *lokshen*, so what other way is there to cook it?" (Of course, she never said this. . . . I'm just putting words into her mouth. . . .) Here is her recipe for "spaghetti." I hope you will enjoy it as much as I always have.

1 lb. spaghetti
2 1/2 cups fresh tomato sauce (p. 6)
1 large yellow onion, peeled and finely
  chopped

1 red onion, peeled and finely chopped
1 clove garlic, peeled and finely chopped
1 green pepper, seeded, cored, and finely
    chopped
1 large carrot, peeled and finely diced
1 large stalk celery, finely diced
2 cups farmer dry cottage cheese
1 tsp. Hungarian hot paprika
1/2 cup sour cream
4 Tblsp. sweet butter
salt and pepper to taste

1. Break the spaghetti in half (I told you Old Country cooks didn't know what to do with Italian pasta!) and cook it in boiling salted water until done. Drain, rinse, and set it aside in a large mixing bowl.

2. Melt 2 Tblsp. of the butter in a quart-size saucepan over medium heat and sauté the onions until translucent and soft. Add the remaining vegetables and sauté until slightly softened.

3. Add the garlic and paprika and cook an additional 5 minutes. Add the tomato sauce and cook until the sauce is heated through.

4. Pour the contents of the saucepan over the spaghetti and mix together well. Mix in the cheese and sour cream and stir together until well blended.

5. Preheat the oven to 350°. Grease a baking pan with a little of the remaining butter. Pour the spaghetti mixture into the prepared pan. Dot with butter bits made of the remaining butter. Bake in the oven for 25 to 30 minutes or until a nice crust forms on top of the spaghetti. Serve directly from the casserole. The tastiest part of this dish is the crisp crust, just as with *lokshen kugel*, so make sure every diner gets some of it. Recipe serves 6 to 8 people.

Serving Suggestions

Serve spaghetti with a plain green salad and, if you like, garlic bread. Any white wine goes well with this.

A *sofer* (scribe) from Russia repairs a Torah Scroll. (Courtesy of YIVO Archives.)

Hungarian Autumn Holiday Menu for Simchas Torah

Galitzianer potato bread

Liver *blintzes* with brandied apple sauce

Rosé

Golden carrot soup

Braised veal shoulder with caraway seed

Galitzianer-style braised red cabbage   Sautéed kohlrabi

Red burgundy

Dried fruit compote with *makos* and *kokos* pastries

Coffee or tea

9

Vegetable Dishes

Greener Maichollim

If you go to bed without eating, you get
up without having slept.

*Az me laigt avek nit gegessen, shtayt men
off nit geshlofen.*

Sautéed Vegetables With Finesse

The simplest way of preparing vegetable side dishes is to sauté them. If you have never tasted a properly sautéed fresh vegetable, you are missing a truly pleasurable experience. Sautéing is a lot like Chinese stir-frying. It makes the texture of the vegetables slightly crisp, keeps the flavor completely intact, and preserves most of the vitamins and nutrients. Sautéed vegetables go well with practically anything. Sautéing is fast and should be done on the spot just as the vegetables are being served.

Some vegetables can be sautéed without any prior preparation. Others require an initial parboiling (a quick boiling that partly cooks the vegetable just to remove its raw taste but not enough to eliminate its crisp texture). The microwave oven is one of the best cooking utensils for parboiling vegetables. It uses only a fraction of the water used by stovetop boiling, and it reduces the cooking time by 50 percent. So if it normally takes 10 to 12 minutes to parboil a particular vegetable on top of the stove, you know it can be done in a microwave oven in 5 to 6 minutes.

In the Jewish kitchen, where milk and meat are kept separate, the sautéing medium (butter or oil) determines whether the dish will be *milchig* or *pareve* and therefore what entrée the vegetable will be served with. I enjoy using the Chinese wok for sautéing vegetables because it cooks them evenly and quickly. If you do not have a wok, a sauté pan or skillet is, of course, quite acceptable.

All sautéed vegetables are prepared in a two- or three-step process, depending on whether or not they need parboiling. The cooking times are different for different vegetables.

Step 1: Parboil the vegetable in lightly salted water. Drain it and rinse it with cold water immediately on order to stop the vegetable from cooking and to preserve its fresh natural color. Drain and dry the parboiled vegetable. This step can be done several hours in advance of sautéing and serving the vegetable. The vegetable may be refrigerated, if necessary, to retain its freshness.

Step 2: Heat the butter or oil in the wok or sauté pan over fairly high heat. Add garlic, if using, and sauté 30 seconds. Add the vegetable. Stir with a spatula constantly as you sauté to make sure it all cooks completely through. Sautéing normally takes about 5 minutes.

Step 3: Add any lemon juice, fresh herbs, salt, and black pepper while the heat is still on. Toss together and then serve the vegetable immediately.

This procedure is the same no matter what vegetable you use. The list of suggestions in the chart includes cooking times and recommended herbs and flavorings for the different vegetables. All recipes are for fresh vegetables with one exception—green peas. I have found that good-quality frozen petits pois are an acceptable substitute for the fresh, which have a very short season.

A Compendium for Sautéed Vegetables

Vegetable	Parboiling Time (in microwave)	Sautéing Fat	Optional Herbs
Asparagus (1 lb.)	3 minutes	Butter or olive oil	Lemon juice
Broccoli (1 lb.)	6–7 minutes (florets) 8–10 minutes (stems)	Butter or olive oil	Garlic (with oil) Lemon juice (with butter)
Brussels sprouts (1 lb.)	10 minutes	Butter or oil	Lemon juice (essential)
Carrots (1 lb.)	8 minutes	Butter or oil	Chives, dill, parsley
Cauliflower (1 lb.)	7–8 minutes	Butter or oil	Lemon juice (essential)
Green beans (1 lb.)	6 minutes	Butter or olive oil	Garlic, dill, savory, fines herbs, parsley
Green peas (10–12 oz.)	3 minutes	Butter	Chives, parsley
Kohlrabi (1 lb.)	8 minutes	Butter or oil	Lemon juice, hot paprika
Spinach (1 lb.)	3 minutes	Butter or olive oil	Garlic (with oil only)
Turnips (1 lb.)	8 minutes	Butter or oil	Lemon juice (essential)
Zucchini or yellow squash (1 lb.)	4–5 minutes	Butter or olive oil	Garlic, chives, parsley, fines herbs

These sautéed vegetables may be used to accompany any entrée. Some suggestions are given with many of the recipes. Herbs and flavorings are optional in all cases except where the word *essential* appears.

Perfect Oven-Roasted Potatoes

Gebrotene Kartoffel

This recipe, my Aunt Ann's, was always a hit. It is a perfect accompaniment to most grilled or roasted meats.

6 to 8 smallish white baking potatoes
1 to 2 Tblsp. corn or peanut oil
salt, pepper, and hot paprika to taste

1. Peel the potatoes and parboil for 8 minutes in boiling salted water on top of the stove or 4 minutes in the microwave oven. Drain and plunge immediately into cold water to stop the cooking.

2. Remove the potatoes from the water when cool, and dry them with paper towels. Preheat the oven to 350°. Oil a baking sheet.

3. Oil your hands with 1 to 2 Tblsp. oil. Lift up each potato and rub it all over with oil. Lay it on the baking sheet. Repeat until all the potatoes are all oiled. Use more oil, if needed.

4. Sprinkle the potatoes with salt, black pepper, and hot paprika. Roast in the oven for 30 minutes on the middle shelf.

5. Turn the potatoes over and sprinkle them again with salt, pepper, and paprika. Roast an additional 30 minutes or until the potatoes are nicely browned. Serve immediately. Recipe serves 6 to 8 people.

Serving Suggestions

Roasted potatoes go well with practically everything, but I think they are at their best served with entrées that are also roasted, grilled, or baked. They are particularly delicious as an accompaniment to roast chicken with prunes (p. 109) or Jewish-style prime rib roast (p. 137).

Butter-Steamed New Potatoes with Dill

Gekochte Nayer Kartoffel Mit Kropp

This dish, which is popular both in Scandinavia and in the Baltic states, has been a part of the Jewish cuisine of those regions for a long time. The art of preparing it correctly lies completely in keeping the temperature of the oven burner very low and in shaking the pot from time to time to prevent the potatoes from sticking to the bottom. It looks very simple, but it takes a little practice to get the technique just right. The result is elegant and delicious.

8 to 12 small unpeeled new potatoes (red or white), washed and dried
4 1/2 Tblsp. sweet (unsalted) butter
1/3 cup chopped fresh dill leaves
salt and black pepper to taste

1. Melt the butter in a deep, heavy saucepan with a tight-fitting lid over medium heat. Enameled cast iron works very nicely. Add the potatoes one at a time, turning them over in the butter so that every side of each potato is covered. The pan should be small enough so that the potatoes fit snugly into it in one layer. This is extremely important because otherwise they will not cook evenly.

2. Reduce the heat to the lowest simmer and cover the pan tightly, with foil in between the pan and the lid if necessary for creating a tight seal.

3. Cook for 1 hour and 15 minutes, shaking the pan every once in a while to loosen the potatoes from the bottom. *Do not remove the lid during cooking* or steam will escape, which affects the result of the dish. You will hear the potatoes sizzle while they are steaming. This is normal.

4. After 1 hour and 15 minutes have passed, uncover the pot and test one potato with a toothpick. It should feel soft but not mushy.

5. Add the dill leaves and re-cover the pot. Steam an additional 10 minutes to help the dill impart its flavor.

6. Uncover the pot, remove the pot from the heat, and stir in salt and pepper to taste. Serve immediately. Recipe serves 6 to 8 people.

Serving Suggestions

Butter-steamed new potatoes are the perfect accompaniment to poached fish. They are also good with baked fish. Try them with poached salmon with dill sauce (p. 85), poached pike with horseradish sauce (p. 86), or my bobbe's baked halibut (p. 84).

Not Your Ordinary Mashed Potatoes

Kartoffel Kasha

Mashed potatoes, called *kartoffel kasha* in Yiddish, are certainly not unique to Jewish cuisine. However, eastern European Jews do have a method of preparing them that is different from the usual. First of all, one must consider the separation of milk and meat. There are both *fleischig* and *milchig* variations of mashed potatoes. The second difference is not as obvious or as well known. It is this second difference that distinguishes how my grandmother and other European Jewish cooks of her generation prepared mashed potatoes from the way they are usually prepared by most American chefs. Yiddish-style mashed potatoes are not supposed to be a fine puree, nor are they ever whipped. Small bits of unmashed potato are supposed to be left in the dish for texture and visual appeal (a slightly different aesthetic sense from the French, I think). Here are my grandmother's recipes for *fleischig* and *milchig* mashed potatoes.

Fleischig Recipe (to be served with meat dishes)

2 lb. red boiling potatoes, peeled and cut into
    chunks
2 Tblsp. chicken *schmaltz*
1 small onion, peeled and finely chopped
salt and black pepper to taste

1. Boil potatoes gently on the stove in plenty of boiling, unsalted water for 25 to 30 minutes (or in the microwave oven for 18 to 20 minutes). Drain and save the water for use in baking bread. This potato water contains potato starch, which adds flavor and texture to breads. It is an essential ingredient in potato breads and in pumpernickel. Do not completely drain the potatoes. Leave approximately 1/4 to 1/3 cup of the potato water in with the cooked potatoes.

2. While the potatoes are boiling, gently sauté the onions in the *schmaltz* until golden brown. Set them aside.

3. Mash the potatoes *loosely* with the leftover 1/4 cup potato water. Use a potato masher and do this by hand rather than in a food processor. The potatoes mash very easily. The potato water will keep the puree loose and prevent the dish from becoming pasty. There should be tiny bits of un-mashed potato left in the mixture. This step is extremely important. Do not mash the potatoes into too smooth a puree, or you sacrifice the rustic character of the dish.

4. After you have finished mashing the potatoes, mix in the sautéed onions together with the *schmaltz* and the salt and pepper to taste. Serve immediately. Recipe serves 6 to 8 people.

Serving Suggestions

Fleischig mashed potatoes are the traditional accompaniment to sautéed liver and onions (p. 157). They are also quite good with stuffed peppers (p. 154), *prakkes* (p. 152), my bobbe's meat loaf (p. 151), and *gedempte fleisch* (p. 129). This is a versatile as well as tasty side dish.

Milchig Recipe (to serve with dairy meals)

Substitute 2 Tblsp. sweet butter for the onions and *schmaltz*. Replace the potato water with 1/3 cup heavy or whipping cream. Serve these potatoes with sautéed or baked fish dishes. It is a perfect accompaniment to sautéed flounder or sole (p. 83) and my bobbe's baked halibut (p. 84). This also makes an excellent filling for *knishes* (p. 48).

Lagniappe

The term *lagniappe* is French for "a little something more." Creole and Cajun cooks from Louisiana apply this term to giving something extra to their guests when they serve a meal or when they add something extra to a recipe. I offer you the following lagniappe to the *milchig* mashed potato recipe.

My grandmother would make a tasty dish with leftover *milchig* mashed potatoes by adding 1/2 cup dry farmer cottage cheese, 1/3 cup *matzoh* meal, and 2 beaten eggs to 2 cups of leftover potatoes. In sweet butter, she would sauté *latkes* (pancakes) made of this mixture until they were golden brown and then serve this with sour cream as a light lunch or supper. She would use about 1/4 cup of the mixture for each *latke*. The name she gave this dish was "*kichelach*," a generic Yiddish term for "something baked or cooked."

Savory Braised Potatoes with Onions and Herbs
Kartoffel mit Tzibbeles

2 lb. red boiling potatoes, peeled and thinly
    sliced
2 medium-size onions, peeled and chopped
5 Tblsp. peanut or corn oil

2 Tblsp. cold water
salt and black pepper to taste
1/4 cup seasonal herbs (parsley, chives, dill,
**   scallions, or a combination. 2 tsp. dried**
**   fines herbs may be substituted for the fresh**
**   herbs.)**

1. Heat 2 Tblsp. oil in a skillet or sauté pan over medium heat. Sauté the onions until soft and translucent. Remove from the skillet and set aside.

2. Add remaining oil. Heat to medium and add potatoes. Cover the skillet and reduce the heat to the lowest simmer. Simmer until tender (about 30 to 35 minutes).

3. Uncover the skillet and return the onions to the pan. Add the water, raise heat to medium, and continue cooking until potatoes start to turn a golden brown. This will take between 10 and 15 minutes.

4. When potatoes and onions have finished cooking, add herbs, salt, and pepper. Cook 2 minutes more and serve. Recipe serves 6 to 8 people.

Serving Suggestions

This versatile dish goes well with a variety of different dishes. Try it with any of the following:

> *Shabbosdige hendel* (p. 101)
> Stuffed peppers (p. 154)
> My bobbe's meat loaf (p. 151)
> Sweet-and-sour meatballs (p. 154)
> Sautéed flounder or sole (p. 83)
> Grilled salmon steaks (p. 82)
> Grilled or broiled fish (any kind) (p. 81)

Savory Braised Potatoes With Paprika

6 medium-size white baking potatoes, peeled
**   and sliced**
1/3 cup peanut or corn oil
1 1/2 tsp. Hungarian sweet paprika
2 Tblsp. cold water
salt and black pepper to taste

Heat oil over medium heat in a large sauté pan with a tight-fitting lid. Add potatoes, turn to cover with oil, and reduce the heat to its lowest simmer.

Sprinkle the water over the potatoes and cover the pan. Cook 30 to 35 minutes, shaking the pan from time to time. Uncover the pan, sprinkle on the paprika, and turn the potatoes to coat them with it. Raise the heat to medium and sauté, turning constantly until potatoes begin to brown. Sprinkle with salt and pepper and serve immediately.

Serving Suggestions

This dish is very versatile. The potatoes go well with any dish that does not contain a sauce featuring paprika. Try it with *weinerschnitzel* (p. 145), turkey *schnitzel* (p. 117), or *Pesachdige hendel* (p. 102).

Stuffed Baked Potatoes, Two Variations
Gefilte Kartoffel

My Aunt Ann often made these as a main-dish dairy supper with a salad for Thursday nights, when she was busy preparing food for the Sabbath and wanted something light and easy. The potatoes were baked the night before and then stuffed and rebaked on Thursday. This was one of those dishes that evolved into "European" and "American" versions (which were named after the ingredients used in the filling).

6 large, white baking potatoes
one recipe Filling 1 or Filling 2
oil for baking

1. Wash potatoes and rub them all over with oil. Preheat the oven to 350° and bake the potatoes for 1 to 1 1/4 hours, depending on the size of the potatoes. Use a conventional rather than a microwave oven to do this or you will not have a crisp potato skin, an essential feature of this dish.

2. Remove the potatoes from the oven and cool to room temperature. This may be done 1 day in advance of the next steps.

3. When the potatoes have cooled sufficiently, cut them in half and scoop out the insides. Leave the shells with their crisp skins intact.

4. Prepare Filling 1 or Filling 2 and stuff the potato shells with the filling mixture. The filling will mound up in the center rather than sit flat. This is the way it should be.

5. Preheat the oven to 350°. Place the potatoes on a well-greased baking sheet and bake for 20 minutes in the oven until tops of the potatoes are nice and brown. Serve immediately. Recipe serves 6 to 12 people, depending on portion size.

Recipe for Filling 1: European Style

the scooped-out insides of the baked potatoes, as prepared in recipe above
6 Tblsp. sweet butter
1 small onion, peeled and finely chopped
1 tin of sprats or good-quality sardines in oil
2 Tblsp. sour cream or plain yogurt
2 Tblsp. freshly squeezed lemon juice
1/2 cup dry farmer cottage cheese
3 Tblsp. chopped fresh dill leaves
salt and black pepper to taste

1. Melt butter in a skillet over medium heat. Sauté onions until soft and translucent. Remove and pour over potatoes. Mix together thoroughly.

2. Add the remaining ingredients and mix together well. Stuff the filling back into the potatoes and proceed with the stuffed baked potato recipe, step 4.

Recipe for Filling 2: American Style

the scooped-out insides of the baked potatoes, as prepared in recipe above
1 8-oz. can tuna fish, packed in oil
1 small onion, finely chopped
1/2 small green bell pepper, cored, seeded, and finely chopped
1/2 small carrot, peeled and finely diced
1/2 cup freshly shelled or frozen petits pois (thawed)
6 Tblsp. sweet butter
2 Tblsp. sour cream or plain yogurt
1/4 cup chopped fresh parsley
1/4 cup dry farmer cottage cheese
salt, black pepper, and hot Hungarian paprika to taste

1. Melt butter in a skillet over medium heat. Sauté onions until translucent. Add carrots and green pepper and continue cooking, stirring from time to time, until all the vegetables are soft (about 10 to 12 minutes). Add peas and cook 1 minute longer.

2. Remove from heat and pour over potatoes. Add the remaining ingredients and mix together thoroughly. Proceed with baked stuffed potato recipe, step 4.

Serving Suggestions

Stuffed baked potatoes are an entrée, not a side dish. Accompany them with a mixed vegetable salad (p. 220), a field green salad (p. 219), or a Boston lettuce salad (p. 220). They are also good as part of a *milchig* buffet.

Baked Spring Asparagus Spears
Gebakte Sparzesche

This is my favorite way of preparing asparagus. The vegetable retains its crispness while cooking very evenly. It also does not lose as many of its nutrients as when it is boiled. The technique is similar to butter-steaming new potatoes (p. 198) except that the cooking is done inside rather than on top of the oven. The technique can be used with many other kinds of vegetables, but I especially like it with asparagus. The dairy version of this dish is made with butter (which is preferable), and the *pareve* version is made with olive oil.

1 lb. fresh asparagus spears
4 Tblsp. sweet butter or olive oil
salt and black pepper to taste
1 to 2 tsp. freshly squeezed lemon juice

1. Preheat the oven to 350°. Wash the asparagus and remove and discard any hard white- or purple-colored pieces at the stem end.

2. Lay the spears flat into a glass or ceramic baking dish. Top with bits of butter, or dribble oil over the asparagus. Cover the pan tightly with tin foil and bake 25 minutes.

3. Remove from the oven and season with salt, pepper, and the lemon juice before serving. Serves 6 to 8 people as a side dish.

Serving Suggestions

Asparagus is wonderful with fresh fish prepared just about any way other than pickled. It is also delicious with simple roasts of poultry. Try it with *hendel mit marantzen* (p. 103) or with either of the stuffed roast chicken recipes (p. 110 and p. 112).

Sautéed Fresh Carrots and Peas with Chives

Mehren mit Frische Arbess

Carrots and peas were once a very popular vegetable side dish. This combination was so popular, in fact, that in the 1940s, the vegetable canning industry picked up on the trend and produced canned carrots and peas in large quantities. This vegetable became synonymous with cafeteria food and was thus given a bad rap by gourmet cooks. This is unfortunate, because the combination is both colorful and tasty. Properly prepared, sautéed carrots and peas hold up well even under a discerning gourmet's scrutiny. They are the ideal accompaniment to sautéed flounder or sole as well as some other fish entrées. The key to preparing them well is to use fresh carrots and, when you can get them, fresh green peas. Fresh sweet butter should always be used to sauté the vegetables, and freshly snipped chives are an essential herb flavoring. Try cooking carrots and peas this way; I am sure you will enjoy them.

1 lb. fresh carrots, peeled and sliced
3 lb. unshelled fresh green peas, shelled, or one
      16-oz. package frozen petits pois, thawed
5 Tblsp. sweet butter
1/4 cup freshly snipped chives
salt and black pepper to taste

1. Parboil the carrots in salted water for 10 minutes on top of the stove or for 6 minutes in the microwave oven. Drain and rinse with cold water to stop the cooking process.

2. Melt the butter in a skillet or sauté pan over medium heat. Add the carrots and sauté for 5 minutes, turning constantly.

3. Add the peas and cook for an additional 4 to 5 minutes, again stirring constantly.

4. Add the chives and cook 1 minute longer, mixing the herbs in as they cook.

5. Remove the pan from the heat, add salt and pepper to taste, and serve immediately as a vegetable side dish.

Serving Suggestions

Carrots and peas have an affinity for fish. They are the ideal vegetable to accompany sautéed flounder or sole (p. 83). Try them also with my bobbe's baked halibut (p. 84) or with any of the grilled-fish dishes (pp. 81–82).

Honey-Glazed Carrots

Mehren mit Honig

Nor in kholem zeinen mehren grois vi bairen.

Only in a dream are carrots as large as bears.
                                    —Yiddish Saying

1 lb. carrots, peeled and sliced
1 Tblsp. honey
1 Tblsp. potato starch
1 tsp. brown sugar
2 Tblsp. peanut or corn oil

1. Parboil carrots in boiling water to cover for 10 minutes on top of the stove or for 5 minutes in the microwave oven. Drain, reserving 1/2 cup of the cooking liquid.

2. Heat the oil in a skillet or sauté pan and add the carrots. Mix honey, sugar, and potato starch into the carrot cooking liquid and pour this over the carrots. Cook over a low flame until the carrots are glazed and tender (15 to 18 minutes).

Alternatively, this can be done in the microwave oven. Parboil for 7 minutes. Drain, reserving 1/2 cup cooking liquid. Glazed carrots will be ready after 10 minutes of final cooking. Proceed as directed in step 2. Cover when cooking for the first 5 minutes and uncover during the last 5 minutes in the microwave.

Serving Suggestions

This is good with braised and roasted meats. Try it with any of the following:

Baked Lemon Chicken (p. 110)
Roast Chicken with Prunes (p. 109)
Roast Duck with Apples and Pears (p. 121)
Braised Sweet-and-Sour Tongue (p. 163)

Carrot-and-Parsnip Tzimmes

Tzimmes mit Mehren und Pasternakken

My grandmother made this to serve alongside the boiled chicken for the *Erev Yom Kippur* prefast meal. It is a tasty vegetable side dish with many other things as well.

1 lb. carrots, peeled and sliced
1/2 lb. parsnips, peeled and sliced
6 Tblsp. peanut or corn oil
6 Tblsp. honey
1 cup cold water
salt and black pepper to taste

1. Preheat the oven to 350°. Mix the honey, oil, and water in a heavy, deep casserole with a tight-fitting lid. Add the carrots and parsnips and mix well to coat the vegetables.
2. Cover the pot tightly and bake in the oven for 2 hours. Remove, add the salt and pepper, and serve. Serves 6 to 8 people.

Serving Suggestions

My grandmother added only the smallest amount of salt when she served this before Yom Kippur, because she claimed that salt and pepper stimulated the taste buds. The dish, served this way, was rather bland (which was what was intended). Outside of the *Erev* Yom Kippur meal, this dish may be served with just about any roast or braised meat.

Sautéed Mushrooms with Sour Cream

Shvammen mit Smetane

2 lb. fresh white mushrooms, wiped clean and sliced
1 large or two medium-size onions, peeled and chopped
1/2 cup sour cream
4 Tblsp. sweet butter
salt and black pepper to taste

1. Melt the butter in a large skillet over medium heat. Sauté the onions until translucent and soft.
2. Add the mushrooms and continue sautéing until they start to give off liquor.
3. Reduce the heat and add the sour cream. Mix in thoroughly and heat through gently without allowing the mixture to come to a boil; this prevents the cream from curdling.
4. Remove from the heat, add salt and black pepper to taste, and serve immediately. Recipe serves 4 to 6 people.

Serving Suggestions

This vegetable side dish is delicious with fish. Try it with any of the following:

Jewish Sole Meunière (p. 83)
Grilled Salmon Steaks (p. 82)
Sautéed Flounder or Sole (p. 83)
Kulebiaka (p. 95)

Creamy Beets with Dill

Burekehs mit Kropp

2 lb. whole beets
4 Tblsp. sweet butter
1/2 cup sour cream or plain yogurt
1/3 cup fresh dill leaves
salt and black pepper to taste

1. Prepare beets as directed in steps 1 and 2 of the recipe for baked-beet salad (p. 224).

2. Melt butter in a saucepan or sauté pan over medium heat and add the beets. Cook until heated through (about 6 to 8 minutes).

3. Reduce the heat to the lowest simmer and add the sour cream and dill. Stir it in gently and heat it through without allowing the ingredients in the pan to come to a boil. Stir in salt and pepper to taste and serve immediately. Recipe serves 8 to 10 people.

Serving Suggestions

This dish is wonderful with fish, but it should be served alongside dishes that do not have a sour cream-based sauce. Try it with fish *kottletten* (p. 93), grilled salmon steaks (p. 82), grilled fish fillets with lemon (p. 81), or *kulebiaka* (p. 95).

Serving Suggestions

This versatile vegetable goes well with practically any meat dish. I love it with sweet-and-sour meatballs (p. 154), my bobbe's meat loaf (p. 151), and roast veal with caraway seeds (p. 142).

Variation

For a variation on this recipe prepared as Jews from Galitzia and Czechoslovakia used to make it, sauté one medium-size onion in the oil before adding the shredded cabbage. At the same time you add the garlic, add 1 Tblsp. caraway seeds. Proceed with the recipe as indicated above. This variation goes exceptionally well with veal *kottletten* (p. 156), *weinerschnitzel* (p. 145), baked veal chops (p. 143), and braised lamb shoulder with beans, Carpathian style (p. 150).

Sautéed Green Cabbage With Garlic

Greener Kroit mit Knobel

Er iz a g'vir! Er farmogt a gantz keppl kroit!

He's a rich man! He has a whole head of cabbage!
— Yiddish witticism

1 small head green cabbage
2 large cloves garlic, peeled and chopped
4 Tblsp. corn or peanut oil
salt and black pepper to taste

Core and finely shred the cabbage. Heat the oil in a deep, wide sauté pan with a tight-fitting lid over medium heat. Sauté the cabbage, turning constantly with a wooden spoon until the cabbage is well coated with oil. When it just begins to soften, add the garlic. Mix it in well, reduce the heat to the lowest possible simmer, and cover the pan tightly, with foil in between the pan and its lid if necessary. Steam the cabbage aproximately 30 minutes. Lift the cover and stir the cabbage well. Cover again and steam another 15 minutes. The cabbage should be well cooked by this time. Season it with salt and black pepper to taste and serve. Recipe serves 6 to 8 people.

Galitzianer-Style Braised Red Cabbage

Gedempte Roite Kroit (Galitzianer)

1 medium-size head red cabbage, finely shredded
boiling water
3 Tblsp. peanut or corn oil
1 medium-size onion, finely chopped
2 tart green cooking apples, peeled, cored, and cut into small chunks
1 Tblsp. sugar
2 tsp. caraway seeds
1 1/2 tsp. Hungarian sweet paprika
1 tsp. salt

1. Place the shredded cabbage into a large mixing bowl and pour boiling water over it. Drain and dry. This prevents the cabbage from turning blue during cooking. If you don't care about the blue color, you may skip this step.

2. Heat oil in a deep, wide sauté pan over medium heat and sauté the onions until soft and translucent. Add the paprika and caraway seeds, reduce the heat slightly, and cook 5 minutes longer.

3. Add the apples, sugar, and cabbage, and mix together thoroughly. Cover the pan and reduce the heat to simmer. Cook for 1 hour, stirring from time

to time. Add water, if necessary, to keep the cabbage moist. When the cabbage is finished cooking, add the salt. Taste for seasoning and add more, if needed. Recipe serves 6 to 8 people.

Serving Suggestions

Galitzianer-style red cabbage goes well with many different meat dishes. Try it with *weinerschnitzel* (p. 145), turkey *schnitzel* (p. 117), my bobbe's meat loaf (p. 151), or any of the *kottletten*.

Litvishe-Style Braised Red Cabbage

Gedempte Roite Kroit (Litvishe)

1 medium-size head red cabbage, finely shredded
2 large tart green apples, peeled, cored, and cut into small chunks
1 medium-size onion, peeled and finely chopped
1/2 cup red wine
1 1/2 Tblsp. red wine vinegar or cider vinegar
2 Tblsp. brown sugar
4 Tblsp. peanut or corn oil
1 tsp. salt

1. Heat oil in a deep, wide sauté pan over medium heat and sauté the onions until soft and translucent.
2. Add the wine, vinegar, and sugar. Mix well before adding the cabbage and the apples. Stir everything together well and lower heat to simmer. Cover tightly and cook, stirring from time to time, for 1 hour.
3. Add salt, and taste for seasoning. Add more if needed, and serve. Recipe serves 6 to 8 people.

Serving Suggestions

This red cabbage dish goes well with meat dishes of all kinds. Try it with *Pesachdige hendel* (p. 102), braised brisket with carrots (p. 132), braised brisket with *chrain* sauce (p. 129), or any of the *kottletten*.

Oven-Roasted Winter Vegetables

This delicious medley of vegetables is one of my favorites. The roasting brings out the full flavor of every ingredient. Although strictly speaking this is a vegetable side dish, one can easily make a full meal of it by itself when it is accompanied by good home-baked bread and cheese.

4 medium-size white baking potatoes, washed and quartered (they may be left unpeeled or may be peeled, as you prefer)
4 large carrots, peeled and cut into 2-inch pieces, halved if they are especially thick
2 large parsnips, peeled and cut into 2-inch lengths
2 large turnips, peeled and quartered
2 bottoms of celery hearts (2 inches in length), washed, quartered, and cut into 2-inch lengths (save the top part of the celery hearts for another use)
4 medium-size red onions, peeled and quartered
2 or 3 kohlrabi, peeled and quartered
1/2 small head white cabbage, washed, cored, and cut into 2-inch wedges
4 to 6 cloves garlic, peeled and left whole
1/2 cup olive oil
salt and black pepper to taste

Preheat the oven to 350°. Use a deep, wide baking pan large enough to hold everything without the contents' being layered too deeply. Lightly oil the pan and mix all the vegetables together in it. Pour the 1/2 cup olive oil over everything and mix again. Bake in the oven for 1 to 1 1/2 hours, turning the vegetables with a wooden spoon a few times during cooking. Vegetables are done when everything is nicely browned and cooked completely through. Season with salt and pepper before serving. Recipe serves 8 to 10 people as a side dish and 4 to 6 as a full entrée.

Serving Suggestions

This goes well with just about anything but especially with roasted meats.

A market in the main square. Lask, 1937. (Photograph by Roman Vishniac.)

Vegetables Braised in Tomato Sauce

Vegetables braised in tomato sauce were prepared by Hungarian and Romanian Jews to accompany grilled and roasted meats and fish, *mamaliga*, and as a meal on their own to be eaten with crusty bread and cheese. I include recipes for three different kinds of vegetables in tomato sauce—green beans, zucchini, and eggplant. The recipes are essentially the same, with minor variations.

Recipe 1: Green Beans in Tomato Sauce
Fassolyes Paprikash

1 lb. fresh green beans, trimmed and ends
   pinched off
1 small onion, peeled and thinly sliced
1 clove garlic, peeled and chopped
1 tsp. Hungarian sweet paprika
1/4 tsp. Hungarian hot paprika
1 cup fresh tomato sauce (p. 6)
2 Tblsp. olive, corn, or sunflower oil
1/4 cup chopped parsley
salt and black pepper to taste

1. Heat the oil in a sauté pan over medium heat. Sauté the onions until soft and translucent.
2. Add the garlic and the paprikas. Reduce the heat slightly and cook 5 minutes longer.
3. Add the tomato sauce and stir everything together until well blended.
4. Add the green beans and stir into the sauce. Cover the pan and cook for 20 minutes.
5. Stir in the parsley, salt, and pepper, and serve. Recipe serves 6 to 8 people as a side dish and 2 to 4 as an entrée alongside *mamaliga*.

Serving Suggestions

This is delicious alongside *kottletten*, *schnitzel*, or *karnotzl* (p. 156).

Recipe 2: Zucchini in Tomato Sauce
Bastaniklach Paprikash

Substitute 1 lb. zucchini, trimmed and cut into round slices, for the green beans. The rest of the ingredients are the same as in the previous recipe.

1. Heat the oil in a sauté pan over medium-high heat and sauté the zucchini slices, a few at a time, until browned on both sides. Remove to a platter.
2. Reduce the heat to medium and proceed as in the previous recipe, steps 1–3. In step 4, return the zucchini to the sauté pan together with the liquid that has accumulated around it. Complete the recipe as outlined above. Recipe provides the same number of servings as Recipe 1. Follow the serving suggestions given for Recipe 1.

Recipe 3: Eggplant in Tomato Sauce
Sinyas Paprikash

Substitute 1 large eggplant for the green beans or zucchini in the previous recipes. The remaining ingredients are the same, but I recommend using olive oil instead of any other kind. Olive oil marries well with eggplant and brings out its full flavor. Increase the oil to a total of 6 to 8 Tblsp. for this recipe. Also, the parsley is optional.

1. Remove the stem end and tip of the eggplant and cut it into 1/4-inch widthwise slices.
2. Layer the eggplant slices in a colander over the sink, salting each layer with coarse or kosher salt. Place 2 or 3 plates on top of the eggplant and allow it to rest for 1 hour. This salting removes any bitter taste from the eggplant.
3. After 1 hour has passed, rinse off the salt and pat the eggplant slices dry with paper towels.
4. Heat 4 Tblsp. olive oil in the sauté pan over high heat and sauté the eggplant slices a few at a time until they are brown on both sides. Add oil as needed. The high heat will sauté the eggplant quickly and prevent it from absorbing too much oil. Lay the slices on a platter as you finish sautéing them.
5. Proceed with steps 1–3 of Recipe 1, using the eggplant slices in place of the green beans. Return to the pan the sautéed eggplant slices together with the liquid that surrounds them, when you get to step 4 of the Recipe 1 plan. This recipe serves the same number of people as do the other two recipes. Serving suggestions are the same as for green beans or zucchini in tomato sauce.

Lesco

This classic Hungarian vegetable dish is much enjoyed by Hungarian Jews. There are many different versions of *lesco*, but every recipe is centered on roasted bell peppers, whose flavor is predominant. As far as seasons go, it is a late summer/early autumn dish, when many different varieties and colors of bell peppers are available in the market. Vary the recipe by choosing what looks most attractive in the vegetable market whenever you are in the mood to make *lesco*.

6 Tblsp. olive oil
3 large onions, peeled and very thinly sliced
3 large red sweet bell peppers, roasted, seeded,
    cored, and cut into thin strips
2 large green bell peppers, roasted, seeded,
    cored, and cut into thin strips
2 large yellow bell peppers, roasted, seeded,
    cored, and cut into thin strips
1/3 medium-size head of green cabbage, cored
    and very thinly shredded
2 tsp. Hungarian sweet paprika
5 large tomatoes, peeled, seeded, and chopped
    (to do this, first parboil the tomatoes in
    boiling water for 3 to 4 minutes and remove
    from the pot; when cool, the skins should
    peel easily)
1/2 cup fresh tomato sauce (p. 6)
2 cloves garlic, peeled and chopped
1 1/2 Tblsp. red wine vinegar
1/2 tsp. sugar
salt and black pepper to taste

1. Heat oil in a large, deep sauté pan over medium heat. Add the onions and sauté until translucent and soft.

2. Stir in the garlic and the paprika and reduce the heat slightly. Cook 5 minutes, stirring every once in a while.

3. Add cabbage and continue to sauté gently, stirring from time to time to prevent burning and scorching. Cook this mixture for 10 minutes. Try not to let the vegetables brown.

4. Add the pepper strips, the chopped tomatoes, the tomato sauce, the vinegar, and the sugar. Stir everything together and bring to a boil.

5. Cover the pot tightly and reduce the heat to simmer. Simmer for 30 to 35 minutes, stirring the vegetables from time to time.

6. When vegetables are finished cooking, add salt and pepper to taste and serve. *Lesco* can be served hot, warm, or cold. It is even better when reheated. Recipe serves 6 to 8 people.

Serving Suggestions

Lesco is a perfect accompaniment to grilled meats or fish that do not have a sauce. Try it with any of the *kottletten*, with *karnotzl* (p. 156), with any of the *schnitzel* recipes, or with plain grilled steaks.

Wild Mushrooms Braised Like *Lesco*

This dish comes from Bessarabia and is also very popular in Romania. Unlike *lesco*, it is a vegetarian entrée rather than a side dish, and it is made by people in this region during the autumn wild mushroom season. Those of us who have never learned how to identify edible mushrooms in the wild can also enjoy the real flavor of this dish because of the wonderful gourmet fresh mushrooms now available in the supermarket. Although the dish can be made with fresh cultivated white button mushrooms, the earthiness and full-bodied flavor of the finished product will be somewhat lacking. Gourmet fresh mushrooms are so expensive that it pays to treat this dish as an entrée. The somewhat prohibitive cost of the raw materials will make you want to serve these mushrooms only as a once-in-a-while special dinner (which is a nice thing to do often with vegetarian foods).

2 lb. fresh gourmet mushrooms (shiitake,
    oyster, gourmet brown, etc.)
8 Tblsp. olive oil
1 1/2 Tblsp. freshly squeezed lemon juice
1 large onion, peeled and very thinly sliced
1 large sweet red bell pepper, roasted, peeled,
    cored, and cut into thin strips
3 large fresh tomatoes, peeled, seeded, and
    chopped
3 extra-large cloves garlic, peeled and chopped
    or thinly sliced
1 1/2 tsp. Hungarian sweet paprika
1 tsp. fresh thyme (or 1/2 tsp. dried thyme)
1 tsp. fresh marjoram (or 1/2 tsp. dried
    marjoram)

1/2 cup chopped fresh parsley leaves
1 Tblsp. unbleached white flour
3/4 cup dry white wine
salt and black pepper to taste

1. Wipe the mushrooms clean with a damp cloth and slice. Heat 4 Tblsp. oil in a skillet or sauté pan over medium-high heat. Sauté the mushrooms until they are browned. Sprinkle with the lemon juice and set aside.

2. In another sauté pan, heat the remaining oil over medium heat and sauté the onions until they are translucent and soft. Add the garlic and paprika and reduce the heat slightly. Cook another 5 minutes. Reduce the heat to the lowest simmer.

3. Add the flour and, stirring all the while, cook for 10 minutes to remove floury taste.

4. Add the wine, tomato chunks, pepper strips, and remaining herbs to the onion mixture. Cook about 15 minutes or until tomatoes begin to soften, stirring all the while.

5. Add to the onion mixture the mushrooms and all the liquid and oil that has accumulated around them. Cook an additional 15 to 20 minutes, partially covered. Stir the vegetables from time to time.

6. Remove from the heat and add salt and pepper to taste before serving. Serve hot or warm. Recipe serves 4 to 6 as an entrée.

Serving Suggestions

Serve the mushrooms alongside a hot *mamaliga* (p. 186), which is the traditional way the dish is served. Precede or follow the entrée with a field green salad (p. 214) or a green bean salad (p. 222). Drink a crisp white wine with the entrée. A chenin blanc or a sauvignon blanc is an excellent choice. This dish may also be served as a side dish to good-quality grilled steaks, in which case the recipe will serve 6 to 8 people.

A New Style of Sweet Potatoes

Sweet potatoes have never been one of my favorite vegetables, especially when they are cooked into a mush and slathered with some kind of sickeningly sweet sauce that contains canned pineapple (or worse, marshmallows and maraschino cherries). Despite this prejudice, I have learned to appreciate a plain baked sweet potato served with nothing other than a little sweet butter and a little salt. Because sweet potatoes are synonymous in many people's minds with Thanksgiving, I created two dishes myself, which offer a simple, tasty sweet potato side dish for this holiday. The recipes are presented in both *milchig* and *pareve* versions so that they can be used in any kosher home. Both of them should be made with the smallest sweet potatoes.

Recipe 1: Sautéed Whole Sweet Potatoes

6 to 8 small sweet potatoes
4 Tblsp. unbleached white flour
6 to 8 Tblsp. corn oil or 3 to 4 Tblsp. corn oil
    mixed with 3 to 4 Tblsp. sweet butter
salt to taste

1. Preheat the oven to 350°. Bake the sweet potatoes in their shells for 1 hour. Remove them from the oven and cool them to room temperature. Up to this point, the sweet potatoes can be prepared in advance, even a day ahead. The next step is even easier if the sweet potatoes have been refrigerated for a day.

2. When the potatoes are completely cool, gently cut a slit lengthwise across the skin of each potato. The skin will peel off easily, leaving the whole potato intact in one piece. You must use a gentle touch when doing this, however, and not push your finger into the potato, or it could fall apart.

3. Have the flour spread out on a large plate next to where you are working. Gently slide the potato into the flour. Roll it gently to coat it lightly, and then roll it gently over to this side of the plate while you repeat this procedure with the other potatoes.

4. In a skillet over high heat, heat the oil or the oil mixed with butter. When the oil is hot and sizzling, slide the potatoes, one at a time, into the pan. Sauté 2 to 3 minutes on each side. The potatoes will develop a crisp brown crust.

5. Remove from the skillet with a slotted spatula or spoon, and drain on paper towels. Sprinkle with salt before serving. Recipe serves 6 to 8, depending on how many potatoes you have made.

Recipe 2: Caramelized Sweet Potatoes

6 to 8 small sweet potatoes
4 Tblsp. unbleached white flour
6 to 8 Tblsp. sweet butter or corn oil plus 4
    Tblsp. melted sweet butter or oil for the
    caramelizing
1/2 cup sugar

1. Bake and prepare the sweet potatoes as directed in steps 1–5 in the previous recipe, but do not sprinkle the potatoes with salt.

2. In a heavy skillet or sauté pan, melt the sugar over low heat. Cook about 6 to 7 minutes or until it begins to caramelize and turn a nice golden brown color. Stir constantly with a wooden spoon and watch the sugar carefully while doing this. The sugar colors quickly once it caramelizes and can burn if left to cook too long. It also should not be too dark or the flavor will be a little bitter.

3. When the sugar has caramelized, stir in the 4 Tblsp. melted butter or oil. When this is well mixed, add the potatoes, one at a time. Do not crowd them. Shake the pan vigorously to turn the potatoes and caramelize them on all sides. Turn over one time with a slotted spoon. Remove the potatoes and serve immediately. Recipe serves 6 to 8 people.

Serving Suggestions

Both of these sweet potato dishes are a wonderful accompaniment to any roast, particularly turkey.

Wine-Braised Sauerkraut

Gedempte Zoyereh Kroit Mit Wein

Sauerkraut (fermented cabbage) is a tasty vegetable side dish. It goes well with any kind of *kottletten*, dry roasted meats, and of course, its traditional culinary partner, charcuterie meats. I love eating sauerkraut with beef *kottletten*, *karnotzl*, and those wonderful butcher-made kosher sausages called *knockwurst*. Although sauerkraut is usually thought of as a German food, it is popular all over central and eastern Europe. A recipe for homemade sauerkraut is given

in chapter 13. The following one is for braising sauerkraut that has already been fermented. The homemade sauerkraut and this recipe for braised sauerkraut come from Galitzia, where there was some German influence on the cooking.

2 lb. fresh sauerkraut, homemade or
    store-bought (good, fresh sauerkraut is sold
    in most supermarkets in the dairy or deli
    section; do not substitute the kind that
    comes in jars or cans, which already has
    some of the "bite" taken out of it)
4 Tblsp. corn or peanut oil
3 cloves garlic, peeled and left whole
10 juniper berries, crushed
freshly ground black pepper to taste
1 bouquet garni, made with 1 bay leaf, 5 sprigs
    parsley, and 4 sprigs fresh thyme (1/2 tsp.
    dried thyme may be substituted)
3 to 4 cups white wine

1. Rinse the sauerkraut well in a colander under cold running water, tossing it with your hands to make sure that all of it gets well rinsed. This needs to be done with fresh sauerkraut (homemade as well as store-bought) to rid it of the excess salt that is left on it from the time when it was fermented.

2. Oil a casserole with 1 Tblsp. of the oil. Layer a third of the sauerkraut into the casserole. Cover it with 3 or 4 juniper berries and 1 clove garlic. Grind a little black pepper over it. Repeat this until all the ingredients are used up, finishing with a layer of sauerkraut. Insert the bouquet garni in the second layer. Grind pepper all over the top layer of sauerkraut.

3. Pour the wine over the sauerkraut. The liquid should come up to the top layer of cabbage. If it does not, add a little more wine.

4. Cover the pot tightly and bring it to a boil on top of the stove. Then reduce the heat to the lowest possible simmer. Braise the sauerkraut at least 2 hours. It can cook longer than this, and the longer it cooks, the better it tastes, so don't worry about overcooking it. Recipe serves 8 to 10 people.

Serving Suggestions

You will develop a new respect for sauerkraut after you serve it this way with *kottletten* or roasted meats and sausages. Warmed corned beef or pastrami is simply delicious with sauerkraut, rye bread, and good-quality mustard. Braised sauerkraut is sensational with baked veal chops (p. 143) too. When you serve it with a variety of smoked and cured meat, accompany the meal with plenty of rye and pumpernickel bread, kosher dill pickles, all kinds of mustards, and if you like, even boiled potatoes. Drink seltzer or beer with the meal.

Latkes

Latkes is the Yiddish word for "pancakes." All *latkes*, but potato *latkes* in particular, are foods that have given generations of Jewish children happy memories. Practically all Jewish adults remember with nostalgia the *latkes* made by their mother or their grandmother or a favorite aunt (in some cases, an uncle). *Latkes* are real homey fare—the kind of food that provides comfort at the end of a long, hard day. *Latkes* are what you make for that "special breakfast" when you are not in a hurry (or for that dinner when you are!). *Latkes* in my childhood home were sometimes even eaten as a spur-of-the-moment snack. *Latkes* of some kind were often on the menu when my grandmother cooked on Thursday nights. "I have to cook for *Shabbos*," she would say, "and anyway, *latkes* are easy to make. And they are fast. And everybody likes them. And everybody wants them. [And so did she.] So don't tell me what you want for supper. I already know." Yes, all this was true. Or so she said. . . .

Because *latkes* are always sautéed in oil, they are customarily served during Chanukah. Jews eat foods cooked in oil during this holiday to celebrate the miracle that occurred in the Hebrew Temple in Jerusalem in 165 B.C.E., when the Maccabbean army recaptured the Temple from the Syrian Greeks and rededicated it to the God of Israel. A single cruse of pure olive oil, which was used to keep the Eternal Light (*Ner Tamid*) burning continuously, lasted 8 days when it should have lasted only 1. Therefore Jews celebrate Chanukah and eat foods cooked in oil to remind them of this miracle.

There are 6 *latke* recipes in this section of the book. All were a part of the cuisine of the Jews of eastern Europe. Those that are modern American inventions (like zucchini *latkes*, for example) were never a part of Yiddish cuisine, so I decided not to include any of them here.

Chanukah Potato *Latkes*

4 large white baking potatoes, peeled and cut
  into chunks
2 medium-size onions, peeled and cut into
  chunks
2 large eggs, beaten
1/3 cup *matzoh* meal
salt and black pepper to taste
corn or peanut oil for sautéing

1. Grate the onions finely, either by hand or using the food processor in a pulse/chop motion. The onions can also be grated using the fine blade of a meat grinder.

2. Grate the potatoes the same way and add them to the onions.

3. Drain carefully in a colander to remove excess moisture but not any of the pulp, and transfer the vegetables to a mixing bowl.

4. Add the *matzoh* meal, beaten eggs, and seasonings. Mix together well until thoroughly blended.

5. In a 9- or 12-inch skillet, heat 6 Tblsp. oil over high heat until sizzling but not smoking. Add 1/4 cup of the batter. It will spread naturally into a small patty. Repeat this three or four more times until you have 4 or 5 *latkes* sizzling in the skillet. Do not crowd the *latkes*. You will be able to make 4 or 5 at the most at a given time. If you have more than one skillet, you can keep 3 or 4 going at once and, in this way, make 12 to 15 at one time.

6. Regulate the heat carefully to prevent the *latkes* from burning as you cook them. Sauté each *latke* at least 3 or 4 minutes before turning it over with a spatula. Sauté the same amount of time on the second side. *Latkes* are through cooking when they are golden brown in color and crisp around the edges.

7. Keep up the same procedure until you have used up all the *latke* batter. To keep it well mixed and free of discoloration stir the batter from time to time as it waits.

8. Have your oven heated to a low temperature (about 175°) to keep the *latkes* warm while you are cooking. The microwave oven also does a good job keeping the *latkes* warm. Drain them on paper towels after they are sautéed, and place them on a baking sheet or platter for keeping warm.

9. This recipe makes between 16 and 20 *latkes*. Serve them as soon as you have finished cooking

them. Make more than you think you will need. Your guests will never be able to eat enough of them, no matter how many you make!

Serving Suggestions

The classical accompaniment to potato *latkes* is sour cream and for some people, applesauce. They may be served as the main entrée of a vegetarian meal or as a *forspeis*, a vegetable side dish, or a snack. If you do not serve them with sour cream, they are *pareve* and can be eaten alongside a meat entrée. Serve at least 6 to 8 *latkes* per person as an entrée, 2 or 3 as a *forspeis*, and 1 or 2 as a side dish with meat. Potato *latkes* may also be part of a vegetarian *latke* medley (see menu, p. 215). This is one of the tastiest vegetarian entrées ever created. Don't forget—potato *latkes* are habit forming, just like French fries and potato chips. Only they taste so much better! If you are indulging in potato *latkes* as a snack, go ahead and enjoy yourself! Eat as many as you want! You only live once!

Bialystock-Style Potato *Latkes*

Bialystoker Latkes

This recipe for potato *latkes*, which comes from the Bialystok area, is rather unusual. I love this dish, although I know that for some people a combination of raisins, potatoes, onions, and cinnamon-sugar is an acquired taste.

4 large white baking potatoes, peeled and cut into chunks
2 medium-size onions, peeled and cut into chunks
1/4 cup dark raisins
1/3 cup unbleached white flour
2 large eggs, beaten
salt and black pepper to taste
1/2 cup sugar mixed with 1 tsp. cinnamon

1. Prepare the *latke* batter exactly as you would for regular potato *latkes* (see directions, steps 1–4 of the previous recipe). Mix the raisins into the batter during step 4. Do not mix the cinnamon-sugar mixture into the batter. It will be used later in a different way.

2. Sauté the *latkes* according to the instructions given in steps 5–7 of the previous recipe.

3. Spread the cinnamon-sugar mixture on a flat plate. Just before you serve the *latkes*, dip them into the cinnamon-sugar mixture on both sides and serve them piping hot with sour cream and, if you wish, applesauce.

Serving Suggestions

These *latkes* may be served as an entrée, a *forspeis*, or a snack. I like them on their own rather than as part of a *latke* medley because their taste is so unusual. I encourage you to try to make this at least once. Don't be put off by the strange combination of flavors. These *latkes* are quite delicious.

Golden Carrot *Latkes*

Mehren Latkes

4 large carrots, peeled and cut into chunks
1 medium-size baking potato, peeled and cut into chunks
1 medium-size onion, peeled and cut into chunks
3 large eggs, beaten
1/3 cup *matzoh* meal
1 pinch freshly grated nutmeg
salt and black pepper to taste
corn or peanut oil for sautéing

1. Finely grate the onion and carrots by hand or in a food processor using a pulse/chop motion. They may also be grated in a meat grinder using the fine blade.

2. Grate the potatoes the same way you have grated the carrots and the onion. Drain the vegetables carefully in a colander to remove excess moisture but none of the pulp, and place them in a mixing bowl.

3. Add all the remaining ingredients and mix together well. If mixture seems too liquid, add 1 or 2 additional Tblsp. of *matzoh* meal.

4. Heat 6 Tblsp. oil in a 9- or 12-inch skillet over high heat until it is sizzling but not smoking. Spoon 1/4 cup of the batter into the skillet. Repeat this 3 or 4 times until you have 4 or 5 *latkes* cooking. Do not crowd the *latkes*. Cook them about 4 minutes on

each side. The *latkes* are ready when they are golden brown on both sides and the edges are crisp. Add oil as needed for sautéing. Drain the *latkes* on paper towels and keep warm in a 175° oven or in the microwave until you have finished cooking. Recipe makes 16 to 20 *latkes*.

Serving Suggestions

Carrot *latkes* may be served as an entrée, a side dish, or as part of a *latke* medley (see menu, p. 215). Serve them with sour cream.

Springtime Spinach *Latkes*

Shpinatz Latkes

2 1/2 lb. fresh spinach
2 large eggs, beaten
1/3 cup unbleached white flour plus more if
    needed
salt and black pepper to taste
corn or peanut oil for sautéing

1. Wash spinach carefully and place in a deep stockpot. Over medium heat until the leaves wilt, cook spinach in the pot with only the water that clings to it. Drain the spinach in a colander and pour cold water over it to stop the cooking process. This keeps the spinach a beautiful bright green color. Drain the spinach and completely dry it.

2. Chop spinach in the food processor using a pulse/chop motion or by hand, and transfer it to a mixing bowl.

3. Mix in all the remaining ingredients, using only 1/3 cup of the flour. If the mixture seems too watery, add a little more flour to the batter by the tablespoonful until the correct consistency is achieved.

4. Heat 6 Tblsp. oil in a 9- or 12-inch skillet over high heat until the oil is sizzling but not smoking. Spoon 1/4 cup of the batter into the oil. Repeat this 3 or 4 times until you have 4 or 5 *latkes* cooking at the same time. Cook about 3 minutes on each side. *Latkes* are golden brown in color and have crisp edges when they are done. Drain on paper towels and keep warm in a 175° oven until you finish cooking the entire amount of batter. Recipe makes 16 to 20 *latkes*.

Serving Suggestions

Spinach *latkes* are served as an entrée, a *forspeis*, or as part of a *latke* medley (see menu, p. 215). Serve with sour cream or fresh lemon wedges.

Zippy Cauliflower *Latkes*

Bloimenkroit Latkes

1 large head cauliflower
1 medium-size onion, peeled and finely
    chopped
1/3 cup *matzoh* meal
2 large eggs, beaten
salt and black pepper to taste
corn or peanut oil for sautéing
hot paprika for sprinkling

1. Break the cauliflower into florets and cut the stems into small chunks. Cook in boiling salted water for 15 minutes on top of the stove or for 7 to 8 minutes in the microwave oven. Cauliflower should be soft and completely cooked through but not mushy. Drain and plunge into cold water to stop cooking. Drain and dry the cauliflower.

2. Process the cauliflower into a coarse puree in the food processor or mash it by hand with a potato masher. Transfer it to a mixing bowl.

3. Heat 2 Tblsp. oil in a small skillet and sauté the onions until soft and translucent. Add this to the cauliflower and cool to room temperature.

4. Add the remaining ingredients (except for the hot paprika) to the cauliflower mixture and mix together well. If the batter seems too liquid, add *matzoh* meal by the tablespoonful to achieve the correct consistency.

5. Heat 6 Tblsp. oil in a 9- or 12-inch skillet over high heat until it is sizzling but not smoking. Spoon 1/4 cup of the batter into the oil. Repeat 3 or 4 times until you have 4 or 5 *latkes* cooking in the skillet. Sauté 3 to 4 minutes on each side. *Latkes* are done when they are golden brown on both sides and the edges are crisp. Add oil as needed for sautéing. Drain *latkes* on paper towels and keep warm in a 175° oven or in the microwave until you have completed using up all the batter. Recipe makes 16 to 20 *latkes*. Sprinkle with hot paprika before serving and serve with sour cream.

Serving Suggestions

Cauliflower *latkes* can be served as an entrée, a *forspeis*, or as part of a *latke* medley (see menu, p.   ).

New York-Style Mixed Vegetable *Latkes*

This recipe was created to use up bits and pieces of leftover vegetables. It has become a popular dish in Jewish dairy restaurants, where it is never thought of in this way.

1/2 lb. fresh mushrooms, wiped clean with a
    damp cloth or paper towel and chopped fine
1 "smallish" medium-size onion, peeled and
    finely chopped
1 large stalk celery, finely chopped
1 very large carrot, peeled and finely grated
1/2 cup fresh green peas or frozen petits pois
2 large eggs, beaten
1/3 cup unbleached white flour
1/4 cup fresh dill leaves, chopped
1/4 cup fresh parsley leaves, chopped
1/4 tsp. Hungarian hot paprika
salt and black pepper to taste
corn or peanut oil for sautéing

1. Heat 1/4 cup oil in a skillet over medium heat. Sauté onions until soft and translucent.

2. Add the mushrooms and celery and continue sautéing until the mushrooms start to give off liquor and the celery begins to soften. Transfer to a mixing bowl and cool to room temperature.

3. Add the rest of the ingredients, except the oil for sautéing, and mix together thoroughly. If the mixture appears too watery, add more flour by the tablespoonful until the correct consistency is achieved.

4. Heat 6 Tblsp. oil in a 9- or 12-inch skillet over medium-high heat until it is sizzling but not smoking. Add 1/4 cup of the batter to the skillet and press it gently with the bottom of a spoon to flatten it into a patty. You may sauté 4 or 5 *latkes*, depending on the size. Sauté 3 to 4 minutes on each side, turning once. *Latkes* are done when they are crisp and golden brown. Drain on paper towels and keep warm in a 175° oven or in the microwave. Stir the batter each time you scoop up some of it to make a *latke*. Add more oil as needed while sautéing. Recipe makes 16 to 18 *latkes*.

Serving Suggestions

Serve these *latkes* with sour cream. They can be a *forspeis*, a vegetarian entrée, or a part of a *latke* medley (see menu, p. 215).

Chanukah Latke Dinner

Creamy wild mushroom soup

Medley of three kinds of *latkes*:

Chanukah potato *latkes*

Golden carrot *latkes*

Zippy cauliflower *latkes*

with sour cream

Chardonnay

Baked apples

American-style cheesecake

Coffee or tea

10

Salads

Tzallaten

If the stomach is empty,
the brain is also empty.

*Az der maigener iz leidik,
iz der moich oich leidik.*

Salads

Tzallaten

It is a common misconception that classical Jewish cuisine does not contain salads. There is only a qualified grain of truth to this. Classical eastern and central European cuisines do not contain recipes for salads made with lettuce. The late Dr. Lucy Dawidowicz, eminent scholar of the Holocaust and author of *The War Against the Jews*, tells the following story about the year she spent in Vilna in 1938 as a research *aspirantur* (research assistant) for the YIVO Institute for Jewish Research:

> We arrived at a large wooden house, surrounded by trees. Waiting on the wide porch to greet us stood Stefania Szabad, a woman about sixty. . . . As we walked up the porch, Stefania immediately introduced herself to me, offered us a cool drink, and presented me to her guests. . . . Minutes later Stefania began questioning me about America, particularly about the foods Americans ate. "They eat lettuce, I hear," she said. I confirmed that it was true. Though she grew lettuce on her farm, she was still skeptical. "Let's see if you're a real American," she challenged me. She soon brought a large plate filled with freshly washed lettuce. "Eat," she commanded. In awe of this formidable woman, I timidly protested, saying I wasn't hungry. But she put me to the test. Everyone watched me, as I set to, attacking the lettuce as if I were a knight defending holy truth. I speared the greens on my fork, chewing, crunching, fiercely determined to prove that I was a true-blue American. I realized I must look comical but I was too intimidated to dare mock Stefania Szabad's peremptory command. Between swallows I ventured to suggest that we never ate such huge quantities of lettuce; besides, it was usually served with salad dressing to make it tastier. But to no avail. . . .

> *From That Place and Time*
> Lucy Dawidowicz

Although classical Yiddish cuisine did not contain any recipes for salads made with lettuce (as this delightful anecdote helps to prove), many other kinds of vegetables were used in salads. The list includes cucumbers, onions, scallions, cabbage, carrots, beets, radishes, and, especially in Romania, bell peppers and eggplant. This chapter offers recipes for all the salads of classical Yiddish cuisine as well as three of my own recipes for lettuce-based salads whose flavors go well with Jewish foods. I also include recipes for several vinaigrette-type salad dressings, some of which were commonly used by eastern and central European Jewish cooks.

Tossed Field Green Salad

6 to 8 leaves each of the following lettuces: romaine, endive, escarole, chicory, Boston
white part of 1 leek, carefully washed and very thinly sliced
1 recipe vinaigrette (your choice)

1. Carefully wash and dry all the lettuce leaves and tear them by hand into small, bite-size pieces. Place them into a deep mixing bowl. Cover with plastic wrap and keep chilled in the refrigerator until 30 minutes before serving. This ensures that the lettuce will remain crisp until it is ready to be eaten.

2. Place the thinly sliced leek into a separate covered container and keep it in the refrigerator as well until 30 minutes before serving.

3. Thirty minutes before you are ready to serve salad, remove the ingredients from the refrigerator. Salads taste best when they are cooler than room temperature but not too chilled, as chilling inhibits their flavor.

4. When ready to serve the salad, add the leeks to the salad bowl. Add whatever vinaigrette you choose. Toss the salad and serve it immediately. Recipe serves 6 to 8 people.

Tossed green salad goes well with any of the following vinaigrette dressings:

Basic vinaigrette (p. 221)
Fresh herb vinaigrette (p. 221)
Dried herb vinaigrette (p. 222)
Egg vinaigrette (p. 222)
Paprika vinaigrette (p. 222)

Serving Suggestions

This salad goes well as part of a meal featuring a savory meat course. (It does not go well with any of the sweet or sweet-and-sour meat entrées like *essig fleisch* or *flommen tzimmes*.)

Boston Lettuce Salad

1 large head Boston lettuce
1/2 small English cucumber or 2 large pickling
    cucumbers
1 cup watercress
1 very small or 1/2 small sweet red onion
1 recipe vinaigrette (your choice)

1. Wash and completely dry the lettuce and tear it into small, bite-size pieces. Place into a deep mixing bowl.

2. Slice the cucumber into very thin (almost paper-thin) slices and add this to the lettuce.

3. Wash and dry the watercress and break it into bite-size pieces. Add it to the lettuce and the cucumber.

4. Cover the vegetables in the mixing bowl with plastic wrap and refrigerate until 30 minutes before ready to serve.

5. Slice the onion into paper-thin slices and place it into a tightly covered container. Refrigerate this as well until 30 minutes before serving.

6. Thirty minutes before serving the salad, remove all the vegetables from the refrigerator. Remember that salad tastes best slightly lower than room temperature but not too chilled. Pour the vinaigrette over the vegetables, toss, and serve immediately. Recipe serves 6 to 8 people.

Boston lettuce salad goes well with any of the following vinaigrettes:

Honey/mustard vinaigrette (p. 222)
Poppy seed vinaigrette (p. 222)
Sour cream vinaigrette (p. 222)

Serving Suggestions

This salad goes very well with a meal featuring sweet or sweet-and-sour meat dishes. When using the sour cream vinaigrette, serve this salad before or after a fish entrée.

Mixed Vegetable Salad

A mixed vegetable salad is composed of many different kinds of vegetables. Its ingredients are flexible and some of its components will vary depending upon the season of the year. Mixed vegetable salads may be dressed with any kind of vinaigrette you like.

All of the vinaigrettes in this book go well with a mixed vegetable salad.

The art of making this salad is to ensure that no one vegetable dominates it and that there are an interesting variety of colors and textures. You should not be able to taste the entire salad by tasting just one mouthful of it; on the contrary, each mouthful of salad should yield new and varied taste experiences.

lettuces: 10 to 12 leaves of two different kinds
    of lettuce; make sure that one variety is
    strong tasting and the other is mild; romaine
    and Boston make a good combination
red color vegetables: 2 medium-size fresh
    tomatoes (late spring to early autumn), or 2
    medium-size sweet red bell peppers (late
    summer to early winter), or 2 medium-size
    carrots or beets, baked and peeled (winter
    until late spring)
onions: 1 leek (white part only), or 3 small
    scallions, or 1 very small sweet red onion
other vegetables (choose any two or three of
    the following):
    1 cup green beans, parboiled but still crisp
    1 cup broccoli florets, parboiled but still
        crisp
    1 cup cauliflower florets, parboiled but still
        crisp
    1 medium-size green or yellow bell pepper
    1 very small English cucumber
    2 pickling cucumbers
    6 to 8 leaves fresh spinach
    1 small zucchini, parboiled but still crisp

1. Wash and dry lettuce (and spinach, if using) and tear into small, bite-size pieces. Place into a deep mixing bowl.

2. Cut the remaining vegetables into bite-size pieces, except for the onions and tomatoes (if using), and add to the greens. Cucumbers should be cut very thin. Carrots and zucchini may be shredded instead of sliced.

3. Cover the vegetables in the mixing bowl with plastic wrap and refrigerate until 30 minutes before serving.

4. If using tomatoes in the salad, do not refrigerate them. Their full flavor is enjoyed best at room temperature. Slice them into the salad just before you toss it and serve it.

5. Slice whatever onions you have chosen and refrigerate them in a separate covered container until 30 minutes before serving.

6. Thirty minutes before you are ready to serve the salad, remove the vegetables from the refrigerator. Pour over 1 portion of the vinaigrette you have chosen and toss. Serve the salad immediately. Recipe serves 6 to 8 people.

The following combinations of vegetables are recommended for their compatible flavors, colors, and textures. You may vary these combinations in any way you choose, but *do not combine carrots and cucumbers in the same salad*, as their flavors are incompatible.

Spring Mixed Vegetable Combination

romaine and Boston lettuce (6 leaves each)
spinach (6 to 8 leaves)
1 small red onion, sliced paper thin
1 small yellow crookneck squash, parboiled
    and sliced very thin
2 medium-size carrots, peeled and shredded
    with the julienne blade of your food
    processor
1 cup green beans, parboiled but left crisp
1 recipe fresh herb vinaigrette

Summer Mixed Vegetable Combination

chicory and Boston lettuce (6 leaves each)
3 scallions, sliced very thin
3 medium-size fresh tomatoes
1 small English cucumber, sliced paper thin
1 medium-size yellow bell pepper
1 recipe dried herb vinaigrette

Autumn Mixed Vegetable Salad

romaine and Boston lettuce (6 leaves each)
2 medium-size fresh tomatoes
1 medium-size red bell pepper
1 small zucchini, parboiled and thinly sliced
1 cup green beans, parboiled but still crisp
1 recipe paprika vinaigrette

Winter Mixed Vegetable Salad

romaine and Boston lettuce (6 leaves each)
1 leek (white only), very thinly sliced
2 medium-size beets, baked and peeled
1 cup cauliflower florets, parboiled but still
    crisp
1 cup broccoli florets, parboiled but still crisp
1 recipe egg vinaigrette

Variation

You can make a light full-course meal out of any mixed vegetable salad by adding bits of leftover cooked chicken, beef, or fish, or very thin pieces of dry kosher salami to the vegetable mixture.

Eight Varieties of Vinaigrette

Vinaigrette means "salad dressing," and each of the recipes below is for a different kind of homemade salad dressing. There is no reason in the world to ever have to use bottled salad dressings, which are loaded with chemical additives and, in some cases, not the best-quality ingredients. And your own vinaigrettes are so simple to make! After you get used to eating salad made with your own homemade vinaigrette, I am sure you will never again want to use any kind of processed bottled salad dressing. Vary your vinaigrette every time you make a salad, and enjoy something different each time you eat one.

Basic Vinaigrette

1/3 cup freshly squeezed lemon juice or wine
    vinegar
2/3 cup extra-virgin olive oil
salt and freshly ground black pepper to taste

Shake these ingredients together in a glass jar and pour over salad before tossing.

Fresh Herb Vinaigrette

1/3 cup freshly squeezed lemon juice
2/3 cup extra-virgin olive oil
1 small clove garlic, peeled and crushed in a
    mortar with 1/2 tsp. salt
1/8 tsp. Dijon mustard
1/4 cup chopped fresh dill leaves
1/4 cup chopped fresh parsley leaves
2 Tblsp. freshly snipped chives
freshly ground black pepper to taste

Combine everything in a glass jar and shake vigorously before pouring over salad.

Dried Herb Vinaigrette

1/3 cup red wine vinegar
2/3 cup extra-virgin olive oil
1 large clove garlic, crushed in a mortar with
    1/2 tsp. salt
1/4 tsp. Dijon mustard
2 tsp. good-quality dried fines herbes
1/8 tsp. sugar
freshly ground black pepper to taste

Combine everything in a glass jar and shake vigorously before pouring over salad.

Paprika Vinaigrette

1/3 cup red wine vinegar
2/3 cup olive oil
1/4 tsp. sugar
1 tsp. Hungarian hot paprika
1/2 tsp. Dijon mustard
1 shake cayenne pepper
salt and freshly ground black pepper to taste

Combine everything together in a glass jar and shake vigorously before pouring over salad.

Honey-Mustard Vinaigrette

1/3 cup freshly squeezed lemon juice
1 Tblsp. honey
1/2 tsp. Dijon mustard
2/3 cup olive oil
salt to taste

Combine everything in a glass jar and shake vigorously before pouring over salad. If honey does not dissolve completely, stir with a spoon to dissolve it and then shake the dressing again.

Egg Vinaigrette

In this day and age when some parts of the country have experienced salmonella contamination from raw eggs, it makes me sad to think that this wonderful vinaigrette cannot be enjoyed without worry. I include the recipe in this book anyhow in the hope that eventually a method will be found to ensure that all raw eggs that are purchased in the average supermarket are free of salmonella contamination.

1/3 cup freshly squeezed lemon juice
1/4 tsp. Dijon mustard
1 raw egg yolk
2/3 cup extra-virgin olive oil
salt and freshly ground black pepper to taste

Combine everything in a glass jar and shake vigorously before pouring over salad.

Poppy Seed Vinaigrette

1/3 cup freshly squeezed lemon juice
1 Tblsp. honey
1/4 tsp. Dijon mustard
1 Tblsp. poppy seeds
1/3 cup olive oil
salt to taste

Combine honey, mustard, and lemon juice in a glass jar. Stir with a spoon until honey is dissolved. Add remaining ingredients and shake vigorously before pouring over salad.

Sour Cream or Yogurt Vinaigrette

1/3 cup freshly squeezed lemon juice
1/4 cup sour cream or plain yogurt
1/2 tsp. sugar
1 Tblsp. freshly snipped chives
1/2 cup olive oil
salt to taste

Combine everything in a glass jar and shake vigorously before pouring over salad.

Savory Green Bean Salad

Fassolyes Tzallat

1 lb. fresh green beans, parboiled but left crisp,
    dried, and cut into 1-inch lengths
1/2 head romaine lettuce
4 scallions, very thinly sliced
1 recipe dried herb vinaigrette (p. 222)

1. Wash and dry the lettuce and tear it by hand into small, bite-size pieces. Place it into a deep mixing bowl. Add the green beans and toss by hand. Cover with plastic wrap and refrigerate until 30 minutes before serving.

2. Wash and slice the scallions and place them into a separate covered container; refrigerate until 30 minutes before serving.

Thirty minutes before ready to serve the salad, combine everything and toss with the vinaigrette. Serve immediately. Recipe serves 6 to 8 people.

Serving Suggestions

This is one of the tastiest and most versatile of all salads. It goes well with practically everything except sweet or sweet-and-sour dishes. You may serve a green bean salad before or after sweet-and-sour entrées as well, but substitute for the scallions 1 very small sweet red onion sliced paper thin, and substitute for the dried herb vinaigrette a honey-mustard or poppy seed vinaigrette.

Hungarian Summer Salad

Ungarische Tzallat

3 medium-size fresh ripe tomatoes, at room temperature
1 medium-size English cucumber (or substitute 3 pickling cucumbers)
2 medium-size green peppers
1 small sweet red onion
1 recipe paprika vinaigrette (p. 222)

1. Roast the peppers on the outdoor grill or broil them in the oven until they blacken on all sides. Turn them every 2 to 3 minutes while they are roasting.

2. Wrap the peppers in a kitchen cloth or place them into a paper bag, folded tightly to keep in the air. When the peppers are cool, peel them, remove the core and seeds, and cut them into 1-inch pieces.

3. Wash and dry the cucumber and slice it paper-thin into rounds.

4. Peel and slice the onion into paper-thin rings. Separate the rings from one another.

5. Cut the tomatoes into 1-inch pieces.

6. Combine everything in a large mixing bowl and pour the vinaigrette over the vegetables. Toss and serve immediately. Recipe serves 6 to 8 people.

Serving Suggestions

This delicious summer salad is at its best served alongside grilled meats or fish. Try it with Romanian-style grilled Cornish hens (p. 116), *karnotzl* (p. 156), grilled whole trout (p. 82), or plain grilled steaks and hamburgers. It is also good with *schnitzel* or *kottletten*. The salad can be made in advance and kept in the refrigerator with no danger of the vegetables' wilting. I think it tastes best when it is freshly made, but it is equally acceptable served after a few hours or even a day or two in the refrigerator.

Baltic-Style Cucumber Salad With Dill

Marinirte Oogerkes mit Kropp

This salad was very popular in all the Baltic states and probably is Scandinavian rather than Russian in origin. Like *oogerkes mit smetana* (p. 224), it is a traditional accompaniment to smoked fish.

2 large English cucumbers (do not substitute any other kind)
3 Tblsp. coarse or kosher salt
3/4 cup white wine or cider vinegar
1 Tblsp. sugar
1/3 cup chopped fresh dill leaves

1. Slice the cucumbers into paper-thin rounds. Place them into a colander over the sink and sprinkle with the coarse salt. Mix the cucumber slices gently with your hands to make sure that they are all well coated with the salt. Put a few plates on top of the cucumbers to weight them down, and allow them to rest for 2 hours.

2. After 2 hours have passed, remove the plates and squeeze the cucumbers gently but firmly to drain them of their excess liquid. Dry them on paper towels.

3. In a glass bowl, beat the vinegar with the sugar to dissolve it. Mix in the chopped dill leaves.

Add the dried cucumbers and toss gently to combine everything.

4. Cover the bowl and chill the salad at least 3 hours before serving it. Just before serving the salad, drain the cucumbers of their excess liquid. Serve the salad well chilled. Recipe serves 8 to 10 people.

Serving Suggestions

This salad traditionally accompanies smoked and pickled fish, but I also like it with *kottletten* and *schnitzel*, especially beef *kottletten*. It is much, much better than sweet pickle relish. Baltic cucumber salad is a fabulous vegetable to serve alongside *gravad lox* (p. 94). The salad keeps very well for several days in the refrigerator.

Creamy Cucumber Salad

Oogerkes mit Smetana

This simple Lithuanian salad was very popular in the *shtetl* during the summer, when fresh cucumbers were abundant.

**1 large English cucumber, washed, trimmed on
   both ends, and diced
1 Tblsp. freshly squeezed lemon juice
1/2 tsp. sugar
1/2 cup sour cream
1/4 cup chopped fresh dill leaves
salt and freshly ground black pepper to taste**

Combine everthing except the cucumbers in a mixing bowl. Beat with a wire whisk until well blended. Add cucumbers and mix with a spoon to combine. Chill well before serving. Recipe serves 6 to 8 people.

Variation

Black Radish with Sour Cream (*Raitechlach mit Smetana*). Substitute 3 cups of peeled, diced black radishes for the cucumbers and prepare as directed above.

Serving Suggestions

Serve this alongside smoked fish, lox, and bagels for a delicious brunch or light dinner.

Baked-Beet Salad

Gebakte Burekeh Tzallat

This recipe is an important one to learn because the baking of the beets is essential to making many different dishes, including *chrain* and several different kinds of salads that use beets.

**2 lb. whole, fresh medium-size beets
juice of 1 lemon
1 tsp. salt
1/2 cup olive or corn oil**

1. Preheat oven to 350°. Wrap each beet individually in aluminum foil and place on a cookie sheet. Bake in the oven for 1 to 1 1/2 hours, depending on the size of the beets. Larger beets take longer to bake. After the required amount of time has passed, remove the beets from the oven and cool to room temperature.

2. Peel the beets and cut into bite-size chunks.

3. In a glass or ceramic bowl, mix the salt, lemon juice, and oil until well combined. Add the beets and toss until everything is well mixed. The salad may be served immediately or refrigerated until ready to serve. I think it tastes best when served at room temperature. This salad keeps very well in the refrigerator for several days. Serves 6 to 8 people.

Serving Suggestions

This is one of those fabulous salads that is so versatile it goes with practically everything. It can accompany grilled or roasted meats, *kottletten*, *schnitzel*, and many, many, other things. It is delicious alongside sweet-and-sour pickled fish (p. 89) or lox and potato casserole (p. 91). Baked-beet salad can suit the occasion whether it is casual or formal.

Litvishe Beet-and-Cucumber Salad

Burekehs mit Oogerkes

**2 medium-size English cucumbers or 4 pickling
   cucumbers, cubed
6 to 8 medium-sizes beets, baked as directed on
   p. 224 and peeled**

1/2 cup sliced scallions
2 Tblsp. freshly snipped chives
1/4 cup freshly chopped parsley leaves
1/4 cup freshly chopped dill leaves
1/4 cup freshly squeezed lemon juice
1 1/4 cups sour cream
2 Tblsp. coarse or kosher salt
1 tsp. sugar

1. Place cucumbers into a colander over the sink and sprinkle with the coarse salt. Mix with your hands to make sure they get covered with the salt. Place 3 or 4 plates on top of the cucumbers and let stand 1 hour. Rinse well and squeeze gently to remove excess liquid. Dry well with paper towels.

2. Place the sour cream, the sugar, and the lemon juice into a deep mixing bowl. With a wire whisk, beat until well blended. Add the herbs and scallions and mix together well.

3. Add the remaining ingredients to the mixing bowl and toss well to combine. Chill at least 2 hours before serving. Recipe serves 6 to 8 people.

Serving Suggestions

This salad is delicious with plain baked, grilled, or sautéed fish as well as smoked fish and herring. I also like it with potato *latkes*.

Galitzianer Beet Salad

Galitzianer Burekeh Tzallat

This delicious beet salad from Galitzia can be served as a salad, a vegetable side dish, or a condiment. It is so flavorful and yet so very simple to make. I like it better than any other beet salad.

2 lb. whole, fresh medium-size beets, baked and
    peeled according to the instructions given
    on p.
1 Tblsp. sugar
1/3 cup *vishnyek* (p. 299) or another
    good-quality cherry brandy

1. Cut the beets into julienne pieces by putting them through the julienne blade of your food processor. Lacking this piece of equipment, you may julienne them by hand using the correct blade of a hand grater. Transfer the beets to a glass or ceramic bowl.

2. In a small cup, dissolve the sugar into the cherry brandy by mixing them together vigorously. Pour this over the beets and mix together thoroughly. The salad may be served immediately or refrigerated until ready to use. Always bring it to room temperature before serving. Recipe serves 6 to 8 people.

Serving Suggestions

This salad may be served with any dish that baked-beet salad is served with. It is a delicious alternative to *chrain* (p. 8) as an accompaniment to *gefilte fisch*. It is also wonderful with *weinerschnitzel* (p. 145), chicken or turkey *schnitzel* (p. 117), or chicken or turkey *kóttletten* (p. 156).

Beet Green Salad

Burekeh Greensen Tzallat

Beet greens are not often thought of as a vegetable by most Americans. Very often, fresh beets are sold in the supermarket without their greens attached, and I know many people who prefer to buy them that way. It is a pity. Those people are missing out on something very special. The flavor of beet greens is unique and quite different from that of the beet roots. Beet greens are highly nutritious as well as very tasty.

For Jews in eastern Europe, the greens of the beets, like spinach, were always an important source of iron and other vitamins. Beet green salad was a common part of the cuisine of eastern European Jews. Polish Jews also put chopped beet greens, together with other vegetables, into beet *borscht* to make *chlodnik* (p. 66).

If you are unused to buying beets with their greens attached or if you have formed the mistaken habit of discarding the greens when you buy beets to make *borscht*, the preparation of this salad will make you feel that you are getting something for free. No supermarket I know of actually sells beet greens. Be sure when you go shopping to always buy your beets with the greens attached, and then you will have two vegetables in one!

Russian Jewish grandmother in traditional dress. St. Louis, 1930s. (Courtesy of Missouri Historical Society.)

1 large bunch beet greens (approximately 2 to 2
   1/2 lb.)
juice of 1 lemon
1 scant tsp. salt
1/2 cup olive or corn oil

1. Separate the stems from the leaves. Carefully wash the stems and put them into a pot of rapidly boiling salted water. Reduce the heat to medium.

2. While the stems are cooking, carefully wash the leaves and when they are all clean, add them to the pot. The stems need to cook a few minutes longer than the leaves.

3. After you have added the leaves to the pot, cook about 7 minutes and drain everything through a colander in the sink. Pour cold water over the vegetables immediately to stop the cooking process. Beet greens will retain a nice color and the stems a slightly crunchy texture by doing this.

4. In a deep glass or ceramic bowl, mix the lemon juice, salt, and oil with a wire whisk to make a vinaigrette.

5. Chop the stems and leaves of the beet greens by hand into small pieces and add them to the bowl. Toss before serving. The salad may be prepared in advance and chilled in the refrigerator. Thirty minutes before it is served, take it out and bring it almost to room temperature. Recipe serves 6 to 8 people.

Serving Suggestions

Beet green salad is almost as versatile as baked-beet salad, but it should not accompany an entrée that has spinach in it or that is served with spinach on the side. This is because of the similarity between the two in texture and, to a degree, flavor. I find that beet green salad goes particularly well with fish. It can be served before, after, or alongside a fish entrée. One of my favorite *forspeizen* is a portion of herring marinated in oil (p. 41) accompanied by a portion of beet green salad.

Carrot-and-Raisin Salad

Mehren Tzallat

2 lb. carrots, peeled
1/2 cup golden raisins

1/2 very small head of green cabbage, washed
   and dried
juice of 1 large lemon
1/4 cup honey
1/3 cup corn oil
3/4 tsp. salt

1. Shred cabbage very finely. Put the carrots through the julienne blade of a food processor (or grate them by hand into juilienne strips using the appropriate blade of a hand grater).

2. With a wire whisk mix the honey, lemon juice, salt, and oil in a deep glass or ceramic bowl. Be sure that all of the honey is dissolved and mixed into the vinaigrette.

3. Add the carrots, the cabbage, and the raisins to the bowl and toss well, making sure the dressing is completely incorporated into the salad. Chill for 2 to 3 hours before serving. This salad tastes good cold or at room temperature. Recipe serves 6 to 8 people.

Variations

For a *milchig* version, add 1/3 cup sour cream or plain yogurt to the recipe, mixing it in at the time the ingredients for the dressing are combined.

For an American-style version, add 1/3 cup mayonnaise instead of the sour cream or yogurt.

For a Southern-style version, add 2 Tblsp. mayonnaise and 2 Tblsp. sour cream to the dressing.

Serving Suggestions

As you may have already guessed, carrot-and-raisin salad is an eastern European version of cole slaw. This salad is used the same way as cole slaw in American cuisine. The difference between the Jewish recipe and the American, though, is that the Jewish one emphasizes the flavor of carrots over that of cabbage. European Jews, as a rule, did not use mayonnaise in salads. Their American offspring started to use mayonnaise as they became more familiar with American foods. This has become so standard, I think, that many American Jews believe, incorrectly, that Jews always used mayonnaise in their salads.

This salad is good to use when an entrée or a menu calls for a vegetable accompaniment that is somewhat sweet. I particularly like the taste of carrot-and-raisin salad alongside sweet-and-sour pickled fish (p.).

Romanian Salad

Romanishe Tzallat

The famous Israeli kibbutz salad is a variation of this Romanian vegetable salad. The trick to making it well is in dicing the vegetables very, very fine, just as in a well-made Middle Eastern vegetable salad.

5 large, meaty ripe tomatoes, finely diced
1 large English cucumber or 4 pickling
    cucumbers, washed and finely diced
2 large green bell peppers, washed, cored,
    seeded, and finely diced
1 large red bell pepper, washed, cored, seeded,
    and finely diced
1 medium-size black radish or several small
    white radishes, peeled and finely diced
12 to 14 black Niçoise or Sicilian olives, pitted
    and halved
1/4 cup chopped parsley
1/2 cup olive oil
1/4 cup red wine vinegar
salt and freshly ground black pepper to taste
6 oz. *brynza* cheese (optional)

Mix all the vegetables and the parsley together in a salad bowl. Mix the remaining ingredients together and pour over the vegetables. Toss the salad again. If using the cheese, mix it in at this point and toss one more time. Recipe serves 6 to 8 people.

Serving Suggestions

This is the ideal summer salad to accompany grilled meats or, when the cheese is added, grilled fish. Try it with *karnotzl* (p. 156). *Mamaliga* (p. 186) or pumpernickel bread and a bottle of wine are all you need to complete the meal. The salad, with the addition of the cheese, is also a wonderful light meal on its own, accompanied, of course, by good dark bread.

Romanian
Roasted-Pepper Salad

Romanische Pfeffer Tzallat

Roasting or grilling brings out the flavor of bell peppers and adds a unique smoky aroma. It also softens the harsh taste of raw pepper and draws out its sweetness. This classical Romanian dish has many variations in the countries around the Mediterranean, where it originated. It may have been brought to Romania by Turkish Jews.

4 large green bell peppers
3 large red bell peppers
3 large yellow bell peppers
1 large sweet red onion, peeled and very thinly
    sliced
4 large cloves garlic, peeled and finely chopped
1/4 cup good red wine vinegar
1/2 cup extra-virgin olive oil
1/2 tsp. sugar
salt and freshly ground black pepper to taste

1. Heat the outdoor grill or the oven and broil the peppers, turning every few minutes, until the peppers are charred and black all over. Wrap them in a kitchen towel or place them into a paper bag and tightly seal it. Allow the peppers to cool completely and then unwrap them. The peel should come off easily. Peel the peppers, remove the cores and seeds, and then cut them into strips lengthwise.

2. Heat 2 Tblsp. of the olive oil and sauté the onions until golden brown. Add the garlic and sauté 1 minute longer, being careful not to burn the garlic. Remove this from the heat and set it aside to cool.

3. Mix the remaining oil, vinegar, salt, sugar, and pepper in a glass jar. Shake it vigorously to make a vinaigrette.

4. Mix the onions and peppers in a glass or ceramic bowl. Pour the vinaigrette over the vegetables and toss. Allow the salad to marinate at least 1/2 hour at room temperature before serving. The salad may also be refrigerated until ready to serve. Bring it to room temperature before you serve it. Recipe serves 6 to 8 people.

Serving Suggestions

This luscious salad is a perfect accompaniment to grilled meats and fish, especially *karnotzl* (p. 156) and Romanian-style grilled Cornish hen (p. 116). It is also delicious with *mamaliga* (p. 186) accompanied by *brynza* or one of the baked *mamaliga* dishes (p. 186).

Romanian Eggplant Salad

Shalloteh

Although there are many kinds of eggplant salads in Mediterranean and Balkan cuisines, there is only one Romanian *Shalloteh*. The key to making this dish correctly lies in roasting or grilling the eggplant before sautéing it in oil. The result is a smoky, savory dish with soft herbal accents. The only other eastern European country to create an eggplant salad was Russia and the Russian dish, called Poor Man's Caviar, also comes from that part of Russia closest to Turkey and the Mediterranean Sea.

1 very large eggplant (about 2 to 2 1/2 lbs.)
2 large green bell peppers
1 large sweet red onion, peeled and finely chopped
2 large, meaty red tomatoes, peeled and finely chopped
2 cloves garlic, peeled
1/3 cup olive oil
2 Tblsp. red wine vinegar
1/4 cup chopped fresh parsley
salt and freshly ground black pepper to taste

1. Preheat the outdoor grill or oven broiler. Pierce the eggplant in several places with a skewer or a toothpick. Grill the eggplant and the peppers on the grill or broiler until they are charred all over. Turn the vegetables every few minutes to ensure even cooking.

2. Wrap the peppers in kitchen towels or place them into a paper bag and seal it tightly. The eggplant does not need to be wrapped. Cool everything to room temperature.

3. Peel, core, and seed the peppers. Then dice them finely.

4. Cut the eggplant in half and scoop out the pulp into a mixing bowl. Mash it well with a potato masher. Any parts that do not mash well should be cut into small dice. Mix the peppers with the eggplant.

5. Heat the oil in a sauté pan and sauté the onions until soft and translucent. Add the garlic and sauté 1 minute longer. Then add the eggplant mixture and cook a few minutes more. Remove from heat.

6. Transfer contents of skillet to a glass or ceramic bowl. Add the tomatoes and remaining ingredients and mix well. Cover and refrigerate the salad for several hours before serving it. To serve, bring to room temperature. Recipe serves 6 to 8 people.

Serving Suggestions

Serve Romanian eggplant salad as a *forspeis* or with any of the grilled meat dishes. This delicious salad should be accompanied by plenty of good dark bread.

Romanian Potato Salad

6 large red boiling potatoes
1/2 cup olive oil
2 large cloves garlic, peeled and finely chopped
1 cup *brynza* cheese (feta cheese may be substituted)
4 scallions, finely chopped
1/4 cup chopped fresh dill leaves
1/4 cup red wine vinegar
salt and freshly ground black pepper to taste

1. Boil the potatoes in their jackets in salted water for 15 to 18 minutes in the microwave oven or for 25 to 30 minutes on top of the stove. Drain the potatoes and plunge them into cold water to cool them off.

2. When they are cool enough to handle, peel them and cut them into 1/2-inch dice. Place them in a heatproof mixing bowl.

3. Heat the olive oil over medium heat and add the garlic. Sauté 1/2 minute—long enough to bring out a little flavor—but be careful not to burn the garlic. Pour it over the potatoes.

4. Add the vinegar, salt, and black pepper to the potatoes. Mix together well and allow to cool to room temperature.

5. Add the remaining ingredients to the bowl, toss, and serve the salad at room temperature. Recipe serves 6 to 8 people.

Serving Suggestions

This dish is excellent as part of a vegetarian meal featuring a variety of Romanian salads. Accompany it with Romanian eggplant salad (p. 229) and Romanian roasted-pepper salad (p. 228), black olives, and lots of dark bread and butter. These salads may also be served with *karnotzl* (p. 156); in that case, do not add the cheese to the potato salad.

Marinated Green Cabbage Salad

Marinirte Greener Kroit Tzallat

1 medium-size head green cabbage, washed,
   cored, and finely shredded
1/2 cup coarse or kosher salt
2 Tblsp. sugar
1/2 cup freshly squeezed lemon juice
1/2 cup corn oil
1/3 cup cold water

1. In a heavy porcelain or glass bowl, layer the cabbage with the salt sprinkled over it. Place several plates on top of the cabbage to weight it down and cover the bowl tightly. Refrigerate for 24 hours.

2. The next day, remove the cabbage from the bowl, drain it in a colander, and rinse it. Dry it thoroughly and place it into a salad bowl.

3. Mix the remaining ingredients and pour them over the cabbage. Toss thoroughly and allow to marinate 1/2 hour before serving. This salad may be refrigerated and brought almost to room temperature starting 1/2 hour before it is served. Recipe serves 6 to 8 people.

Serving Suggestions

This salad is delicious with a meat entrée that pairs well with cabbage. I like to serve it alongside a bowl of *cholent* (p. 139) or with Carpathian-style braised lamb (p. 150) as something light and cooling to balance the heaviness of the meat dish. This salad is also quite good with *kottletten*.

Tzallat Vinegret

Tzallat vinegret is the Yiddish name for a main-dish herring salad that is popular with Jews from Litteh and Russia. This salad is a traditional way of using up leftover vegetables.

2 *schmaltz* or *matjes* herrings, soaked and
   prepared according to the instructions given
   on p.
12 medium-size red boiling potatoes, boiled in
   their jackets and peeled
8 medium-size beets, baked and peeled
   according to the instructions given on p.
1 tart green apple, peeled and cored
3 hard-boiled eggs
1 small sweet red onion, peeled and finely
   chopped
1 large or 2 small kosher dill pickles (p. 291),
   diced
1/2 cup chopped fresh dill leaves
1/4 cup freshly squeezed lemon juice
1/4 cup corn oil
1 1/2 cups sour cream
freshly ground black pepper to taste and salt, if
   needed

1. Fillet the prepared herrings and cut them into small pieces. Place them into a deep ceramic or glass bowl.

2. Dice the potatoes, beets, apples, and hard-boiled eggs, and add them to the herring. Toss together.

3. Add the finely chopped onion, dill leaves, and dill pickles. Toss together again.

4. In a bowl, whisk together the lemon juice, oil, and sour cream. Pour this over the other ingredients and mix together thoroughly. Sprinkle the pepper over this and toss again. Taste for seasoning and, if necessary, mix in a little salt. Cover the salad and chill it for 2 hours before serving. Recipe serves 6 to 8 as an entrée.

Serving Suggestions

Accompany the salad with good rye or pumpernickel bread and butter. If you wish, drink beer with the meal. This salad may also be part of a *milchig* buffet. It is customary to serve a hot dessert after *tzallat vinegret*. *Milchig lokshen kugel* (p. 171) and *challah* bread pudding (p. 246) are both excellent choices. So is apple *schalet* (p. 245).

Spring Salad

Freilingtzeit Tzallat

This delicious salad comes directly from the eastern European *shtetlach*, where it was formerly prepared for lunch on Shevuos. It included some of the first vegetables of the new harvest as well as the new fresh spring herbs of the season, hence its name. Because it is so easy to make and keeps so well under refrigeration, *freilingtzeit tzallat* was almost immediately adopted as a standard offering by some of the Jewish dairy restaurants in the United States. When this happened, the traditional recipe was changed considerably. Some outlandish recipes came to include just about every vegetable that could be eaten raw—the greater the variety, it seemed, the "fancier" the salad. What was originally a simple, sensible dish with a few ingredients that complemented each other well came to be a kind of catchall salad that was made of anything that happened to be found in the vegetable market. My recipe for *freilingtzeit tzallat* goes back to the original concept. The following *freilingtzeit tzallat* is a familiar old favorite of the Yiddish kitchen.

1 large English cucumber, washed and cut into fine dice

6 red radishes, trimmed and cut into fine dice

1 small black radish, peeled and cut into fine dice

6 scallions, trimmed and finely chopped

1/3 cup chopped fresh parsley

2 Tblsp. freshly snipped chives

2 Tblsp. chopped fresh dill leaves

1 lb. farmer dry cottage cheese

1 cup plain yogurt

salt and freshly ground black pepper to taste

Mix everything together in a glass or ceramic bowl and serve immediately. Spring salad should be served right away rather than refrigerated because, contrary to popular belief, it does lose its fresh flavor rapidly. It will, however, keep fairly well for 2 days in the refrigerator and still be edible but not at its best. Recipe serves 6 to 8 people.

Serving Suggestions

The traditional accompaniment to spring salad is Russian eggs (p. 43) or plain hard-boiled eggs, smoked fish, and rye or pumpernickel bread with butter. Spring salad makes a wonderful *milchig* buffet dish.

Roast Goose Dinner for Shabbos Chanukah

Challah

Stuffed *helzel*

Golden carrot soup

Roast goose with Hungarian sweet *challah* stuffing

Litvishe-style braised red cabbage

Zinfandel

Fresh pineapple compote with almond macaroons

Coffe or tea

11

Compotes and Light Desserts

Kompotten und Zisse Maichollim

Food gets cooked by the pot, but all the
honor goes to the plate!

*Shpeiz kocht men in teppl, un der koved
krigt der teller!*

Compotes and Other Light Desserts

European Jewish cuisine has always been well known for its desserts and baked goods. What is not as well known, however, is that cakes, tarts, *babkas*, and other baked sweets were never everyday fare. These kinds of rich, flavorful sweet dishes were always reserved for the Sabbath, festivals, and special occasions. Particularly among the more affluent classes, baked sweets were never consumed at the dinner table. Once the main meal was concluded, it was followed by a rest period for which everyone retired to the parlor or sitting room. Eventually, tea and some kind of baked sweet dish were served in this room some time after the main meal had been digested. The only baked goods ever eaten with dinner were things like *mandelbroit* or *makarondelach* to accompany a fruit compote or *kissel*. In central Europe, particularly Hungary and Vienna, coffee was favored over tea as an after-dinner drink, but the procedure for concluding the meal was exactly the same. Instead of concluding the meal with a rich slice (or two) of pastry, the dinner finished with a light fruit dessert such as a compote or a *kissel*. These kinds of desserts were standard fare everywhere in the Yiddish-speaking world except some parts of Romania, where plain fresh fruit was usually preferred to a cooked compote.

Americans could learn a great deal from these forgotten old European customs. Our regular meals would be much lighter and more nutritious and the sweet pastries would be much more appreciated if they were eaten less often. I am a strong advocate of eating fresh fruit at least twice a day. Fruits, fresh or cooked, are really the best way to conclude a meal because they cleanse the palate as well as leave a sweet taste in your mouth.

The recipes in this chapter are, for the most part, all light, fruit-based desserts. Although most of them are found in traditional Yiddish cuisine, I have modified the old recipes in most cases to include wines and liqueurs, because I think they add a great deal to the overall flavor of a compote or *kissel*.

Uncooked Fruit Compotes

Almost any fruit can be turned into a delicious and refreshing compote with the addition of sugar, fruit juice, wine, or liqueur. The method of preparing most of the uncooked fruit compotes is the same for every recipe. The proportions of sugar, juice, and alcohol vary from recipe to recipe because of the differences in sugar content of the various fruits. The wines and liqueurs have been chosen for the compatibility of their flavors with the different fruits.

Strawberry Compote

Pozenikes Kompot

Make this compote only in the spring, when fresh, locally grown strawberries are in season. Do not waste money or time on those insipid-tasting, out-of-season strawberries that have flooded the supermarkets in recent years. Nothing short of collective consumer disinterest will make this product disappear from the supermarket shelves.

4 cups hulled fresh strawberries
1/3 cup sugar
1/3 cup freshly squeezed orange juice
1/4 cup Grand Marnier
sour cream for garnish (optional)

1. Wash and dry the strawberries and cut three quarters of them in half. Place these into a deep glass bowl.
2. Puree the remaining strawberries in the blender or food processor together with the sugar. Pass this mixture through a fine sieve into a mixing bowl, pressing down hard on the fruit to separate the pulp from the seeds.
3. Mix the orange juice and the Grand Marnier into the strawberry puree. Blend well and pour over the sliced strawberries.
4. Mix together well, cover the bowl, and chill 2 hours in the refrigerator before serving. Serve well chilled. I also recommend serving this compote the same day it is made. Its fresh flavor and consistency change slightly the longer the compote is kept. It does keep for several days in the refrigerator, but the texture of the fruit gets mushier, like that of frozen strawberries. Recipe serves 6 to 8 people.

Serving Suggestions

For a meat meal, serve the compote exactly as it is, accompanied by almond *makarondelach* (p. 258). For a dairy meal, a small dollop of sour cream is a welcome addition.

Summer Berry Compote With Peaches

Yogges Kompot

The key to a successful dish here is the ripeness of the peaches and the blackberries, both of which should be very sweet and ripe and without a trace of sourness.

2 cups fresh blueberries
1 cup fresh blackberries
2 cups fresh raspberries
2 very ripe fresh peaches
1/2 cup sugar
1/3 cup fruity white wine
1/4 cup kirsch
heavy or whipping cream (optional)

1. Wash and dry the blueberries and place them into a glass bowl.
2. Peel and pit the peaches and cut them into small pieces. Add them to the blueberries.
3. Carefully wash and dry the blackberries and 1 cup of the raspberries. Add this to the rest of the fruit.
4. Puree the remaining cup of raspberries in the blender or food processor together with the sugar. Pass this puree through a fine sieve. The seeds will remain in the sieve while a lovely, brilliant red puree passes through into the mixing bowl. This puree is the classic sauce cardinale of French cuisine.
5. Mix the wine and the kirsch into the rasberry puree and add this to the fruit in the glass bowl. Gently mix all ingredients, being careful not to crush the delicate raspberries or blackberries. Cover the bowl and chill in the refrigerator for 1 1/2 to 2 hours before serving. Recipe serves 6 to 8 people.

Serving Suggestions

With a meat meal, serve the compote as is, accompanied by any of the various *makarondelach*. With a dairy meal, a little splash of unwhipped heavy or whipping cream is a terrific addition. Let every diner mix some cream into the compote.

Winter Citrus Compote

Pommerantzen Kompot

This compote is made with a sugar syrup that is cooked and cooled to room temperature. The fruit is then set into the cooled syrup to marinate. It is refrigerated and served chilled. The optional kiwi fruit adds a nice contrasting green color to an otherwise rather monochromatic dish.

4 large seedless navel oranges plus the grated zest of one of the oranges
2 small ruby red Indian river grapefruits
1/2 small pineapple, cored, peeled, and cut into chunks
2 small kiwi fruit
juice made from the other half of the pineapple
1 cup rosé or white zinfandel wine
1 cup sugar
1/4 cup triple sec or Cointreau

1. Make the pineapple juice by grinding the entire core and the pulp of half the pineapple in the juicer attachment of a blender/juicer. Lacking this appliance, make a puree of the pineapple in the blender or food processor and push it through a fine sieve. You should have 1 to 1 1/2 cups juice. Place this into a saucepan.
2. Add enough of the rosé wine to make 2 1/2 cups liquid. Stir in the sugar and bring to a boil on top of the stove. Cook until the mixture is reduced to 1 1/2 cups liquid. Then remove it from the heat and cool it to room temperature.
3. While the syrup is cooling, prepare the orange zest. Make sure it is zested into thin, delicate strips by cutting it with a citrus zester. Bring a small amount of water to boil in another saucepan and add the zest. Cook it 5 minutes and then drain it.
4. Peel the oranges and the grapefruit. With a very sharp paring knife, separate the flesh of the fruit from the white pith into segments. Place these segments of fruit, together with the pineapple chunks, into a glass bowl.
5. Peel the kiwi fruit, if using, and cut it into wedges or rounds. Add it to the other fruit.
6. Mix the cooled syrup, orange zest, and triple sec or cointreau together and pour it over the fruit. Mix gently and carefully. Cover the bowl and let it chill in the refrigerator for 2 to 3 hours before serving. Recipe serves 6 to 8 people.

Serving Suggestions

Serve the compote accompanied by *mandelbroit* (p. 256), Aunt Ann's sugar cookies (p. 260), or any of the *makarondelach* (p. 258).

American-Style Peach-and-Blueberry Compote

Pershkes Kompot

The combination of peaches and bourbon whiskey is uniquely American. It is the basis of one of America's most delicious liqueurs—Southern Comfort. This summer compote is one of my favorites—a special way to celebrate the American peach and blueberry crops.

6 large very ripe peaches
2 cups fresh blueberries
1/2 cup (heaping) sugar
1 cup cold water
1/2 cup Kentucky bourbon whiskey
1/4 cup Southern Comfort

1. Make a sugar syrup out of the sugar and the water by dissolving the sugar into the water in a saucepan and bringing it to a boil over medium-high heat. Cook the syrup until it cooks down to 3/4 cup. Cool to tepid.

2. Pit and peel the peaches. Slice them into attractive, wedge-shaped slices and place them into a glass bowl.

3. Wash and dry the blueberries and add them to the peaches.

4. In a small mixing bowl, dissolve the sugar syrup into the whiskey using a fork or a wire whisk. Whisk in the Southern Comfort and pour this over the fruit. Cover the bowl and chill it 2 hours before serving. Serve well chilled. Serves 6 to 8 people.

Serving Suggestions

This compote is delicious by itself. You do not need to add any cream, even if you serve it with a *milchig* meal. I like to accompany this compote, if serving *milchig*, with Aunt Ann's sugar cookies (p. 260) or Aunt Ann's peanut butter cookies (p. 261) rather than the traditional *mandelbroit* or *makarondelach*.

Fresh Pineapple Compote

Ananas Kompot

Fresh pineapple is available all year but I like to serve this compote in the winter, when citrus fruit is in season and when you are looking for something festive as a reminder of the sunnier seasons. The pineapple is a traditional folk symbol of welcome. The custom goes back to the time when pineapple was rather exotic and difficult to obtain. Having a pineapple on the table when guests were visiting indicated to them that the host or hostess had gone to great trouble to extend correct and proper hospitality.

Among Jews in eastern Europe, the pineapple was extremely costly and considered even more of a delicacy than oranges. In some Jewish homes, pineapple was eaten only once a year, on Rosh Hashanah, when tradition requires the making of a special blessing over a fruit that has not been eaten for an entire year.

To make pineapple compote, use only a well-ripened pineapple. This is sometimes difficult to obtain. Underripe, second-rate merchandise always seems to be available at the supermarket, so shop carefully. A well-ripened fresh pineapple is one of the most delicious of all fruits—it is sensuously sweet and juicy. And it has none of the sour, astringent taste or the woody texture of the underripe variety that has given the pineapple a bad rap.

The other truly special ingredient in this compote is dried tart cherries, one of the newest products to come on the market in recent years. Dried tart cherries are quite expensive and generally available only in gourmet specialty shops, although I have seen them in a few supermarkets. The flavor of this dried fruit has no equal, and it is well worth the extra trouble and expense.

The combination of good-quality fresh pineapple and tart cherry with kirsch is delicious. Like citrus compote, this one is made with a sugar syrup that is cooked and then cooled to room temperature.

1 large fresh pineapple
1/2 cup dried tart or sour cherries
3/4 cup sugar
1/2 cup cold water
1/3 cup kirsch

1. Peel and core the pineapple. Cut the core into chunks and put it into the juicer attachment of a

juicer/blender and make juice from it. Lacking this appliance, puree it in a blender or food processor and put it through a fine sieve. The result will be fresh pineapple juice. This should make about 1/2 cup of juice. You will need about 1 1/2 cups of liquid, so cut a little of the pineapple into chunks and do the same with them. Make enough of this to give you 1 cup of fresh pineapple juice.

2. Pour the juice into a saucepan and add the water and the sugar. Bring it to a boil and cook for 7 minutes, stirring to dissolve the sugar. Reduce the liquid to about 1 cup.

3. Remove the saucepan from the heat and add the cherries to it. Cool, with the cherries in it, to room temperature.

4. Cut the remaining pineapple into chunks and place it into a glass bowl. When the liquid has cooled to room temperature, add the kirsch to it and pour it over the pineapple. Mix well, cover the bowl, and chill in the refrigerator for 2 to 3 hours before serving. Recipe serves 6 to 8 people.

Serving Suggestions

Serve pineapple compote with almond *makarondelach* (p. 258) or *mandelbroit* (p. 256).

Cooked Fruit Compotes

The cooked fruit compotes are made mainly with autumn fruits like apples and pears. The exception is rhubarb compote, which is made in the springtime during the rhubarb season.

Apple Compote

Eppl Kompot

3 lb. tart green apples, peeled, cored, and cut into wedge-shaped slices
1/2 cup golden raisins
1/2 cup light brown sugar
thinly zested zest of 1 lemon
1 cinnamon stick
1 tsp. whole cloves
1 1/3 cup cold water
2/3 cup brandy

1. Dissolve the sugar in the water in a saucepan and bring it to a boil over medium heat. Cook for 5 minutes until the mixture begins to get syrupy.

2. Add the lemon zest, the spices, and the raisins, and cook 5 minutes longer.

3. Add the apples, reduce the heat to simmer, and cook 15 minutes longer.

4. Remove from the heat and stir in the brandy. Cool to room temperature and transfer the compote to a glass bowl. Cover the bowl and chill for 2 to 3 hours in the refrigerator before serving. Recipe serves 6 to 8 people.

Serving Suggestions

Serve apple compote with any of the *makarondelach* (p. 258) or with *mandelbroit* (p. 256). For a *milchig* meal, you may top each portion of compote with whipped cream, if you wish.

Springtime Rhubarb Compote

Rabbarber Kompot

1 1/2 lb. fresh rhubarb stalks, cut into 1/2-inch lengths
2 cups hulled fresh strawberries, halved
1 1/2 cups vanilla sugar (or 1 1/2 cups regular sugar plus 1 tsp. vanilla extract)
2 1/2 cups water
1/4 cup brandy

1. Dissolve the sugar into the water in a large saucepan and bring to a boil. Cook 5 minutes.

2. Add the rhubarb and the strawberries. Reduce the heat to medium and cook the fruit for 10 to 15 minutes or until the rhubarb is completely cooked and begins to break apart. Do not let it cook too long because, since this is compote, you want to keep some of the rhubarb whole. The strawberries will mostly disintegrate during cooking but will lend a marvelous flavor.

3. Remove the saucepan from the heat, stir in the brandy, and cool, partially covered, to room temperature. Transfer to a glass bowl, cover, and refrigerate for 2 to 3 hours before serving. Recipe serves 6 to 8 people.

Serving Suggestions

Serve rhubarb compote with almond *makarondelach* (p. 258) or *mandelbroit* (p. 256). With a *milchig* meal, serve the compote with a dollop of whipped cream on each portion.

Cranberry Compote

Broznitzel Kompot

Cranberries are extremely tart and need more sugar than other fruits. They also need the flavors of other sweeter, complementary fruits to balance out their strong, robust flavor. Each of the two compote recipes below achieves this with totally different results. The first is a traditional recipe for cranberry compote from Lithuania. The second is my own creation, which pairs cranberries with oranges, a combination that has been appreciated by gourmet cooks everywhere.

Recipe 1: Lithuanian Cranberry Compote

4 cups fresh cranberries
2 pears, peeled, cored, and cut into pieces
2 tart green apples, cored, peeled, and cut into pieces
2 cups sugar
2 cups water
1/2 cup pear brandy

1. Dissolve the sugar in the water in a saucepan and bring to a boil. Cook 5 minutes.
2. Add the cranberries, pears, and apples. Reduce the heat to medium and cook until the berries soften and begin to break apart (about 15 to 20 minutes).
3. Remove from the heat, stir in the pear brandy, and cool, partially covered, to room temperature. Transfer to a glass bowl when cooled, cover, and chill in the refrigerator for 2 to 3 hours before serving. Recipe serves 6 to 8 people.

Serving Suggestions

Serve with *mandelbroit* (p. 256), oatmeal cookies (p. 261), or Aunt Ann's sugar cookies (p. 260).

Recipe 2: Cranberry/Orange Compote

4 cups fresh cranberries
2 seedless navel oranges
2 cups sugar
2 cups freshly squeezed orange juice
1/2 cup cold water
thinly zested zest of 1 orange
1/3 cup brandy
1/3 cup triple sec

1. Dissolve the sugar into the water in a saucepan. Add the orange juice and bring to a boil. Cook 5 minutes.
2. Add the cranberries and orange zest and reduce the heat. Cook until the berries begin to burst (about 15 to 20 minutes).
3. Remove from the heat and stir in the brandy and triple sec and partially cover the pot to cool.
4. While the cranberries are cooling, peel and segment the oranges. With a sharp paring knife, separate the fruit from the membrane and add it to the cranberries. Mix the fruit well.
5. When the compote has cooled to room temperature, transfer it to a glass bowl. Cover the bowl and refrigerate it for 2 to 3 hours before serving. Recipe serves 6 to 8 people.

Serving Suggestions

Serve the compote with *mandelbroit* (p. 256), Aunt Ann's sugar cookies (p. 260), or oatmeal cookies (p. 261).

Pears Poached in Red Wine

Baren in Wein

Unlike any of the other compotes, this compote leaves the fruit whole. It is a classical dish that is common to many cuisines, including Yiddish cuisine.

6 to 8 whole Anjou pears, not too ripe
1 cup sugar
1 1/4 cups cold water
1 1/4 cups red wine
1 cinnamon stick
thinly zested zest of one lemon

1. Core the pears from the bottom up, leaving the stem at the end of each pear. Then peel the pears.

2. In a large saucepan with a tight-fitting lid in which all the fruit will be able to fit standing up, dissolve the sugar in the water. Bring to a boil and cook 5 minutes.

3. Add the wine, zest, and cinnamon stick and boil 5 minutes longer. Reduce the heat to simmer.

4. Arrange the pears in the saucepan and cover with the lid. Cook 10 minutes. Uncover the pot and baste the pears with the liquid in the pan.

5. Cook a total of 15 to 20 minutes longer, basting with the syrup every 5 minutes, or until the pears are cooked through. Be careful not to overcook them or they will be mushy.

6. Remove the saucepan from the heat and cool to room temperature, partially covered. Cover the pot and chill the pears for 2 to 3 hours in the refrigerator before serving. Serve 1 pear, with some of the syrup, to each diner. The pears will absorb the flavor of the wine and attain a beautiful rose-colored blush as they cool. Recipe serves 6 to 8 people, depending on how many pears you poach.

Serving Suggestions

Poached pears taste good with all of the *makarondelach*, but I prefer them with hazelnut *makarondelach* (p. 258).

Dried Fruit Compote

Getrukente Frucht Kompot

1 1/2 lb. dried mixed fruit
1/2 cup sugar
1 cinnamon stick
1 medium-size lemon, sliced
1 1/2 cups cold water
2 cups red wine

1. Dissolve the sugar in the water in a large saucepan. Bring to a boil and cook 5 minutes. Add the wine, the cinnamon stick, and the lemon slices and cook 5 minutes longer.

2. Add the fruit and reduce the heat to a gentle simmer. Partly cover the pot and cook 20 minutes or until the fruit fluffs up and cooks through. Cool to room temperature partially covered.

3. Transfer to a glass bowl, cover, and chill in the refrigerator for 2 to 3 hours before serving. Recipe serves 6 to 8 people.

Serving Suggestions

Serve this classic dessert dish with *mandelbroit* (p. 256), its traditional accompaniment.

Kissel

Kissel is a fruit puree pudding that is popular in Russia and in Litteh. The thickening for the pudding is always potato starch. *Kissel* may be served as a change of pace from compote. The recipes given here are all traditional except for my usual addition of wine or liqueur. *Kissel* can be made out of pretty much any kind of fruit except citrus. The *kissel* recipes I include in this book were selected to create alternatives for each season.

Recipe 1: Strawberry-Rhubarb *Kissel* (Springtime)
Pozenikes mit Rabbarber Kissel

2 cups hulled, sliced fresh strawberries
2 cups rhubarb stalks, cut into small pieces
2 1/2 cups cold water
1/2 cup vanilla sugar (or substitute 1/2 cup
    sugar and 1/8 tsp. vanilla extract)
1/3 cup Grand Marnier
2 Tblsp. potato starch mixed into a paste with
    1/2 cup cold water

1. In a saucepan, dissolve the sugar in the 2 1/2 cups cold water and bring to a boil over medium heat.

2. Add the rhubarb and the strawberries and cook until the fruit disintegrates. Break the rhubarb pieces apart with a fork as the fruit cooks to help speed the process along.

3. Add the potato starch mixture to the saucepan and simmer until the fruit puree is thick.

4. Remove saucepan from the heat and stir in the Grand Marnier.

5. Pour the fruit puree into individual dessert bowls. Cover the bowls and chill until ready to serve. Recipe makes about 6 servings of *kissel*.

Serving Suggestions

Serve strawberry-rhubarb *kissel* with almond *makarondelach* (p. 258) or *mandelbroit* (p. 256). If serving the *kissel* with a *milchig* meal, top it with unwhipped heavy or whipping cream. Let each diner pour his or her own cream over the *kissel*.

Recipe 2: Summer Berry **Kissel**
Zummerdige Yogges Kissel

4 cups summer berries (a combination of
    raspberries and blueberries is excellent)
2 1/2 cups cold water
1/3 cup sugar
3 Tblsp. potato starch mixed into a paste with
    1/3 cup cold water
1/3 cup raspberry liqueur, crème de cassis, or
    blackberry vodka (p. 299)

1. Dissolve sugar in 2 1/2 cups cold water in a saucepan and bring to a boil over medium heat. Add berries and cook until they are broken up into a puree.

2. Pass the fruit puree through a sieve to separate the fruit pulp from the seeds. It will pass through quite easily and leave a beautifully colored fruit puree.

3. Return the puree to the saucepan and reheat at a low temperature. Add the potato starch mixture to the puree and cook until thickened.

4. Remove the saucepan from the heat and add the liqueur. Pour the *kissel* into individual dessert bowls. Cover the bowls and chill for several hours before serving. Recipe makes about 6 portions of *kissel*.

Serving Suggestions

This type of *kissel* tastes best accompanied by cream. Serve it with whipped or unwhipped heavy cream. Devon cream is also delicious with this *kissel*. A butter cookie like Aunt Ann's sugar cookies (p. 260) should accompany the pudding.

Recipe 3: Cranberry **Kissel** (Autumn)
Broznitze Kissel

2 cups cranberries
1 tart green apple, peeled, cored, and cut into
    chunks
1 large pear, peeled, cored, and cut into chunks

2 1/2 cups unsweetened apple juice
1 cup sugar
3 Tblsp. potato starch mixed into a paste with
    1/3 cup cold water
1/3 cup calvados or applejack

1. Dissolve the sugar into the apple juice in a saucepan and bring to a boil over medium heat. Add the fruit and cook until everything disintegrates. Help this along by mashing the cranberries against the sides of the saucepan with a wooden spoon as they cook.

2. Pass the contents of the saucepan through a sieve, pressing down hard on the fruit to separate the pulp from the skins of the berries. The puree will be a beautiful bright red color.

3. Return the puree to the saucepan and reheat over a low flame. Add the potato starch mixture and cook until the mixture thickens.

4. Remove the saucepan from the heat and stir in the liqueur. Pour the *kissel* into individual dessert bowls and chill in the refrigerator several hours before serving. Recipe makes about 6 portions of *kissel*.

Serving Suggestions

This *kissel* can be served with or without heavy cream. Accompany the *kissel* with oatmeal cookies (p. 261).

Recipe 4: Prune **Kissel** (Winter)
Getrukente Flommen Kissel

2 cups pitted prunes
1 cup red wine
1 1/2 cups prune juice
grated zest of 1 lemon
1/4 cup sugar
2 Tblsp. freshly squeezed lemon juice
1/4 tsp. ground cinnamon
1/8 tsp. ground cloves
pinch freshly grated nutmeg
2 Tblsp. potato starch mixed into a paste with
    1/2 cup cold water
2 Tblsp. brandy

1. Soak the prunes in the wine for 1 hour.

2. Pour the prune juice, sugar, and lemon juice into a saucepan and bring to a boil over medium heat. Add the prunes, wine, spices, and lemon zest

and cook until prunes are very soft and cooked through enough to break apart.

3. Puree the contents of the saucepan in a blender or food processor and pass the puree through a sieve. Return this mixture to the saucepan and reheat over a low flame. Add the potato starch mixture and cook until the mixture is thick.

4. Remove the saucepan from the heat and add the brandy. Pour the *kissel* into individual dessert bowls. Cover the bowls and chill in the refrigerator several hours before serving. Recipe makes 6 portions of *kissel*.

Serving Suggestions

Prune *kissel* may be served with any of the cookies whose recipes are given in this book or with *mandelbroit* (p. 256). The *kissel* tastes good with or without whipped cream.

Schnay

Schnay is the Yiddish word for "snow." *Schnay* is another type of fruit puree pudding that was popular in Litteh. Similar dishes are made in Russia and Scandinavia. *Schnay* is made with egg whites, and it has the appearance of colored snow, hence its name.

Recipe 1: Strawberry *Schnay*
Pozenikes Schnay

4 cups fresh strawberries, hulled and sliced
1/2 cup vanilla sugar (or substitute 1/2 cup
    sugar and 1/4 tsp. vanilla extract)
1 cup freshly squeezed orange juice
1 Tblsp. Grand Marnier
2 egg whites

1. Dissolve the sugar into the orange juice in a saucepan and bring to a boil. Add the strawberries and cook until the fruit disintegrates.

2. Pass the fruit through a fine sieve into a mixing bowl. Press down hard and scrape the sieve to remove as much of the fruit puree as possible. Stir in the Grand Marnier and cool to room temperature.

3. Beat the egg whites into stiff peaks and fold this into the fruit puree.

4. Spoon the *schnay* into individual glass serving bowls and cover. Chill for at least 2 hours before serving. Recipe makes 6 portions of *schnay*. Serve with *mandelbroit* (p. 256) or almond *makarondelach* (p. 258).

Recipe 2: *Eppl Schnay*

2 lb. tart green apples, peeled, cored, and cut
    into chunks
1 cup cold water
2/3 cup sugar
1/2 tsp. ground cinnamon
1/4 tsp. freshly grated nutmeg
2 egg whites
1 Tblsp. calvados, applejack, or brandy
1 Tblsp. sugar mixed with 1/4 tsp. cinnamon

1. Place the apples, sugar, spices, and water into a saucepan and bring to a boil over medium heat. Cook 25 to 30 minutes or until the fruit is completely cooked through.

2. Puree the contents of the saucepan in a blender or food processor and pass through a sieve into a mixing bowl. Stir in the liqueur or brandy and cool to room temperature.

3. Beat the egg whites until stiff and fold into the apple puree. Place in individual glass serving bowls and chill in the refrigerator for 2 hours before serving.

4. To serve, mix together the sugar and cinnamon and sprinkle over each portion of *schnay* before serving. Serve with *mandelbroit* (p. 256).

Baked Apples
Gebakte Eppl

When you're not in the mood for compote or *kissel* but you'd like a light, tasty, easy dessert, nothing fills the bill better than baked apples. I like mine baked with Jonathan apples, but practically any variety of apple will do for baking except the Delicious or Macintosh varieties, which I find disintegrate when they bake.

6 to 8 Jonathan apples
1 cup cold water
1 cup red or white wine

1 cup sugar or vanilla sugar
1/4 cup raisins
1/4 cup chopped walnuts

1. Dissolve the sugar or vanilla sugar in a saucepan and bring it to a rapid boil. Boil 5 minutes.

2. Add the wine and continue boiling until a thinnish syrup is formed (about 15 minutes). Test the syrup for thickness periodically with a spoon. It should be rather thin but still have the consistency of syrup and not plain liquid. When the syrup reaches the correct consistency, set it aside.

3. Cut the tops (stem ends) off the apples and set them aside. Remove the cores and seeds of the apples, using an apple corer and the tip of a vegetable peeler. Discard cores and seeds.

4. Preheat the oven to 350°. Pour some of the syrup into a flat glass or ceramic baking dish. Set the apples, without their tops, into the syrup.

5. Mix the raisins and the walnuts, and then fill the center of each apple with some of this mixture. Ladle some syrup over the apples and into their filled cavities.

6. Replace the tops of the apples, pressing them gently into the apple. Ladle the remainder of the syrup over the apples. Bake on the middle shelf of the oven for 35 to 45 minutes or until the apples are well baked through. Baste them from time to time as they cook with the syrup. The syrup will thicken slightly as the apples bake, but it will never become so thick that it caramelizes.

7. When the apples are through baking, remove them from the oven and cool them to room temperature. Serve the apples at room temperature, with some of the syrup poured over each portion. Recipe serves 6 to 8 people, depending on how many apples you bake. If you wish, you may serve *makarondelach* or cookies with the apples.

Apple *Schalet*

Apple *schalet* is one of the richest and most elegant of the apple-based desserts despite the fact that it was probably created as a way of using up leftover bread. It is Russian in origin but found its way into Jewish cuisine in the Ukraine and in the Baltic states. This recipe is *milchig*. I do not recommend making a *pareve* version by substituting margarine for the butter.

1 loaf day-old *challah* (choose a plain *challah* or a sweet raisin *challah* that is made without a topping of sesame or poppy seeds; when I bake *challah*, I always make at least one of the loaves plain and I bake it in a loaf pan so that I can use it in making this and other dishes)
up to 2 sticks sweet butter
8 cups homemade applesauce (or substitute good-quality store-bought applesauce)
1/2 tsp. ground cinnamon
1 extra-large egg, beaten
1 1/2 cups apricot preserves
2 Tblsp. cold water
1/4 cup apricot brandy or brandy

1. Put the applesauce into a saucepan and simmer it, stirring from time to time, until it cooks down to 6 cups of thickened apple puree. Remove from the heat and cool to room temperature.

2. Remove the ends of the *challah* and save them for some other purpose. Cut the *challah* into 16 slices. Cut 13 of these slices in half on the diagonal to form bread triangles. Set aside 6 of the triangles. Cut the remaining *challah* into cubes.

3. Grease well with butter a 1 1/2-quart round baking dish or a ceramic mold that is 3 1/2 inches deep.

4. Melt 1 stick of the butter in a skillet over low heat. When the butter is melted, remove it from the heat. Dip the bread triangles into the melted butter and line the bottom and sides of the baking dish. Some of the bread will sit higher than the baking dish but this is not a problem, so do not be concerned about it. If there is any butter left, leave it in the skillet and set it aside.

5. Melt 4 more Tblsp. butter in the skillet. Drop the *challah* cubes into the butter and sauté on all sides until golden in color. Repeat until all of the *challah* cubes are sautéed. Add more butter only if needed.

6. Mix the sautéed *challah* cubes and the cinnamon into the apple puree. Beat the egg and mix this into the same mixture. Pour this mixture into the *challah*-lined baking dish. Do not be alarmed about how high the filling rises. It cooks down during baking.

7. If necessary, add more butter to the skillet and melt it over low heat. Dip the remaining bread triangles into this and cover the top of the baking dish with them.

8. Preheat the oven to 350°. Bake the *schalet* in the oven on the middle shelf for 1 hour or until the top is golden brown. Remove from the oven and cool to room temperature.

9. Put a flat platter on top of the *schalet* and turn it over to unmold. It should unmold quite easily.

10. Just before serving the *schalet*, make a sauce. Put the apricot preserves through a sieve into a saucepan. Stir in the 2 Tblsp. water and heat it for 10 minutes. Stir in the brandy and pour the sauce into a sauceboat. To serve the *schalet*, bring it to the table to cut. Spoon a portion of the sauce over each wedge of apple *schalet*.

Serving Suggestions

A dessert this elegant calls for an equally elegant entrée. Try it as a dessert following an entrée of grilled salmon steaks (p. 82) or poached salmon with dill sauce (p. 85).

Challah Bread Pudding

This recipe is an old Creole dish that tastes even better made with *challah* than it does with white French bread. The dish was probably created as a way of using up leftover bread. The sauce is optional but makes an already scrumptious dessert extra-special. The recipe is *milchig*. I do not recommend making it with *pareve* ingredients.

1 loaf day-old *challah* (without poppy or
    sesame seeds sprinkled on it)
1 stick plus 2 Tblsp. sweet butter
1 quart whole milk
4 eggs
1 1/2 cups vanilla sugar (or substitute 1 1/2 cups
    regular white sugar plus 1 tsp. vanilla
    extract)
1 cup regular white sugar
3/4 cup golden raisins
1/2 cup bourbon whiskey or brandy

1. Cut the *challah* into 1 × 1-inch cubes. Mix with the raisins in a deep mixing bowl. Pour the milk over the *challah* and raisins and mix gently until it is completely absorbed.

2. Spread the 2 Tblsp. butter all over the bottom and sides of a 9 x 13 inch baking pan that is 2 inches deep.

3. Beat 3 of the eggs together with the vanilla sugar (or sugar plus extract) with an electric beater or by hand until the mixture is very smooth and thick. Pour it over the bread mixture and mix gently until everything is well combined.

4. Preheat the oven to 350°. Transfer the contents of the mixing bowl to the baking pan. Place the baking pan into a large, deep roasting or baking pan into which it will fit comfortably, leaving at least a 1-inch border around the edges. This pan will provide a water bath for the pudding to steam in. Pour boiling water into the larger roasting or baking pan, and surround the pudding with the water. Make sure that the water comes at least 1 inch up the sides of the pudding pan. Place this into the oven and bake the pudding for 1 hour or until a toothpick inserted into the center of the pudding comes out clean. Add boiling water to the water bath, if necessary.

5. While the pudding is baking, prepare the sauce. Do this about 20 minutes before the pudding is done. Melt the stick of butter in a double boiler set on top of the stove at medium heat.

6. Stir the remaining cup of sugar into the boiling water.

7. Beat the remaining egg and add it to the double boiler. Cook this mixture about 5 minutes or until the sugar dissolves. Make sure that the mixture never comes to a boil or the egg will curdle, spoiling the sauce. Remove the sauce from the heat and let the mixture in the double boiler cool to room temperature.

8. Stir in the whiskey or brandy just before you are ready to serve the sauce.

To serve the pudding, cut the pudding into squares and place each square onto its own serving plate or dessert bowl. Spoon some of the sauce over the pudding and serve the remaining sauce in a sauceboat.

Serving Suggestions

Challah bread pudding is excellent following a meal featuring fish. Just about any of the fish recipes in this book is delicious with this dessert except *kulebiaka*, which is extremely rich and requires a somewhat lighter finish. I also think this is a delicious alternative to the traditional *lokshen* course that is served after sweet-and-sour pickled fish (p. 89).

Palaschinken

Palaschinken are Hungarian dessert *blintzes*. They are a little larger in size than regular *blintzes*, because the crepes are made in an 8-inch rather than a 6-inch crepe pan. Although the recipe below is *milchig*, you may substitute water and oil for the milk and butter with no significant loss of flavor and make the dish *pareve*.

1 cup unbleached white flour
3 eggs
1 cup whole milk or cold water
1/3 cup club soda or seltzer
3 Tblsp. sugar
pinch salt
1/4 cup good-quality imported cocoa
3/4 cup apricot jam
1 cup ground walnuts
butter or peanut oil for sautéing
icing or confectioner's sugar for sprinkling

1. Beat the eggs with the milk or water in a mixing bowl. Add the club soda and mix well.

2. Add the pinch salt and stir in the flour and the sugar. Stir the batter until it is smooth and without any lumps. You will have a rather thin batter.

3. Melt a small amount of the butter, or heat a little oil, in an 8-inch crepe pan over medium-high heat. When the fat is sizzling, add 1/4 cup batter and spread it across the pan. Cook 2 to 3 minutes on one side, then flip it over and lightly brown on the other side. The crepe will puff up slightly because of the club soda in it. When the crepe is cooked through, remove to a platter.

4. Spread a heaping tsp. of the jam over the crepe, sprinkle it with a little cocoa, and roll it into a loose cylinder. Put it into a well-greased baking pan and keep warm in a low (175°) oven while you make the rest of the crepes.

5. Repeat steps 3 and 4 until all the batter is used up. You should have about 16 to 18 crepes.

6. To serve *palaschinken*, place two of the crepes on a dessert plate. Drop ground walnuts onto them and sprinkle confectioner's sugar over everything. Repeat with each portion. Recipe serves 8 to 10 people as a dessert.

Serving Suggestions

Palaschinken go well with *milchig* or *fleischig* meals, especially those that feature a Hungarian dish as an entrée. They also make a delicious light supper dish. In this case, serve 3 rather than 2 *palaschinken* per person. A fruity white wine goes very well with *palaschinken* when they are served as an entrée. To balance the meal, begin it with a bouquet of fresh vegetables soup (p. 62).

Varenikes

Varenikes are Polish fruit *kreplach* that are served as a dessert or a light supper. They are made mostly with summer fruits like plums, cherries, and berries. My recipe calls for either a plum or a blueberry filling.

1 recipe *kreplach* dough (p. 188)
12 to 16 Italian prune plums or 2 1/2 cups fresh
**   blueberries**
3/4 cup sugar
6 Tblsp. sweet butter, melted
1/3 cup bread crumbs
sour cream

1. Prepare *kreplach* dough as directed on p. 59 as if you were preparing meat or cheese *kreplach*. Each piece of dough should be cut into a 2-inch square, just as for any other kind of *kreplach*.

2. If using the plums, pit them and cut them in half. Lay half a plum on the middle of a square of dough. Sprinkle it with a tiny bit of sugar and cover it with the other half. If using the blueberries, place 1 1/2 Tblsp. berries onto the middle of a square of dough and sprinkle them with a little sugar.

3. Fold the square of dough over the fruit diagonally to make a triangle. Seal the triangle by pinching it together and then pressing it all along the edges with the tines of a fork. Repeat this until all the dough and fruit have been used up. You should have used up no more than 1/3 cup of the sugar.

4. Bring a large pot of salted water to boil on top of the stove. When it is boiling rapidly, add a few *varenikes* and lower the heat to a gentle, rolling boil. Cook the *varenikes* about 20 minutes and remove with a slotted spoon. Transfer to a platter or baking dish and keep warm in a low oven (175°) or in the microwave while you finish making the remaining *varenikes*.

5. In a skillet, melt the butter over medium-low heat. Add the remaining sugar and stir it in well.

A chasidic deli in Montreal, 1992.

6. Add the bread crumbs to the butter and stir together again until well mixed.

7. To serve the *varenikes*, place 3 or 4 on each dessert plate. Spoon over some of the melted butter and the bread crumbs. Serve immediately with sour cream on the side. Recipe serves 6 to 8 as a dessert and 4 as a light supper.

Serving Suggestions

Varenikes may be served the same way as *blintzes* (p. 188) or cheese *kreplach* (p. 185).

Hungarian Fruit *Knaidelach*

Hungarian fruit *knaidelach* are one of the most elegant and beautiful desserts one can make. They are a *milchig* dessert and should never be made *pareve* because the taste of the melted butter topping is

essential to the flavor of the dish. These *knaidelach* are traditionally made with apricots in the late spring/early summer and with plums in the late summer/early autumn. Although other fruits may be substituted for these, I do not find this dough quite as versatile as that for *varenikes*. I prefer to stick to the classical recipes with this dish.

2 pkg. active dried yeast
1/2 cup plus 1 tsp. sugar
1/2 cup lukewarm water
1/2 tsp. grated lemon zest
1/4 tsp. freshly grated nutmeg
1/4 tsp. salt
3 egg yolks
2 cups unbleached white flour
12 fresh Italian prune plums or apricots, pitted
1 stick sweet butter
1/2 tsp. ground cinnamon with 1/3 cup sugar mixed together in a small cup

1. Mix the 1 tsp. sugar into the lukewarm water and dissolve the yeast in it. Place in a warm, draft-

free place to proof. After about 10 minutes, the yeast should be bubbly and frothy.

2. Mix the flour, 1/4 cup sugar, salt, lemon zest, and nutmeg together in a small bowl. Make a well in the center of the flour.

3. Add the yeast mixture and the egg yolks to the dry ingredients. Mix together and knead by hand until smooth dough is formed. The dough should be elastic and slightly moist. If it is too dry, add a little more water. If it is too wet, add a little more flour.

4. Roll the dough into a ball and place it into a greased bowl. Cover with a damp kitchen towel and set aside in a draft-free place to rise until double in bulk. This will take approximately 1 hour.

5. When the dough has risen sufficiently, punch it down and roll it out flat onto a board. Roll the dough until you have a rectangle 1/4 inch thick.

6. With a pastry cutter or a knife with serrated edges, cut the dough into 12 equal 4-inch squares.

7. Lay one fruit in the center of each square of dough. Sprinkle the insides of the fruit with a little sugar.

8. Fold the dough over the fruit to completely enclose it and then roll each package into a ball. Set the balls of filled dough onto a platter or baking sheet. Up to this point, the recipe can be made in advance.

9. The dough now needs to rise about 15 minutes before it gets cooked. If you are going to proceed immediately, cover the balls of dough with a damp kitchen cloth and set them aside to rise. If you wish to wait, cover them with wax paper and then with plastic wrap. Place in the refrigerator and bring to room temperature when ready to cook.

10. To cook the *knaidelach*, bring a large pot of salted water to a rapid boil on top of the stove. There should be at least 5 to 6 cups of water in it and more will not hurt.

11. Using a large slotted spoon, carefully lower each *knaidel* into the boiling water up to 6 *knaidelach*. Keep the heat high and boil the *knaidelach* 6 to 7 minutes.

12. Turn them over with the slotted spoon and boil an additional 6 minutes on the other side. Transfer the cooked *knaidelach* to paper towels to dry. Repeat with the remaining *knaidelach*.

13. Have the cinnamon-sugar mixture ready at your side. Melt the butter over low heat. To serve the *knaidelach*, place one or two of them onto a dessert plate. Dribble melted butter over each *knaidel* and sprinkle with the cinnamon-sugar mixture. Recipe serves 6 to 12 people.

Serving Suggestions

This elegant dessert goes well after an elegant fish entrée. Try it following a cold summer supper featuring *gravad lox* (p. 94) as the entrée.

Photographic still life by Henrietta Komras Sternberg.

Early Spring Dinner to Celebrate Tu B'shevat

Challah

"Old Country" Chopped Liver

Bouquet of fresh vegetables soup

Golden orange roast chicken

Orange-scented fruit *kugel*   Baked asparagus with lemon

Chardonnay

Prune *kissel* with almond macaroons

Assorted dried fruits and nuts from Israel
(figs, dates, carob), chocolates

Coffee or tea

12

Baked Goods

Gebakte Zisse Maichollim

They say: A fool loves sweet things.
This brilliant idea the smart people
came up with!

*Me zogt: A naar hot lieb zisse zachen. Dos
hobben di kluggeh mentschen oisgetracht!*

BAKED GOODS

Yiddish cuisine has always been well known for its delicious pastries and sweets. There is such a tremendous variety of Jewish bakery specialties that I found it necessary to subdivide this chapter in order to make it manageable. The recipes I selected to include here by no means represent the totality of what the Yiddish kitchen has to offer. They are a sampling of almost every type of pastry specialty that Yiddish cuisine contains. I use eight general categories:

Kichelach (cookies) are standard accompaniments to compote or *kissel*. They are also enjoyed as a between-meal snack with tea. *Ayer kichelach*, *mandelbroit*, *makarondelach*, and *tzimshterner* all are types of *kichelach*.

Small pastries are baked for special occasions only. Some of them, such as *hamantaschen* and *taigelach*, are associated with specific Jewish holidays.

Shabbos cakes are made with baking powder or baking soda to help them rise. I chose the name *Shabbos* cakes for this category because in my home these are the pastries most often prepared in honor of the Sabbath.

Sponge cakes, in Yiddish cuisine, are associated mainly with Passover baking. This is because they use no leavening agents like yeast or baking powder, which are strictly forbidden on Passover. Eggs are separated and the whites stiffly beaten in sponge cakes to help them rise during baking. There is a strong possibility that sponge cakes were introduced into Yiddish cuisine by Sephardic Jews from Spain who found refuge from persecution in Poland.

A large variety of pastries that figure prominently in Yiddish cuisine are made with yeast dough. This includes the various *babkas*, *kuchen*, Jewish apple tart, and the Hungarian *makos*, *dios*, and *kokos*.

Flourless tortes are the exquisite creations of Hungarian and Viennese bakers. They have always been enjoyed by the Jews who come from this region as well as by non-Jewish Hungarians and Austrians. The flourless tortes are the only pastries in Yiddish cuisine that traditionally are iced. Because they are made without flour or any kind of leavening agent, flourless tortes are excellent alternatives to sponge cakes on Passover.

There are four different cheesecake recipes in this book. One of them is the familiar American-style cream cheese cake, which is often thought of as a Jewish dish because of its popularity in Jewish deli-type restaurants. This cake, however, is purely American, even though it may be Jewish American.

Shtrudel is in a category all by itself. The dough for *shtrudel* is somewhat time consuming and difficult to make, but don't let that deter you. Homemade *shtrudel* is well worth the trouble it takes to make, and no kind of store-bought *shtrudel* tastes anything like the homemade. Make *shtrudel* once a year and enjoy it as a truly special treat. In our home, that time of year is Sukkos.

Some of the pastry recipes in this book are *pareve*, others are *milchig*, and a few others may be prepared both ways. The most important factor in deciding whether or not to use dairy products in baking is the need for sweet butter. Sweet butter imparts a distinct flavor that cannot be replicated by anything else. Margarine and vegetable shortening, which some people claim are flavorless, in point of fact do have their own aromas and flavors. In my opinion, those flavors are decidedly chemical. Anything baked with margarine or vegetable shortening tastes as if has been baked with margarine or vegetable shortening. My *pareve* recipes all use peanut oil. But, as any experienced cook knows, oil does not work well for every kind of baking. I have experimented a great deal in my kitchen in order to prepare the recipes for this cookbook. I draw my conclusions about which pastries may be made *pareve* and which should be made only *milchig* based on hours and hours of testing and retesting. Experiment for yourself and see if you agree or disagree with my choices.

COOKIES
KICHELACH

Mandelbroit

Mandelbroit, called by Ukrainian Jews *kamishbroit*, was practically a staple in my childhood home. We had two tin cookie containers in the kitchen. One was always filled with *mandelbroit* and the other with some other kind of cookie. The second kind of cookie varied from week to week. But the *mandelbroit* was always there. It was even there during Passover, except that *matzoh* cake meal was used instead of flour and the baking powder was left out of the recipe. This recipe for *mandelbroit* was handed down in my family through I don't know how many generations. The only change I have made to the original recipe is the optional substitution of whiskey, amaretto, or brandy for 1/4 cup of the orange juice.

There is one little secret my grandmother shared with me about making *mandelbroit*, and I think this makes her recipe a little different from the others I have seen. She felt that good *mandelbroit* required the use of both ground almonds and sliced almonds. This gave the cookie a flavor of the nut in every bite. Well-made *mandelbroit* should also always be crispy and somewhat brittle.

It is possible that *mandelbroit* originated with Sephardic rather than Ashkenazic Jews, who use liberal quantities of almonds in their cooking and baking.

4 eggs plus 1 large egg white beaten with 1
    Tblsp. cold water
1 1/2 cups sugar
1 cup corn or peanut oil
1 tsp. baking powder
1/2 cup freshly squeezed orange juice or 1/4 cup
    orange juice plus 1/4 cup whiskey, brandy,
    or amaretto liqueur
finely grated zest of 1 orange
4 1/2 to 5 cups unbleached white cake flour
3/4 cup finely ground almonds (this can be
    done in the food processor)
1 1/2 cups sliced unblanched almonds
1/2 tsp. ground cinnamon

1. In a mixing bowl, cream the eggs and 1 cup of the sugar with an electric mixer or a hand mixer.

2. Add the oil and beat until well incorporated.

3. Add the juice or juice and liquor and beat in lightly but completely.

4. Add the orange zest, 4 1/2 cups flour, baking powder, and ground almonds. Beat in lightly but thoroughly until well incorporated. Finish doing this in a kneading motion by hand.

5. Knead in the sliced almonds. The dough should be dry enough to work with easily. It should be soft, pliant, and not sticky. If it seems too loose or too sticky, add up to 1/2 cup additional flour.

6. Preheat the oven to 350°. Place the oven rack on the middle shelf. Mix the remaining sugar and cinnamon together in a bowl and set aside. You will need several well-greased cookie sheets.

7. Divide the dough into 3 parts and shape each part into a log about 2 inches in diameter. Place each of these on a well-greased baking sheet.

8. Bake 1 or 2 of the logs at one time on the middle shelf of the oven for 30 to 35 minutes or until nicely browned. When each log has baked sufficiently, remove it from the oven and cool it slightly.

9. Using a well-sharpened serrated bread knife, slice each log into 1/2-inch-thick slices and lay each slice carefully on a well-greased cookie sheet. Each slice should reveal almonds attractively floating in the dough.

10. Beat the egg white with the water. Mix the remaining sugar with the cinnamon. Set each of these next to you with a pastry brush while you work on the next steps.

11. Lay the slices of *mandelbroit* across the cookie sheet so that one of the cut sides faces upward.

12. When you fill up a cookie sheet with *mandelbroit* slices, place it in the oven and bake it for 5 minutes.

13. Remove the *mandelbroit* from the oven and turn each slice over. Brush with the beaten egg white the side facing upward and sprinkle with cinnamon-sugar. Return the *mandelbroit* slices to the oven and bake another 5 minutes. Repeat this until all of the *mandelbroit* have been baked twice, once with the cinnamon-sugar coating.

14. Cool to room temperature and store in tins. Recipe makes about 4 dozen *mandelbroit*.

Serving Suggestions

Mandelbroit make a perfect accompaniment to fruit compotes and *kisselen*. They are also delicious on their own with coffee or tea. I love them as a change of pace from the traditional amaretti (Italian almond cookies) that accompany Italian espresso coffee.

Cinnamon Toast

Cinnamon toast is an alternative to *mandelbroit* that was very popular among Jews from Litteh and Russia to eat with their glass of tea. Cinnamon toast is actually a bread that is made with "raisin water," which my grandmother used to call *m'zonos challah*.

M'zonos challah is a term that requires a little explanation. In Jewish tradition, bread is considered the most important food. Before eating a piece of bread, one is required to wash one's hands, make a blessing over the hand washing, and then recite the blessing over the bread. This is the customary way a meal is begun. The ritual is called the "grace before meals." However, there are breads that can be baked that do not require this elaborate ritual because they are made with fruit juice instead of water in the dough. According to Jewish law, this renders them "cake" instead of "bread." One does not recite the blessing for bread over such bread. Instead, one recites the blessing for cake: *Borei minay m'zonos*. *M'zonos challah*, therefore, means "bread that is considered cake" and over which one does not recite the blessing for bread. My grandmother, and many other Jewish women from eastern Europe, made *m'zonos* breads using "raisin water" as the fruit juice or flavored liquid. Cinnamon toast is a kind of *m'zonos* bread that is turned into a tasty cookie or sweet.

Recipe for Raisin Water

1 cup raisins
2 cups cold water

Place the water in a saucepan and bring it to a boil. Add the raisins and cook for 3 minutes. Cool to lukewarm. Drain the raisin water through a sieve into a container. Dry the raisins and eat them as a snack or use them in some kind of baking. Store them in the refrigerator to prevent spoilage. The raisin water may now be used for baking.

Recipe for Cinnamon Toast

5 1/2 to 6 cups unbleached white bread flour
2 pkg. freeze-dried yeast
1 1/2 cups raisin water
3/4 cup sugar
3 eggs
2/3 cup peanut oil
1 tsp. salt
1/2 cup sugar mixed with 1 tsp. cinnamon
1 large egg white beaten together with 1 Tblsp.
**   cold water**

1. Heat raisin water to lukewarm. Stir in 1 tsp. of the sugar and proof the yeast by dissolving it in the water. Set aside in a draft-free place, such as an unlit oven, to proof (about 10 minutes). The proofed yeast will be bubbly and puffy.

2. Place 5 1/2 cups flour, sugar, and salt into a deep mixing bowl and make a well in the center. Place the eggs and yeast mixture into the well. Beat in and then knead the dough by hand until it is smooth and elastic. The kneading can also be done in a food processor or with the dough hook of an electric mixer. Use up to 1/2 cup additional flour to correct the consistency of the dough, if necessary.

3. Place the dough in a well-oiled bowl and cover with a damp kitchen towel. Set in a draft-free place to rise until doubled in bulk (about 1 to 1 1/2 hours).

4. Punch down dough and divide into 4 equal parts. Roll each of these into a very long oblong loaf that is 1 1/2 times the length of a standard-size loaf pan (about 18 inches). Set each loaf onto a well-greased baking sheet. Cover again with damp kitchen towels and set aside to rise again until doubled in bulk.

5. Preheat the oven to 350°. After the loaves have risen sufficiently, bake them two at a time on the middle shelf of the oven for 35 to 40 minutes. To test for doneness, tap the bottoms of the loaves. If they sound hollow when tapped, they are done. Cool the loaves on wire racks to room temperature.

6. When the loaves have cooled, slice them into 1/2-inch slices.

7. Mix together the cinnamon and the sugar in a mixing bowl. Have the beaten egg white and the cinnamon-sugar mixture next to you while you work.

8. Toast the slices on one side in a 350° oven until well browned. Turn each slice over, brush lightly with the beaten egg white, and sprinkle with the cinnamon-sugar mixture. Return to the oven and toast again until the cinnamon-sugar forms a glaze. Cool cinnamon toast slices on wire racks and store in paper or cloth bags instead of tins or plastic, because this will affect the crispness of the toast. The cinnnamon toast keeps fresh and crisp for weeks at a time in paper or cloth bags. The crumbs of cinnamon toast are delicious sprinkled over *lokshen* before it is baked.

Variation

M'zonos challah can be made from this recipe and eaten as bread. Just braid the loaves as you would *challah*, brush them with an egg wash, and sprinkle them with poppy or sesame seeds. The loaves are ready at the end of step 5 of this recipe.

Macaroons

Makarondelach

Macaroons were a popular cookie with Jews from eastern Europe. Their Sephardic origin is obvious, even though most Yiddish-speaking Jews would huffily claim them as their own. Like many of the most interesting Jewish recipes, the recipe for macaroons was most probably brought to Poland and Russia by Jewish immigrants from Italy, Greece, Turkey, and Holland. Or perhaps it was brought directly from Spain itself by Jews who found sanctuary from persecution in Poland during the exodus of 1492. The word *macaroon* is Italian, from the word *maccarone*, an Italian cookie made out of ground almonds. The Yiddish name for these cookies, *makarondel* (plural: *makarondelach*), sounds a lot like the Italian name.

Whatever their origin, *makarondelach*, after *mandelbroit*, are the second most popular cookie that the Jews in eastern Europe made. *Makarondelach* are simple confections, made almost exclusively of ground nuts and sugar bound together with lightly beaten egg white. Unlike that other famous egg-white cookie, meringues, *makarondelach* should be somewhat soft and chewy. The most classical recipes for *makarondelach* are those made with almonds, but they actually can be made out of almost any kind of nut. The basic recipe never varies, no matter what kind of nut you use.

My own recipes for *makarondelach* call for 1/2 tsp. liqueur as well as the usual ground nuts, sugar, and egg whites. The liqueur gives the cookie a little extra zip without affecting its texture. I also recommend finishing the grinding of the nuts by hand, using a mortar and pestle rather than doing it all in the food processor. This little extra effort will give you better control over the final texture of the nut paste, which is very important in the dish. The paste has to be granular and moist but not too oily, or the dough will not cohere well. You will obviously need a very large mortar and pestle to do this. These are not difficult to obtain.

Almond *makarondelach*

4 cups blanched almonds, whole or in pieces
2 1/2 cups sugar
5 egg whites
1/2 tsp. amaretto

parchment paper for baking cookies on
whole blanched almonds for garnish

1. In the food processor, coarsely grind the nuts, using a pulse/chop movement. Transfer half the nuts to a large mortar and pestle.

2. Add half the sugar and continue to grind the nuts until it is well incorporated.

3. Add the remaining nuts and grind again. Add all but 1/2 cup of the sugar and finish the grinding. The texture of the mixture should be granular and moist but not too oily.

4. Beat the egg whites until foamy but not stiff and pour half of them into the nut paste with the amaretto liqueur. Mix well in the mortar, using the pestle until well incorporated.

5. Add the remaining sugar and egg white and continue mixing and grinding until the mixture is just soft enough to drop from a spoon without losing its shape or separating. Test this on a dish. Be sure to add the egg whites slowly as you work.

6. Transfer the contents of the mortar to a mixing bowl and refrigerate it for 15 minutes. Meanwhile, preheat the oven to 350°.

7. Line 3 or 4 baking sheets with parchment paper. Remove the paste from the refrigerator. Using a teaspoon, drop a spoonful of the nut paste onto the parchment paper. Continue doing this, leaving about 2 inches of space between each teaspoonful of paste.

8. Bake each sheet of cookies for 10 minutes. The cookies will spread out and flatten a little.

9. Remove from the oven and press a whole blanched almond into each cookie and return them to the oven. Bake 5 to 7 minutes longer. Remove from the oven and cool on the baking sheets. Do not attempt to remove the macaroons from the baking sheets until they have cooled completely. If you do this, there is a good chance they will fall apart.

10. When the macaroons have completely cooled off, gently and carefully separate them from the parchment paper. They may be served at any time or stored in tins, where they keep very well. Recipe makes about 2 1/2 dozen cookies.

Variations

For walnut macaroons, substitute 4 cups walnuts for the almonds. Substitute whole walnuts for the whole almonds. Substitute frangelico liqueur for the amaretto. Follow the recipe as directed above.

For hazelnut macaroons, substitute hazelnuts for

the almonds and frangelico liqueur for the amaretto. Follow the recipe as directed above.

For pecan macaroons, subsitute pecans for the almonds and frangelico liqueur for the amaretto. Follow the recipe as directed above.

Tzimshterner Kichelach

These honey-spice cookies are a little like ginger-bread. Their name means "cookies for the stars." They got this unusual name because they are baked with spices that are also used in the *Havdallah* cere-mony at the conclusion of the Sabbath. The Sab-bath ends when the first three stars come out in the evening sky on Saturday night. *Tzimshterner ki-chelach* were customarily served in some Jewish homes, particularly in central Europe, at the conclu-sion of *Shabbos*.

4 Tblsp. sweet butter
1/2 cup vanilla sugar (or substitute 1/2 cup
    white sugar and 1/8 tsp. vanilla extract)
5 cups unbleached white cake flour
1 cup honey
3 eggs
1/2 tsp. baking soda
1 tsp. ground cinnamon
1 tsp. ground ginger
1/2 tsp. ground cloves
1/4 tsp. freshly grated nutmeg
1 egg white mixed with 1 Tblsp. cold water
    (egg-white wash)

1. Cream the butter with the sugar, using an electric beater or mixer at medium speed.
2. Add the eggs and the honey and beat in until well blended.
3. Mix the remaining ingredients together in a separate mixing bowl. Beat this into the egg mixture by hand or with an electric mixer at low speed a little at a time. You will have to finish the mixing by hand because it will form itself into a soft dough.
4. Wrap the cookie dough in wax paper and refrigerate it for 2 hours.
5. After 2 hours have passed, roll out the dough on a floured board to a 1/8-inch thickness and cut it into rounds or any other shape you desire. You may use cookie cutters or a narrow-mouthed glass. Place

the cookies on well-greased baking sheets. Brush the tops of the cookies lightly with the egg-white wash.

6. Preheat the oven to 350°. Bake the cookies for 15 minutes. Cool them to room temperature and serve, or store them in tins, where they will keep well for quite a while. Recipe makes about 36 cookies.

Egg Crackers or Cookies
Ayer Kichelach

This was one of my grandmother's prize recipes. *Ayer kichelach*, when properly made, are light as a feather. As unsweetened crackers, they are delicious with appetizers. The sweet sugar-coated *ayer kichelach* are delicious with tea. *Ayer kichelach* are one of those inimitable little delicacies that seem as if they are made of absolutely nothing at all. To the inexperi-enced cook, they appear so simple and easy to make that "anyone can do it." But oh, the moans and the groans and the intense disappointment when time after time the cook struggles and still they don't curl up or they burn on the bottom or generally don't turn out "right!" *Ayer kichelach*, in my opinion, are a true gourmet food. Just like the proverbial soufflé (that horror that can sink in the middle at the slightest motion around the stove), there is an art to making the *ayer kichel*, which must be practiced and practiced until it is perfected. A properly baked *ayer kichel* has curled-up edges and is practically all air when you bite into it. More so, even, than a me-ringue. The process of making *ayer kichelach* is full of tricks, but don't despair. Do it anyway and proceed without fear. *Ayer kichelach* may be tricky but they are not at all time consuming or complicated. The ingredients are simple and really quite nutritious, even the sweet ones. They are much better for you than any kind of chips, crackers, or store-bought cookies.

These simple rules tell you all you need to know to master the art of baking *ayer kichelach*:

1. Always bake them on a heavy, *ungreased* baking sheet.
2. Always place the oven rack on the *middle* shelf of the oven when you bake.
3. If you are baking a large quantity of dough that must be done in batches, *never remove* the baking sheet from the oven during the baking time. This keeps it at a sufficiently high temperature, as

required for the *kichelach* to rise and curl up at the edges.

4. Don't use too much flour, only enough to make a *smooth* dough. Practice and time will give you a feel for the right texture.

5. If you can get them, wear cloth gloves while cooking the *kichelach* to avoid getting burns on your fingers.

6 eggs
1/2 tsp. salt
2 1/2 Tblsp. peanut oil
2 1/2 to 2 3/4 cups unbleached white *bread* flour

1. Beat the eggs, 2 Tblsp. oil, and salt with a fork or a wire whisk until well beaten and blended.

2. Add the flour gradually, up to 2 1/2 cups, mixing constantly with the whisk and then by hand until the dough is smooth. Avoid adding the last 1/4 cup flour unless you absolutely need it to get the correct consistency. Knead the dough for a few minutes by hand to make it soft and pliable.

3. Place the oven rack on the middle shelf and place the ungreased baking sheet on top of the rack. Preheat the oven to 450°.

4. Roll out the dough on a floured board to about 1/8-inch thickness. Brush the top of the dough with the last 1/2 Tblsp. oil.

5. Cut the dough into 2-inch squares.

6. Open the oven and, using a kitchen mitt glove on one hand, slide the rack out slightly, just enough to give you access to the cookie sheet. Place 4 to 6 squares of dough on the baking sheet, oiled side down, and slide the rack back in place. Close the oven door.

7. Bake the *kichelach* 6 to 7 minutes. They will puff up and curl as they bake and be light brown on the bottom.

8. Open the oven and turn the *kichelach* over onto the other side. Bake an additional 6 to 7 minutes. The underside of the *kichelach* will brown at this time.

9. Remove *kichelach* and cool on a wire rack. Repeat this procedure until all the dough is used up. Recipe will make about 18 to 20 *ayer kichelach*.

Variation: Sweet *Ayer Kichelach*

1 recipe plain *ayer kichelach* dough (see above)
1 egg, beaten with 1 Tblsp. cold water (egg wash)
white granulated sugar for sprinkling

Prepare the *ayer kichelach* as directed above. Then brush the egg wash onto the turned-up bottom of each *kichel*. Sprinkle this with sugar and pop the *kichelach* in the oven, sugared side up, for 2 minutes. Remove and cool, sugared side up, on a wire rack. The *kichelach* will have a beautiful, shiny sugar glaze.

To store *ayer kichelach*, do not use the usual cookie tins, ceramic jars, or plastic bags, as the *kichelach* will lose their crispness. Store them in paper or cloth bags, just like cinnamon toast (p. 257).

Serving Suggestions

Plain, unsugared *ayer kichelach* should be served alongside *forspeizen* like chopped herring (p. 41) or *liptavsky kayz* (p. 47). They are wonderful with herring but genuinely good with practically any appetizer. The sweet *ayer kichelach* make a great alternative to *makarondelach* or cookies alongside compote or *kissel*. They are also wonderful alone with tea or coffee. Sweet *ayer kichelach* are almost always served at a traditional eastern European tea table.

Aunt Ann's Sugar Cookies

My Aunt Ann loved these simple butter cookies, and she made them very well. This cookie lends itself easily to any shape cookie cutter, but I like to make them the way she did, simply taking a standard-size juice glass with a narrow mouth and using it to cut out the cookie shapes. This recipe is hers, exactly as she used to prepare it. The variations are also hers.

1 3/4 sticks sweet butter
1 cup vanilla sugar (or substitute 1 cup white sugar plus 1 tsp. vanilla extract)
1 egg
2 cups unbleached white cake flour
pinch salt
1/3 cup regular white sugar mixed with 1 tsp. cinnamon

1. Cream the butter and vanilla sugar (or regular sugar), using an electric mixer, until pale and fluffy.

2. Beat in the egg and vanilla extract (if using).

3. Stir in the flour very gradually until it is well incorporated. Roll the dough into a ball and wrap it in wax paper. Refrigerate for at least 1 hour.

4. Roll out the dough to the thickness of 1/4 inch.

5. Use a juice glass or whatever cookie cutter you prefer. Press the glass or cookie cutter firmly into the dough to make a clean cut. Transfer the cut cookies with a clean metal spatula to a well-buttered baking sheet. Reroll the remaining dough and continue to cut out cookies until the dough is all used up. Place all the cookies on baking sheets as you make them.

6. Preheat the oven to 350°. Make sure that the 1/3 cup regular sugar and the cinnamon are well mixed together. Sprinkle each cookie with a little of this cinnamon-sugar mixture. Bake 12 to 15 minutes or until the cookies are a pale golden color. Cool to room temperature before storing in tins. Recipe makes about 2 to 3 dozen cookies, depending on how small or how large they are cut.

Variations

For variety in taste, add any of the following to the basic cookie dough as you prepare it:

3 Tblsp. poppy seeds
3 Tblsp. anise or fennel seeds
3 Tblsp. caraway seeds

Do not sprinkle any of these variations with cinnamon sugar, and with the caraway seeds, use regular sugar instead of vanilla sugar. Do not use vanilla extract in caraway cookies.

Serving Suggestions

Serve these cookies as you would *mandelbroit* or any of the other *kichelach*, with tea or coffee or with compote or *kissel*.

Aunt Ann's
Oatmeal Cookies

My Aunt Ann, the cookie baker in the family, also loved to make these cookies as a lunchtime or snack-time treat. This recipe and the one following it for peanut butter cookies are called drop cookies because the dough is dropped onto the cookie sheet instead of being rolled and cut out. My bobbe called them *Amerikanische kichelach* (American cookies).

2 cups unbleached white cake flour
1 tsp. baking soda
1/2 tsp. salt
1 1/2 sticks sweet butter

1 cup brown sugar
2 eggs
2 cups old-fashioned rolled oats
1 cup dark raisins
1/2 cup chopped walnuts

1. Mix the flour, baking soda, and salt in a small bowl. Mix the oatmeal and the nuts in a second mixing bowl.

2. In a third mixing bowl, cream the butter and the sugar until smooth and fluffy, using an electric mixer.

3. Beat the eggs into the butter and sugar.

4. By hand, stir in 1/3 of the flour mixture, followed by 1/3 of the oatmeal mixture. Alternate until all of both mixtures are thoroughly incorporated into the butter and sugar.

5. Add the raisins and mix well. Preheat the oven to 350°.

6. Drop the batter by the scant tablespoonful onto well-greased baking sheets. Bake the cookies 12 to 15 minutes or until firm and golden brown. Cool to room temperature before storing in tins. Recipe makes about 3 dozen cookies.

Serving Suggestions

These cookies go well with compote or *kissel*, particularly those made with cranberries and apples. They are also delicious on their own with coffee or tea as a snack. Very healthy too!

Aunt Ann's
Peanut Butter Cookies

These were a childhood favorite of mine. They are "American all the way!" The cookies are made especially attractive by the imprinted crisscross pattern imprinted on them by the tines of a fork.

1/2 cup natural unsalted chunky peanut butter
1 stick sweet butter
1 cup brown sugar
1 egg
1/4 tsp. salt
1/2 tsp. baking soda
1 1/3 cups unbleached white cake flour plus 2 Tblsp.

1. Cream the butter and the sugar with an electric mixer until fluffy and smooth.

2. Beat in the egg and the peanut butter. Mix in the remaining ingredients except for the extra 2 Tblsp. flour. Place this onto a small plate.

3. Drop heaping teaspoonfuls of the batter 2 inches apart onto well-greased baking sheets.

4. Dip a fork into the 2 Tblsp. flour on the plate and press a crisscross pattern into each cookie. Preheat the oven to 350°.

5. Bake the cookies at 350° for 10 to 12 minutes or until firm. Cool and store in tins to preserve crispness. Recipe makes about 3 dozen cookies.

SMALL PASTRIES

Roggelach (Cookie Dough)

Roggelach are a crescent-shaped cream cheese pastry that is traditionally eaten during the week of Chanukah or on Shevuos. They can be made with either a cookie dough or a yeast dough.

2 cups unbleached white cake flour
1 3/4 sticks sweet butter
one 8-oz. pkg. cream cheese
1/2 cup chopped walnuts
1/2 cup dark raisins
2 Tblsp. sugar
1 Tblsp. cinnamon
1 egg white mixed with 1 Tblsp. cold water
   (egg-white wash)

1. The evening before baking, mix the flour, butter, and cream cheese and blend together by kneading until smooth. Roll this into a ball and wrap in wax paper. Refrigerate overnight.

2. The next day, combine in a mixing bowl all the remaining ingredients for the filling.

3. Remove the dough from the refrigerator and cut it into 3 equal parts. Roll the first piece of dough into a circle about 1/4 inch thick and cut the circle of dough into 6 or 8 triangular-shaped wedges.

4. Place a small amount of the filling onto a wedge of dough and roll it up jelly roll style, starting with the wide end and finishing at the narrow end. The pointed narrow end of the dough wedge should be in the center of the rolled dough when finished.

5. Bend the pastry slightly so that it forms a crescent shape, and place it on a well-greased baking sheet. Repeat until all the wedges of dough are used up. Repeat this entire process until all of the dough and all of the filling have been used up.

6. Preheat the oven to 350°. Brush the *roggelach* lightly with the egg-white wash. Bake the *roggelach* for 15 minutes or until they have turned a golden brown. Cool on wire racks. Recipe makes 18 to 24 *roggelach*.

Roggelach (Yeast Dough)

Yeast dough *roggelach* are made with sour cream instead of cream cheese.

1 envelope freeze-dried yeast
1/2 cup lukewarm whole milk
2/3 cup sugar plus 2 Tblsp.
1/4 tsp. salt
1 stick sweet butter, cut into bits
2 eggs, separated plus 1 egg white mixed with
   1 Tblsp. cold water (egg-white wash)
3 cups unbleached white bread flour
1 cup sour cream
1 Tblsp. cinnamon
2/3 cup chopped walnuts
2/3 cup dark raisins

1. Combine milk with 1 Tblsp. of the 2/3 cup sugar and stir in the yeast. Set aside in a draft-free place until the yeast is proofed (about 10 minutes). When ready, it will be bubbly on top.

2. Mix the flour with the reminder of the 2/3 cup sugar and the salt in a deep mixing bowl or in the bowl of the food processor. If using the food processor, you should fit it with the dough blade. Add the yeast mixture, egg yolks, butter, and sour cream to the flour and knead together. This can be started in the food processor. Finish the kneading of the dough by hand. This will take about 10 minutes. The dough should be smooth and moist, like bread dough.

3. Place the kneaded dough into a well-greased bowl. Cover with a damp cloth and set aside in a draft-free place to rise until doubled in bulk (about 1 1/2 hours).

4. When the dough has risen sufficiently, divide it into 4 pieces. In a separate bowl, beat the 2 egg

whites together with the remaining sugar and the cinnamon until foamy but not stiff. Mix the raisins and walnuts in a separate bowl.

5. Roll out one section of the dough into a round circle about 1/4 inch thick. Cut the circle into 6 or 8 triangle-shaped wedges.

6. Brush one wedge with the beaten egg white and sprinkle some of the raisins and walnuts over this.

7. Roll the wedge up, jelly roll style, starting at the wide bottom end and ending with the pointed top. The point of the wedge should be in the center when you finish rolling.

8. Bend the pastry into a crescent shape and lay it onto a well-greased baking sheet.

9. Repeat this procedure with the remaining wedges of dough. Then repeat all of the steps with all the remaining dough and filling ingredients until everything is used up. As you fill a baking sheet, cover it with a damp towel so that the pastries will rise a second time. You will need about 3 or 4 baking sheets, and the second rising will take about 45 minutes.

10. Preheat the oven to 350°. Brush the pastries with the egg-white wash and bake each sheet of *roggelach* in the oven for 15 to 20 minutes or until they are golden brown. Cool on a wire rack. Recipe makes about 24 to 32 *roggelach*. The *roggelach* may be sprinkled with confectioner's sugar before serving.

Taiglach

Taiglach are a strange and luscious confection that is served by eastern European Jews on Rosh Hashanah. The main feature of this delicacy is the sticky honey syrup in which it is simmered after it is baked and which clings to each piece of the confection. Because of its intense sweetness and its reliance on a syrup for sweetening, I am inclined to believe that *taiglach* are Sephardic in origin. Sephardic cooking is influenced by that of the Moslem world, of which Spain was a part before 1492, the year when its Jews and Moslems were exiled or forcibly baptized. One of the special features of the North African and Middle Eastern cuisines is their use of sugar syrups to sweeten pastries. Greek baklava, Moroccan m'hanncha, and Syrian khadaifi are all examples of pastries that are made very sweet by being drenched in a honey or sugar syrup. The baked goods of northern and central European cuisines, to my knowledge, have never made use of this technique.

There is a lovely tradition associated with *taiglach*. Like other Rosh Hashanah foods, its sweet flavor is considered a blessing that will usher in a sweet year. *Eretz Yisroel* (the Land of Israel) is called in the Hebrew Scripture *Eretz zovas cholov u'dvash* (a land flowing with milk and honey). This was the term used to describe the land the Jewish people would inherit. The honey evoked an image of something comfortingly sweet. Sweet dishes are eaten on Rosh Hashanah, particularly dishes made with honey, to remember the land of our ancestors. Eating *taiglach* was an important part of the tradition among the Jews of eastern Europe, exiled from their ancestral homeland and victims of periodic oppression and persecution. *Taiglach* reminded them of *Eretz Yisroel*, the land flowing with milk and honey.

4 cups unbleached white cake flour
2 tsp. baking powder
6 eggs, beaten
2 Tblsp. peanut oil
1/4 tsp. salt
2 cups honey
2 cups sugar
2 tsp. ground ginger
finely grated rind of 1 lemon
1 cup chopped walnuts

1. Mix together the flour, eggs, oil, baking powder, and salt. Knead the dough for 10 to 15 minutes. Roll into a ball, wrap in wax paper, and chill in the refrigerator for 1 hour.

2. On a floured board, roll the dough into ropes 1/2 inch thick and cut them into 1/2-inch size pieces. Roll these pieces into balls and place on well-greased cookie sheets.

3. Preheat the oven to 350° and bake for 5 to 7 minutes or until the cookie balls are golden brown in color. Do not allow them to get too brown. Shake pan, if necessary, to prevent the cookie balls from sticking together.

4. Mix honey, ginger, lemon zest, and sugar together in a deep soup pot and bring to a boil. Reduce heat, cover, and simmer for 5 minutes.

5. Drop the cookie balls into the syrup and add the walnuts. Simmer 5 to 10 minutes, stirring constantly with a wooden spoon until the *taiglach* are coated with the honey and nuts and are a golden brown.

6. Moisten a large wooden, marble, or formica board or slab with ice-cold water. Remove the *taiglach* with a slotted spoon and transfer to this board to cool. Recipe makes about 60 to 70 *taiglach*.

Serving Suggestions

Taiglach are traditionally served mounded on top of one another and each one stuck with a toothpick for easy, nonmessy handling. Delicious with coffee or tea. You'll love them, but don't eat too many at once!

Hamantaschen

Hamantaschen are a special pastry baked once a year in honor of the holiday of Purim. Legend has it that the shape of the *hamantaschen* resembles the three-cornered hat worn by Haman, minister to King Ahasuerus (Artaxerxes) of Persia.

The Book of Esther records that Haman had convinced the king to order the murder of all the Jews living in the Persian Empire because they would not declare him a god and bow down to him. (The religious injunction of refusing to recognize flesh-and-blood rulers as gods put Jews in conflict with their neighbors many times in the ancient world.) Haman was exposed by the Jewish Queen Esther, with whom Ahasuerus was madly in love. Esther reminded the king about the loyalty of her uncle Mordecai, who had foiled an assassination plot against the king by two members of his court some months earlier. Ahasuerus, best remembered as an avowed hedonist and a glutton, was considered by history a rather benign and unintelligent monarch. Since his priorities were limited to self-indulgences like food and romance, he did not at first comprehend how he had been tricked by Haman. But once he understood, he ordered that instead of the Jews, Haman and his family be hung on the gallows. After this happened, Jews all around the world began to celebrate the holiday of Purim as a reminder of the triumph of justice over the evil of the idolatrous Haman and his family.

In all truth, it is highly unlikely that Haman wore a three-cornered hat. This was a fashion in 18th-century Europe, where this folktale originated, and not in ancient Persia. Remember that *hamantaschen* is a Yiddish word, not Hebrew or Persian. In the Hebrew language, *hamantaschen* are called *Oznei Haman*, which means "Haman's ears." This implies a conclusion even more bizarre than believing that the triangle-shaped cakes were created to resemble Haman's hat. Surely Haman's ears were no more triangular in shape than those of other human beings.

In all fairness, it should be pointed out that Purim, in Jewish tradition, is the "holiday of nonsense," and the spreading of silly little fairy tales like the above two is really very much in keeping with the old Yiddish custom of saying "Purim Torah." "Purim Torah" means clowning around with the traditions by giving them nonsensical meanings and off-the-wall interpretations. For all we know, both of these stories began as Purim Torah and over time became enshrined by the Jewish community as plausible explanations for how *hamantaschen* were created.

The true origin of the word *hamantaschen* comes from the medieval German term *mohn taschen*. *Mohn taschen* means "poppy seed pockets" and was the name of an old recipe for pastries filled with a poppy seed filling. The pockets may or may not have been triangular in shape when the recipe was first conceived. But this dish was adopted and brought east by Jews from Germany into what would become Yiddish-speaking Europe (the Yiddish language is similar to medieval German). Because the expression *mohn taschen* reminded the Jews of Haman's name, the name *hamantaschen* ("Haman's pockets") was given by Jews to this pastry and it came to be baked in honor of Purim.

There is another silly bit of Purim Torah that I must share regarding *hamantaschen*. *Hamantaschen* are not made exclusively with poppy seed filling. Prune filling is also traditional. When I was 3 1/2 years old, I was sent to Hebrew school, and one of the stories I heard in school from my *rebbe* (teacher) was this absurd explanation for why we eat *hamantaschen* made with prune filling. When Queen Esther made a feast for Haman and King Ahasuerus (the feast at which she exposed Haman to the king), she served them *hamantaschen*. All the *hamantaschen* but one were made with poppy seeds. The remaining one had a prune filling. The prune-filled *hamantasch* was served to Haman. After Haman ate the prune-filled *hamantasch*, Esther pointed out to the king that there was an evil person who had plotted to murder off all her people and that the king would receive a sign pointing out to him who that evil person was. By this time, the *hamantasch* was digested and had entered Haman's bloodstream. The pits of the prunes were showing through his veins. The king took this to be the sign that Haman was the evil person who had plotted the murder of the Jews. Today we Jews eat *hamantaschen* filled with prunes to remind us of how prunes helped to expose Haman.

Although *hamantaschen* can be baked and eaten all year, my grandmother was adamant about reserving this name and her recipe for these cakes for the holiday of Purim alone. When she baked similar pastries at other times of the year, she would vary the fillings and call the pastries *pireshkes*, a Yiddish pronunciation for the Polish word *pierogi* or the Russian word *pirozhki*. *Pierogi*, or *pirozhki*, are filled pastries (sweet fillings or savory fillings) that are an important part of the Polish and Russian cuisines. *Pirozhki* are usually cigar shaped rather than triangular shaped. This was, of course, one thing my grandmother pointed out to me in her insistence that there was a fundamental difference between *pireshkes* and *hamantaschen*. The irony was that when she made *pireshkes*, they always had the same triangular shape as *hamantaschen*. She would go only to the extent of varying her fillings when she made *pireshkes*, but she never varied the shape of the two pastries. While a *pireshkeh* and a *hamantasch* were definitely not the same thing to my grandmother, I must concede that the only real difference between *pireshkes* and *hamantaschen* is that special ingredient called "Purim."

Here are recipes for both *hamantaschen* and *pireshkes*, as my Grandmother Miriam made them.

Hamantaschen, Cookie Dough

2 1/2 cups unbleached white cake flour
2 1/2 tsp. baking powder
1 tsp. salt
1/2 cup sugar
4 Tblsp. melted sweet butter
1 egg, beaten
3/4 cup whole milk
1 egg yolk mixed with 1 Tblsp. honey and 1
   1/2 Tblsp. cold water (egg-honey wash)
1 recipe prune or poppy seed filling

1. Mix together the flour, baking powder, salt, and sugar. Add melted butter, egg, and milk. Mix together and knead a minute or two. Cut the dough in half.

2. Roll out each half to a thickness of 1/8 inch. Using a glass or 2-inch cookie cutter, cut 2-inch rounds out of the dough.

3. Fill each round with 1 tsp. of the prune or poppy seed filling. Place the filling in the center of the circle.

4. Fold three sides of the piece of dough up over the filling and pinch together. This will form a triangular pocket. Pinch together well to make sure the *hamantaschen* are sealed, or they will break open during baking. Place each *hamantasch* on a well-buttered cookie sheet as you finish filling and shaping it.

5. Repeat this with the remaining dough until all the dough and all the filling are used up. Make new *hamantaschen* out of the dough that remains from cutting out the first rounds by rerolling and recutting it.

6. Preheat the oven to 350°. Brush the *hamantaschen* with the egg-honey wash, using a pastry brush. Bake the *hamantaschen* for 20 to 25 minutes or until they are golden brown. Cool on wire racks before serving. Recipe makes about 36 *hamantaschen*.

Hamantaschen, Yeast Dough

I personally like these *hamantaschen* better than those made with a cookie dough, but they are definitely more time consuming to make. The advantage is that these can be made pareve with absolutely no loss of flavor.

1 recipe yeast pastry dough, *pareve* or *milchig*
   (p. 273)
1 recipe prune or poppy seed filling
1 egg yolk mixed with 1 Tblsp. honey and 1
   1/2 Tblsp. cold water (egg-honey wash)

1. Divide the yeast pastry dough into 3 parts. Roll out one part into a circle or rectangle 1/8 inch thick. Using a glass or a 2-inch cookie cutter, cut out 2-inch rounds.

2. Fill each round with 1 tsp. of the prune or poppy seed filling. Place the filling in the center of the round of dough.

3. Pinch together 3 sides of each round of dough to form a triangular shape. Pinch the pieces together tightly so that they won't break apart during baking.

Using a pastry brush, brush the seal with a little cold water to fix it. Place each filled *hamantasch* on a well-greased cookie sheet.

4. Repeat this procedure until you have used up all the dough and all the filling. As you fill a cookie sheet with *hamantaschen*, cover them over with a damp kitchen cloth and set aside to rise until they are doubled in bulk (about 45 minutes).

5. Preheat the oven to 350°. Brush the *hamantaschen* with egg-honey wash and bake 25 to 30 minutes. To test for doneness, lift up one *hamantasch*. Tap it on the bottom. If it sounds hollow, it is ready. Cool *hamantaschen* on wire racks before serving. Recipe makes about 36 *hamantaschen*.

Fillings for *Hamantaschen*

Filling 1: *Mohn* (Poppy Seed) Filling

1 cup poppy seeds
3 Tblsp. sugar
1/3 cup honey
1/2 cup brandy or whiskey
1/4 cup freshly squeezed lemon juice
finely grated zest of 1 lemon
1/4 cup raisins
1/4 cup blanched almonds, ground
1 egg white
boiling water

1. Place poppy seeds in a heatproof mixing bowl. Pour enough boiling water over them to cover them by 1 inch. Let them soak for 3 hours. Drain off excess water after 3 hours have passed.

2. Place sugar, honey, lemon juice, and whiskey or brandy in a saucepan. Stirring constantly, bring almost to a boil over medium heat. Stir until all the sugar and honey are dissolved, but do not let the mixture come to a boil.

3. Add drained seeds, raisins, lemon zest, and almonds to the saucepan. Reduce the heat to the lowest simmer, and simmer the ingredients 10 to 12 minutes or until all the liquid has evaporated. Cool to room temperature.

4. Beat the egg white until it forms stiff peaks. Fold this into the poppy seed mixture.

Filling is now ready. Use in *hamantaschen* as directed in the recipes on p. 265.

Filling 2: Prune Filling

1 lb. pitted prunes, cut into bits
1/2 lb. dark raisins
1 cup walnuts
juice and zest of 1 orange
juice of 1 lemon
1/3 cup honey
1/2 cup sweet red wine

Soak the prune pieces and the raisins in the wine for 1 hour. Place everything into a food processor and, using a pulse/chop motion, grind into a paste. If the filling seems too liquid, increase the quantity of nuts until the consistency is correct. It should be a thick, compact paste.

Filling is now ready. Use in *hamantaschen* as directed in the recipes on p. 265.

Pireshkes

Pireshkes are made exactly the same way as *hamantaschen*, but the fillings are different. These two fillings were my grandmother's favorites for *pireshkes*. Use them instead of the *hamantaschen* fillings and enclose them in either a cookie or yeast pastry dough.

Filling 1: Nut Filling for *Pireshkes*

1 1/2 cups walnuts
1 1/2 cups almonds
1/2 cup golden raisins
grated zest of 1 orange
1/2 cup sugar
1/4 cup freshly squeezed orange juice
1/4 cup whiskey or brandy

Into a food processor, place all the ingredients. Pulse/chop until the mixture becomes a coarse paste. If the mixture seems too dry, add a little more orange juice.

The filling is now ready. Prepare the *pireshkes* exactly as you would *hamantaschen*, using the recipes on p. 265.

Filling 2: *Lekvar* or *Povidl* Filling for *Pireshkes*

1 1/2 cups *lekvar* or *povidl* (p. 294)
1 cup walnuts, coarsely ground in food
    processor
grated zest of 1 orange
1 Tblsp. freshly squeezed orange juice
1 Tblsp. brandy

Mix everything together in a mixing bowl and fill *pireshkes* as directed in the recipes on p. 265.

SHABBOS CAKES

Rosh Hashanah Honey Cake

Yomtovdige Medyvnik

Honey cake is traditional during the High Holy Days of Rosh Hashanah and Yom Kippur, and there are two different kinds. One is a honey *lekach* (p. 272), which is a honey-flavored sponge cake. The other is leavened with baking powder and baking soda and is called a *medyvnik*. *Medyvnik* is actually the Ukrainian name for honey cake, but my grandmother used this name to distinguish it from the honey *lekach*, which had an entirely different texture and method of preparation.

Honey *medyvnik* is a spicy, rich, and very satisfying cake I always looked forward to at Rosh Hashanah time. It really can and should be eaten at other times of the year, too, because it is easy to prepare as well as delicious.

5 large eggs, at room temperature
1 cup brown sugar
1 cup honey
2 Tblsp. peanut or corn oil plus oil for greasing
    pan
1/2 cup golden raisins
1/2 cup walnut pieces
1 tsp. ground ginger
1/2 tsp. ground allspice
1/2 tsp. ground cinnamon
1/4 tsp. ground cloves
3 1/2 cups unbleached white cake flour
1 tsp. baking powder
1 tsp. baking soda
juice and grated zest of 1 orange
1/2 to 3/4 cup strong black coffee, cooled to
    room temperature
1/3 cup Sabra liqueur

1. Mix raisins and walnuts with 2 Tblsp. of the flour and set them aside. This is done to prevent the raisins and nuts from sinking to the bottom of the cake during baking.

2. Preheat the oven to 300°. Grease a 9 x 5 x 3 1/2 inch loaf pan with oil. Line the bottom and sides of the pan with wax paper and grease the paper with oil as well. Set pan aside.

3. Beat the eggs with the sugar until well blended. This should be done by hand or using an electric mixer at the lowest speed.

4. Add honey and orange rind and thoroughly mix into the eggs and sugar.

5. In a separate bowl, mix together the flour, spices, baking powder, and baking soda. In a measuring cup, mix the orange juice, coffee, and liqueur. The total liquid mixture should be no more than 1 1/3 cups. Add extra coffee or orange juice if necessary to make up this amount.

6. Mix the flour mixture and the liquid mixture into the egg mixture in small amounts, alternating between the dry and the liquid ingredients. It is best to do this by hand. Do not overmix. If you prefer to do this with the electric mixer, use the lowest speed. Too much mixing and too rapid mixing result in a dry cake. The ingredients must be completely and thoroughly blended while using a minimum of mixing motion.

7. Gently fold in the nuts and raisins, using a rubber spatula. Mix this only enough to make sure that no flour adheres to the fruit and nuts. It should be completely mixed into the cake batter. This is a little tricky, so do it carefully.

8. Immediately pour the batter into the loaf pan and bake the cake for 1 hour or until it is done. To test for doneness, poke a toothpick or a cake tester into the center of the cake. If it comes out clean with no batter clinging to it, the cake has baked long enough. Cool the cake completely to room temperature. Then, to unmold it, turn it upside down onto a board. Gently peel off the wax paper. The flavor of this cake actually improves after 2 or 3 days.

Jewish Apple Cake

Eppl Kuchen

This is a *pareve* cake that, like *medyvnik*, seems to get better and better after the second or third day.

1 cup peanut oil plus oil for greasing the pan
1 1/2 cups brown sugar
3 eggs
2 cups unbleached white cake flour
1 tsp. baking soda
1 tsp. ground cinnamon
1/2 tsp. salt
2 Tblsp. brandy
4 tart green apples, peeled, cored, and finely
 diced
1/2 cup chopped walnuts or hazelnuts
confectioner's sugar for sprinkling

1. Preheat the oven to 350°. Grease a 9-inch cake pan (regular round or tube shaped) with oil and set it aside. A springform pan is an excellent choice.

2. Cream the eggs together with the sugar in a deep mixing bowl, using an electric mixer. The mixture should be thick and fluffy.

3. Add the oil and the brandy and continue to mix until well incorporated.

4. Add the flour, salt, baking soda, and cinnamon and beat into the egg mixture lightly but thoroughly. This is best done by hand but may also be done with the mixer at low speed. Do not overmix.

5. Fold in the apples and the nuts, using a rubber spatula.

6. Pour the cake batter into the prepared cake pan.

7. Bake the cake at 350° for 55 to 60 minutes. To test for doneness, poke a toothpick or a cake tester into the center of the cake. If it comes out clean with no batter clinging to it, the cake is done. Cool it to room temperature before removing it from the pan. Sprinkle with confectioner's sugar before serving.

Sour Cream Coffee Cake With Streusel Topping

Streusel Kuchen

This rich, mocha-flavored marble cake has always been one of my favorites. It is a *milchig* recipe and should not be made into a *pareve* one. You will need several mixing bowls to prepare the separate batters.

Dark mocha batter

2 cups unbleached white cake flour
1 cup dark brown sugar
1/2 cup honey
1 1/2 tsp. ground cinnamon
1/2 tsp. ground cloves
1 Tblsp. unsweetened cocoa
1/2 tsp. freshly grated nutmeg
1 tsp. baking soda
1 cup sour cream
1/4 tsp. salt
1 stick sweet butter
1/2 cup dark black coffee, cooled to room
 temperature
4 egg yolks

Light vanilla batter

2 1/2 cups unbleached white cake flour
2 tsp. baking powder
1/4 tsp. salt
1 stick sweet butter
1 cup vanilla sugar (or substitute 1 cup regular
 white sugar plus 1 tsp. vanilla extract)
3/4 cup whole milk
4 egg whites

For streusel topping

1/2 cup sugar
1/2 cup unbleached white cake flour
4 Tblsp. sweet butter

1. Preheat the oven to 350°. Grease a 10-inch springform tube cake pan with butter. Sprinkle it with a little flour. Tip the pan from side to side to cover the bottom and sides with flour. Then tap out the excess. Set the pan aside.

2. To prepare the dark mocha batter, combine the flour, baking soda, salt, cocoa, and spices together in one mixing bowl.

3. In another bowl, using an electric mixer or by hand, cream the brown sugar and the butter together, mashing it against the sides of the bowl. When you are finished doing this, the mixture should be creamy and fluffy.

4. Beat in the egg yolks and then the honey and the coffee.

5. Lightly mix in the sour cream and the dry ingredients in small amounts. Do this by hand or with the electric mixer at low speed. Mix everything together thoroughly, but do not overmix the batter. It should be well blended and smooth when you finish.

6. To prepare the light vanilla batter, combine the flour, salt, and baking powder in a small mixing bowl.

7. Cream the butter and vanilla sugar (or regular sugar) with an electric beater or by hand, mashing it against the sides of the bowl. When you are finished, the mixture should be creamy and fluffy. If using vanilla extract, add it at this point.

8. Mix in the dry ingredients and the milk in small amounts, alternating between one and the other. Do this by hand or with the electric mixer at low speed. Mix everything thoroughly but do not overmix.

9. In a deep mixing bowl, beat the egg whites until they form into stiff peaks. Make sure you are using perfectly clean blades on your egg beater when you do this or the whites won't stiffen properly.

10. Fold the egg whites into the vanilla cake batter, using a rubber spatula. Fold them thoroughly until no trace of egg white remains but, again, do not overmix.

11. In a small mixing bowl, prepare the streusel topping by rubbing the sugar, flour, and butter together by hand. It should have the consistency of coarse crumbs when you are finished.

12. To create a proper marbled effect, use 2 ladles or 1/4-cup scoops. Spoon 1/4 cup of each batter into the prepared pan, alternating scoops. Place each scoop of batter next to its opposite in color. As the cake becomes layered, repeat this pattern again and again until you have used up all of both batters. After it has baked, the cake will take on a marbled rather than a checkerboard pattern, even though it looks a little like a checkerboard when you are spooning the batters into the baking pan.

13. When you have finished doing this, sprinkle the streusel topping over the cake.

14. Bake the cake in the oven for 55 to 60 minutes. To test for doneness, insert a toothpick or cake tester into the center of the cake. If it comes out clean, the cake is ready. Cool to room temperature before unmolding. This cake keeps moist and delicious for several days after it has been baked.

Hungarian Sour Cherry Cake

Ungarische Karschkuchen

This cake should be made only in the springtime and early summer, when fresh sour cherries are in season. It is a wonderful way to mark this season every year and is just as delicious as strawberry shortcake!

1 cup pitted fresh sour cherries
4 Tblsp. sweet butter
1 cup sour cream
1 1/2 cups sugar
3 large eggs, beaten
1/2 cup chopped almonds
3 Tblsp. kirsch or cherry brandy
2 3/4 cups unbleached white cake flour
1 1/2 tsp. baking powder
pinch salt
powdered sugar for sprinkling

1. Preheat the oven to 350°. Prepare a 9-inch springform round cake pan by greasing it with sweet butter. Then sprinkle a little flour into it. Tip it from side to side to cover the bottom and sides of the pan. Tap out the excess flour and set the pan aside.

2. Process the cherries in the food processor using the pulse/chop motion until coarsely pureed.

3. In a mixing bowl, cream the butter and the sugar with an electric mixer or by hand, mashing it against the sides of the bowl, until it is creamy and fluffy.

4. Add the eggs, liqueur, sour cream, and cherries. Mix together well but do not overmix. This is best done by hand but may be done with the electric mixer at low speed.

5. Add the dry ingredients and the nuts in small amounts. Stir in gently by hand or at low speed with the electric mixer. Blend completely but do not overmix the cake batter.

6. Pour the batter into the prepared cake pan and bake at 350° for 40 to 45 minutes. To test for doneness, insert a toothpick or a cake tester. If it comes out clean, the cake is done. Cool to room temperature before unmolding. Sprinkle with powdered sugar before serving.

Serving Suggestions

For a rich and luscious dessert, mix pitted, halved, fresh sweet bing cherries with sour cream and a little cherry brandy or kirsch. Spoon this over each slice of cake for a special presentation. Unbelievably delicious!

Galitzianer Plum Cake

Galitzianer Flommenkuchen

This lovely little cake from Galitzia is unbeatable during the short season in late summer and early autumn when fresh Italian prune plums are found in the market. It should be eaten fresh the day it is baked because it does not keep well.

1 stick sweet butter
1 cup vanilla sugar (or substitute 1 cup regular
    white sugar plus 1 tsp. vanilla extract)
1 1/2 cups unbleached white cake flour
1 1/2 tsp. baking powder
1/4 tsp. salt
2 large eggs
1/4 tsp. freshly grated nutmeg
1/2 cup sour cream
12 or 13 Italian prune plums, pitted and halved

For streusel topping

4 Tblsp. sweet butter
1/2 cup brown sugar
4 Tblsp. unbleached white cake flour

1. Preheat the oven to 350°. Prepare a 9-inch springform cake pan by greasing it with sweet butter and sprinkling it with flour. Tip the pan from side to side to make sure the bottom and sides of the pan are covered with flour. Tap out the excess and set aside.

2. Cream the butter with the vanilla sugar (or white sugar) using the electric mixer or by hand mashing it against the sides of the mixing bowl. When you are finished, the mixture should be creamy and fluffy.

3. Add the eggs and continue mixing until well blended.

4. Mix the flour, nutmeg, salt, and baking powder in a small bowl.

5. Add the sour cream and the dry ingredients to the cake batter in small amounts, alternating between the two until everything is incorporated into the batter. This is best done by hand but may also be done with the electric mixer at low speed.

6. Pour the batter into the prepared cake pan. Lay the plum halves gently on top of the batter, skin side down, in concentric circles or a spiral pattern until the entire cake is covered with the plums.

7. Prepare the streusel topping by mixing the ingredients by hand until they are formed into a coarse, grainy meal. Sprinkle this over the plums.

8. Place the cake into the oven and bake for 1 hour or until the cake starts to pull away from the sides of the pan and the top is golden brown.

9. Remove from the oven and cool to room temperature before removing from springform pan. The cake will deflate slightly due to the weight of the plums on top of the batter, but this is typical of the dish. Serve the cake right away after it has cooled sufficiently to room temperature. It is perfect with coffee or tea or as part of an eastern European tea table.

Fluden

My grandmother used to call *fluden* the lazy *balaboosteh's* (homemaker's) *hamantaschen*. This was because the fillings she most often used resembled those used for *hamantaschen*. In point of fact, *fluden* can be made using any type of filling. My Aunt Ann once made one filled with a thickened rhubarb compote. *Fluden* is essentially 2 or 3 layers of cookie dough with a filling or two sandwiched in between the layers. It is an excellent way of using leftover filling. When served, *fluden* is cut into squares. It is a wonderful treat with tea or coffee.

1 stick sweet butter or 1/2 cup peanut oil
finely grated zest and juice of 2 oranges
2 large eggs
3/4 cup sugar
1/2 tsp. salt
1 tsp. baking powder
1/2 tsp. baking soda
3 1/2 cups unbleached white cake flour
1/3 recipe poppy seed filling for *hamantaschen*
    (p. 266) or
1/3 recipe prune filling for *hamantaschen*
    (p. 266) or
1/3 recipe apple filling for apple strudel (p. 285)
    or
1/3 recipe nut filling for *pireshkes* (p. 266)
1 egg yolk mixed with 1 Tblsp. honey and 2
    Tblsp. cold water (egg-honey wash)

1. In a large mixing bowl, cream the butter or oil with the sugar. Beat with the electric mixer until the mixture is creamy and fluffy.

2. Beat in the eggs, orange juice, and orange zest. Lightly beat in the remaining ingredients except the fillings and the egg-honey wash. Allow the dough to rest for 1/2 hour. It will be very thick but still pourable.

3. Grease a deep, rectangular baking pan like the kind used for brownies or squares (10 × 10 × 2 inches is a good size).

4. Pour half of the dough into the pan and spread it across the bottom. Make sure it covers the entire pan.

5. Spread the filling across this but do not go completely to the edge of the pan.

6. Pour and spread the remaining dough over the top.

7. Preheat the oven to 350°. Brush the egg-honey wash over the top of the *fluden* and bake it on the middle shelf of the oven for 45 to 50 minutes or until the top is golden brown.

8. Cool to room temperature before cutting the *fluden* into squares.

SPONGE CAKES

Sponge Cake

Lekach

There is a theory that sponge cakes became popular among Jews because they have always been eaten on Passover when yeast, baking powder, and other leavening agents are prohibited. A cake that rises because the egg whites in it are separated from the yolks and beaten stiff before being folded into the other ingredients is not considered, according to Jewish law, *chometz* (leavened) and is therefore kosher on Passover.

I have another theory to add to this one. Desserts that use large amounts of eggs have always been popular in Spain and Portugal, where Sephardic Jews originally came from. Among these egg-based confections are various kinds of sponge cakes. This type of dessert is still popular in Sephardic cuisine today. It is highly probable that the popularity of sponge cakes among Polish and Russian Jews was due to their ancestors having migrated eastward from Spain (or to the contact between the Sephardic Jews and the Jews already living there).

Whatever their origins, sponge cakes have been so much a standard part of Yiddish cuisine that the sponge cake was given a Yiddish name—*lekach*. *Lekach* is eaten all year, not only on Passover. The non-*pesachdig* variety was typically consumed with a shot of vodka or schnapps after the synagogue services were over.

I include three variations on *lekach* in this book. Recipe 1 is a basic *lekach* that is eaten all year. Recipe 2 is a Passover nut *lekach*. Recipe 3 may have been the earliest version of the famous Jewish honey cake, called "honey *lekach*." Each kind of *lekach* can be eaten by itself or made more elaborate when it is glazed or filled.

Some cooks advocate using ungreased cake pans to bake sponge cakes, but I find that the cakes really unmold much better if the pans are greased and floured.

Basic Sponge Cake

Poshetteh Lekach

9 eggs, separated (make sure the eggs are very fresh; eggs that are not fresh will not work well for sponge cake)
2 cups sugar
pinch salt
grated zest of 1 lemon and orange
2 cups unbleached white cake flour plus 2 Tblsp. flour for flouring the cake pan
2 Tblsp. peanut oil plus 2 Tblsp. oil for greasing the cake pan

1. Preheat the oven to 350°. Set aside a 10-inch tube cake pan. A springform pan in which the center with the tube comes out is excellent. Grease it with the 2 Tblsp. peanut oil set aside for this purpose, and then sprinkle it with flour. Tap the flour all over the bottom and sides of the pan, then tap out the excess.

2. In a deep mixing bowl, beat the egg yolks, 1 cup of the sugar, and the remaining 2 Tblsp. oil. Beat the mixture until it is thick and frothy, using an electric mixer.

3. Gently mix in the citrus peel and the flour by hand. Mix it in completely but do not overmix or the cake will be too dry.

4. In a separate, very deep mixing bowl, using a clean beater attachment, mix the remaining sugar, the pinch salt, and the egg whites. Whip this until it forms itself into rather stiff, high peaks. It is important that the blades of the egg beater attachments be very clean when you do this. Make absolutely sure that no egg yolk has attached itself to any white when the eggs were separated. Otherwise, the whites will not whip and the cake will not rise properly.

5. Gently fold the egg-white mixture into the egg-yolk mixture with a rubber spatula. Make sure that everything is well folded and that no trace of white remains.

6. Gently pour the batter into the prepared baking pan. Bake the cake at 350 ° for 55 to 60 minutes. The cake will feel springy to the touch. *Do not open the oven* or move around very much in the kitchen while the cake is baking or it will fall. Sponge cakes, like soufflés, are tricky in this way.

7. Remove the cake from the oven only when you are certain that it has baked completely. It may fall slightly when it cools but not enough to label it a "fallen cake." Don't get discouraged if it doesn't work well the first time. Sponge cakes take a little practice to get right.

8. To remove cake from pan, invert it onto a board and cool it completely in the pan turned upside down. When it is cool, it should unmold very easily. If it doesn't, run a knife gently around the edges.

Passover Nut Sponge Cake

Pesachdige Mandel Lekach

This cake may be made as a non-Passover dish by substituting unbleached white cake flour for the *matzoh* cake meal.

10 eggs, separated (fresh eggs only)
1 cup sugar
1/3 cup *matzoh* cake meal (*matzoh* cake meal is very finely ground *matzoh* meal that resembles flour and is found during Passover on the kosher food shelf of the supermarket) or 1/2 cup unbleached white cake flour plus enough *matzoh* cake meal or flour to flour the cake pan
2 Tblsp. amaretto or frangelico liqueur
2 cups almonds, walnuts, or hazelnuts, finely ground

2 Tblsp. sunflower oil plus 2 Tblsp. oil for greasing the cake pan (2 Tblsp. almond oil or hazelnut oil may be used instead of the sunflower oil to give a special flavor to the cake; use sunflower oil for greasing, however, as these other oils are quite expensive. Almond oil and hazelnut oil are both available in health food stores and specialty shops.)
grated zest of 1 orange
pinch salt

1. Preheat the oven to 350°. Prepare a 10-inch tube cake pan by greasing it with 2 Tblsp. sunflower oil and then flouring it with the 2 Tblsp. *matzoh* cake meal or flour. Tap the meal or flour all around the sides and bottom of the pan and then tap out the excess. A springform pan with a removable tube center works very well.

2. Beat the egg yolks, oil, and half of the sugar in a deep mixing bowl, using the electric mixer until the mixture is frothy and thick.

3. Add the liqueur, orange peel, cake meal or flour, and ground nuts to this. Mix these ingredients in by hand. Mix them well but do not overmix or the cake will be too dry.

4. In a separate deep mixing bowl, mix the remaining sugar, the pinch salt, and the egg whites together. Beat them well with an electric beater, using very clean blades, until they form into stiff peaks.

5. Gently fold the egg-white mixture into the egg-yolk mixture, using a rubber spatula. Mix well, making sure that the egg whites are well folded into the egg yolk mixture.

6. Pour the batter into the prepared cake pan and bake the cake in the oven for 55 to 60 minutes. *Do not open the oven* during baking and do not move around too much in the kitchen or there is a chance that the cake might fall.

7. Remove the cake from the oven. It should feel springy to the touch. Turn it over onto a board and cool to room temperature before unmolding. It should unmold very easily after it is cooled.

Honey *Lekach*

9 eggs, separated (use fresh only)
1 cup unbleached white cake flour
1/2 cup brown sugar
1 cup honey
1 tsp. ground cinnamon

1/2 tsp. ground allspice
1/2 tsp. ground ginger
2 gratings fresh nutmeg
1/4 cup whiskey or brandy
2 Tblsp. peanut oil plus 2 Tblsp. oil for
   greasing the pan
pinch salt

1. Preheat the oven to 350°. Prepare a 10-inch tube cake pan by greasing it with 2 Tblsp. oil and then sprinkling flour over the pan, tapping it all over the sides and bottom. Set the prepared pan aside.

2. In a large mixing bowl, beat the egg yolks together with the sugar and the honey, using an electric mixer, until the mixture is thick and frothy.

3. Mix in the spices, the whiskey or brandy, and the flour by hand. Mix completely but do not overmix or the cake will be too dry.

4. In a separate deep mixing bowl, beat the egg whites together with the salt until they form stiff peaks.

5. Fold the egg whites into the egg-yolk mixture, using a rubber spatula. Fold well until all traces of white disappear into the batter.

6. Pour the batter into the prepared cake pan. Bake the cake for 55 to 60 minutes. *Do not open the oven* during baking or move around too much in the kitchen or the cake may fall.

7. Remove the cake from the oven. It should feel springy to the touch. Turn it over onto a board and cool to room temperature before unmolding. It should unmold quite easily. If it doesn't, gently run a knife around the edges. The cake will deflate slightly after it cools but not enough to warrant calling it a "fallen cake."

Glazed *Lekach*

A glazed *lekach* is a fancier presentation than a plain one. Both variations of glazed *lekach* make attractive presentations at a tea table. Each of the recipes below is easy to make and elevates the ordinary *lekach* to an elegant and beautiful after-dinner dessert with coffee or tea.

Recipe 1: Orange-Glazed *Lekach*

1 basic *lekach*, cooled and unmolded
1/4 cup triple sec
1/4 cup sugar
1/3 cup freshly squeezed orange juice

Dissolve the sugar in the orange juice while heating it in a small saucepan over medium heat. Remove the pan from the heat and stir in the triple sec. Poke holes all over the *lekach* with a toothpick and spoon the warm syrup over it. Let the cake steep for 1 hour before serving it.

Recipe 2: Glazed Honey *Lekach*

1 honey *lekach*, cooled and unmolded
1/4 cup sugar
1/4 cup coffee-flavored liqueur (e.g., Tía María or Sabra)
1/4 cup water

Dissolve the sugar in the water in a small saucepan while heating it over medium heat. Remove the saucepan from the heat and stir in the liqueur. Poke holes all over the *lekach* and spoon the warm syrup over it. Let the *lekach* steep for 1 hour before serving it.

Recipe 3: Glazed Nut *Lekach*

Substitute amaretto or frangelico for the coffee-flavored liqueur in the previous recipe, and prepare and glaze a nut *lekach* exactly as directed for glazed honey *lekach*.

YEAST DOUGH PASTRIES

Yeast Pastry Dough

This yeast pastry dough is used in many different kinds of Jewish baked goods, including *kuchen*, *makos*, *dios*, *kokos*, and Lithuanian cheesecake. It may be made *milchig* or *pareve* depending on how you wish to serve it or on your own personal preference. Both kinds of yeast pastry dough are excellent.

1 envelope freeze-dried yeast
1 1/4 cups raisin water (p. 257) or whole milk
3/4 cup plus 1 Tblsp. sugar
1 tsp. salt
1 cup peanut oil or 1 stick sweet butter
2 eggs, beaten
4 1/2 to 5 cups unbleached white bread flour

1. Heat the raisin water or milk to lukewarm. Dissolve the yeast with 1 Tblsp. of the sugar. Set aside in a draft-free place to proof. Yeast will be proofed in about 10 minutes, when the yeast will bubble up to the top of the glass in which it has been proofed.

2. This next step may be done in a food processor, with an electric mixer, or by hand. Place 4 1/2 cups of the flour into a mixing bowl or the bowl of the food processor. Add all of the ingredients into the flour, mix, then knead either by hand or in the machine. Add more flour, if necessary, to achieve the correct texture, which should be smooth and moist but not sticky. Finish kneading the dough by hand. Shape it into a ball and cover it with a damp cloth to begin the first rising. *This is the first step in making any of the yeast dough pastries in the recipes that follow.*

Kuchen

Kuchen in Yiddish simply means "something baked," but here it refers to a specific type of yeast dough pastry that was popular all over the Yiddish-speaking world. There are many different recipes for this dish, but mine, which comes from my grandmother, was probably typical of how it was made in the area of Poland she came from.

For pastry

1 recipe *milchig* yeast pastry dough (p. 273)
1/2 cup melted sweet butter
3/4 cup vanilla sugar (or substitute 3/4 cup
    regular white sugar plus 1/2 tsp. vanilla
    extract
4 tsp. cinnamon
3/4 cup raisins
3/4 cup chopped walnuts
1 egg white mixed with 1 Tblsp. cold water
    (egg-white wash)

For streusel topping

1/2 cup sugar
1/2 cup unbleached white flour
4 Tblsp. sweet butter

1. Roll out half of the pastry dough on a floured pastry board after it has gone through its first rising. The dough should be rolled into an oval shape about 1/8 inch in thickness.

2. Spread this with half of the melted butter. Mix the vanilla sugar with the cinnamon and sprinkle half of this mixture over the dough.

3. Sprinkle half of the raisins and half of the walnuts over this. Roll the dough up jelly roll fashion until it forms a long cylinder. Pinch the ends of the cylinder together tightly and shape the pastry into a round ring shaped somewhat like a bagel. Place it on a well-greased baking sheet and cover it with a damp kitchen cloth. Set it aside to rise.

4. Repeat steps 1 through 3 with the remaining dough and remaining ingredients.

5. After the pastries have risen (about 1 hour) until doubled in bulk, mix the ingredients for the streusel topping by hand until they are formed into a grainy meal.

6. With a serrated knife, cut the pastry ring into 1/2-inch slices, but do not make complete slices. Slice 3/4 of the way into each slice you make. After you have sliced all the way around the pastry ring, take one slice and gently rotate it upside down into the middle of the pastry ring. Try to do this without losing any of the filling. Repeat this with every alternate slice you have made. The pastry ring will have been formed into an attractive wreath with slices jutting out both outward and inward. Gently turn the slices so that their filling faces slightly upward and you are able to see the jelly roll pattern.

7. Brush the entire pastry with the egg-white wash and then sprinkle it with half the streusel topping.

8. Repeat steps 6 and 7 with the second pastry ring. Preheat the oven to 350°.

9. Bake the *kuchen* for 30 to 35 minutes or until it is golden brown. To test for doneness, lift one up gently and tap the bottom. If it sounds hollow, it is ready. Cool on wire racks before serving. Delicious with coffee or tea.

Makos, Kokos, Dios

Makos, kokos, and *dios* are three wonderful Hungarian pastries that every Hungarian Jewish cook knows how to make. As with every recipe of this kind, there are many different ways of making these pastries. These are my favorites.

Makos

1 recipe *pareve* yeast pastry dough (p. 273)
2 cups poppy seeds
1 cup orange juice
1/2 cup sugar
3 Tblsp. honey
3/4 cup golden raisins
grated zest of 1 orange
2 Tblsp. peanut or corn oil
2 egg whites
1 egg yolk mixed with 1 Tblsp. cold water (egg wash)

1. In the microwave oven or on top of the stove, bring the orange juice to a boil and pour it over the poppy seeds. Allow to rest for 5 minutes and then pour off all but a few tablespoonfuls of the liquid.

2. In a food processor or blender, grind the soaked poppy seeds into a coarse paste and then mix them in a bowl with the rest of the ingredients except for the egg wash and the yeast pastry dough.

3. On a well-floured board, roll out half of the dough into a rectangle or oval about 18 inches in length and about 1/8 inch thick.

4. Spread half of the filling over this, leaving a 1-inch border all around the oval or rectangle of dough.

5. Roll the pastry up jelly roll fashion until it is formed into a long cylinder. Place it on a well-greased baking sheet and cover with a damp kitchen towel. Set it aside to rise until doubled in bulk (about 1 hour).

6. Repeat steps 3 through 5 with the remaining dough and filling.

7. When pastries have risen sufficiently, preheat the oven to 350°. Brush each pastry with egg wash and bake in the oven for 30 to 35 minutes or until golden brown. To test for doneness, gently tap the bottom of one *makos*. If it sounds hollow, it is ready. Cool on wire racks before serving. With coffee or tea, serve the *makos* cut into slices.

Kokos

1 recipe *pareve* or *milchig* yeast pastry dough (p. 273)
1 egg yolk mixed with 1 Tblsp. cold water (egg wash)

8 oz. semisweet baker's chocolate
3 Tblsp. very strong coffee
1/4 tsp. cinnamon
1 Tblsp. sugar
1 Tblsp. coffee or chocolate liqueur (e.g., Tía María or Kahlúa)

1. To prepare filling, melt the chocolate in a double boiler on top of the stove or in the microwave oven according to microwave instructions. Mix the remaining ingredients into the chocolate after removing it from the heat.

2. To make *kokos*, follow steps 1 through 7 in the recipe for *makos*, substituting the *kokos* filling for the *makos* filling.

Dios

1 recipe *pareve* yeast dough pastry (p. 273)
1 egg yolk mixed with 1 Tblsp. cold water (egg wash)
3 cups ground walnuts
1/2 cup sugar
1/3 cup raisins
1/4 tsp. cinnamon
1/4 cup rum
1/4 cup frangelico or amaretto liqueur
2 large egg yolks

1. Mix together all the ingredients listed above except for the pastry dough and the egg wash. This is the *dios* filling.

2. Prepare *dios* as you would *makos* or *kokos*, using the filling made from the above ingredients. Follow steps 1 through 7 in the recipe for *makos* to make the *dios*.

Jewish Apple Tart

1 recipe *milchig* or *pareve* yeast pastry dough (p. 273)
9 tart green apples, peeled, cored, and thinly sliced (3 apples per tart)
9 Tblsp. brown sugar
3 tsp. cinnamon
freshly grated nutmeg
1/2 cup sweet butter, cut into bits (if using *milchig* dough)

1. Divide the yeast pastry dough into 3 parts. Roll them out and spread them onto well-buttered 9-inch pie plates or rectangular baking pans.

2. Arrange apple slices in the baking pans. If using round pie plates, arrange them in concentric circles or a spiral pattern. If using rectangular pans, arrange them in attractive rows.

3. Mix sugar and cinnamon and sprinkle this over the top of the apples. Grate a little nutmeg over each tart after you have sprinkled the cinnamon-sugar over it. Then dot each tart with the butter bits, if using. Cover with a damp cloth and let rise in a cool, dry place about 45 minutes.

4. Preheat the oven to 350°. Bake the tarts 25 to 30 minutes or until they look ready. Cool before serving. Recipe makes 3 tarts.

Variation

For a delicious variation, sprinkle the tarts with a streusel topping, as directed in the recipe on p.274, instead of dotting the tarts with butter bits.

Babka

Babka is a not-too-sweet but absolutely scrumptious yeast cake that is made all over Poland and Russia. It has always been a favorite of Jewish bakers from eastern Europe. The richness of babka derives from the eggs and sweet butter used in the dough. Many different kinds of babka were devised by Jewish bakers in the Old Country. The plain babka always had citrus peel and raisins in it. The fancier kinds had marbled layers of cocoa, mocha, and cinnamon-sugar flowing through them. The most elegant of all was the shikkereh babka, "drunk" with rum, whiskey, or brandy and served with the hamantaschen on Purim.

Every babka is milchig. It must be made only with sweet butter, or the essence of the dish is lost. A properly kneaded babka slightly resembles French brioche in texture, but there the similarity ends. Babka is richer and, for some unknown reason, seems to have a longer shelf life than brioche.

I include in this book recipes for five kinds of babka—Polish babka, lemon-flavored babka from Vilna, chocolate babka, layered babka from Vilna, and shikkereh babka.

Polish Babka

9 to 9 1/2 cups unbleached white bread flour
2 pkg. freeze-dried yeast
1/2 cup sugar
6 eggs plus 2 egg yolks
2 sticks sweet butter plus butter for greasing the rising and baking pans
1/2 tsp. salt
1 1/2 cups golden raisins
grated zest of 1 lemon and 1 orange
3/4 cup freshly squeezed orange juice
3/4 cup whole milk

1. Heat the milk to lukewarm and mix the yeast and 1 tsp. sugar into it. Set this aside in a draft-free place to proof (about 10 minutes). When proofed, the mixture will be bubbly.

2. Place 6 cups of the flour, the remaining sugar, and the salt into a deep mixing bowl. Make a well in the center of the bowl and pour in the yeast mixture, the orange juice, and the eggs. Beat together by hand or with the dough hook of an electric mixer.

3. Add the butter in small bits, beating and kneading all the while. Babka requires quite a lot of kneading, and the electric mixer both simplifies this process a great deal and saves wear and tear on one's arms and hands. The kneading takes about 30 to 35 minutes. Note that the resulting dough will not be exactly like bread dough. Babka dough is much stickier than bread dough. Nonetheless, the dough should hold together well. If it appears as though it will not, add up to 1/2 cup additional flour. Do not add too much flour or the texture of the babka will be too heavy. Practice will give you a feel for the correct consistency.

4. Grease a deep bowl well with sweet butter and place the sticky dough into it. Cover the bowl with a damp kitchen towel and set aside to rise in a draft-free place for 1 hour or until the dough is doubled in bulk.

5. When the dough has risen the first time, it will be a little easier to handle. Place it on a well-floured board or mixing bowl and knead in the lemon and orange zest and the raisins.

6. Grease one or two large kugelhopf, bundt, or tube cake pan(s) with butter. Then sprinkle a little flour into it (them). Tip the pan(s) from side to side in order to coat all sides of the pan(s) with flour. Tap out the excess flour.

7. Pat the dough into the pan(s), making sure that all sides are even. The dough should come up no

higher than 3/4 the height of the pan(s). You will probably have enough dough to make 2 *babkas*, which is why you have prepared the second pan. Cover the pan(s) with the damp cloth and set the *babka(s)* aside for a second rising. This, too, will take about an hour. The dough will have risen to the top of the pan and be doubled in volume.

8. Preheat the oven to 350°. Bake the *babka(s)* in the oven for 40 to 45 minutes or until they are golden brown. Turn them out just like a bread to cool on a wire rack before serving. To test for doneness, tap as you would a bread. If it sounds hollow, it is ready. Serve *babka* with coffee or tea after it has cooled sufficiently. It keeps well for days.

Lemon-Flavored *Babka* From Vilna

I first tasted this *babka* at the home of a friend of my in-laws, Mrs. Mary Gerstein of Montreal and formerly of Niemencin, Lithuania, in the area of Vilna. Mrs. Gerstein claimed that the secret to making any *babka*, including this one, was to beat the dough 100 strokes with a wooden spoon. This little bit of food lore probably grew up among *babka* makers as a way of quantifying the long kneading process in making a *babka*. Do not be alarmed! This recipe does not require beating the *babka* 100 strokes with a wooden spoon. The electric mixer with its dough hook does a very adequate job of beating and kneading the *babka* to produce all the right results.

This recipe is almost identical to Polish *babka*, but it has a couple of variations that make the difference in flavor quite significant. To make lemon-flavored *babka*, replace the orange juice in the Polish *babka* recipe with an additional 3/4 cup whole milk. Delete the grated orange zest. Add 3/4 cup candied lemon peel at the same time you add the lemon zest and the raisins. Follow the same procedure as for making Polish *babka*. This *babka* is absolutely delicious with coffee or tea.

Chocolate *Babka*

This *babka* has a marbled layer of filling that flows through it. It is baked in a loaf pan rather than a round tube cake pan.

1 recipe Polish *babka* dough, raisins left out (p. 276)
8 oz. baker's semisweet chocolate
3 Tblsp. strong black coffee
1 tsp. cinnamon
confectioner's sugar for sprinkling

1. Prepare a Polish *babka* dough up to the second rising (see p. 276 up to step 5).
2. Melt the chocolate in a double boiler on top of the stove or in the microwave oven. Mix in the coffee and cinnamon after the chocolate is melted and removed from the heat source. Cool it down to lukewarm.
3. After you have kneaded in the citrus peel, roll out the dough into a large rectangle or oval about 12 x 9 inches. Spread the chocolate mixture all over the dough, leaving a 1/2-inch margin around the edges.
4. Roll up the *babka* jelly roll fashion and pinch the edges together to seal in the filling. Place it into a large, well-buttered loaf pan and cover with a damp kitchen towel to rise.
5. Preheat the oven to 350° and bake the *babka* for 35 to 40 minutes or until it is golden brown in color. Remove and cool on a wire rack to room temperature. To test for doneness, tap the bottom of the *babka* as you would a bread. If it sounds hollow when tapped, it is done. When the *babka* has cooled down to room temperature, sprinkle with confectioner's sugar before serving. The marbled slices are very attractive. This *babka* is delicious with coffee.

Layered *Babka* from Vilna

This *babka* is my own attempt to re-create a dish described to me by my mother-in-law, Mrs. Nelly Komras, as having been made by her own mother-in-law, my wife's paternal grandmother, who lived in Vilna and perished during the Holocaust.

The layers are formed by separating the *babka* dough into pieces and placing a different kind of filling between each piece of the dough before baking. This *babka* demonstrates very well the refinement and sophistication of Jewish baking in eastern Europe.

1 recipe Polish *babka* dough (p. 276) with raisins left out

1 recipe of each of the following fillings:
   a. 1/2 cup golden raisins mixed with 1/2 cup dark raisins, 1 Tblsp. sugar, and 1/4 tsp. cinnamon
   b. 1/3 cup sugar mixed with 1/2 tsp. cinnamon, and 1/2 cup ground almonds
   c. 1/3 cup sugar mixed with 1/2 tsp. cinnamon and 2 Tblsp. unsweetened cocoa
   d. 1/2 cup mixed candied fruit peels
   e. 1/3 cup sugar mixed with 1/2 tsp. cinnamon and 1/2 cup ground walnuts

1. Follow the recipe for Polish *babka* through step 5. Just knead in the citrus peels and leave out the raisins. Then divide the dough into 7 equal pieces.

2. Layer the *babka* in the prepared tube or bundt cake pan starting with a layer of dough followed by a layer of one of the fillings and finishing with a last layer of dough.

3. Proceed with the baking of the *babka* as directed in the Polish *babka* recipe. Cool the *babka* to room temperature before serving it. Each slice of *babka* will have a layer of each kind of filling. Delicious with either tea or coffee.

Shikkereh Babka

Ven a shikker hot nit ken bronfin, redt er chotsh fun bronfin.

When a drunk has no liquor, he talks at least about liquor.

— Yiddish saying

Shikker in Yiddish means "drunk." This *babka* is "drunk" with a liquor-flavored syrup that makes each bite tastes like a little piece of heaven. You may use the liquor of your preference in preparing *shikkereh babka.* My first choice is rum.

1 Polish *babka,* baked but not cooled (p. 276)
2 cups sugar
1 1/2 cups cold water
1 cup rum, brandy, or whiskey

1. Prepare the Polish *babka* as directed on p. 276. Bake it but do not cool it. As the *babka* is baking, prepare the syrup.

2. Mix the sugar with the water in a saucepan and bring to a boil, stirring all the while with a wire whisk to dissolve the sugar. Let it come to a boil over high heat.

3. Cook the syrup down at a brisk boil for about 5 minutes or until it is thick enough to coat a spoon lightly. Pour the syrup into a heatproof bowl and stir in the liquor.

4. When the *babka* has finished baking, unmold it and set it onto a plate. Poke holes all over it with a toothpick. Slowly spoon the syrup over and into the *babka* as it cools, taking care that all the syrup gets absorbed before you pour more on the cake. As the cake cools down, it will absorb more and more of the syrup until all of it is completely absorbed. The cake will be wetly moist, which is exactly the way you want it to be. Cool completely before serving. The longer it waits, the better it gets. Splendid!

FLOURLESS TORTES

Hungarian Flourless Tortes

Hungarian pastries are world renowned, and one of the sweets that Hungarian bakers are best known for is the flourless cake called a torte. Tortes are both light and airy and at the same time made rich and luscious by the addition of fillings and icings. In the elegant baroque *kaffeehausen* of Vienna and Budapest, flourless tortes are made of hazelnuts, walnuts, and chocolate. They are traditionally served with aromatic European roast coffee and, in Vienna, topped with a dollop of whipped cream called "schlag." Flourless tortes are also the one kind of cake that European Jewish bakers invariably prepared with fillings and icings.

I offer recipes for four different flourless tortes in this cookbook — hazelnut, walnut, carrot-and-almond, and poppy seed. The last two tortes are exclusively Jewish recipes that will not be found in any books on Hungarian or Viennese cuisine.

Hazelnut Torte

Hazzennissel Torte

For torte

3 cups hazelnuts or filberts, shelled
6 eggs, separated
1/4 tsp. salt
1 cup vanilla sugar (or substitute 1 cup regular
    white sugar plus 1 tsp. vanilla extract)
1 Tblsp. frangelico liqueur

1. Grease 3 9-inch round springform cake pans with sweet butter. Line these with wax paper cut out to fit the bottom and sides. Butter the wax paper after it is inserted into the cake pans. Preheat the oven to 350°.

2. Coarsely grind the nuts in the food processor so that they are ground but not pureed into a nut butter. Use the pulse/chop motion for doing this.

3. Set the egg yolks aside for making the butter cream filling and icing. Beat the whites together with the sugar, liqueur, and salt until the mixture forms peaks. The peaks should be stiff but not dry.

4. Fold the nuts into the egg-white mixture, using a rubber spatula. Make sure they are completely mixed together.

5. Divide the batter evenly between the three baking pans. Bake the tortes for 1 to 1 1/2 hours or until the cakes look brown and the tops are no longer sticky.

6. Remove pans from the oven and cool 5 minutes. Unmold from the springform pans. Gently peel off the wax paper and set the cakes aside to cool while you prepare the butter cream. If the paper still seems to stick to the cakes, let them cool off a little more until they are ready to be peeled.

Butter cream filling and icing

3 sticks sweet butter
the 6 reserved egg yolks
1/3 cup heavy or whipping cream
1/3 cup strong black coffee
2 Tblsp. frangelico liqueur
2 Tblsp. unsweetened cocoa
1/2 cup sugar

1. This butter cream can be prepared the conventional way on top of the stove or it can be prepared in the microwave oven. The microwave cuts the cooking time by 10 minutes. To do this the conventional way, follow these steps:

1. Cut the butter into bits and place it into a mixing bowl. Set it aside to soften.

2. In a saucepan over medium heat, place the egg yolks, the cream, the coffee, the cocoa, and the sugar. Beat with a wire whisk constantly as the mixture cooks and thickens to a creamy consistency. This will take about 15 to 20 minutes, and the change from liquid to thick will happen very suddenly as you cook the ingredients.

3. When this happens, remove the saucepan from the heat, pour its contents into a mixing bowl, add the liqueur, and continue beating until the mixture cools down a little.

4. Beat in the butter, a small amount at a time. The icing will first appear thin, then grainy, and finally silky smooth. This process can be done well in an electric mixer. When the butter cream is ready, you may fill and frost the torte.

The microwave oven can be used for step 2. Cook at 50 percent power for 8 to 10 minutes, beating the mixture with a wire whisk after each minute of cooking.

Assembling the Torte

Place one of the 3 cakes onto a plate. Spread some of the butter cream over it. Top it with the second cake. Spread more butter cream over this. Top it with the third cake. Spread the remaining butter over the top and sides of the torte. Decorate the top of the torte with whole hazelnuts, their skins removed. To remove the skins of hazelnuts, roast them in a 400° oven for 10 minutes. The skins will rub off easily when the nuts have cooled.

Serve this elegant torte with good European roast coffee.

Hungarian Walnut Torte

Weltschannernuss Torte

For the torte

3 cups walnuts
6 eggs, separated
3/4 cup sugar

finely grated zest of 1 lemon
juice of 1 lemon
1/4 tsp. salt

1. Preheat the oven to 350°. Grease 2 spring-form round cake pans with butter. Line them with wax paper cut to fit the bottom and the sides. Grease the paper with butter and set the pans aside.

2. Beat the egg yolks and the sugar until the mixture is light and foamy. Mix in the lemon zest and juice.

3. Grind the walnuts in the food processor, using a pulse/chop motion to achieve a coarse grind.

4. Beat the egg whites with the salt until they form stiff peaks. Fold this into the egg-yolk mixture thoroughly but gently, using a rubber spatula.

5. Fold the ground nuts into the rest of the ingredients after the egg whites have been folded in.

6. Divide the batter between the two prepared cake pans. Bake in the oven for 55 to 60 minutes or until the cakes start to brown and pull away from the sides of the pans. Remove from the oven and cool to room temperature before unmolding and peeling off the paper.

Mocha icing and apricot filling

8 oz. semisweet chocolate squares
1 stick sweet butter cut into bits
1 Tblsp. extra-strong black coffee
1 Tblsp. coffee-flavored liqueur (e.g., Tía María)
1/2 cup apricot preserves
whole walnuts for decorating

Melt the chocolate squares in a double boiler over medium heat or in the microwave oven. When the chocolate is melted, add the butter bits to it. Mix them together until the butter disappears into the chocolate. Stir in the coffee and the liqueur. Remove from the heat and let the icing cool.

Assembling the Torte

Place one of the baked, unmolded cakes on top of a plate. Spread the apricot preserves over it and top it with the other cake. Spread the mocha icing over the top and sides of the torte. Decorate the torte with whole walnuts.

Serve this delicious torte with good European roast coffee.

Carrot-and-Almond Torte

Mehren und Mandlen Torte

6 eggs, separated
1 3/4 cups sugar
juice and zest of 1 large orange
1 lb. carrots, peeled and grated in food processor
3 cups almonds, ground in food processor
4 Tblsp. *matzoh* meal
1/4 tsp. salt
1/3 cup raisins
3 Tblsp. triple sec or other orange-flavored liqueur
1/2 cup orange marmalade

1. Preheat the oven to 350°. Grease a 9-inch springform cake pan with oil and set aside. Beat the egg yolks with half of the sugar to a froth and add the orange juice and zest. Continue beating until mixture is smooth and fluffy.

2. Add the remaining ingredients except for the marmalade, 2 Tblsp. of the liqueur, the egg whites, the remaining sugar, and the salt. Mix gently but thoroughly until well blended.

3. Beat the egg whites together with the salt and the remaining sugar until it forms into stiff peaks.

4. Fold the egg-white mixture into the egg-yolk mixture with a rubber spatula. Fold gently but thoroughly until no trace of the egg whites remains visible.

5. Pour the batter into the prepared cake pan and bake for 1 hour. If the cake seems to need it, bake 15 minutes longer. Remove cake from the oven and cool it completely before unmolding.

6. When the cake has cooled, unmold it and set it on a plate. Prepare the glaze by heating the marmalade in a saucepan over medium heat. Remove the saucepan from the heat and add the remaining

2 Tblsp. liqueur. Spoon the glaze over the top and sides of the torte. Cool to room temperature before serving.

Hungarian Poppy Seed Torte

Mohn Torte

5 eggs, separated
1/2 cup peanut or corn oil
1 1/2 cups sugar
juice and grated zest of 1 large, juicy lemon
2 cups poppy seeds
1 cup bread crumbs or *matzoh* cake meal

1. Grease a 9-inch tube baking pan with oil. Line it with wax paper, and grease the paper with oil. Set aside and preheat the oven to 350°.
2. Cream the egg yolks, sugar, and oil until thick and fluffy in a mixing bowl, using the electric mixer.
3. Add the lemon juice, zest, poppy seeds, and bread crumbs or *matzoh* cake meal, and mix in thoroughly but gently.
4. Beat the egg whites in another deep mixing bowl until they form stiff peaks.
5. Fold the egg whites into the egg-yolk mixture gently but thoroughly with a rubber spatula until no trace of white is showing.
6. Pour the batter into the prepared baking pan and bake 1 hour or until the cake feels springy to the touch. Cool on a wire rack for a few minutes before unmolding. Unmold the cake as soon as it has cooled sufficiently and gently remove the wax paper. Cool the cake completely before glazing.

For glaze

1/4 cup sugar
1/4 cup brandy
1/4 cup cold water

Heat the sugar and water over medium heat, stirring until the sugar dissolves. When it begins to boil, remove it from the heat and stir in the brandy. Poke holes into the torte with a toothpick, and spoon the glaze over the torte. Let it steep at least 1 hour before serving the torte.

CHEESECAKES

European-Style Cheesecake

Europsche Kayzkuchen (Gomolke)

Mit schnay ken men mit machen gomolkes!

With snow you cannot make cheesecakes!
— Yiddish saying

This cheesecake is the authentic Jewish one that eastern European immigrants brought over with them. It is much lighter in texture than the more familiar New York–style cheesecake.

Crust

1/2 cup sweet butter
1/4 cup sugar
1 1/3 cups unbleached white flour
2 to 3 Tblsp. cold water

Cheese filling

3/4 lb. farmer dry cottage cheese
1/3 cup plus 1 Tblsp. sugar
4 eggs, separated
2 Tblsp. freshly squeezed lemon juice
1/3 cup unbleached white flour
1/2 tsp. baking powder
1/2 tsp. salt

1. Prepare crust by cutting the butter into small bits. Mix the flour into the butter by hand, rubbing the mixture between your fingers to produce a grainy texture. Mix in the sugar the same way. Add 2 Tblsp. water and mix dough by hand. If it seems too dry to roll into a ball, add 1 more Tblsp. water. Roll the dough into a ball and wrap it in wax paper. Refrigerate for at least 1 hour.
2. Preheat the oven to 375°. After 1 hour, remove the dough from the refrigerator and roll it out into a 12-inch circle. Grease a 9-inch springform cake pan with butter and line it with the dough. Make sure the dough comes all the way up the sides of the pan.

3. Cover the dough with aluminum foil and fill it with dried beans. This makes sure the dough holds its shape during baking.

4. Bake the crust for 15 minutes. Remove it from the oven. Remove the tin foil and return the dried beans to their storage jar.

5. Prepare the cheese filling by mixing the farmer cheese with 2 Tblsp. of the sugar, the egg yolks, and the lemon juice, either by hand or with an electric mixer at low speed.

6. When this is well mixed, add the flour, baking powder, and salt.

7. In a separate deep mixing bowl, beat the egg whites with the remaining sugar until they form stiff peaks.

8. Fold the egg-white mixture into the cheese mixture with a rubber spatula, mixing gently but thoroughly until it is well incorporated.

9. Pour the cheese filling mixture into the prepared pan with the partially baked crust. Reduce the oven temperature to 350° and place the cake into the oven. Bake 50 to 55 minutes. Remove cake from the oven and cool. When the cake has cooled to room temperature, open the springform and gently remove it from the pan. It should remove quite easily as long as you are careful.

Variations

You can make many interesting variations to this basic recipe. It can be topped with strawberry or berry compote when it is served or sprinkled with cinnamon-sugar before it is baked. You may also add 2 Tblsp. of your favorite liqueur to the filling before baking. It is also very delicious glazed with an apricot or orange glaze made with heated preserves.

Lithuanian Cheesecake

Litvishe Kayzkuchen

This cheesecake, popular in the Baltic area, was prepared both summer and winter. In summer, fresh blueberries were mixed in with the cheese, and in the winter, raisins.

1/2 recipe *milchig* yeast pastry dough (p. 273)
2 cups farmer dry cottage cheese
1/2 cup sugar

grated zest of 1 small lemon
2 Tblsp. sour cream
2 1/2 cups fresh blueberries (or, in winter, 1 cup golden raisins; those left over from making raisin water are perfect for this dish)
1 large egg yolk plus 1 egg yolk mixed with 1 Tblsp. cold water (egg wash)

1. In a mixing bowl, mix together well the cheese, sugar, lemon zest, sour cream, and egg yolk.

2. Fold the blueberries or raisins into the cheese mixture.

3. On a floured pastry board, roll out 3/4 of the pastry dough into a circle about 13 inches in diameter. Fit this into a well-buttered 10-inch springform pie pan, letting the excess hang over the rim.

4. Fill the pie with the cheese and blueberry (or raisin) mixture.

5. Roll out the remaining dough into a 10-inch circle. Cut the circle into strips about 1/2 inch wide. Weave these strips into a lattice pattern on top of the pie.

6. Fold the excess dough over the ends of the lattice top from the dough that was left hanging over the edges of the pan. Pinch it tightly so that it all holds together. Cover the cake with a damp kitchen cloth and let it rise 30 minutes.

7. Preheat the oven to 350°. Brush the top of the cake with the egg wash and bake it for 30 to 35 minutes or until it is golden brown. Remove the cake from the oven to cool. When cool, unmold from the springform pan and serve.

Bialystok-Style Cheesecake

Bialystoker Kayzkuchen

This is a variation of the Lithuanian-style cheesecake and was a specialty of the Bialystok area. It may be served warm or at room temperature.

1 recipe *milchig* yeast dough pastry (p. 273)
2 lb. farmer dry cottage cheese
1 cup sugar plus 1/3 cup
2 large eggs
1 tsp. cinnamon plus 1/4 tsp.
1/2 cup raisins
1/2 cup melted sweet butter

1 egg white mixed with 1 Tblsp. cold water (egg-white wash)

1. Roll out half of the yeast pastry dough into a very large rectangle on a large, well-floured board. The dough needs to be very thin, almost but not quite like strudel dough. The thickness should be no more than 1/16 inch. If you do not have a large enough board to do this with half of the dough, use a quarter or a third of it. The finished rectangle of dough should be about 18 x 12 inches.

2. To make the filling, mix together everything except the egg-white wash, the 1/3 cup sugar, and the 1/4 tsp. cinnamon.

3. Brush the rolled dough with melted butter. Place half, a third, or a quarter of the filling onto the dough (depending on how much of it you have used to make the rectangle of dough) and spread the filling all over, leaving a 1-inch margin around the edges.

4. Roll the pastry up jelly roll fashion and place it on a well-buttered baking sheet. Cover it with a damp kitchen towel and set it aside to rise until doubled in bulk.

5. Repeat steps 1 through 4 with the remaining dough.

6. Preheat the oven to 350°. When the pastries have risen sufficiently, mix the remaining cinnamon and sugar together. Brush each pastry with the egg-white wash and then sprinkle it with cinnamon-sugar.

7. Bake the pastries for 30 to 35 minutes or until well browned. Serve warm or at room temperature. If serving warm, accompany the slices of cheesecake with sour cream and preserves. Delicious with tea!

American-Style Cheesecake

The main difference between European *kayzkuchen* and American-style cheesecake is lightness versus heaviness. American-style cheesecake is dense, creamy, and so rich that it is almost a meal in itself instead of a dessert. The most famous American-style cheesecake was created by Clara and Leo Lindemann, the original owners of Lindy's Restaurant. This famous restaurant on Broadway and Forty-ninth Street in New York City was a central meeting place of actors, writers, and theater buffs. Since the time Lindy's first introduced its cheesecake in the 1930s, every American-style cheesecake has been measured against this original.

My own recipe for American-style cheesecake calls for a short crust pastry rather than the more commonly used graham cracker crust. This basic recipe can also entertain an infinite number of variations. I give you two—one plain and the other with a fresh strawberry topping.

Crust

1 cup unbleached flour
2 Tblsp. sugar
1 stick sweet butter
1 pinch salt
2 to 3 Tblsp. ice water

Cheese filling

2 lb. Philadelphia cream cheese (3 16-oz. packages)
1 lb. farmer dry cottage cheese
2 cups vanilla sugar (or substitute 2 cups regular white sugar and 1 1/2 tsp. vanilla extract)
4 Tblsp. unbleached white flour
grated zest of 1 orange and 1 lemon
5 large eggs
powdered sugar and cinnamon for sprinkling

1. Prepare the crust by cutting the butter into bits and rubbing the flour and butter together between your fingers until it becomes a coarse and grainy meal. Mix in the sugar, salt, and 2 Tblsp. of the water. If the dough seems too dry to roll into a ball, add 1 more Tblsp. water. Roll it into a ball, wrap it in wax paper, and chill for 1 1/2 to 2 hours.

2. Grease a 9-inch springform cake pan with butter. Roll out the dough into an 18-inch circle.

3. Place the cake pan over the center of the circle of dough and cut out a piece to fit into the bottom of the pan. Place it into the pan.

4. Wrap the remaining dough around the sides of the pan. Pinch the bottom together all around the pan so that the dough will be tightly sealed and not break apart after the cake is baked.

5. In a large mixing bowl, beat the cheeses together with the sugar, flour, vanilla extract if using, and the zests.

6. Beat in the eggs one at a time. Make sure that the mixture is well beaten and very smooth.

7. Preheat the oven to 400°. Pour the filling into the dough-lined cake pan, smooth out the top, and put it into the oven. Bake for 15 minutes and lower the oven temperature to 300°. Bake the cake 1 hour more.

8. Cool the cheesecake in its baking pan on top of a rack. Then refrigerate it overnight.

9. Remove it from the refrigerator and carefully release the springform of the pan. The cake should unmold easily. Sprinkle it, if you wish, with confectioner's sugar and cinnamon before serving.

Variation: Cheesecake with Fresh Strawberry Topping

To make this variation, replace the lemon zest with additional orange zest in the previous recipe and add 1/4 cup Grand Marnier to the filling before you bake it. Follow the procedure previously outlined but do not sprinkle the cake with the confectioner's sugar or cinnamon. Instead, prepare the following topping.

2 cups fresh strawberries
1/2 cup apricot preserves
2 Tblsp. Grand Marnier

Wash, dry, and hull the strawberries. Place them, bottoms facing upward, in concentric circles or a spiral on top of the cake. Heat the preserves in a saucepan on top of the stove. Remove from the heat and stir in the Grand Marnier. Cool to lukewarm and spoon this over the strawberries. Before serving, chill the cake for 2 hours in the refrigerator.

Shtrudel

Bronfin vert nit zoyer un shtrudel vert nit fartrukent!

Brandy never gets sour and strudel never gets stale!
— Yiddish folk saying

Strudel, called *shtrudel* in Yiddish, is really in a category by itself as a kind of pastry. Real *shtrudel* takes time, patience, and a great deal of love to make, but the effort is well worth it. Some people claim that commercially made filo dough is an adequate substitute for *shtrudel* dough, but I do not agree. Real *shtrudel* dough is not as thin as filo, nor is it supposed to flake the way filo does.

My grandmother made *shtrudel* only once or twice a year because it was so time consuming. When she made it, the dough was rolled all across the kitchen table and she used the broomstick she made *lokshen* with to stretch the dough to the correct degree of thinness. Her theory was that *shtrudel* dough should be thin enough that you are able to see your hand through the dough. Accomplishing this was no mean achievement. It took great talent to stretch and roll, stretch and roll. . . . But the result was something that compares with nothing else I have ever eaten.

I have tried to use the pasta machine to see if it could help me achieve the correct consistency more efficiently, but it doesn't work because most pasta machines make long and narrow pieces of dough that are cut into noodles. However, I have found a way to make real *shtrudel* dough that, while it takes quite a bit of time, does help you do the job at least in a manageable way with smaller pieces of dough. Essentially, it is this. One recipe of yeast pastry dough (which is what you use to make *shtrudel* dough) provides enough for 9 *shtrudels* of the correct size and consistency. Simply divide the dough into 3 parts and then divide each third into 3 more parts. Place the portions of dough under a damp towel while you work so they won't dry out, and prepare your fillings beforehand. This way you can devote all your time and energy to the rolling and stretching of the dough on a small, normal-size board.

I always recommend making different kinds of *shtrudel* at the same time. That way you can make this dish no more than once a year but still enjoy several different kinds in one sitting. A sampler of *shtrudels* makes a wonderful, tasty, and rather light dessert.

1 recipe yeast pastry dough (p. 273)
melted butter (optional, only if using *milchig* pastry dough)
1 recipe apple *shtrudel* filling
1 recipe walnut *shtrudel* filling
1 recipe prune *shtrudel* filling (same as filling for *pireshkes*, p. 267)

To prepare *shtrudel*, just divide the yeast pastry dough into 9 equal pieces. Set them aside under a damp kitchen towel to keep them from drying out. Then prepare the fillings in separate bowls. You will make 3 of each kind of *shtrudel*. Work with the dough on a floured board, rolling and stretching it carefully so that it does not break open (which takes patience). When you have rolled the piece of dough to the correct thickness, it will be an oval or a rectangle approximately 18 × 12 inches in size and adequately thin. Spread some melted butter, if you wish, over the dough and then spread a third of the filling over it, leaving a 1-inch margin all around. Then, gently roll it up, jelly roll fashion, and pinch the ends together to hold the seal. Finally, gently roll it onto a well-greased baking dish, cover it with a damp towel, and let it rise for about 20 minutes before baking. Just remember to do this patiently and carefully, and I am certain you will be very happy with the results. I am especially sure that you will notice the big difference between *shtrudel* dough and the convenience substitute, filo dough.

To bake the *shtrudel*, brush it with egg wash (1 egg yolk mixed with 1 Tblsp. cold water) or egg-white wash (1 egg white mixed with 1 Tblsp. cold water), and then bake it for about 30 to 35 minutes in a 350° oven. Cool it to room temperature before slicing.

Filling 1: Apple filling

9 tart green apples
1 cup sugar
2 tsp. cinnamon
1/2 cup raisins
2 or 3 gratings nutmeg
4 Tblsp. bread crumbs

Peel, core, and cut the apples into fine dice. Mix the rest of the ingredients into the apples and set aside.

Filling 2: Walnut filling

1 lb. walnuts
2 tsp. cinnamon
1 1/2 cups sugar
1 1/2 cups raisins
1/2 cup bread crumbs
2 whole seedless oranges, cut into pieces

Process the oranges into a coarse puree in the food processor, using a pulse/chop movement. Add the remaining ingredients and pulse/chop them as well until the mixture turns into a coarse puree. Set aside in a bowl.

Filling 3: Prune filling (p.267)

(This is the same as the filling for *pireshkes*.)
To prepare the *shtrudel*, simply follow the direc-

tions given above. You may use any of the other fillings given in this book to make *shtrudel*, or be creative and invent some of your own. Practically anything works well with *shtrudel* dough. Make at least three kinds when you make it. The more variety, the more fun it is!

Lemon Meringue Pie

Lemon meringue pie is definitely not a part of Yiddish cuisine. I include this recipe for it because it was my Aunt Ann's favorite dessert and one that, more than any other dish, represented American cooking to her. She loved making it, and she made it often. This recipe is completely her own, unaltered by me in any way.

Crust

1 heaping cup unbleached white cake flour
6 Tblsp. sweet butter, cut into small bits
pinch salt
1 Tblsp. sugar
2 to 3 Tblsp. ice water

Filling

7 large egg yolks
1 cup sugar
juice and grated zest of one large lemon

Meringue

7 large egg whites
2 Tblsp. sugar

1. Make the crust by rubbing the flour, butter, sugar, and salt together with your fingertips until they form into coarse, grainy meal.

2. Add 2 Tblsp. of the ice water and knead/roll the dough into a ball with your hands. If the mixture seems too dry, add one more tablespoonful of the water.

3. Wrap the ball of dough in wax paper and put it into the refrigerator to chill for 2 hours.

4. Unwrap the dough and roll it into a 12-inch circle. To do this properly, roll it from the center outward, turning the dough 90° clockwise after each roll. The result will give you a circle about 1/8 inch

thick. Line a pie plate with the circle of dough, pressing it into the plate tightly. Make sure there are no holes. Using the edge of a knife, trim off any excess dough.

5. Preheat the oven to 400°. Cover the dough with aluminum foil and fill the center with dried beans. These keep the dough weighted down as it bakes.

6. Bake the pie crust in the oven for 10 minutes to set the dough. Remove the pan from the oven and gently lift out the foil with the beans in it.

7. Lightly prick the dough with the tines of a fork and put it back into the oven. Bake 10 to 15 more minutes or until the crust is crisp and golden in color.

8. In the top of a double boiler, beat the egg yolks with a wire whisk together with the sugar, lemon juice, and lemon zest. Beat this until everything is very well mixed.

9. Insert the top of the double boiler into the bottom, which has been filled with water that is simmering. Stir constantly as the mixture cooks until it is very thick. Remove from the heat and cool.

10. Beat the egg whites vigorously in a deep mixing bowl with the electric mixer and very clean blades until they form soft peaks (not stiff peaks).

11. With a rubber spatula, fold 1/3 of the egg whites into the egg yolk mixture.

12. Add the remaining 2 Tblsp. of sugar to the egg whites and beat until they are glossy but not too stiff. Preheat the oven to 350°.

13. Pour the egg-yolk mixture into the baked pie shell. Then pile the egg-white mixture on top of the filling. You can do this by spooning scoops of the egg-white meringue all over the filling. It should look like a fluffy cloud.

14. Bake the pie for 10 minutes or until the meringue begins to turn a light brown. Cool the pie to room temperature before serving.

Purim Tea Table

Farmer cheese finger wedge sandwiches on sugar bialys

Rum-soaked *shikkereh babka*

Hamantaschen with poppy seed and prune fillings

Jewish apple cake

Sugar-glazed *Ayer Kichelach*

Assorted cookies and fresh fruit

Coffee, tea, wine, fruit-flavored vodkas, and liqueurs

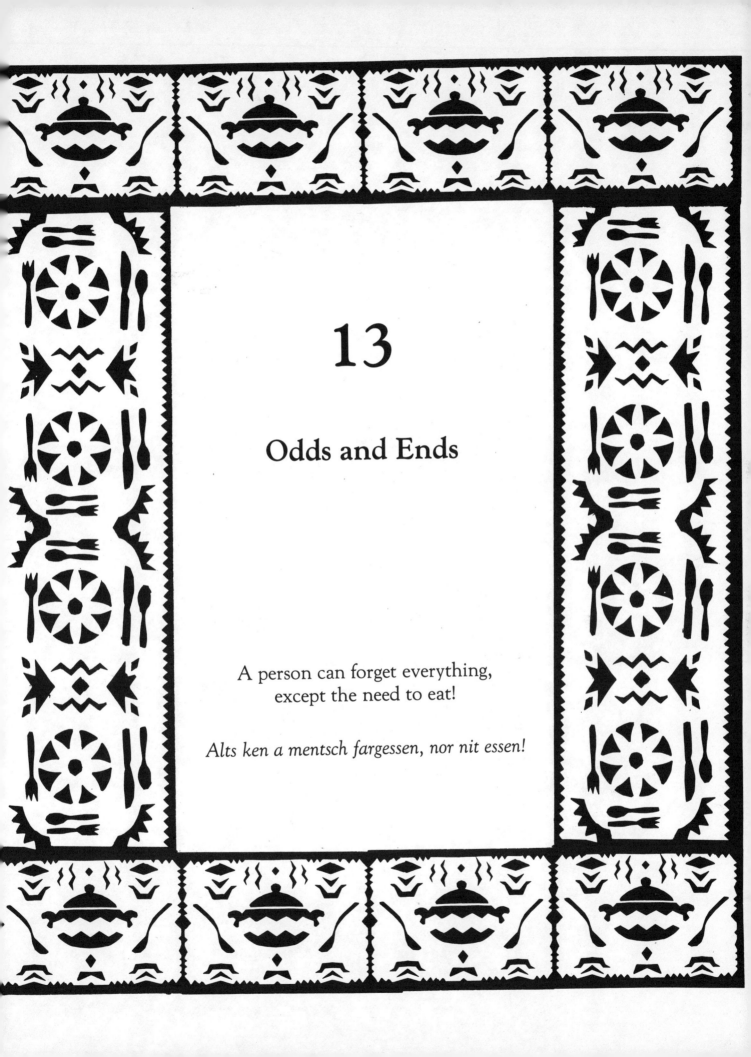

13

Odds and Ends

A person can forget everything,
except the need to eat!

Alts ken a mentsch fargessen, nor nit essen!

Odds and Ends

No book on Yiddish cuisine would be complete without a few odds and ends. This chapter contains a variety of different things. Unlike the sections of recipes in the previous chapters, I do not try to place these dishes into specific categories. Here you will find recipes for all the preserves, beverages, candies, and pickles that were important parts of the everyday fare of European Jews. The fruit-flavored vodkas like *vishnyek*, and assorted dishes like *matzoh brei* and *smetana latkes*, which are hard to place in any category, also appear here.

Kosher Dill Pickles

Koshereh Marinirte Oogerkes

This is my grandmother's recipe. She was very insistent that dill pickles never be made with vinegar. Hers were pickled in a garlicky, spicy salt brine.

16 to 20 pickling cucumbers
4 flat Tblsp. coarse or kosher salt
4 tsp. pickling spice
8 large cloves garlic, peeled
4 dried, whole hot red chili peppers
16 to 20 large sprigs fresh dill plus 4 or 5 dill
     heads, if you can get them
cold water

1. Thoroughly wash 4 quart-size mason jars and then put them through one cycle of your dishwasher to sterilize them (or, alternatively, plunge them for a few seconds into boiling water if you do not have a dishwasher, and wipe them dry with a clean kitchen cloth). Thoroughly wash and dry the lids of the mason jars.

2. Into each jar, place 1 Tblsp. of the salt, 1 tsp. of the pickling spice, 2 cloves garlic, and 1 of the peppers.

3. Place 4 or 5 cucumbers into each jar. Then add 4 or 5 sprigs dill and 1 dill head, if you can get it.

4. Fill each jar to the top with cold water. Make sure that all the cucumbers and dill are completely covered by water. Tightly cover each jar and shake it gently, turning it upside down, to disperse all the ingredients.

5. Place the jars in a cool, dry place (a cupboard in your basement is good). In approximately 3 weeks, you will have half-sour pickles; in six weeks, you will have fully pickled dill pickles. Refrigerate the pickles before opening, and serve them with cold cut sandwiches or anything else you like. They are a wonderful garnish to chopped liver (p. 43) and chopped egg and onion with *schmaltz* (p. 42). They are also an ingredient in herring salad vinaigrette (p. 230).

Pickled Beets

Marinirte Burekehs

2 lb. fresh, whole medium-size beets, baked and
     peeled according to the instructions given
     on p. 224
1 cup cider vinegar
1 cup cold water
1 cup brown sugar
1 heaping tsp. coarse or kosher salt
6 whole peppercorns

1. In a saucepan, combine the water, vinegar, sugar, and salt and bring to a boil. Stir constantly with a wire whisk until the sugar is completely dissolved.

2. Add the peppercorns and boil the mixture for 4 minutes. Remove from the heat.

3. Slice the beets thin and place them into a glass or ceramic bowl, or, alternatively, into glass mason jars.

4. Ladle the hot marinade over the beets and let them cool, uncovered, to room temperature.

5. Cover with plastic wrap or lids and refrigerate at least 12 hours before using. The jars may be shaken or the mixture stirred periodically to keep the beets moist.

Serving Suggestions

Pickled beets are a delicious accompaniment to cold cuts, smoked fish, herring dishes, hamburgers, and frankfurters. They keep fresh for quite a long time. Use them with kosher dill pickles to go with any of the dishes mentioned.

Homemade Sauerkraut

Zoyereh Kroit

10 lb. fresh green cabbage
8 heaping Tblsp. coarse or kosher salt
3 tart green apples, peeled and cored

Prepare a large glass or enamel Crockpot by washing it and drying it very carefully. Shred the cabbage very fine. Shred the apples as well. Mix the cabbage, apples, and salt together in a large mixing bowl and then press this mixture down into the crock. Cover the top of the crock with several layers of cheesecloth. Wrap a heavy weight or a bunch of plates in a very clean white kitchen cloth and place this over the cabbage. Make sure it is heavy enough to weight down the cabbage. The cabbage will marinate for about 3 1/2 to 4 weeks. Every week, change the cheesecloth and the cloth that wraps the weight. Let the cabbage marinate in a cool, dark place. In 3 1/2 to 4 weeks, you will have sauerkraut. The sauerkraut can be processed and stored in the pantry or refrigerated and kept several weeks. Before using the sauerkraut, be sure to rinse it off well to remove the excess salt.

Cranberry-Orange Relish For Turkey

In Litteh, the berry most resembling the American cranberry is the lingonberry, called *kliuvka* in Russian or *broznitzel* in Yiddish. The traditional cranberry (or lingonberry) sauce made by European Jews greatly resembles my recipe for cranberry compote. I prefer this American-style cranberry-orange relish with my turkey and veal to the traditional Jewish one. I share it with you here.

4 cups fresh cranberries
2 cups sugar
2 large seedless oranges

Wash and dry the cranberries and the oranges. Put 2 cups berries, 1 cup sugar, and 1 orange cut into pieces into the food processor. Pulse/chop this until it turns into a coarse puree. Place this into a mixing bowl. Repeat with the remaining ingredients and add this to the first mixture. Mix everything together and refrigerate for at least 2 hours before serving with roast turkey, roast veal, veal chops, or *kottletten* made of veal, turkey, or chicken. Relish keeps well in the refrigerator for a couple of weeks.

Applesauce

Epplzoss

This basic recipe for applesauce comes from my grandmother. Not every kind of apple is good for making sauce. My grandmother liked to use a combination of tart green apples and sweet apples, which created a sauce that was balanced in flavor and interesting in texture. The green apples did not cook down into a mush, but pieces of green apple remained in the sauce. The sweet apples, on the other hand, cooked down into an almost perfect puree. The use of two kinds of apples also cut down on the quantity of sugar that was used in the sauce. My grandmother also spiced her sauce with cinnamon, but nutmeg is just as good a flavor for those who do not like cinnamon.

The two important things to remember about making good applesauce are not to use too much water, as the apples themselves contain quite a bit, and not to put in the sugar until almost the end of the cooking. That way, you will be able to tell just how much you need by tasting the sauce.

8 lb. apples (4 lb. tart green apples and 4 lb. sweet apples like golden delicious or Jonathan)
1 cup cold water
2 sticks cinnamon
sugar to taste
juice of 1 lemon

1. Peel and core the apples. Cut them into wedges and place them in a nonreactive pot containing water and lemon juice. Let the apples sit in this until all of them are peeled and cut. The lemon juice prevents the apples from discoloring.

2. When all the apples have been peeled and sliced, place them in a nonreactive stockpot on top of the stove. Add 1 cup of water to the pot and bring it to a boil over medium heat.

3. Add the cinnamon sticks and reduce the heat slightly. Partially cover the pot and let cook at a gentle simmer until the fruit is almost soft.

4. Taste and add sugar. Taste again and add as much as you think you need to sweeten the sauce. There is no set quantity. Stir the sugar in to dissolve it completely.

5. Continue to cook the sauce another 10 to 15 minutes. Remove the cinnamon sticks and discard.

6. The applesauce will look like a coarse puree with some small pieces floating in it. I like the texture this way but if you wish a smooth puree, you may puree the sauce in a blender or food processor.

7. Cool the applesauce and then pour it into mason jars. It may be stored in the refrigerator or processed and stored on the pantry shelf. Recipe makes 6 to 8 jars of applesauce.

Variation

For a supersmooth puree, pass the pureed applesauce through a fine sieve before putting it in jars.

Fruit Preserves

Frucht Eingemachts

Several fruit preserves were popular among Jewish immigrants. The three favorites were apricot, plum, and cherry. They were used in baking as well as eaten with bread and tea. All of the *eingemachts* were jams rather than jellies. Although Jewish immigrants used only fruit and sugar in preparing their preserves, I have included some optional liqueurs as additions for each of the recipes. The technique for preparing the preserves is the same for every kind of fruit, but the quantities of sugar will vary from fruit to fruit. The ratio of sugar to fruit is given below:

For 6 lb. fresh apricots, use 8 cups sugar.
For 6 lb. red or green plums, use 9 cups sugar.
For 6 lb. tart sour cherries, use 10 cups sugar.

6 lb. fruit
sugar (proportions indicated above)
1/2 cup optional liqueur (for cherries, kirsch; for apricots, brandy or apricot brandy; for plums, brandy or cognac)

1. Pit and halve the fruit and place it with the sugar into a heavy stockpot. Bring to a boil, stirring constantly, and reduce the heat to medium as soon as the mixture starts to boil. Cook, stirring and mashing the fruit every once in a while for 1 1/2 to 2 hours or until the preserve is quite thick. Remove from the heat and stir in the liqueur, if using.

2. Ladle the preserves into 2-cup-size mason jars that have been carefully sterilized by either pouring boiling water over them or running them through a complete cycle of the dishwasher. Screw the lids of the jars on tightly, and process the preserves by boiling the jars for 15 minutes in boiling water to cover in a canning pot or a stockpot fitted with a wire rack. After the jars have been processed, store on the pantry shelf. Recipe makes 4 or 5 pint-size jars of preserves.

Beet Preserves

Burekeh Eingemachts

This was a specialty made by Ukrainian Jews for Passover. It may be eaten like any other kind of preserves, with sweet *bialys* or some other kind of bread. Or it can serve as a relish for roasted or grilled meats.

4 lb. whole beets, baked (see instructions, p. 224)
8 cups sugar
2 lemons, sliced
one 2-inch-piece fresh ginger
1 cup chopped almonds
3 cups cold water

1. Peel the baked beets and coarsely grate them by hand or in the food processor using the julienne blade. Place the beets into a large, heavy saucepan.

2. Add the sugar and the water and bring to a boil, stirring constantly with a wooden spoon until the sugar is completely dissolved. Reduce the heat to the lowest simmer.

3. Peel and finely grate the ginger and add it, together with the lemon slices, to the simmering beet mixture.

4. Partially cover the pot and simmer for 2 to 2 1/2 hours, stirring every once in a while, until the mixture is very thick.

5. Add the almonds and stir them in well. Cook 15 minutes longer and remove from the heat.

6. Cool the preserves to room temperature and store in the refrigerator or in mason jelly jars. Recipe makes 4 to 6 small jelly jars of *eingemachts*.

Povidl

Povidl is a luscious fresh plum butter. It is an eastern European specialty made by both Jews and non-Jews of the Slavic countries during August, when fresh plums are in season. *Povidl* is used in the same way any other kind of preserves is used. My grandmother used it to prepare a special filling for *pireshkes* and for *fluden*.

9 lb. Italian prune plums, pitted
4 Tblsp. corn or peanut oil
2 Tblsp. finely zested lemon zest
2 Tblsp. finely zested orange zest
5 cups sugar

1. In a deep, large, heavy saucepan or stockpot (enameled cast iron is ideal), place the 4 Tblsp. oil and coat the bottom and sides of the pot with it. This will prevent the *povidl* from burning during the initial cooking stage.

2. Add the pitted plums and cook over low heat for 20 minutes or until they are soft enough to disintegrate and separate from their skins. Stir constantly to prevent scorching.

3. Remove the plums and put them through a fine sieve, which will separate the pulp from the skins.

4. Wash out the pot, dry it carefully, and return the plum puree to it. Mix in the zest and the sugar. Cook over very low heat, stirring from time to time, until the mixture is very thick and dark. The pulp will reduce to little more than half its original bulk. This will take several hours.

5. When the *povidl* is thick enough, remove it from the heat and ladle it into sterilized pint-size mason jars. Process the preserves as directed on p. 7. Recipe yields 5 or 6 pint-size jars of *povidl*.

Lekvar

Lekvar is a delicious Hungarian prune butter. It is used the same way as *povidl*. Although *lekvar* is traditionally made with water, I have varied the classic recipe and substituted red wine for the water, which gives the preserves an unusual richness and brings out its full-bodied flavor much better than water does. It may, of course, be made both ways.

5 lb. pitted prunes
1 quart-size bottle red wine and 1 quart cold water
2 large seedless navel oranges
1 cup golden raisins
4 cups sugar

1. Cut the prunes into chunks and soak them overnight in the wine mixed with water.

2. Zest the oranges, cutting the peel into very thin strips, and set the orange zest aside. Then peel the flavorless white membrane off the oranges, revealing the pulp of the fruit.

3. Cut the oranges in half to make sure that there are no seeds in them and then cut them into chunks. Set aside in a mixing bowl.

4. Into a large, deep, heavy saucepan or stockpot (enameled cast iron is best), put the prunes and their soaking liquid together with the sugar. Bring this to a boil, stirring constantly to dissolve the sugar. Then reduce the heat to a low simmer.

5. Add the remaining ingredients and simmer until the mixture is heavy and thick. This will take several hours. Stir from time to time.

6. When the mixture is very thick, remove from the heat and ladle into sterilized jelly jars. Cover the jars tightly and process as directed on p. 7. Recipe makes 4 or 5 jars of *lekvar*.

Sesame Candies

2 cups sesame seeds
2 cups sugar
2 Tblsp. water

1. Preheat the oven to 400°. Spread the sesame seeds on a baking sheet and toast them in the oven until they are light brown (about 15 minutes). Remove from the oven.

2. Place the water in a heavy saucepan and add

the sugar. Cook over medium heat until the sugar melts and starts to caramelize. It will first crumble and then melt.

3. When it starts to caramelize, add the toasted sesame seeds. Mix very quickly and remove from the heat. Turn the contents of the saucepan into a 9 × 13-inch baking pan and pat into a smooth rectangular shape with the back of a large spoon dipped in water.

4. Cut the candy into small rectangular pieces while it is still hot. Make sure the pieces are separated, and let them cool to room temperature. Wrap the candies in cellophane and store in tins or jars. They will keep indefinitely and make beautiful gifts.

Poppy Seed Candies

Mohnelach

1 lb. poppy seeds
1/2 cup sugar
2 cups honey
2 cups chopped pecans or walnuts
boiling water

1. Pour boiling water over the poppy seeds to cover by 1 inch and allow to stand overnight. Drain the seeds completely in the morning.

2. Grind the seeds in the food processor or blender until they are a coarse puree.

3. Bring the sugar and honey to a boil over medium heat in a saucepan. Reduce the heat to low and add the poppy seed puree. Cook this mixture until very thick, stirring frequently (about 40 to 45 minutes). Test for doneness by dropping a spoonful onto a wet wooden, marble, or formica board. If it holds its shape, it is done cooking.

4. Stir in the nuts. Cook 5 minutes longer and turn the mixture out onto a wet board. Marble is best but formica or wood works almost as well. Dip your hands into cold water and pat the mixture into a rectangular shape that is 1/2 inch thick. Cut the mixture into small rectangular pieces with a knife that has been dipped into hot water. Cool the candies to room temperature before wrapping in cellophane. Store the candies in tins or jars. They keep indefinitely and make lovely gifts.

Matzoh Brei

Matzoh brei is a classic Passover breakfast dish. It is delicious to eat all year round and does not have to be eaten only at breakfast. It is also good as a light lunch or supper or even as a late-night, after-theater snack.

3 whole *matzos*
2 extra-large eggs
salt and pepper to taste
sweet butter for sautéing
preserves and/or sour cream

1. Break up the *matzos* into small pieces in a mixing bowl. Pour cold water over them to cover and let them stand for 1 minute. Drain completely and gently squeeze dry.

2. In another mixing bowl, beat the eggs until foamy and add the *matzoh* pieces. Mix together well. Add salt and pepper to taste and mix again.

3. Melt a little butter in a small, 8-inch skillet over medium heat and add the *matzoh* mixture. Sauté on one side about 2 to 2 1/2 minutes. Turn over with a spatula. Do not be concerned if the *matzoh brei* breaks apart during turning. It does this sometimes. Sauté on the other side until crisp. Serve with preserves and sour cream. Recipe serves 1 person. Increase portions of egg and *matzoh* for more people. If you wish a smaller portion of *matzoh brei*, this recipe may serve as two small portions.

Note: For attractive *matzoh brei*, do not cook more than the above amount in one skillet. If you increase the recipe, use the same quantity of *matzoh* mixture in each skillet. You may cook a larger quantity of the mixture in a bigger skillet (e.g., a 12-inch skillet) but it is almost guaranteed that the *matzoh brei* will break apart during turning if you do this. There is a possibility that if you are able to obtain an oversized spatula, you will be able to successfully turn a large *matzoh brei* in a 12-inch skillet without breaking it.

Serving Suggestions

If serving *matzoh brei* as a light meal, accompany it with a carrot-and-raisin salad (p. 227) or a beet-and-cucumber salad (p. 224). It makes a delicious vegetarian entrée served this way. A glass of white wine turns this meal into something very elegant, almost like a French meal featuring an omelet as its main course.

A cooking school in Vilna, 1930s. Yiddish signs read (*left to right*), *Milchig* (dairy) and *Fleischig* (meat). (Courtesy of YIVO Archives.)

Chremslach

Chremslach are *latkes* made of *matzoh* meal. They are another traditional Passover food that is delicious all year round. My grandmother made two kinds of *chremslach*—light ones and extra-light, puffy ones. Both were wonderful. She also made stuffed *chremslach* with meat filling. I include a recipe for each of these here.

Recipe 1: Light *Chremslach*

4 large eggs
3/4 cup cold water
1/2 tsp. salt
1 cup *matzoh* meal
peanut oil or butter for sautéing

1. With a wire whisk, beat the eggs well in a mixing bowl until frothy. Add the salt and water, beating all the time.
2. Add the *matzoh* meal and keep beating until the mixture is smooth. Allow this batter to rest for 1 hour in the refrigerator.
3. Heat 3 to 4 Tblsp. oil or butter in a 12-inch skillet over medium-high heat until the oil or butter is sizzling but not smoking.
4. Ladle a scant 1/4 cup batter into the skillet. Repeat until you have 4 *chremslach* frying. Sauté until golden brown on both sides, turning once. Repeat until all the batter is used up. Add oil or butter as needed. Recipe makes 16 to 18 *chremslach*. They will puff up very slightly during cooking but deflate immediately when removed from the heat. You can tell when the time comes to turn the *chremslach* because the edges will be nicely browned. Serve with sour cream and preserves or with a seasonal fruit compote.

Recipe 2: Extra-Light, Puffy *Chremslach*

4 eggs, separated
3/4 cup club soda or seltzer

1/2 tsp. salt
1 cup *matzoh* meal
peanut oil or butter for sautéing

1. Beat the egg yolks in a mixing bowl with the salt and the club soda. Add the *matzoh* meal and mix well until completely incorporated. Allow to rest for 45 minutes in the refrigerator.

2. In a separate large mixing bowl, beat the egg whites until stiff and standing in peaks.

3. Fold the egg whites into the *matzoh* meal mixture with a rubber spatula. Make sure that it is well incorporated and no trace of white is showing, but do not overfold.

4. Heat 4 Tblsp. oil or butter in a 12-inch skillet over medium-high heat until sizzling but not smoking. Ladle 1/4 cup batter into the skillet. Repeat this 4 times until 4 *chremslach* are frying at the same time. Sauté on both sides until golden brown, turning once. Repeat until all the batter is used up. Add oil or butter as needed. Recipe makes 16 to 18 *chremslach*. These will puff up during cooking and remain puffy after they are removed from the skillet, but they should be eaten right away. They are as light as miniature soufflés. Serve with preserves and sour cream.

Recipe 3: Stuffed *Chremslach*

4 eggs, beaten
1/2 cup cold water
1 1/2 cups *matzoh* meal
1 recipe meat filling for *kreplach* (p. 59)
salt and black pepper to taste

Mix the eggs, water, *matzoh* meal, salt, and pepper together well and allow this batter to rest in the refrigerator for 1 to 1 1/2 hours. Preheat the oven to 350°. Remove from the refrigerator, and ladle 1/4 cup batter onto a well-greased baking sheet. It should spread but hold its shape well. Spread it out a little to the size of a hamburger patty. Spoon 1 Tblsp. meat filling into the center of this, and ladle 1/4 cup batter over the filling. Repeat until you have used up all the batter and, it is hoped, all of the filling. Do not exceed 1 Tblsp. filling per *chremsl*. Place the baking sheet with the *chremslach* on it into the oven and bake for 10 minutes. Turn the *chremslach* over with a spatula and bake an additional 10 minutes. The *chremslach* will be beautifully browned on both sides and well cooked through. Serve as a *forspeis*, a main dish, or a snack. If served

as a *forspeis*, one or two *chremslach* are quite sufficient. Serve a small portion of beet green salad (p. 227), *shalloteh* (p. 229), or Romanian roasted-pepper salad (p. 228) alongside the *chremslach*. If serving as a main dish, serve at least 3 per person and accompany the meal with one or two salads; *Romanishe tzallat* (p. 228) is an excellent choice.

Cottage Cheese *Latkes*

Kayzel Latkes

1/2 lb. farmer dry cottage cheese
4 extra-large eggs
2 Tblsp. sugar
1/4 tsp. salt
1/2 cup *matzoh* meal
butter or butter mixed with peanut oil for
    sautéing

1. Beat the eggs and sugar together in a mixing bowl with a wire whisk until well incorporated.

2. Put the cheese through a sieve into the egg mixture and whisk again. The cheese will be well pureed and will blend completely into the *latkes*.

3. Add the remaining ingredients except for the butter or butter and oil. Mix everything well again. The batter should hold together well during cooking. If it does not look as if it will, add up to 1 more Tblsp. *matzoh* meal.

4. Heat 6 Tblsp. butter or 3 Tblsp. oil and 3 Tblsp. butter in a 12-inch skillet over medium-high heat until it is sizzling but not smoking. Drop 1/4 cup batter into the skillet. Repeat 4 times until 4 *latkes* are frying. Sauté until golden brown on both sides. You will have to sauté for about 3 minutes on the first side and then lift the *latkes* up gently to test before turning over. Repeat this until all the batter is used up, adding butter or oil as needed. Remember that cottage cheese *latkes* can be a little tricky, and they'll sometimes stick to the bottom of the pan if there is not enough oil in it. This is the reason for taking more care than normal in testing for doneness. Turn the *latkes* over only once during cooking, when you are abolutely certain that the underside is done enough. The *latkes* are ready when they are golden brown on both sides. Recipe makes 16 to 18 *latkes*. Serve with sour cream and preserves. These may be eaten as a breakfast dish or a light lunch or dinner. Follow the suggestions given for *matzoh brei*.

Sour Cream *Latkes*

Smetane Latkes

Smetane latkes are the basic Jewish pancake. This is what eastern European Jews, especially those from Litteh, serve when in the mood for griddle cakes. They are made small, just like Scandinavian pancakes.

1 cup unbleached white flour
2 Tblsp. melted sweet butter
1/2 tsp. salt
2 large eggs
2 cups sour cream
1 Tblsp. sugar
butter for sautéing

1. Beat the eggs together with the sugar in a mixing bowl, using a wire whisk until it is well mixed.
2. Beat in the sour cream with the whisk, mixing thoroughly until everything is well incorporated.
3. Add the remaining ingredients and whisk together well to form a smooth batter.
4. Melt 4 Tblsp. butter in a 12-inch skillet over medium-high heat. Ladle 1/4 cup batter into the skillet. Repeat 4 times until you have 4 *latkes* frying at the same time. Sauté until golden brown on both sides. Repeat until all the batter has been used up. Add butter as needed. Recipe makes 16 to 18 *latkes*. Serve with preserves and sour cream.

Challah French Toast

The best French toast in the world is made out of *challah*, and the best *challah* to make it with is day-old *challah* left over from Shabbos. I offer you two recipes here. One is traditional. The other is the kind of French toast, "pain perdu," that is made in New Orleans by Creole chefs. Of course, in New Orleans they make their pain perdu with day-old French bread and I make mine with *challah*. There is nothing better than this to start off your Sunday morning. Have it with good, strong New Orleans–made chicory coffee.

Recipe 1: Traditional French Toast With *Challah*

2 extra-large eggs
1/4 tsp. salt
2/3 cup whole milk
8 to 12 slices day-old *challah* or sweet *challah*
butter for sautéing

1. Beat the eggs, milk, and salt together in a mixing bowl.
2. Melt 4 Tblsp. butter in a 12-inch skillet over medium-high heat. You can sauté 2 slices of French toast in one skillet.
3. Dip each slice of *challah* into the egg mixture. Let it soak for 30 seconds to absorb some of the egg before you remove it. Let the excess drip back into the bowl and place the *challah* into the sizzling butter. Repeat with second slice. Saute 2 slices at a time until each piece of French toast is golden brown on both sides. Serve immediately with preserves or syrup. Serve 2 slices of French toast per diner.

Recipe 2: Creole Pain Perdu With *Challah*

4 extra-large eggs
1/3 cup sugar
grated zest and juice of 1 orange
3 Tblsp. brandy
1/3 cup coffee cream or half-and-half
6 to 8 very thick slices of day-old *challah*
butter for sautéing
confectioner's sugar for sprinkling

1. Mix everything but the *challah*, butter, and confectioner's sugar together in a large bowl.
2. Add the *challah* slices to the egg mixture to coat them evenly. Soak them about 10 to 15 minutes to make sure the bread absorbs the liquid ingredients.
3. Melt 4 to 6 Tblsp. butter in a 12-inch skillet over medium-high heat and sauté the *challah* slices 2 at a time on both sides until golden brown. Sprinkle with confectioner's sugar before serving. Serve 1 slice of pain perdu per diner. Do not serve syrup or preserves with pain perdu. It is rich enough as is and very sophisticated in flavor. For a real treat, serve it with freshly brewed New Orleans chicory coffee.

Vishnyek and Other Flavored Vodkas

Vishnyek is a homemade cherry liqueur made out of tart sour cherries, sugar, and vodka. It is served the same way as brandies and American cordials—as an after-dinner drink or for special occasions. Jews also drank a shot of this after eating a *forspeis* of fish if the entrée were to be meat. The other flavored vodkas in this recipe are all variations on *vishnyek* and all were a part of Yiddish cuisine.

To make these liqueurs, you will need a 1-liter bottle of vodka. Follow the proportions given below for fruit and sugar.

Vishnyek, use 1 lb. tart sour cherries and 2 1/2 cups sugar

Shlivovitz (plum vodka), use 1 lb. ripe plums and 2 cups sugar

Blackberry vodka, use 1 lb. blackberries and 2 cups sugar

Cranberry vodka, use 1 lb. cranberries and 3 cups sugar

Pit the fruit (in the case of *vishnyek* and *shlivovitz*, cut them in half or into small pieces). In the case of cranberries, coarsely chop them in the food processor. Blackberries may be left whole. Place the fruit into a large glass canning jug with a clamp-seal top. Add the appropriate amount of sugar. Pour the bottle of vodka over this. Clamp down the lid of the jug and shake vigorously to dissolve the sugar. Place the jug in a cool, dark place and allow it to ferment for at least 6 to 8 weeks. Shake the jar once a day. At the end of this time, uncover the jar and through a funnel lined with cheesecloth, strain the liqueur into a decanter. Cork or cover the decanter and serve the liqueur as you would any liqueur or cordial.

Coffees and Teas

One doesn't usually consult a Jewish cookbook to learn how to correctly brew coffee or tea. However, there are some special ways of preparing these beverages that are a traditional part of Yiddish cuisine and, therefore, warrant some mention in this book.

Coffee is the beverage of central Europe. Both Vienna and Budapest were famous for their coffee-houses as well as for some unique ways of preparing this drink. Coffee was much less popular in eastern Europe because it was very expensive. However, it caught on quite well with middle- and upper-middle-class Jews in the large cities. My father, whose family came from Novogrod-Wolinsk, a small village in the Kiev area of the Ukraine, told me that his father (my grandfather) used to break an eggshell into his coffee whenever he made it in order to clarify the brew. As an adult, I tried this and found that it worked very well. I also found recipes in many old eastern and northern European cookbooks for egg-clarified coffee, which used not only an eggshell but a whole egg. I experimented with this as well and found that it made a delicious brew.

Here are two interesting variations on regular coffee for you to try in your own kitchen. Enjoy them courtesy of the Jewish immigrants who passed them on to me.

Egg-Enriched Coffee

Use an old-fashioned coffee percolator for making this. I have a percolator made out of Pyrex that I use especially for making this kind of coffee. My recipe makes 8 cups of coffee, but the same recipe works just as well for 6 or up to 10 cups. All you need to do is increase or decrease the amount of coffee grounds in the recipe. Remember that coffee tastes best when the beans are freshly ground and, if possible, freshly roasted. The standard rule for making coffee is to use 1 Tblsp. ground coffee for every cup of water and 1 extra Tblsp. "for the pot." More than this amount will probably make too strong a brew. Less coffee grounds than this will give you weak coffee—unfortunately a very common problem with some of the coffee made in this country. A family friend who was born in Poland calls weak American coffee by the caustic name of "fookoo mookoo." (My grandmother had another name for weak coffee which, regrettably, is not printable.)

9 Tblsp. medium-ground coffee (use your favorite bean)
1 egg
8 cups cold water
pinch salt

Pour the cold water into the coffeepot. Fill the container that holds the coffee grounds with 4 Tblsp. of the coffee. Break the egg and place it in a small bowl. Crush the eggshell and place this on top of the 4 Tblsp. coffee. Add the remaining 5 Tblsp. coffee grounds to the container. Beat the egg well and pour it over the coffee grounds. Place the percolator on top of the stove and heat up the water over medium heat. When the coffee begins to perk, adjust the heat so that it perks steadily but not too rapidly, for about 20 minutes. Serve.

Egg-enriched coffee may be drunk black, with cream, or as café au lait (with hot milk). Delicious!

Hungarian Mocha Coffee

This is one of the many different methods of preparing coffee that comes from the elegant coffeehouses of Budapest. It is easily prepared in your own kitchen. The traditional way of doing this is to brew it in an old-fashioned coffeepot that is brought to a boil on top of the stove and then filtered into a serving pot or individual cups. The correct technique is very important in this recipe and makes all the difference in the resulting flavor of the coffee. I own an ibrik (which is used to make Turkish coffee), and I find it the perfect pot for making Hungarian mocha coffee.

**7 Tblsp. freshly ground coffee (the coffee
should be ground slightly more fine than a
medium grind; the texture used for
automatic drip coffee is just right)
10 tsp. sugar
6 tsp. unsweetened cocoa
6 cups cold water**

Put the coffee grounds, sugar, and cocoa into the coffeepot or ibrik. Pour the water over it and heat it slowly over low heat. It will take at least 30 minutes (less if your coffeepot has a lid). When 25 minutes have elapsed, start to watch the coffee carefully. Do not let it come to a boil. You will see the coffee start to bubble up as it heats up. If it boils, the boiling liquid will burst the bubble, which you do not want to do. The second it reaches this point,

you must remove the coffee from the heat source and pour it through a filter into a serving pot or individual cups. If your coffeepot has a filter built into it, you may pour directly from the pot into cups. Serve the coffee with cream or, if you like, whipped cream. Recipe makes 6 regular cups of coffee or 12 demitasses.

Tea

My grandmother held a regular bingo game in her house every two weeks. On bingo evenings, more than a dozen of her friends would be there to play, gossip, and, most important of all, drink many *gleizelach varms* (glasses of warm liquid). Tea was the universal drink of the Yiddish-speaking world, and no day in the life of a self-respecting Yiddish-speaking Jew (except Yom Kippur and other fast days, of course) went by without at least five or six glasses of tea being drunk. Tea was always drunk in a glass—never a cup! Cups made out of china were for drinking coffee. A glass of tea was drunk in almost ritualistic style—sipped from the glass with a lump of sugar between the teeth (provided, of course, that one had teeth—many of my grandmother's friends didn't). Sugar for drinking tea always came in lumps. No other kind was acceptable. For a "fancier" glass of tea, one could put a spoonful of preserves into it, stirring this in before drinking the tea.

On bingo night in my grandmother's house, every guest would come armed with her "special order" of the evening. Some wanted sugar alone with the tea, some wanted preserves alone, others wanted both. A few would want lemon and sugar. Others, strangely enough, wanted no "sense" in their tea. "Sense" is the term used to describe the strongly brewed infusion made with tea leaves and mixed with boiling water for a glass of tea. They wanted preserves mixed with hot water, or lemon with hot water, or milk with hot water (milk was never put into tea, just hot water), and believe it or not, there was always one lady who wanted nothing more than plain hot water! The tea, by the way, never came in bags. Loose tea was used to brew "sense" in a ceramic teapot, and the glass of tea was made by mixing the "sense" in the glass with the hot water. One could mix whatever proportion of "sense" to water one liked. The glass was extremely important because only by looking through the glass could you tell if the tea were as strong as you liked it. The only thing that was missing from our tea table was a samovar—an outdated appliance my grandmother sometimes reminisced about. Tea made with water from the *tcheinik* (teakettle) never quite tasted the same to her. Or so she said.

One vestige of this childhood experience remains with me in my home. We drink our coffee out of cups and our tea out of cups made of glass. Psychologically, I have always maintained, absurd as it may be, that tea drunk from a glass tastes better than tea drunk from a cup. The exceptions, of course, are Chinese and Japanese teas, which always taste better in the cups made especially for them.

Although I can offer you nothing more unusual as an example of Yiddish cuisine than this description of how tea was drunk in our house, I do have one recipe to give you for "fruit tea," which my grandmother prepared for special occasions.

My Bobbe's Fruit Tea

**9 tsp. loose tea leaves (Darjeeling and orange
    pekoe are my favorites)**
zest of 1 orange
zest of 1 lemon
8 to 10 sweet cherry pits
2 or 3 peach or plum pits
8 cups boiling water

Heat up and rinse out the teapot with boiling water by pouring a little water in and pouring it out again. Place the tea leaves, citrus zest, and fruit pits into the pot. Pour the boiling water over this and steep for 4 or 5 minutes. Serve the tea immediately, as is or with preserves. Recipe makes 8 cups of fruit tea. You may also let the infusion steep for a while until it gets very dark and becomes "sense." Then you can mix it with boiling water at whatever strength you prefer. This is even better than drinking the brew as straight tea because the fruit peels and pits impart more flavor when the tea steeps longer.

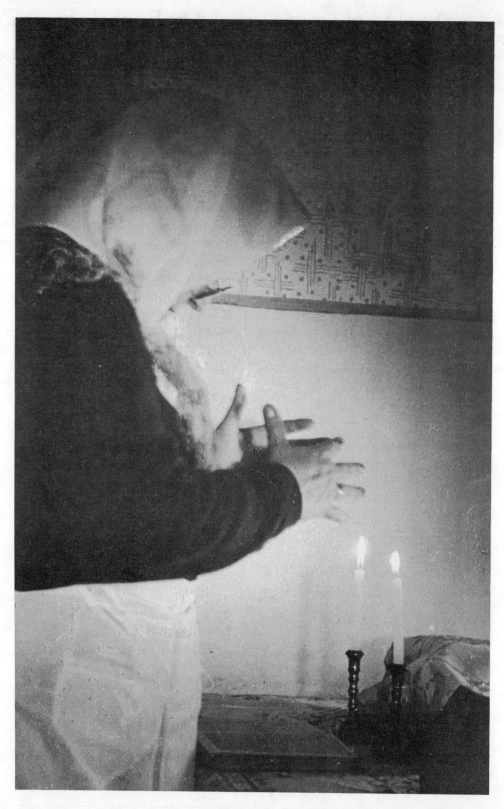

A woman in Poland lights the Sabbath candles. (Courtesy of YIVO Archives.)

Sabbath Cholent Lunch

Challah

Winter mixed vegetable salad with egg vinaigrette

Cholent

Kosher dill pickles

Pickled beets

Spanish rioja

Cranberry compote with walnut macaroons

Coffee or tea

Afterthought

Nochwort

A thing of beauty is a joy forever
   its loveliness increases, it will never
pass into nothingness . . .
                  John Keats
                  "A Thing of Beauty"

How often do we experience a moment—such as a brilliant autumn sunset, the warm caress of someone we love, or the drama and passion of a great performance—and wish that time would stop and suspend us permanently in the presence of that experience? Moreover, how often do we wish that the things we treasure and value most in life could last forever? For me, the creation of this book has been that kind of moment in time. The joy I have experienced in being involved with the process—documenting and testing the recipes, researching the folklore and foodlore, and above all, reliving some of the more pleasant memories of my childhood—all of this has been incredibly uplifting for me. And yet I know, too, that I must bring the work to a close and go on to other things.

As I ponder what I would like to say to conclude this book, I am struck by a sensation that is both sad and exhilarating. It is something like the feeling that comes over me once in a while at twilight on a Saturday afternoon when I sense that the Sabbath is just about to end. I watch the daytime colors in the sky gently recede and become overshadowed by the more luminescent shades of evening. My thoughts begin to turn inward and I whisper a quiet good-bye to the last lingering rays of sunlight.

When the first three stars come out in the evening sky, the Jew performs the *Havdalah* ceremony, a beautiful ritual that was created to say good-bye to the Sabbath and to welcome the workweek. This short prayer includes wine, a large braided candle, a box of aromatic spices, and the singing of hymns that cry out longingly for the Messianic Age to come. We Jews are taught that when the Messiah comes, every day of the week will be just like *Shabbos*. Every day will be a day free of care and worry, and the entire world will be at peace with itself.

I find myself being drawn into another childhood memory. My grandmother used to sing two Yiddish melodies at the conclusion of the Sabbath. One was a Yiddish prayer she said before reciting

Havdalah entitled *Gott fun Avrohom*. The second was called *Dem Seudanyu* ("The Feast"), and it tells what will happen at the coming of the Messianic Age, when a special meal (*seudah*) will be held in the court of the Almighty. At this *seudah*, people will drink wine that was consecrated for the anointing of kings, King David will sing the Psalms, Moses will teach Torah to the people, and wise King Solomon will be the judge over every human matter. The souls of all good people everywhere, from time immemorial, will be gathered together to share in this glorious messianic feast. And all the souls will be united forever and ever with the Creator.

In the spirit of extending *Shabbos* just a little bit longer, my grandmother would light a small candle about the size of a Chanukah candle with the flame of the braided *Havdalah* candle before she extinguished it. She would say in Yiddish, "*Zol zein a lichtige voch*" ("May the week be filled with peace and with light"). Until this little candle burned out (about 30 minutes), the laws of *Shabbos* would still be kept in our home. The humble beauty of my grandmother's *Havdalah* ceremony always had the power to distract me from the inevitable feeling of sadness that came with saying good-bye to the Sabbath.

We all know that beautiful moments in time ultimately fade, and when they do, a new reality rushes in with a relentlessness that cannot be controlled. So we cling all the harder to the moments we love and we savor their sweetness for as long as we can. In doing this, we help ourselves to accept the ultimate transformation of the experience into a memory.

The Jews of the Yiddish-speaking world, impoverished as they may have been in terms of material goods, lived their lives with vigor, spiritedness, and full-hearted enthusiasm. Such zest for life is a quality we rarely encounter today. Most people are too technical minded, too eager to do things quickly and in the most convenient way possible. Then these same people search constantly for those perfect moments in time, but satisfaction eludes them. Yet such perfect moments are often found in ordinary things—things that have always been there for everyone to enjoy. Perfect moments in time exist for us in the simplest pleasures, such as enjoying a good home-cooked meal with the people we love. We have the power inside ourselves to create perfect moments in time for ourselves and to make them be whatever we want them to be—if we just allowed ourselves to put forth the effort.

This cookbook is all about making that extra effort—the effort to bring beauty into our lives by way of something as ordinary and mundane as a meal. If we try to teach ourselves to stop being satisfied with what is convenient or with what is acceptable but only mediocre, we can turn so many of the ordinary experiences of everyday life into extraordinary moments in time. The recipes and the overall approach I have tried to develop in working with food in *Yiddish Cuisine* give me the ability to both create joyous moments in time right in my own home and to constantly reexperience Jewish cooking in the way I believe it was meant to be experienced. I hope that *Yiddish Cuisine* will do this for you too. Or, if you are trying Jewish cooking for the first time, I hope that what you have learned from working with this book will make your first experience with Jewish cooking an unforgettable one.

Ha-olom k'minhago nohaig. Di sheynkeit fargeyt, di chochmeh bashteyt. Nit dos iz sheyn vos iz sheyn, nor dos vos gefailt zich aleyn iz sheyn.

The world goes its usual way. Beauty subsides while wisdom abides. The things that have beauty are not in and of themselves beautiful. It is that which gives pleasure that is truly beautiful.

—Yiddish saying

Appendix A

Cooking to Suit
the Season

Passover we can eat where we like but not what we like.
Sukkos we can eat whatever we like but not wherever
we like.
The nicest holiday is Shevuos because on Shevuos we can eat
whatever we like wherever we like!

— Yiddish folk saying

Pesach esst men vi mir vilt ober nit vos mir vilt.
Sukkos esst men vos mir vilt ober nit vi mir vilt.
Di shainsteh Yom Tov iz Shevuos—mir esst vos mir vilt vi mir vilt!

In biblical times, the Hebrews were an agricultural people. Social and religious life revolved around the turning of the seasons and the impact of this cycle on the survival of the community. The Mediterranean region has essentially two seasons (a dry one and a rainy one) and two harvests (one in the early summer and one in late summer/early autumn) just before the rainy season begins. The rainy season lasts from approximately November to March. Biblical and rabbinic literature, including the Talmud, provides historians with detailed information about the agricultural practices of the Jewish community living in ancient Israel. Although the biblical Jewish nation basically ceased to exist after the destruction of the Second Temple by the Romans in the year 70 C.E., the Jewish religion that followed it, created by the *Anshei Knesset Hagedolah* (the Rabbis of the Great Assembly), retained many of the ancient traditions that had agricultural origins. This was to have a long-lasting effect on everything in Jewish life, including Jewish cuisine.

When Jews migrated from the Mediterranean region to temperate climates that had four seasons instead of two, they quickly adopted the culinary habits of their new neighbors. However, they held on to some of the old ways of doing things, especially if something had religious significance or was connected to some religious custom or tradition. Unfortunately, precise information that might have been helpful in tracing the origins of certain Jewish dishes has been lost in obscurity. But there is enough material in folklore and traditional literature that can teach us something about at least some of the foods connected with the Sabbath and Jewish festivals. The chart on the next pages lists each of the festivals in the Jewish calendar for which there are culinary traditions. In this chart, I include only the traditions of the Jews of the Yiddish-speaking world. Jews from Mediterranean and Middle Eastern countries have different traditions and with these, a very different cuisine from that of eastern European Jews.

Spring

Holiday	Historical/Seasonal Meaning	Culinary Traditions
Passover	Celebrates the Exodus of the Hebrews from Egypt. Celebrates the arrival of spring.	1. Foods made with *matzoh* and *matzoh* products 2. Spring greens and herbs such as chives and dill 3. The first asparagus 4. The first strawberries 5. Hard-boiled eggs
Lag B'Omer	Celebrates the survival of rabbinic tradition after the Temple was destroyed. On this day, no students of Rabbi Akiva died during a plague (second century B.C.E.) that struck ancient Judea. Celebrates the final departure of cold weather and ability to spend time outdoors.	Picnics
Shevuos	Celebrates the Jews' receiving the Torah on Mount Sinai. Celebrates the first harvest of the year and the arrival of summer.	1. Dairy foods 2. Early vegetables, herbs, and fruits 3. *Schav* 4. Sour cherry soup 5. *Blintzes* 6. *Challas* shaped like Tablets of the Law

Summer

Holiday	Historical/Seasonal Meaning	Culinary Traditions
Tisha B'Av, the Three Weeks, and Shabbos Nachmu (the Sabbath of Comfort), immediately after Tisha B'Av	A fast day in mourning for the First and Second Temples and the disappearance of biblical Jewish life. Entry into the autumn season of repentance. Saying good-bye to summer.	1. Three weeks before Tisha B'Av—light meals 2. Nine days before Tisha B'Av—frugal dairy and vegetarian meals 3. The meal before the fast—a hard-boiled egg dipped in ashes 4. *Shabbos Nachmu*—a meat feast to mark the end of mourning

Autumn

Holiday	Historical/Seasonal Meaning	Culinary Traditions
Rosh Hashanah	The Jewish spiritual New Year. The first two days of the ten days of Repentance. The beginning of the season of spiritual renewal. The turning of the season from summer to autumn.	1. Sweet *gefilte* fish 2. *Kreplach* 3. Sweet meat dishes 4. Dishes cooked with honey 5. Apples dipped in honey 6. Round-shaped sweet *challas* 7. Honey cake and *taiglach* 8. All sweet foods to symbolize a sweet year.
Yom Kippur	The last of the ten days of Repentance. A day of fasting and prayer when Jews experience the strongest sense of their relationship to the Creator.	1. A bland meal—usually poached chicken and plain vegetables to avoid stimulating the taste buds 2. A light dairy meal to break the fast and ease the body gently back into eating and drinking
Sukkos	Celebrates the wandering of Jews in the Sinai Desert and the booths (*sukkos*) they built to live in while they were there. Celebration of the autumn harvest.	Rich dishes like chopped liver, liver *blintzes*, *tzimmes*, *lokshen kugels*, stuffed cabbages, rich, sweet desserts, and sweet *challas* to celebrate the joy and abundance of the harvest

Winter

Holiday	Historical/Seasonal Meaning	Culinary Traditions
Chanukah	Celebrates the victory of the Maccabean army over the Syrian Greeks (164 B.C.E.) and the miracle of the cruse of oil that burned for eight days in the Temple. Chanukah celebrates Jewish resistance to assimilation. The bringing of light into the season of darkness (winter).	1. Foods cooked in oil 2. Potato *latkes* 3. Foods made with cheese in them
Tu B'Shevat	The end of the old and the beginning of the new growing season in biblical Israel. The running of sap in the trees, marking the beginning of the end of winter.	1. Vegetarian foods 2. Foods made with fruits that grow in Israel 3. Dried fruits from Israel (dates, figs, carob)
Purim	Celebrates the events recorded in the Book of Esther. The triumph of the Jewish people over persecution and the saving of the Jews from genocide. The end of the winter season and the beginning of preparations for spring.	Tea tables, baked goods, *hamantaschen*, *lokshen* dishes, *kreplach*—all of which are made with flour; this uses up the last flour before the house is cleaned for Pesach

Appendix B

Some Formal and Casual Menus

The various menus given below are a representative sampling of some of the best of Yiddish cuisine. I have tried to include examples of casual and formal dinners for every season of the year and something from every kind of regional cooking. Use this as a general guide to meal planning on your own, and be creative. I am sure you will come up with dozens of other interesting combinations yourself.

Rainy Day Spring Dinner from Litteh

Pumpernickel and *pletzel* breads with butter
Matjes herring in olive oil with beet green salad
Litvishe fish soup
Sauvignon blanc
Apple *schalet* with apricot sauce
Coffee or tea

Ukrainian Autumn Harvest
Sabbath Dinner

Challah and Jewish rye bread
Chopped herring with apples
Cherry brandy (*vishnyek*)
Golden carrot soup
Braised brisket with fresh horseradish sauce
Oven-roasted *kasha*
Sautéed green beans with herbs
Fruity red burgundy
Cranberry *kissel* with walnut macaroons
Coffee or tea

Summertime Lunch, Polish Style

Pumpernickel and Jewish rye bread
Chlodnik (chilled beet and summer vegetable soup)
Chilled Polish-style carp with lemon slices
and *chrain*
Sauvignon blanc
Blueberry *varenikas*
Coffee or tea

Casual Midweek Winter Dinner

Jewish rye and *pletzel* breads
Chopped egg salad with onions
Galitzianer beef and cabbage *borscht*
Baked apples
Coffee or tea

Elegant Midsummer's Evening Dinner

Pumpernickel and Vienna bread
Hungarian sour cherry soup
Gravad lox with mustard sauce
Cucumber salad with dill
Baked-beet salad
Fumé blanc
European-style cheesecake
Coffee or tea

Viennese *Schnitzel* Dinner

Vienna bread
Bouquet of fresh vegetables soup
Weinerschnitzel with egg and capers
Galitzianer beet salad
Chardonnay
Palaschinken (Hungarian crepes)
Coffee or tea

Romanian Outdoor Grill Dinner

Pumpernickel
Shalloteh (Romanian eggplant salad)
Karnotzl (Romanian spiced ground beef cutlets)
Sautéed *mamaliga*
Romanian roasted-pepper salad
Romanian salad
Black Niçoise olives
Spanish rioja
Summer berry compote with hazelnut macaroons
Coffee or tea

Sabbath Hungarian Goulash Dinner

Challah and Vienna bread
Savory green bean salad
with dried herb vinaigrette
Hungarian goulash with potato *knaidelach*
Red bordeaux
Jewish apple tart with fresh plum sauce
Coffee or tea

Polish-Style Roast Duck Dinner

Litvishe potato bread
Boston lettuce salad
Chicken soup consommé
Polish-style roast duck with brandied apples
and pears
Honey-glazed carrots
Sautéed turnips with lemon and chives
Rosé
Prune *kissel* with walnut macaroons
Coffee or tea

Jewish Thanksgiving Dinner

Bulkes (assorted dinner rolls)
Liver pâté à la Rothschild
Roast turkey with potato stuffing
Honey-glazed carrots
Sautéed green beans with lemon
Cranberry orange relish
Rosé
Poached pears in red wine
with hazelnut macaroons
(after an appropriate waiting period)
Aunt Ann's lemon meringue pie
Coffee or tea

Fleischig Buffet for a Bar Mitzvah

Pumpernickel, Jewish rye bread, onion bialys
Assorted cold cuts
(kosher corned beef, pastrami, salami)
Old Country chopped liver
Kosher dill pickles, pickled beets,
green cabbage salad
Assorted mustards and mayonnaise
Fleischig lokshen kugel
Soft drinks and beer
Glazed carrot-almond torte
Jewish apple cake
Assorted fresh fruit
Coffee or tea

Milchig Buffet for a Sunday Brunch

Bagels, pumpernickel, Jewish rye bread
Lox and assorted smoked fish
Marinated herring in sour cream with dill
Spring salad
Chopped egg and summer vegetables salad
Beet greens salad
Milchig lokshen kugel
Roggelach
Sour cream coffee cake with streusel topping
Assorted fresh fruit
Coffee and tea

Appendix C

An Explanation of
the Artwork

The artwork in *Yiddish Cuisine* includes black-and-white photographs and line drawings. The photographs are both historical and modern. The historical photographs were taken in Russia, Poland, Lithuania, the Ukraine, and the United States and come from a variety of sources—the YIVO Archives, the photographic archives of Roman Vishniac (who documented Jewish life in eastern Europe before the Nazis and their collaborators destroyed it), the Missouri Historical Society, and the family album of Robert and Henrietta Sternberg. The modern photographs are mostly the work of Henrietta Komras Sternberg, except for the two photographs taken in Montreal, which were made by Shirley Snitzer.

The line drawings, prepared by Lisa Goffstein under the supervision of Robert Sternberg, are based on two artistic traditions of the Jews of eastern Europe. One of these is ornate, decorative paper-cut patterns that were a popular folk art in all the eastern European countries and adopted by the Jews of these regions. They were called *raizelach* in Yiddish. The border pattern used for the title page of each chapter of *Yiddish Cuisine* is made from a paper-cut pattern. *Raizelach* were used for preparing patterns for wood and embroidery as well as by themselves to decorate homes. On the holiday of Shevuos, *raizelach*, as well as greens, were used to decorate Jewish homes and were also called *Shevuoselach*.

The artistic plates that appear before the special holiday menus at the end of each chapter of the book incorporate the Hebrew words of biblical and rabbinic texts into designs. This art form was uniquely Jewish and resembles Islamic art, which does the same thing with verses from the Koran. Both traditional Jewish and Islamic art avoid using the human form. This is a way of affirming their

religious stand against idolatry and therefore many of the oldest pieces of Jewish art contain only geometric and animal shapes.

Following are explanations of the symbolism in the artistic plates created for this book:

1. Passover: Verses from the text of the Passover *Haggadah* are incorporated into the borders of this traditional *seder* plate. The outermost verse translates as, "In every generation, each person is obligated to see himself or herself as if he or she has been newly liberated from slavery in Egypt." The words of the inner circle contain two separate verses: (left side of the circle) ". . . not only were our ancestors redeemed from slavery by the Holy One but also we [in our generation] were redeemed together with them"; (right side of the circle) "Slaves were we to Pharaoh in Egypt, and God brought us out with a strong hand an an outstretched arm." The Hebrew word in the center of the plate is Pesach, which is Hebrew for Passover. The five food symbols around the circle represent the five ritual foods of the *seder* meal. Clockwise, from the top, they are the bitter herbs, represented by the horseradish root; the spring herbs, represented by parsley; the shankbone of the Passover lamb; the roasted egg, symbolizing the *korban haggigah* (the holiday sacrifice in the ancient Hebrew Temple); and the *charoses*—a mixture of wine, nuts, apples, and honey representing the mortar of the bricks manufactured by the Hebrew slaves.

2. Lag B'Omer: The artistic plate for Lag B'Omer is a photograhic still life of a picnic, because in Jewish tradition, this holiday is the time for picnics.

3. Shevuos: The symbol of the Tablets of the Law is the central theme of this artistic plate, because Shevuos commemorates the giving of the

Torah on Mount Sinai to the Jewish people. The verse at the top of the page translates as, "From Zion shall go forth the Law and the Word of God from Jerusalem." These words are recited during the part of the synagogue service when the Torah scrolls are removed from the ark before the reading of the Scripture. In this drawing, they are placed directly above the inner set of tablets, which represents the biblical tradition in Judaism. The Hebrew letters inscribed on the tablets are the numbers 1 to 10 and symbolize the Ten Commandments, which are the essence of the entire Jewish biblical tradition. The verse above the tablets is written onto an open Torah scroll, symbolizing both that the meaning of the entire Torah is contained within the Ten Commandments and that the Ten Commandments themselves are an opening to one's understanding of the entire Torah. The eye is drawn toward these tablets, from which radiates the Divine Light of Wisdom, and intentionally draw the viewer closer toward the Creator.

The verse at the bottom of the drawing is taken from the prayer recited at the end of the reading of the Scripture in the synagogue service, when the Torah scrolls are returned to the ark. It translates as "Its ways are the ways of pleasantness and its paths are the paths of peace." The verse appears here as a kind of road sign, which indicates the road one takes on the journey toward enlightenment, wisdom, and oneness with the Creator. The path just above it leads invitingly toward the tablets of the Torah.

The outer shape of the drawing is also that of the Tablets of the Law and it represents the rabbinic tradition in Judaism. The rabbinic tradition completely envelopes and encircles the biblical tradition, symbolizing the Jewish belief that the wisdom of the Torah is best understood through developing an understanding of rabbinic thought and literature.

The season of the journey is set in the summer, when the trees are in full bloom and the nurturing warmth of the sun is greatest. Just as sunlight nurtures the physical body of all creation, Torah nurtures the soul of every Jew.

4. Tisha B'Av: The artistic plate for Tisha B'Av shows a Jew praying at the Western Wall in Jerusalem. On this day, Jews mourn for the destruction of the First (586 B.C.E.) and the Second (70 C.E.) Hebrew Temples. The verses surrounding the drawing come from the Book of Psalms, chapter 137. Translated, they read (counterclockwise from right to left), "If I forget you, oh Jerusalem, let my right hand lose its cunning. . . . There we sat and also wept, remembering Jerusalem. . . ."

5. Rosh Hashanah: The *shofar*, or ram's horn, is the most important ritual symbol of this holiday, the Jewish spiritual New Year. Three verses from the prayer service for this holiday surround the *shofar*. From the top, counterclockwise, the verses translate as ". . . And the great *shofar* shall be blown. . . . On Rosh Hashanah the great judgments are written and on the fast of Yom Kippur the decree is sealed. . . . Repentance, Prayer, and Acts of Charity can repeal an evil decree. . . ."

6. Yom Kippur: The artistic plate for Yom Kippur is a photographic still life, which displays the ram's horn, the prayer shawl, an old-fashioned black skullcap, and an open High Holy Day prayer book, which was printed in Warsaw in 1880 on a synagogue bench. These are the symbols of the day, which is spent entirely at the synagogue fasting and praying.

7. Sukkos: The abundance of the autumn harvest is shown inside the *sukkah*, a booth built outdoors of wood and covered by branches. The *sukkah* is used for eating meals and for other things during this holiday. The corn, gourds, pumpkin, and sheaves of wheat are traditional North American harvest symbols, which many American Jews have adopted for decorating their *sukkah*. A simple verse on a banner summarizes all that needs to be said about this holiday. In translation, it reads, "And you shall be happy on your festival and, above all, rejoice fully in it!" The symbols displayed on the Sukkos menu are the *lulav* and the *esrog*. The four Mediterranean plant species that are used for special blessings on Sukkos are the palm branch, the citron, the willow branches, and the myrtle branches. The use of these plants underscores the Mediterranean origin of the Jewish religion.

8. Simchas Torah: Simchas Torah is celebrated at the end of Sukkos because at that time the congregation completes the reading of the entire scroll of the Torah in the synagogue (from Genesis to Deuteronomy). The last verses are read, followed immediately by the first verses of the Torah, indicating that Torah study never comes to an end but is an eternal, continual cycle. This is a very happy holiday, and all the Torah scrolls are removed from the ark and paraded out into the sanctuary of the synagogue amid much singing and dancing. Sometimes the festivities spill out into the street. The artistic plate for this holiday is a historical photograph from Russia of a scribe repairing a Torah scroll so that it can be read in the synagogue. The photograph of Reb Elye, the Sofer of Annopol, comes from the YIVO Archives.

9. Chanukah: The eight-branched Chanukah candelabra, called in Yiddish the Chanukah *menorah* and in Hebrew the *Chanukiah*, is lit for 8 consecutive days to commemorate the miracle of the small cruse of oil that miraculously burned for 8 days in the Temple. Four traditional verses are used to form the branches of the candelabra. From top to bottom, they translate as follows: (1) "A great miracle happened there [in Israel]." The first Hebrew letter of each of these words is also one of the four letters on the spinning top, called a *dreydl* in Yiddish, which is used in a Chanukah game. The *dreydl* is shown on the Chanukah menu. (2) ". . . And all 8 days of Chanukah these candles are holy. . ." (from a prayer recited after the Chanukah candles are lit). (3) "We light these candles to remember the great wonders and miracles. . ." (from the same prayer as the verse above). (4) ". . . And they purified the Temple and established the 8 days of Chanukah in order to give thanks and praise to the Lord. . ." (from a prayer added during Chanukah to the silent meditation recited daily by Jews).

10. *Shabbos* Chanukah: On the Sabbath that falls during Chanukah, both Sabbath candles and Chanukah candles are lit before the evening meal.

11. Tu B'Shevat: The Jewish New Year for the trees celebrates the connection of the Jewish people to the land of Israel and its growing seasons. Fruits from the Holy Land, invariably dried ones, graced every Jewish table in eastern Europe at this time of the year. The photographic still life, which is the artistic plate for this holiday, shows pomegranates and citrus fruit from Israel, dried apricots, dates, figs, and almonds, as well as tea served in a traditional eastern European tea glass. A sunbeam falls gently over the fruit, reminding us of the sunny days that will be coming at the end of winter.

12. Purim: Purim is a type of Jewish Mardi Gras or carnival. Adults as well as children dress up in costumes and read the story of how Queen Esther saved the Jewish people in Persia from being hung on the gallows by the wicked Haman, court servant of the Persian king. In the villages of eastern Europe, Jews used to put on plays, called *Purim shpielen*, in which a burlesque version of the story of Queen Esther is acted out. The masks in the drawing represent the king, the queen, and Haman. In the lower right-hand corner there is a *grogger*—a noisemaker used in the synagogue service to drown out the name of Haman every time it is uttered during the reading of the Book of Esther. The scroll in the drawing is one of the traditional eastern European forms used in making a special scroll for the Book of Esther, called the *megillah*. The words printed on the scroll in this drawing do not come from the *megillah* but from a song sung after it is read at the synagogue service. The words of the first line of this scroll, in translation, read, "Cursed be Haman, who sought to destroy us. Blessed by Mordecai the Jew. . . ." The remaining words on the scroll are shown only in part but they are a continuation of the same theme: "Cursed be Zeresh, Haman's evil wife. . . . Blessed be Esther. . . ." The image of the Hebrew letters flying off the scroll is a kind of Purim enigma. There is a tradition on this holiday that allows a person to drink more alcohol than usual in order to liberate the soul from any inhibitions and allow it to rejoice in the triumph of good over evil. According to rabbinic tradition, one may drink enough so that "he or she can no longer distinguish between the meaning of the words 'Cursed be Haman' and 'Blessed be Mordecai.'" The words of this scroll appear to lift themselves off the earthbound pages of the scroll and frolic playfully in midair. The higher they ascend above the scroll, the more they begin to draw apart and separate from one another, making it difficult to read the words and thus fulfilling the rabbinic injunction.

13. Shabbos: The last artistic plate is perhaps the most important in the series, because the Sabbath is the most important of all Jewish holidays. It is fitting that *Yiddish Cuisine* conclude with the kindling of the Sabbath candles, because these symbolize Jewish continuity. The lighting of the Sabbath candles is an eternal commandment that links every generation of Jews to the communities of the past and to those of the future. When the Spanish Inquisition forcibly baptized all Jews and Muslims remaining in Spain in 1492, the Jewish religion went underground among many who remained. Many members of the Jewish community held on in secret to some of the practices of the Jewish religion while outwardly pretending they were Christians. One of the practices that continued among these secret Jews (called by Jewish historians the *Anusim*, or "forced ones," and by the Spaniards "Marranos" or "pigs") was the lighting of Sabbath candles. Discoveries have been made in recent years in Mexico, in Peru, and even in some isolated Hispanic communities in Texas and New Mexico of people who have believed themselves Catholic through many generations but are members of secret societies where rituals are observed such as the lighting of candles on a Friday night. Could it be that the kindling of Sabbath lights is a link between these people and long-forgotten Jewish ancestors?

This poignant, beautiful photograph of a Jewish woman lighting the Sabbath candles was taken in pre-World War II Poland at a time when Poland had the largest Jewish community in the world. It comes to *Yiddish Cuisine* courtesy of the YIVO Archives and is a permanent reminder of Jewish continuity through the traditions that all generations of Jews share.

Index

About the Author

Robert Sternberg is the executive director of the St. Louis Center for Holocaust Studies. He received his bachelor of arts degree from Roosevelt University in Chicago, Illinois, his master of arts from Concordia University in Montreal, Quebec, and his rabbinic ordination from Machon Harry Fischel, Jerusalem. Rabbi Sternberg is a member of many organizations, including the International Association of Culinary Professionals (IACP), The James Beard Foundation, and the St. Louis Culinary Society.